Lecture Notes in Computer Science   7383

Commenced Publication in 1973
Founding and Former Series Editors:
Gerhard Goos, Juris Hartmanis, and Jan van Leeuwen

Klaus Miesenberger   Arthur Karshmer
Petr Penaz   Wolfgang Zagler (Eds.)

Computers Helping People with Special Needs

13th International Conference, ICCHP 2012
Linz, Austria, July 11-13, 2012
Proceedings, Part II

 Springer

Volume Editors

Klaus Miesenberger
Universität Linz, Institut Integriert Studieren
Altenbergerstraße 69, 4040 Linz, Austria
E-mail: klaus.miesenberger@jku.at

Arthur Karshmer
University of San Francisco
2130 Fulton St., San Francisco, CA 94117, USA
E-mail: arthur@lakeland.usf.edu

Petr Penaz
Masaryk University, Support Centre for Students with Special Needs
Botanická 68A, 602 00 Brno, Czech Republic
E-mail: penaz@fi.muni.cz

Wolfgang Zagler
Vienna University of Technology, Institute "Integriert Studieren"
Favoritenstr. 11/029, 1040 Vienna, Austria
E-mail: zw@fortec.tuwien.ac.at

ISSN 0302-9743   e-ISSN 1611-3349
ISBN 978-3-642-31533-6   e-ISBN 978-3-642-31534-3
DOI 10.1007/978-3-642-31534-3
Springer Heidelberg Dordrecht London New York

Library of Congress Control Number: 2012940983

CR Subject Classification (1998): K.4.2, H.5.2-3, H.5, H.4, K.3, H.3, J.3

LNCS Sublibrary: SL 3 – Information Systems and Application, incl. Internet/Web
and HCI

Typesetting: Camera-ready by author, data conversion by Scientific Publishing Services, Chennai, India

Printed on acid-free paper

Springer is part of Springer Science+Business Media (www.springer.com)

Preface

Welcome to the ICCHP 2012 Proceedings

The information society is moving towards eAccessibility and eInclusion around the world, facilitated by better and user-friendlier assistive technologies. Research and development are important drivers in moving the sector forward and also in implementing accessibility as a key feature of today's mainstream systems and services. Evidence of this trend can be seen in new

July 11-13, 2012
Pre-conference July 9-10

International Conference on Computers
Helping People with Special Needs
Johannes Kepler University Linz

free and commercial products, such as screenreader software, working seamlessly on all up-to-date smartphones, pads and tablets.

ICCHP is proud of being an active force in this process since the 1980s. Scientific conferences, besides showcasing the newest ideas and developments, facilitate exchange and cooperation. They are indispensable ingredients of innovation and progress.

This year, as in the past, we are proud to welcome more than 500 participants from over 50 countries from around the world; 112 experts selected 147 full and 42 short papers out of 364 abstracts submitted to ICCHP. They form the core of the program of ICCHP 2012. Each paper was reviewed by three expert reviewers and every submission was then further evaluated in a meeting of the international Program Committee. The acceptance ratio of about 50% of the submissions demonstrates our strict pursuit of scientific quality both of the program and in particular of the proceedings in your hands.

The concept of organizing "Special Thematic Sessions" helped to structure the proceedings and program. The process supports focusing on selected topics of high interest in the field as well as bringing new and interesting topics to the attention of the research community. This approach makes the 13th edition of ICCHP proceedings a valued and interesting contribution to the state of the art and a reference in our domain of study.

ICCHP, for the first time, features and includes the conference "Universal Learning Design (ULD)". This part of the ICCHP program invites experienced practitioners and users to present their ideas, problems, experiences and concepts in an open forum, allowing us to learn from and advance our work based on experience and best practice. Most of these contributions are of a practical nature and are therefore included in a special publication of the ULD hosting partner Masaryk University Brno, Czech Republic. We recommend referring to them when reading these proceedings. With ULD, ICCHP will advance more rapidly towards a platform facilitating the exchange and cooperation of a diverse set of stakeholders allowing deeper and more sustainable impact.

ULD complements ICCHP very well. Together with the "Young Researchers Consortium", the "Summer University on Math, Science and Statistics for Blind and Partially Sighted Students", the finals of the international coding event "SS12 – Project:Possibility", intensive workshops, meetings and an exhibition including presentations and demonstrations of major software and assistive technology producers and vendors, ICCHP will once again be the international meeting place and center of advanced information exchange.

ICCHP 2012 is held under the auspices of Dr. Heinz Fischer, President of the Federal Republic of Austria, an honorable Committee of Honor and under the patronage of the United Nations Educational, Scientific and Cultural Organization (UNESCO), and of the European Disability Forum (EDF).

We thank the Austrian Computer Society for announcing and sponsoring the ICCHP Roland Wagner Award, endowed in 2001 in honor of Roland Wagner, the founder of ICCHP.

Former Award Winners:

- Award 5: Handed over at ICCHP 2010 in Vienna to:
  - Harry Murphy - Founder, Former Director and Member of Advisory Board of the Centre on Disabilities, USA
  - Joachim Klaus - Founder, Former Director of the Study Centre for the Visually Impaired at Karlsruhe Institute of Technology (SZS - KIT), Germany
- Award 4: George Kersher, Daisy Consortium, ICCHP 2008 in Linz
- *Special Award 2006:* Roland Traunmüller, University of Linz
- Award 3: Larry Scadden, National Science Foundation, ICCHP 2006 in Linz
- Award 2: Paul Blenkhorn, University of Manchester, ICCHP 2004 in Paris
- *Special Award 2003:* A Min Tjoa, Vienna University of Technology
- Award 1: WAI-W3C, ICCHP 2002 in Linz
- Award 0: Prof. Roland Wagner on the occasion of his 50th birthday, 2001

Once again we thank everyone for helping with putting ICCHP in place and thereby supporting the AT field and a better quality of life for people with disabilities.

Special thanks go to all our sponsors and supporters.

July 2012

Klaus Miesenberger
Arthur Karshmer
Petr Penaz
Wolfgang Zagler

Organization

ICCHP 2012 General Chair

A. Karshmer   University of San Francisco, USA

Program Board

D. Burger   INSERM, France
J. Klaus   Karlsruhe Institute of Technology (KIT),
                                   Germany
H. Murphy   California State University, Northridge, USA
M. Suzuki   Kyushu University, Japan
A.M. Tjoa   Vienna University of Technology, Austria
R. Wagner   University of Linz, Austria

Program and Publishing Chairs

K. Miesenberger   University of Linz, Austria
W. Zagler   Vienna University of Technology, Austria
P. Penaz   Masaryk University Brno, Czech Republic

Young Researchers Consortium Chairs

D. Archambault   Université Paris 8, France
D. Fels   Ryerson University, Canada
D. Fitzpatrick   Dublin City University, Ireland
M. Kobayashi   Tsukuba College of Technology, Japan
M. Morandell   AIT Austrian Institute of Technology GmbH,
                                   Austria
E. Pontelli   New Mexico State University, USA
S. Trewin   IBM, USA
G. Weber   Technische Universität Dresden, Germany

Workshop Program Chair

F. Pühretmair   KI-I, Austria

Program Committee

J. Abascal	Euskal Herriko Unibertsitatea, Spain
C. Abbott	King's College London, UK
S. Abou-Zahra	W3C Web Accessibility Initiative (WAI), Austria
A. Abu-Ali	Philadelphia University, Jordan
I. Abu Doush	Yarmouk University, Jordan
R. Andrich	Polo Tecnologico Fondazione Don Carlo Gnocchi Onlus, Italy
A. Arató	KFKI-RMKI, Hungary
P. Arató	TU Budapest, Hungary
L. Azevedo	Instituto Superior Tecnico, Portugal
M. Batusic	University of Linz, Austria
C. Bernareggi	Università degli Studi di Milano, Italy
I. Bosse	Technische Universität Dortmund, Germany
H.-H. Bothe	Hochschule für Technik und Wirtschaft Berlin, Germany
J. Bu	Zhejiang University, China
C. Bühler	TU Dortmund University, FTB, Germany
J. Coughlan	Smith-Kettlewell Eye Research Institute, USA
G. Craddock	Centre for Excellence in Universal Design, Ireland
D. Crombie	Utrecht School of the Arts, The Netherlands
H. Cui	China Disabled Persons' Federation, China
M. Cummins Prager	California State University Northridge, USA
A. Darvishy	Zurich University for Applied Sciences, Switzerland
J. Darzentas	University of the Aegean, Greece
M. Debeljak	University of Ljubljana, Slovenia
F. DeRuyter	Duke University Medical Centre, USA
R. Diaz del Campo	Antarq Tecnosoluciones, Mexico
A.D.N. Edwards	University of York, UK
P.L. Emiliani	Institute of Applied Physics "Nello Carrara", Italy
J. Engelen	Katholieke Universiteit Leuven, Belgium
G. Evreinov	University of Tampere, Finland
Ch. Galinski	InfoTerm, Austria
J. Gardner	Oregon State University, USA
G.-J. Gelderblom	Zuyd University, The Netherlands
V. Hanson	University of Dundee, UK
S. Harper	University of Manchester, UK
A. Holzinger	Medical University of Graz, Austria
E.-J. Hoogerwerf	AIAS Bologna, Italy
T. Inoue	The National Rehabilitation Center for Persons with Disabilities, Japan

M. Jemni	University of Tunis, Tunisia
L. Kalinnikova	Pomor State University, Russia
A. Koronios	University of South Australia, Australia
G. Kouroupetroglou	University of Athens, Greece
W. Kremser	OCG, HSM, Austria
V. Lauruska	Siauliai University, Lithuania
D. Leahy	Trinity College Dublin, Ireland
A. Leblois	G3ict, USA
M. Magnussen	Stockholm University, Sweden
R. Manduchi	University of California at Santa Cruz, USA
K. Matausch	KI-I, Austria
N.-E. Mathiassen	Danish Centre for Assistive Technology, Denmark
Ch. Mayer	Austrian Institute of Technology, Austria
E. Mendelova	Comenius University of Bratislava, Slovak Republic
Y. Mohamad	Fraunhofer Institute for Applied Information Technology, Germany
H. Neveryd	Lund University, Sweden
L. Normie	GeronTech - The Israeli Center for Assistive Technology & Aging, Israel
G. Nussbaum	KI-I, Austria
T. Ono	Tsukuba University of Technology, Japan
M. Paciello	The Paciello Group, USA
P. Panek	Vienna University of Technology, Austria
P. Penaz	University of Brno, Czech Republic
H. Petrie	University of York, UK
A. Petz	University of Linz, Austria
G. Quirchmayr	University of Vienna, Austria
R. Raisamo	University of Tampere, Finland
D. Rice	National Disability Authority, Ireland
A. Salminen	KELA, Finland
C. Sik Lányi	University of Pannonia, Hungary
D. Simsik	University of Kosice, Slovak Republic
D. Sloan	University of Dundee, UK
M. Snaprud	University of Agder, Norway
C. Stephanidis	University of Crete, FORTH-ICS, Greece
R. Stiefelhagen	Karlsruhe Institute of Technology, Germany
B. Stoeger	University of Linz, Austria
Ch. Strauss	University of Vienna, Austria
O. Suweda	The Hyogo Institute of Assistive Technology, Japan
Y. Takahashi	Toyo University, Japan
M. Tauber	University of Paderborn, Germany
R. Traunmüller	University of Linz, Austria
P. Trehin	World Autism Organisation, France

J. Treviranus	University of Toronto, Canada
E. Vlachogiannis	Fraunhofer Institute for Applied Information Technology, Germany
C.A. Velasco	Fraunhofer Institute for Applied Information Technology, Germany
N. Vigouroux	IRIT Toulouse, France
K. Votis	CERTH/ITI, Greece
G. Wagner	Upper Austria University of Applied Sciences, Austria
H. Weber	ITA, University of Kaiserslautern, Germany
J. Weisman	Rehab Technology Service, USA
W. Wöß	University of Linz, Austria

Organising Committee

Austrian Computer Society (OCG), Masaryk University (MU),
Johannes Kepler University of Linz (JKU)

Bieber, R. (OCG, CEO)
Damm, Ch. (MU)
Feichtenschlager, P. (JKU)
Göbl, R. (OCG, President)
Heumader, P. (JKU)
Kremser, W. (OCG, Working Group ICT with/for People with Disabilities)
Miesenberger, K. (JKU)
Ossmann, R. (JKU)
Penaz, P. (MU)
Petz, A. (JKU)
Pölzer, S. (JKU)
Schult, Ch. (JKU)
Wagner, R. (JKU)
Zylinski, I. (JKU)

Table of Contents – Part II

Portable and Mobile Systems in Assistive Technology

Assistive Technology, HCI and Rehabilitation

Sign 2.0: ICT for Sign Language Users: Information Sharing, Interoperability, User-Centered Design and Collaboration

Computer-Assisted Augmentative and Alternative Communication (CA-AAC)

Easy to Web between Science of Education, Information Design and (Speech) Technology

Smart and Assistive Environments: Ambient Assisted Living (AAL)

Text Entry for Accessible Computing

Tactile Graphics and Models for Blind People and Recognition of Shapes by Touch

Mobility for Blind and Partially Sighted People

Human-Computer Interaction for Blind and Partially Sighted People

Table of Contents – Part I

ULD - Universal Learning Design

Putting the Disabled Student in Charge: User Focused Technology in Education

Access to Mathematics and Science

Policy and Service Provision

CDI - Creative Design for Inclusion

Virtual User Models for Designing and Using Inclusive Products

Web Accessibility in Advanced Technologies

Website Accessibility Metrics

Entertainment Software Accessibility

Document and Media Accessibility

Inclusion by Accessible Social Media

PDF/UA – A New Era for Document Accessibility. Understanding, Managing and Implementing the ISO Standard PDF/UA (Universal Accessibility)

Human – Computer Interaction and Usability for Elderly (HCI4AGING)

A Multimodal Approach to Accessible Web Content on Smartphones

Lars Emil Knudsen and Harald Holone

Østfold University College, Halden, Norway
{larseknu,h}@hiof.no

Abstract. Mainstream smartphones can now be used to implement efficient speech-based and multimodal interfaces. The current status and continued development of mobile technologies opens up for possibilities of interface design for smartphones that were unattainable only a few years ago. Better and more intuitive multimodal interfaces for smartphones can provide access to information and services on the Internet through mobile devices, thus enabling users with different abilities to access this information at any place and at any time. In this paper we present our current work in the area of multimodal interfaces on smartphones. We have implemented a multimodal framework, and has used it as a foundation for development of a prototype which have been used in a user test. There are two main contributions: 1) How we have implemented W3C's multimodal interaction framework on smartphones running the Android OS, and 2) the results from user tests and interviews with blind and visually impaired users.

1 Introduction

This project has been created in relation to the SMUDI project. The project looks at how Norwegian speech recognition can be used in a multimodal interface to achieve universal design. The goal of the SMUDI project is to see how the users perceive different interaction methods, with dyslectics, visually impaired and mobility impaired users. The mobile multimodality project relates to the SMUDI project in that it looks at some of the same subjects, i.e. multimodality and disabled users. The main difference is that this project mainly focuses on visually disabled and blind users, and multimodality on smartphones instead of desktop. The SMUDI project is run by MediaLT, a company specializing in universal access, innovation and education.

1.1 Multimodality

Modalities describe the different paths of communication between a human and the computer. The term *modality* in human-computer interaction (HCI) refers to the sensor or device with which a computer can receive input from a human, for example touch, audio or visual. It also refers to a sensory perception of the output a computer gives.

K. Miesenberger et al. (Eds.): ICCHP 2012, Part II, LNCS 7383, pp. 1–8, 2012.

Different modalities can be combined in a richer multimodal interface. For example, visual output can be supplemented with audio (sound and/or speech), while touch input can be augmented with spoken data with the use of automatic speech recognition (ASR). There are also more advanced options available, like gaze tracking or gesture recognition.

1.2   Multimodality and Smartphones

The smartphones have many different capabilities which can be used to create multimodal interfaces where the users can choose between different input and output methods depending on their abilities, context and preferences. By utilizing these possibilities, we can give people with different abilities the opportunity to access information and services they might not have been able to before. With the use of multimodality the user can be given the opportunity to choose the most convenient interaction method available at any given time, which in turn can help overcome challenges of having to use a small mobile device [9].

We have implemented a multimodal framework based on W3C's Multimodal Interaction Framework on the Android OS. Secondly we have created a prototype of a multimodal interface on top of the framework, which have been tested with four blind and visually disabled users. Each test consisted of a number of predefined tasks, and were followed by interviews with each of the participants.

The rest of the paper is structured as follows. In the next section we present related work. Section 3 describes background and our implementation of W3C's multimodal framework, and the method are presented in Section 4. The results from the prototype evaluation is described in Section 5, and selected implications are discussed in Section 6. We conclude the paper and suggest future work in Section 7.

2   Related Work

In this section, we present some of the related work in the field of universal access, multimodal interaction and mobile devices. According to Oviatt, given the right context, temporal disability applies to everyone [7]. For example when a person drives a car, he need to be focused on the road and what happens around him.

A multimodal interface which makes it possible for him to be able to navigate and use the phone with the use of speech input and output would enable him to use the phone and drive at the same time, thus reducing the need to look at the phone's screen.

Kranjc et al. [3] studied how one can approach design of mobile applications with a focus on visually impaired and blind users. Turunen et al. has conducted a study of three different approaches to a mobile transport information services, both speech based and multimodal [10], with visually impaired and blind users. The evaluation looked at users preference, with regards to speech or tactile interface, how age and gender influenced the expectations of the system and how the experience was compared to their expectations [11]. The conclusion of the report states that multimodality generally improves performance, but that it's important to know that the users need training to be able to use the system, these findings are also supported by Krüger et al. [4].

Several multimodal frameworks have been created as a result of different research projects like MONA [1], MIRANDA [8], and others [5]. Most of these are either server based, or for the desktop. Few, if any of these are currently available for Android, the platform of choice for development of our prototype. We decided to adapt the W3C's Multimodal Interaction Framework [13], together with the use of EMMA[1] [12]. EMMA is a description of a XML markup language for representing the semantics and meaning of data, specifically made for multimodal communication.

Users are adaptable. If they encounter errors when using an application, they will typically try to solve them, by improvising or negotiating [2]. A multimodal interface may help users to use a system more fluently. If an interaction method doesn't work, they have the opportunity to use another one which can enable them to continue to use the system. A multimodal interface could also make the application less error prone [6], since the different modalities can complement each other.

3 Framework

The framework we have implemented is based on W3C's Multimodal Interaction Framework [13]. The framework consists of four main components. The *recognition component* recognizes the user input and translates it to a form that's useful for later processing. The *interpretation component* takes care of the semantic interpretation of the information sent from the recognition component. The *integration component* takes care of combining the data received from the different interpretation components. The *interaction manager* decides the appropriate output to give based on all the information gathered from the different components, context and the status of the system.

An outline of the input components that W3C specifies can be seen in figure 1. And the outline of our implementation can be seen in figure 2. The different modalities has each been implemented through two different input components. The first component is responsible for recognition of the user input. For example, the speech recognition component will recognize the words "Oslo Monday Morning" from the speech input given by the user. The second component takes care of the semantic interpretation of the recognized words and converts them to the equivalent EMMA notation. The interaction manager analyses and responds to the data received from the input components and gives the appropriate output to the user. The integration component has been implemented as part of the interaction manager.

The system and environment component has not been implemented yet. Android handles some of the tasks that the system and environment component

---

[1] EMMA: "Extensible MultiModal Annotation markup language".

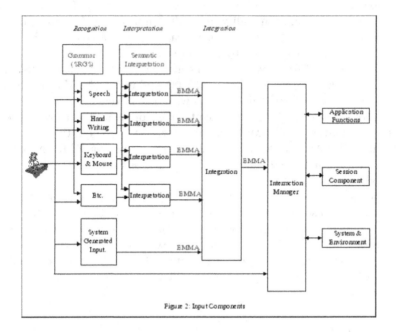

Fig. 1. Input Components specified på W3C, source: http://www.w3.org/TR/ mmi-framework/

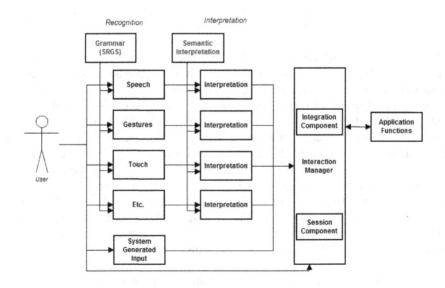

Fig. 2. Input Components - Our implementation

usually should do, e.g. scaling for different resolution displays. The session component is currently integrated in the interaction manager.

EMMA is a description of a XML markup language for representing the semantics and meaning of data, specifically made for multimodal communication. It describes the markup for representing interpretations of user inputs. EMMA [12] can be used as an output from the interpretation and integration component. Our EMMA implementation has been implemented on a need to have basis, and would have to be expanded to envelop all of the markup that EMMA describes. We have used SimpleXML for serialization and deserialization of objects and EMMA. SimpleXML is a framework that provides XML serialization and revolves around adding annotations to classes to be able read and write objects to and from XML. Each of the nodes in the EMMA has it's own class. To expand the implementation, one would have to create the new classes needed based on the nodes, and SimpleXML would do the rest of the transition to and from XML.

Based on our experience from this project, such an implementation is feasible, also with new modalities. By adding the appropriate recognition and interpretation components, the framework can easily be extended and used for new applications and prototypes.

4   Method

To test our framework implementation and evaluate multimodal mobile interfaces, we have developed a prototype and tested it with a small user group. We recruited users through MediaLT's homepage[2], and through contact in Norges Blindeforbund (Norwegian Blind Association).

The tests were conducted with four blind and visually impaired users, and consisted of two phases. One practical, where the user were given tasks to carry out with the prototype, i.e. "Find the weather in Oslo on Wednesday evening". The second phase with each participant consisted of a semi-structured interview where we focused on the users own experiences of the multimodal interface and which modalitites they preferred. There were two test administrators present at each test. One giving the users their tasks, as well as assisting the user with any technical issues. The other test administrator which took notes and conducted the semi-structural interview. The whole test was also recorded with sound and later transcribed. The notes, transcriptions and observations of the user test were used as a basis for the analysis.

Next, we give a description of the prototype and results from the prototype evaluation.

5   Prototype and Evaluation

We have developed a prototype of a multimodal interface for the Android platform. This prototype were built on top of, and in parallel to, the multimodal

---

[2] http://www.medialt.no

framework. It gives access to yr.no, a Norwegian weather service. The input modalities available to the user are touch input, navigation keys, speech recognition, touch gestures, orientation and acceleration gesture. The type of multimodality is uncoordinated simultaneous, the user has several input modalities to choose from, but only one input modality is analyzed at a time, . Voice recognition were available in Norwegian with the use of Nuances Dragon Mobile SDK through their mobile development program. The user has the possibility to search for a place, date and time of the day to get a weather forecast, either with speech, or with a form and a touch keyboard. It was also possible to search for weather in a given distance and direction, where, including the two aforementioned modalities, direction could be given with both touch gestures and orientation. With the acceleration gesture, the user could shake the phone to get the information entered in one of the input fields read out to them.

The test consisted of a practical user test where the user was given different tasks to perform with the prototype. After the practical test a semi-structured interview was conducted.

What follows is a summary of findings for each of the modalities of the prototype.

Speech input was preferred if the context allowed them to, because it was perceived as faster and more convenient to use, even though the speech interpretation wasn't always correct.

Touch gestures and orientation were perceived as more fun than actually useful by the users. But users are different and one of them saw gestures as very nice way of giving direction. Another saw the potential in using touch gestures in an extended form, where one could use them as shortcuts.

Acceleration gesture input was seen as simple to use, and as a good way to get what's in the input field. While one user wanted the content of the input field to be read when it got focus, instead of having to use the acceleration gesture.

Touch keyboard was perceived as a nice, but slow way to interact when they couldn't use speech input. They especially liked that the letters were read out when they touched them, and written when they let go.

The navigation keys were perceived as an OK method for navigating in the user interface, but several of the users also wanted the ability to use the touchscreen in a similar way as on the iPhone, where the label of the touched element is read out.

All of the users gave examples of how context affected them, even though the the user test took place in a controlled environment. They explained that they preferred to use speech if the context allowed them to. If the context didn't allow them to use speech, they needed other usable input methods instead. Several of them gave examples of sitting on the train or outside, where the use of speech would either not work properly due to ambient noise, or be embarrassing and interfering to use.

6   Discussion

We have demonstrated that it is feasible to implement W3C's Multimodal Interaction Framework, and use it as a foundation for making a multimodal application on a smartphone with Android.

Some of the more technical users naturally wanted to see this kind of multimodal interaction for the whole platform, more like the way it works with iOS and iPhone, where the accessibility and interaction is more closely integrated into the OS. These observations make sense from a developers view as well.

A multimodal interface can help to support universal access. As one user said: *"with the help of a multimodal interface the user is given a feeling of accomplishment when he's able to use the system because of the universal access and being able to use at least one, if not more of the input methods."*

Speech as an input method was preferred by all of the users, if the context they were in allowed them to use it. They said that it was simplest to use speech for the search. Speech was also perceived as faster than writing, although the users also thought it was OK to use the touch keyboard as well. Users appreciated the ability to have something to fall back on if the speech failed, or the context didn't allow them to use it properly. These findings correlate somewhat with those of Turunen et. al. [11], although the focus of the evaluation is a bit different, with different prerequisites. Turunen looked at how being introduced to a multimodal interface as either tactile or speech based would influence their impression, how age and gender influenced their expectations and how expectations differed from the actual experience. The group using the tactile interface where more positive towards speech, both in performance and interpretation, than they expected. While the other group where disappointed with the speech only system, and felt the system was slow, more so than the tactile group.

Our user test, interview and observations shows that multimodality on smartphones can help visually impaired and blind access web services with the help of their smartphone. All the users where positive towards the multimodal interface. They thought it could benefit them greatly if they had access to all the web services and information they wanted through a multimodal interface.

7   Conclusion and Future Work

We have presented our implementation of W3C Multimodal Interaction Framework on Android and smartphones, as well as the results from our user test of a multimodal prototype for the Android platform, with blind and visually impaired users. Our implementation of the framework to develop an multimodal application, and it should be possible to use it to make more multimodal applications. Based on our experience with the development, it is possible to make a more complete implementation of both W3C Multimodal Interaction Framework, and the integration of EMMA with SimpleXML in Java. A multimodal interface can help to support universal access and it is beneficial for visually impaired and blind users, since it enables them to adapt to the context their in by using fitting modalities, and handle errors in a better way. Speech input was a well perceived modality, while touch gestures and orientation were perceived as more fun than useful by the users.

We welcome anyone who want to do any further development with the source code to send an email request to the lead author.

References

1. Anegg, H., Niklfeld, G., Schatz, R., Simon, R., Wegscheider, F.: Multimodal interfaces in mobile devices–the mona project. In: MobEA II-Emerging Applications for Wireless and Mobile Access Workshop at the 13th International World Wide Web Conference. Citeseer (2004)
2. Hedvall, P.O.: Towards the Era of Mixed Reality: Accessibility Meets Three Waves of HCI. In: Holzinger, A., Miesenberger, K. (eds.) USAB 2009. LNCS, vol. 5889, pp. 264–278. Springer, Heidelberg (2009)
3. Krajnc, E., Feiner, J., Schmidt, S.: User Centered Interaction Design for Mobile Applications Focused on Visually Impaired and Blind People. In: Leitner, G., Hitz, M., Holzinger, A. (eds.) USAB 2010. LNCS, vol. 6389, pp. 195–202. Springer, Heidelberg (2010)
4. Krüger, A., Butz, A., Müller, C., Stahl, C., Wasinger, R., Steinberg, K.E., Dirschl, A.: The connected user interface: Realizing a personal situated navigation service. In: Proceedings of the 9th International Conference on Intelligent User Interfaces, pp. 161–168. ACM (2004)
5. Nardelli, L., Orlandi, M., Falavigna, D.: A multi-modal architecture for cellular phones. In: Proceedings of the 6th International Conference on Multimodal Interfaces, pp. 323–324. ACM (2004)
6. Oviatt, S.: Ten myths of multimodal interaction. Communications of the ACM 42(11), 74–81 (1999)
7. Oviatt, S.: Designing robust multimodal systems for universal access. In: Proceedings of the 2001 EC/NSF Workshop on Universal Accessibility of Ubiquitous Computing: Providing for the Elderly, pp. 71–74. ACM (2001)
8. Paay, J., Kjeldskov, J.: Understanding and modelling built environments for mobile guide interface design. Behaviour and Information Technology 24(1), 21–36 (2005)
9. Ringland, S.P.A., Scahill, F.J.: Multimodality - the future of the wireless user interface. BT Technology Journal 21(3), 181–191 (2003)
10. Turunen, M., Hakulinen, J., Salonen, E.P., Kainulainen, A., Helin, L.: Spoken and multimodal bus timetable systems: design, development and evaluation. In: Proceedings of 10th International Conference on Speech and Computer (SPECOM 2005), pp. 389–392 (2005)
11. Turunen, M., Hurtig, T., Hakulinen, J., Virtanen, A., Koskinen, S.: Mobile Speech-based and Multimodal Public Transport Information Services. In: Proceedings of MobileHCI 2006 Workshop on Speech in Mobile and Pervasive Environments. Citeseer (2006)
12. W3C. Emma: Extensible multimodal annotation markup language,
    http://www.w3.org/TR/emma/
13. W3C. W3c multimodal interaction framework,
    http://www.w3.org/TR/mmi-framework/

Mobile Vision as Assistive Technology for the Blind: An Experimental Study

Roberto Manduchi

Department of Computer Engineering,
University of California, Santa Cruz
manduchi@soe.ucsc.edu

Abstract. Mobile computer vision is often advocated as a promising technology to support blind people in their daily activities. However, there is as yet very little experience with mobile vision systems operated by blind users. This contribution provides an experimental analysis of a sign-based wayfinding system that uses a camera cell phone to detect specific color markers. The results of our experiments may be used to inform the design of technology that facilitates environment exploration without sight[1].

1 Introduction

There is increasing interest in the use of computer vision (in particular, mobile vision, implemented for example on smartphones) as assistive technology for persons with visual impairments [7]. Advances in algorithms and systems are opening the way to new and exciting applications. However, there is still a lack of understanding of how exactly a blind person can operate a camera-based system. This understanding is necessary not only to design good user interfaces (certainly one of the most pressing and as yet unsolved problems in assistive technology for the blind), but also to correctly dimension, design and benchmark a mobile vision system for this type of applications.

This paper is concerned with a specific mobile vision task: the detection of "landmarks" in the environment, along with mechanisms to guide a person towards a detected landmark without sight. Specifically, we consider both the *discovery* and *guidance* components of this task. Consider for example the case of a blind person visiting an office building, looking to find the office of Dr. A.B. He or she may walk through the corridor (while using a white cane or a dog guide for mobility), using the camera phone to explore the walls in search of a tag with the desired information. This is the *discovery* phase of sign-based wayfinding. Suppose that each office door has a tag with the room number and

---

[1] The project described was supported in part by Grant Number 1R21EY021643-01 from NEI/NIH and in part by Grant Number IIS-0835645 from NSF. Its contents are solely the responsibility of the author and do not necessarily represent the official views of the NEI, NIH, or NSF.

the occupant's name. The vision algorithm implemented in the camera phone can be programmed to identify tags and read the text in each tag.

Once a target has been detected, and the user has been informed (via acoustic or tactile signal) of its presence, the user may decide to move towards the target guided by the vision system. In some cases, only the general direction to the target is needed (e.g., the entrance door to a building). In other cases, more precise guidance is required, for example to reach a specific item on a supermarket's shelf, a button on the elevator panel, or to get closer to a a bulletin board in order to take a well-resolved picture of a posted message which can then be read by OCR. This *guidance* task calls for the user to maintain appropriate orientation of the camera towards the target as he or she moves forward, ensuring that the target remains within the camera's field of view so that its presence and relative location can be constantly monitored. Although trivial for a sighted person, this operation may be surprisingly challenging for a blind person.

This paper presents a user study with eight blind volunteers who performed discovery and guidance tasks using a computer vision algorithm implemented in a cell phone. Specific "markers", designed so as to be easily detectable by a specialized algorithm, were used as targets. Since the goal of this investigation is to study how a blind person interacts with a mobile vision system for discovery and guidance tasks, the choice of the target to be detected is immaterial: similar results would be obtained with a system designed to find other features of interest, such as an informational sign, an office tag, or an elevator button. The experiments described in this paper were inspired by a previous user study that was run on a smaller scale [8]. These previous tests turned out to be inconclusive, due to the small sample size and poor experimental design, which resulted in experiments that were too challenging for the participants to complete. The new user study presented here was more carefully designed: all participants were able to complete all tasks, yet the tasks were challenging enough that informative observations were obtained.

We note here that vision-based landmark detection is not the only technology available for blind wayfinding. Other approaches considered include the use of

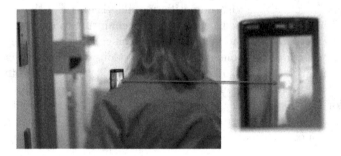

Fig. 1. Our color marker system, tested in the Env3 environment. The right image shows the view from the viewfinder; the pie-shaped color marker is displayed in yellow, signaling that detection has occurred.

active light beacons such as TalkingSigns [4], GPS [2], indoor positioning systems (e.g. Wi-Fi triangulation), inertial navigation [6] and RFID [5].

2 Experiments: Design and Outcomes

2.1 System Design

For our wayfinding tests, we selected the system proposed in [3] that uses carefully designed, pie-shaped color markers, easily detected by a camera phone with a minimal amount of computation. We used the implementation of the color marker detector for the Nokia N95 by Bagherinia and Manduchi [1]. Equipped with an ARM 11 332 MHz processor, the Nokia N95 is certainly not a state of the art platform; however, its processing rate (about 8 frames per second on VGA-resolution images) was fast enough for our experiments. The system can reliably detect markers with diameter of 16 cm at a distance of about 3.5 meters, and is insensitive to rotations of the cell phone around the camera's optical axis by up to $\pm 40°$. We observed virtually no false alarms during our tests. By printing the same color marker with spatially permuted colors, we were able to obtain a variety of markers with ID embedded in the color permutation.

The feedback provided by the detection system to the user is in the form of an acoustic signal (a sequence of "beeps"). There are two distinct beeping rates: a slower rate (about 2 beeps per second) at distances beyond 1 meter, and a faster rate (about 5 beeps per second) at closer distances. The pitch of the beep is kept constant, while its volume depends on whether the target is within the central third of the image (higher volume) or in the left or right third of the image (lower volume). This allows the user to figure out the approximate bearing angle to a detected marker. In previous preliminary tests we experimented with richer types of interface (e.g., multiple sound pitch), but the feedback we received from blind users led us to select the simple and "minimalistic" interface described above. Indeed, all participants to this user study commented positively on the chosen interface. Finally, the cell phone vibrates if the user rotates the cell phone by more than $30°$ around its optical axis. This provides a discreet warning and reminds the user to keep the cell phone straight up.

2.2 Experiment Design

We considered three environments that were representative of a variety of realistic indoor situations. The first environment (Env1) was a wide (4 meters by 5 meters) hall opening onto a corridor with the markers attached to two opposing walls. The starting position for each trial was in the middle of the open side of the hall. Note that some of the markers could be detected (if aiming in the correct direction) already from the starting point. The second environment (Env2) was a fairly wide corridor (about 2 meters in width), with markers placed flat on just one wall at several meters of distance from each other (some but not all located near office doors). The participants were informed of which wall the

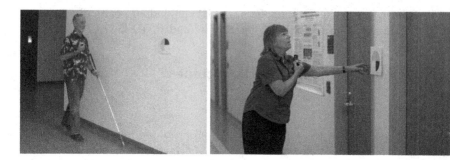

Fig. 2. Bind volunteers during our experiments in the Env1 (left) and Env2 (right) environments

markers were attached to. The starting position was at either end (alternating) of a stretch about 20 meters long. Two markings ("fiducials") were taped to the floor at a distance of 3.25 meters from each other at one end of the test stretch, defining a "probe" segment. The walking speed of each participant during the tests was measured by recording the time at which he or she crossed each fiducial. The third environment (Env3) was a narrower corridor (1.6 meters wide), with markers attached by velcro strips so that they would jut out orthogonally from the wall (see Fig. 1). Copies of the same marker were attached to both faces of a piece of cardboard, allowing it to be seen in fronto-parallel view from either side of the corridor. The participants were instructed to start walking from either end (alternating) of a 15 meters long stretch. As in the previous case, fiducials were placed on the floor to measure the participant's walking speed.

Eight blind volunteers (two men and six women, aged 50 to 83) participated in our experiments. Only one of them was congenitally blind; the others lost their sight at various stages in life. All but one of the participants had only at most some light perception; the remaining participant had enough sight to recognize a marker at no more than a few centimeters of distance. Two participants were already familiar with the system, having tried it one year earlier, while the other six were new users. Three participants used a guide dog during the experiments; everyone else used a white cane, except for one who elected to walk without any assistance.

Each participant was read the IRB-approved informed consent form and was given the opportunity to ask questions afterwards. The participants demographic details were filled in by the investigators, and the participant signed the consent form (which included permission to use pictures taken of them in scientific publications). After these preliminary instructions, the participant was taken to each one of the chosen environments in turn (the order of the environments in the test was chosen randomly for each participant). The participant was explained the correct usage of the system and was given ample time to experiment with a test marker at a known location within each environment. The participant then completed a "dry run" sequence of at least eight trials. During the dry run, the participant was allowed to ask questions; some general recommendations were also offered by the investigator supervising the experiment. Each participant was allowed to continue the dry run trials until he or she felt comfortable with the system.

After the dry run phase, the official test began. Each test comprised eight trials. In each trial, the participant was led by hand to the starting location for the current environment and asked to search, using the cell phone, the camera pointing forward, for one specific marker (whose location was unknown to the participant). Rather than manually changing the location of the marker at each trial, we placed five markers in different position of the wall at the beginning of the experiment, and programmed the cell phone so as to only detect one specific marker at each trial. The sequence of marker IDs to be detected during the trials was chosen randomly for each environment (the same sequence was used for all participants at that environment).

At each trial, the investigator used a stopwatch to record the time at which the phone first beeped after detecting a marker, and the time at which the participant touched the marker (which concluded the trial). The walking speed of the participant during the trial was also measured in Env2 and Env3 using the fiducials on the floor, as explained earlier. If a participant was not able to complete a trial in Env1 within a period if five minutes, or walked past the designated marker without finding it in Env2 or Env3, the trial was declared unsuccessful. The total experiment (including initial training) took between three and four hours per participant.

2.3   Results

Results from the tests are shown in Fig. 3 for the three different environments considered. Each figure reports the median *guidance time*, defined as the time between the first beep (when the system first detected the marker) and the time at which the participant touched the marker. The number of unsuccessful trials (if any) is also reported in each figure. For Env2 and Env3, we also reported the average *probe time*, that is, the time it took to each participant to walk trough the 3.25 meter probe.

One thing that results apparent from the plots is that the median probe time was, in general, quite smaller than the median guidance time. Considering that the target was detected at no more than 3.5 meters of distance, and often at a shorter range[2], it results clear that the participants walked faster during the "discovery" phase (as measured by the probe time) than during the "guidance" phase. In fact, guidance often proved to be a long and painstaking process.

Different environments called for different search strategies. In the case of Env1, a few participants methodically explored all walls in the hall (keeping at an approximate constant distance from the wall) until they came upon the marker. Others participants would move towards the center of the room, slowly rotating the camera to obtain a panoramic view of the space. One participant (who did not use a cane or guide dog during the trials) experienced serious difficulty in this environment, as she would soon get disoriented. Indeed, self-location awareness is important for successful exploration and discover (as noted

---

[2] This was especially the case for the case of markers placed flat on a corridor's wall (Env2), and thus seen from a slanted angle.

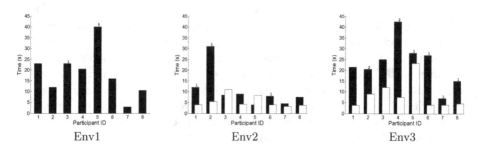

Fig. 3. The median guidance time (black bars) and median probe time (white bars) for the environments considered. The number of unsuccessful trials (if any) for each participant is shown by a number on top of the bar.

in the post-test interview by two other participants). This seems to be less of a concern during the guidance phase, in which case only one's relative location with respect to the marker needs to be controlled.

Env2 had markers only on one side of the corridor, placed flat on the wall. Successful detection required walking at a specific distance to the wall, holding the cell phone at an approximately constant angle. Due to the geometry of this environment, the target was typically detected at a closer distance than in Env1 or Env3 (in which case the marker could be found facing the participant). This explains why guidance time was in most cases smaller for Env2 than for the other environments. One participant using a guide dog pointed out that maintaining the desired location in the corridor was challenging, as the dog was trained to walk at a specific distance from the wall. At the same time, this participant remarked that the guide dog helped her maintaining a straight directions, often a difficult task (even in a corridor) without sight.

Env3 was considered the most challenging by five participants (while five participants considered Env2 to be the easiest one). This came somewhat as a surprise, as we originally thought that the fronto-parallel geometry of the marker placement would simplify both detection and guidance. In fact, median guidance times in Env3 were almost always higher than for the other environments (with a median value of 23 seconds, versus 18.25 seconds for Env 3 and 8 seconds for Env2). The probe times in Env3 were also higher than in Env2 (with a median value of 6 seconds, compared to 4.12 seconds for Env2), showing that the participants preferred to walk slower in this environment. Part of the difficulty was that in Env3 the markers were found on both walls, and participants were asked to explore both walls as they proceeded. This required methodically scanning the scene by rotating the cell phone around its vertical axis, an operation that several participants found challenging. Once the cell phone beeped signaling a detection, some participants had trouble understanding whether they should keep searching on the left or on the right wall. This is not surprising, given the relatively large field of view of the camera compared width the small width of the corridor.

From the answers to the post-test questionnaire, several common themes emerged. Participants seemed to think that the system worked well for what it was supposed to do: on a scale from 0 to 5 (where 0 meant "did not work" and 5 meant "worked perfectly"), the average score was 4.25. This was certainly very encouraging. Two participants commented that they would prefer a wider field of view. The need for rotating the cell phone to search for a target was also commented negatively by some. These two aspects are clearly related: a larger field of view would require less active interaction, since the marker could be found without having to constantly rotate the phone. Several participants commented positively on the fact that the markers were all at the same height. Indeed, earlier experiments [8] with markers at different heights resulted in very poor performance.

Several participants commented on the importance of keeping the phone at the correct height and orientation. Indeed, we observed that at least two participants had serious difficulty with holding the phone properly. For example, Participant 5 found that she had to hold the cell phone "locked" onto her shoulder (see Fig. 2), and thus would rotate her whole body when looking for a target. Other participants, however, showed good wrist control, which enabled effective discovery and guidance. Understanding the correct direction to a detected target was also challenging for some participants. For example, one participant observed that she was constantly misestimating the location of the marker by two feet or so.

Finally, almost all participants commented positively on the chosen interface, but noted that it may be impractical to use it if other people were nearby (who could be annoyed by the beeping). Most participants appreciated the information provided by the interface: approximate distance to the target (through the beeping rate) and bearing angle (through beeping loudness). Indeed, when asked to describe their guidance strategy in words, most participants said that they tried to always aim the cell phone so that the beeping was loud (signaling that the marker was seen straight ahead). However, at least two participants seemed to confuse the role of two features (beeping rate and volume). This confirms our previous observations that rich interfaces may easily become too complex, especially when one is already concentrated in other mobility tasks (e.g., avoiding obstacles).

3   Conclusions

Our experiments have resulted in a number of interesting (and at times unexpected) observations, which may inform the design of future wayfinding systems mediated by computer vision. We summarize our main conclusions below.

Field of view: The limited field of view of typical camera phones forces the user to actively explore the environment in search of a target, an operation that may be challenging for some people. A natural solution would seem the use of shorter focal lengths (and thus wider field of view). It should be noted, however, that a wider field of view reduces the angular resolution of each pixel and thus the distance at which a target of given size can be found.

Camera placement: Several participants found the use of a hand-held camera to explore the environment difficult, and some observed that they would prefer the camera to be attached to their body or their garment. Further investigation is necessary to establish whether a wearable camera could be used for effective exploration

Target location: Our experiments have shown that, even with an "ideal" system with carefully designed targets, detection and guidance can be difficult and time-consuming in some environments. This suggests that the environment layout and target location have an important role in the success of vision-based systems for information access and wayfinding without sight.

References

1. Bagherinia, H., Manduchi, R.: Robust real-time detection of multi-color markers on a cell phone. Journal of Real-Time Image Processing (June 2011)
2. Brabyn, J., Alden, A., H.-P. G., Schneck, M.: GPS performance for blind navigation in urban pedestrian settings. In: Proc. Vision 2002 (2002)
3. Coughlan, J., Manduchi, R.: Functional assessment of a camera phone-based wayfinding system operated by blind and visually impaired users. International Journal on Artificial Intelligence Tool 18(3), 379–397 (2009)
4. Crandall, W., Bentzen, B.L., Meyers, L.: Talking signs®: Remote infrared auditory signage for transit, intersections and ATMs. In: Proceedings of the CSUN, Los Angeles, CA (1998)
5. Kulyukin, V., Gharpure, C., Nicholson, J., Pavithran, S.: RFID in robot-assisted indoor navigation for the visually impaired. In: Proc. IEEE/RSJ International Conference on Intelligent Robots and Systems, IROS 2004 (2004)
6. Ladetto, Q., Merminod, B.: An alternative approach to vision techniques - pedestrian navigation system based on digital magnetic compass and gyroscope integration. In: Proc. WMSCI (2002)
7. Manduchi, R., Coughlan, J.: (Computer) vision without sight. Commun. ACM 55(1) (2012)
8. Manduchi, R., Kurniawan, S., Bagherinia, H.: Blind guidance using mobile computer vision: A usability study. In: ACM SIGACCESS Conference on Computers and Accessibility, ASSETS (2010)

Camera-Based Signage Detection and Recognition for Blind Persons

Shuihua Wang and Yingli Tian

Department of Electrical Engineering,
The City College, City University of New York,
160 Convent Ave., New York, NY 10031
{swang15,ytian}@ccny.cuny.edu

Abstract. Signage plays an important role for wayfinding and navigation to assist blind people accessing unfamiliar environments. In this paper, we present a novel camera-based approach to automatically detect and recognize restroom signage from surrounding environments. Our method first extracts the attended areas which may content signage based on shape detection. Then, Scale-Invariant Feature Transform (SIFT) is applied to extract local features in the detected attended areas. Finally, signage is detected and recognized as the regions with the SIFT matching scores larger than a threshold. The proposed method can handle multiple signage detection. Experimental results on our collected restroom signage dataset demonstrate the effectiveness and efficiency of our proposed method.

Keywords: Blind people, Navigation and wayfinding, Signage detection and recognition.

1   Introduction

There were about 161 million visually impaired people around the world in 2002, which occupied 2.6% of the entire population according to the study of World Health Organization (WHO). Among these statistics, 124 million were low vision and 37 million were blind [5]. Independent travel is well known to present significant challenges for individuals with severe vision impairment, thereby reducing quality of life and compromising safety. Based on our survey with blind users, detecting and recognizing signage has high priority for a wayfinding and navigation aid. In this paper, we focus on developing effective and efficient method for restroom signage detection and recognition from images captured by a wearable camera to assist blind people independently accessing unfamiliar environments.

Many disability and assistive technologies have been developed to assist people who are blind or visually impaired. The voice vision technology for the totally blind offers sophisticated image-to-sound renderings by using a live camera [10]. The Smith-Kettle well Eye Research Institute developed a series of camera phone-based technological tools and methods for the understanding assessment, and rehabilitation of blindness and visual impairment [14], such as text detection [12], crosswatch [4] and wayfinding [8].

K. Miesenberger et al. (Eds.): ICCHP 2012, Part II, LNCS 7383, pp. 17–24, 2012.

To help the visually impaired, Everingham *et al.* [1] developed a wearable mobility aid for people with low vision using scene classification in a Markov random field model framework. They segmented an outdoor scene based on color information and then classified the regions of sky, road, buildings etc. Shoval *et al.* [13] discussed the use of mobile robotics technology in the Guide-Cane device, a wheeled device pushed ahead of the user via an attached cane for the blind to avoid obstacles. When the Guide-Cane detects an obstacle it steers around it. The user immediately feels this steering action and can follow the Guide-Cane's new path. Pradeep *et al.* [11] describes a stereo-vision based algorithm that estimates the underlying planar geometry of the 3D scene to generate hypotheses for the presence of steps. The Media Lab at the City College of New York has been developed a number of computer vision based technologies to help blind people including banknote recognition [7], clothing pattern matching and recognition [16], text extract [18], [19], and navigation and wayfinding [15], [17]. Although many efforts have been made, how to apply this vision technology to help blind people understand their surroundings is still an open question.

In this paper, we propose a computer vision-based method for restroom signage detection and recognition. The proposed method contains both detection and recognition procedures. Detection procedure gets the location of a signage in the image. Recognition procedure is then performed to recognize the detected signage as 'Men", "Women", or "Disabled". The signage detection is based on effective shape segmentation, which is widely employed and achieved great success in traffic signage and traffic light detection [10]. The signage recognition employs SIFT feature-based matching, which is robust to variations of scale, translation and rotation, meanwhile partially invariant to illumination changes and 3D affine transformation.

Our proposed method in this paper is one component of a computer-vision based wayfinding and navigation aid for blind persons which consists of a camera, a computer, and an auditory output device. Visual information will be captured via a mini-camera mounted on a cap or sunglasses, while image processing and speech output would be provided by a wearable computer (with speech output via a Bluetooth earpiece). The recognition results can be presented to blind users by auditory signals (e.g., speech or sound).

2   Methodology for Restroom Signage Detection and Recognition

2.1   Method Overview

The proposed restroom signage recognition algorithm includes three main steps: image preprocessing, signage detection, and signage recognition as shown in Fig. 1. Image preprocessing involves scale normalization, monochrome, binarization, and connected component labeling. Signage detection includes rule-based shape detection by detecting head and body parts of the signage respectively. Finally, the characteristic of restroom signage (e.g., for "Men", "Women", or "Disabled") is recognized by SIFT feature based matching distance between the detected signage region and restroom signage templates.

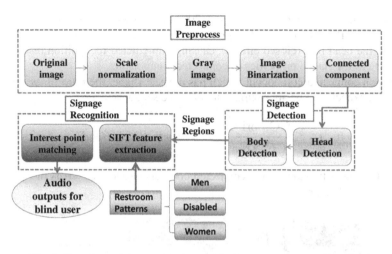

Fig. 1. Flowchart of the proposed method of restroom signage detection

2.2 Image Preprocessing for Signage Detection

To effectively detect signage from an image, an image preprocessing is first conducted which includes three main steps: 1) convert input image to gray image; 2) binarize gray image to a binary image; and 3) perform connected component processing on binary images to find the connected pixels and eliminate small noises.

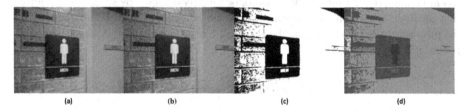

Fig. 2. Image Preprocessing for restroom signage detection. (a) Original image, (b) Gray image; (c) Binary image; (d) Labeled connected components.

2.3 Signage Detection Based on Shape and Compactness

We observe that most of images are upright and with relative stable illumination. Most important, the shape of the restroom signage in USA does not change much, which involves a circle-shaped "head" part and a more complicated "body" part as shown in Fig. 2. In this section, we describe an effective rule-based method to locate restroom signage in images using shape information.

Detecting Head Part of a Restroom Signage: As shown in Fig. 2., the restroom signage of all "Men", "Women", and "Disabled" has a circle-shaped head part. The most popular circle detection method is Hough transform. However, Hough transform detects circles by voting procedures based on *a-b-R* space]. Suppose processing a

200-by-200 image, the size a-b-R space is $200*200*100=4*10^6$, which has high computation cost [10]. Meanwhile, Hough transform accept open circles, which do not represent the head part (closed circles), causing unpredicted recognition results. Thus we detect circles via the properties of connected components.

For each connected component which has a circle shape, the ratio of its perimeter and area is expected to be approximate to 4π. We set the rule as:

$$\text{If} \quad \alpha_2 \le \frac{\text{CC.peri\^{}2}}{\text{CC.Area}} \le \alpha_1, \text{ then the CC is } \textbf{Head}. \tag{1}$$

where CC.Area is the area of the connected component and CC.Peri is the perimeter of the connected component.

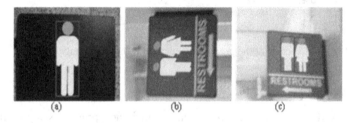

Fig. 3. Example results of signage detection

Detecting Body Part of a Restroom Signage: The body part of a restroom signage has more complicated shape which cannot be directly detected by simple shape detection method. Therefore, we detect a connected component if a body part based on the positions of the body part and head part of a restroom signage. A connected component is a body part if:

$$\beta_2 \le \frac{\text{CC.Area}}{\text{Head.Area}} \le \beta_1 \ \& \ \delta_2 \le \frac{\text{CC.Peri}}{\text{Head.Peri}} \le \delta_1. \tag{2}$$

where *CC.Area* and *CC.Peri* are the area and the perimeter of the connected component which is nearest the detected head part. All the parameters in the above equations are set by training of good quality sampled images from a restroom image database.

Fig. 3 shows some example results of restroom signage detection. The green components indicate the detected "head" part, and yellow components indicate the "body" part, and red boxes show the signage locations in images which will be used for recognition.

2.4   Signage Recognition Based on SIFT Matching

SIFT Feature Extraction and Representation: SIFT features have been widely employed for object detection and recognition due to the robustness to variations of scale, translation, rotation, illumination, and 3D affine transformation. In order to perform signage recognition, we employ SIFT features and descriptors. SIFT feature extraction and representation contains two phases: (1) detect interest feature points and (2) feature point descriptor.

First, potential feature points are detected by searching overall scales and image locations through a difference-of-Gaussian (DoG) function pyramid. The DoG is a close approximation to the scale-normalized Laplacian-of-Gaussian to find the most stable image features [6], [7]. Hence, the locations of the points correspond to these most stable features are identified as interest feature points.

Second, the feature descriptor is created for each interest point by sampling the magnitudes and orientations of image gradients in a 16x16 neighbor region. The region is centered at the location of the interest point, rotated on the basis of its dominant gradient orientation and scaled to an appropriate size, and evenly partitioned into 16 sub-regions of 4x4 pixels. For each sub-region, SIFT accumulates the gradients of all pixels to orientation histograms with eight bins [9]. A 4x4 array of histograms, each with eight orientation bins, captures the rough spatial structure of the neighboring region. This 128-element vector, i.e. the feature descriptor for each interest point, is then normalized to unit length.

Signage Recognition by SIFT Matching: In order to recognize the detected signage, SIFT-based interest points are first extracted from the template images of restroom signage patterns which are stored in a database. Then, the features of the image region of the detected signage will be matched with those from the template signage patterns based on nearest Euclidean distance of their feature vectors. From the full set of matches, subsets of key points that agree on the object and its location, scale, and orientation in the new image are identified to filter out good matches. If two or more feature points in another image match a single point in the image, we assign the pair as the best match. In our method, two criteria are required for matching points (1) similar descriptors for corresponding feature; and (2) uniqueness for the correspondence.

Provided the number of matches between the signage template images and detected signage, the signage gets the maxima feature matches are selected as the most possible pattern.

3   Experimental Results

To validate the effectiveness and efficiency of our method, we have collected a database which contains 96 images of restroom signage including patterns of "Women", "Men", and "Disabled". There are total 50 "Men" signage, 42 "Women" signage, and 10 images of "Disabled" signage. As shown in Fig. 4, the database includes the changes of illuminations, scale, rotation, camera view, perspective projection, etc. Some of the images contain both signage of "Men" and "Women", or both signage of "Men" and "Disabled", or "Women" and "Disabled".

Our method can handle signage with variations of illuminations, scales, rotations, camera views, perspective projections. We evaluate the recognition accuracy of the proposed method. As shown in Table 1, the proposed algorithm achieves accuracy of detection rate 89.2% and of recognition rate 84.3% which correctly detected 91 and recognized 86 signage of total 102 signage in our dataset. Some examples of the detected restroom signage from different environments are shown in Fig. 4. The red boxes show the detected signage region, while the letter above each red box indicates the recognition of the signage: "W" for "Women", "M" for "Men", and "D" for "Disabled".

Fig 5 demonstrates several signage examples which our method fails to detect and recognize. We observe that the failures are mainly caused by the following three reasons: 1) large camera view changes which can cause large shape distortion; 2) image blurry due to camera motion; and 3) low image resolution when the user is far from the signage.

Table 1. Restroom signage detection and recognition accuracy

Classes	No. of Samples	Correctly Detected	Recognition		
			Men	Women	Disabled
Men	50	44	**41**	3	0
Women	42	38	2	**36**	0
Disabled	10	9	0	0	**9**

Fig. 4. Sample images with signage detection and recognition in our database include changes of illuminations, scale, rotation, camera view, and perspective projection, etc. The red boxes show the detected signage region, while the letter above each red box indicates the recognition of the signage: "W" for "Women", "M" for "Men", and "D" for "Disabled".

Fig. 5. Examples of Failures

We further verify the computation time of the proposed method. The experiments are carried on a computer with a 2GBHz processor and 1GB memory. The proposed algorithm is implemented in Matlab without optimization. The average time for detecting and recognizing signage from 30 testing images is 0.192s. This ensures real-time processing for developing navigation and wayfinding systems to help blind and vision impaired users.

4   Conclusion and Future Work

To assist blind persons independently accessing unfamiliar environments, we have proposed a novel method to detect and recognize restroom signage based on both shape and appearance features. The proposed method can handle restroom signage with variations of scales, camera views, perspective projections, and rotations. The experiment results demonstrate the effectiveness and efficiency of our method. Our future work will focus on detecting and recognizing more types of signage and incorporating context information to improve indoor navigation and wayfinding for blind people. We will also address the significant human interface issues including auditory displays and spatial updating of object location, orientation, and distance.

Acknowledgement. This work was supported by NIH 1R21EY020990, NSF grants IIS-0957016 and EFRI-1137172, DTFH61-12-H-00002, and City SEEDs grant.

References

1. Everingham, M., Thomas, B., Troscianko, T.: Wearable Mobility Aid for Low Vision Using Scene Classification in a Markov Random Field Model Framework. International Journal of Human Computer Interaction 15, 231–244 (2003)
2. Hasanuzzaman, F., Yang, X., Tian, T.: Robust and Effective Component-based Banknote Recognition for the Blind. IEEE Transactions on Systems, Man, and Cybernetics–Part C: Applications and Reviews 41(5) (2011), 10.1109/TSMCC.2011.2178120
3. Seeing with Sound – The voice, http://www.seeingwithsound.com/
4. Ivanchenko, V., Coughlan, J., Shen, H.: Crosswatch: A Camera Phone System for Orienting Visually Impaired Pedestrians at Traffic Intersections. In: Miesenberger, K., Klaus, J., Zagler, W.L., Karshmer, A.I. (eds.) ICCHP 2008. LNCS, vol. 5105, pp. 1122–1128. Springer, Heidelberg (2008)
5. Kocur, I., Parajasegaram, R., Pokharel, G.: Global Data on Visual Impairment in the Year 2002. Bulletin of the World Health Organization 82 (2004)
6. Lindeberg, T.: Scale-space theory: A basic tool for analyzing structures at different scales. J. Appl. Statist. 21, 224–270 (2004)
7. Mikolajczyk, K., Schmid, C.: An Affine Invariant Interest Point Detector. In: Heyden, A., Sparr, G., Nielsen, M., Johansen, P. (eds.) ECCV 2002. LNCS, vol. 2350, pp. 128–142. Springer, Heidelberg (2002)
8. Manduchi, R., Coughlan, J., Ivanchenko, V.: Search Strategies of Visually Impaired Persons Using a Camera Phone Wayfinding System. In: Miesenberger, K., Klaus, J., Zagler, W.L., Karshmer, A.I. (eds.) ICCHP 2008. LNCS, vol. 5105, pp. 1135–1140. Springer, Heidelberg (2008)

9. Matsui, Y., Miyoshi, Y.: Difference-of-Gaussian-Like Characteristics for Optoelectronic Visual Sensor. Signal Processing & Analysis 7, 1447–1452 (2007)
10. Omachi, M., Omachi, S.: Traffic light detection with color and edge information. In: 2nd IEEE International Conference on Computer Science and Information Technology, Beijing, pp. 284–287 (2009)
11. Pradeep, V., Medioni, G., Weiland, J.: Piecewise Planar Modeling for Step Detection using Stereo Vision. In: Workshop on Computer Vision Applications for the Visually Impaired (2008)
12. Shen, H., Coughlan, J.: Grouping Using Factor Graphs: An Approach for Finding Text with a Camera Phone. In: Escolano, F., Vento, M. (eds.) GbRPR. LNCS, vol. 4538, pp. 394–403. Springer, Heidelberg (2007)
13. Shoval, S., Ulrich, I., Borenstein, J.: Computerized Obstacle Avoidance Systems for the Blind and Visually Impaired. In: Teodorescu, H.N.L., Jain, L.C. (eds.) Invited chapter in Intelligent Systems and Technologies in Rehabilitation Engineering, pp. 414–448. CRC Press (2000)
14. The Smith-Kettlewell Rehabilitation Engineering Research Center (RERC) develops new technology and methods for understanding, assessment and rehabilitation of blindness and visual impairment, http://www.ski.org/Rehab/
15. Wang, S.H., Tian, Y.L.: Indoor signage detection based on saliency map and Bipartite Graph matching. In: International Workshop on Biomedical and Health Informatics (2011)
16. Yang, X., Yuan, S., Tian, Y.: Recognizing Clothes Patterns for Blind People by Confidence Margin based Feature Combination. In: International Conference on ACM Multimedia (2011)
17. Yang, X., Tian, Y., Yi, C., Arditi, A.: Context-based Indoor Object Detection as an Aid to Blind Persons Accessing Unfamiliar Environment. In: International Conference on ACM Multimedia (2010)
18. Yi, C., Tian, Y.: Text Detection in Natural Scene Images by Stroke Gabor Words. In: The 11th International Conference on Document Analysis and Recognition, ICDAR (2011)
19. Yi, C., Tian, Y.: Text String Detection from Natural Scenes by Structure-based Partition and Grouping. IEEE Transactions on Image Processing 20(9) (2011), PMID: 21411405

The Crosswatch Traffic Intersection Analyzer: A Roadmap for the Future

James M. Coughlan and Huiying Shen

The Smith-Kettlewell Eye Research Institute, San Francisco, CA
{coughlan,hshen}@ski.org

Abstract. The "Crosswatch" project is a smartphone-based system developed by the authors for providing guidance to blind and visually impaired pedestrians at traffic intersections. Building on past work on Crosswatch functionality to help the user achieve proper alignment with the crosswalk and read the status of Walk lights to know when it is time to cross, we outline the direction Crosswatch should take to help realize its potential for becoming a practical system: namely, augmenting computer vision with other information sources, including geographic information systems (GIS) and sensor data, to provide a much larger range of information about traffic intersections to the pedestrian.

Keywords: visual impairment, blindness, assistive technology, traffic intersection, pedestrian safety.

1   State of the Art and Related Technology

Crossing an urban traffic intersection is one of the most dangerous activities of a blind or visually impaired person's travel. Several types of technologies have been developed to assist blind and visually impaired individuals in crossing traffic intersections. Most prevalent among them are Accessible Pedestrian Signals, which generate sounds signaling the duration of the Walk interval to blind and visually impaired pedestrians [2]. In addition, Talking Signs® [4] allow blind travelers to locate and identify landmarks, signs, and facilities of interest, at intersections and other locations, using signals from installed infrared transmitters that are converted to speech by a receiver carried by the traveler.

However, the adoption of both Accessible Pedestrian Signals and Talking Signs® is very sparse, and they are completely absent in most cities. More recently, Bluetooth beacons have been proposed [3] to provide real-time information at intersections that is accessible to any user with a standard mobile phone, but like Talking Signs® this solution requires special infrastructure to be installed at each intersection.

The current version of the prototype Crosswatch system provides information to a visually impaired traveler using computer vision to interpret existing visual cues, such as crosswalk patterns and Walk signal lights, which has the advantage of not requiring any additional infrastructure for each intersection. Experiments with blind subjects are

K. Miesenberger et al. (Eds.): ICCHP 2012, Part II, LNCS 7383, pp. 25–28, 2012.
© Springer-Verlag Berlin Heidelberg 2012

reported in [5,6], and also in a related project using a similar smartphone-based system [1], demonstrating the feasibility of the computer vision-based approach for helping visually impaired travelers find and align themselves to crosswalks and detect the status of Walk signals.

2   Proposed Approach

We propose extending the Crosswatch system to obtain a broader range of information about traffic intersections, which may be categorized as "what", "where" or "when" information:

- "What" information includes not only the presence of crosswalks in an intersection and the type of intersection (e.g., four-way or T-junction) but also the presence of any signal lights (which may include traffic lights), important signs such as Stop signs, walk buttons, median strips and a variety of other important features.
- "Where" information includes the location of any crosswalks or other features listed above, which can be obtained from smartphone sensors in absolute geographic terms (i.e., latitude/ longitude coordinates and bearing relative to North). To be useful to the traveler, it must be translated in terms relative to the user's location and bearing at each moment (e.g., to guide him/her to the entrance of the crosswalk).
- "When" information specifies the real-time status of "Walk" lights or other traffic lights.

Previous work on Crosswatch has attempted to answer some of the "what" and "when" questions on a smartphone platform using computer vision algorithms. However, many "what"-type features are extremely challenging to determine solely through computer vision alone. For instance, walk buttons appear in a great variety of forms: some are small, recessed buttons while others are large and protruding; the signs labeling them appear in different colors and may contain text, graphics or both. Similarly, a median strip is hard to discern without detailed knowledge of the three-dimensional surface geometry (since the strip is elevated relative to the road surface but otherwise looks similar to the road surface), and failure to detect the median strip can cause gross confusion about the length of the crosswalk. We note that complex intersections pose the biggest challenge to visually impaired pedestrians – and these are also the intersections where assistive technology such as Crosswatch is most needed. Unfortunately, it is precisely these intersections that pose the biggest challenge to computer vision algorithms!

Accordingly, we plan to focus on augmenting computer vision with other information sources, especially geographic information systems (GIS), which associate data with a given geographic location, and sensor data. For instance, given the pedestrian's current location (GPS specifies location with enough accuracy to determine the nearest intersection) and bearing (indicated by the smartphone compass), a GIS can look up a host of information associated with that specific intersection, such as the intersection layout (including crosswalk lengths and directions), the presence and location of signs, crosswalks, signals, walk buttons and median strips (or other specific features). We are currently researching the types of GIS data already available about traffic intersections (e.g., through municipal/transit data sources, Google Maps and other commercial sources). Crowd-sourcing approaches may be the most practical way of adding to this data in the future, which would allow volunteers to contribute information about the intersections they are familiar with (and to focus on the intersections that are the most challenging to navigate).

Computer vision is still indispensable for certain information provided by the system, specifically, the pedestrian's orientation relative to the crosswalk (i.e., detailed location information which GPS resolution is insufficient to determine), and the status of a Walk (or traffic) light, for which no reliable non-visual cues exist. The detailed location information provided by computer vision can also be combined with GIS and sensor information to deduce information such as where the user is standing relative to the walk button, and thereby help the user find the button.

3 Conclusion

We propose to extend the functionality of Crosswatch to encompass a wide range of "what," "where" and "why" information about traffic intersections. This information can be obtained by augmenting computer vision with other information sources, including GIS and smartphone sensor data. Ongoing testing with blind and visually impaired volunteer subjects will be needed to devise effective user interfaces for obtaining the desired information, and for communicating it to users.

Acknowledgments. The authors acknowledge support by the National Institutes of Health from grant No. 2 R01EY018345-04 and by the Department of Education, NIDRR grant number H133E110004. We would like to thank Dr. Megan Lawrence for several helpful conversations about GIS, which were instrumental in helping the authors formulate the current research approach. Dr. Ender Tekin and Dr. Vidya Murali also provided useful feedback on drafts of the paper.

References

1. Ahmetovic, D., Bernareggi, C., Mascetti, S.: Zebralocalizer: identification and localization of pedestrian crossings. In: Proceedings of the 13th International Conference on Human Computer Interaction with Mobile Devices and Services (MobileHCI 2011). ACM, New York (2011)
2. Barlow, J.M., Bentzen, B.L., Tabor, L.: Accessible pedestrian signals: Synthesis and guide to best practice. National Cooperative Highway Research Program (2003)
3. Bohonos, S., Lee, A., Malik, A., Thai, C., Manduchi, R.: Cellphone Accessible Information via Bluetooth Beaconing for the Visually Impaired. In: Miesenberger, K., Klaus, J., Zagler, W.L., Karshmer, A.I. (eds.) ICCHP 2008. LNCS, vol. 5105, pp. 1117–1121. Springer, Heidelberg (2008)

4. Crandall, W., Bentzen, B., Myers, L., Brabyn, J.: New orientation and accessibility option for persons with visual impairment: transportation applications for remote infrared audible signage. Clinical and Experimental Optometry 84(3), 120–131 (2001)
5. Ivanchenko, V., Coughlan, J., Shen, H.: Staying in the Crosswalk: A System for Guiding Visually Impaired Pedestrians at Traffic Intersections. In: Association for the Advancement of Assistive Technology in Europe (AAATE 2009), Florence, Italy (September 2009)
6. Ivanchenko, V., Coughlan, J., Shen, H.: Real-Time Walk Light Detection with a Mobile Phone. In: Miesenberger, K., Klaus, J., Zagler, W., Karshmer, A. (eds.) ICCHP 2010. LNCS, vol. 6180, pp. 229–234. Springer, Heidelberg (2010)

GPS and Inertial Measurement Unit (IMU) as a Navigation System for the Visually Impaired

Jesus Zegarra and René Farcy

Laboratoire Aimé Cotton, bat 505
91405 Orsay Cedex France
jesus.zegarra-flores@u-psud.fr, rene.farcy@lac.u-psud.fr

Abstract. The current GPS (Sirf 3) devices do not give the right heading when their speed is less than 10 km/h. This heading is also less reliable when the GPS is used in the big cities where it is surrounded by buildings. Another important problem is that the change of orientation of the visually impaired needs a long delay to be detected by the GPS due to the fact that the GPS must reach certain speed for obtaining the new heading. It can take from 2 seconds to 15 seconds depending on the GPS signal conditions. In order to avoid these problems, we have proposed the use of one GPS coupled to the IMU (inertial measurement unit). This IMU has one 3 axis compass, a one axis gyroscope and one 3 axis accelerometer. With this system, we can update the heading information every second. The user Interface is developed in the Smart Phone which gives the information of heading and distance to the destination. In this paper, we are also going to describe the advantages of using the heading and distance to the final destination, updated every second, to navigate in cities.

Keywords: GPS, IMU, visually impaired, Smart Phone.

1   Introduction

Among the GPS devices for blind people, we have the Wayfinder system, the Trekker system, the Kapten system, the GPS Braille note etc. The Wayfinder system has not been specifically designed for blind people [1]. It is used with Symbian mobile phones and gives the same instructions as for cars [1]. The Trekker and the GPS Braille Note systems also reproduce the automatic path determination and guidance mode used for cars (the pedestrian mode do not take into account the prohibited directions for cars) [2]. The Kapten was developed for pedestrian navigation but not specifically for blind people [3].

The technology GPS Sirf 3 has some problems. We have conducted different tests that show the limitations. First of all, there is a strong dependence between the quality of the heading given by the GPS and the instantaneous speed. The heading is more stable when the speed is more than 10 km/h. On the other hand, the heading, in pedestrian navigation is not stable and more susceptible to interferences. Another main problem is that it is known that the person has to move for updating the information of the direction. This updating time is variable. It can take from 2 seconds when the signal GPS is not blocked to 12 seconds when the signal GPS is blocked or if the person walks slowly.

K. Miesenberger et al. (Eds.): ICCHP 2012, Part II, LNCS 7383, pp. 29–32, 2012.

2   Materials

Taking into consideration the problems described before; we have proposed to join to the GPS an IMU (inertial measurement unit). We have developed the IMU in the laboratory with a one 3-axis compass (HMC1052 and HMC1051Z from Honneywell), one 1-axis gyroscope (EMC-03RC from Murata Manufacturing) and one 3-axis acce-lerometer (LIS 331AL from ST microelectronic), a microcontroller (DSPIC 30F6012A from Microchip) and a module Bluetooth (ARF 32 from ADEUNIS). The IMU is connected to a Smart Phone using the Bluetooth transmission. This IMU is placed on the right side of the belt of the person. The calibration and programming were developed for this case (Fig. 1, left).

The user interface is developed in the Smart Phone under the Windows Mobile oper-ating system. It gives the information about destination using directions and distances. The unit system for the distances is meters and for the directions is time dial i.e. : from 1 o'clock to 12 o'clock with one hour of precision; for instance, 12 o'clock means go straight, nine o'clock means turning left, three o'clock means turning right, etc. All this spoken information is given by clicking on the corresponding destination button.

We have proposed six buttons on the screen like the Braille system point 1 to 6. In order to locate the buttons easily; we have put some small glue balls on each button like in the Fig. 1, right. A short click will vocalize the content of the button and a long click will confirm the selection.

There are three ways of saving the information (specifically the latitude and longi-tude of the destination). The first one is being in the place of interest and clicking on the button for saving the information with the GPS, Fig. 2 ("enregistrer position cou-rante" point 5). The second one is typing the address of the place with the twelve buttons system. It includes numbers and letters which are the most used by blind people, Fig. 2. The system will search on Internet the coordinates GPS. Finally, it is possible to type directly the coordinates GPS and save them. The option of vocal identification will be shortly implemented.

Fig. 1. The figure on the left shows IMU placed to the right side; on the right, screen of the interface

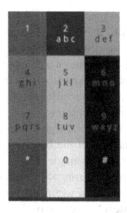

Fig. 2. The figure on the left, screen of mode navigation; on the right, screen for typing address

3   Method

The different tests were conducted in Paris in the twelfth, thirteenth and the first neighborhood in hard receptions conditions for the GPS. There was 1 km in between the destinations, and each subject had to complete three different paths. The total distance was about 3 km. The tests were done with ten subjects (visually impaired and blind people), who belong to categories three (3), four (3) and five (4) according to the World Health Organization. The subjects of categories 3 and 4 had one hour of training. The subjects of category 5 had about 10 hours of training. The difference of training for category 5 is justified by the total impossibility to analyze visually any intersection; therefore, the locomotion tasks and the analysis of the situations are more difficult.

4   Results

- All the subjects arrived to the destination points alone (except one who was not confident enough after training to make the tests).
- The benefits about the use of GPS seem to be proportional to the initial autonomy of the visually impaired. One person who does not go out by himself since a long time will not solve his problem by using the GPS, without taking a mobility course. Teaching the way of using the device is faster for the subjects in category 3 than for those in category 4 and 5. This is mainly because the visually impaired from category 3, most of the time, do not use the white cane and they have both hands free.
- The main problem is keeping the security for the user that suddenly increased his autonomy in unknown environments. The risk was the same for the three categories, even two persons of category 3 were too confident and made dangerous crossing.
- The advantage of using only the final destination point in a city is the following: it is impossible to find automatically the best route for a blind person with only cartographic information. Even the best route could depend on the person. There are a

lot of different possible routes to join a point. With a good heading and distance information, the blind person can chose the intersections and the routes where he feels more confident. This way of giving information was appreciated by all the users, even by the two people who were currently using other GPS devices.

- One system of recalibration in situ was programmed due to the fact that the compass could be uncalibrated, if it is exposed to a strong magnetic field (for example a long metallic bridge).
- The compass could give wrong information (direction) if it is not well placed on the right side of the belt. For solving this problem; extra information is giving to the user. For example; if it is not completely vertical, the system will say; <<vertical position wrong>>; if it is not completely horizontal, the system will say <<horizontal position wrong>>.
- The battery autonomy of the smart phone is about six hours and the battery autonomy of the IMU is about seven hours.

5   Conclusions

- The GPS system coupled to IMU is better because the heading is more stable in the pedestrian navigation and, the person does not have to walk for knowing the direction to go.
- The information about heading and distance is important because it lends us to arrive to the final destination with only the coordinates GPS of the final destination. It also works even when the cartography of the place is not well elaborated because the person can take any direction and the system can guide him until the destination. It seems to be one reliable guiding system option for the blind people in the cities.

References

1. Wayfinder (2005), http://www.wayfinder.com
2. Denham, J., Leventhal, J., McComas, H.: Getting from Point A to Point B: A Review of Two GPS Systems: Trekker and GPS Braille; Note, AccessWorld, vol. 5(6). American Foundation for the Blind, AFB Press (November 2004)
3. Kapten (2009), http://www.rdtronic.com/?q=node/168

Visual Nouns for Indoor/Outdoor Navigation

Edgardo Molina[1], Zhigang Zhu[1], and Yingli Tian[2]

[1] Department of Computer Science
[2] Department of Electrical Engineering,
Grove School of Engineering, The City College of New York,
138th Street and Convent Avenue, New York, NY 10031
{molina,zhu}@cs.ccny.cuny.edu
ytian@ccny.cuny.edu

Abstract. We propose a local orientation and navigation framework based on visual features that provide location recognition, context augmentation, and viewer localization information to a human user. Mosaics are used to map local areas to ease user navigation through streets and hallways, by providing a wider field of view (FOV) and the inclusion of more decisive features. Within the mosaics, we extract "visual noun" features. We consider 3 types of visual noun features: signage, visual-text, and visual-icons that we propose as a low-cost method for augmenting environments.

1   Introduction: Idea and Impact

Local indoor and outdoor navigation and localization remains a challenging problem. Various solutions have been proposed with varying degrees of success. GPS and GPS combined with image registration works well outdoors and for large area localization, but can be problematic in dense urban environments and indoors since devices require a direct view of the sky. Augmented indoor positioning systems have been proposed [8] using RFID or sonar sensors. Such systems require extensive and expensive environment augmentation, and can suffer from interference in noisy (from both radio-frequencies and acoustic) environments and power restrictions. A vast amount of research has focused on robot navigation and SLAM (Simultaneous Localization And Mapping). A smaller subset of work has focused on adapting the research to human users, in particular users that are blind or low-vision.

Here we propose a local orientation and navigation framework based on visual features that provide location recognition, context augmentation, and viewer localization information to a human user. Although it seems counter-intuitive to use visual features for blind and low-vision user navigation, we note that signs, icons, and text in images are among the most common ways of providing humans context information. The key is being able to perform object-recognition and text recognition from video reliably so that it can be communicated to a blind or low-vision user with text-to-speech software. Furthermore, these features in the scene could also provide the user accurate location information in the 3D world. If we consider the image features traditionally used in robotics for localization: image edges, corners, SIFT/SURF

K. Miesenberger et al. (Eds.): ICCHP 2012, Part II, LNCS 7383, pp. 33–40, 2012.

descriptors and so on, we realize that while they work well in algorithms it would have almost zero benefit to communicate such information to a human user.

In Section 2 we review related work. In Section 3 we fully describe what visual nouns are. Section 4 presents our visual noun based algorithms. Section 5 shows experiments and results. Conclusions and a discussion of further work are in Section 6.

2   Related Work

A lot of work has been done in object detection and recognition. For object detection a useful method has been the MSER blob detector [14]; it has been extended to handle color [12], and text [3]. Saliency maps are another method employed in detecting objects and areas of interest [1]. Both MSER and Saliency map methods provide regions of interest that are consistent with characteristics we expect in visual features, such as signs and text, mainly because they highly contrast with their backgrounds. Object matching has been well studied, with simple methods such as template matching, to machine learning based methods. Object detections can often be distinguished from one another readily, but to be truly informative to human users we must recognize the sign from a labeled database to communicate its meaning to the user.

We use the visual features to perform localization of the user in their environment. Methods such as 3D reconstruction [16] can be employed, or methods with a sparse set of features can also be used, such as the PnP algorithm [15]. The PnP algorithm requires some knowledge or mapping of the signs in 3D space.

The typical camera view is not wide enough to cover enough visual features for a user to perform localization. A sighted user usually looks around to find recognizable features around them. Similarly the blind and low-vision do the same to get an understanding of sounds around them. Using a panorama of a user's surroundings provides more visual features that can help localize the user. Visual navigation using panoramic images have been studied by us [6] and others [5], and here we leverage our past experience and integrate visual nouns as local features for user localization using panoramic images.

The system presented here differs from the typical SLAM approaches in that we are not interested in automatically mapping entire scenes, but rather providing salient local orientation and localization information to a human user, who is using their own cognitive abilities to make decisions.

3   Visual Nouns in Context: Our Approach

A primary goal in this work is to use and detect features that naturally provide human users context information, not only what they see, but also as to where they are in the 3D world. Below we describe the 3 types of features we call Visual Nouns:

Text appearance is a rarely used feature in video and image matching and retrieval applications. Traditionally, OCR algorithms reduce and map text in imagery to ASCII character codes, occasionally with some minimal formatting/layout information. Visually, text provides richer features such as: font styling, color/texture, its geometric alignment, and size relative to other text. In addition, each text sign may contain unique markers due to age, weathering, damage, and vandalism. In outdoor and indoor navigation scenarios, users encounter such text on storefronts, signs, postings, and doors. Since, typically these are static and on planar surfaces, we may wish to use visual text as fiducial features for localization. Recent work [2, 3] has presented methods for extracting visual text for better performance in information retrieval and matching. The results in these works provide motivation to further extend the work in particular for 3D localization, when building visual navigation systems for the blind.

In addition to aiding navigation, combining Text with other signage provides users (the blind especially) location context information. When combined with a text-to-speech component, blind users can be alerted as they approach and arrive at known locations, such as health facilities, restaurants or friends and family homes.

Visual-icons denote universal symbols that are in use throughout the world that convey a particular meaning. The Department of Transportation in the US has a set of vehicle and pedestrian symbols that are similar to those used in other countries to depict where a user can find a train, taxi, elevators, escalators, etc. Figure 1 shows 5 sample icons. Such symbols are not universally standardized, but there are efforts to create databases of such symbols [9,10].

Fig. 1. Five Aiga & US DOT symbols from [9]

Augmenting an environment with electronic positioning devices (RFID, NFC) is always a costly endeavor. Using symbols is more cost effective since they can be printed and only requires cameras for detection, which are already widely available. Additionally, these signs can be further augmented as the price of electronic tags and receivers fall.

Signage as used in our paper refers to those signs that are not already covered by Text or Visual Icons. In general signs are natural for matching as they are found both indoors and outdoors. Signs contain logos, text, and symbols that in addition to serving as localization markers also provide contextual information. These especially become useful in recognition and verbal translation for the blind and visually impaired. Here we differentiate visual-icons as those we are matching against a known database of universal symbols, and we restrict it to binary image symbols. With signage we refer more generally to all signs (grayscale and colored), including previously unseen signage (not in a DB of symbols) and logos and brand marks, such as a pizza image outside of a pizzeria or car brand mark at a car dealership.

4   Visual Noun Based Localization: Algorithms

We propose the use of Visual Noun features to aide blind and low-vision users in orientation and navigation tasks. Our system considers a user with a wearable camera (either on the frame of glasses or on a cap). They arrive at a place that is new to them, has recently changed or they have not immediately recognized. The user may survey the area around them by panning their head; blind and low-vision users may also do this as they try to locate distinct sounds or lighting in their surroundings. Our system:

1. captures video of the panned area;
2. registers video image frames to the first frame (will serve as reference);
3. generates a wide field-of-view panorama (see Figures 3 and 4);
4. extracts and matches visual-noun features; and
5. localizes the user in 3D space relative to the visual nouns.

Figure 2 shows a workflow of the entire process. The output available to the user is the detected visual nouns and their meaning through matched visual-icons and text in the surrounding panorama. Further, the user's location relative to the visual nouns can be estimated using the PnP algorithm. The final step is using an interface and text-to-speech so that the user can utilize the discovered information, here we have made no attempt for this final step but we plan to explore it further.

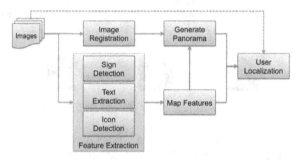

Fig. 2. Visual-noun based navigation framework

4.1   Mapping

To assist users in navigation tasks we must first obtain or build a mapping of the environment they are navigating in. In the US, Google has the StreetView service and Microsoft has a similar service, which they both continue to grow. Google's Street-View provide panoramic views of major city streets. Microsoft's Bing maps provide route-panoramas like the ones in [11] of many major city streets. For indoor and outdoor environments where no pre-existing mappings exist, local mosaic maps can be built using various existing techniques [7,11] which all produce aligned panoramas. In the City College Visual Computing Lab, we have developed software packages to generate panoramic mosaics in real-time with a hand-held camera [7]. Visual nouns in both the conventional images and panoramic images are be annotated with their 3D location information and therefore these visual nouns and their images can be used as the scene model for both recognition and localization.

4.2   Visual Nouns Extraction

Visual-noun features are extracted from images by locating areas where high contrast changes occur. The intuition being that signage, text, and icons used to alert users should have enough contrast so that they catch the viewer's attention. In this work we have used the MSER blob detector [13] which performs well at segmenting regions with high contrast from their backgrounds, as proposed by Chen et. al. [3]. It was found that MSER does not deal well with blurry regions and so the Edge Enhanced Maximally Stable Extremal Regions (EE-MSER) algorithm was proposed in [3] to detect text in natural images. We found a sharpening procedure corrected some of the issues that occur due to motion blur in video.

4.3   Localization

By combining multiple visual nouns with known 3D locations, the viewer's pose can be determined, using a typical pose estimation algorithm such as the PnP algorithm [4] we have used in multi-robots navigation tasks.

A panorama view allows us to match both reliable visual-nouns and traditional features that are common among multiple views. It may be the case that the visible visual-nouns are not enough to perform localization using the PnP algorithm. In these cases we augment the visual-nouns with traditional features that are consistent with the panoramic view and with the projections of the visual-nouns. We use RANSAC to check that all features provide consistent projections onto the panorama.

With the panoramic view we can take 3 algorithmic approaches to assist blind users.

1. Through visual noun detection we can provide the user contextual information about their surroundings. (User can be told what resources/facilities are around them.)
2. The panoramic view provides the user orientation information, which can be used to tell a user in which direction they should turn. (User can be told which sign they are facing.)
3. When the visual noun locations are known and panoramas constructed we can localize the user in 3D space using the PnP algorithm. (User can be told how far from a sign they are.)

5   Experiments and Results

In our experiment we augmented an indoor hallway with 4 visual-icon printouts and we captured a 5 second video recording of the surroundings. Figure 3 shows 3 original video frames. Few visual nouns are often seen in any single view. Figure 4 shows the result from registering the video frames and generating a wide field-of-view panorama of the scene. The panorama contains many more visual-noun features which provide both context and allow us to localize a user.

Fig. 3. Three original frames from the 5 seconds of video

Fig. 4. Wide field-of-view panorama generated from video

Using the panorama we are able to identify signs and text markings across the entire scene. We then use MSER to detect regions of high contrast. Figure 5 shows the resulting detections on various signs. Some false positives are also detected by the MSER algorithm, but can be reduced by matching against a database of visual-icons, and applying geometric text filters as described in [3].

Fig. 5. MSER results on signs

Figure 6 shows a single view and a panorama with markings to the right of the features used in the localization experiment. The red circle markings denote visual nouns, and the green square markings denote additional selected points.

Table 1 shows the results from our localization experiment. The test video was captured with a hand held camera by a viewer at head height. For the single frame, the *Estimated Pose* row gives our manually measured camera pose. The *Single View* row shows the results of using the 4 marked features, showing that we were up to 3 feet off in any one axis, and a few degrees off from the estimate. Using the panorama (with the same reference frame as the single view) we located 8 features which gave us a better overall pose estimate. Using the 8 features from the panorama, our translation result was only 6 inches off from the estimated pose (along the Y axis, the distance to the wall).

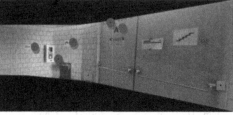

Fig. 6. A single view and a panorama marked with detected visual-nouns in red circles, and additional features in green squares (markings are to the right of features)

Table 1. Visual-Noun localization experiment results

	(Tx, Ty, Tz) inches	(θx, θy, θz) degrees
Estimated Pose	(-30, 140, 65) manual est.	(-90, 20, 180) manual est.
Single View	(3.043, 136.23, 73.39)	(-98.07, 6.05, 179.79)
Panorama	(-29.90, 143.30, 66.29)	(-94.28, 17.59, -179.04)

The green square markings denote feature points which were manually measured and used in localization. With a single view, often insufficient features are detected to robustly run localization. The panorama provides us more features, but we are exploring the use of matched SIFT points as secondary features to the Visual-Nouns to make localization more robust.

6   Conclusions and Discussions

In this paper we have proposed the use of Visual Noun features as a way of providing users, particularly the blind and low-vision, context information that is otherwise difficult for them to obtain. Visual-noun features such as signage, visual-text, and visual-icons, are already found throughout human indoor and outdoor environments. And with the availability of inexpensive cameras and improved vision algorithms, we can readily detect them without significant infrastructure investment. We present a workflow that adapts core robotics and vision algorithms for use with a human user that will be using their own cognitive skill in making navigation decisions. We have presented preliminary experiments and results that demonstrate the capabilities of using Visual Nouns for navigation and localization tasks.

There are many open questions we are still exploring in making this system useful to a user. The first is the interface the user would interact with. We recognize that this is crucial to successfully aide users and we have focused in this paper on ensuring that the contextual and 3D location information available is in a human understandable format.

Acknowledgments. This work is supported by US National Science Foundation Emerging Frontiers in Research and Innovation Program under Award No. EFRI-1137172, and City SEEDs: City College 2011 President Grant for Interdisciplinary Scientific Research Collaborations.

References

1. Wang, S., Tian, Y.: Indoor Signage Detection Based on Saliency Map and Bipartite Graph Matching. In: Intl. Workshop on Biomedical and Health Informatics, BHI (2011)
2. Schroth, G., Hilsenbeck, S., Huitl, R., Schweiger, F., Steinbach, E.: Exploiting Text-related Features for Content-based Image Retrieval. In: IEEE Intl. Symposium on Multimedia (ISM), Dana Point, CA, USA (December 2011)
3. Chen, H., Tsai, S.S., Schroth, G., Chen, D.M., Grzeszczuk, R., Girod, B.: Robust Text Detection in Natural Images with Edge-enhanced Maximally Stable Extremal Regions. In: 2011 IEEE Intl. Conference on Image Processing, Brussels (September 2011)
4. Feng, Y., Zhu, Z., Xiao, J.: Self-Localization of a Heterogeneous Multi-Robot Team in Constrained 3D Space. In: IEEE/RSJ Intl. Conference on Intelligent Robots and Systems, San Diego, CA, USA, October 29-November 2 (2007)
5. Binding, D., Labrosse, F.: Visual Local Navigation Using Warped Panoramic Images. In: Proceedings of Towards Autonomous Robotic Systems, Guildford, UK, pp. 19–26 (2006)
6. Zhu, Z., Karuppiah, D.R., Riseman, E.M., Hanson, A.R.: Keep Smart, Omnidirectional Eyes on You - Adaptive Panoramic Stereo Vision for Human Tracking with Cooperative Mobile Robots. Robotics and Automation Magazine, Special Issue on Panoramic Robots 14(11), 69–78 (2004)
7. Zhu, Xu, G., Riseman, E., Hanson, A.: Fast Construction of Dynamic and Multi-Resolution 360° Panoramas from Video Sequences. Image & Vision Computing Journal 24(1), 13–26 (2006)
8. Zhu, Z., Huang, T.S. (eds.): Multimodal Surveillance: Sensors, Algorithms and Systems. Artech House Publisher (July 2007)
9. Symbol-Signs, http://www.aiga.org/symbol-signs/
10. The Noun Project, http://www.thenounproject.org/
11. Zheng, J.Y.: Digital Route Panoramas. IEEE Multimedia 10, part 3, 57–67 (2003)
12. Forssen, P.-E.: Maximally Stable Colour Regions for Recognition and Matching. In: IEEE Conference on Computer Vision and Pattern Recognition, CVPR 2007, June 17-22, pp. 1–8 (2007)
13. Vedaldi, A., Fulkerson, B.: VLFeat, An Open and Portable Library of Computer Vision Algorithms (2008), http://www.vlfeat.org
14. Matas, J., Chum, O., Urban, M., Pajdla, T.: Robust wide baseline stereo from maximally stable extremal regions. In: Proc. of British Machine Vision Conference, pp. 384–396 (2002)
15. Quan, L., Lan, Z.: Linear N-point camera pose determination. IEEE Transactions on Pattern Analysis and Machine Intelligence 21(8), 774–780 (1999)
16. Hartley, R., Zisserman, A.: Multiple View Geometry in Computer Vision. Cambridge University Press (2003)

Towards a Real-Time System for Finding and Reading Signs for Visually Impaired Users

Huiying Shen and James M. Coughlan

The Smith-Kettlewell Eye Research Institute, San Francisco, CA
{hshen,coughlan}@ski.org

Abstract. Printed text is a ubiquitous form of information that is inaccessible to many blind and visually impaired people unless it is represented in a non-visual form such as Braille. OCR (optical character recognition) systems have been used by blind and visually impaired persons for some time to read documents such as books and bills; recently this technology has been packaged in a porta-ble device, such as the smartphone-based kReader Mobile (from K–NFB Read-ing Technology, Inc.), which allows the user to photograph a document such as a restaurant menu and hear the text read aloud. However, while this kind of OCR system is useful for reading documents at close range (which may still re-quire the user to take a few photographs, waiting a few seconds each time to hear the results, to take one that is correctly centered), it is not intended for signs. (Indeed, the KNFB manual, see knfbreader.com/upgrades_mobile.php , lists "posted signs such as signs on transit vehicles and signs in shop windows" in the "What the Reader Cannot Do" subsection.) Signs provide valuable loca-tion-specific information that is useful for wayfinding, but are usually viewed from a distance and are difficult or impossible to find without adequate vision and rapid feedback.

We describe a prototype smartphone system that finds printed text in clut-tered scenes, segments out the text from video images acquired by the smart-phone for processing by OCR, and reads aloud the text read by OCR using TTS (text-to-speech). Our system detects and reads aloud text from video images, and thereby provides *real-time feedback* (in contrast with systems such as the kReader Mobile) that helps the user find text with minimal prior knowledge about its location. We have designed a novel audio-tactile user interface that helps the user hold the smartphone level and assists him/her with locating any text of interest and approaching it, if necessary, for a clearer image. Preliminary experiments with two blind users demonstrate the feasibility of the approach, which represents the first real-time sign reading system we are aware of that has been expressly designed for blind and visually impaired users.

Keywords: visual impairment, blindness, assistive technology, OCR, smart-phone, informational signs.

1 Introduction and Related Work

OCR is designed to process images that consist almost entirely of text, with very little non-text clutter, such as would be obtained from a picture (e.g., acquired by a flat-bed

K. Miesenberger et al. (Eds.): ICCHP 2012, Part II, LNCS 7383, pp. 41–47, 2012.

image scanner) of a single page of a book. A growing body of research [2] has focused on the complementary problem of finding text in cluttered images, such as are encountered by a person searching for a sign, so that the text can be isolated in each image in order to be processed effectively by OCR. Some research [4] has specifically tackled the added challenge of finding and reading text on a portable device, and smartphone apps such as Word Lens (http://questvisual.com/) have been developed, which are able to find and read scene text at several video frames per second, but are intended for use by people with normal vision.

A comparatively small amount of work has addressed the specific problem of finding and reading signs or other non-document text for blind or visually impaired people. Yi and Tian [6] have focused on computer vision algorithms for finding text in complex backgrounds (e.g., found in typical indoor and outdoor urban scenes), training their algorithms on an image dataset collected by ten blind users, but have not yet addressed the formidable user interface issues posed by a full system that helps a visually impaired user find text and have it read aloud to him/her. The "Smart Telescope" SBIR project from Blindsight Corporation (www.blindsight.com) is a novel system to help a person with low vision find and read text by automatically detecting text regions in a scene acquired by a wearable camera and presenting the regions one at a time to the user, using a head-mounted display that zooms into the text to enable him/her to read it. Finally, [3] reports studies with three blind users of a real-time computer vision-based smartphone system for locating special "color marker" signs, describing the strategies employed by the users to find each marker, walk towards it and touch it. While color markers are specially designed for ease of detection by the system, and are therefore much easier to find and read than the kinds of text signs considered in our application, the search strategies adopted by the users underscore the challenges of finding any kind of sign with a camera-based system.

2   Finding Text in Images and Performing OCR

The foundation of our prototype system is a processing pipeline that includes a computer vision algorithm for finding text in images, followed by a standard OCR package run on the text regions identified by this algorithm.

The text detection algorithm, which builds on previous work by the authors [5], processes a video frame (which has 640x480 resolution, see Fig. 1a) and converts it to grayscale for subsequent processing. "Blob"-like structures in the image (Fig. 1b) are detected in the image, one blob typically being extracted for each character of text (in addition to many other blobs corresponding to non-text clutter in the image). Blobs whose shape and/or size are incompatible with that of text characters are removed, and the remaining blobs are searched for groups of consistently sized ones that are aligned in a way that is consistent with a horizontal word or line of text. This procedure is applied to the image at both polarities (for detecting light text on a dark background and vice versa), yielding blob groups that are classified as text groups, which form candidate text regions demarcated by rectangles (Fig. 1c), referred to as "text boxes."

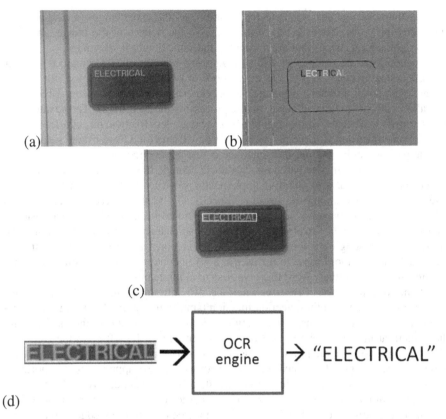

Fig. 1. Main stages of text detection and recognition. (a) Sample indoor image taken by smartphone. (b) "Blob" regions detected in image (each blob is given a separate, random color for visibility). (c) Detected text region drawn as a "text box" (in yellow). (d) When this text region is input to OCR it is correctly read as "ELECTRICAL."

Each text box forms a cropped portion of the image that is sent to the Tesseract OCR engine (http://code.google.com/p/tesseract-ocr/), an open source OCR package that runs in real time on the smartphone (Fig. 1d). Some OCR output contains errors, either because it results from a false positive text box (i.e., it is reported incorrectly as a text region), or because the text box is valid but OCR is unable to process it correctly. To reduce the number of spurious or incorrect OCR output strings to communicate to the user, we apply a simple filtering procedure to discard strings with unlikely characters or character combinations.

3   System and User Interface

Our software was programmed in C++ and implemented on an LG-P990 Android smartphone processing video frames using the smartphone's camera. After processing each video image frame as described above, we read aloud each text string using TTS.

If more than one text string is detected in an image, the text strings are read aloud in the following order: from the top of the image to the bottom of the image, and from left to right among strings that are at roughly the same height in the image.

Depending on the complexity of the images and amount of text contained in them, the processing proceeds at a rate as high as one or two frames per second (for simpler images with small amounts of texture). After experimentation we chose a TTS setting that allows all text to be read aloud, before processing the next frame. The advantage of this setting is that scenes with longer strings of text are less likely to be cut off, but at the cost of sometimes delaying the processing of a new frame for a few or more seconds.

The philosophy behind our user interface is that some errors are inevitable with any OCR system, especially one based on a handheld camera; the simplest way to overcome the errors is for the user to obtain multiple readings of each text sign over time and arrive at a consensus among the readings. Specifically, spurious readings (e.g., due to false positives from background clutter) can be ignored because of their inconsistency over time; minor reading errors (e.g., a few misread characters in a word) can often be "repaired" by waiting for a correct reading (which is more likely to be read consistently, and usually makes more sense to the user in a given context, than an incorrect reading) or inferring the most likely word that gives rise to multiple misreadings.

To improve the basic TTS user interface, we introduced three novel functions. First, we implemented a tilt detection function (similar to that in [1]), using the smartphone accelerometer to sense the direction of gravity, which allows the user to point the camera arbitrarily above or below the horizon and to the left or to the right, but issues a vibration warning if the camera is rotated clockwise or counterclockwise about its line of sight. This maximizes the chances that text appears roughly horizontal in the image (as required for successful detection). Second, any text string that originates from a text box that is close to the border of the image is read aloud in a low pitch, to warn the user that important text may be cut off at the edge of the image. (For instance, a "No smoking permitted" sign may be detected as "smoking permitted" if the first word falls outside of the image.) Finally, any text string corresponding to text that is sufficiently small in the image is read aloud in a high pitch, which warns the user that such text may be incorrectly recognized (and that the user should approach closer if possible to get a more reliable reading).

4   Experimental Results and User Testing

We explained the purpose and operation of the system to two completely blind volunteer subjects. Particular emphasis was placed on the importance of moving the camera slowly to avoid motion blur, ensuring the camera lens was not covered (e.g., by the user's fingers), and thoroughly sweeping the desired target region to accommodate the camera's limited field of view. After a brief training session with a handheld sign, we took the subjects to a conference room in which ten text signs were posted along two adjoining walls. The signs were high contrast (black and white), of varying font, font size and polarity (i.e., dark text on light background or vice versa), and were placed at approximately chest level; they contained the type of text that might be expected in an office building, such as "Room 590" or "Main entrance." The subjects were told to search both walls for an unknown number of signs, standing a few meters away from the signs (i.e., out of reach), and to tell the experimenter the content of each sign detected.

Fig. 2. Scene from experiment shows signs posted on wall with blind volunteer holding system

The first subject took under six minutes to search for the signs, and reported six of them perfectly correctly. Of the remaining four signs, two were completely missed, the sign labeled "Dr. Samuels" elicited a TTS response of "Samuels" (which was audible to the experimenter but not the subject) and the "Meeting in Session" sign gave rise to the words "Meeting" and "section" (though they were not uttered together). The second subject searched for the signs in about the same length of time, but only reported three of them perfectly, in part because he moved the camera quickly while searching for them. The pattern of errors he encountered among the other seven signs is telling: for instance, the sign labeled "Exam Room 150" was detected and read aloud correctly, but he was unable to understand the word "exam" (perhaps because there was no context to prepare him for it); and he reported "D L Samuels meeting in session" as a sign, which is an incorrect combination of two signs, "Dr. Samuels" (in which the system misread "Dr.") and "Meeting in Session." Of the three special user interface functions we devised, the tilt sensor appeared to be most consistently useful to the subjects, while the situations requiring the use of the low/high pitch signals were less common.

While the results show that the system needs to be improved substantially before it becomes practical, the study provides proof of concept of the approach and provides insight into the most important problems to be addressed. First, the main challenge in using the system was finding text in an unknown location, which required the user to patiently scan large areas. Slow processing speeds (especially on images of high-texture regions), combined with motion blur (exacerbated by low lighting conditions where the experiment was conducted), forced the user to scan slowly. False positive text detections created a significant amount of spurious TTS responses, which further slowed down the process. Somewhat surprisingly, even when the system functioned perfectly, the TTS output was not always interpreted correctly by the user. Finally, the simple procedure we used for deciding the order in which to announce multiple text lines was helpful, but did not address the need to announce the contents of each sign separately from the others. We discuss possible solutions to these problems, which we are currently implementing, in the next section.

5   Conclusion

We have demonstrated a novel smartphone system to find and read aloud text signs for blind and visually impaired users. A prototype system has been implemented on the Android smartphone, which includes special user interface features to help guide the search for text. We have conducted preliminary experiments with blind volunteers to test the system, demonstrating its feasibility.

We are planning several future improvements and extensions to the system. First and foremost, speed and accuracy improvements to the text detection algorithm will make the system faster and create fewer false positive readings; a faster algorithm may also permit processing of higher resolution video images, which would enable signs to be detected from farther away. The ability to detect text that is poorly resolved (because of small size or motion blur) would also permit text detection in some cases when the text is not clear enough to be read. A more efficient user interface might then signal the presence of text with a brief audio tone, help the user center and/or approach the text and then have it read aloud. Multiple text lines will be clustered into distinct sign regions, which will help both with centering of signs and intelligibility of the TTS output, and the user will be able to hear the TTS output repeated for any given sign upon request. Eventually we envision a system that analyzes an entire scene as an image panorama (i.e., mosaic), acquired by panning the camera back and forth, which is able to seamlessly read lines of text that extend beyond the borders of any individual image frame.

Acknowledgments. The authors acknowledge support by the National Institutes of Health from grants No. 1 R21 EY021643-01, 1 R01 EY018210-01A1 and 1 R01 EY018890-01, and by the Department of Education, NIDRR grant number H133E110004. We would like to thank Dr. Ender Tekin and Dr. Vidya Murali for many helpful conversations about the paper.

References

1. Ivanchenko, V., Coughlan, J., Shen, H.: Real-Time Walk Light Detection with a Mobile Phone. In: Miesenberger, K., Klaus, J., Zagler, W., Karshmer, A. (eds.) ICCHP 2010. LNCS, vol. 6180, pp. 229–234. Springer, Heidelberg (2010)
2. Liang, J., Doermann, D., Li, H.: Camera-based analysis of text and documents: a survey. International Journal on Document Analysis and Recognition 7, 83–200 (2005)
3. Manduchi, R., Kurniawan, S., Bagherinia, H.: Blind Guidance Using Mobile Computer Vision: A Usability Study. In: ACM SIGACCESS Conference on Computers and Accessibility, ASSETS (2010)

4. Pilu, M., Pollard, S.: A light-weight text image processing method for handheld embedded cameras. In: British Machine Vision Conference (2002)

5. Sanketi, P., Shen, H., Coughlan, J.: Localizing Blurry and Low-Resolution Text in Natural Images. In: 2011 IEEE Workshop on Applications of Computer Vision (WACV 2011), Kona, Hawaii (January 2011)

6. Yi, C., Tian, Y.: Assistive Text Reading from Complex Background for Blind Persons. In: Iwamura, M., Shafait, F. (eds.) CBDAR 2011. LNCS, vol. 7139, pp. 15–28. Springer, Heidelberg (2012)

User Requirements for Camera-Based Mobile Applications on Touch Screen Devices for Blind People

Yoonjung Choi and Ki-Hyung Hong

Department of Computer Science, Sungshin University, Seoul, S. Korea
li31122@naver.com
kihyung.hong@gmail.com

Abstract. This paper presents user requirements for camera-based mobile applications in touch screen devices for blind people. We conducted a usability testing for a color reading application on Android OS. In the testing, participants were asked to evaluate three different types of interfaces of the application in order to identify user requirements and preferences. The results of the usability testing presented that (1) users preferred short depth of menu hierarchy, (2) users needed both manual and automatic camera shooting modes although they preferred manual to automatic mode, (3) the initial audio help was more useful for users than in–time help, (4) users wanted the OS supported screen reader function to be turned off during the color reading, and (5) users required tactile feedback to identify touch screen boundary.

Keywords: Accessibility, User Requirements, Camera-Based Mobile Applications, Visual Impairment.

1 Introduction

Touch screen-based mobile devices with cameras become increasingly prominent in the consumer market. Especially, camera-based mobile applications are very useful to blind people in their daily lives. The camera-based applications[1-4] such as color, patternand object reading typically consist of two different modes: the camera (main function) mode and the application setting/help mode. The main function mode usually consists of the following four steps: (1) focusing on the target object, (2) taking the snapshot, (3) identifying the designated properties and then (4) talking back the identified properties. The application setting/help mode includes the following three components: (1) initial and in-time helps, (2) audio feedback controls, and (3) language selections. However, those applications are still inconvenient for blind people to operate independently. In this study, we examined the user requirements of those camera-based applications for blind people based on a user study.

2 Related Works

There have been a lot of works [5], [6] to enhance accessibility of touch screen. Most of them focus on how to support accessible touch gestures to navigate list-based

K. Miesenberger et al. (Eds.): ICCHP 2012, Part II, LNCS 7383, pp. 48–51, 2012.

information, how to make a selection among the listed items, and how to activate the selected item. Kane and colleagues [5] proposed the Slide Rule, which is a set of multi-touch gestures to enhance accessibility for list-based information applications such as e-mail, phone, and music selection. In this study, we put more focus on the accessible usage flow than the accessible touch gesture of the camera-based applications. In the setting/help mode, accessibility of camera-based applications depends mostly on the screen reader function embedded in OS such as iOS's Voice Over and Android's Eyes-free (Talk-back). Using OS supported accessibility functions for camera-based applications is uncomfortable since the simultaneous audio feedbacks from OS and the application especially from step (4) of the main function are mixed up frequently.

3   User Study

3.1   Participants

In order to identify accessible user interface requirements for camera-based mobile applications on touch screen devices, we conducted a user study in which 5 blind people (3 female and 2 male) participated. All participants had used a mobile device on a daily basis. But only one of them had an experience of using a touch screen device (iPhone). All participants had used a screen reader function on their PCs for more than 8 hours a day.

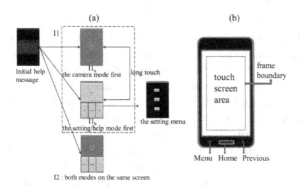

Fig. 1. (a) is three interface for user study and (b) is front side of typical mobile device.Procedures

For the user study, we implemented two different interfaces (I1 and I2 as shown in Fig.1(a)) for a color reading application on an Android mobile device. Each of them provided their own initial help message to explain how to operate the application. The main difference between these two interfaces was the way to change modes (i.e., from the main function to the setting/help mode.) In I1, users use a long touch (tab and hold more than a specific time period) to move from main function mode to the setting/help mode presented on the same screen, thus users can select one of the modes using their finger navigation on the screen. With these two interfaces, we prepared 3 usage scenarios - two scenarios (Il_a and Il_b) from I1 and one scenario from I2. After playing the initial help message (it might be skipped depending on the application's setting), Il_a presented the main function (camera) mode as a default, while Il_b presents the setting/help mode as a default.

In the camera mode, each interface had two different shooting methods: automatic and manual. In the automatic shooting mode, the camera took snapshots automatically at a predefined time-interval. On the other hand, in the manual shooting mode, the camera took a shot only when the user tabbed on the screen.

3.2   Results : User Requirements Analysis

After each participant performed 6 tasks (3 scenarios and 2 manual/automatic modes) twice using a Samsung Galaxy Player, all participants were asked to answer a questionnaire to identify user requirements and preferences. Based on the results of the questionnaires and the user performance observations, we found the following accessibility requirements for camera-based applications.

Table 1. Preference priorities

Preference Priority	First	Second	Third
Il_a	0	2	3
Il_b	1	2	2
I2	4	1	0

- *Prefer I2.* : Four participants selected I2 as the most preferable interface (Table 1). They felt uncomfortable for explicit change of modes. The shorter depth of menu hierarchy the interface had, the more comfortable people felt.
- *Prefer manual mode to automatic mode, but want to support both.* : All participants preferred manual to automatic shooting mode, but they mentioned that the automatic shooting mode would be useful in some situations.
- *Initial audio help message are more important than in-time help.* : All participants were satisfied with the initial audio help message. We also provided in-time help for each menu. The color reading application was relatively simple to use, so the compact but specific initial audio help was sufficient for users to use the application.
- *Turn off the OS supported screen readers.* : Most camera-based applications have their own audio feedback. If the OS supported screen reader is running simultaneously with the applications, users hardly recognize the sound from the applications be-cause audio feedbacks from both the OS supported screen reader and the applications are mixed up frequently.
- *Require tactile feedback for touch screen boundary.* : There is no physical boundary between the touch screen and the frame area on almost all smart devices, and that is the major barrier for blind people to use the smart devices. Usually, there are three buttons ("Menu", "Home", and "Previous") at the bottom of the Android devices. "Menu" and "Previous" buttons cannot be identified by blind people

(see Fig. 1(b)) without tactile or auditory feedback. Eventually, participants made many unwanted selections of these buttons during the navigation of (menu) items on the screen.

4   Conclusion and Future Work

Through this study, we found important user requirements of camera-based mobile applications for blind people. We are currently designing a new user interface for people who are blind by applying the results of this study, and we have a plan to conduct a usability testing for the new interface.

Acknowledgments. This work was supported by the Technology Innovation Program (100036459, Development of center to support QoLT industry and infrastructures) funded by the MKE/KEIT, Korea.

References

1. Kutiyanawala, A., Kulyukin, V.: Eyes-Free Barcode Localization and Decoding for Visually Impaired Mobile Phone Users. In: 2010 International Conference on Image Processing, Computer Vision and Pattern Recognition, vol. 1, pp. 130–135 (2010)
2. VOICEYE (2010), http://www.voiceye.com/eng
3. ColorIdentifier (2010), http://www.greengar.com/apps/color-identifier
4. Sudol, J., Dialameh, O., Blanchard, C., Dorcey, T.: LookTel-A Comprehensive Platform for Computer-Aided Visual Assistance. In: Computer Vision and Pattern Recognition Workshops 2010, pp. 73–80 (2010)
5. Kane, S., Bighanm, J., Wobbrock, J.: Slide Rule: Making Mobile Touch Screens Accessible to Blind People using Multi-Touch Interaction Techniques. In: 10th International ACM SIGACCESS Conference on Computers and Accessibility 2008, pp. 73–80 (2008)
6. Kane, S., Bighanm, J., Wobbrock, J., Ladner, R.: Usable Gestures for Blind People: Understanding Preference and Performance. In: CHI 2011, pp. 413–422 (2011)
7. Oliveira, J., Guerreiro, T., Nicolau, H., Jorge, J., Gonçalves, D.: Blind People and Mobile Touch based Text-Entry: Acknowledging the Need for Different Flavors. In: 10th International ACM SIGACCESS Conference 2011, pp. 179–186 (2011)
8. Tian, Y., Yuan, S.: Clothes Matching for Blind and Color Blind People. In: Miesenberger, K., Klaus, J., Zagler, W., Karshmer, A. (eds.) ICCHP 2010, Part II. LNCS, vol. 6180, pp. 324–331. Springer, Heidelberg (2010)
9. Shaik, A., Hossain, G., Yeasin, M.: Design, Development and Performance Evaluation of Reconfigured Mobile Android Phone for People Who are Blind or Visually Impaired. In: SIGDOG 2010, pp. 27–29 (2010)
10. Lee, H.P., Huang, J.T., Chen, C.H., Sheu, T.F.: Building a Color Recognizer System on the Smart Mobile Device for Visually Impaired People. In: 6th International Multi-Conference on Computing in the Global Information Technology 2011, pp. 95–98 (2011)

A Route Planner Interpretation Service
for Hard of Hearing People

Mehrez Boulares and Mohamed Jemni

Research Laboratory of Technologies of Information and Communication
& Electrical Engineering (LaTICE),
Ecole Supérieure des Sciences et Techniques de Tunis,
5, Av. Taha Hussein, B.P. 56, Bab Mnara 1008, Tunis, Tunisia
mehrez.boulares@gmail.com,
Mohamed.jemni@fst.rnu.tn

Abstract. The advancement of technology over the past fifteen years has opened many new doors to make our daily life easier. Nowadays, smart phones provide many services such as everywhere access to the social networks, video communication through 3G networks and the GPS (global positioning system) service. For instance, using GPS technology and Google maps services; user can find a route planner for traveling by foot, car, bike or public transport. Google map is based on KML which contains textual information to describe streets or places name and this is not accessible to persons with special needs like hard of hearing people. However, hearing impairment persons have very specific needs related to the learning and understanding process of any written language. Consequently, this service is not accessible to them. In this paper we propose a new approach that makes accessible KML information on android mobile devices. We rely on cloud computing and virtual agent technology subtitled with SignWriting to interpret automatically textual information on the map according to the user current position.

Keywords: Android, SignWriting, Cloud Computing, Virtual Agent, Google map, GPS.

1 Introduction

In the world, there are around 70 million people with hearing deficiencies (information from World Federation of the Deaf http://www.wfdeaf.org/). Most of them prefer to communicate with sign language rather than with words [11] because they have many difficulties related to the learning process [8]. Consequently, all services based on textual information are not accessible to them. In our context, we focused on the route planner information based on the Google map service. We use this service to find a route planner for traveling by foot, car, bike or public transport. However, the Google map service[1] gives us the route information as textual form

---

[1] KML is a file format used to display geographic data in an Earth browser such as Google Earth, Google Maps, and Google Maps for mobile.

K. Miesenberger et al. (Eds.): ICCHP 2012, Part II, LNCS 7383, pp. 52–58, 2012.

(as shown in Figure1) to be used by developers to place markers, to draw the route path on the map and to give us the route planner as audio indication. Consequently, hearing impairment persons cannot use this kind of services.

In order to make this service accessible to the hearing impairment persons, we built a solution that allows android devices users to use a route planner based on sign language interpretation. In this context, this paper presents a new approach that allows an automatic interpretation of the KML route planner information using sign language. We rely on virtual agent technology [1] as artificial signer with a SignWriting [9] subtitling for automatic interpretation of textual information.

This paper is organized as follow: the next section is dedicated to the previous works. The section 3 is devoted to describe the benefits of our automatic sign lan-guage interpretation service. In section 4, we describe our contribution, the approach used and the architecture of our system. Finally, we give a conclusion and some perspectives.

Fig. 1. Part of KML route planner information from Edinburgh to Sunderland United Kingdom.

2   Previous Works

Up today, there are many works for people with special needs. For example, a mobile navigation and orientation system for blind users in a Metrobus Environment [7]. This is a mobile assistant to spatially locate and orient passengers of a Metrobus system in the city of Mexico. In our context, we are interested on hearing impairment people. However, most of previous works on sign language interpretation are based on two main techniques: pre-synthesized animation and generated animation. The first one relies on motion capture pre-recorded animation using avatar technology or video interpretation [4 - 5]. For example, Mathsigner or DIVA framework [2], are based on pre-recorded animation using virtual agent technology. This approach depends on expensive material to build signs and decreases the user interactivity to create new signs according to the chosen community. Also there are some works deployed on mobile phones which use video support such as ASL dictionary application or sign language idioms application on android OS which includes 70 idioms/phrases and sentence examples in American Sign Language to teach sign language.

The second one consists on automatic and real-time generation of animations. In this area there are some works as eSIGN, signSMITH [10]. ESIGN (see Fig1B) is based on synthetic signing works by sending motion commands in the form of written codes for the Avatar to be animated. SignSMITH provides a gesture builder to create signs with elementary movement. In general, these works are not dedicated to interpret automatically written text on mobile devices. In other words, there are no mobile services which provide an automatic sign language interpretation of textual information as the route planner. Consequently, if we want to interpret the route planner information, we must purchase dedicated devices such as GPS Ranger gadget. This gadget provides a GPS touring in American Sign Language ASL; it allows a way finder and directional information in Austin, Texas based on video support. This kind of gadget is expensive and depends on specific sign language interpretation such as ASL. Therefore, for example French or Arabic hearing impairment persons cannot use this kind of devices.

3   The Benefits of Our Automatic Sign Language Interpretation Service

Our automatic sign language interpretation service is based on WebSign project developed on our laboratory. This is a Web application that relies on virtual agent technology to interpret automatically written text to sign language. However, this approach uses a dictionary of words and signs saved on Sign modeling language SML format (as shown on Figure 2b) [6]. The SML is created to describe the gesture sequence and to create signs to be saved on dictionary. The dictionary can be made in an incremental way by users who propose signs corresponding to words. The originality of our approach is the collaborative approach used to enrich our multiple-community dictionary.

3.1   Multi-community Approach

As the primary communication means used by members of deaf community, sign language is not a derivative language. It is a complete language with its own unique grammar [3]. However, some specific words are interpreted differently from community to another. Consequently, if users share a global dictionary the interpretation lost the truth information meaning. To resolve this problem, we introduced the concept of community. A community is a group of users that can build and share a common sign language dictionary. User can create his signs on his own community and he can share signs with others.

3.2 Collaborative Approach

Our service relies on a collaborative approach to enrich dictionary. Using this strategy, every user can contributes in the creation of new signs according to his region. Our aim is to cover all route planner information in the map. Consequently, we make available a path finder service based on sign language interpretation that allows hard of hearing persons to navigate on the mobile phone map. The creation process of signs is based on WebSign interface. User can create his sign through our web interface [6]. As shown in Figure2a, we rely on virtual agent technology to create animation in SML format.

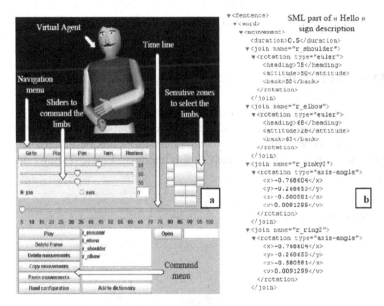

Fig. 2. (a) Web tool to create signs (b) SML description

3.3 Mobile Solution

The route planner service relies primarily on mobility. For this reason we built a mobile service that allows a real time route planner interpretation. This service allows a current position localization using Global Positioning System GPS. User introduces his destination using our input SignWriting interface (as shown in Figure3) and the system generates the route planner interpretation based on virtual agent subtitled with SignWriting.

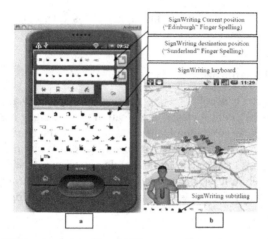

Fig. 3. (a) The SignWriting input interface (b) The route planner interpretation interface on the map

4   Our Contribution

In order to create a route planner interpretation system, we have developed first a web service. The aim of this service is to ensure interaction between the mobile client and our interpretation server. Second, we have implemented a mobile solution on Android OS that provides an accessible and easy to use interface. Figure 4 shows our system architecture.

4.1   Architecture

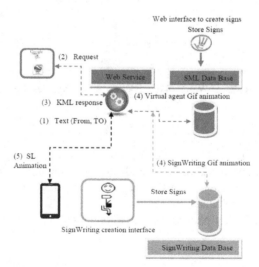

Fig. 4. Our system architecture

4.2 Web Service Interpretation System

Our approach relies on a web service interpretation system using cloud computing technology and android client application. Cloud computing refers to the on-demand provision of computational resources (data, software) via a computer network, rather than from a local computer. This approach is adapted to be used by minimal computational resource. Users or clients can submit task to our service provider without knowing either the location or the type of background processing.

In our context the computational resource are dedicated to sign language computational processing. However, our service depends mainly on 3D rendering and this kind of processing is closely related to CPU computing power. As shown in Figure 4, this approach gives us opportunity to use mobile device as a client and to take advantage of computing power offered by this service. However, the idea is based on textual information extracted from KML file. The android client detects automatically the user current position using GPS. User introduces the destination address in SignWriting format to be converted in textual information and submitted to our web service. This service sends a request to the Google map web service to obtain the KML file. The received response will be parsed and generated as a GIF animation format subtitled with SignWriting. The generation process is based on the conversion of SML animation to GIF 3D rendering format. However, the output animation will be sent to the client as a GIF animated file which integrates the sign language virtual agent interpretation subtitled with SignWriting. Figure 4 shows also that user can create signs using Web Sign and SignWriting creation interfaces to be stored in data bases.

4.3 Android Client

We developed a mobile client application under android operating system. This application uses mainly the GPS service to detect the current user position. As shown in figure 4, our application interprets the route planner information received from our service using HTTP protocol. We use the Google map technology to draw the path from the current to destination position. Our sign language interpretation changes according to the current user position.

The virtual agent allows a real time interpretation of the nearest next position to in-form user that he must turn right or left etc. Our application allows also a finger spelling interpretation of places name if there is no sign language translation. Furthermore, this solution chooses automatically the community according to the local mobile phone language and offers a virtual agent interpretation subtitled with SignWriting to improve the translation meaning.

5   Conclusion and Future Works

In this paper we presented a system to make a route planner information accessible to hard of hearing persons with low English literacy. This system is based on a real time interpretation service that allows a virtual agent interpretation subtitled with sign writing. We showed that our solution offers the possibility to create signs from our WebSign interface and SignWriting interface. We have tested this system in our laboratory and we have succeeded to introduce a set of signs in the dictionary according to some places in Tunisia. During the evaluation of our work, we have seen that we need to add other signs and some new functionalities. In particular, we can improve the 3D rendering quality. Also we can optimize the HTTP interactions between the mobile solution and the web service to reduce the bandwidth use. In future work, we will focus on improvement of the virtual character quality to support facial and body expression and we will develop other client versions on other mobile operating systems such as Iphone OS and Black Berry OS.

References

1. Albert, L.H.: Web 2.0 and Virtual World Technologies: A Growing Impact on IS Education. Journal of Information Systems Education 20(2), 137–144 (2009)
2. Annelies, B., Jean-Paul, S., Jean-Claude, M., Cyril, V.: Diva, une architecture pour le support des agents gestuels interactifs sur internet. Technique et Science Informatiques 29(7), 777–806 (2010)
3. Bouchard, D.: Sign Languages & Language Universals: The Status of Order & Position in Grammar. Sign Language Studies 91, 101–160 (1996)
4. Dreuw, P., Stein, D., Deselaers, T., Rybach, D., Zahedi, M., Bungeroth, J., Ney, H.: Spoken Language Processing Techniques for Sign Language Recognition and Translation. Technology and Disability 20(2), 121–133 (2008)
5. Efthimiou, E., Fotinea, S., Hanke, T., Glauert, J., Bowden, R., Braffort, A., Collet, C., Maragos, P., Goudenove, F.: DICTA-SIGN: Sign Language Recognition. In: The Representation and Processing of Sign Languages: Corpora and Sign Language Technologies (CSLT 2010), Valletta, Malta, pp. 172–178 (May 2010)
6. Jemni, M., Elghoul, O.: A System to Make Signs Using Collaborative Approach. In: Miesenberger, K., Klaus, J., Zagler, W.L., Karshmer, A.I. (eds.) ICCHP 2008. LNCS, vol. 5105, pp. 670–677. Springer, Heidelberg (2008), doi:10.1007/978-3-540-70540-6_96
7. Mata, F., Jaramillo, A., Claramunt, C.: A mobile navigation and orientation system for blind users in a metrobus environment. In: Tanaka, K., Fröhlich, P., Kim, K.-S. (eds.) W2GIS 2011. LNCS, vol. 6574, pp. 94–108. Springer, Heidelberg (2010), doi:10.1007/978-3-642-19173-2_9
8. Marschark, M., Harris, M.: Success and failure in learning to read: The special case of deaf children. Journal: Reading Comprehension Difficulties: Processes and Intervention, 279–300 (1996)
9. Official SignWriting web site, http://www.signwriting.org
10. Official Sign Smith web site, http://www.vcom3d.com
11. Wheatley, M., Pabsch, A.: Sign Language in Europe. In: 4th Workshop on the Representation and Processing of Sign Languages: Corpora and Sign Language Technologies, LREC, Malta, pp. 251–255 (2010)

Translating Floor Plans into Directions

Martin Spindler[1], Michael Weber[2], Denise Prescher[1], Mei Miao[1],
Gerhard Weber[1], and Georgios Ioannidis[2]

[1] Chair of Human-Computer Interaction,
Technische Universität Dresden,
Nöthnitzer Straße 46, D-01187 Dresden, Germany
{spindler,presche,mm33,gw9}@mail.zih.tu-dresden.de
[2] IN2 search interfaces development Ltd,
Fahrenheitstrasse 1, D-28359 Bremen, Germany
{mw,gi}@in-two.com

Abstract. Project Mobility supports blind and low-vision people in exploring
and wayfinding indoors. Facility operators are enabled to annotate floor plans to
provide accessible content. An accessible smartphone app is developed for presenting spatial information and directions on the go, regarding the user's position. This paper describes some of the main goals and features of the system
and the results of first user tests we conducted at a large airport.

Keywords: accessibility, blind, low-vision, indoor, localization, directions,
floor plans, annotation, mobile, Mobility.

1   Introduction

Project Mobility[1] addresses blind and low-vision people and their need for more independence in indoor exploration and wayfinding. Within unfamiliar public buildings,
such as unknown airport terminals, large train stations, hotels or administrative buildings, vision impaired visitors need an adequate knowledge supply as they can't read
posted signs and floor plans. Our goal is to offer a solution for users who, besides following routes to reach destinations, want to understand the arrangement of areas and
interior in public buildings to discover more possibilities were to go and what to do.

Spatial information is valuable for all visitors as it helps to get an overview of directions and major facilities within buildings. Other research projects like BAIM[2]
have shown that especially mobility impaired people need more and better data about
stations, like detailed interchange maps [1]. But blind and visually impaired people
face even more challenges due to lack of appropriate GIS data and insufficient accessibility of maps or floor plans or relevant applications. Many blind people do not even
know the layout of the cities and streets they live in, a problem that also applies to
indoor areas. Although many graphical digital floor plans for large buildings are

---

[1] http://www.mobility-projekt.de
[2] http://www.baim-info.de

K. Miesenberger et al. (Eds.): ICCHP 2012, Part II, LNCS 7383, pp. 59–66, 2012.
© Springer-Verlag Berlin Heidelberg 2012

offered for download, most of them are inaccessible for the blind. As a first approach, graphical floor plans could be converted to tactile floor plans. In interviews we conducted [2], blind users liked the idea of exploring tactile floor plans in theory but in practice it took a long time to gather an understanding of a graphical tactile representation and it was even more difficult to mentally map virtual to real world perception on the way. This approach may need much training to be effective. Furthermore, the manual translation of detailed graphical content to more abstract tactile graphics with braille captions is very time-consuming. Also, new revisions have to be printed and delivered when construction or furniture changes.

Timely map production and digital delivery is an approach that benefits from web technologies. WCAG recommends the development of alternative descriptions for images in order to make them accessible to blind people. Until now, it remains difficult to provide an alternative description for images showing maps as the development of orientation or formation of routes is an activity based on the graphical representation. Some early notes on accessibility of SVG [3] refer to some useful techniques, but still nearly no assistive technology supports SVG. A new framework for tagging indoor areas is also provided by Google, which allows overlying their existing maps with bitmaps and place tags[3]. Currently, this approach is in beta state and requires a long-lasting approval of Google. The floor plans themselves are not accessible for blind and low-vision users as they are just raster images.

Mobility supports facility operators in making floor plan information easily accessible by adding annotations and storing the data on a web server. A web application, based on SVG, is provided for this purpose.

Former approaches like HapticRiaMaps already investigated how to provide tactile and multimodal exploration of online digital maps with audio-tactile feedback [4]. But the usage of specialized and expensive hardware-supported systems is usually not appropriate for mobile applications. Mass-market smartphones are affordable and easy to carry and natural language is easy to understand. The Mobility project focuses on presenting floor plan data as textual or spoken descriptions, comparable to audio guides, but more dynamic and interactive. Our accessible client is a smartphone application (app) that processes relevant spatial annotations into directional descriptions for a certain area, which is selected by indoor localization methods. As a second client a web-app provides access for desktop and tablet PC users, e.g. for preparing a visit in advance.

2   Mobile Client User Requirements

The Mobility smartphone app is under development following a user-centred design method [5]. Requirements of blind users were analysed in a first study to identify needs for appropriate route description and for the app's functionality and usability. For that purpose literature research, user profile analysis, environment analysis, mobility training with a professional mobility coach and interviews with blind users were conducted. The resulting requirements were verified in pilot tests with blind users.

---

[3] http://google-latlong.blogspot.de/2011/11/new-frontier-for-google-maps-mapping.html

For example, the system has to summarize routes to present an overview, respect the user's preferences in how to transfer between levels when selecting routes and it has to declare changes in direction in an intuitive way like "left" and "right" when following routes [2].

In a next step, annotations for a common real world scenario in Frankfurt Airport (Germany), Terminal 1, were prepared as a basis for upcoming evaluations (see section 5). Subjects had to get from the adjacent railway station to the security zone in Terminal 1, including multiple intermediate destinations within different parts of the complex of buildings. The scenario was reviewed with help of a blind expert in a Wizard of Oz experiment in which descriptions and directions were read aloud manually, depending on the expert's location. This provided helpful feedback for enhancing the annotations and also resulted in further requirements that had to be verified in the user tests. We identified three priority levels for annotations:

1. Essential, security relevant annotation.
2. Helpful annotation to get one's bearings within the environment.
3. Optional annotation for situations in that people feel uncertain.

This supports an adaptation of presenting annotations to the user. For example, a person who already knows the building may only want to know a minimum of information, while a first time visitor is interested in much more explanations.

Also, the order of detailed information at a certain position should follow their importance:

1. Name and type of the point of interest (POI) reached or region entered.
2. Overview when entering a region (dimensions, shape, position ... of the interior).
3. Primary directions to other areas (if relevant) or directions to the next significant waypoint when following a route.
4. Special characteristics, e.g. environmental patterns, provided guidance etc.

3   Indoor Localization

Currently most smartphones enable localization due to an onboard GPS receiver. This is e.g. used by the Haptimap[4] project, which intends to provide a navigator for visual impaired people in outdoor domains [6]. In indoor environments, where hardly any GPS signals can be retrieved, current state of the art solutions, as offered by Skyhook[5] or Fraunhofer's awiloc[6], allow this on the basis of Wi-Fi signals, which are received by a smartphone's onboard Wi-Fi receiver. The mobile device utilizes a database of pre-collected fingerprints, that represent stored Wi-Fi signal strengths at a position, and computes its position, by comparing it's on the fly received Wi-Fi signals with the ones of the database and finally triangulating the best matching database's fingerprints' positions. Mobility makes use of these indoor localization possibilities,

---

[4] http://www.haptimap.org
[5] http://www.skyhookwireless.com
[6] http://www.awiloc.de

to allow rough localization features, which support a user on the go and to provide navigation instructions, specifically in case, one walks into certain wrong or critical areas. The Wi-Fi accuracy heavily depends on the Wi-Fi access points, their number and their signal strengths, which differ in larger buildings. Current tests in Frankfurt Airport indicate an accuracy level of approximately 3 to 15m.

4   Spatial Descriptions

Mobility intends to provide spatial descriptions to various different user groups, such as blind, low-vision or elderly people. Due to the limitations of Wi-Fi positioning methods, one cannot provide step-by-step instructions (as provided by common navigation solutions), but those would anyhow limit the freedom while walking in an (un-)known area. E.g. imagine a visually impaired person having to listen to direction instructions on the go, which would disturb their own navigation methods (e.g. listening to acoustic sounds of the environment). That is why Mobility addresses the need, to provide spatial descriptions of the current targeted environment, with some indications on how to walk through this area to reach a specific desired point.

5   Annotation

To benefit blind users with spatial information, some clues can be extracted from graphical floor plans (SVG) if modelling rules for the plan are known. In the best case this helps to collect information about how rooms, walls or doors are situated, with the advantage of keeping the correct map scale, which allows mapping graphical items correctly to real world conditions. More content information about areas, certain POIs with labels, descriptions and attributes, as well as the connectivity of rooms and buildings have to be added by manual annotation.

A GUI-based web application is under development to assist sighted operators in doing so. It outputs XML data containing structured annotation that references graphical elements in an SVG floor plan. Since the client is developed with user centred design methods, early testing in mock-up stages caused the need for annotated data with location references way before a new productive annotation tool could be provided. To overcome this issue, available software was looked for, that produces output in a format that could be processed afterwards for first annotations. The software tool had to offer the abilities to work with floor plan images, map them to real world geo coordinates, place areas and POI markers within these plans graphically and to add some descriptions to annotated elements. Google Earth[7] complies with these requirements.

In areas, in which no original floor plans are available escape and evacuation plans following ISO 23601 [7] that are posted at the walls all over public buildings are simply photographed, allowing enough accuracy for our purposes. They are cut out with ordinary photo software, saved as raster graphic and then graphically aligned to satellite photos in Google Earth, providing georeferenced floor plans (see Figure 1).

---

[7] http://www.google.com/earth

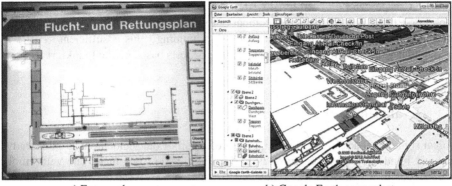

a) Escape plan.   b) Google Earth screenshot.

Fig. 1. A Photo of an escape plan (a) and a Google Earth screenshot (b), showing the escape plan as ground overlay image and some manually annotated POIs

With the help of XSL processing, annotated data (areas, POIs) exported from Google Earth in the open KML[8] format can be transformed directly into the DAISY XML format DTBook [8], containing all names and descriptions and encoding geospatial references too. Another converter was built for extracting SVG images and XML annotation data from KML, allowing annotations made in Google Earth to be imported into our Mobility annotation web-app later, for further editing and structuring. A final conversion, still under development, will allow transforming the structured XML annotation data into DTBook content by dynamically generating text phrases out of the structured data and the current mobile context (position, direction, route...).

6   Client Presentation of Directions

Our multimodal interactive smartphone app presents the spatial descriptions of environment and directions, utilizing text to speech (TTS), audio signals and vibration patterns. The user can browse information via gestures and through the smartphone's default screen reading features to access the platform's widget toolkit. The first prototype is implemented as an Android app. DAISY[9] is a well-proven accessible document standard and multiple smartphone apps are already available[10] for reading DAISY books. Besides other purposes the Digital Talking Book format can also be used for tour guides. It may fit our goal of presenting indoor overview and directions. Yet two major issues have to be overcome. The first thing to consider is that descriptions of areas and POIs have to be related to their spatial location. Therefore the standard either is extended or a third format can be used to add geo-references to DTBook-Items [9]. By adding elements from a custom XML namespace, geographical position

---

[8] http://www.opengeospatial.org/standards/kml
[9] http://www.daisy.org/daisy-standard
[10] http://www.daisy.org/tools/mobile-applications

and even shape can be coded directly into the DAISY book to be interpreted by the Mobility Client, while sustaining compatibility with standard DAISY players. For predefined tours - as most important routes in a building - this is sufficient to offer a talking tour guide which was used in our prototype tests based on the Frankfurt Airport scenario.

7   Evaluation

To get some feedback on the style and level of detail of our annotations, a pilot study with six blind subjects (aged from 29 to 54, five female / one male, one with guide dog / five with white cane) was conducted. Their task was to use our first smartphone app prototype with the generated DTBook, based on annotations following the afore-mentioned user requirements. The corresponding description of an area was read to the subjects via speech output, followed by directions to the next significant waypoint or region. At the time of testing the output was not initiated automatically by location, but manually by the test supervisor (wizard of Oz technique). Our scenario in Frank-furt Airport consisted of 34 descriptions (1 summary, 18 areas, 15 route sections). The test included two different types of triggering output: either the description of an area was presented when entering the area, or already on the way towards the area. Our experimental setup was as follows: the test supervisor handled the smartphone to trigger TTS output and warnings. The output was logged and transmitted to the sub-ject via a Bluetooth headset. To support the subsequent analysis of the subject's movement, a spy cam was attached to the headset. In addition, the whole scene was recorded by an external camera and a manual protocol was written.

The rating of our prototype, based on post-test interviews, is shown in Table 1. In Table 2 the measured behaviour of the subjects is summarized. In general, the sub-jects stated to approve our application as the given descriptions allowed a good im-agination of the areas. However, the amount of information was rated too high. Most of the subjects would prefer to get more details on demand only. Since orientation and mobility skills already mean a lot of mental load for blind people, four of the subjects would prefer to get the descriptions not until reaching an area, which implies to stop walking and listening before entering areas with much annotated information. In our scenario such intermediate stops took about 36% of the total time (see Table 2). Pre-senting the route information as soon as possible and minimizing the length of the area description would be beneficial. Another requirement pointed out in interviews is that descriptions of route sections should contain distances (especially on long sec-tions without new landmarks) and also information on significant hazards to increase the user's confidence. The test has also shown insufficient feasibilities for some route instructions, leading to difficulties, especially when crossing large halls with only few clear orientation points. In such cases, a more accurate description of the route was necessary, for example indications like floor cover, airstream or even smell informa-tion can be helpful. Otherwise, the description should be as short as possible and it should not contain too many orientation points at once. If there are no unique land-marks for describing a clear route description from point A to point B, a position based announcement should be given when arriving at B.

Table 1. Average rating of the our prototype (5 = very good, 1 = very bad)

rating criterion		Average	standard deviation
general rating of the app		4.2	0.8
area description	level of detail	3.7	1.0
	precision	4.1	0.7
	way of description	3.8	1.1
route description	level of detail	3.7	1.2
	precision	3.5	0.5
	feasibility	3.5	0.8

Table 2. Analysis of subject behaviour

measuring factor	average	standard deviation
duration of the scenario	25min 23s	4min 19s
duration of intermediate stops (listening)	9 min 22s	2min 57s
count of intermediate stops (listening)	18	4.6
count of repeating an announcement	3	2.7
count of self-correction a route	1	–
count of correction a route with help	3	2.5

As shown in Table 2, subjects sometimes lost their way and had to correct their route. In most of these cases help of the test conductor was necessary. Thus, our system needs an appropriate backup strategy in future revisions. As part of our test, we provoked such a situation two times with each participant, offering more or less options how to get back to the route. The less options were listed and the less interaction was necessary, the better it was accepted by our blind subjects. Furthermore, in contrast to the results of our requirement analysis [2], some subjects preferred to get more detailed direction angles (not only simple left/right orientation, but also a clock-based or degree system). Therefore a configurable presentation of orientation seems useful to meet the needs of all users.

8   Conclusion and Outlook

The ongoing Mobility project is still a work in progress but has proven to be well accepted by our test participants. Our next prototype will enable users to operate more independently on the move, instead of strictly following predefined routes. Information will be selected and sorted more dynamically, therefore the DAISY book contents has to be generated based on the user's position and direction, classes of POIs the user is interested in and the user profile. Still, a predefined route can be used, especially when using the web client at home to gather information in advance.

Extensive user tests with more subjects will follow this year. In these studies we want to learn more about intermediate stops to increase the efficiency of our descriptions. For example, we will analyse the user's behaviour of listening to the descriptions and how he interacts independently with the application. Therefore we will measure the time from starting an announcement till the user stops for listening.

Acknowledgments. The Mobility project is sponsored by the German Federal Ministry of Education and Research (BMBF) under the grant number FKZ 01IS11005. Only the authors of this paper are responsible for its content. The consortium consists of IN2 search interfaces development Ltd, spring techno GmbH & Co. KG and the Chair of Human-Computer Interaction at Technische Universität Dresden. The project is being supported by Fraport AG (Frankfurt Airport Services World-wide in Frankfurt, Germany).

References

1. Bühler, C., Heck, H., Becker, J.: How to Inform People with Reduced Mobility about Public Transport. In: Miesenberger, K., Klaus, J., Zagler, W.L., Karshmer, A.I. (eds.) ICCHP 2008. LNCS, vol. 5105, pp. 973–980. Springer, Heidelberg (2008)
2. Miao, M., Spindler, M., Weber, G.: Requirements of Indoor Navigation System from Blind Users. In: Holzinger, A., Simonic, K.-M. (eds.) USAB 2011. LNCS, vol. 7058, pp. 673–679. Springer, Heidelberg (2011)
3. W3C: Accessibility Features of SVG (August 2000),
   http://www.w3.org/TR/SVG-access (accessed January 2012)
4. Kaklanis, N., Votis, K., Moschonas, P., Tzovaras, D.: HapticRiaMaps: towards interactive exploration of web world maps for the visually impaired. In: Proceedings of the International Cross-Disciplinary Conference on Web Accessibility (W4A 2011). ACM, New York (2011)
5. ISO 9241-210, Ergonomics of Human-System Interaction. Part 210: Human-centred design (2010)
6. Magnusson, C., Tollmar, K., Brewster, S., Sarjakoski, T., Sarjakoski, T., Roselier, S.: Exploring future challenges for haptic, audio and visual interfaces for mobile maps and location based services. In: LOCWEB 2009 Proceedings of the 2nd International Workshop on Location and the Web, Boston, MA, USA (2009)
7. ISO 23601, Safety identification – Escape and evacuation plan signs (2009)
8. Kerscher, G.: Theory Behind the DTBook DTD. DAISY Consortium (September 2001),
   http://data.daisy.org/publications/docs/theory_dtbook/
   theory_dtbook.html (accessed January 2012)
9. Pöhland, R.: Location-Based Services for the Blind. Student Thesis (in German), TU Dresden, Institute of Applied Computer Science (2011)

Harnessing Wireless Technologies for Campus Navigation by Blind Students and Visitors

Tracey J. Mehigan and Ian Pitt

Dep't Computer Science, University College Cork, Ireland
{t.mehigan,i.pitt}@cs.ucc.ie

Abstract. Navigating around a university campus can be difficult for visitors and incoming students/staff, and is a particular challenge for vision-impaired students and staff. University College Cork (UCC), like most other universities and similar institutions worldwide, relies mainly on sign-posts and maps (available from the college website) to direct students and visitors around campus. However, these are not appropriate for vision-impaired users. UCC's Disability Support Service provides mobility training to enable blind and vision-impaired students and staff to safely and independently navigate around the campus. This training is time-consuming for all parties and is costly to provide. It is also route-specific: for example, if a blind student who has already received mobility training is required to attend lectures in a building they have not previously visited, they may require further training on the new route. It is not feasible to provide this kind of training for blind/visually-impaired visitors. A potential solution to these problems is to provide navigation data using wireless and mobile technology. Ideally this should be done using technologies that are (or will shortly be) widely supported on smart-phones, thus ensuring that the system is accessible to one-time visitors as well as regular users.

A study was conducted in order to identify user-requirements. It was concluded that there is no off-the-shelf system that fully meets UCC's requirements. Most of the candidates fall short either in terms of the accuracy or reliability of the localization information provided, ability to operate both indoors and outdoors, or in the nature of the feedback provided. In the light of these findings, a prototype system has been developed for use on the UCC campus. This paper describes the development of the system and ongoing user-testing to assess the viability of the interface for use by vision-impaired people.

Keywords: Accessibility, Navigation, HCI & Non-Classical Interfaces, Design for All, User Centered Design and User Involvement.

1   Introduction and Background

Navigating around a university campus can be difficult for visitors and incoming students/staff, and is a particular challenge for vision-impaired students and staff. Most universities and similar institutions worldwide rely on sign-posting and maps to direct students and visitors around campus. However this is not appropriate for vision-impaired users. UCC's Disability Support Service provides mobility training to enable

K. Miesenberger et al. (Eds.): ICCHP 2012, Part II, LNCS 7383, pp. 67–74, 2012.

blind and vision-impaired students and staff to safely and independently navigate around the campus. This training is time-consuming for all parties and is costly to provide. It is also route-specific: for example, if a blind student who has already received mobility training is required to attend lectures in a building they have not previously visited, they may require further training on the new route. It is not feasible to provide this kind of training for blind/visually-impaired visitors.

A potential solution to these problems is to provide navigation data using wireless and mobile technology. Ideally this should be done using technologies that are (or will shortly be) widely supported on smart-phones, thus ensuring that the system is accessible to one-time visitors as well as regular users.

1.1   Review of User Requirements

In order to develop an understanding of the needs of vision-impaired students navigating the UCC campus, a series of interviews and walkabouts were undertaken. The students involved were studying a range of courses and had varying levels of familiarity with the campus - some were newly-arrived whilst others were in their final year. The group included both guide-dog and white-cane users. An interview and campus walkabout with UCC's mobility trainer was also conducted. Participants were asked to comment both on general issues regarding navigation around campus, on issues associated with particular routes, and on the strengths and weaknesses of existing mobility training and support. During the walkabouts, participants were asked to describe their thought processes and the cues and techniques they used to determine their position and orientation at each stage of the journey.

The study highlighted differences between the long-cane users, who need to check and correct their position every few steps, and guide-dog users, who require less frequent position checks but must be able to identify route decision-points with great accuracy if they are to instruct the dog to follow a route with which it is not familiar. It also illustrated the extent to which both groups make use of environmental sounds either as a primary means to determine position or to confirm information obtained through other means. For example, many of those interviewed reported using manholes as route-markers: they were able to distinguish aurally between the different manholes (silence, various degrees of water flow, etc.), whilst walking across a manhole is easily distinguishable from walking over solid ground. The river which flows through campus also provides a useful auditory cue for many. Most participants reported that the area which causes them most difficulty is the Honan Plaza, a large, open space with little variation in terrain and few useful sources of sound.

1.2   Review of Previous Work

There have been a number of attempts in recent years to develop efficient and cost-effective systems that enable blind and vision-impaired pedestrians to safely and independently navigate spaces with which they are not familiar. These include the Drishti system [5], and other care-giving monitoring systems for location-based information such as that proposed by Tee et al [9]. Researchers have developed navigation solutions tailored for use at exhibitions [1], museums [8], and universities [9]. Several commercial systems are also available, such as the Trekker Breeze GPS System [6] and the Mobile Geo [3].

Most of these systems are based on one or more of the following technologies: Radio Frequency Identification (RFID) [4], Bluetooth, Dead–Reckoning systems using accelerometer devices, and Global Positioning Systems (GPS). Nokia Research Labs have developed a high-accuracy indoor positioning system delivered via Bluetooth 4.0 [7].

As an example, Bellotti et al [1] developed a tour-guide system for exhibitions, using RFID tags to identify the user's location, transmitting the information to a PocketPC handheld device which provides Text-to-Speech (TTS) feedback. The information provided includes the generalities of the exhibition, the guide itself, and available services. Descriptions of the selected interest points are also provided in an event-driven fashion. The User Interface (UI) provides a four level structure including an extended title of an exhibit, a description of the points of interest, extended descriptions and information, and spatial guidance to exhibits. The UI also provides the user with information about service areas, for example restaurants etc. Users are supported in developing mental maps of their surroundings through the inclusion of reference points within descriptions, for example: you are near (here) and the identification of key decision points. Visual information is also provided for sighted users including animations and static images. Device control for the UI is via hardware buttons.

Considering these and similar systems in the light of the review findings, it was concluded that there is no off-the-shelf system that fully meets UCC's requirements. Most of the candidates fall short either in terms of the accuracy or reliability of the localization information provided, ability to operate both indoors and outdoors, or in the nature of the feedback provided by the interface. There are also issues with power-drain and battery life. While some of the experimental systems mentioned above have been shown to offer improvements over earlier systems, it is clear that there are still significant problems, e.g., in successfully conveying an impression of terrain and environment via hearing and touch. Most of these systems use TTS to provide navigation cues to users, and there are problems in providing the information in ways that don't overload sensory channels or conflict with other demands on these channels. There are issues concerning the use of such systems alongside other mobility aids, such as a long cane. In many cases these systems are cumbersome and can isolate the user.

2   Developing the 'WayFinding' Navigation System

In view of the review findings, we are currently developing a system that has two distinct layers - a navigation layer that obtains data on position and orientation, and an interface layer that makes this information available to the user. Separation of the two layers allows development to proceed independently, and will also make it easier to upgrade or replace one layer at a later date without unnecessarily affecting the other.

2.1   The Navigation Layer

The navigation layer will initially be based on ULP Bluetooth 4.0 [2] combined with Wireless Inertial Measurement Units (WIMU). Bluetooth 4.0 offers many benefits over technologies such as RFID. It is aimed at the same application-area as RFID, in that it can be used to provide location-based information at bus-stops, etc., but it also offers a low energy wireless solution with average and idle mode power consumption, the ability to run for years on standard coin-cell batteries, is low cost, and offers an enhanced range. Bluetooth 4.0 also offers multi-vendor interoperability. WIMUs typically provide data from accelerometer, gyroscope and magnetometer sensors. Pedestrian Dead Reckoning (PDR) alone is not sufficient for positioning, but it provides incremental, relative position information to complement any system that can provide absolute location estimates. WIMUs capture tilt, force and timings and represent an optical 3D motion capture system to provide a complete kinematic model of a subject (Walsh et al [10]). Bluetooth 4.0 technology is currently included in the iPhone 4S and is due to be included in most modern mobile devices by the end 2012, thus allowing the development of a low cost and highly accurate navigation system accessible via any smart-phone.

It became clear during the review that positioning technology is developing at a rapid pace, and that while ULP Bluetooth appears the most appropriate choice at present, other systems might soon overtake it. For example, GPS might be considered at a later stage as GPS accuracy levels increase. This informed our decision to separate the navigation layer from the interface. The focus of this paper is the development of the User Interface layer.

2.2   The User Interface Layer

In designing the user interface, the aim has been to address issues apparent in other systems while at the same time retaining beneficial elements of those systems. Thus while many existing systems (e.g., that described by Bellotti et al [1]) only provide TTS and visual feedback, we have extended the feedback facility to include optional audio and haptic components. Consideration has also been given to user control. As most modern devices (for example the iPhone) use touch-screens, gesture based system controls have been implemented.

Attention has been paid to the needs of users with differing levels of experience (casual/one-off user, beginner, expert), and of the differing requirements of guide-dog users and long cane users. It is important not to create any features that would constitute isolating factors for specific user groups. As some vision-impaired users rely on environmental sounds and use echo-location techniques to gather information on their surroundings, it is important that any audio interaction used is optional, controlled by the user, and is not totally reliant on the use of headphones.

Based on these considerations, the interface will incorporate three audio options: speech-based, simple and spatial audio. Simple audio will present beeping with a repetition-rate that is proportional to landmark distance. Spatial sound will use directional cues so that it appears to come from the direction of the landmark. Orientation could also be facilitated, whereby the audio response varies as the device is turned relative to a landmark.

Other key components of the user interface include:

- A 'You are Here' facility to inform the system user of their exact location on campus at the time requested
- A 'Route' marking facility to explain to the user the best route from their current location or a particular building to their required destination
- A 'Near me' facility allows access to services on campus.
- An 'Orientation' facility to aid users should they become disorientated while on campus; it gives feedback on current location, the direction in which the user is facing, and the nearest building in that direction and /or the nearest building / service in any direction requested.

These facilities rely on speech based feedback in the first instance, but a text-based option is available on request. Different text options are available to the user, such as color and size options. Map-based visual feedback is included for sighted users. Users are provided with the option to select any combination of these facilities, and to switch off any they find unhelpful or intrusive.

A compass facility has been be implemented using speech, providing 'You are Facing...' information. Decision Points, for example, directional information, are included, e.g., "Turn right to building 1 / turn left to building 2".

Haptic components include varying levels of pulsed vibration to indicate external key features, such as buildings. For example, the device will vibrate once as a user approaches a building. The haptic interface also provides various levels of pulsed vibration in respect of stepped / ramped entrances, (e.g. device vibrates twice for steps / thrice for ramped entrances, etc). It is intended that this will be extended to include other potential obstacles including areas of traffic and to indicate crossings.

2.3   Developing a Prototype System

An initial prototype navigation system was developed, incorporating the key components outlined above. The system was developed for use with mobile phones / devices running the Android OS. The prototype system includes a user interface layer and a Bluetooth connectivity layer. The connectivity layer represents a prototype navigation layer and facilitates the transmission of navigation-based data to the user interface layer from a second Bluetooth enabled device. The system was programmed in Java and developed using Eclipse IDE.

The prototype user interface layer comprises the key components outlined in Section 2.2.

Fig. 1. Prototype System – Sample User Interface Screens

3   User Testing

3.1   Pilot Study

A short pre-test pilot study was conducted using the WayFinder system. The study involved two blind UCC students, one guide-dog and one long-cane user. Each student was instructed on how to use the system. The students then traversed a short route across campus using WayFinder in conjunction with their existing mobility aid.

Having completed the route, the students were each asked a series of questions relating to the usability of the system. The test results were mixed. One student (a guide-dog user) reported that he had no difficulty in using the system and indicated that he would be interested in using it regularly as a navigation aid. The second student (a long-cane user) reported that her previous knowledge of the route made it difficult for her to use the system effectively. She found that she was constantly anticipating the system's feedback, much of which was therefore redundant and distracting. In retrospect, it is possible that these problems would not have arisen had she had more opportunity to familiarize herself with the system and select appropriate feedback options. It also highlights the differing needs of those who are new to a particular route, and those who are familiar with it and require less feedback. These issues were taken into account in the design of the next phase of user-testing.

3.2   Main Study

A 'Wizard of Oz' study is being conducted to test the viability of the pilot user interface for use by vision-impaired people for navigation purposes. The testing focusses on the use of Android Devices and Bluetooth connectivity to assess user actions in relation to information received by the user via a handheld device.

Six blind / vision-impaired students will take part in the study. They have been contacted through the Disability Support Services (DSS) Office at UCC, and all are students attending courses at the university. All are experienced in using smart phones. The subjects vary in their level of familiarity with the UCC campus familiarity.

Three Hypotheses will be tested as part of the user study:

1. Subjects will accurately react to instructions posed to them via the UI.
2. Subjects will complete the route independently based on information received from their interaction with the UI running on an Android device.
3. Based on their interaction with the system subjects (both guide-dog and long cane users) will exhibit a high level of satisfaction with the system.

All subjects will interact with the Way-Finder system on a specific UCC campus route, from the Boole Library to the Clock Tower. Subjects will be instructed on the planned route, and on how the system works and how to interact with it. After instruction, students will receive no help or prompting from the test coordinator, and will receive instruction on the route only via the mobile device. Subjects will be required to use their normal mobility aids in conjunction with the system.

For safety purposes subjects will be accompanied on route. Subjects' reaction to instruction will be observed by the test coordinator. The coordinator will walk behind the subject during the test, but no communication will take place between the subject / test coordinator unless the subject becomes disorientated during the test. If a subject fails to complete the test, it is only necessary to replace that one subject's contribution to the test.

On completion of the route subjects will be asked a number of questions to assess usability and user satisfaction with the system.

Data will be analyzed in respect of the user's reaction to instruction received from the device, user satisfaction with the application and overall usability of the system. Results will be presented at the ICCHP 2012 conference.

4   Future Work

On completion of the evaluation of the user interface via the pilot study, work will commence to address any issues encountered and reported by subjects. Further work will be conducted on the user interface to include other elements, such as spatial sound feedback which was outlined above. Work will also commence on the development of the Navigation Layer through the incorporation of a Bluetooth RF-based system and the inclusion of WIMUs to gather specific user location data based on inertial movement. It is also intended to advance this work to include a facility for the measurement of inertial movement.

5   Principle Benefits of This Work

Maintaining spatial orientation can be a challenge for vision-impaired people, especially in relation to their awareness of landmarks in the surrounding environment. A campus navigation system that makes use of mobile and wireless technologies could provide a more accessible and flexible navigation system than is currently available, allowing blind and vision-impaired people to accurately orientate themselves and navigate independently to and from key points on UCC's campus. The use of a student's own mobile device for this purpose will address some of the inclusion issues faced by vision-impaired students. Such a system will make navigation on campus easier not only for blind/vision-impaired students and staff, but also for visitors and new students (both vision-impaired and sighted). Once in place and tested at UCC, such a system could also be piloted at other universities / institutions.

References

1. Bellotti, F., Berta, R., De Gloria, A., Margarone, M.: Guiding visually impaired people in the exhibition. In: Virtuality 2006, Mobile Guide Workshop, Turin, Italy (2006), `http://hcilab.uniud.it/sigchi/doc/Virtuality06/Bellotti&al.pdf`
2. Bluetooth SIG, `http://www.bluetooth.com/Pages/Low-Energy.aspx`
3. Mobile Pocket Speak, `http://www.codefactory.es/en/products.asp?id=336`
4. D'Atri, E., Medaglia, C.M., Serbanati, A., Ceipidor, U.B.: A System to Aid Blind People in Mobility: A Usability Test and Results. In: Second International Conference on Systems (ICONS 2007), Sainte-Luce, Martinique, p. 35 (2007)
5. Helal, A.S., Moore, S.E., Ramachandran, B.: Drishti: An Integrated Navigation System for Visually Impaired and Disabled. In: Fifth International Symposium on Wearable Computers, Zurich, Switzerland, pp. 149–156 (2001)
6. Humanware, `http://www.humanware.com/en-usa/products/blindness/talking_gps/trekker/_details/id_88/trekker_talking_gps.html`
7. Kalliola, K.: High Accuracy Indoor Positioning System on BLE. Nokia Technical Report (2011), `http://hermia-fi-bin.directo.fi/@Bin/b85924038a216224b987d81d837f0959/1327586874/application/pdf/865170/HighAccuracyIndoorPositioningBasedOnBLE_Kalliola_270411.pdf`
8. Santoro, C., Paterno, F., Ricci, G., Leporini, B.: A Multimodal Mobile Museum Guide for All. In: Mobile Interaction with the Real World (MIRW 2007), pp. 21–25 (2007)
9. Tee, Z., Ang, L.M., Seng, K.P., Kong, J.H., Lo, R., Khor, M.Y.: SmartGuide System to Assist Visually Impaired People in a University Environment. In: Third International Convention on Rehabilitation Engineering & Assistive Technology (ICREAT 2009), Singapore, IETE Technical Review, pp. 455–464 (2009)
10. Walsh, M., Gaffney, M., Barton, J., O'Flynn, B., O' Mathuna, C., Hickey, A., Kellett, J.A.: Medical study on wireless inertial measurement technology as a tool for identifying patients at risk of death or imminent clinical deterioration. In: Pervasive Health 2011, Dublin, Ireland, pp. 214–217 (2011)

Eyesight Sharing in Blind Grocery Shopping: Remote P2P Caregiving through Cloud Computing

Vladimir Kulyukin, Tanwir Zaman,
Abhishek Andhavarapu, and Aliasgar Kutiyanawala

Department of Computer Science,
Utah State University,
Logan, UT, USA
vladimir.kulyukin@usu.edu

Abstract. Product recognition continues to be a major access barrier for visually impaired (VI) and blind individuals in modern supermarkets. R&D approaches to this problem in the assistive technology (AT) literature vary from automated vision-based solutions to crowdsourcing applications where VI clients send image identification requests to web services. The former struggle with run-time failures and scalability while the latter must cope with concerns about trust, privacy, and quality of service. In this paper, we investigate a mobile cloud computing framework for remote caregiving that may help VI and blind clients with product recognition in supermarkets. This framework emphasizes remote teleassistance and assumes that clients work with dedicated caregivers (helpers). Clients tap on their smartphones' touchscreens to send images of products they examine to the cloud where the SURF algorithm matches incoming image against its image database. Images along with the names of the top 5 matches are sent to remote sighted helpers via push notification services. A helper confirms the product's name, if it is in the top 5 matches, or speaks or types the product's name, if it is not. Basic quality of service is ensured through human eyesight sharing even when image matching does not work well. We implemented this framework in a module called EyeShare on two Android 2.3.3/2.3.6 smartphones. EyeShare was tested in three experiments with one blindfolded subject: one lab study and two experiments in Fresh Market, a supermarket in Logan, Utah. The results of our experiments show that the proposed framework may be used as a product identification solution in supermarkets.

1   Introduction

The term teleassistance covers a wide range of technologies that enable VI and blind individuals to transmit video and audio data to remote caregivers and receive audio assistance [1]. Research evidence suggests that the availability of remote caregiving reduces the psychological stress on VI and blind individuals when they perform various tasks in different environments [2].

A typical example of how teleassistance is used for blind navigation is the system developed by Bujacz et. al. [1]. The system consists of two notebook computers: one

K. Miesenberger et al. (Eds.): ICCHP 2012, Part II, LNCS 7383, pp. 75–82, 2012.
© Springer-Verlag Berlin Heidelberg 2012

is carried by the VI traveler in a backpack and the other used by the remote sighted caregiver. The traveler transmits video through a chest-mounted USB camera. The traveler wears a headset (an earphone and a microphone) to communicate with the caregiver. Several indoor navigation experiments showed that VI travelers walked faster, at a steadier pace, and were able to navigate more easily when assisted by remote guides then when they navigated the same routes by themselves.

Our research group has applied teleassistance to blind shopping in ShopMobile, a mobile shopping system for VI and blind individuals [3]. Our end objective is to enable VI and blind individuals to shop independently using only their smartphones. ShopMobile is our most recent system for accessible blind shopping that follows RoboCart and ShopTalk [4]. The system has three software modules: an eyes-free barcode scanner, an OCR engine, and a teleassitance module called TeleShop. The eyes-free barcode scanner allows VI shoppers to scan UPC barcodes on products and MSI barcodes on shelves. The OCR engine is being developed to extract nutrition facts from nutrition tables available on many product packages. TeleShop provides a teleassistance backup in situations when the barcode scanner or the OCR engine's malfunction.

The current implementation of TeleShop consists of a server running on the VI shopper's smartphone (Google Nexus One with Android 2.3.3/2.3.6) and a client GUI module running on the remote caregiver's computer. All client-server communication occurs over UDP. Images from the phone camera are continuously transmitted to the client GUI. The caregiver can start, stop, and pause the incoming image stream and to change image resolution and quality. Images of high resolution and quality provide more reliable detail but may cause the video stream to become choppy. Lower resolution images result in smoother video streams but provide less detail. The pause option is for holding the current image on the screen.

TeleShop has so far been evaluated in two laboratory studies with Wi-Fi and 3G [3]. The first study was done with two sighted students, Alice and Bob. The second study was done with a married couple: a completely blind person (Carl) and his sighted wife (Diana). For both studies, we assembled four plastic shelves in our laboratory and stocked them with empty boxes, cans, and bottles to simulate an aisle in a grocery store. The shopper and the caregiver were in separate rooms. In the first study, we blindfolded Bob to act as a VI shopper. The studies were done on two separate days. The caregivers were given a list of nine products and were asked to help the shoppers find the products and read the nutrition facts on the products' packages or bottles. A voice connection was established between the shopper and the caregiver via a regular phone call. Alice and Bob took an average of 57.22 and 86.5 seconds to retrieve a product from the shelf and to read its nutrition facts, respectively. The corresponding times for Carl and Diana were 19.33 and 74.8 seconds, respectively [3].

In this paper, we present an extension of TeleShop, called EyeShare, that leverages cloud computing to assist VI and blind shoppers (clients) with product recognition in supermarkets. The client takes a still image of the product that he or she currently examines and sends it to the cloud. The image is processed by an open source object recognition software application that runs on a cloud server and returns the top 5 matches from its product database. Number 5 was chosen, because a 5-item list easily fits on one Google Nexus One screen. The matches, in the form of a list of product names, are sent to the helper along with the original image through a push notification service. The helper uses his or her smartphone to select the correct product name from the list or, if the product's name is not found among the matches, to speak it into the smartphone. If speech recognition (SR) does not work, the helper types in the product's name. This framework is flexible in that various image recognition algorithms can tested in the cloud. It is also possible to use no image recognition, in which case all product recognition is done by the sighted caregiver.

The remainder of our paper is organized as follows. In Section 3, we present our cloud computing framework for remote caregiving with which mobile devices form ad hoc peer-to-peer (P2P) communication networks. In Section 4, we describe three experiments in two different environments: a laboratory and a local supermarket where a blindfolded individual and a remote sighted caregiver evaluated the system on different products. In Section 5, we present the results of our experiments. In Section 6, we discuss our investigation.

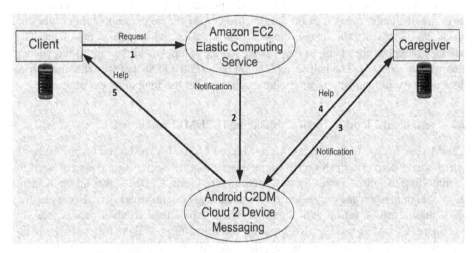

Fig. 1. Cloud Computing Framework for Remote Caregiving

2   A Cloud Computing Framework for Remote P2P Caregiving

The cloud computing framework we have implemented consists of mobile devices that communicate with each other in an ad hoc P2P network. The devices have Google accounts for authentication and are registered with Google's C2DM (cloud to device messaging) service (http://code.google.com/android/c2dm/), a push notification service that allocates unique IDs to registered devices. Our framework assumes that the cloud computing services run on Amazon's Elastic Computing Service (EC2) (http://aws.amazon.com/ec2/). Other cloud computing services may be employed. We configured an Amazon EC2 Linux server with 1 GHz processor and 512 MB RAM. The server runs an OpenCV 2.3.3 (http://opencv.willowgarage.com/wiki/) image matching application. Product images are saved in a MySQL database. The use of this framework requires that clients and helpers download the client and caregiver applications on their smartphones. The clients and helpers subsequently find each other and form an ad hoc P2P network via C2DM registration IDs.

Figure 1 shows this framework in action. A client sends a help request (Step 1). In EyeShare, this request consists of a product image. However, in principle, this request can be anything transmittable over available wireless channels such as Wi-Fi, 3G, 4G, Bluetooth, etc. The image is received by the Amazon EC2 Linux server where it is matched against the images in the MySQL database.

Our image matching application uses the SURF algorithm [5]. The matching operation returns the top 5 matches and sends the names of the corresponding products along with the URL that contains the client's original image to the C2DM service (Step 2). Thus, the image is transmitted only once – in the help request. C2DM forwards the message to the caregiver's smartphone (Step 3). The helper confirms the product's name by selecting it from the list of the top 5 matches. If the top matches are incorrect, the helper uses SR to speak the product's name or, if SR does not work or is not available, types it in on the touchscreen. If the helper cannot determine the product's name from the image, the helper sends a resend request to the client. The helper's message goes back to the C2DM service (Step 4) and then on to the client's smartphone (Step 5). The helper application is designed in such a way that the helper does not have to interrupt its smartphone activities for too long to render assistance.

2.1   Android Cloud to Device Messaging (C2DM) Framework

C2DM (`http://code.google.com/android/c2dm/`) takes care of message queuing and delivery. Push notifications ensure that the application does not need to keep polling the cloud server for new incoming requests. C2DM wakes up the Android application when messages are received through intent broadcasts. However, the application must be set up with the proper C2DM broadcast receiver permissions. In EyeShare, C2DM is used in two separate activities. First, C2DM forwards the message from the server to the helper application. This message consists of a formatted string of the client registration ID, the names of the top 5 product matches, and the URL containing the client's image. Clients' images are temporarily saved on the cloud-based Linux server and removed as soon as the corresponding help requests are processed. Second, C2DM is used when helper messages are sent back to clients.

2.2   Image Matching

We have used SURF (Speeded Up Robust Features) [5] as a black box image matching algorithm in our cloud server. SURF extracts unique key points and descriptors from images and later uses them to match indexed images against incoming image. SURF uses an intermediate image representation called Integral Image that is computed from the input image. This intermediate representation speeds up the calculations in rectangular areas. It is formed by summing up the pixel values of the x,y co-ordinates from the origin to the ends of the image. This makes computation time invariant to change in size and is useful in matching large images. The SURF detector is based on the determinant of the Hessian matrix. The SURF descriptor describes how pixel intensities are distributed within a scale dependent neighborhood of each interest point detected by Fast Hessian. Object detection using SURF is scale and rotation invariant and does not require long training. The fact that SURF is rotation invariant makes the algorithm useful in situations where image matching works with object images taken at different orientations than the images of the same objects used in training.

3   Experiments

We evaluated EyeShare in product recognition experiments at two locations. The first study was conducted in our laboratory. The second and third studies were conducted at Fresh Market, a local supermarket in Logan, Utah.

3.1   A Laboratory Study

We assembled four shelves in our laboratory and placed on them 20 products: bottles, boxes, and cans. The same setup was successfully used in our previous experiments on accessible blind shopping [3, 4]. We created a database of 100 images. Each of the 20 products on the shelves had 5 images taken at different orientations. The SURF algorithm was trained on these 100 images. A blindfolded individual was given a Google Nexus One smartphone (Android 2.3.3) with the EyeShare client application installed on it. A sighted helper was given another Google Nexus One (Android 2.3.3) with the EyeShare helper app installed on it.

The blindfolded client was asked to take each product from the assembled shelves and recognize it. The client took a picture of the product by tapping the touchscreen. The image was sent to the cloud Linux server where it was processed by the SURF algorithm. The names of the top 5 matched products were sent to the helper for verification along with the URL with the original image through C2DM. The helper, located in a different room in the same building, selected the product's name from the list of the top matches and sent the product's name back to the client. If the product's name was not in the list, the helper spoke the name of the product or, if SR was not recognized after three attempts, typed in the product's name on the virtual touchscreen keyboard. The run for an individual product was considered completed when the product's name was spoken on the client's smartphone through TTS. Thus, the total run time (in seconds) for each run included all five steps given in Fig. 1.

3.2   Store Experiments

The next two experiments were executed in Fresh Market, a local supermarket in Logan, Utah. Prior to the experiments we added 270 images to our image database used in the laboratory study. We selected 45 products from 9 aisles (5 products per aisle) in the supermarket and took 6 images at different rotations for every product.

The products included boxes, bottles, cans, and bags. We biased our selection to products that an individual can hold in one hand. SURF was retrained on these 370 images (100 images from the lab study and 270 new ones).

The same blindfolded subject who participated in the laboratory study was given a Samsung Galaxy S2 smartphone (Android 2.3.6) with the EyeShare client application installed on it. The client used a 4G data plan. The same helper who participated in the laboratory study was given a Google Nexus One (Android 2.3.6) with the Eye-Share helper application installed on it. The helper was located in a building approximately one mile away from the supermarket. The helper used a Wi-Fi connection. The first set of experiments was confined to the first three aisles of the supermarket and lasted for 30 minutes. In each aisle, three products from the database and three products not from the database were chosen by a research assistant who went to the supermarket with the blindfolded subject. The assistant gave each product to the subject who was asked to use the EyeShare client application to recognize the product. There was no training involved, because it was the same blindfolded subject who did the laboratory study. The subject was given 16 products, one product at a time, by the assistant. One experimental run began at the time when the subject was given a product and went on until the time when the subject's smartphone received the product's name and read it out to the subject through TTS.

The second set of experiments was conducted in the same supermarket on a different day with the same subject and helper. The experiments lasted 30 minutes. Since, as explained in the discussion section, the image matching did not perform as well as we hoped it would in the first supermarket study, we did not do any image matching in the second set of experiments. All product recognition was done by the remote sighted helper. The subject was given 17 products, one product at a time, taken from the next three aisles of the supermarket by the assistant. The experimental run times were computed in the same way as they were in the first supermarket study.

4   Results

The results of the experiments are summarized in Table 1. Column 1 gives the environments where the experiments were executed. Column 2 gives the number of products used in the experiments in the corresponding environments. Column 3 gives the mean time (in seconds) of the experimental runs. Column 4 gives the standard deviations of the corresponding mean time values. Column 5 gives the number of times the correct product was found in the top 5 matches. Column 6 gives the mean number of SR attempts. Column 7 gives the number of SR failures when the helper had to type the product names on the touchscreen keyboard after attempting to use SR three times. In all experiments, all products were successfully recognized by the blindfolded subject. As can be seen in Table 1, in supermarket study 1, after our image database had grown in size, there were no correct product names in the top 5 matches. Consequently, we decided not to use SURF in supermarket study 2. In supermarket study 1, there were three cases when the helper requested the client to send another image of a product because he could not identify the product's name from the original image. In supermarket study 1, there was one brief (several seconds) loss of Wi-Fi connection on the helper's smartphone.

Table 1. Experimental results

Environment	# Products	Mean Time	STD	Top 5	Mean SR	SR Failures
Lab	16	40	.00021	8	1.1	0
Store 1	16	60	.00033	0	1.2	2
Store 2	17	60	.00081	0	1.1	3

5   Discussion

Our study contributes to the recent body of research that addresses various aspects of independent blind shopping through mobile and cloud computing (e.g., [6, 7, 8]). Our approach differs from these studies in its emphasis on dedicated remote caregiving. Our approach addresses, at least to some extent, both image recognition failures of fully automated solutions and the concerns about trust, privacy, and basic quality of service of pure crowdsourcing approaches. Dedicated caregivers alleviate image recognition failures through human eyesight sharing. Since dedicated caregiving is more personal and trustworthy, clients are not required to post image recognition requests on open web forums, which allows them to preserve more privacy. Interested readers may watch our research videos at www.youtube.com/csatlusu for more information on our accessible shopping experiments and projects.

The experiments show that the average product recognition is within one minute. The results demonstrate that SR is a viable option for product naming. We attribute the poor performance of SURF in the first supermarket study to our failure to properly parameterize the algorithm. As we gain more experience with SURF, we may be able to improve the performance of automated image matching. However, database maintenance may be a more serious long-term concern for automated image matching unless there is direct access to the supermarket's inventory control system.

Our findings should be interpreted with caution, because we used only one blindfolded subject in the experiments. Nonetheless, our findings may serve as a basis for future research on remote teleassisted caregiving in accessible blind shopping. Our experience with the framework suggests that telassistance may be an feasible option for VI individuals in modern supermarkets. Dedicated remote caregiving can be applied not only to product recognition but also to assistance with cash payments and supermarket navigation. It is a relatively inexpensive solution, because the only required hardware device is a smartphone with a data plan.

As the second supermarket study suggests, cloud-based image matching may not be necessary. The use of mobile phones as the means of caregiving allows caregivers to provide assistance from the comfort of their homes or offices or on the go. As data plans move toward 4G network speeds, we can expect faster response times and better quality of service. Faster network connections may, in time, make it feasible to communicate via streaming videos.

References

1. Bujacz, M., Baranski, P., Moranski, M., Strumillo, P., Materka, A.: Remote Guidance for the Blind - A Proposed Teleassistance System and Navigation Trials. In: Proceedings of the Conference on Human System Interactions, pp. 888–892. IEEE, Krakow (2008)
2. Peake, P., Leonard, J.: The Use of Heart-Rate as an Index of Stress in Blind Pedestrians. Ergonomics (1971)
3. Kutiyanawala, A., Kulyukin, V., Nicholson, J.: Teleassistance in Accessible Shopping for the Blind. In: Proceedings of the 2011 International Conference on Internet Computing, July 18-21, pp. 190–193. ICOMP Press, Las Vegas (2011)
4. Kulyukin, V., Kutiyanawala, A.: Accessible Shopping Systems for Blind and Visually Impaired Individuals: Design Requirements and the State of the Art. The Open Rehabilitation Journal 2, 158–168 (2010), 10.2174/1874943701003010158, ISSN: 1874-9437
5. Bay, H., Tuytelaars, T., Van Gool, L.: SURF: Speeded Up Robust Features. In: Leonardis, A., Bischof, H., Pinz, A. (eds.) ECCV 2006. LNCS, vol. 3951, pp. 404–417. Springer, Heidelberg (2006)
6. Sam, S., Tsai, S., Chen, D., Chandrasekhar, V., Takacs, G., Ngai-Man, C.:
7. Vedantham, R., Grzeszczuk, R., Girod, B.: Mobile Product Recognition. In: Proceedings of the International Conference on Multimedia (MM 2010), pp. 1587–1590. ACM, New York (1873), http://doi.acm.org/10.1145/1873951.1874293, doi:10.1145/1873951.1874293
8. Girod, B., Chandrasekhar, V., Chen, D.M., Ngai-Man, C., Grzeszczuk, R., Reznik, Y., Takacs, G., Tsai, S.S., Vedantham, R.: Mobile Visual Search. IEEE Signal Processing Magazine 28(4), 61–76 (2011), doi:10.1109/MSP.2011.940881
9. von Reischach, F., Michahelles, F., Guinard, D., Adelmann, R., Fleisch, E., Schmidt, A.: An Evaluation of Product Identification Techniques for Mobile Phones. In: Gross, T., Gulliksen, J., Kotzé, P., Oestreicher, L., Palanque, P., Prates, R.O., Winckler, M. (eds.) INTERACT 2009. LNCS, vol. 5726, pp. 804–816. Springer, Heidelberg (2009)

Assessment Test Framework for Collecting and Evaluating Fall-Related Data Using Mobile Devices

Stefan Almer[1], Josef Kolbitsch[1], Johannes Oberzaucher[2], and Martin Ebner[1]

[1] Institute for Information Systems and Computer Media,
Graz University of Technology,
Inffeldgasse 16c, 8010 Graz, Austria
`stefan.almer@student.tugraz.at`,
`{josef.kolbitsch,martin.ebner}@tugraz.at`
`http://www.iicm.edu`
[2] Institute for Rehabilitation and Ambient Assisted Living Technologies,
CEIT RALTEC,
Am Concorde Park 2, 2320 Schwechat, Austria
`j.oberzaucher@ceit.at`
`http://www.ceit.at`

Abstract. With an increasing population of older people the number of falls and fall-related injuries is on the rise. This will cause changes for future health care systems, and fall prevention and fall detection will pose a major challenge. Taking the multimodal character of fall-related parameters into account, the development of adequate strategies for fall prevention and detection is very complex. Therefore, it is necessary to collect and analyze fall-related data.

This paper describes the development of a test framework to perform a variety of assessment tests to collect fall-related data. The aim of the framework is to easily set up assessment tests and analyze the data regarding fall-related behaviors. It offers an open interface to support a variety of devices. The framework consists of a Web service, a relational database and a Web-based backend. In order to test the framework, a mobile device client recording accelerometer and gyroscope sensor data is implemented on the iOS platform. The evaluation, which includes three mobility assessment tests, demonstrates the sensor accuracy for movement analysis for further feature extraction.

Keywords: fall detection, fall prevention, mobile devices, restful Web service.

1 Introduction

The demographic change by [8] shows that the average age of the European inhabitants will increase. A recent projection by [9] shows that in 2060, the number of people aged 80 or over is three times larger than in 2008 and the rate of people aged 65 and over will double. With the rising age of the population also the

K. Miesenberger et al. (Eds.): ICCHP 2012, Part II, LNCS 7383, pp. 83–90, 2012.

number of falls and fall-related injuries rise [10]. According to [10] approximately 28-35% of people aged 65 and over fall each year about 2 to 4 times while 32-42% of the people aged 70 fall. Therefore, falls are a relevant factor in the society especially in the in group of older and disabled people and will raise new challenges for the healthcare, care systems and retirement plans.

Therefore, fall prevention and fall detection will become a major challenge. To perform fall detection, it is important to distinguish between activities of daily living and a fall. Current approaches deal with the fact that a fall-like behavior has a higher acceleration than normal activities [12]. Consequently, it is possible to define an acceleration threshold where a fall is detected [12]. According to [11], also the position of the sensor leads to different body accelerations which makes it more difficult to identify a fall-like behavior. Taking all the facts into account, fall prevention and fall detection is a complex task.

With the growing success of mobile devices, especially smartphones, it can be observed that such devices are becoming more accepted among older people. Moreover, modern mobile devices are equipped with the necessary hardware sensors as well the required software capabilities for performing automatic fall detection. Using smartphones has the advantage of cost effectiveness, robust and stable hardware as well as the form factor, which makes them well-suited for pervasive fall detection.

In order to develop an adequate algorithm for automatic fall detection and prevention by using smartphones, an assessment-based test framework has been implemented. The purpose of the framework is to collect (fall-related) motion data in order to evaluate and analyze them regarding fall detection, taking different activities and positions of the smartphone into account. The framework uses an open and easy to use interface while supporting different devices with their sensors. This paper shows the development of a Web-based test framework, used by a variety of mobile devices in order to record motion data. Furthermore, the architecture and the poof-of-concept is discussed.

2   Related Work

Fall detection methods are divided into three main approaches using a wearable device, camera-based or ambience device [4]. This paper focuses on the wearable device approach by using mobile devices and its embedded sensors such as accelerometer and gyroscope for measuring body movement. The advantage of this approach is that it is independent of the user's location and a fall-like behavior can be directly assigned to the user.

[5], [6] and [7] use mobile phones equipped with accelerometers to detect a fall. The application by [5] monitors the X, Y and Z acceleration in order to detect a fall. [6] developed an application running on Google's Android mobile platform and presented a fall detection algorithm. The system proposed by [7] focuses on the advantages and disadvantages of using mobile phones for fall detection.

Fall prevention is a wide research topic and varies in the ways a fall is prevented or predicted and differentiates between usage based on context such as nursing home, hospital, home or living in the community. According to [14], [15], [16], [17], and [10] the following most common fall prevention methods can be identified:

– Assessment tests: By performing common clinical mobility assessment tests, the fall risk of a user can be determined.
– Adjustment of environment and walking aids: Potential tripping hazards can be removed and by using walking aids the risk of falling can be reduced.
– Gait Analyses: Based on the analysis of the gait pattern, a potential fall can be predicted and the user is alarmed.
– Education: By clarifying the fall risk factors to the involved parties, fall risks can be reduced.
– Exercise/training: Specifically developed training sessions and exercises strengthen the patient's body and thus reduce the risk of falling.
– Medications: The use of the wrong medication can lead to reduced alertness, balance and gait.

3   Framework Architecture

In order to evaluate and analyze fall-related data gathered by devices during assessment-based tests, a framework for collecting motion data is required. The described framework provides an open interface to support a variety of devices. The framework is designed to offer great flexibility and extensibility in order to integrate different types of devices and sensors. The recorded motion data is saved in a consistent way on a consolidated database backend and analyzed afterwards.

The framework consists of three main components: database, interface and client as depicted in Fig. 1. A client-server architecture based on a 3-tier architecture is chosen. This architecture offers a clean separation of the presentation, application and data layer.

The data layer consists of a database for storing test-related data as well as the device types with their configured sensors. The relational database ensures integrity and consistency of the data. The application layer resides on the server side and implements the Application Programming Interface (API). The interface is implemented as a Web service according to the Representational State Transfer (REST) architectural style [13]. This approach offers best flexibility for implementing the client regardless of the programming language. Therefore, different kinds of devices used for measuring motion can be integrated into the framework. The client layer is responsible for recording motion data and uses the Web service API for storing test-related data.

3.1   Features of the Framework

The framework features an assessment test-based approach. With an assessment test, the following properties are assigned:

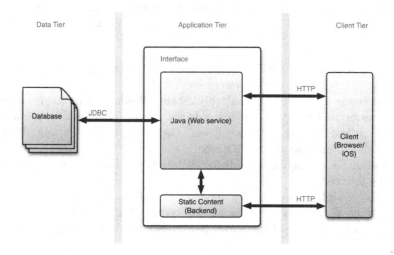

Fig. 1. 3-tier Framework Architecture

– the user who actually performs the test;
– the researcher who observes the test;
– location, start and end time of the test;
– the performed test type, e.g., "Timed Up and Go";
– the device sensors and their data types;
– the used devices with its position and sample rate.

After the test is finished, the client transfers the recorded motion data to the database backend using the Web service and is assigned to the performed assessment test. This allows to access the recorded data later on for performing the required evaluation. The framework offers the possibility to assign various results of different evaluation methods to the test. This makes it possible to compare the result of the performed evaluations.

To provide a better user experience, a Web-based administrative tool has been developed. This tool allows the creation of tests, users, devices and their related sensors.

4   Mobile Device Client

A mobile device client for the iOS platform, especially the iPhone 4, has been implemented. The client is used to demonstrate the functionality of the framework as well as the capabilities and sensor accuracy of the iPhone 4. The application uses the possibility to receive high-rate continuous motion data with the "Core Motion" framework. The framework provides access to raw accelerometer data, raw gyroscope data, and processed device-motion data. Motion data is obtained by requesting the data at the given interval and saved locally on the device during the assessment test.

The communication with the Web service API is achieved by using HTTP requests. First, the user is authenticated and the current device information is loaded to identify the used device. Subsequently, the client periodically requests for the currently running tests issued for the current user and device. After a running test has been found, the device starts recording motion data and periodically requests the status of the test in the background. If the test is finished, the recorded data is transmitted to the Web service.

The iOS application depicted in Fig. 2 consists of several easy-to-use interfaces which are designed to require as little user interaction as possible. Fig. 2a shows the main view and displays current user and device information. A running test is indicated by the green background in the first cell with the appropriate status description as seen in Fig. 2b. Moreover, the device settings used (position and sample rate) for the current test are shown.

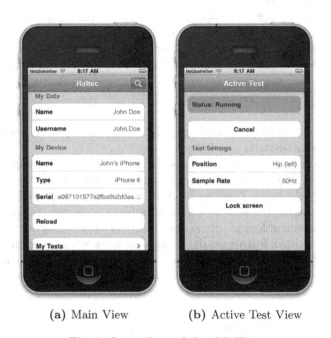

(a) Main View   (b) Active Test View

Fig. 2. Screenshots of the iOS Client

5   Evaluation

The framework and the iOS client were evaluated by running three common clinical mobility assessment tests. The "2-Minute Walk" (2MWT), "Sit-to-Stand 5" (STS5) and "Timed Up and Go" (TUG) tests were performed [3], [2], [1]. The evaluation proved the flexibility, availability and integrity of the framework as well as the recorded gait data of the iPhone 4 regarding movement analysis and feature extraction.

The test scenarios comprised creating the tests and their dependencies using the administrative backend. For each test two iPhones using the implemented client were used for recording the motion data during the test to demonstrate the capabilities of the framework. During the assessment, the motion data was stored locally on the devices and was transmitted to the Web service after the test was finished. Finally, the recorded data was analyzed.

5.1   Test Settings

The tests were performed in a well equipped room for assessment testing. A notebook using the Mozilla Firefox browser was used for performing backend relevant tasks such as creating assessment tests, users, devices and its sensors. The notebook as well as the two mobile phones were connected though Wi-Fi with the Internet. As mobile devices running the client application, an iPhone 4 (using accelerometer and gyroscope) and an iPhone 3 (using accelerometer only) have been connected to the Web service using the proband's user credentials. Both devices were running all the tests with a sample rate of 50Hz. The iPhone 4 was located on the right hip and the iPhone 3 on the left hip height.

5.2   Analysis

The gait data recorded by the iPhone 4 has been visualized and analyzed regarding movement analysis and feature extraction.

In Fig. 3, data recorded during the performance of a classical *2-Minute Walk* test can be seen. The test was performed on a 10 meter straight walk passage. During the test, the test-subject had to walk with "normal" (self-chosen) speed. As depicted in Fig. 3, the iPhone 4 data promises a good base for ongoing data analysis and movement feature extraction (based on simple peak detection as well as more sophisticated feature analysis, such as knowledge-based methods and statistical analysis). Single movement passages (for example 10m straight walk, turn around) are distinguishable by performing a simple Support Vector Machine

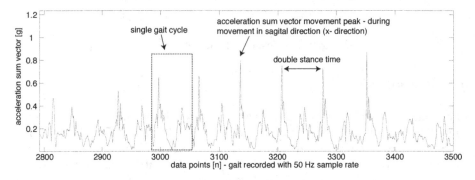

Fig. 3. Detailed Gait Signal During 2-Minute Walk with Normal Gait Speed (Single Steps)

(SVM) calculation and following peak detection. A calculation of peak distances offers the opportunity to extract important and fall risk describing parameters (for instance gait cycle times, variances over time) in the time domain.

After the 2 minutes of normal walking, a walking phase with an increased speed can be seen, which is characterized by a well increased value of the acceleration sum vector peaks during the movement in x-direction (sagittal plane).

The evaluation of the *Sit-to-Stand* test shows a good base for feature extraction of classical assessment parameters like STS5 performance time as well as an expanded set of features like single movement times. The *Timed Up and Go* test evaluation shows a base for feature extraction. Moreover, parameters for classical assessments like TUG performance time can be extracted as well as an expanded set of features (single movement times, gait cycle times, variances over time).

6 Conclusion

Developing a fall detection algorithm is a complex task. A fall must be differentiated from activities of daily living. Moreover, also the position of the used motion tracking device influences the fall detection behavior. In order to perform fall detection and fall prevention analysis, an assessment test framework has been developed. The framework is based on a 3-tier architecture consisting of a data layer for storing motion data, an application layer which implements an open interface and the client layer for recording motion data.

The application layer offers a RESTful Web service with the ability to integrate various devices with their sensors into the framework. This approach makes it easy to create new assessment tests taking all the different fall parameters into account. The collected data is analyzed after the test with the possibility to save and compare results.

In order to demonstrate the functionality of the framework, a mobile device client was implemented. This proof-of-concept implementation runs natively on iOS devices, particularly the iPhone 4, and records motion data using accelerometer and gyroscope sensors. The evaluation was done by performing three clinical assessment tests. The visualization and evaluation of the recorded iPhone 4 motion data showed that the framework fulfills the requirements for data storage and processing as well as flexibility regarding the integration of new devices into the framework. Moreover, the iPhone 4 is well-suited for movement analysis regarding the sensor data and accuracy.

References

1. Podsiadlo, D., Richardson, S.: The Timed "Up & Go": A Test of Basic Functional Mobility for Frail Elderly Persons. American Geriatrics Society 39, 142–148 (1991)
2. Whitney, S.L., Wrisley, D.M., Marchetti, G.F., Gee, M.A., Redfern, M.S., Furman, J.M.: Clinical Measurement of Sit-To-Stand Performance in People With Balance Disorders: Validity of Data for the Five-Times-Sit-To-Stand Test. Physical Therapy 85, 1034–1045 (2005)

3. Lewis, C., Shaw, K.: Benefits of the 2-Minute Walk Test. Physical Therapy & Rehab Medicine 16 (2005)
4. Yu, X.: Approaches and Principles of Fall Detection for Elderly and Patient. In: 10th International Conference on e-Health Networking, Applications and Services, pp. 42–47. IEEE, Singapore (2008)
5. Lopes, I.C., Vaidya, B., Rodrigues, J.J.P.C.: SensorFall - An Accelerometer Based Mobile Application. In: 2nd International Conference on Computer Science and its Applications, pp. 1–6. IEEE, Jeju (2009)
6. Dai, J., Bai, X., Yang, Z., Shen, Z., Xuan, D.: PerFallD: A Pervasive Fall Detection System using Mobile Phones. In: 8th IEEE International Conference on Pervasive Computing and Communications Workshops, pp. 292–297. IEEE, Mannheim (2010)
7. Sposaro, F., Tyson, G.: iFall: An Android Application for Fall Monitoring and Response. In: Annual International Conference of the IEEE Engineering in Medicine and Biology Society, pp. 6119–6122. IEEE, Minneapolis (2009)
8. van den Broek, G., Cavallo, F., Odetti, L., Wehrmann, C.: Ambient Assisted Living Roadmap. VDI/VDE-IT AALIANCE Office (2009)
9. Eurostat: Population Projections 2008-2060, http://europa.eu/rapid/pressReleasesAction.do?reference=STAT/08/119
10. World Health Organization: WHO Global Report on Falls Prevention in Older Age. World Health Organization (2007)
11. Kangas, M., Konttila, A., Winblad, I., Jämsa, T.: Determination of Simple Thresholds for Accelerometry-Based Parameters for Fall Detection. In: 29th Annual International Conference of the Engineering in Medicine and Biology Society, pp. 1367–1370. IEEE, Lyon (2007)
12. Noury, N., Fleury, A., Rumeau, P., Bourke, A.K., Laighin, G., Rialle, V., Lundy, J.E.: Fall Detection - Principles and Methods. In: 29th Annual International Conference of the Engineering in Medicine and Biology Society, pp. 1663–1666. IEEE, Lyon (2007)
13. Fielding, R.T.: Architectural Styles and the Design of Network-based Software Architectures. University of California, Irvine (2000)
14. Todd, C., Skelton, D.: What are the main risk factors for falls among older people and what are the most effective interventions to prevent these falls? WHO Regional Office for Europe, Copenhagen (2004)
15. Tremblay Jr., K.R., Barber, C.E.: Preventing Falls in the Elderly (2005), http://www.ext.colostate.edu/pubs/consumer/10242.pdf
16. LeMier, M., Silver, I., Bowe, C.: Falls Among Older Adults: Strategies for Prevention. Washington State Department of Health (2002)
17. Bridging Research in Ageing and ICT Development: Automatic Wearable Fall Detectors (2008), http://capsil.braidproject.eu/index.php?title=Automatic_wearable_fall_detectors&oldid=1738

NAVCOM – WLAN Communication between Public Transport Vehicles and Smart Phones to Support Visually Impaired and Blind People

Werner Bischof[1], Elmar Krajnc[2], Markus Dornhofer[1], and Michael Ulm[2]

[1] FH JOANNEUM – EVU, Austria,
Werk VI-Street 46, A8605 Kapfenberg
werner.bischof@fh-joanneum.at
[2] FH JOANNEUM Internet-Technologies, Austria

Abstract. Visually impaired and blind people want to move or travel on their own but they depend on public transport systems. This is sometimes challenging. Some problems are to find the right vehicle, signalling their wish to enter or leave the vehicle and getting information of the upcoming stations. To solve these problem very specialized equipment was develop. In this paper we show a solution with standard WLAN components and a standard smart phone, that might solve these problems. Hopefully this raises the life quality for the people with special needs.

Keywords: Mobility, accessibility, vehicle communication, WLAN, smart phone, IBIS, public transport.

1   Introduction and Motivation

Mobility is a very important factor for a self-determined life. People want to move or travel on their own whenever and wherever they want. Most people can use their car, their bike or just go by foot to nearly any place they want. But not everyone is able to move or travel independently.

People with special needs depend on travelling by public transport like trains, busses, subways and trams. For seeing persons travelling by public transport isn't a big challenge. They can see an arriving bus, can choose the rights train on a crowded railway station or recognize the next stop when they are in the vehicle. Visually impaired and blind people don't have these options. Visually impaired and blind people want to be able to choose the right bus choose to leave on the suiting station. To find the right platform or to move in public places on their own is substantial.

In the project series Ways4all [1] the aim is to create a barrier-free system for orientation and movement in public space for people with special needs. The concept includes components which allows indoors and outdoors navigation, communication with public transport and public infrastructure to ensure safe travel. Several parts of this system are already implemented, like for instance the consultation of numerous sources of public transport schedules, the concept of indoor guidance [2] and the implementation of a barrier-free user interface for smart phones [3].

K. Miesenberger et al. (Eds.): ICCHP 2012, Part II, LNCS 7383, pp. 91–98, 2012.

In this paper we describe the communication between a public transport vehicle and the person's smart phone, the project NAVCOM.

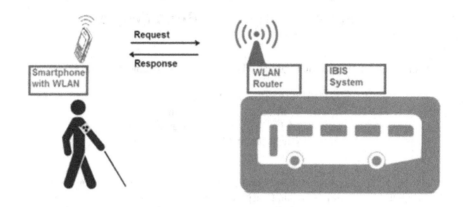

Fig. 1. Overview of NAVCOM System

1.1   Related Work

The projects of the ways4all series are not the only research projects that support people with reduced mobility.

The PAVIP system allows visually impaired users with a portable hand-held device (Milestone) communication and interaction with the corresponding counterpart. There is a radio module installed in the handset, where data between vehicles or appropriate information points and the handset can be exchanged. Every component (i.e. vehicle or check-in points) requires one PAVIP box. The PAVIP box can transmit various information to the user's devices, like the bus number, the direction or the next stop. [4] The user must log on with an RFID chip with 13.56 MHz at the bus stop (check in). This chip provides the essential information to find the suitable public transport vehicle. A disadvantage of this system is only that static information is specified at check-in points. These points are also difficult to locate. The range of passive RFID tags is only a few centimeters and must be found by the user at each bus stop.

Apex Prague TYFLOSET® is designed as a unified system for all types of acoustic information and orientation in the Czech Republic. The blind person uses a command station where he or she can activate all voice information and the guidance systems. The blind person can request an acoustic report on the number of the bus and the driving direction of the arriving vehicle at a public bus stop. As far as the blind person wants to break into the vehicle, he/she confirms his/her intention to the driver with his command through a key transmitter. The feedback from the system will also be given via the external speaker of the vehicle (same like PAVIP). The blind person can use additional annexes to TYFLOSET® system such as the acoustic position marking on buildings, in sunsets, at intersections with traffic signals operate, and so on in a similar way. Following the introduction of visual information systems for passengers in the form of large-area displays, the system TYFLOSET® allows providing audible information with identical content for blind and partially sighted people. The company Apex GmbH uses the frequency 433.95 MHz for TYFLOSET®, so a reach of 100m can be made possible. [5]

The Digital Speech (DISA) should make acoustically accessible the visual information displayed on billboards to blind and visually impaired persons. Therefore stations are equipped with appropriate devices which visually displayed information can translate into language. "For the spatial detection of the speech output, which can be integrated into existing systems in a simple manner, there is a signal that can be requested by the visually impaired through a separate radio transmitter in the wider area of a station."[6]. The system provides assistance to get knowledge about punctuality of transport and driving off the stop lines for the visually impaired. Unfortunately, it is not possible that the transmitter, communicate with the vehicle, to localize this, or to issue a stop request.

RAMPE Project – Interactive Auditory Information System for the Mobility of Blind People in Public Transports – extended mobility in public transport is made possible to blind and visually impaired people. The system makes use of Personal Digital Assistants (PDA) with wireless support. This system can be used at bus and tram stops and major towns for the use of public transport. The user is given the major route information by the PDA that is Wi-Fi router connected to the RAMPE at the stop (Lines, schedules or additional information, such as delays, or vehicle arrival notifications of the operator). This information is given by the RAMPE access point (hotspot) and can be played back using the application on the PDA. The RAMPE system provides no way of user interaction with the vehicle. [7]

1.2   Summarizing

All these projects help people with special needs to find their way in public transport. But at a closer look we can find some advantages and also disadvantages. All these related projects have a wide range and a fast signal transmission. But there are also some dis advantages. These projects are using specialized hardware for the hand tool and also for the vehicle. There are also now standards in the used radio system (Apex and DISA 434MHz,   PAVIP 868MHz, RAMPE 2.4 GHz)

2   Implementation of the NAVCOM System

The project NAVCOM tries to bring together the best features of each of these projects. As a wireless radio technology Wi-Fi is used, which is normally available on most smart phones. Based on wireless technology a standard wireless router with open source software could be used as IBIS slave. The user has the opportunity to communicate directly to the vehicle by using his personal mobile phone with a special application. Each request of the user will be confirmed by feedback of the system and by voice output. So passers-by are harassed by outside speakers of the vehicle no longer. Direct wireless connection via socket allows transferring only relevant information. A connection to the Internet would be possible, but was not currently enabled.

2.1   System Architecture

Nowadays public transport systems are connected by an Intermodal Transport Control System (ITCS)[1] . Data between the public transport vehicles and a control unit can be exchanged over an air interface. Inside the vehicles, the IBIS bus supplies all components with information. By example, the outdoor display receives the right destination and the line number from the IBIS bus. The IBIS bus is an old fashioned and low speed protocol. It is designed as master and slave system and the main activity is to transmit information to all components. This information can be easy received with an IBIS-to-RS232 Connector.   Unfortunately it is impossible to transmit data back to the IBIS Master, without a change in the IBIS system. With the help of a USB-to-serial converter the information can be analyzed by a wireless LAN Router. On the wireless LAN Router the default firmware was replaced by a Linux-Distribution for Embedded devices called OpenWrt [8]. This step is required to run customized services on the Router. Some available Routers have just one USB Interface, so a USB Hub is used to connect multiple devices. With an USB audio stick different sounds can be triggered by the Router. Visually impaired people should localize the vehicle with the help of acoustics. These sounds can be enabled by a USB-Relay-Board. A second relay triggers a stop request. It has the same function as the button in the bus, which visualizes the driver the stop request by a signal lamp. The lamp is switching off on the next bus stop. Multiple wireless LAN Clients (i.e. smart phones) can connect to the Router and use the custom service on the router to trigger the following actions:

- Play the bird sound to localize the bus
- Request the next bus stop
- Entry request to enter the bus
- Exit request to leave the bus

2.2   Router Operating System

The Linux distribution OpenWrt [8] supports more than 100 different Router devices. A well-structured software developing kit can be downloaded from the Internet. After the selection of the router model the software developing kit generates the right cross-compiler for the Router CPU.   Now services on the router can be developed. With the packaging system opkg on the programs can be easily installed on the router. It also takes care of all dependencies of the program and the libraries.

All components are standard devices and available on the market. This enables a low cost solution.

2.3   Client Components

The Communication between the bus and blind people will be done by a mobile application. This application was first created for Nokias mobile operation system Symbian, because it's the most popular system for Blind People. New requirements and because of the missing Symbian support in the near future we migrated our basis

---

[1] Former known as Rechnergestütztes Betriebsleitsystem RBL.

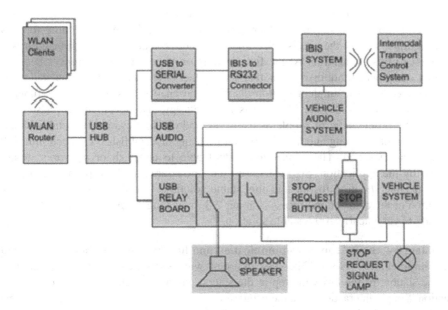

Fig. 2. System overview of vehicle components

application to the widely spread system Android. Another main reason for the Android system was the wide open architecture which allows activating a lot of features for disabled people. The bus and the application communicate over a wireless LAN connection. On this connection we enable a socket connection between the router (bus) and the application (blind people). By this connection we send commands to each device. Each Command will be connected to a sequence of simple messages. In general it sounds like a simple process but in detail there are a lot of problems.

Problem 1 – Finding possible WLAN connections. Each WLAN has its own name, called SSID (Service Set Identifier). It's impossible to connect with the first founded SSID because in city areas the possibility to find more than one WLAN connection is nearly by 100%. So we need to define our own SSID Schema. Why we need a Schema and can't use exactly one SSID? The reason is because there will be more than one bus using this system in the future. So it's also possible that more than one bus can cross meeting point of blind people and we can't identify on a quick way which bus is the correct one for their journey. So we defined a Schema with a Prefix "NAVCOM" to filter all founded SSIDs to a qualified amount of possible SSIDs. Combined with the Number of the Bus and the name of last bus stop we can define the bus line and the driving direction.

Problem 2 – Establish new Connection. Connecting with a wireless network is a simple user process. First the user selects a wireless connection and the second step is that the device will connect to the selected connection. The technical problem hap-pens at the android framework because enabling, disabling, connecting and disconnecting wireless connections are asynchronous processes. The implemented solution is doing one step by another step. First the application is searching for new connections, second the use is selecting a connection and third the application will connect to this connection. At the first description there are no differences between theory and practice, but there is another special fact of connecting to the needed wireless connection. Our implementation disabled and enables first the wireless functionality of the user's device. Many tests at the design and development phase have shown the problematic of problems using the android framework. Re-establishing a connection or selecting another connection by using an established connection hasn't worked as expected. The connection wasn't able to establish or networks wasn't found by the application. So we focused the source area of those problems and we were trouble shooting to find out this stable solution. One disadvantage is that the duration of the connection process is about 2-3 times longer than without our "workaround" to get a nearly 100% stable solution.

Problem 3 – client / router communication and how we can tell blind people what will happen now. "Normal" people can use all wits. So they can see the bus is coming to the station, or the bus will stop at the station and also when the bus is leaving the station. Simple interactions like the using of the entry button of the bus are not the same for Blind people. Blind People can use our "Entry Button" for telling the busdriver that they want to entry the bus, but Blind People need a feedback for this action, that the system is working properly or not. So we designed our communication with a feedback process that each command will get an answer from the other site of communication. In this example the application will send the message "EW" to the router and the router will answer with the message "EW-A". The Letter "A" is our "Acknowledged" Part of an answer message. This schema of original message and acknowledged extension will be used at all command sequences between the router and the client.

Problem 4 – losing wireless connection. Blind people will also leaving. Our concepts integrated the possibility of using an Exit-Button, but we want to get a proper usage of our system. So the router needs to know which client "is alive" and which client leaved or "died". The solution for this problem is the usage of solution nr 3. The Router sends a Heartbeat to the client and the client will send an answer back. Each site will accept a timeout of 5 seconds. By overrunning this timeout the router and the client will close the connection. The Client also will tell the user that the connection was killed because of missing communication to the router in a user friendly way.

3   First Test Results

To confirm our system implementation we tested three different scenarios.

- **Scenario 1:** The person is inside the moving public transport vehicle. The main goals are to get the upcoming stops and to request a stop at the next station.

- **Scenario 2:** The communication between a slowly moving person and a non moving vehicle. The target of the person is to find the right transport vehicle on a public place.
- **Scenario 3:** The person is waiting on a station and wants to send a request for entering the vehicle to the driver.

For the test setup we installed a WLAN Router in a car (VW Touran). The router (Cisco Linksys WRT160NL) was arranged in the trunk and also near the windscreen. The test for scenario 1, was done on an 12.5 km track in the city of Kapfenberg. The vehicle was moving between 0 and 50 km/h. The traffic was medium. The test for scenario 1 worked very well. The person and the WLAN route have a fixed distance, and are moving with the same speed. There were no problems to establish a connection and the test person got all messages and was able to send stop-request. The test for scenario 2 and 3 were done in the parking place of the FH Joanneum and a nearby industrial area.

The results for scenario 2 were also very satisfying. The connection to the router was established without problems. After the connection with the right line, the request for bird twitter was send and the person was able to hear the vehicle. There were no problems with the signal strength.

For the test scenario 3 are the results not satisfying. About 50% of the tests ended with a failure. We recognized that the timing for the WLAN search and the connection to the route is not well organized. To get a suitable result the timing of the search process and the start of the connection should be automated form data as the right arrival time and the position of the person.

4   Outlook and Conclusion

In our test of the system we showed that this solution based on standard component, is a practical approach to solve the problems of visually impaired and blind people with public traffic vehicles. One existing problem is the delay of the WLAN connection. Scanning the networks and establishing a connection requires about 4 to 7 seconds. For scenario 1 and 2 is this time sufficient, but for fast moving public transport vehicles this could be a problem. For further development we are using special antennas and better accessible spots for the router on the vehicle. Also some improvements of the software settings will provide a better timing of the connection process.

Acknowledgements. The project NAVCOM started in May 2010. The overall project manager is the University of Applied Sciences FH-JOANNEUM in Kapfenberg, Austria. Project participants are "Wiener Linien", "ÖBB", TU Graz - Institute of Building Informatics and the Österr. Blinden- u. Sehbehindertenverband. The Project is subsidized by the Austrian Federal Ministry for Transport, Innovation and Technology (BMVIT) and the Austrian Research Promotion Agency (FFG).

References

1. Ways4all (2012), http://www.ways4all.at (visited January 2012)
2. Kiers, M., Bischof, W., Krajnc, E., Dornhofer, M.: Evaluation and Improvements of an RFID Based Indoor Navigation System for Visually impaired and Blind People. In: 2011 International Conference on Indoor Positioning and Indoor Navigation; Paper, Guimarães, Portugal (September 2011)
3. Krajnc, E., Knoll, M., Feiner, J., Traar, M.: A Touch Sensitive User Interface Approach on Smartphones for Visually Impaired and Blind Persons. In: Holzinger, A., Simonic, K.-M. (eds.) USAB 2011. LNCS, vol. 7058, pp. 585–594. Springer, Heidelberg (2011)
4. PAVIP (2012), PAVIP Transport Flyer,
   http://www.bones.ch/bones/media/downloads-ger/
   pavip/Flyer%20PAVIP%20Transport.pdf (visited January 2012)
5. APEX (2012). System TYFLOSET® – Ein elektronisches Orientierungs- und Informations-system für Blinde und Sehbehinderte,
   http://www.apex-jesenice.cz/tyfloset.php?lang=de (visited January 2012)
6. CAT: DISA – Digitale Sprachausgabe – Fahrgastinformationssystem für Blinde und Sehbe-hinderte im öffentlichen Personennahverkehr (2012), http://www.cat-traffic.de/
   DE/06_html_oepnv/06_oepnv_1.php
7. Baudoin, G., Venard, O., Uzan, G., Rousseau, A., Benabou, Y., Paumier, A., Cesbron, J.: The RAMPE Project: Interactive, Auditive Information System for the Mobility of Blind People in Public Transports. In: Proc. of the 5th International Conference on ITS Telecom-munications, Brest, France (2005)
8. OpenWrt (2011), OpenSource WLAN router firmware, https://openwrt.org/
   (visited January 2012)

Mobile-Type Remote Captioning System for Deaf or Hard-of-Hearing People and the Experience of Remote Supports after the Great East Japan Earthquake

Shigeki Miyoshi[1], Sumihiro Kawano[1], Mayumi Shirasawa[1], Kyoko Isoda[1],
Michiko Hasuike[1], Masayuki Kobayashi[1], and Midori Umehara[2]

[1] National University Corporation Tsukuba University of Technology,
4-3-15 Amakubo, Tsukuba 305-8520, Japan
`{miyoshi,kawano,shirasawa,isoda,mhasuike,`
`masayuki}@a.tsukuba-tech.ac.jp`
[2] CSR Division, SOFTBANK MOBILE Corp.,
1-9-1 Higashi-shimbashi, Minato-ku, Tokyo 105-7317, Japan
`midori.umehara@tm.softbank.co.jp`

Abstract. Mobile-type Remote Captioning System which we proposed is to realize advanced support for sightseeing tours using an uttering guide or practical field trip outside of class. Our syetem utilizes the mobile phone network provided by Japanese mobile phone carriers, the monthly flat-rate voice call and data transfer services. By using these services, deaf or hard-of-hearing student could use real-time captioning while walking. On March 11, 2011, the Great East Japan Earthquake shook Japan. After the quake, there was a great lack of the volunteer students(captionists) inside of the affection areas. Universities outside of the affection areas supported remotely to cover the volunteer work. In order to realize such remote support, the system reported by this paper was used.

Keywords: Remote Caption, Real-time, Deaf or Hard-of-Hearing, the Great East Japan Earthquake.

1 Introduction

Currently, there are over 1,100 deaf or hard-of-hearing students enrolled at universities around Japan. Naturally, this is exceeded by the number of pupils and students at schools for the deaf or ordinary schools at the primary and secondary levels. In order that these students can fully experience the learning activities in class, it is necessary to provide them with information access that transcribes the speech of teachers and the peripheral sound information into sign language or text. As a method of providing information access to deaf or hard-of-hearing students, handwriting notetaking is widely used to transmit what the teacher is saying. Meanwhile, computer-assisted notetaking is also becoming popular recently and can be anticipated to become a major method in the future. In general, this computer-assisted notetaking method is characteristic in that it allows much more information to be transmitted to deaf or hard-of-hearing students than when the handwriting notetaking method is used.

K. Miesenberger et al. (Eds.): ICCHP 2012, Part II, LNCS 7383, pp. 99–104, 2012.

There are two ways in the computer-assisted method. The first is where information input is made by people taking turns, one person for 20 minutes at a time. The second way is to assign two people to turn given part of spoken content into text. The latter is unique to Japan (cooperate typing). Incidentally, notetaking in Japan denotes the use of a captioning device to transmit the content of a lecture and the surroundings (such as comments by someone or the bell ringing inside the classroom). It is a method that provides real-time transmission of information and does not provide summarized notes of the lecture content.

There is a freeware called IPtalk[1] developed by Shigeaki Kurita that is suited for implementing this cooperative typing method. This program has made it possible for a single person to work with many words that would have conventionally been difficult to handle. There is also a free server software ITBC2[2] developed by Naoya Mori that distributes caption data created on IPtalk within a local network (wired LAN and wireless LAN) to PCs connected to that network.

The National University Corporation Tsukuba University of Technology with which the authors are affiliated is the only university in Japan that provides everything to accommodate deaf, hard-of-hearing, or visually impaired people. While there are services such as C.A.R.T. provided in Japan, they are extremely expensive and our university is the only one that uses such services for usual lectures[3]. Meanwhile, there are no products or services such as Remote C.A.R.T. in Japan, and the only similar thing available is the correspondence system we have uniquely developed that is now being used for lectures at the university. The characteristics of this system are such as the high caption displaying speed and the high quality of the captions. This is thanks to efforts made to ensure that no definition quality is lost in the video images showing the lecture room scene (presentations given by lecturers or the whiteboard used by lecturers for explanations) or in the captions. In order to bring these advantages to reality, each class will require one to two technical staff members (not someone to input text), which means high personnel cost.

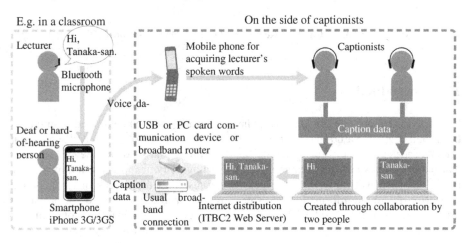

Fig. 1. Configuration of Mobile-type Remote-captioning System using a mobile phone (iPhone 3G, 3GS, 4, or 4S)

At present, there are limits to handwriting notetaking when using information access while walking, which prevents advanced support through cooperate typing. For this reason, we cannot anticipate advanced support for sightseeing tours using an uttering guide or practical field trip outside of class. To ameliorate this situation, we are proposing a mobile-type remote captioning system, whose system makeup is shown in Fig. 1.

Under this system, a deaf or hard-of-hearing person holds an iPhone that is connected to a hands-free microphone via Bluetooth. Fig. 2 shows an iPhone and a Bluetooth hands-free microphone. The deaf or hard-of-hearing person would use the smartphone to make a call (usual voice call) to the smartphone held by the people inputting the captions. By doing this, the voice of the lecturer will be transmitted to the people making the captions via the hands-free microphone, who will then change the voice information immediately into text on their notebook computers. The captions will then be displayed immediately on the smartphone. Deaf or hard-of-hearing students would read captions this way. Fig. 3 depicts how the service is used.

The system we are proposing have the following characteristic:

- It is built from accessible commercial products and a freeware programs;
- It uses mobile phone network;
- It utilizes the multitasking functionality of smartphones, while reducing the number of devices required and simplifying device operation (using caption displaying and updating functions through voice call function and web browser at the same time);
- It utilizes monthly flat-rate voice call and data transfer service provided by a mobile phone carrier.

These four characteristics mentioned above will provide the following advantages:

- A deaf or hard-of-hearing person can freely move about anywhere and receive advanced support regardless of where the person is indoors or outdoors
- Sharing of high-level skills of people handling text input;
- Continual operation is possible through cutback on labor and communication costs.

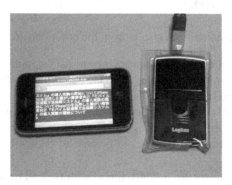

Fig. 2. iPhone 3G and Bluetooth mic-speaker

Fig. 3. Situation where our system was used

2   Methods

This system was used to test information accessing under various conditions with people creating captions as subjects. The conditions of use tested were: lessons or field trips for elementary school and junior high school students, lectures or field trips for university students who are deaf or hard-of-hearing, and indoor seminars or outdoor activities (guided sightseeing tour) for working people who are deaf or hard of hearing.

With such usage of this our system under various conditions being tested, we then asked test subjects with experience making captions through the conventional computer-assisted notetaking method to answer a questionnaire individually. The questionnaire was conducted after the testing of the system and there were a total of seventeen test subjects.

3   Summary of Results

The following were obtained from results from the questionnaire:

- This system does not distribute video footage to the captionists. The lack of video footage may likely stress captionists. Also, the possibility of deteriorated quality of the captions was also being pointed out.
- Technical staff is not required on the side of deaf or hard-of-hearing people, making it possible for the people using this system (only deaf of hard-of-hearing people, or together with the lecturer) to prepare or pack up during the break between classes.
- Compared with other existing systems, this system isn't all better, but it is useful as a method for outdoor support, or as a tool that allows the sharing of captionists among campuses.

4   The Experience of Remote Supports to the Universities in a Damaged Area after the Great East Japan Earthquake

On March 11, 2011, the Great East Japan Earthquake shook Japan, causing great tsunamis and crippling the Fukushima nuclear plants. This also caused great chaos in class scheduling at universities located at disaster-affected regions and where deaf or hard-of-hearing students were enrolled at the time. Japanese universities begin the academic year in April, but the earthquake forced the universities to delay the start to May. During the period immediately after the quake to the end of April, we worked with universities in affected areas to discuss about students' needs for support.

Before March 11, training of volunteer students who were scheduled to create captions for classes in the new semester starting from April was being conducted at universities of affected areas. However, after the quake the students were unable to go ahead with their volunteer work and there was a great lack of people to create captions.

This resulted in discussions about asking universities outside of the affection areas to support remotely to cover the volunteer work. In order to realize such remote support, the system reported by this paper was used.

There were thirteen universities that took part in the support. These universities ranged from one in Japanese northernmost Hokkaido all the way to Kyushu in the south. The total number of volunteering students from the supporting universities was 627. These students have been providing remote real-time captioning for seventeen deaf or hard-of-hearing students enrolled at four universities in earthquake hit areas. There have been 262 supported classes up to now (as of November 2011), with each class lasting ninety minutes. This remote support volunteer work is scheduled to continue into 2012.

This kind of trial was implemented through PEPNet-Japan[4] (the Japanese version of the PEPNet organization in the U.S.). In addition, SOFTBANK MOBILE Corp. (a major mobile carrier in Japan) also lent many smartphones for this trial to supporting universities and those in disaster-affected areas free of charge. The trial was possible thanks to this free lending service by Softbank.

5   Conclusions

On proposing this system, we also paid attention to ensure the system makeup could be easily imitated by other groups of people. Furthermore, in order for ongoing operation of the system, efforts and choices were made to cut back on communication and labor costs. Consequently, we were able to make clear of the merits and demerits of the system. In particular, we found that this system would be useful under conditions where existing methods fail to deliver.

Meanwhile, we have been able to harness the merits of this system to contribute to the restoration efforts after the Great East Japan Earthquake, with the trial currently ongoing.

We plan to recommend this system to universities, which we hope will allow the universities to share volunteer students between campuses and to implement outdoor activities and field trips for deaf or hard-of-hearing students. Further, as the next step we hope to see the sharing of student volunteers between universities. If such sharing becomes a reality, then we should be able to immediately respond to the needs after natural or man-made disasters. The remote support provided to disaster-struck areas this time has been a contribution in such situations.

References

1. Kurita, S.: IPtalk (2011), http://www.geocities.jp/shigeaki_kurita/
2. Mori, N.: ITBC2 (2012), http://www2.wbs.ne.jp/~condle/ITBC2.html
3. Miyoshi, S., et al.: A Basic Study on Supplementary Visual Information for Real-Time Captionists in the Lecture of Information Science. IEICE Trans. Inf. & Syst. (Japanse Edition) J91-D(9), 2236–2246 (2008)
4. PEPNet-Japan (The Postsecondary Education Programs Network of Japan) (2005), http://www.pepnet-j.org/

Handheld "App" Offering Visual Support to Students with Autism Spectrum Disorders (ASDs)

Bogdan Zamfir[1], Robert Tedesco[2], and Brian Reichow[1,3]

[1] Southern Connecticut State University, New Haven, CT, United States
zamfirb1@southernct.edu
[2] HandHold Adaptive, LLC, Shelton, CT, United States
robtedesco@handholdadaptive.com
[3] Yale Child Study Center, New Haven, CT, United States
brian.reichow@yale.edu

Abstract. iPrompts® is a software application for handheld devices that provides visual support to individuals with Autism Spectrum Disorders (ASDs). Caregivers use the application to create and present visual schedules, visual countdown timers, and visual choices, to help individuals with ASDs stay organized, understand upcoming events, and identify preferences. The developer of the application, HandHold Adaptive, LLC, initially introduced iPrompts on the iPhone and iPod Touch in May of 2009. The research team from the Center of Excellence on Autism Spectrum Disorders at Southern Connecticut State University conducted a study of iPrompts in 2010, investigating its use by educators working with students with ASDs. Among other findings, educators indicated a desire to present visual supports on a larger, "tablet"-sized display screen, leading the developer to produce an iPad-specific product, iPrompts® XL. Described in this paper are the research effort of iPrompts and subsequent development effort of iPrompts XL.

Keywords: autism spectrum disorder, ASD, iPad, iPhone, smartphone, tablet, handheld device, application, app, iPrompts.

1 Introduction to the Technology and Supporting R&D Effort

In May of 2009, HandHold Adaptive introduced the iPrompts application [1] for sale as the first special education application available on Apple's iTunes App Store. The founders of HandHold Adaptive, themselves the family of a young boy on the autism spectrum, designed a tool that would provide customizable, portable visual supports using the iPhone and iPod Touch. Subsequent to the introduction of this early version of iPrompts, the company received in 2010 a Phase I research award from the U.S. Department of Education's Institute of Education Sciences Small Business Innovation Research (SBIR) program in collaboration with a research team from the Center of Excellence on Autism Spectrum Disorders at Southern Connecticut State University (hereafter, SCSU Autism Center).

K. Miesenberger et al. (Eds.): ICCHP 2012, Part II, LNCS 7383, pp. 105–112, 2012.

iPrompts® XL is an iPad-specific version of iPrompts®, an "app" that provides a suite of visual supports for individuals with autism spectrum disorders (ASDs) and other developmental delays. The application allows users to create visual supports, including visual schedules, visual countdown timers, and visual choices, to present to individuals with ASDs. Both iPrompts and iPrompts XL include four main features: Schedules, Countdown, Choices and Library. Each feature is customizable, allowing educators and related personnel to respond quickly to unexpected situations that arise in educational settings. Using the Schedules feature, educators present sequences of images, which can help explain to individuals with ASDs any routines or multi-step tasks occurring during the day (e.g., a schedule for "Tuesday's Classes"). The Countdown feature includes both graphical and numeric timers that are presented alongside any image, to help convey to students that the pictured activity will soon occur (e.g., "In two minutes, it will be time to pack your book bag"). The Choices feature is used to present choices between any two or more images (e.g., "Would you like pretzels or yogurt for a snack?"), and allows users to highlight their choice. Images used in these visual supports are accessed from a Library of stock illustrations, which users can expand and customize by: 1) taking pictures with the built-in camera, 2) transferring digital pictures from a personal computer, and/or 3) downloading images from the Internet using a search tool available within the application. Thus, millions of images are rapidly available, ranging from familiar images from the proximate environment to abstract images downloaded from the Internet.

Fig. 1. Screenshots of iPrompts XL (from left to right: Schedules in portrait orientation, Schedules in landscape orientation, Countdown Timer in portrait orientation, and Choices in landscape orientation)

The goal of the Phase I study (hereafter, the "Feasibility Study") was to investigate using iPrompts in an education setting. iPrompts XL was the direct result of the collaborative research and development effort between HandHold Adaptive, LLC (the developer and commercial rights owner of the application), and a team of researchers from the SCSU Autism Center. As described further below, educators enrolled in the study were each provided with either an iPhone or iPod Touch pre-loaded with the iPrompts application. Among other findings from the study, educators indicated a desire for a larger, "tablet"-sized display screen when presenting visual supports in academic environments. This, combined with the launch of the iPad earlier in 2010, led the developer to hasten production of an iPad-optimized software application (iPrompts XL).

2 ASDs and the State of the Art in Visual Supports

The most recent prevalence estimates for ASDs from the US Center for Disease Control and Prevention (CDC) is 1 in 88 children [2]. ASDs comprise a triad of challenges, encompassing difficulties in social competence, communication, and restricted and repetitive behavior, all of which compromise an individual's ability to function effectively and independently. There are now many evidence-based treatments that capitalize on the visual strengths of individuals with ASDs, such as visual supports [3], visual activity schedules [4], video modeling [5], and Social Stories™ [6]. However, these treatments are currently made and delivered using mostly low-tech devices. Low-tech visual supports are typically created by teachers and parents using a personal computer, which involves printing the visual supports onto paper, cutting out the supports, and laminating the visual supports to increase durability. This process can be time consuming, and produces large physical products (e.g., notebooks containing printed symbols) that may be cumbersome to carry and stigmatizing to use. Moreover, these visual supports often use graphics that are generic, rather than representative of the actual social or physical environment in which the student is expected to function. While research has validated the use of low-tech visual supports [7], little has been done to analyze the utility and appropriateness of high-tech assistive technology, which are being used more frequently in education settings [8].

Since the introduction of iPrompts in May of 2009, a variety of handheld applications designed to provide visual supports have become available, including *First Then Visual Schedule, iCommunicate*, and *Time Timer*. iPrompts has differentiated from these offerings through its unique blend of features, enabling users to create many visual supports, including visual schedules, visual timers, and visual choices. As shown by Fig. 2, commercial iPrompts users have accessed each of these core features with regularity over a period of nearly two years. Users can access the unique mix and presentation of these features by performing just one application download, and by learning a single user interface.

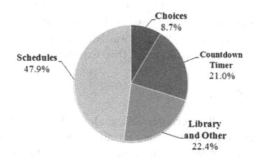

Fig. 2. While the Schedules feature is most popular (48% of occurrences), users of iPrompts® access each of its four major features with regularity. (Source: *Flurry Analytics* application data, contributed by author, 12/10 through 3/12).

3   The Feasibility Study and Its Methodology

3.1   Research Questions

Beginning in June of 2010, the research team from the SCSU Autism Center conducted the Feasibility Study. The goal of the research was to analyze the general feasibility and promise of using iPrompts in educational settings. Specifically, the Feasibility Study evaluated the following research questions:

1. What professional development is needed for teachers to gain the knowledge necessary to use iPrompts appropriately with their students in educational settings?
2. Can teachers use iPrompts to support students with ASDs feasibly within the confines of a typical school setting?
3. When used by teachers in educational settings, do students show interest in the application and are changes in student behavior evident after its use?
4. When used by teachers in educational settings, can the iPhone or iPod Touch platform be used to deliver visual supports for students with ASDs?

3.2   Sample

Twenty-nine teachers used the iPrompts application with 88 students (ages 5- to 16-years-old) with ASDs in Bridgeport Public Schools and Connecticut Region 15.

3.3   Measures

The research team from the SCSU Autism Center developed four measures to evaluate the feasibility and promise of using iPrompts in authentic educational settings. The *Professional Development Evaluation Index* was a nine-question evaluation of the teachers' knowledge of the different features of iPrompts. The *Self-Reflection on Teaching Index* was a self-report measure created to capture the teachers' reflections on using iPrompts in educational settings. The *Observation Rubric* was used during direct observation to evaluate teachers' use of iPrompts and the students' behavioral responses. Finally, a *Focus Group Protocol* was administered to the teachers to foster a group discussion among participants about their experiences using iPrompts.

3.4   Procedures and Results

All participants evaluated the Schedules, Countdown Timer and Choices features. Hands-on training sessions were provided for all teachers, and the *Professional Development Evaluation Index* was administered at the end of the training. The results showed most teachers strongly agreed that (1) the training was effective (94%), (2) assistive technology is a tool that can be used to help students with ASDs (88%), (3) the training demonstrated teaching strategies that are relevant to the backgrounds and skills of their students (71%), and (4) the training demonstrated teaching strategies that can be easily implemented in educational settings (71%).

After the training, the teachers were videotaped and/or observed using iPrompts with their students. Sixty-one observations were scored using the *Observation Rubric*, which showed very few system defects were encountered. In over 65% of the observations, the student was rated as using the application as intended and 87% of the sessions showed the students to have shown a keen interest in the device by moving closer to it or making an effort to handle it. The data from the observations also provide strong support that the application had a positive impact on the learning and development of the students. Eighty-two percent of observations identified a positive impact on student behavior with respect to both on-task behavior and attentiveness.

Results obtained from the *Observation Rubric* also suggested that while teachers were able to correctly use iPrompts, some had difficulty determining when and under what conditions to implement assistive technology with their students (only 23% of teachers were rated as having used the Choices feature correctly and 12% of teachers were rated as having used iPrompts correctly to prepare a student for a transition). Thus, while teachers felt they had received the knowledge necessary to use iPrompts, the observational data highlight the need for better training with respect to general assistive technology strategies. Specifically, the teachers needed training targeted toward helping them to understand situations in which it is appropriate to use the iPrompts app, situations in which it is inappropriate to use the app, and which tools within the app might be most appropriate in given situations. This training to knowledge gap was also apparent during the *Focus Group*, in which two additional opportunities for future training were identified: (1) training on implementing assistive technology in general in the classroom, and (2) training on the difference between the device (i.e., iPod Touch or iPhone) on which the app runs and the iPrompts app.

The *Self-Reflection on Teaching Index* was administered to the teachers during the final week of the Feasibility Study. Every teacher (100%) felt iPrompts was not too complex to set up and that he or she had figured out how to use iPrompts. Most teachers (81%) felt there was enough time to set up iPrompts for use with students and a majority of teachers felt their students liked the Countdown Timer (94%) and Choices features (59%). However, the teachers acknowledged that they occasionally did not have enough time to set up iPrompts. Forty-five percent agreed that in the middle of their educational activities "It takes too much time to set up iPrompts and I have to give my attention to the students," although this finding could be an artifact of student behavior, as 45% of teachers also noted that there was not sufficient time to set up iPrompts because "The student does not have enough self-control over his/her behavior." Collectively, these data suggest that teacher discretion in determining when and whether to use the app is important, both to the success of the use of the app and the success of the student.

Responding to the *Focus Group Protocol*, teachers commented on the ease of using the Schedules feature, the amount of time and effort that was saved using iPrompts to create Schedules, and the convenience of creating Schedules "on the fly" as needs arose. The teachers indicated a preference for using the iPrompts Schedules feature over a computer program such as Boardmaker to create hard copy visual schedules. Teachers indicated that being able to take photos and incorporate them into the iPrompts app was an important feature, and for this reason, they preferred using the iPhone to the iPod Touch (newer iPod Touch models, released after the Feasibility Study, now include cameras). The teachers also commented during the Focus Group Protocol on the utility of the Countdown Timer feature, which they reported to be the most used feature during the feasibility study. This tool was utilized to help with both whole group transitions and for transitions for individual students. The Countdown Timer tool helped students to stop working at an appropriate time and also to keep working until the allotted time had elapsed. Several teachers commented on the effectiveness of the Countdown Timer tool in helping with group transitions.

4   Impact of the Feasibility Study

4.1   Iterative Software Development

After considering the results of the Feasibility Study, requests from iPrompts customers, and the introduction of the iPad in April of 2010, HandHold Adaptive expedited development of an iPad-optimized product in hopes of introducing a tool that accommodated educators' desire for visual supports presentable via a larger, "tablet"-sized handheld device. The development process included several modifications to the software, such as adjusting layouts, type sizes, image sizes, and allowing the screen to be rotated or oriented in any direction.

The results at market have been positive. Since its introduction, iPrompts XL has outsold iPrompts by a unit sales ratio of 3:1; since its release, iPrompts XL has accounted for 75% of iPrompts sales. The historic composition of iPrompts sales (including both iPrompts and iPrompts XL) reveals that within 2 months after the release of iPrompts XL, it had surpassed iPrompts in sales. Sales of iPrompts XL through Apple's Volume Purchase Program (which provides discounts and a large-scale software deployment option for educational institutions) have also exceeded sales of iPrompts through this mechanism, demonstrating demand for tablet compatibility in the realm of visual supports for students with ASDs. But if not for the results of the Feasibility Study (specifically, the strong recommendations of teachers responding to the *Focus Group Protocol*), HandHold Adaptive may not have hastened development of a tablet-specific product, and may have lost an opportunity to capture share of this market. Thus, the research effort behind iPrompts helped guide broader software development priorities for HandHold Adaptive, and might serve as a model for other software developers seeking to align their products with consumer demand.

4.2   Contributions to the Research Field

There are hundreds of thousands of apps available for iOS devices like the iPhone, iPod Touch and iPad. Many of these apps may be useful to individuals with ASDs and their caregivers. A keyword search in February of 2012 revealed more than 580 autism-related apps available on the Apple iTunes Store and 250 on the Android market, many of which have been developed by parents of individuals with ASDs, and without the guidance of research [9]. However, very few empirical studies documenting the effects of these apps have been published to date. Thus, HandHold Adaptive and the research team from the SCSU Autism Center have made a unique contribution to the field by researching the efficacy of iPrompts in authentic education delivery settings. The Feasibility Study was one of the first ever to investigate handheld visual supports on Apple handheld devices (including the iPhone and iPod Touch). As described above, our research has confirmed that iPrompts can have a positive impact on the behavior of students with ASDs, and has features which are well-liked by individuals with ASDs. Additionally, our research has confirmed that teachers can use iPrompts within the confines of a school setting to positively impact student behaviors that support academic and other important school related outcomes. Given these positive findings, we feel more research on how best to use smartphone and tablet applications in educational settings is highly warranted.

In addition to documenting the positive effects that can be achieved by using iPrompts, we feel that our Feasibility Study contributes a template for future research endeavors investigating the effectiveness of smartphone and tablet applications. We also hope to guide small businesses toward utilizing local research expertise, and feel that an iterative research and development process involving a combination of private industry and public research expertise can produce better-informed product development efforts for smartphone and tablet applications serving individuals with ASDs.

5 Conclusions and Planned Activities

Collectively, it is clear from the data obtained during the Feasibility Study that iPrompts is feasible for use in educational settings. Teachers were able to incorporate iPrompts into their classroom, iPrompts was preferred by the teachers, and the application was of great interest to the students. The data also indicated that iPrompts had a positive impact on students' behavior, including time-on-task and attentiveness, which are two prerequisite skills for learning. Finally, the majority of teachers agreed that they would use iPrompts in their classrooms, clearly demonstrating the feasibility and promise of the product for use by teachers in educational settings.

Since the conclusion of the Feasibility Study in 2010, HandHold Adaptive and SCSU Autism Center have been awarded Phase II follow-on research award from the U.S. Department of Education's IES SBIR program. With the goal of increasing the application's utility, usability, and commercial potential, HandHold Adaptive intends to improve iPrompts the following ways: (1) extend the brand onto new platforms (e.g., the Android operating system), (2) addition of enhanced features (e.g., Visual Checklists, cloud storage and syncing), (3) make the software accessible outside of the handheld device itself (e.g., through projectable and/or printable screens), and (4) production of training materials for using the product and assistive technology in classroom settings. New technologies will be developed and tested iteratively in authentic education delivery settings to ensure the product operates as intended, is easily incorporated into educational practices, and effectuates positive outcomes in students with ASDs. If research indicates that these goals are achieved, the software improvements may be released (via online marketplaces for handheld applications, such as the iTunes App Store and Google Play), and supported by marketing initiatives.

HandHold Adaptive has also begun development of a Beta version of StoryMaker, an application for iOS devices which will allow teachers and other caregivers to create and present narrative visual supports (e.g., Social Stories [6]) using large pictures and editable text (e.g., a teacher creates a multi-page story explaining how to eat lunch in a cafeteria, explaining the nuances of how to stand in a lunchline, order food, sit down at a table in a cafeteria, and make appropriate conversation with friends). In addition to using pictures taken with the built-in cameras of iOS devices, StoryMaker will allow user to download images from other sources, such as Facebook, Flickr, Google, and Bing. The research team from the SCSU Autism Center is currently completing a Feasibility Study on teachers' use of StoryMaker in schools, which, will help refine and guide the development of the commercial release.

Acknowledgments. This research and development was funded by contract #ED-IES-11-C-0040 through the SBIR Program of the IES within the US Department of Education. The opinions expressed are those of the authors and do not necessarily represent views of the US Department of Education. The authors gratefully acknowledge the contributions of Michael Ben-Avie, Deborah Newton, Ruth Eren, and of the SCSU Autism Center research team for their assistance with the Feasibility Study. The authors also wish to thank Bridgeport Public Schools and Connecticut Region 15 Schools for their participation and assistance during the Feasibility Study. Finally, the authors thank AT&T for the donation of iPhones and cellular service used during the Feasibility Study.

References

1. iPrompts, http://www.handholdadaptive.com/iprompts.html
2. Centers for Disease Control and Prevention. Prevalence of autism spectrum disorders—Autism and developmental disabilities monitoring network, 14 sites, United States (2008), Surveillance Summaries, MMWR, 61, 1–19, SS3, March 30 (2012)
3. Quill, K.: Instructional considerations for young children with autism: The rationale for visually-cued instruction. J. Autism Dev. Disord. 27, 697–714 (1997)
4. McClannahan, L.E., Krantz, P.J.: Activity schedules for children with autism: Teaching independent behavior. Woodbine House, Bethesda (2010)
5. Nikopoulos, C., Hobbs, S., Keenan, M.: Video modeling and behaviour analysis: A guide for teaching social skills to children with autism. Jessica Kingsley, London (2006)
6. Gray, C.: The New Social Story Book. Future Horizons, Arlington (2010)
7. National Autism Center. National standards report. Author, Randolph, MA (2009)
8. Gray, L., et al.: Teachers' use of educational technology in U.S. public schools: 2009 (NCES 2010-040). National Center for Education Statistics, Washington DC (2010)
9. Davis, K.: Parents herald rise in apps to help treat autism but proof of therapeutic benefits is lacking. PC World, February 10 (2012), http://www.pcworld.com/article/249775/parents_herald_rise_in_apps_to_help_treat_autism_but_proof_of_therapeutic_benefits_is_lacking.html (obtained on April 19, 2012)

Cloud-Based Assistive Speech-Transcription Services

Zdenek Bumbalek, Jan Zelenka, and Lukas Kencl

R&D Centre for Mobile Applications (RDC),
Department of Telecommunications Engineering,
Faculty of Electrical Engineering, Czech Technical University in Prague,
Technicka 2, 166 27 Prague 6, Czech Republic
{bumbazde,zelenj2,lukas.kencl}@fel.cvut.cz
http://www.rdc.cz

Abstract. Real-time speech transcription is a service of potentially tremendous positive impact on quality of life of the hearing-impaired. Recent advances in technologies of mobile networks, cloud services, speech transcription and mobile clients allowed us to build eScribe, a ubiquitiously available, cloud-based, speech-transcription service. We present the deployed system, evaluate the applicability of automated speech recognition using real measurements and outline a vision of the future enhanced platform, crowdsourcing human transcribers in social networks.

Keywords: Hearing-Impaired, Cloud Computing, Voice Recognition.

1 Introduction

Speech is one of the most natural means for sharing ideas, information or feelings. However, speech may also become a communication barrier for those not knowing the language or unable to use it, like the hearing-impaired or the foreign-language speakers. For those hearing-impaired who lost hearing during their life, transcription is a natural way of receiving information. Motivated by the growing number of the hearing-impaired in the Czech Republic (ca 500.000) and the fact that only 1.2% of them use sign language, the Czech Technical University in Prague (CTU) and the Czech Union of the Deaf (CUD)[4] have embarked on a joint project called eScribe [2], with the goal of reducing communication barriers and improving quality of life of the hearing-impaired. As part of the project we have designed and built a prototype cloud-based assistive speech-to-text services platform, providing ubiquitously available real-time speech transcription. The actual transcription may either be provided by real transcribers or by Automated Speech Recognition (ASR) engines.

2 Related Work

Today's speech-to-text services (STTS) are generally provided by one of the following methods: 1. physically present transcribers; 2. remote-transcription

K. Miesenberger et al. (Eds.): ICCHP 2012, Part II, LNCS 7383, pp. 113–116, 2012.

carried out by human transcribers [1][2]; 3. concepts based on ASR [4]; 4. ASR combined with human error-correction [3]. Physically present transcribers are highly limiting because there is shortage of educated transcribers, costs of these services are high and they are restricted to particular locations. An alternative is using ASR. Yet, ASR is limited in recognition accuracy, especially of colloquial speech and of difficult national languages such as Czech. Today, ASR systems are largely trained on literary texts. Dictionaries and hypotheses for national colloquial languages are missing. ASR techniques are sensitive to many miscellaneous characteristics of the input signal. From fundamental signal attributes (signal input level, sample frequency) across disturbing influences (background noise, other voices, music) to the culture of idea formulation (fluent speech with minimal unfinished sentence fragments). Remote transcription and ASR combined with human error-correctors is limited by costs and human resources too.

3   eScribe Implementation and Architecture

The currently operational eScribe platform utilizes the widespread Voice-over-Internet-Protocol (VoIP) telephony. Asterisk, a simple but powerful system for VoIP communication, acts as the core server. Audio and text transmission are controlled by the Session Initiation Protocol (SIP). In the eScribe architecture, Asterisk operates as a transparent gateway between the ASR server and Google Cloud. To interconnect eScribe with the ASR server, a modified SIP MESSAGE method is used. The Cloud part of eScribe is based on the Google App Engine, and communication with Asterisk is carried out by the Jabber protocol. The Cloud environment is used as a text editor, represented by Google Docs, as well as storage space for the transcribed texts. Some of eScribe internal logic is deployed in the Google Cloud too. There are several options how to deliver the audio signal to the system: using a cell phone, a fixed phone, a SIP phone or a webphone. From the user perspective, eScribe is used in two modes: *1. Lecture mode* (one speaker - many listeners), *2. Face-to-face communication mode*. Practical tests have shown that a DECT (Digital Enhanced Cordless Telecommunications) phone used as a wireless microphone by the speaker and a laptop (usually connected to a beamer) as a display is the best arrangement for the Lecture mode. For the Face-to-face communication, tablets or smartphones were the user equipment alternatives.

4   Performance Evaluation and User Experience

One of the key criteria impacting the quality of ASR is the choice of codec and its related parameters. eScribe uses ASR provided by Newton Technologies [9]. Fig. 1 shows recognition success rates comparing various audio codecs at different sample frequencies. The success rate was evaluated according to the methodology described in [6]. Final results were obtained as an arithmetic mean of simple results from a set of 13 utterances. The spectrum of utterances was not optimized in any way, so the utterance set consisted of audio records including many disturbances

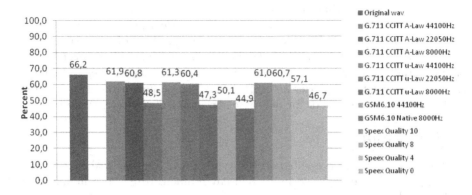

Fig. 1. Recognition Success Rates for Several Codecs and Different Settings. Recognition success rate of the original wav file, using a 44 kHz sample frequency at 8bit coding, is used as reference. The results can be grouped around two success-rate levels. The first group includes utterances with sample frequency higher than 8 kHz (quality parameter higher than 4 in SPEEX codec). Success rates of this group vary at about 60 %. The second group is characterized by success rates of around 50 %. Unfortunately, the common sample frequency for telecommunication audio signals is 8 kHz, which provides perceptibly worse performance than in the case of the other group.

such as background noise, voices, unintelligible parts etc., just as in ordinary everyday speech. In our scenario, the performance of ASR was quite independent of the general type of audio codec, but considerable improvement can be reached by using a wideband codec such as SPEEX or G.722 in VoIP telephony or AMR-WB in mobile telephony. Other methods to enhance results of the recognition process exist, e.g. text correctors or trained shadow speakers [4]. Nevertheless, the role of human transcribers is essential for a number of real-life situations where the accuracy of sentence understanding does play a crucial role in the life of an individual, such as at courts of law. Although eScribe was developed as a prototype and a proof of concept, we have arranged several events, where eScribe provided speech transcription to hearing impaired people. In the Lecture mode, several lectures at CTU were transcribed. Also CUD uses eScribe at their conferences or meetings. Using eScribe in the Face-to-face mode was firstly demonstrated in February 2012 in a cafe at Vodafone headquarter in Prague and later at a Vodafone shop in communication between a shop assistant and a hearing impaired client. [7]

5   Future Work

The limiting factors of today's systems for speech transcription are lack of well-educated transcribers or shadow speakers, and associated financial costs. Until the ASR systems are able to reliably recognize colloquial language or speech in noisy environment, the role of humans will remain irreplaceable. The boom of social networks brings a potential tool to attract transcribers. As demonstrator, we aim to interconnect our cloud-based transcription solution with a crowdsourcing

platform using gadgets built upon G-Talk, which can easily be integrated into social networks or webpages. The platform will support continuous improvement of
transcription capabilities by developing a learning database of transcribed texts.
Among the challenges to be addressed remain algorithms matching users to groups
of appropriate transcribers, techniques of collecting the transcribed data and of
creating colloquial dictionaries for ASR, anonymization algorithms for the transcribed speech, and methods for real-time auctioning of transcriber services.

6   Conclusion

In this paper, we have presented a prototype of a ubiquitous real-time speech-
transcription service deployed in a cloud environment using both human transcribers and ASR technology. The wide availability of access to this real-time
speech-transcription service will enable providing it to a much larger community
of hearing-impaired people. High usage is expected in face-to-face communication, where the service of a physically present transcriber (assistant) is difficult
to arrange from both financial and logistical point of view. The eScribe solution
has a huge potential to minimize communication barriers and to make cultural,
educational, social or other events more accessible to the hearing-impaired people. We have also proposed to reduce the limitations of the current solution -
the shortage of well educated transcibers or shadow speakers - by crowdsourcing
these services within social networks. This approach would help popularize the
eScribe project and last but not least provide valuable scientific data for future
research and development in the area of assistive voice services.

References

1. Miyoshi, S., Kuroki, H., Kawano, S., Shirasawa, M., Ishihara, Y., Kobayashi, M.:
   Support Technique for Real-Time Captionist to Use Speech Recognition Software.
   In: Miesenberger, K., Klaus, J., Zagler, W.L., Karshmer, A.I. (eds.) ICCHP 2008.
   LNCS, vol. 5105, pp. 647–650. Springer, Heidelberg (2008)
2. Bumbalek, Z., Zelenka, J., Kencl, L.: E-Scribe: Ubiquitous Real-Time Speech Transcription for the Hearing-Impaired. In: Miesenberger, K., Klaus, J., Zagler, W., Karshmer, A. (eds.) ICCHP 2010. LNCS, vol. 6180, pp. 160–168. Springer, Heidelberg (2010)
3. Wald, M.: Captioning for Deaf and Hard of Hearing People by Editing Automatic
   Speech Recognition in Real Time. In: Miesenberger, K., Klaus, J., Zagler, W.L.,
   Karshmer, A.I. (eds.) ICCHP 2006. LNCS, vol. 4061, pp. 683–690. Springer, Heidelberg (2006)
4. Forman, I., Brunet, T., Luther, P., Wilson, A.: Using ASR for Transcription of
   Teleconferences in IM Systems. In: Stephanidis, C. (ed.) Universal Access in HCI,
   Part III, HCII 2009. LNCS, vol. 5616, pp. 521–529. Springer, Heidelberg (2009)
5. Czech Union of Deaf, http://www.cun.cz
6. IDIAP Research Institute - On the Use of Information Retrieval Measures for Speech
   Recognition Evaluation,
   http://publications.idiap.ch/downloads/reports/2004/rr04-73.pdf
7. http://www.kochlear.cz
8. http://htk.eng.cam.ac.uk
9. http://www.newtontech.cz/

Developing a Voice User Interface with Improved Usability for People with Dysarthria

Yumi Hwang[1], Daejin Shin[2], Chang-Yeal Yang[3], Seung-Yeun Lee[4], Jin Kim[5],
Byunggoo Kong[5], Jio Chung[6], Sunhee Kim[7], and Minhwa Chung[8]

[1] Interdisciplinary Program in Cognitive Science, Seoul National University, Korea
yumi4395@snu.ac.kr
[2] Weavers TnC, Seoul, Korea
djshin@weavers.co.kr
[3] GO Design Studio, Seoul, Korea
severo@gostudio.co.kr
[4] E-ROOM Consulting, Seoul, Korea
eroomcon@gmail.com
[5] Infinity Telecom, Seoul, Korea
{kimjin,kongbgkong}@infinity.co.kr
[6] HCILAB , Seoul, Korea
jio@hcilab.co.kr
[7] Center for Humanities and Information, Seoul National University, Korea
sunhkim@snu.ac.kr
[8] Department of Linguistics, Seoul National University, Korea
mchung@snu.ac.kr

Abstract. This paper describes the development of a voice user interface (VUI) for Korean users with dysarthria. The development process, from target application decisions to prototype system evaluation, focuses on improving the usability of the interface by reflecting user needs. The first step of development is to decide target VUI application and its functions. 25 dysarthric participants (5 middle school students and 20 adults) are asked to list the devices they want to use with a VUI interface and what purposes they would use VUI devices for. From this user study, SMS sending, web searching and voice dialing on mobile phones and tablet PCs are decided as the target application and its functions. The second step is to design the system of the target application in order to improve usability. 120 people with dysarthria are asked to state the main problems of currently available VUI devices, and it is found that speech recognition failure (88%) is the main problem. This result indicates high speech recognition rate will improve usability. Therefore, to improve the recognition rate, an isolated word recognition based system with a customizable command list and a built-in word prediction function is designed for the target VUI devices. The final step is to develop and evaluate a prototype system. In this study, a prototype is developed for Apple iOS and Android platform devices, and then the system design is modified based on the evaluation results of 5 dysarthric evaluators.

Keywords: VUI, Dysarthria, Usability.

K. Miesenberger et al. (Eds.): ICCHP 2012, Part II, LNCS 7383, pp. 117–124, 2012.
© Springer-Verlag Berlin Heidelberg 2012

1   Introduction

As technology in the IT industry continues to advance, the types of IT devices incorporated into our daily lives are increasing. However, individuals with disabilities demonstrate difficulty using a majority of these devices. One of the reasons is that this group of users is not always well taken into consideration during the development phase of these devices. Even when a product is designed specifically for users with certain disabilities, it is not easy to satisfy all of the various needs as these users vary in their kind and severity of disabilities.

People with dysarthria are one representative user group that face continuous struggles with IT device usage due to their physical limitations caused by neurological deficits [1]. An interface that runs on speech recognition is proposed as a possible solution for improving usability among them [2], because it is not physically exhausting and not as time consuming as other alternatives. However, there are limitations with using commercial speech recognition systems targeting normal speech, because speech production problems associated with dysarthria results in speech recognition accuracy significantly lower than that of normal speech [2-5]. Therefore, when developing a voice user interface (VUI) for people with dysarthria, an emphasis should be placed not only on improving the recognition accuracy of dysarthric speech, but also on enhancing the usability of the application in order to satisfy user needs with the available speech recognition technology.

This paper describes the development of a VUI for Koreans with dysarthria that runs on various products including smartphones and tablet PCs. This paper does not focus on improving the speech recognition accuracy itself, but on reflecting user requirements and feedback into the VUI system design for improving usability. Various user studies have been conducted in each phase of the development process, and the results of systematic user-needs analyses have played a significant role in developing the VUI for people with dysarthria.

2   The State of the Art in VUIs for People with Dysarthria

Because of the low speech recognition accuracy of dysarthric speech, recent studies, well summarized in [6], focus mostly on improving the recognition accuracy, but not on the development of application systems. There are two recent studies that focus on the development of applications. Hamidi, et al. [7] describe the development of "CanSpeak", a customizable speech interface which aims to run on various applications for people with dysarthria. CanSpeak uses a set of keywords, consisting of a small number of words that are produced easily for dysarthric users. The recognition accuracy is increased as a result. Hosom, et al. [8] describe the development of a speech recognition system that has word prediction functions. This approach is expected to reduce the number of trials required for recognition and to increase speech recognition accuracy.

The two studies have significance in developing voice recognition application systems for dysarthric users with current technology resources. However, the studies did not conduct or reflect systematic user studies, which are essential for improving usability of systems.

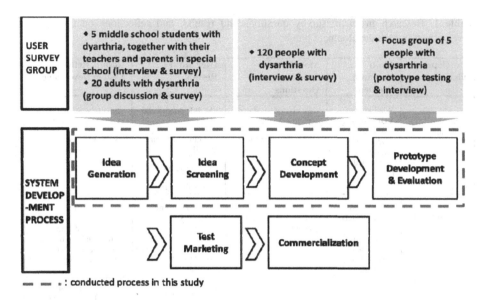

Fig. 1. The system development process and corresponding user survey group

3   The System Development

The entire development process of a VUI system for Korean people with dysarthria consists of six phases. Since the development is still in progress, this paper shows the details up to "prototype development and evaluation phase" and describes how the results of the user studies are integrated into the system development. User studies are conducted through the use of questionnaires for various user groups corresponding to each phase. Figure 1 shows the system development process and user survey groups corresponding to each phase. Table 1 describes details of how the results of the user surveys are applied to the system development.

3.1   Idea Generation and Idea Screening

During the first step of the development, a survey is conducted to analyze user needs. 5 middle school students and 20 adults with dysarthria are chosen for this user study. The participants are asked to list the devices they want to use with a VUI interface and what purposes they would use VUI devices for. The data is collected through interviews, paper questionnaires, and group discussions. The results indicate that the use of mobile phones and PCs are a necessity for the majority of the participants. Consequently, smartphones and tablet PCs are determined as target platforms, and SMS, Web searching, and voice dialing are decided as target applications.

Table 1. Research problem, survey questions and results, and reflections on the system development in each development phase

Development Phase	Main Research Problem	Main User Survey Questions	User Survey Results	Results Reflected on System Development
(1) Idea Generation and (2) Idea Screening	What kind of VUI system should be developed in order to assist people with dysarthria?	· Which devices do you hope to use with VUI? · What do you want to do with a device with VUI?	· Mobile phones and PCs · Sending SMS and E-mail · Web searching · Voice dialing	· Smartphones and tablet PCs as target platforms · SMS, Web searching, and voice dialing as target applications
(3) Concept Development	How should a VUI system be designed in order to improve usability for people with dysarthria?	· What are the main problems of currently available VUI devices?	· Speech recognition failure (88%) · Speech adaptation takes a long time and devices are not portable (10%)	· Individual alphabets should be recognized upon the production of a customizable command word correlated with a certain alphabet · Provide word/sentence prediction functions to reduce the number of utterances and trials. · The system should be in a mobile/portable device application form for portability
(4) Prototype Development and Evaluation	What should be provided in the prototype VUI system?	· Which words do you prefer to use as commands for a VUI system? · How often would you use a VUI system over another alternative interface? · Which function needs most improvement in currently available VUI systems?	· Word list consisting of words that are frequently used by each user · Mostly and Often (80%) · Rarely and Never (20%) · Reducing the number of utterance trials	· Provide a default command word list with a customization function so the default command word list can be adjusted upon request · Develop a new keyboard type to reduce the number of utterance trials

3.2   Concept Development

After determining the target platforms, a research on detailed methods of voice user interface design which aims to improve usability is performed. In this step of the developmental process, 120 people with dysarthria are asked about the problems of existing voice recognition interface systems. 20% of the people have experience using VUI and most of them (88%) report that speech recognition failure is the main problem. Based on this result, isolated word recognition based voice interface is chosen as it usually outperforms continuous speech recognition based systems. Customizable command list based recognition for identifying individual alphabets is also considered as an effective way of dealing with speech variance among users with dysarthria. Word prediction system is also chosen to be applied to the system, since the method is

Table 2. Prototype system information and performance

Application Devices and S/W Information					
(Apple) **·iPhone4** **·iPad**	Developed as App available from Apple App Store -APPLE iPhone4/iPad optimized GUI -iOS 4.3.2 , C++ based VUI -iOS 4.3.2 based speech recognizer optimization				
(Samsung) **·Galaxy S** **·Galaxy Tab**	-Developed as App for mobile platform available from Android Market -Available on most Android smart mobile and tablet PC platforms including SAMSUNG Galaxy S and Galaxy Tab -Android OS 2.2 Froyo , Java based VUI -Android OS 2.2 Froyo based speech recognizer optimization				
System Performance					
Speech Recognition Rate	Severity level	Number of subjects	Number of words	SNR	Word Accuracy (%)
	Mild	33			72.64
	Moderate	49	100	20dB	51.29
	Severe	18			38.33
Real Time Factor(RTF)	Normal Speech			0.1~0.3	
	Dysarthric Speech			0.2~0.35	

revealed to be an efficient way for speech recognition as shown in [8]. Additionally, for portability of the system, we decide to develop the system in the form of a mobile/portable device application that users can easily download to their portable devices.

3.3   Prototype Development and Evaluation

System Information. The Prototype system is developed for four application devices based on Apple iOS (iPhone4, iPad) and Android platform (Galaxy S, Galaxy Tab). The detailed information of the prototype software and the speech recognition efficiency is shown in Table 2.

System Image. The developed system concept is reflected to the prototype design as shown in Figure 2. This image is the first version of a prototype application layout for VUI SMS sending. Users can enter speech recognition mode by touching the touch area. This area is relatively larger than other areas considering motion difficulties of people with dysarthria. The default command word list for each target letter, located on the left side, is developed based on the preference words of 120 target users. The command list can be replaced with other user-friendly words by selecting the "setting" key on the bottom of the application screen. Other function keys (to keyboard, remove all, switching target letters, and sending SMS) are also located on the bottom. The touch-activated keyboard is also accessible for those users with normal motor abilities.

Prototype Evaluation and Modification. The initial prototype system is evaluated by a focus group of five people with dysarthria. Users are asked to perform several tasks using the system, and then to report the difficulties with using the system. Four of them state they are willing to use the system in their everyday life, but all five users indicate that too many trials are required for the system to recognize a target phrase despite the word prediction function. That might be a result of the word prediction system's performance as it is still being developed. The number of trials can be reduced by modifying the keyboard structure. The participants are not satisfied with the way that the command list is shown in the prototype system because there are too many words on the command list, making it difficult when searching for commands.

Based on the prototype evaluation, the prototype is modified by integrating command list into the keyboard. Figure 3 shows the modified keyboard. The keyboard includes the three main elements of Korean alphabet (initial consonant, vowel, final consonant), in accordance with Korean orthography; consonant-vowel (CV) and consonant-vowel-consonant (CVC). The keyboard is transformed automatically according to Korean orthography, so users can complete their words without having to change the layout themselves. With this keyboard, diphthongs and consonant clusters can be recognized with a single utterance, reducing speaking trials. Having three different types of keyboards can reduce the number of words included in the command list. Consequently, users can find target commands more quickly and remember these commands better than in the previous version because fewer commands are displayed on each keyboard. Additionally, the keyboard is also activated by touch, for those with normal motor abilities.

The third version prototype is currently under development. The voice-activated keyboard in this version functions not only in SMS sending environments but in all keyboard-requiring situations in the target devices (smartphones and tablet PCs). Figure 4 shows images of the third prototype version.

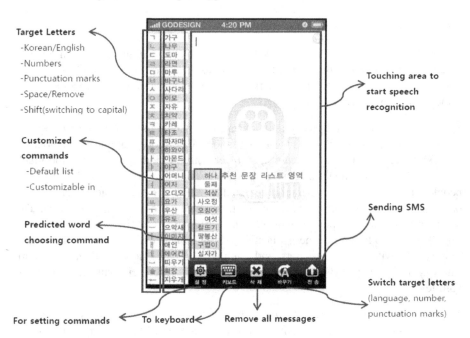

Fig. 2. The image of the first prototype system's SMS sending layout

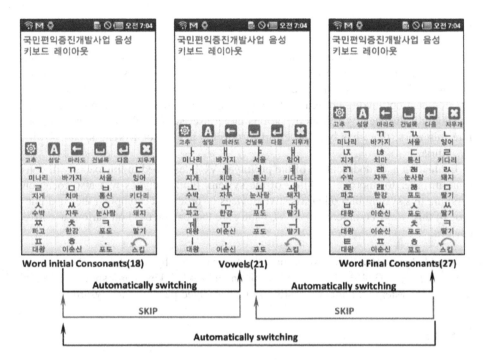

Fig. 3. The second version prototype image of SMS sending: Automatic transformation of the keyboard including specific commands in accordance with Korean orthography

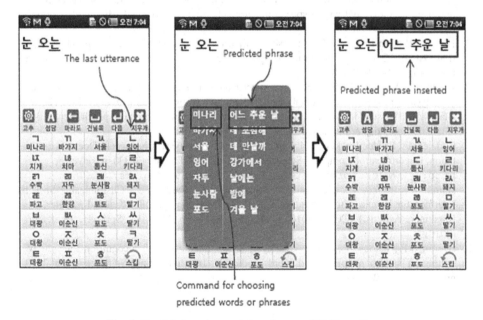

Fig. 4. The third version prototype image of SMS sending

4   Conclusion

This paper describes the development of a smartphone/tablet PC voice user interface designed to improve usability and accessibility for users with dysarthria. The contributions of this paper are: this is one of the few cases of voice user interface system development optimizing present technology resources, and each developmental phase is heavily influenced by results of various target user studies. We also note that, before this work, there has been no effort to develop a VUI for Korean speakers with dysarthria.

Evaluation and modification of the prototype VUI described in this paper will continue in order to improve usability of the system. Future studies will also focus on applying this system into other assistive devices in order to accomplish the final purpose of this work: commercialized VUI software that can be used on various assistive devices.

Acknowledgements. This work has been supported by the R&D Program of MKE/KEIT (10036461, Development of an embedded key-word spotting speech recognition system individually customized for disabled persons with dysarthria)

References

1. Darley, F.L., Aronson, A.E., Brown, J.R.: Differential diagnostic patterns of dysarthria. Journal of Speech and Hearing Research 12, 246–269 (1969)
2. Kotler, A., Thomas-Stonell, N.: Effects of speech training on the accuracy of speech recognition for an individual with a speech impairment. Augmentative and Alternative Communication 13, 71–80 (1997)
3. Hux, K., Rankin-Erickson, J., Manasse, N., Lauritzen, E.: Accuracy of three speech recognition systems: Case study of dysarthric speech. Augmentative and Alternative Communication 16(3), 186–196 (2000)
4. Rosen, K., Yamplosky, S.: Automatic speech recognition and a review of its functioning with dysarthric speech. Augmentative and Alternative Communication 16(1), 48–60 (2000)
5. Blaney, B., Wilson, J.: Acoustic variability in dysarthria and computer speech recognition. Clinical Linguistics & Phonetics 14, 307–327 (2000)
6. Rudzicz, F.: Production knowledge in the recognition of dysarthric speech. Doctoral dissertation, Department of Computer Science of University of Toronto (2011), retrieved, http://www.cs.toronto.edu/~frank/Download/Papers/
7. Hamidi, F., Baljko, M., Livingston, N., Spalteholz, L.: CanSpeak: a Customizable Speech Interface for People with Dysarthric Speech. In: Miesenberger, K., Klaus, J., Zagler, W., Karshmer, A. (eds.) ICCHP 2010. LNCS, vol. 6179, pp. 605–612. Springer, Heidelberg (2010)
8. Hosom, J.P., Jakobs, T., Baker, A., Fager, S.: Automatic speech recognition for assistive writing in speech supplemented word prediction. In: Proceedings of Interspeech 2010, pp. 2674–2677 (2010)

Wearable Range-Vibrotactile Field: Design and Evaluation

Frank G. Palmer[1], Zhigang Zhu[1], and Tony Ro[2]

[1] City College Visual Computing Laboratory
[2] Department of Psychology,
Grove School of Engineering, City College of New York,
138th Street at Convent Avenue, New York, NY 10031
{fpalmer00,zzhu,tro}@ccny.cuny.edu

Abstract. Touch is one of the most natural methods of navigation available to the blind. In this paper, we propose a method to enhance a person's use of touch by placing range sensors coupled with vibrators throughout their body. This would allow them to be able to feel objects and obstacles in close proximity to them, without having to physically touch them. In order to make effective use of this vibrotactile approach, it is necessary to discern the perceptual abilities of a person wearing small vibrators on different parts of their body. To do this, we designed a shirt with small vibrators placed on the wrists, elbows, and shoulders, and ran an efficient staircase PEST algorithm to determine their sensitivities on those parts of their body.

1 Introduction

Blindness is a disability that affects millions of people throughout the world. According to the World Health Organization, there are 285 million people who are visually impaired worldwide [1]. Performing normal navigational tasks in the modern world can be a burdensome task for them. In this paper, we introduce a wearable range-vibrotactile field approach that can be useful for aiding in blind navigation. In addition, we wish to further develop a theory of optimal of range-field navigation to aid in the development of both alternative perception for the blind and non-visual sensors for robots, which have the promise of being cheaper, easier, and more efficient to develop than those that rely on some forms of computer vision.

The paper is organized as the following. Section 2 discusses related work and some background information. In Section 3, we present our approach in both design and evaluation. Section 4 provides some experimental results. Finally we conclude our work and discuss potential implications and applications in Section 5.

2 Background and the State of the Art

One of our collaborating consultants is equipped with an Argus II from Second Sight [2], a retinal prosthesis for patients blinded from outer retinal degenerations.

K. Miesenberger et al. (Eds.): ICCHP 2012, Part II, LNCS 7383, pp. 125–132, 2012.

The Argus II provides a novel opportunity to understand various kinds of alternative perception for the blind. The device consists of a tiny camera and transmitter that are mounted in eyeglasses, as well as an implanted receiver and an electrode-studded array (6x10) that is secured to the retina with a microtack that is the size of the width of a human hair. With assistance from Lighthouse International, our consultant reports that implanted perception is improving: she could see motion (cars driving by) when she is stationary, black and white patterns, but trees and poles appear the same.   What she wants most are (1) depth, (2) information about when people are approaching, (3) higher contrast, and (4) color perception, all of which cannot be easily provided by the Argus II system.

A recently-blind student in our lab reports the necessity of two important characteristics from navigational aid devices: (1) easy, intuitive use and (2) minimal interference with the other senses. This student uses a white cane and a dog as primary navigational aids. He says that the main benefit of those aids is that they are very easy to understand and use. They have a minimal learning curve and provide easily understood cues to understanding the spatial environment. However, he says that the white cane and the dog also require a large commitment of mental and physical resources that decrease the attractiveness of their use. The white cane requires sweeping of the area in front of its user, while the dog requires nudges and commands to go to the right place.

The blind student has also tried the Brainport system [3], a tongue-based device that conveys information regarding the presence of light and dark areas in front of the user through an electrode array pressed against the tongue. A camera worn on the user's forehead scans the area in front of him/her and translates the resulting light and dark pixels into voltages across electrodes on the user's tongue. The advantages of this device are: it conveys a large amount of information by virtue of the fact that its input is taken from a camera and translated into a matrix of corresponding "pixels", without any surgery as in [2]. It also doesn't occupy the user's arms or hands, instead using their mouth, which isn't used for spatial navigation. However, this student has pointed out that there are a number of drawbacks to using the Brainport. For one, having the device in his mouth at all times is inconvenient, especially since he sometimes needs to talk to people and give commands to his dog. He has also found that images of light and dark shadows in the real world are difficult to correlate with tongue stimuli, thus producing a steep learning curve, and that the constant stimulus to the tongue can produce an acrid taste in the mouth.

Other devices have been developed, such as the one developed at AIC [4]. The AIC device uses a camera to create a depth map of the area in front of the user, which is then translated into a series of sounds that can be interpreted by the user to understand the world in front of them. Another device has been developed by EPFL [5]. This device uses an array of sonar sensors mounted on the chest to convey spatial information to an array of vibrators also mounted on the chest. A similar device was developed at the University of Toronto [12], which consisted of a Microsoft Kinect mounted on a helmet that relayed information about distances of objects in its field of view to vibrators surrounding the face.

All of these devices suffer from a number of problems, which we will try to address. Some problems include steep learning curves, overloading of the senses, interference with other functions, and the need for surgery. As mentioned, the Brainport interferes with the user's ability to speak and can leave an acrid taste in the mouth, making it difficult to use for long periods of time. It is also difficult for users to learn to use their tongue for spatial navigation. The AIC device suffers from similar setbacks: one can imagine that the constant barrage of new sounds can become annoying to the wearer and those around them, making it difficult to communicate and to hear other important sounds in the environment. Also, training the user to interpret sounds for spatial navigation could require significant mental effort. The EPFL and University of Toronto devices both possess a less intrusive method of conveying spatial information, but this information is limited and also not intuitive to interpret.

There is currently much interest in using haptic vibrational feedback as a means of helping people perform tasks that require spatial and temporal acuity. There have been many investigations of the prospect of using an array of vibrators to provide a novel means of increasing the bandwidth of information available to the wearer. This was investigated in [8], where a rugged vibrotactile suit was designed to aid soldiers performing combat-related tasks. In addition, arrays of vibrotactile stimulators have been paired with optical motion tracking systems [11] and inertial measurement units [10] to aid in teaching people new motor-learning tasks and facilitate their recovery in physical therapy. This combination has been shown to provide a noticeable improvement in the ease and speed of the wearer's ability to learn a new task. In addition, the tactile detection abilities of people wearing many of the same kinds of vibrators we are using were investigated in [9].

While it is clear that the idea of using spatially oriented vibrotactile feedback is not new, none of these devices convey range information with respect to objects that are orthogonal to the skin of the wearer at the point of vibration. Furthermore a systematic approach to optimize the number of sensor- vibrator pairs and their locations is missing. The novel design and evaluation method of using full-body range-vibrotactile field is the contribution of this paper.

3   Our Approach: Design and Testing

With the design of our device, we hope to address most, if not all of these concerns. One of the most intuitive forms of navigation used by anyone who is blind is his/her sense of touch. We seek to enhance a blind wearer's use of touch by allowing them to "feel" with their skin the spatial environment around them. Our non-visual sensor network consists of very cheap (~$10 a pair) IR range-vibrotactile pairs and sonar-vibrotactile pairs that are worn on the whole body, using vibrotactile transducing for direct range sensing and obstacle detection. Range information around the whole-body will be created so that the user can use the vibration "display" on different body parts to directly feel the range perpendicular to the surface of that part to plan his/her route and avoid obstacles. We have successfully developed small prototypes, for example, hand sensor-display pairs for reaching, arm and leg sensor sets for obstacle avoidance, and a foot sensor set for stair detection. Figure 1 shows an early prototype of the arm sensor-vibrotactile sets tested in the lab and inside a building. An initial testing with a blind individual indicated that she liked the small device since it is light, direct and can be used without any need to learn.

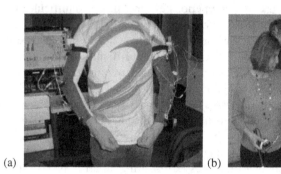

(a)   (b)

Fig. 1. Early prototype for the arm sensor-vibrotactile sets. (a) Two sets on two arms of one of the authors, each having three pairs of sensors. (b) One set of sensor-vibrotactile pairs tested by our consultant, a visually impaired person.

Our work has the following four major objectives:

1. Designing modular interchangeable sensor/vibrator pairs for use and wearability;
2. Designing comfortable and effective clothing for carrying sensor/vibrator pairs;
3. Designing circuitry for testing and controlling sensor/vibrator pairs; and
4. Designing software for testing vibratory sensitivity of different body parts.

The methodology is quick prototyping using Arduino and Java with a variety of sensors and vibrators placed in different configurations on the body. We imagine the sensation will be similar to having a "range field" around the wearer, causing sensation whenever a part of their body is near a wall or obstacle. By using parts of the body which are normally covered up by clothes, we also hope to minimize potential interference to senses that could be used for other tasks.

Our prototype for design and testing of a practical range-vibrotactile field will consist of an array of different kinds of vibrators and sensors, wires for interconnecting them, clothing for housing them on different parts of the body, and control electronics for controlling them. The evaluation experiments will run in three available modes.

In the first set of experiments, just the vibrators will be activated one at a time in order to find "thresholds" of perception for different vibrators on different parts of the body. In the second set of experiments, all or subsets of the vibrators are activated all at the same time in conjunction with input from virtual sensors as the wearer navigates a virtual environment. In the third set of experiments, the vibrators are connected to input from corresponding sensors as the wearer navigates a real environment. At the time of writing this paper, we have mainly performed the first set of experiments, which will be described in Section 4.

4   Experimental Results

We conducted the first experiment with vibrators individually activated to discern the sensitivities of various parts on the body where we thought placing range-based vibrotactile sensors would be most useful. In the first stage, we tested six locations. These were the elbows, shoulders, and wrists. Each of them is connected to a corresponding IR distance sensor, using pockets sewn into a specially designed shirt (Figure 2). This will allow the user to perceive a "force field" around their arms. In the next stage we will test other parts of the body, such as the legs, waist, chest, back, etc. The vibrators will be controlled through a transistor connected to the output from an Arduino microcontroller. The microcontroller will output a pulsed width modulation signal, which will take advantage of the inductive nature of the vibrators in order to average the pulses into a corresponding equivalent voltage as seen by the vibrator.

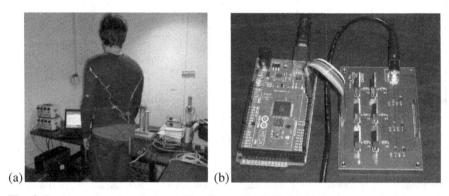

Fig. 2. Design and testing the wearable vibrotactile field. (a). A subject wearing the specially designed shirt. (b) The Arduino microcontroller.

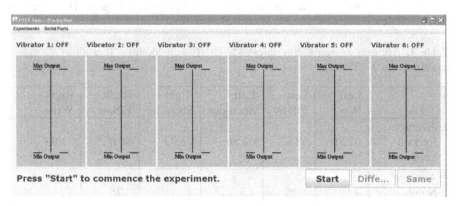

Fig. 3. A user interface for the PEST approach

At the moment, we have completed our design of the prototype shirt with six vibrators to be worn by the user, and an algorithm based on the PEST approach [6] for finding intensity discrimination thresholds on different parts of the body of a given user. Figure 3 shows a user interface for the PEST approach. The PEST algorithm presents the user with two vibrations of increasing similarity, until the user indicates that they feel the same. The PEST algorithm operates in a manner similar to binary search.

Approximately 45 minutes were required to discern the thresholds for all six locations that we were testing. Further work is in progress to improve the speed with which the algorithm converges to find a given discrimination threshold. We hope to cut the time down to a minute or two for each location so that we could perform full body vibration sensitivity evaluation in a reasonable amount of time, for example, within an hour for 100 locations.

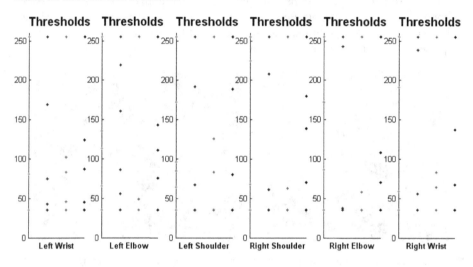

Fig. 4. Vibrotactile thresholds of six locations for four human subjects. Four different colors (green, blue, pink and black) correspond to four different human participants. The vertical axes are the voltages of vibration strengths, quantized from 0 to 255.

Table 1. Averages of vibrotactile thresholds on six arm locations (Length of intervals as quantized on a 0 -255 scale)

	Left Wrist	Left Elbow	Left Shoulder	Right Shoulder	Right Elbow	Right Wrist
Average Interval Length	62.86	58.67	62.86	73.33	80.0	73.33
Average Number of Thresholds	4.5	4.75	4.5	4	3.75	4

We have performed experiments with six human subjects. Figure 4 shows the experimental results of the discerning thresholds with four of the six human subjects, whose data were completely collected for our purpose. In the figure, for each location, each column of color dots represents the threshold locations for each person. The average interval distance and the average number of thresholds for each location along the arms are shown in Table 1. These results show:

1. Similarity and differences across locations. We found that on average, the sensitivity of various locations of human arms is very similar. In our experiment, human arms can discern about 3-4 levels of vibration whose voltage is from 0 to 5 Volts. However we found that the left arms are more sensitive to vibration than the right arms. This might be due to the sensor setup, the real discerning power of humans, or the combination of both. More experiments are needed to verify this difference, but if this laterality effect is real, it may be related to handedness as all of our subjects were right-handed and may therefore be less sensitive to somatosensory input on their more frequently used arm.
2. Similarity and differences among human subjects. We have found that the range of thresholds of the four participants varies from 3 to 6. However on average, the number is about 4.

Statistical tests of the experimental results will be conducted after more participants are test. However, these preliminary results indicate that three to four different distance ranges can be conveyed to users through vibration. Adding no vibration for a safe range, this would be sufficient to inform a user about ranges that are safe, far, medium, close, and very close, so that the user can respond accordingly.

Once we have systematically established an average threshold number and value for each body part, we will switch our attention to the second set of experiments in testing the design using a virtual reality based approach similar to [7], followed by connecting the sensors to the vibrators and testing the device in a real environment (the third set of experiments). All the while we will continue testing different kinds of vibrators and sensors to find the optimal combination of each.

5   Conclusion

Anyone who closes their eyes and tries to navigate their way around a room can attest to how quickly they begin to feel their way around, reaching out with their hands and arms, as their primary means of determining where they are. By allowing a person to feel their environment without touching it, we allow them to essentially "see" with their body. This paper describes the concept of a full-body wearable range-vibrotactile field approach for achieving this goal. As a first step, the experiments to determine the vibrotactile discrimination thresholds of perception on different parts of the body have moved us closer to creating this novel form of spatial navigation.

Acknowledgments. This work is supported by US National Science Foundation Emerging Frontiers in Research and Innovation Program under Award No. EFRI-1137172, and City SEEDs: City College 2011 President Grant for Interdisciplinary Scientific Research Collaborations. We would also like to thank Ms Barbara Campbell and Mr. Ben Humphreys for their consultation and feedback in designing and testing our systems.

References

1. World Health Organization, Visual impairment and blindness,
   http://www.who.int/mediacentre/factsheets/fs282/en/
2. Second Sight, http://www.2-sight.com
3. Wicab, Inc., Brainport Vision Technology,
   http://vision.wicab.com/technology/
4. Gonzalez-Mora, J.L., et al.: Seeing the world by hearing: Virtual Acoustic Space (VAS) a new space perception system for blind people. In: Information and Communication Technologies, pp. 837–842 (2006)
5. Cardin, S., Thalmann, D., Vexo, F.: A wearable system for mobility improvement of visually impaired people. Vis. Comput. 23(2), 109–118 (2007)
6. Lieberman, H.R., Pentland, A.P.: Microcomputer-based estimation of psychophysical thresholds: the best PEST. Behavior Research Methods & Instrumentation 14(1), 21–25 (1982)
7. Torres-Gil, M.A., Casanova-Gonzalez, O., González-Mora, J.L.: Applications of virtual reality for visually impaired people. WSEAS Transactions on Computers 9(2), 184–193 (2010)
8. Lindeman, R.W., Yanagida, Y., Noma, H., Hosaka, K.: Wearable vibrotactile systems for virtual contact and information display. Virtual Reality, 203–213 (2006)
9. Sch, S. & Hulin, T.: Evaluation of vibrotactile feedback to the human arm. Configurations 3–6 (2006), http://lsc.univ-evry.fr/~eurohaptics/upload/cd/papers/f78.pdf
10. Lee, B.-C., Chen, S., Sienko, K.H.: A Wearable device for real-Time motion error detection and vibrotactile instructional cuing. IEEE Trans. Neural Systems and Rehab. Eng. 19(4) (2011)
11. Lieberman, J., Breazeal, C.: TIKL: Development of a wearable vibrotactile feedback suit for improved human motor learning. IEEE Transactions on Robotics 23, 919–926 (2007)
12. Mann, S., et al.: Blind navigation with a wearable range camera and vibrotactile helmet. In: Proceedings of the 19th International Conference on Multimedia (2011)

System Supporting Speech Perception
in Special Educational Needs Schoolchildren

Adam Kupryjanow, Piotr Suchomski, Piotr Odya, and Andrzej Czyzewski

Multimedia Systems Department, Gdansk University of Technology,
Narutowicza 11/12, Gdansk, Poland
{adamq,pietka,piotrod,andcz}@sound.eti.pg.gda.pl

Abstract. The system supporting speech perception during the classes is presented in the paper. The system is a combination of portable device, which enables real-time speech stretching, with the workstation designed in order to perform hearing tests. System was designed to help children suffering from Central Auditory Processing Disorders.

Keywords: special education needs, Central Auditory Processing Disorders, time-scale modification.

1   Introduction

Children with special education needs (SEN) provide a large group of pupils. In Europe, the number of children with SEN can be estimated to be about 4% [1]. Hence, the development of effective methods for helping them to reduce any inequities becomes a priority task. At the Multimedia Systems Department of the Gdansk University of Technology, research devoted to the problem of helping people, especially children, with various types of hearing disorders, has been carried out for many years [2], [3]. However, it appears that in addition to well-known problems associated with hearing loss, many children suffer from impaired perception related to the Central Auditory Processing Disorders (CAPD). As a result, children belonging to this group are not able to understand speech being articulated too fast for them. The problem arises in degraded listening conditions e.g. in noisy, reverberant rooms like classrooms. In case of hearing problems presence correlated with the CAPD, it was shown that the speech intelligibility could be improved by the usage of time scale modification (TSM) of speech signal (i.e. time-expansion). One of the main challenges in this context is the development of algorithms capable to operate in real-time. Such algorithms were implemented in the developed system. The engineered system consists of two basic modules: PC application, which allows for performing hearing tests and training, as well as a portable device that stretches speech signal in real-time.

2   Pre-existing Solutions

One of the most widely known methods devoted to the speech perception improvement is the FM system [1]. It is composed of a wireless microphone worn by the

K. Miesenberger et al. (Eds.): ICCHP 2012, Part II, LNCS 7383, pp. 133–136, 2012.

teacher and a signal receiver with headphones, which is used by the child. The purpose of the system is to increase the signal to noise ratio (SNR) by eliminating of the classroom acoustical field influence. Less known approaches are those presented by Nakamura [5] and Nejime [6]. Both methods are based on the assumption that it is significant to adjust not only the SNR of the received speech, but also its speed. As a solution they designed devices performing the time scale modification (TSM) of speech signal in the real-time. Nakamura had proposed to combine their device with the TV set. That solution is dedicated to stretching speech signal for the person watching TV. Nejime's system was designed as a small device stretching the signal captured by the microphone and reproducing it through headphones. The microphone was wired to the device, so the captured speech was distorted by the reverberation of the room. A user had to specify the moments when speech should be modified.

3   Proposed Solution

3.1   Overview

In Fig. 1 general diagram of the proposed system was presented. The system is supervised by the multimedia application. The software was designed in order to: perform diagnosis of hearing disorders, prepare and manage auditory training, configure and interact with the portable device.

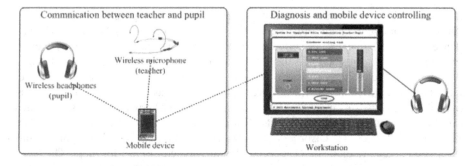

Fig. 1. General diagram of the system

Before the first usage of the system, every user has to perform hearing tests. As a result, hearing characteristics of the pupil are obtained. In the next step, all collected parameters are sent to a portable device. The key assumption is that the child could use the device during all lessons. To acquire signal without additional noise and reverberation, the teacher has to use a wireless microphone transmitting speech signal to the device. The device processes (in a real-time) speech signal according to the child's needs. As a result, the child could participate in classes with normal hearing children. All lessons could be recorded in order to listen to them at home using a PC computer.

A vital functionality of the PC application is hearing training. It can be conducted using practically any sounds stored on the computer, including material recorded at school.

3.2 Mobile Device

As a mobile device typical smartphone was used. The device receives (by the Bluetooth) speech captured by the teacher's microphone and reproduces stretched speech through child's headphones. The time-scale modification of speech signal is performed by the usage of the dedicated stretching algorithm developed by the authors of this paper [6].

3.3 Workstation

In the PC application two types of hearing diagnosis methods were implemented: peripheral auditory system tests and central auditory system tests. The first group of tests includes air conduction tonal audiometer and loudness scaling test. The second group includes: dichotic digits test (DDT), duration pattern sequence test (DPST), pitch pattern sequence test (PPST), random gap detection (RGD) and distorted speech perception test. Based on the results of the diagnostic application will calculate the adequate hearing aid dynamic characteristic, which should compensate the hearing impairment (compression curves - virtual hearing aid) and to appoint the initial slow rate of speech, in the case of central hearing problems.

An important function is preparing and performing of hearing training. With this application the user (pupil) will be able to systematically carry out various types of auditory system trainings. The application will have all the data that are needed for this type of training. In addition to the predefined sets of training signals, such as pre-recorded words, phrases, expressions, sentences, the application will also be able to process the recorded lessons. The computer application gives also opportunity to track the progress of the pupil, which in turn will facilitate the proper control of the training process.

4   Target Group

The preliminary tests of the designed TSM algorithm had shown that the main improvement in the speech intelligibility could be achieved by the group of children with the low hearing resolution threshold. This threshold was measured using TCT_{50} value (50% Time-Compressed speech Threshold). TCT_{50} value was obtained during the time compressed speech test. It defines the threshold for which person could understand 50% of the words in a typical sentence [8]. In our research we have found that speech intelligibility was improved for the children with the TCT_{50} lower than 6 [vowels/s]. The average rate of the input speech was equal to 7.57 [vowels/s] and the average improvement in speech intelligibility tests, was equal to 20 %.

5   Conclusions

It is expected that the proposed system could reduce difficulties during the lessons. Consequently, children's social isolation may decrease and their school results might be improved. The tests of the whole developed system will be continued in the future.

Acknowledgements. Research funded within the project No. POIG.01.03.01-22-017/08, entitled "Elaboration of a series of multimodal interfaces and their implementation to educational, medical, security and industrial applications". The project is subsidized from the European Regional Development Fund by the Polish State budget".

References

1. European Agency for Development in Special Needs Education: Special Needs Education Country Data 2010 (2010)
2. Kosikowski, R., Kosikowski, L., Odya, P., Czyzewski, A.: SENSES - WHAT U SEE? Vision screening system dedicated for iOS based devices. Development and screening results. In: SIGMAP, Sevilla, Spain (2011)
3. Kostek, B., Czyzewski, A., Skarżyński, H., Kochanek, K.: Internet-Based Automatic Hearing Assessment System. In: 46 Internationales Wissenschaftliches Kolloquium Ilmenau, Ilmeanu, Germany, September 24-27, pp. 87–89 (2001)
4. Kupryjanow, A., Czyzewski, A.: A non-uniform real-time speech time-scale stretching method. In: Proc.of International Conference on Signal Processing and Multimedia Applications (SIGMAP), Sewilla, pp. 1–7 (2011)
5. Nakamura, A., et al.: Real Time Speech Rate Converting System For Elderly People. In: IEEE Int. Conf. Acoust., Speech, Signal Proc. (ICASSP), Adelaide (1994)
6. Nejime, Y., Aritsuka, T., Imamura, T., Ifukubei, T., Matsushima, J.: A portable digital speech-rate converter for hearing impairment. IEEE Trans. Rehabil. Eng. 4(2), 73–83 (1996)
7. Phonak Hearing System, EduLink: Improves speech understanding in noisy classroom, Field News, pp. 1–2 (2004)
8. Versfeld, N.J., Dreschler, W.A.: The relationship between the intelligibility of time-compressed speech and speech in noise in young and elderly listeners. J. Acoust. Soc. Am. 111(1), 401–408 (2002)

Designing a Mobile Application to Record ABA Data

Silvia Artoni[1], Maria Claudia Buzzi[1], Marina Buzzi[1], Claudia Fenili[1],
Barbara Leporini[2], Simona Mencarini[1], and Caterina Senette[1]

[1] CNR-IIT, via Moruzzi 1, 56124 Pisa, Italy
{Silvia.Artoni,Claudia.Buzzi,Marina.Buzzi,Claudia.Fenili,
Simona.Mencarini,Caterina.Senette}@iit.cnr.it
[2] CNR-ISTI, via Moruzzi 1, 56124 Pisa, Italy
Barbara.Leporini@isti.cnr.it

Abstract. Applied Behavior Analysis (ABA) is a scientific method for modelling human behavior, successfully applied in the context of educating autistic subjects. ABA's scientific approach relies on recording measurable data derived from the execution of structured programs. In this paper we describe an application designed to support the work of ABA tutors with autistic subjects. Specifically, we describe an Android application for gathering data from ABA sessions with a patient and sharing information among his/her ABA team. Tablets allow mobility and ease of interaction, enabling efficient data collection and processing, and automating tasks previously carried out by recording notes on paper. However, reduced screen size poses challenges for user interface design.

Keywords: Autism, ABA, mobile, android, data recording.

1   Introduction

Applied Behavior Analysis (ABA) is a scientific method for modelling human behavior, successfully applied in several contexts, including work safety and education. It is currently adopted for effective educational training, especially with autistic children. The ABA intervention consists of a sequence of programs and trials of increasing difficulty. ABA's scientific approach relies on measurable data and programs, so data related to each trial are recorded on a paper form in order to monitor and assess each subject's progress in the intervention.

ABA methodology is based on Augmentative and Alternative Communication (AAC) and Discrete Trial Training (DTT). AAC provides an alternative method for communicating (usually by images or gestures) used in treating learning disabilities and neurological pathologies [1]. DTT is used for teaching and fixing concepts in subjects with learning disabilities. It consists of trials of increasing difficulty, repeated several times, according to the subject's needs. Basic ABA programs operate using articles of common categories (colors, shapes, numbers, food, vehicles, clothes, etc.) according to the following sequence:

- Matching: 1) image with image; 2) word with word; 3) image with word; 4) word with image

K. Miesenberger et al. (Eds.): ICCHP 2012, Part II, LNCS 7383, pp. 137–144, 2012.
© Springer-Verlag Berlin Heidelberg 2012

- Receptive: 1) image 2) word
- Expressive: 1) image.

Each program is executed according to DTT. An article is considered mastered after the correct independent execution of the following learning sequence of trials:

1. Mass Trial (MT): basic trial ensuring subject's success
2. Distracter phase: first a neutral (of different category, size, color, etc.) distracter is added to the item on acquisition (MT+Dn); next the same trial is executed with two neutral distracters (MT+2 Dn). Then a non-neutral distracter (MT+D) and next two non-neutral ones (MT+2D) are introduced in the trial
3. Extended Trial (ET): a choice of three items, two previously mastered and the third on acquisition
4. Random Rotations (RR) of three learned (mastered) items.

Usually a subject moves on to the next program when 80% of articles in the category are mastered. Different types of prompts can be provided to a subject to help him/her to successfully complete the trial (avoiding mistakes), as required by the ABA error-less principle. The generalization process consists in proposing new ways to acquire each mastered item, for instance changing the stimulus (e.g. image color), the position of the article (e.g. bringing it closer) and/or the discriminative stimulus (e.g. the directive). The autistic subjects involved in our study are children between 2 and 10 years old. An example of trial data collected by tutors is shown in Fig. 1. FP indicates the use of a full prompt to help the child, PP a partial prompt.

Program: matching image/image
Article: Red
SD: Combine
Level: MT   MT+ND   MT+2ND
             MT+D   MT+2D   ET   RR

N.	Prompt Type %	Rein-forcement	Notes
1	FP 100%	3-D book	
2	PP 80%		
3	PP 50%		
4	PP 20%		
5	PP 20%		
6	0%		
...	...		
Messages:			

Fig. 1. Paper form for recording trial data

The ABA approach requires different tutors to rotate for didactic sessions with the same child (another kind of generalization, necessary for testing the learning), so considerable time is spent by the ABA team (usually 1 consultant, 1 senior tutor, 2-3 tutors, and child's parents) on exchanging information on executed programs and trials. In a 3-hour session, at least 10 minutes are spent reading comments of previous tutors and 20 minutes writing comments on the on-going session. Furthermore, copying data of each session in an Excel file to analyze the subject's progress is time-consuming and prone to error. The proposed application, moving from paper to electronic data, optimizes tutors' time by allowing rapid access to previous ABA data, providing better time scheduling for the child's caregivers (tutors, teachers, parents).

In this paper we describe the design of an Android application for supporting tutors in data collection from ABA sessions. The targets of our application are ABA tutors and people involved in the child's education (e.g., parents, teachers). A touch-screen mobile device facilitates data collection and offers simple interaction, while enabling efficient data processing; however, reduced screen size poses challenges for user interface (UI) design and usability, as discussed in the following. The paper is organized into four sections. After this introduction, related work in the field is briefly described. Next, the focus moves to the design and implementation of the application. Last, the paper ends with conclusions and future work.

2   Related Work

Recent studies have confirmed the efficacy of educational therapy delivered by electronic devices for autistic children. Specifically, mobile devices are an emerging field in Augmentative and Alternative Communication research. Although many digital products are available for AAC (e.g., GoTalk, Tango, Dynavox, Activity Pad) they are expensive and not very usable or flexible: training is required for set-up and customization, making it difficult for parents to use it at home [2]. The use of a mobile platform can offer many advantages: lower cost, greater flexibility, simpler and faster customization, smaller size enabling ubiquity, and a familiar environment (mostly cell phone) for the children.

Pervasive technologies are also investigated for monitoring the subject's behavior. To enhance the social skills and abilities of persons with ASD, Kaliouby and Goodwin built a suite of wearable technologies (cameras, microphones, sensors) for capturing, analyzing, and sharing (via wireless network) their social-emotional interactions, in a fun and engaging way [3].

A large branch of research on autism is devoted to providing usable tools to assist tutors during therapy sessions and to analyze related data. Several researchers have based their studies and software development on participatory design (Kientz et al., 2007), [2], [4]. Kientz et al. designed and developed two systems for facilitating efficient child monitoring (both progress and behavior): 1) Abaris, the supporting team executing Discrete Trial Training therapy, building indices into videos of therapy sessions and allowing easy data search; 2) CareLog, for collecting and analyzing behavioral data ("problem behaviors"). Furthermore sensors were used to monitor stimming behavior (self-stimulatory movements) in order to understand the cause of an uncomfortable situation [5]. However, few details are available concerning the software design and implementation; specific software (SW) is proprietary while research prototypes are not publicly and freely available, so paper forms are still widespread.

Concerning DTT, Tarbox et al. compared a commercial software program for recording the outcome of discrete trials (mTrial) and other subject behavior data on a personal data assistant (PDA) with traditional pen-and-paper data recording systems, both in terms of the accuracy of gathered data and therapist efficiency in filling out paper or electronic forms by means of a stylus. Results showed equal data accuracy for both formats but traditional data collection was faster [6]. However the rapidity of filling out data mainly depends on the software user interfaces and also on the subjective ability and rapidity of the therapist to type data. Today modern tablets and smart phones favor data entry efficiency allowing natural interaction with touch screen interfaces via fingers: drag and drop, taps and gestures. In the proposed application, trial-related data are rapidly inserted in the user interfaces using different gestures for signaling prompted or independent trials. Furthermore, the availability of electronic data stored in a database makes their processing faster and easier.

3   The Application

From the beginning of the project, the design of the application has involved senior ABA tutors and psychologists, according to participatory design principles. All members of the design team have participated in ABA sessions with autistic children in order to observe and better understand the natural environment where the application has to run. With this aim, the original data collected was also optimized, integrating new parameters related to the child (e.g., non-collaboration on the part of the child or problem behavior) or set-up errors (tutor error) that can be useful for co-relating data collected from the ABA sessions with the child antecedent or consequent behaviours.

As previously described, ABA sessions can take place in various environments such as the child's home, school, hospital or other places (e.g., association headquarters). For this reason, portable and ubiquitous solutions are needed, considering that the success of ABA intervention relies on its regular and frequent execution.

We selected the Android operating system, which is open source and offers the advantage of Android's developer community that contributes to improving its functionalities. For deploying the application, we used a Tablet device with Android 3.0 O.S. (Honey Comb, optimized for Tablets) with display WXGA (1280x 800 pixels; 150 pixels/inch), HD 720p touch screen and excellent processing capability (memory up to 32 GB on board and Processor speed: 1GHz Dual Core). The application is optimized to run with functionalities specifically designed for tablets. The recently released Android version 4.0 brings together smart phone and tablet features, allowing the SW tools to run even on cell phones with a few adjustments for adapting the visual rendering to a smaller screen (including reducing the amount of widgets placed on the UI). When designing for a small touch-screen device offering a virtual keyboard, it is important take into account factors such as the distance between text box and push button to facilitate data entry, font size and color, and contrast level, to ensure readability for all. A path should be found regarding flexibility in inserting new elements when selecting items from a pull-down menu in order to make the process more efficient. Furthermore, a usable way to aggregate large quantities of data should be adopted in order to effectively manage the enormous amount of data recorded by the application.

Data entry during an ABA session must be executed very quickly and smoothly so that it is not source of environmental disturbance for the child. Often tutors do not record data in a timely way if circumstances do not allow it (e.g. to avoid breaking the child's rhythm) and they must follow mentally, requiring considerable effort. Entering data quickly is also fundamental. To limit writing/editing, both signs and gestures may be implemented, but to be very useful they must be clear and fast. For this the application UI allows tutors to act in a natural way using gestures to reproduce the signs that they used to fill out the paper forms, so the time spent is comparable. Fortunately, touch-screen devices facilitate data entry (compared to mouse-based interactions) reducing coordination efforts to focus on any UI widgets.

As shown in Table 1, the typical form used by a tutor during an ABA program requires detailed data for each trial performed. The tutor frequently has to fill out more than 3-4 paper sheets for each program, having to rewrite the same information (session, program and article) several times. Furthermore, for each trial (s)he has to insert the type (indicative, positional or physic) and percentage of prompt provided to the child, and the type of errors occurring if any. In the SW these data are automatically set up by the program according to the previous one inserted.

3.1   The User Interfaces

As previously mentioned, before an ABA intervention the tutor needs to read all the forms of previous sessions carried out by the child with other tutors, in order to choose the best program according to the present status of his/her learning. The main interface is designed to enable tutors to record trial data with only a few clicks, from 1 to max 5-6 for each trial, depending on how much information must be collected.

When the application is launched, a Login Page for user authentication appears, since different subjects may be taught to each child. A new account can be created if one is not available. After user authentication, the Main page makes some software functions available including: 1) Selection of a child; 2) Insertion of a new child's account (if not present); 3) Accessing Session History (partial or full) in order to monitor a child's progress; 4) Recording Data Session (Fig. 2).

The tutor selects a child 'nickname' from a combo box. A new child may be added using the window activated by pressing the New Child Account push button (Fig. 2).

The History button provides a complete overview of past sessions and the child's progress. The tutor can choose/examine the number of previous sessions as well as the filters to apply, depending on the type of information (s)he is looking for. The tutor can obtain further details by just clicking on the level. An example of the Summary is shown in Fig. 3. An additional function for showing a child's data in graphic format will be provided, in order to make the child's progress and response to the methodology more understandable.

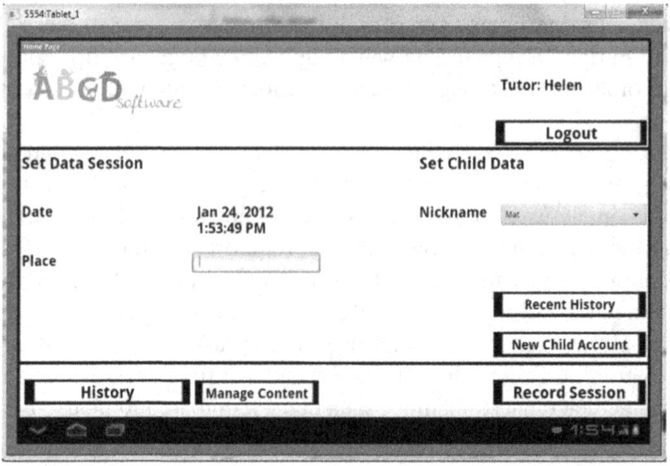

Fig. 2. Main user interface

Selecting the *Record Session* button in the Main user interface, the tutor moves on to the child's Recent History page, enabling access to the child's last sessions (details of one trial shown in Fig. 3) and then to the *Trial Evaluation Form*, the core of the application (Fig. 4).

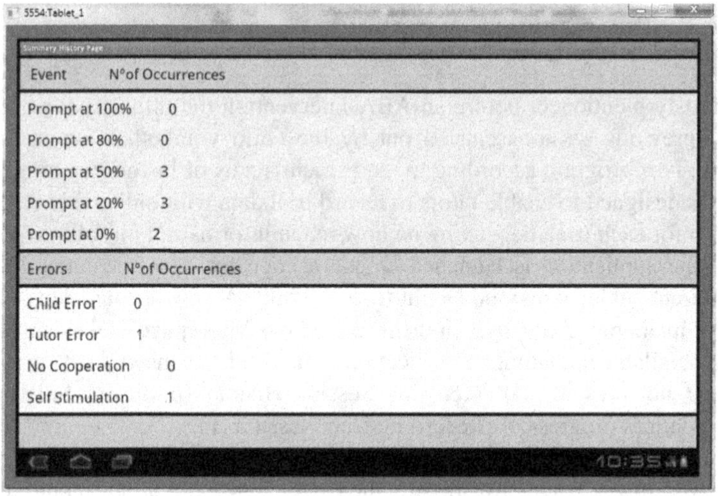

Fig. 3. Summary of one trial's data

General data such as the ABA program, the article in acquisition, the trial level, and the stimulus provided to the child, are automatically set by the system to those from the last program (done in the last session) if the article involved had not been mastered. Of course, all these default values can be changed by the Tutor to perform another program or to repeat an executed level if the child needs a refresh. The UI proposes an initial group of 8 trials (that can be doubled repetitively) to be filled in with data from each trial: the type and percentage of prompt, additional information as to whether the set-up was smooth or if an external error occurred (e.g., child distraction, tutor or set-up error, etc.). If information on an error is inserted, a text field appears for inserting any tutor comments.

If more than 8 trials are needed for the child to execute a successful independent trial in that combination of program, level and article, the *Trial Continue* button can be pressed to add a new set of 8 trials' data (9-16).

Fig. 4. Evaluation Activity UI

The *Next Program* and *Next Level* buttons allow the tutor to automatically jump to the next program (when an ABA program is completed) or to the next level of the selected program (when the previous level is successfully accomplished) respectively. For each level the same UI is shown, with only a slight difference in background color to help tutors better identify the different levels.

4   Conclusion and Future Work

In this paper we describe an Android application for mobile devices aimed at recording data from ABA sessions with autistic children. The application, developed in the context of the ABCD SW project, was designed involving two ABA senior tutors, a psychologist, and a pedagogy and ABA consultant. The ABA approach requires different tutors who rotate during the didactic sessions with the same child; thus considerable time was spent by the ABA team exchanging information. The proposed application moving from paper to electronic data optimizes tutor time, allowing rapid access to previous data, also in aggregated format, and better management of time for the child's team/family (eliminating the need to copy session data).

A mobile platform offers many advantages: it is cheap, flexible, simple to use (touch screen), small-sized so easily transportable, it can be used in a familiar environment, and especially it can replace most of the paper-based forms usually used by tutors.

Future work will include user tests with autistic children and data processing to further refine the proposed software. The created software will be shared in the public domain, under the Creative Commons licence. The possibility of sharing the app with the Internet community will favor faster and better improvement.

Acknowledgments. We thank the Regione Toscana, which funded this project within the framework of the "FAS 2007 2013 Delibera CIPE 166/2007 PAR FAS Regione Toscana Action Line 1.1.a.3" (14 Feb 2011-13 Feb 2013).

References

1. Drager, K., Light, J., McNaughton, D.: Effects of AAC interventions on communication and language for young children with complex communication needs. Journal of Pediatric Rehabilitation Medicine 3(4) (2010)
2. Hayes, G.R., Hirano, S., Marcu, G., Monibi, M., Nguyen, D.H., Yeganyan, M.: Interactive visual supports for children with autism. Springer Personal and Ubiquitous Computing, 18p (2010), doi:10.1007/s00779-010-0294-8
3. el Kaliouby, R., Goodwin, M.S.: iSET: Interactive Social-Emotional Toolkit for Autism Spectrum Disorder. In: Interaction Design and Children (IDC 2008), pp. 77–80 (2008)
4. Monibi, M., Hayes, G.R.: Mocotos: Mobile Communications Tools for Children with Special Needs. In: Interaction Design and Children (IDC 2008), pp. 121–124 (2008)
5. Kientz, J.A., Hayes, G.R., Westeyn, T.L., Starner, T., Abowd, G.D.: Pervasive Computing and Autism: Assisting Caregivers of Children with Special Needs. IEEE Pervasive Computing 6(1), 28–35 (2007)
6. Tarbox, J., Wilke, A.E., Findel-Pyles, R.S., Bergstrom, R.M., Granpeesheh, D.: A comparison of electronic to traditional pen-and-paper data collection in discrete trial training for children with autism. Research in Autism Spectrum Disorders 4(1), 65–75 (2010)

Creating Personas with Disabilities

Trenton Schulz and Kristin Skeide Fuglerud

Norsk Regnesentral – Norwegian Computing Center,
Gaustadallen 23a/b, Kristen Nygaards hus, NO-0373 Oslo, Norway
{Trenton.Schulz,Kristin.Skeide.Fuglerud}@nr.no
http://www.nr.no

Abstract. Personas can help raise awareness among stakeholders about users' needs. While personas are made-up people, they are based on facts gathered from user research. Personas can also be used to raise awareness of universal design and accessibility needs of people with disabilities. We review the current state of the art of the personas and review some research and industry projects that use them. We outline techniques that can be used to create personas with disabilities. This includes advice on how to get more information about assistive technology and how to better include people with disabilities in the persona creation process. We also describe our use of personas with disabilities in several projects and discuss how it has helped to find accessibility issues.

Keywords: personas, accessibility, universal design, inclusive design.

1 Introduction

Personas are a great way of raising awareness of user needs throughout a project. A persona is a rich description of a potential user of your system and consists of several stereotypical traits, such as preferences, needs, attitudes, habits, and desires, composed into a realistic, but fake, person with a name and picture. Instead of arguing for the needs of a generic user that can morph from being a complete novice in one situation to an experienced expert in another, stakeholders ground themselves in the facts of the personas in front of them. The idea is that the resulting system will be more successful when it is designed with specific users in mind rather than a vague idea of an average user.

Since personas help focus on the concrete facts about your potential users, it would be beneficial if the needs of people with disabilities are included among the personas. While this has been encouraged and used in different places, there is little information on how one should create personas with disabilities. This results in a risk of creating personas that do not capture the needs of people with disabilities or that are based on incorrect information. We introduce a methodology for creating personas with disabilities that minimizes this risk by providing ways of collecting information and opinions from the people with disabilities and taking into account the different Assistive Technology (AT) they use. This methodology can be easily included in a standard persona creation methodology contributing to systems that are designed for all.

K. Miesenberger et al. (Eds.): ICCHP 2012, Part II, LNCS 7383, pp. 145–152, 2012.

2   State of the Art

Input from users is important to ensure that new systems can be usable and cover their needs. Participation from the users is one of the principles behind Scandinavian Design [1]. Yet, having constant access to users is resource-intensive and may be too costly for a project. Using personas helps ensure that users' perspectives are included. Lindgren, Chen, Amdahl, and Chaikiat [2, p. 461] describe personas as "... a hypothetical archetype of real users described in great detail and defined by their goals and needs, rather than just demographics." Personas are usually presented in a persona description, this usually includes a picture of the persona; background information including family, tasks, motivations, attitudes to technology and technical knowledge.

Personas were popularized by Cooper [3] in his book *The Inmates are Running the Asylum*. Cooper presents personas as a way to include viewpoints from different user groups without falling into the trap of using a generic user. He stresses that designing something for specific people will be more successful than trying to create something that works for generic users. Cooper then uses the persona technique to aid in designing an entertainment system for an airline. While one of the personas is an elderly man with some vision problems, there is little information about how Cooper created these personas.

Personas are normally used to keep the focus on the users on the project, but it is also possible to find out about your users based on the personas you have created. Chapman, Love, Milham, ElRif, and Alford [4] have demonstrated a novel use of personas. They took personas' properties and found how prevalent each property was among their user groups.

To ensure that systems we design are accessible, we should also create personas that have disabilities. Zimmermann and Vanderheiden [5] point out that using personas with impairments help make the accessibility requirements real. Using personas with disabilities gives us an opportunity to include their needs without the resource intensive task of recruiting disabled people for all stages of the project. Although he does not provide detailed instructions on how to create personas, Henry [6] encourages the use of personas with disabilities in the design of ICT, but reminds us that everything that is true for one person with one disability is not necessarily applicable to all people with that disability. This advice, however, is useful for all kinds of personas.

The use of personas with disabilities has gained traction in the industry and in several recent EU research projects like ACCESSIBLE [7] and ÆGIS [8]. The Ubuntu operating system has also adapted personas in guiding its accessibility development [9]. These projects have provided their personas online. Others have encouraged people to use these specific personas for other projects [10]. This may seem like a shortcut for creation, but recycling personas is not recommended [11]. This is because an equally important aspect is to engage the stakeholders and the development team, to let them get to know the personas and to empathize with them. This part is lost when recycling personas from another project. Knowledge of creating personas can be recycled, however.

Pruitt and Grudin [12] list several problems with personas in projects. The personas are not believable, because they were not based on real data; that they are not presented well, and then not used; no understanding of how to use the personas; and finally that only part of the group is interested in using personas and there are no resources to make personas come alive. There are several methods for combating these problems and we will present some in Section 4.

Even though personas have become a popular method for raising awareness of users' needs in a project, it is important to remember that personas are *not* a replacement for actual users. That is, one should not create personas out of thin air to replace gathering input from users. This may allow stakeholders to think about the users, but it will be problematic when creating personas with disabilities. This is because many people have misconceptions about how people with disabilities interact with technology and this can lead to these personas having extra powers or disadvantages that they may not have. As pointed out by Grudin and Pruitt [13] personas can be used poorly and for most people "... a more solid foundation will prove necessary." In particular, Grudin and Pruitt recommend basing personas on user research and facts.

3   Methodology

As mentioned in the Section 2, even though personas are fictional, they should be based on experiences with and information from real users [14]. We underscore that personas cannot replace contact with real users altogether, but rather be used as a supplement, and as a way of keeping a continual focus on the users throughout the project life-cycle. There are many ways that one can go about collecting information about real users and, depending on the resources available, selecting more than one method may be useful.

One way that can be useful for collecting information about users is by simply asking them. This includes methods like using focus groups, interviews, and surveys. Observation is another good method. As Gould [15] points out, you may not have any idea about what you need to know about users and their environment until you see them. It is useful to study information from case studies and other user research. Market information may be another source to consider including.

When it comes to recruiting people with disabilities, having contacts inside the user organizations that support people with disabilities is a good start. User organizations can contact members for you and provide opportunities for you to talk to users at meetings or provide a location to host a focus group: a well-known location can make it easier for people with visual or physical impairments to participate rather than traveling to your site, which is unlikely unknown to them. Using surveys can also be a way of gathering information. An online survey can help you reach a wider audience that might have been impossible or cost prohibitive otherwise, but it is important that the tools for gathering the information are usable for your audience. For example, using a web survey tool may create a survey that is inaccessible to people using certain types of AT like screen readers [16]. A plain text email with the questions may be an alternative for getting these voices heard. Getting more information will help create more well-rounded personas and highlight different issues that will need to be taken into a system.

Looking at the AT used by people with disabilities also helps in creating personas with disabilities. Some personas will be using AT for accessing information. It is important to know how these technologies work and how people work with them. It is vital that someone in the design team has actual experience working with people with disabilities, either from user tests or from teaching them to use technology. You should at least include people with this kind of experience in the process of creating personas. One way to do this could be to invite them to a persona workshop.

As an example of how to involve users, in one project, the UNIMOD project [17], a navigation system for drivers working at a rehabilitation center was to be developed. A persona workshop was arranged on the premises of the rehabilitation company. Employees at the company with ample experience with the target population were invaluable during the persona workshop. As various aspects of the target population were discussed during the persona creation process, the employees could fill in with related real-life stories. The stories were told in connection to discussions of traits, needs, attitudes, and habits of the various personas. Later in the project, project participants remembered several of these stories; they were referred to when using the personas, and they were useful for keeping the personas alive.

As outlined by Pruitt and Adlin [11], a persona workshop gathers the stakeholders to generate personas based on assumptions and factoids. Assumptions are quotes, opinions, or goals that these potential personas would have along with a possible name for the persona. Factoids are small facts or news items from literature, research, or data from your own user research. During the workshop, participants re-read through the collected research and writes out factoids (e.g., on post-it notes). This can also be repeated for assumptions. Starting first with the assumptions, stakeholders build groups of similar assumptions to see if there are any patterns that emerge. This could be done digitally with mind-mapping software or in analog with post-it notes and a clear wall or whiteboard. This process is repeated with the factoids usually resulting in a rearrangement or new groups being created. These groups are the starting point for creating persona skeletons.

Persona skeletons are the outlines of the actual personas. They consist of the assumptions and factoids that were collected earlier, but they also are where sketches of information about the personas start to emerge. One way of organizing this information is to use a template with all the different areas of the final persona description. Start by filling in information first as keywords and continue until you have fleshed-out the entire section. A mind map is another good way of creating the "bones" of the skeletons before adding "flesh."

Once everyone agrees on the persona skeletons, writing up of the actual personas can begin. The outcome is usually what most people see when they are presented personas, the persona description as detailed in Section 2. If the persona has a disability, this information is also presented along with information about the AT the persona uses. Since others in the project may not have an understanding about how a person with a disability works with an AT, it may be necessary to include information about how a disability affects a persona or how particular AT plays a part in the persona's life. After this, the personas are ready to become active participants in the project.

How many personas should be created for a project? If we want to aim for universal design, targeting the four main groups of disabilities is a good start. That is, create personas with vision, hearing, movement, and cognitive impairments. Yet, as mentioned in Section 2, one should keep in mind that each of these impairments group are diverse and have different abilities. Another option to consider is to create an elderly persona. Elderly personas usually have a combination of several milder versions of impairments from these groups. In our experience, we have found that three to six personas is a manageable amount of work and covers important aspects of our target groups.

4   Work and Results

This technique has been used in several of our projects. Currently we are using it in researching the Internet of Things (IoT) and Ambient Assisted Living (AAL). We wanted to ensure that the needs of users with disabilities were included in the requirements and prototypes. For the IoT project, we wanted to examine the issues that people with vision impairment and those with dyslexia have when interacting with the Internet of Things. Of our five personas, one has twenty percent vision, another has dyslexia, and another is elderly and has begun to suffer from mild dementia. We have documented the different AT these personas use and tried to describe real issues. For example, our persona with vision impairment uses a screen reader and magnifier, but has one version at work and another at home; the different software results in our persona sometimes forgetting which keyboards shortcuts work where.

The AAL project focuses on elderly people's use of mobile phones and getting help on them. We want to make sure that we can reach the largest group of the elderly as possible. All the personas for this project have a slight vision impairment and other disabilities like hearing loss or problems remembering information. Since the project is about using mobile phones and asking for assistance, we made sure that the elderly personas have similar attitudes to technology and to learning new information that match the different focus groups we held when gathering user requirements. This is also reflected in our personas choice of mobile phone.

We have found that including disabilities in the persona creation phase has helped in raising awareness for universal design and accessibility both during the creation process and in many other areas of the project. One of the most obvious places was in the creation of the user scenarios. Our personas became the performers in these scenarios and it was necessary to ensure that the different actions in the scenarios could be accomplished by the specific persona. This bubbled up into later requirements work such as selecting technology, defining use cases, and in recruiting informants for evaluations. It is important to keep the personas in project participants' thoughts. This has been done in different ways. Each month we get an email message with a story from one of the personas explaining an issue that persona faced with technology or some other aspect that is related to the project. The task of writing such a story is distributed among the project participants. During the process of creating these stories and describing in detail how a persona interacts with the technology may raise questions for the story's author. Is the story realistic for the actual persona? Would the persona actually do it in this way? If the project participant authoring the story does not have experience with how people with the particular type of disability interacts with technology, the story should be presented to someone who has this experience, or even users themselves. The process of writing the story and getting it validated either by experts or by users, helps to reveal potentially wrong assumptions among the project participants. Because the process is creative and active, it encourages learning about the issues this persona, and people with similar disabilities, have. Project participants also received gifts related to the personas, such as a chocolate Advent Calendar with their pictures, reminding project participants about the personas every day in December. Pruitt and Grudin [12] list many additional ideas that can keep personas alive.

Another valuable method to utilize the personas is to do *persona testing* with prototypes as an analog to user testing. Tasks for the personas to perform are created as in a user test. The personas are divided between members of the project team according to their experience and familiarity with the disability that the persona has. Then, the team member acts as the persona while doing the tasks with the prototype. The more experience the team member has, either from user tests with or training people with the type of disability that the persona has, the easier it is to do a realistic and credible acting performance when persona testing the prototype. If none of the team members have this experience, one should consider inviting someone who does. The person performing the persona test may take notes, but we advise to have another team member to be observer and to takes notes during the persona testing. This approach is informal and relatively quick to do. It can be done in between user testing with real users. We have also used persona testing to pilot user tests, to identify potential problems that can be corrected before the user test, and to see how many and what types of tasks would be fruitful to do in the user test.

5   Impact

As more countries have started to create requirements that new ICT targeting the public be universally designed or accessible, including the needs of people with disabilities will be increasingly needed for projects. The methodology outlined above is useful for others that want to include the perspectives of people with disabilities in their work. It requires some initial work upfront to build competence and knowledge about AT and people with disabilities, but this work would be needed in any sort of work for universal design. Once this knowledge is acquired, it can easily be incorporated into any persona creation process. Rather than using personas to replace user research, it can be used as a means to elicit knowledge and experience from people in your team or network that do have experience with people who have the type of disability the persona has.

6   Conclusion

We have presented the state of the art for persona creation and outlined a methodology for creating personas with disabilities. In our own work, we have found that using this methodology has helped raise awareness among partners about the needs of people with disabilities and has ensured that the personas' needs are included in all steps in the project. We hope that this methodology will result in more universally designed ICT and that others will use this technique themselves. We also have found that it is important that to involve people in the project who have experience with how people with disabilities use technology. This can either be with people with disabilities themselves or others who aid people with disabilities or research issues in the universal design of ICT. Including these people can only help ensure that a project focuses on the needs for universal design.

Finally, it is not sufficient to simply create personas. They need to be used in order for them to be alive. This can include things like creating stories to document things that are happening in a persona's life and remind everyone that they should keep these personas in mind in the work that they do. A persona walkthrough using the proper AT is also a concrete way to remind everyone about what type of users will actually be using the final product or service. Following this advice should ensure that personas you create will capture the needs of people with disabilities and capture the attention of the project members.

Acknowledgments. This research is funded as part of the uTRUSTit project. The uTRUSTit project is funded by the EU FP7 program (Grant agreement no: 258360).

References

1. Ehn, P.: Scandinavian Design: On Participation and Skill. In: Schuler, D., Namioka, A. (eds.) Participatory Design. Principles and Practice, pp. 41–77. Lawrence Erlbaum (1993)
2. Lindgren, A., Chen, F., Amdahl, P., Chaikiat, P.: Using Personas and Scenarios as an Interface Design Tool for Advanced Driver Assistance Systems. In: Stephanidis, C. (ed.) UAHCI 2007 (Part II). LNCS, vol. 4555, pp. 460–469. Springer, Heidelberg (2007)
3. Cooper, A.: The Inmates Are Running the Asylum. Macmillan Publishing Co., Inc., Indianapolis (1999)

4. Chapman, C.N., Love, E., Milham, R.P., Elrif, P., Alford, J.L., Way, M.: Quantitative Evaluation of Personas as Information. Human Factors and Ergonomics Society Annual Meeting Proceedings 52(16), 1107–1111 (2008),
   http://www.ingentaconnect.com/content/hfes/hfproc/2008/
   00000052/00000016/art00002
5. Zimmermann, G., Vanderheiden, G.: Accessible design and testing in the application development process: considerations for an integrated approach. Universal Access in the Information Society (2007),
   http://dx.doi.org/10.1007/s10209-007-0108-6
6. Henry, S.L.: Just Ask: Integrating Accessibility Throughout Design, 1st edn. Lulu.com (2007), http://www.uiaccess.com/accessucd/
7. Isacker, K.V., Votis, K., Soergel, P.: ACCESSIBLE Project presentation (2008),
   http://www.accessible-eu.org/tl_files/documents/
   deliverables/ACCESSIBLE_D8.1c.pdf
8. Isacker, K.V., Gemou, M., Bekiaris, E., Korn, P.: Ægis Project Presentation & project description leaflet (2008)
9. Bell, A.: Accessibility/Personas (2011),
   https://wiki.ubuntu.com/Accessibility/Personas
10. Korn, P.: AEGIS Personas - free for the world to use (2010),
   http://blogs.oracle.com/korn/entry/aegis_personas_free_for_the1
11. Pruitt, J., Adlin, T.: The Persona Lifecycle. Morgan Kaufmann, San Francisco (2006)
12. Pruitt, J., Grudin, J.: Personas: practice and theory. In: Proceedings of the 2003 Conference on Designing for User Experiences, San Francisco, California. ACM (2003)
13. Grudin, J., Pruitt, J.: Personas, Participatory Design and Product Development: An Infrastructure for Engagement. In: The Participatory Design Conference, pp. 144–161 (2002)
14. Calabria, T.: An introduction to personas and how to create them (2004),
   http://www.steptwo.com.au/papers/kmc_personas/index.html
15. Gould, J.D.: How to design usable systems. In: Baecker, R.M., Grudin, J., Buxton, W.A.S., Greenberg, S. (eds.) Human-computer Interaction: Toward the Year 2000, pp. 93–121. Morgan Kaufmann Publishers, Inc., San Francisco (1995)
16. Wentz, B., Lazar, J.: Email Accessibility and Social Networking. In: Ozok, A.A., Zaphiris, P. (eds.) Online Communities. LNCS, vol. 5621, pp. 134–140. Springer, Heidelberg (2009)
17. UNIMOD: Universell Utforming i Multimodal Grensesnitt (2007),
   http://www.nr.no/pages/dart/project_flyer_unimod

Eye Controlled Human Computer Interaction for Severely Motor Disabled Children

Two Clinical Case Studies

Mojca Debeljak, Julija Ocepek, and Anton Zupan

University Rehabilitation Institute, Republic of Slovenia, Ljubljana, Slovenia
{mojca.debeljak,julija.ocepek,anton.zupan}@ir-rs.si

Abstract. This paper presents two case studies of two children with severe motor disabilities. After years of no effective feedback from them, an interdisciplinary approach had been explored with the use of an eye controlled computer. A multidisciplinary team in clinical environment included a specialist in physical and rehabilitation medicine, an occupational therapist, a speech therapist and an engineer. Several applications were tested to establish feedback from the users, using the only movement they were capable of: eye movement. Results have shown significant improvement in interaction and communication for both users. Some differences were present, possibly due to the age difference. Preparation of content for augmented and alternative communication is in progress for both users. We realized that awareness of the existent advanced assistive technology (AT) is crucial for more independent and qualitative life, from parents or care givers to all AT professionals, working in clinical environment.

Keywords: assistive technology, augmentative and alternative communication, human computer interaction, eye control, case study.

1 Introduction

Spinal muscular atrophy is a chronic disease characterized by loss of motor function [1]. There is a widespread perception that spinal muscular atrophy (SMA) type 1 children have a poor quality of life [2]. It is diagnose, where a person is not capable of autonomous breathing, feeding or moving. Generally the only feedback parents or care givers get from them is the frequency of breathing, frequency of cleaning of aspirator and movement of the eyes. Children and adolescents with SMA have a general intelligence in the normal range [3]. Even though eye tracking has a long history, only recently have the systems matured to a level usable and robust enough to be commercially available and used beyond the lab [4]. There are some case studies already presented by COGAIN project [5], however none of them in clinical environment. As there is still a lack of knowledge about modern assistive technology (AT), parents or care givers and even some AT professionals are not aware neither of the already commercially available eye control AT nor of the fact that national insurance company in Slovenia covers the

K. Miesenberger et al. (Eds.): ICCHP 2012, Part II, LNCS 7383, pp. 153–156, 2012.

expenses for eye controlled AT if that is the only possibility for a patient to communicate. There are many commercially available eye controlled devices on the market, from which some are appropriate and used also for augmentative and alternative communication (AAC). Fourteen of eye controlled AAC devices are listed at the COGAIN project's wiki site [6], (last time modified on 21st March 2012).

In Slovenia, at University Rehabilitation Institute, a smart home project called IRIS has been successfully carried out in 2008 [7]. It has developed to a higher level of everyday treatments in testing and advising about various AT within a multidisciplinary team, covered by health insurance. The demonstrative smart home is equipped with various AT, from the most simple to the most advance, including AT for computer access.

2   Methods and Materials

In this research two case studies are included: two boys, both with the most severe motor disability - Spinal Muscular Atrophy Type 1, aged 3 (PS) and 6 (RB). Three sessions were performed for each individually as a part of treatment in Smart Home IRIS. Each session lasted approximately 1 hour; sessions were performed within a period of two weeks. A standardized occupational test Canadian Occupational Performance Measure (COPM) [8] was performed in the first sessions. Both parents had to speak for their children due to the lack of possibilities for communication of PS and RB. For both cases, parents exposed one problem: lack of communication and feedback from their children.

A multi-function eye controlled communication device MyTobii P10 [9] was used as a HCI, since among eye-gazed AAC systems this was the only one available in the Smart Home IRIS. The functioning (interaction) of the system was explained to PS and RB. A standard 10 seconds calibration from MyTobii P10 with dots in five locations of the screen was used to calibrate the system. Various applications were tested to establish feedback from the users. First a simple game IT Mouse Skills [10] was used to move the mouse pointer among balloons of different colors. Afterwards, it was used to train the confirmation of the selected item/location. Grid Size Test from Tobii and individually prepared content in ChooseIt! Maker 2 [11] and in BoardMaker with Speaking Dynamically (BM with SPD) [12] by a speech therapist. AAC content was prepared entirely in BM with SPD. A Slovenian speech synthesis Proteus TTS by Alpineon was used for computer voice.

Instructions were given orally and included directions for better calibration as well as for interaction and confirming the selected item.

3   Results

The COPM showed the same results for both PS and RB in assessing the problem of communication - performance and satisfaction were graded with the lowest grade, meaning no performance and total dissatisfaction.

PS had at the first session some problems in understanding the instructions, possibly because of his young age, as well as problems because of his individually made resting wheelchair, which had had an unmovable handle right above his eyes. Therefore, at the beginning he had to control the device only with his left eye, which took him more time than afterwards in the other two sessions, when the handle was shifted to another position. In the first session he needed more time to figure out how to interact with the computer and had problems with the content of the described games. The grid size test in Tobii software showed that he was capable of selecting items in a grid 2x3, when pointed out with a finger. However, he proved to understand the content, individually prepared by a speech therapist, who started to train him for using AAC in a grid of 2x3 items in the 3rd session.

On the other hand, RB succeeded in calibration perfectly already the first time. He played the game IT Mouse Skills as if he had already been training before. The grid size test from Tobii showed that he is capable of confirming items in a grid of 4x5 items. Already in the second session the speech therapist has started to introduce him to AAC, which he succeeded to operate perfectly. For the 3rd session RB has been practicing with individually prepared basic AAC.

For both users, confirmation (click) was performed with dwell, as an intentional blink of the eyes was too motor pretentious. The best results were acquired when the dwell was set to 1.5 seconds.

4   Conclusion and Planned Activities

Seeing the results, RB had performed better than PS possibly due to his older age. He could confirm smaller areas and understood better instructions, if we base on the feedback from the eye movement. Based on the report, insurance approved the financing for both users. The speech therapist and the rest of the multidisciplinary team are preparing and completing AAC content upon the patients' needs on a regular basis, which is important for greater inclusion of both users in society.

The described case studies show a great potential of technology, especially eye-controlled HCI for the most severely motor disabled children with SMA type 1.

Eye controlled communication aid, based on a computer, like MyTobii P10 and many other similar commercially available systems can besides communication enable also control of home environment and therefore more independence, inclusion and better quality of life. The advancing availability of mainstream AT shows potential for better quality life in the future. However, if the end-users or the AT professionals do not know about those, or in our case about eye controlled systems, they will not acquire them. Therefore, it is quite important to inform the end-users, the AT professionals and the public [13], which we are and will keep doing, as well as follow all the emerging AT.

References

1. Carter, G.T., Abresche, R.T., Fowler, W.M., Johnson, E.R., Kilmer, D.D., McDonald, C.M.: Profiles of neuromuscular diseases: spinal muscular atrophy. Am. J. Phys. Med. Rehabil. 74, 150–159 (1995)
2. Bach, J.R., Vega, J., Majors, J.B., Friedman, A.: Neuromuscular Disease, Spinal Muscular Atrophy Type 1 Quality of Life. Am. J. Phys. Med. Rehabil. 82(2), 137–142 (2003)
3. von Gontard, A., Zerres, K., Backes, M., Laufersweiler-Plass, C., Wendland, C., Melchers, P., Lehmkuhl, G., Rudnik-Schöneborn, S.: Intelligence and cognitive function in children and adolescents with spinal muscular atrophy. Neuromuscul. Disord. 12(2), 130–136 (2002)
4. Hansen, D.W., Ji, Q.: In the eye of the beholder: a survey of models for eyes and gaze. IEEE Transactions on Pattern Analysis and Machine Intelligence 32(3), 478–500 (2010)
5. Bates, R., Donegan, M., Istance, H.O., Hansen, J.P., Räihä, K.J.: Introducing COGAIN: communication by gaze interaction. Universal Access in The Information Society 6(2), 159–166 (2007)
6. COGAIN Project Wiki, http://www.cogain.org/wiki/Eye_Trackers
7. Smart Home IRIS project, http://www.dom-iris.si/en
8. Law, M., Baptiste, S., Carswell, A., McColl, M.A., Polatajko, H., Pollock, N.: Canadian Occupational Performance Measure, http://www.caot.ca/copm/
9. Tobii Technologies, MyTobii P10, http://www.tobii.com/en/assistive-technology/global/products/hardware/mytobii-p10/
10. IT Mouse Skills, Inclusive Technology, http://www.inclusive.co.uk/it-mouse-skills-p2295
11. ChooseIt Maker, Inclusive Technology, http://www.inclusive.co.uk/chooseit-maker-2-p2281
12. Boardmaker® with Speaking Dynamically Pro v.6, Mayer-Johnson, http://www.mayer-johnson.com/boardmaker-with-speaking-dynamically-pro-v-6/
13. Communication by Gaze Interaction (COGAIN), IST-2003-511598, D 7.2. Report on a market study and demographics of user population, 4, (2005), http://www.cogain.org/w/images/7/7f/COGAIN-D7.2.pdf

Gravity Controls for Windows

Peter Heumader[1], Klaus Miesenberger[1], and Gerhard Nussbaum[2]

[1] University of Linz, Institut Integriert Studieren, Austria
[2] KI-I, Linz, Austria
{peter.heumader,klaus.miesenberger}@jku.at,
gerhard.nussbaum@ki-i.at

Abstract. This paper presents the concept and a prototype of "Gravity Controls". "Gravity Controls" makes standard Graphical User Interface (GUI) controls "magnetic" to allow overcoming impacts of motor problems (e.g. tremor of users leading to unsmooth movements and instable positioning of the cursor (e.g. for clicking or mouse over events). "Gravity Controls" complements and enhances standard or Assistive Technology (AT) based interaction with the GUI by supporting the process of reaching a control and better keeping the position for interaction.

Keywords: assistive technology, software for people with special needs.

1 Introduction and Idea

The standard GUI is based on a set of controls which can be manipulated by navigating the mouse cursor over the desktop and interacting with controls and content placed on the desktop. The universal applicability of this concept of interaction, know and Graphical User Interface (GUI) and invented in the 1960ies of last century [4], has contributed considerably to the ICT success and revolution pushing towards the information society. Its flexibility allows adapting the interaction to the needs of users, engaging a broad variety of devices for handling the cursor, navigating the interface and interacting with controls of applications as well as the content. Besides the mouse, which became the standard tool for interaction, a broad spectrum of alternative interaction devices has become available to accommodate a diverse set of needs of individuals and specific situations of use. This includes a broad spectrum of Assistive Technology (AT) for people with disabilities [3].

These alternative input devices provide all functionalities supporting the user in moving and positioning the cursor ("pointing device") and to activate clicks. Due to physical constraints of alternative methods to move the cursor (e.g. track ball, head or eye movements) and physical constraints of the user like e.g. tremor, ataxia or spasm, these alternative interaction modalities are restricted in terms of accuracy, speed and linearity of movements as well as the stability of keeping the cursor in a certain position. In particular the need to perform clicking events tends to instability of the cursor position due to unintended movements of the cursor. The state of the art methods to overcome these constraints focus on smoothing the movements what allows to

K. Miesenberger et al. (Eds.): ICCHP 2012, Part II, LNCS 7383, pp. 157–163, 2012.

stabilize the position of the cursor itself (e.g. tremor reduction, smoothing algorithms) [1]. On the GUI controls side the standard methods to overcome interaction problems have been enlarging and adapting the spacing between controls with according impact and restrictions in terms of size and quality of the displayed information, navigation and interaction elements and accordingly reduced usability of the interface.

"Gravity Controls" introduces a complementary and supporting feature of adapting the behavior of the cursor and controls helping to overcome these impacts of physical constraints of users with motor problems. "Gravity Controls" is a concept that tries to make the controls of Microsoft Windows "magnetic". This means that the cursor is automatically attracted by controls in range.

This increases the accessibility of the GUI for people having problems with controlling the cursor. At the same time "Gravity Controls" will not only increase the accessibility of standard input devices but also ease the use of alternative input devices like head- or eye-trackers. Every shaking and unintended movement of the user has negative effects on handling the cursor while using those input devices. Above all it is extremely difficult to select small controls. Therefore "Gravity Controls" provides the potential to significantly increase the accuracy and the speed of controlling the cursor with alternative input devices.

Thereby "Gravity Controls" complements the already existing ATs as well adaptation mechanisms provided by the operating system. It adds an additional layer of adaptability which increases accessibility and in particular allows keeping the available or intended level of usability of the standard design of the interface.

2   State of the Art and Related Research

Intense desktop research and studies have shown that similar concepts like "Gravity Controls" have been considered only a few times so far by Robert Pastel [1] from the Michigan Technological University in 2004. In his attempt the cursor is attracted by a control when it is moved towards this control. Pastel uses the direction vector of the actual movement to determine a subset of all controls visible on the screen that lie within a conical space alongside the direction vector. The geometry of the graphical user interface and the system is used to select a target control from the subset. If the target control lies within a certain range and the direction vector of the last cursor movement aims directly at the target control, the cursor is instantly attracted by the center of the target control. After such an erratic movement of the cursor the probability that the user moves out of the area of the control is very high. To prevent that the cursor has to succeed a certain velocity before it is able to leave the control.

Pastel implemented a test suite of this concept called "Gravity Mouse" allowing a number of user test. These tests did not include users with motor disabilities. The tests showed that users were able to reduce the average time to click a button by 100 to 200 milliseconds. On the other hand the tests also showed that users resist the full benefit of "Gravity Mouse" because they became irritated by the un-intended gravitation and arbitrary movement of the cursor.

Since then, despite the promising test results, no effort has been made to implement a real prototype of this concept. Based on those results we created our own approach and implemented a prototype of "Gravity Controls".

3   Concept and Prototype Implementation

The basic principle of "Gravity Controls" is to calculate the force of attraction between controls and the cursor and to move the cursor depending on the attraction. To achieve this, the prototype has to accomplish three tasks:

1. Determine the current cursor position on the screen and the current cursor movements caused by user interaction with the Human-Computer interface (HCI).
2. Determine the currently visible controls on the screen.
3. Calculate the gravitation between cursor and controls and move the cursor according to that gravitation.

To determine the current cursor position on the screen a low level mouse-hook is used. A hook in general is a instance in the system message-handling mechanism where an application can monitor the traffic of messages in the system and process certain types of messages before they reach the target window procedure. In the case of a mouse-hook only messages changing the mouse position are observed. The hook in this tool also prevents that those messages reach the operating system. This guarantees that "Gravity Controls" is able to control the mouse independently and without interfering with other applications and the operating system.

Another important task of the prototype is to locate visible controls on the desktop. This is achieved with the help of Microsoft's accessibility frameworks "Microsoft Active Accessibility [5]" (MSAA) and "User Interface Automation [6]" (UI). Those frameworks allow applications to expose information about their user interface in a standardized way to the operating system. If an application implements the interfaces of the accessibility frameworks, Assistive Technologies like a Screen-reader and therefore also "Gravity Control" get detailed information about the controls used in the graphical user interface of the application. This information includes position, type and bounding rectangle of each control. However, if an application does not implement the MSAA or UI, the prototype does not work for the controls of that application, because it cannot gather information about the controls of that application. "Gravity Controls" therefore in a similar way as other assistive devices depends on accessible software development.

To collect the information of all currently visible controls on the screen a special parser, which uses the previous mentioned frameworks, has been implemented. The result of the parsing is a list of all currently visible controls representing a model of the desktop. If the user-interface changes, the parser is called again and builds an adapted model. This is achieved with several User Interface Automation Listeners and a WinEventHook. These tools, available from MSAA and UI, react when the user interface changes (e.g. a window has closed) and inform the parser to update the model.

The parser also attaches a factor called enhancement to each control it finds. The enhancement factor, later in the process, determines how much the control is considered then in the calculation of the gravitation and can be defined in two modes:

- **Normal Mode:** The user is able to set the enhancement factor for each type of control. A large enhancement for the button control type and a small enhancement for the text field control type would mean that buttons would exert more gravitational attraction on the cursor then text fields.
- **Inverted Mode:** The enhancement is calculated automatically for each control. Controls with a large area are given a low enhancement factor whereas small controls are given a large enhancement factor. By this small, hard to reach controls should get more gravitational attraction then big easy to reach controls.

The enhancement factor is crucial for the next task: the calculation of the force of attraction of controls. Three basic concepts to calculate the attraction of controls were implemented to allow better adaptation to the individual skills of users with motor problems:

- **Gravity Concept:** The force of attraction between cursor and control is calculated with Newton's law of universal gravitation. Cursor and controls are assigned with a virtual mass and the gravitational force between those masses is calculated with a slightly adapted Newton's formulae:

$$K_{grav} = \frac{m1*m2*G}{h^2} * enhancement \qquad (1)$$

The variables "m1" and "m2" in this formula represent the virtual mass of the cursor and controls. "G" is the universal gravitational constant and h defines the distance between cursor and control. The result of the formula is then multiplied with the "enhancement" factor which is determined in one of the previously mentioned modes. A small enhancement factor will therefore reduce the force of attraction between cursor and control at a bigger scale.

As shown in figure 1, the gravitational force in this concept is very high when the cursor position is close to the control

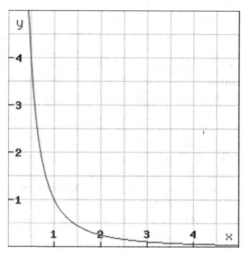

Fig. 1. Gravitational Concept Effect

- **Exponential Concept:** The force of attraction between cursor and controls is calculated with the help of an exponential function. Based on some experiments the following formulae provides best results:

$$F_{grav} = (1 - 0.001 * h^{exp}) * enhancment \qquad (2)$$

The variable "h" in the formula describes the distance between cursor and control. "Exp" is a variable that can be modified by the user during runtime, allowing the user to adjust the force of attraction.

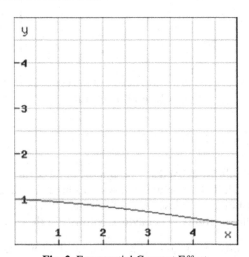

Fig. 2. Exponential Concept Effect

The attraction force rises exponentially when the distance between cursor decreases. Therefore near controls apply the most force of attraction to the cursor.

- **Linear Concept:** The calculation of the force of attraction between cursor and controls is based on a linear function:

$$F_{grav} = \left(\frac{-slope}{GravityRange} * h + slope \right) * enhancment \qquad (3)$$

The user is able to adapt the force of gravitation by changing the variables "slope" and "GravityRange" during runtime to adjust the concept for his needs.

As seen in Figure 3 the force of attraction is rising linearly using this concept, so the cursor is drawn in a very linear speed towards a near control.

Calculating the force of attraction and the set of currently visible controls on the screen is very resource demanding. Therefore, the gravitation is restricted to controls on the desktop, the taskbar and the currently focused window.

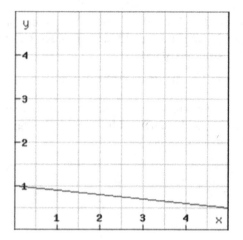

Fig. 3. Linear Concept Effect

4   User Testing

Applicability and usefulness as well as the impact on accessibility and usability of "Gravity Controls" are tested at the moment with a sample of 12 end users including users with motor disabilities. In these tests subjects use different input devices to gain data for comparing the suitability of "Gravity Controls" for these devices:

- Mouse: A normal two Button mouse with a mouse-wheel was used.
- Head-tracker: With a head-tracker the user is able to control the cursor on the screen with head movements. The user performs a mouse click when the cursor is not moved for a specified amount of time ("dwelling function").
- Joystick: For this test a simple 2-axis joystick with two buttons is used.

During these tests subjects had to solve two simple tasks in a test suite. In the first task users had to perform a single click on a randomly marked button a matrix of buttons as fast as possible.

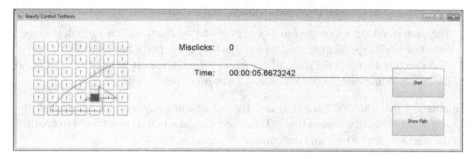

Fig. 4. First User Test

As seen in Figure 5 participants of the user tests had to perform a click on a very small black spot as fast as possible to finish the second test.

Fig. 5. Second User Test

Subjects have to run each test twice: One time with the help of the "Gravity Controls" prototype and one time without the help of the prototype. To compare the results the trajectory of the cursor is recorded as well as the time the user needs to perform the task.

The results of the user tests so far are quite promising. Above all, tests with the head-tracker and the joystick are quite successful. With activated "Gravity Controls" the user can activate controls faster and besides that these controls were also easier to reach for the user because of the gravitation force. In tests with a head-tracker users are not much faster, but they had better control over a more stable cursor when intending to perform a click. User tests with the mouse tend to be not that successful, because the user experiences the attraction of the controls to be rather disturbing than helpful. In all test cases when subjects suffered from tremor or other unintended movement "Gravity Controls" increased the speed and success of interaction.

References

1. Pastel, R., Himes, P., Harper, P., Helton, W.S.: Gravity mouse
2. Design and Evaluation: Effects of distracters and taget size. In: Human Factors and Ergonomics Society Annual Meeting Proceedings, pp. 444–448. Human Factors and Ergonomics Society, Santa Monica (2007)
3. Miesenberger, K.: Best practice in design for all. In: The Universal Access Handbook, pp.58-1 – 58-19. Lawrence Erlbaum Associates Inc. (LEA), Mahwah (2008)
4. Myers, B.A.: A brief history of human-computer interaction technology. J. Interactions 5, 44–54 (1998)
5. Sinclair, R.: Microsoft Active Accessibility: Architecture,
   http://msdn.microsoft.com/en-us/library/ms971310.aspx
6. Microsoft Developer Network.: UI Automation Overview,
   http://msdn.microsoft.com/en-us/library/ms747327.aspx

Addressing Accessibility Challenges of People with Motor Disabilities by Means of AsTeRICS: A Step by Step Definition of Technical Requirements

Alvaro García-Soler[1], Unai Diaz-Orueta[1], Roland Ossmann[2], Gerhard Nussbaum[2], Christoph Veigl[3], Chris Weiss[3], and Karol Pecyna[4]

[1] INGEMA, Spain
{alvaro.garcia,unai.diaz}@ingema.es
[2] Kompetenznetzwerk KI-I, Austria
{ro,gn}@ki-i.at
[3] FHTW, Austria
{veigl,weissch}@technikum-wien.at
[4] Harpo, Poland
kpecyna@harpo.com.pl

Abstract. The need for Assistive Technologies in Europe is leading to the development of projects which aim is to research and develop technical solutions for people with long term motor disabilities. The Assistive Technology Rapid Integration & Construction Set (AsTeRICS) project funded by the 7th Framework Programme of the EU (Grant Agreement 247730) aims to develop a supporting multiple device integrated system to help people with upper limbs impairment. To this end, AsTeRICS is following the User Centred Design methods to gather the user requirements and develop solutions in an iterative way. This paper reports requirements prioritization procedures. These procedures are described in order to illustrate the user requirements transformation into technical requirements for the system development.

Keywords: User Centred Design, motor disabilities, assessment, requirements, non-classical interfaces.

1 Introduction

In Europe there is a strong need for Assistive Technologies (AT) supporting people with reduced motor capabilities. A Eurostat statistic [1] from 2005 shows that between 1.7% (Hungary) and 17.5% (Norway) of people with long term disabilities have problems with their arms or hands. In absolute figures there were about 2.6 million persons in Europe with problems with their arms or hands.

Over the last decades a considerable number of information and communication technology based Assistive Technology devices have become available for people with disabilities. These AT devices often ask for adaptation of software and/or hardware to fit the user's abilities before they can be used. All too often, assistive tools that have been optimized for particular applications cannot be used in other situations

K. Miesenberger et al. (Eds.): ICCHP 2012, Part II, LNCS 7383, pp. 164–171, 2012.

out-of-the-box. Additionally some people cannot be supplied with AT devices at all, due to the limits of adaptability or unaffordable costs of the necessary adaptations.

The aim of the AsTeRICS project [2] is to reshape this situation substantially. As-TeRICS will provide a flexible and affordable construction set for user driven Assistive Technologies or assistive functionalities. Sensors and actuators are linked together via an embedded computing platform and a configuration suite offers the interface to set up and configure them. Therefore the AT released with AsTeRICS facilities can be tailored to the user with severe reduced motor capabilities and within several contexts of use.

In the following pages, we provide an overview of what the construction of As-TeRICS meant from the first steps of gathering user requirements to the setup of the first integrated prototype, by means of a step by step transformation of users' capabilities into technical functionalities of the system that may response to technological accessibility challenges faced by a heterogeneous range of users with motor disabilities in their upper limbs.

2   Material and Methods

An initial sample of 33 participants (increased to 46 in the first prototype evaluation stage), 23 male and 10 female, on an age range between 18 and 91 (x=34.55, sd=15.23), were interviewed in Spain (n=13), Austria (n=10) and Poland (n=10). In terms of educational level, the participants showed homogeneous features: 48.5% finished the secondary school, 21.2% completed primary studies, 18.2% is graduated in University, 6.1% completed technical education and only the 3% did not receive any education. With regard to the disability, more than half of the participants (54.5%) suffered from tetraplegia, 21.5% paraplegia, 9.1% spastic tetraparesis, 6.1% hemiplegia, and 8.8% from other type of mixed motor disabilities. For these evaluations, a common extensive questionnaire, which included the following sections was administered: sociodemographic variables, activities of daily living, information about users' motor diagnosis (condition plus etiology); occurrence of tremors, muscular weakness, spasms, and use of wheelchair; fine motor abilities, including where possible eye-hand coordination; perceptual abilities; psychological evaluation questionnaires; architectural barriers; leisure activities and acceptability issues. In addition to this, some of the most interesting sections from this comprehensive interview included questions about users' motor interactions with frequent-use technology and preferred uses for smart home environments and internet based assistive technologies. We will refer to those as the core issues for the user requirement definition in the following section.

2.1   User Requirements Definition

Information collected in the individual interviews showed that almost all of the users used a PC in one or other way, regardless of their disability (97%). Regarding the specific PC use, figure 1 presents different uses that the participants give to their PCs in their daily lives, most of them using it for more than one thing simultaneously.

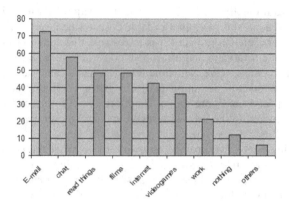

Fig. 1. PC usage preferences in total sample

In term of specific computer interfaces (i.e. keyboard and mouse), most of the participants can use a QWERTY keyboard, but only some people without any difficulties. A significant percentage of the participants cannot use a keyboard. Half of the participants already uses the keyboard with some difficulties, and just one out of ten with no difficulty at all. Altogether, nearly three quarters of the participants use the keyboard in one way or another. They show different speed at writing a single word such as ASTERICS between 3 sec and 30 seconds. Half of the keyboard users point out that it is not tiring and more than half stated that using it is harmless.

Regarding the standard mouse, near to third part of the PC users cannot use it, but other third part can use it with no difficulties and the other third can use it with problems. The PC users' problems related to the mouse usage were that between 30% and 43% of the users cannot click without moving the mouse; cannot double click; cannot use the mouse wheel, cannot "drag and drop"; the sensibility of the mouse must be set between 25-75% for optimal use.

In terms of more familiar interfaces, the regular Remote Control for the TV could be used without difficulties by near to half of the participants, while some users showed some difficulties, near to 20% showed lots of difficulties and 15.2% could not use it at all. Near to half of the users use it most of the time (42%).

For phone calls, a mobile phone was preferred and easily used. Most of the participants can use it, but from them just some users can use the numeric pad. When coming to send SMS, a significant part of the users cannot send SMS, while more than half can actually send them, but with difficulties. The mobile phone is mostly used to speak with the family (40%).

Other technological applications like videogame devices, were performed by a minority. Most of the participants never used a videogames pad, near to half cannot use one, and just a little percentage can use one with no difficulty. Regarding the use of the Wii pad only one user stated that he could use it without difficulty. Near 3 out of 4 users never had any contact with touch screens, and EEG/EMG technology was unknown for most of the participants. The exposure to smart home environments was also minor. However, their preferences in potential applications for this kind of technology included: opening doors and blinds, controlling lights, heating, etc.

Table 1. User ability related to interfaces

Interfaces User Ability	%	Interfaces User Ability	%
Keyboard use		Mobile phone	
Can use a keyboard	78.8	Can use and prefer mobile phone	81.8
Can use a keyboard with some difficulties	50	Can use numeric pad	21.2
Can use a keyboard with no difficulties	18	Can send SMS	57.6
Cannot use a keyboard	21.2	Can send SMS without difficulties	24.2
Mouse use		Non classical interfaces	
Can use a mouse	67.8	Can use videogames pad	69.7
Can use a mouse with some difficulties	35.5	Never used a videogames pad	45.5
Can use a mouse with no difficulties	32.3	Can use a videogame pad without difficulties	12.2
Cannot use a mouse	32.3	Never had contact with touchscreens	75.8
Cannot click without moving the mouse	30	Don't know about EEG/EMG	87.9
Cannot double click	31	Don't know about Smart Home Environments	72.7
Cannot use the mouse wheel.	43	TV Remote Control	
Cannot drag and drop	34.5	TV Control use without difficulties	54.2
		TV Control use some difficulties	12.2
		TV Control use several difficulties	18.1
		Cannot use TV control	15.2
		TV control frequent use	42

2.2   User Requirements Prioritization

The requirements captured in the user requirements and needs' stage were based on ad hoc questionnaires. At this phase, the values, requirements and needs of the target users were obtained. This led to the following prioritised list of functional requirements. The prioritisation is based on making a judgment about the requirements obtained in terms of High, Medium, and Low Priority. The different categories are established using the frequency to which the main topics were addressed as a need by the users (Fig.2).

The requirements prioritization will be split in the following sections:

- Requirements and needs: What the users do and what they are not able to do: (ADLs), fine motor abilities and Technology use.
- Wishes: What the users would expect to receive as a benefit from a new system.

The percentage based criteria for prioritization is related to the aimed statistic validity of the user statements within the sample. The criteria could be changed in order to address the importance of different statements. For example we could want to define what could be the most important requirement that is stated by 100% of the participants, but probably this highly specific percentage can bring us one obvious

(H) High Priority (More than 60% of the users have stated the need)
• The finding is highly relevant. If it is not accomplished, the product will fail. • Frequent and re-occurring. • It is broad and will have interdependences with other requirements.
(M) Medium Priority (Between 40% - 60% of the users have stated the need)
• The finding, if not accomplished, will be difficult for some participants. • Not to cope with this finding can cause frustration or confusion in the majority of the users. • The requirement might affect other tasks.
L (Low) (Less than 40% of the users have stated the need)
• A few participants might experience frustration if this requirement is not addressed. • This specific requirement is not related to others.

Fig. 2. Prioritization categories

statement (100% of the sample with hip fracture stated that they have problems with the hips and legs movement) or even not any statement because the sample is still heterogeneous in their responses, especially when the sample is broad. The criteria should be defined and specified by the researchers based on the scope of the research.

In AsTeRICS study we fit to a frequency criteria, and then defined three categories percentage based (high, medium and low). Then for a more comprehensive under-standing of the descriptive results, they were assigned to one of the three categories.

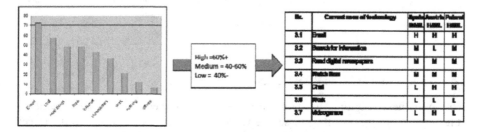

Fig. 3. Example of first data transformation procedure

In this way we can have the results prioritized by frequency in each country. This is a simple way to address the user requirements and establish a hierarchy. This process can be very useful to focus the efforts in finding and developing solutions for the most important needs of the users.

Due to the EU projects joint nature, user requirements phase is often carried out simultaneously in several countries. This makes possible to analyse the differences between countries if interesting, but sometimes it could be a source of confusion. Taking, for example, the case that three countries differs in the results of the evaluation. In our study, users showed differences in their ability to use the mobile phone due to the heterogeneous disability profiles: in Spain it was evaluated as a high prior-ity requirement, in Austria as low and in Poland as a medium priority requirement. In these cases separated analysis can be done taking into account each country by itself, but many times addressing the sample as a whole is needed. In this case we could develop a criterion to establish joint sample-as-a-whole prioritized requirements.

Taking into account the priority definitions scheme, we decided to assign a top priority when just a single country results showed the requirement as high priority. In the rest of the cases, we assign the priority that two out of three countries pointed out. In the case that the three countries coincide we assigned the priority as it was. Thus, the final prioritized requirements list as high and medium importance can be checked in the following table:

Table 2. Prioritized requirements and needs list

Regarding motor abilities	Regarding technologies	Current technology use
Cannot tie up their shoes	Difficulties to use QWERTY kb.	E-mail
Cannot dress up	Difficulties to use a fixed phone.	Chat
Cannot button up	Difficulties to use a mobile phone	Videogames
Cannot get up or go to bed	Do not know about EEG devices	Search for information
Cannot get up or sit down	Do not know about robotic devices	Read digital newspapers
Cannot eat with fork or knife	Difficulties using TV remote control	Watch films
Cannot use a spoon		
Cannot insert coins		

2.3   Transformation of User Requirements into Technical Requirements

Once we had the list of requirements prioritized, the search for a technical solution is a process that should be done by technical partners and user oriented partners working together. Achieving a solution for the users' desires and needs is a complex task that requires discussion between developers and user's partners, especially reassuring ethical issues in this phase is a crucial step to avoid failing respect the human rights and specific country laws. The developed solution should take into account issues such as: privacy, dignity, non-exclusion, security, etc. In AsTeRICS project, ethical issues have a main role during the project development, and make up a whole task that lasts throughout the project. The technical requirements are the technological aims the future system should develop to cope with the user requirements. AsTeRICS project solutions include the implementation of supporting devices as:

- Sip-puff sensor: this sensor allows detection of very fine sip/puff activities. It can be used for mouse control, clicking actions or selections. The sensor consists of a washable mouth-piece with built-in membrane, and a pressure sensor which measures breathing and blowing in order to perform the desired interactions.
- Enobio [3]: wireless electro-physiology sensor system for the reception and transmission of ElectroEncephaloGram (EEG), ElectroMyoGram (EMG) and ElectroOculoGram (EOG) signal.
- Webcam-mouse [4]: It provides a head tracking-controlled mouse for a remote computer. It consists of a high resolution Logitech webcam and associated Camera Mouse software.

- IRTrans [5]: This device enables Infrared remote control of different electronic devices (for example, it was used to connect a Radio CD player).
- OSKA [6]: The On-Screen Keyboard Adapter it is a virtual keyboard software and includes a settings-editor and a grid layout designer. OSKA features a built-in scanning (row/column scan), word prediction and different input methods. This is displayed in the MIMO (Nanovision Mimo Screen) an LC-Display with touch screen.

As a result of this transformation of user requirements into models of sensor combinations for AsTeRICS, a series of models available for the first evaluation was developed. Most of these models were developed in order to allow the users to face three general scenarios: (1) mouse substitution with other accessible devices, (2) QWERTY keyboard substitution and (3) environmental control (i.e. using a radio CD player without using their hands).

For most of the user tests, the basic equipment was: (1) the AsTeRICS platform connected to a mini touch screen (Nanovision Mimo Screen), (2) a laptop or computer where the actions (either mouse cursor control or keyboard substitution) from the user would take place; (3) sensors specified in each model to be tested and connected to the AsTeRICS platform via USB or GPIO/ADCM connectors: switches, accelerometer, sip/puff sensor, flex sensor, Enobio, IRtrans, and webcam.

2.4   Iteration Process. First Evaluation Results and Adjustment of Requirements

In terms of preferred models, the models integrating the camera mouse were liked by many users, even by those that could use other means of input. Also, environmental control (i.e. IR control of the Radio CD player) was considered as a tool which could enhance users' independent living. Due to the specificities of motor problems in different countries, Spanish users, probably the ones with more mobility in general terms, preferred both models that integrated the camera and the switches, as well as Enobio. In general, for those users for which the tests with Enobio were possible, it was considered a real solution either "now" or "in the future" (the latter, thinking of future events in their life when their mobility will be severely reduced when compared to the current moment, i.e. due to a neurodegenerative disease).

In terms of motor conditions which need further adaptations within the AsTeRICS project, the ones in need of models more suitable for them were spastic and cerebral palsy users, mainly due to their involuntary movements. For some of them, only models accessed with one switch worked correctly, due to the need of coordination abilities that sometimes were beyond the capabilities of these users. The sip/puff sensor was a good idea for those with most reduced mobility, but it also became a problem for cerebral palsy patients due to breathing problems they usually showed. Flex sensor and the accelerometer appeared as very promising devices in need of further adjustments. As in other models tested in these first integrated prototype evaluations, there is a need to refine parameters that allow adjustment of speed and sensitivity for these specific devices.

3   Conclusion

As a general conclusion, it can be stated that most of the Austrian, Polish and Spanish users reacted very positively to the AsTeRICS prototype and wanted to use it, even if some models needed improvement for them. Even those users who were experienced with other existing assistive technologies considered it was a good idea and believed it could improve the quality of their life.   Some of the users also mentioned the wish to use their usual assistive technologies (e.g. wheelchair control) to control their PC or cell phone, so the basic concept of integrating different devices in an accessible unique device was highly accepted. Future integration of additional devices, such as further environmental control, cell phone, voice recognition, etc. will probably provide a clearer picture of the potentiality of AsTeRICS to become the "one-device-for-all" in terms of the amount of different technological devices with different purposes that can be integrated on it on a plug-and-play manner. All these considerations will be taken into account in future developments within the project in order that AsTeRICS reaches a successful outcome.

References

1. Population and Social Conditions: Percentual Distribution of Types of Disability by Sex and Age Group. Luxembourg: Eurostat, October 21 (2010),
   http://appsso.eurostat.ec.europa.eu/ (cited September 1, 2011)
2. AsTeRICS, http://www.asterics.eu/
3. ENOBIO (Internet). Barcelona, ES: Starlab,
   http://www.starlab.es/products/enobio (cited September 1, 2011)
4. Lin, Y.P., Chao, Y.P., Lin, C.C., Chen, J.H. (eds.): Webcam mouse using face and eye tracking in various illumination environments. IEEE: Engineering in Medicine and Biology 27th Annual Conference, Shanghai. China, September 27-30 (2005)
5. IRTrans (Internet). Germany: IRTrans, http://www.irtrans.com/en/main.php (cited September 1, 2011)
6. OSKA Onscreen Keyboard Application (Internet). Preston, UK: Claro Interfaces, http://www.OSKAworld.com (cited September 1, 2011)

Indoor and Outdoor Mobility
for an Intelligent Autonomous Wheelchair

C.T. Lin, Craig Euler, Po-Jen Wang, and Ara Mekhtarian

Mechanical Engineering Department, California State University, Northridge, CA, USA

Abstract. A smart wheelchair was developed to provide users with increased independence and flexibility in their lives. The wheelchair can be operated in a fully autonomous mode or a hybrid brain-controlled mode while the continuously running autonomous mode may override the user-generated motion command to avoid potential dangers. The wheelchair's indoor mobility has been demonstrated by operating it in a dynamically occupied hallway, where the smart wheelchair intelligently interacted with pedestrians. An extended operation of the wheelchair for outdoor environments was also explored. Terrain recognition based on visual image processes and multi-layer neural learning network was demonstrated. A mounted Laser Range Finder (LRF) was used to determine terrain drop-offs and steps and to detect stationary and moving obstacles for autonomous path planning. Real-time imaging of the outdoor scenes using the oscillating LRF was attempted; however, the overhead in generating a three-dimensional point cloud exceeded the onboard computer capability.

1 Smart Wheelchair Research and Development for Indoor and Outdoor Mobility

Conventional wheelchairs are often employed by physically-challenged, disabled or elderly persons. Depending on the extent and the type of disabilities—physical, perceptive or cognitive—as well as the ability to perform everyday tasks, wheelchair users may show a various level of dependency on the assistance provided by family members or healthcare providers. The goal for smart wheelchair users is to minimize or entirely eliminate the need for such caregivers. This not only reduces healthcare costs, but increases the independence and flexibility of the wheelchair user. It is expected that a computer-assisted wheelchair can increase independence and accomplishment in the lives of people with disabilities and the aging population.

Previously, there have been wheelchairs developed, which have drawn on forms of brain control to generate their mobility. The development of these wheelchairs was either based on a neurophysiological protocol using electroencephalogram (EEG) electrodes to monitor brainwaves or based on a neurological signal translation from the brain into spoken words or commands for a power wheelchair.

The research team from the California State University, Northridge (CSUN) has designed an intelligent wheelchair and developed its software algorithm, which can be operated autonomously or controlled by a user's thoughts. The hybrid nature of the

K. Miesenberger et al. (Eds.): ICCHP 2012, Part II, LNCS 7383, pp. 172–179, 2012.
© Springer-Verlag Berlin Heidelberg 2012

wheelchair operation addresses the issues of discontinuity in the chair mobility that all previously developed "smart" wheelchairs have encountered. The autonomous mode of this newly developed wheelchair allows for it to respond in real-time based on changes in its immediate environment. This smart wheelchair also has considerable mobility that can cope with indoor and outdoor environments.

2   The State of the Art in This Field of Study

Previous research on brain-computer interface (BCI) controlled wheelchairs includes industrial development, individual effort, but mostly university research projects. Most of the smart wheelchairs being developed were operable in relatively simplified and well-structured environments. The video demonstration clips being released showed movements of their wheelchairs in an empty hallway where there was no interference from pedestrians [1], in an empty room where a few chairs were presented and strategically set up [2], on a paved driveway in front of a house garage, or, at most, in a university student study room where a smart wheelchair moved through a doorway [3]. Those wheelchair demonstrations do not involve a dynamically changing environment or a crowded furnished indoor space. In other words, real-world mobility was not properly addressed. The wheelchair developed by the group from the University of Illinois [1] claimed 70% accuracy in translating neurological signals into spoken words or commands. In the case of Toyota-RIKEN wheelchair [2], stopping of the wheelchair was actually activated by the user puffing his cheeks—a muscular process—to trigger an electromyogram (EMG) signal. The brain-actuated wheelchair developed at University of Zaragoza, Spain [3] performed discrete movements using P300 potentials in EEG activity at a latency of approximately 300 milliseconds, which were collected by a cap with an ensemble of wires.

On those videos, it is clear that there was an inherent lag in generating a motion command, which, in turn, delayed the generation of motion execution. The same was observed by the CSUN research team using an EEG headset to control their smart wheelchair. This delay may become critical when the wheelchair user decides to turn and instead, bumps into a corner of the wall. If the wheelchair misses the optimal turning moment, the execution will become awkward and ineffective, and possibly even dangerous. The cause for such errors in these BCI controlled wheelchairs stems from a delay in processing, resulting in lurching motions. The discontinuity can be much improved by having the wheelchair operate in an autonomous mode where on-board sensors continuously react in real time to their immediate environment; in the meantime, the user may still generate motion commands, which can be compensated as needed by the autonomous cognition and navigation for motion safety considerations.

The CSUN research team has worked on smart wheelchair research and development since July 2010. They have co-authored several papers [4-6] on their wheelchair development, which has focused on indoor mobility that may be autonomously and BCI controlled. Their earlier work has demonstrated that the developed smart wheelchair is able to cope with a busy hallway with pedestrians. Recently, the CSUN research group has expanded their work on the smart wheelchair to the realm of extended outdoor mobility over a variety of terrains as well as the wheelchair's ability to cope with dynamic and static outdoor obstacles.

3   The Methodology

3.1   Retrofitting for a Smart Wheelchair

A motorized wheelchair was retrofitted with a Laser Range Finder (LRF), a digital camera, and a laptop computer, which provides autonomy and intelligence (Figure 1). The LRF sensor and the camera may scan and generate an instant local map of its environment to provide cognitive information needed for planning a movement trajectory for the wheelchair to navigate in a dynamically changing environment. Software algorithms have been developed and tested for the wheelchair to fine tune its robotic mobility. The National Instruments' LabVIEW is used to develop the measurements, motion control, and cognitive path planning needed for the wheelchair. Its drive train had been modified to include a pair of QuickSilver motors and their controllers.

The laptop on-board of the wheelchair can receive motion commands generated separately by the human brain and the sensor-based wheelchair intelligence, by which its cognitive algorithm will finalize an optimally planned path and execute movements using its motion control loop.

Fig. 1. CSUN smart wheelchair with onboard sensors

3.2   BCI vs. Autonomous vs. Hybrid Control Modes

The primary target consumers are persons with limited use of their legs and arms such as amputees or quadriplegics; and persons with limited cognitive or perceptive abilities, such as low vision wheelchair users. A non-invasive Emotive EPOC EEG headset with 16 electrodes is used to read brainwaves given off by the user and to decipher these inputs as commands for the wheelchair.

As a result of inherent delay between the generation of one's thoughts and the time required for motion execution when the wheelchair is BCI-controlled, it is crucial that a safety factor is built into the real-time operation of the chair. The real-time decision-making ability, or the autonomous mode of operation, may be provided by the on-board sensors that can continuously detect the immediate environment and allow the chair to react to its surroundings accordingly. The motion compensation created for the wheelchair based on the constant sensing can guarantee that the time delay will not result in any moment when the wheelchair is not being continuously controlled by brain. Any uncontrolled state of the wheelchair may result in a momentary lack of interaction with its environment.

It has become apparent that the effort needed for the headset reading of the brainwaves and the endeavor required for the interpretation of motion commands should not overtax the user. Fatigue and energy consumption can easily wear out the user, which would cause the smart wheelchair to quickly become a burden. An effective solution to this inherent problem is to operate the smart chair in the hybrid mode. While it allows the user to take control of the chair navigation, the autonomous mode will always be running in parallel simultaneously. Any command the user gives will be analyzed by the wheelchair, and that command will only be executed if the wheelchair sees it as a safe command. Otherwise, the autonomous algorithm will compensate for any time lag or avoid a potential collision. In this manner, the smart chair will continually evaluate the safety of its environment and will avoid dangers regardless of whether the user provides a command. The user-generated motion command can be overridden by the onboard autonomous intelligence as a result of a safety consideration. This will provide safety to the user in the case that there is any latency or misread signals from the EEG headset while maneuvering the smart chair. Thus, the continuously running autonomous mode maintains the safety of its operation while also preventing the overtaxing the user. On the other hand, an onboard emergency stop is also installed to allow for stopping the wheelchair in a danger situation at the discretion of a user.

4 The Research and Development Work and Results

The indoor mobility of the wheelchair has been demonstrated by operations in both autonomous and BCI modes in a dynamically occupied hallway, where the smart chair intelligently and successfully interacted with pedestrians. Concurrently, extended mobility of the wheelchair for outdoor environments has been explored.

For outdoor mobility, the on-board intelligence was developed to cope with a variety of outdoor challenges. Outdoor motion planning and strategy involves GPS navigation, and vision-based feature detection and extraction. Colors and textures are features used to differentiate a variety of terrains, using computer vision.

4.1 Terrain Recognition

One of the major challenges for the smart wheelchair in the outdoor setting is to have an ability of recognizing and differentiating a variety of terrains and to be able to use a discretion to stay on a preferred terrain, such as a cement pavement, unless it has no other choice but to maneuver temporarily around less preferable terrains, such as a grass field or a dirt or gravel surface.

The algorithm developed for terrain recognition is based on a classification problem, which consists of taking a large number of image pixels from several visual images of various terrains and grouping those terrain image examples into different classes. By using the definition of each terrain, the algorithm is learning to adapt to an artificial neural network training, so that its ability to recognize a specific class of terrain improves. The definition of a terrain, such as that of a grass field, is characterized by color parameters, like hue, saturation and luminance (HSL) in Figure 2(a), of the grass field.

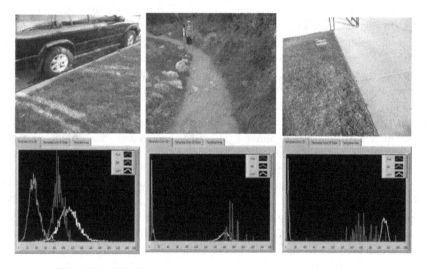

Fig. 2. The HSL Histograms of (a) Grass, (b) Dirt, and (c) Cement

Based on the training from the examples or the training set of each class, the algorithm has learned to become smart in recognizing a new terrain of such a class when the new terrain in question is among several unknown terrains faced by the wheelchair in an outdoor setting.

The classification problem employing a multi-layer perceptron (MLP) network, which has been developed in the machine learning field, was used to configure for the terrain recognition algorithm. For terrain recognition training, many examples of images of cement, grass, dirt, and other undetermined surfaces (such as gravel, bush, wood, tile, metal, etc.) were used to train the classifier. The outdoor lighting conditions were taken into consideration for learning the HSL parameters of each terrain.

Typically, for terrain recognition, about 5,000-10,000 pixels from each image sample were used to define the HSL parameters of the terrains in question, which were needed for the MLP network (Figure 3).

Terrain Learning

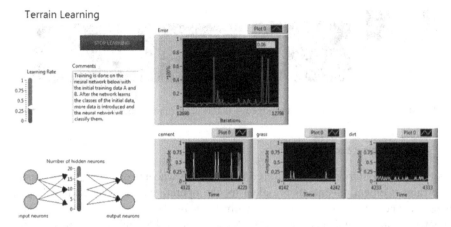

Fig. 3. Terrain Learning Neural Network

From the hue, saturation and luminance distribution curves in the histogram of a sampled terrain, its mean, variance and amplitude values at the distinctive single peak (i.e. unimodal), respectively, could be determined. However, the peak amplitude depends on the pixel sample size. Yet, the mean and variance values did not seem to change much when the pixel sample size was varied. Therefore, it was determined that only the mean and variance parameters were needed to characterize a terrain for terrain classification. As a result, a total of six parameter values from an HSL histogram would be fed into the MLP learning network. The input layer of the MLP network used six input nodes that took in hue, saturation and luminance parameter values of the terrain image. The number of nodes included in the hidden layer was determined experimentally by training the network that would give the best results. There were three output nodes in the output layer, which would generate the learned or interpreted class of the terrain in question, in terms of cement, grass, and dirt terrains. Any other terrain class would be regarded as undetermined and would not be attempted by the wheelchair.

4.2   Image Processes

Various terrains and changing lighting conditions in the outdoor present a broad range of dynamic scenes and images. Visual interpretation and feature extraction from a raw image captured by a CCD camera is an extremely challenging problem. Image processing of a terrain sampled with computer vision often involves filtering, thresholding, and edge detection before pixels can be correlated and grouped for analysis. Desired features of the terrains, such as HSL parameters, can then be extracted in real time as the wheelchair moves through its environment.

Once the edges had been outlined, a selected number of adjacent pixels across each edge contour would be taken from both sides of the edge, and the color parameters associated with these adjacent pixels would be used to determine the different terrain classes from both sides, using the MLP learning network, as in Figure 4.

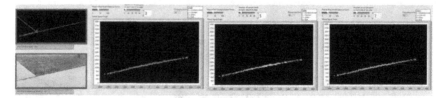

Fig. 4. Detected pixels along a terrain edge that reveals pixels ranging from dirt to grass

4.3   Wheelchair Excursion

Another major outdoor challenge faced by the smart wheelchair is the uneven surface of terrains. Cement pavements are ideal for the operation of a wheelchair. However, there are uneven surfaces associated with grass fields, dirt roads, gravel grounds, wheelchair ramps, and roadside curbs. Some are tolerable and others are off-limits. Examples among the off-limit or restrained areas are steps and drop-offs, such as stairs, roadblocks, exposed tree roots, ledges, scale obstacles, and roadside curbs. The governing factors for the restrained areas are vertical changes between the levels of two adjacent surfaces in the area, and the sizes of castor and drive wheels of a wheelchair. On the other hand, the wheelchair ramps that involve a vertical change should not be regarded as one of the restrained areas. The maximum permissible gradient set by the Americans with Disabilities Act (ADA) requires a 1:12 slope for wheelchairs and scooters for business and public use. This gradient amounts to a slope of 4.8 degrees, which can be set as a threshold in determining whether a vertical change in a surface level be regarded as a restrained area or not.

While the wheelchair navigates about in a busy outdoor environment, it also needs intelligence to avoid all static or dynamic obstacles in its surroundings. An onboard Laser range finder (LRF) is an ideal ranging sensor to provide two key functions needed for its navigation: scanning a terrain for its gradient changes and detecting obstacles surrounding the wheelchair.

By moving the wheelchair, the LRF scans of the terrain and the surrounding obstacles could generate gradients in x, y and z directions. This required the most recently recorded Cartesian coordinates of the scene be stored momentarily for calculating the gradients. As a result, the vertical changes in a terrain were determined and checked against the preset critical threshold for height change in order to detect any possible drop-offs or steps. In Figure 5, the mounted LRF, with an incline angle of 20 degrees, at its given height on the wheelchair approaching a roadside curb, measured the drop-off of the curb to be 14.7 centimeters, or 5.8 inches, which was very close to the nominal 6-inch curb height above the road.

Fig. 5. The inclined LRF detecting and measuring the drop-off of a roadside curb

5 Contributions to the Field

The completed prototype of the functional smart wheelchair will be evaluated by the Los Angeles District Assessor of the California Department of Rehabilitation. The assessor will evaluate the functionality and safety features of the chair to make sure the chair design has complied with the government requirements and regulations.

6 Conclusions and Planned Activities

The successful development and demonstration of indoor and outdoor mobility for a smart wheelchair, which can be operated autonomously or be controlled by a BCI EEG headset, depends heavily on computer-assisted and Internet technologies. Wireless sensing also plays a key role in facilitating the technology development in this field. This technology will relieve the ever-increasing healthcare budgets and expenses that society is facing, in terms of the shortage of care givers and the financial burden for a long-term care.

References

1. Callahan, M.: Mind-Controlled Wheelchair. PN (Paraplegia News) Magazine 61(8) (August 2007)
2. BSI-Toyota Collaboration Center (BTCC): Real-time control of wheelchairs with brain waves. TOYOTA News Release, June 29 (2009)
3. Iturrate, I., Antelis, J.M., Kuebler, A., Minguez, J.: A Noninvasive Brain-Actuated Wheelchair Based on a P300 Neurophysiological Protocol and Automated Navigation. IEEE Transaction on Robotics 25(3) (June 2009)
4. Lin, C.T.: A Non-Invasive Brain-Computer Interface for Autonomous Wheelchair Mobility. In: 26th Annual International Technology and Persons with Disabilities Conference, San Diego, California, March 14-19 (2011)
5. Lin, C.T., Euler, C., Mekhtarian, A., Gil, A., Hern, L., Prince, D., Shen, Y., Horvath, J.: A Brain-Computer Interface for Intelligent Wheelchair Mobility. In: Pan American Health Care Exchanges (PAHCE) 2011 Conference, IEEE, Paper No. 201, Rio de Janeiro, Brazil, March 28-April 1 (2011)
6. Lin, C.T., Euler, C., Wang, P., Mekhtarian, A., Horvath, J.: Improved and Extended Mobility and Machine Learning for an Intelligent Wheelchair. In: 27th Annual International Technology and Persons with Disabilities Conference, San Diego, California, February 27-March 2 (2012)

Comparing the Accuracy of a P300 Speller for People with Major Physical Disability

Alexander Lechner[1], Rupert Ortner[1], Fabio Aloise[2,3], Robert Prückl[1], Francesca Schettini[2,3], Veronika Putz[1], Josef Scharinger[4], Eloy Opisso[5], Ursula Costa[5], Josep Medina[5], and Christoph Guger[1]

[1] g.tec Guger Technologies OG, Schiedlberg, Austria
lechner@gtec.at
[2] Neuroelectrical Imaging and BCI Lab, Fondazione Santa Lucia IRCCS
[3] Department of Computer Science, University of Rome "Sapienza", Rome, Italy
[4] The Department of Computational Perception, Johannes Kepler University, Linz, Austria
[5] Fundació Privada Institut de Neurorehabilitació Guttmann, Barcelona, Spain

Abstract. A Brain-Computer Interface (BCI) can provide an additional option for a person to express himself/herself if he/she suffers a disorder like amyotrophic lateral sclerosis (ALS), brainstem stroke, brain or spinal cord injury or other diseases affecting the motor pathway. For a P300 based BCI a matrix of randomly flashing characters is presented to the participant. To spell a character the person has to attend to it and to count how many times the character flashes. The aim of this study was to compare performance achieved by subjects suffering major motor impairments with that of healthy subjects. The overall accuracy of the persons with motor impairments reached 70.1% in comparison to 91% obtained for the group of healthy subjects. When looking at single subjects, one interesting example shows that under certain circumstances, when the patient finds difficult to concentrate on one character for a long period of time, reduce the number of flashes can increase the accuracy. Furthermore, the influence of several tuning parameters is discussed as it shows that for some participant's adaptations for achieving valuable spelling results are required. Finally, exclusion criteria for people who are not able to use the device are defined.

Keywords: brain-computer interface (BCI), Stroke, Amyotrophic Lateral Sclerosis, P300, Locked-In Syndrome, Visual Evoked Potentials, Spinal Cord Injury.

1   Introduction

For the realization of a brain-computer interface (BCI) system the P300 event-related potential can be used [1 - 3]. Such systems are mostly used as spelling devices because a high number of different characters enhance the BCI communication speed [4].

Conversely assess BCIs performance with people who have motor impairments and compare the results with the healthy subjects ones is of special interest to determine optimal settings and what constraints affect device performance.

K. Miesenberger et al. (Eds.): ICCHP 2012, Part II, LNCS 7383, pp. 180–183, 2012.

In a previous study we examined the overall accuracy of our P300 speller for healthy subjects [5].

2   Methods

2.1   Participants

The data of 15 persons with motor impairments (9 male, 6 female, age: 45.20 ± 17.12) are compared to results obtained by the group of 81 healthy subjects.[5] They participated in the study at two different institutions, applying slightly different signal processing methods explained below. Ten subjects (S1-S10; group 1) EEG data were recorded at the Fundació Privada Institut de Neurorehabilitació Guttmann, Barcelona, Spain. Inclusion criteria were:

Cervical Spinal Cord Injury (SCI) (between C2 and C6) or massive subcortical stroke patients with preserved cognitive function. Subjects S2 and S10 suffered locked-in syndrome (LIS). They also presented moderate visual impairment such as binocular diplopia and optical nerve lesions. Subject S6 suffered a sacral pressure score.

The other five subjects (S11-S15; group 2) data were recorded at Thuiszorg Het Friese Land of Leewarden, Netherlands.

Table 1 shows the pathology of each patient according to the scales mentioned above and the spelling accuracy achieved.

Table 1. Information about participants and their achieved accuracy. The impairment degree is described by the scale of the American Spinal Injury Association (ASIA), the ALS Functional Rating Scale – Revised (ALSFRS-R), the Kurtzke Expanded Disability Status Scale (EDSS), and the Rankin Scale for Stroke Disability. The achieved accuracy during the copy spelling run is shown in the last column.

Group	Patient ID	Age (years)	motor impairment	since (months)	ASIA	ALSFRS-R	EDSS	Rankin Scale for Stroke Disability	Accuracy (%)
	S1	37	SCI (C3)	0	A				80
	S2	42	Stroke (LIS)	3				V	0
	S3	24	SCI (C6)	10	A				100
	S4	21	SCI (C4)	39	A				60
1	S5	24	SCI (C6)	36	A				80
	S6	60	SCI (C4)	5	A				20
	S7	31	SCI (C6)	102	B				100
	S8	40	SCI (C5)	267	A				100
	S9	46	SCI (C2)	6	B				80
	S10	31	Stroke (LIS)	4				V	0
	S11	68	FSHD	240		10			100
	S12	64	MS	120			3		40
2	S13	59	MS	108			3		100
	S14	64	MS	264			8		100
	S15	67	Stroke	48				IV	100

2.2   Paradigm and Experimental Procedure

A matrix was shown (dimension 10x5 for group 1 and 6x6 for group 2) consisting of several characters on the computer screen. To select one character, each row and column was flashed several times in a random order before classification. The BCI user focused on a specific character to select it and a P300 was elicited whenever the row or column containing the character flashed.

2.3   Experimental Setup and Data Processing

The EEG data were acquired using active electrodes. Electrode positions were: Fz, Cz, P3, Pz, P4, PO7, Oz, PO8 for group 1 and Fz, FCz, Cz, CPz, Pz, Oz, F3, F4, C3, C4, CP3, CP4, P3, P4, PO7, PO8 for group 2. The ground electrode was located on the forehead or mastoid; the reference was mounted either on the right or on the left earlobe. The amplifier (g.USBamp, g.tec medical engineering GmbH, Austria) measured the EEG data at 256 Hz sampling frequency.

3   Results

Table 1 shows the accuracy results of the subjects. Seven of them (S3, S7, S8, S11, S13, S14, S15) achieved an accuracy of 100%. S4 had strong muscle activation in the neck due to a lack of control of the main breathing muscles (diaphragm). S6 stayed in bed during the measurement and the accuracy was poor (20%). The two patients suffering LIS (S2 and S10) were innaccurate with the predefined settings. With different parameter settings (i.e., flashing time: 150 ms, dark time: 100 ms) the subjects reached an accuracy of 40% and 20%, respectively.

Table 2 compares the averaged accuracy of the current study to a previous study that included 81 healthy subjects.

Table 2. Comparison of achieved accuracy of the 15 patients to the healthy subjects (N=81)

Classification Accuracy in %	Percentage (N=15)	Percentage (N=81)
100	46,7	72,8
80-100	20,0	88,9
60-79	6,7	6,2
40-59	6,7	3,7
20-39	6,7	0,0
0-19	13,3	1,2
Average accuracy of all subjects	70,7	91,0

4   Discussion and Suggestions to Improve the Spelling Accuracy

In this study we collected data from 15 people with various motor disabilities. The aim of the study was to compare the results obtained by these subjects to the accuracy obtained by healthy subjects.

Excluding subjects 2, 4, 6, and 10 mean accuracy was 89%. This level of accuracy is comparable to the 81 healthy subjects (accuracy: 91%) in the previous study. Of special interest is S9 who suffers a lesion at C2. Unfortunately - because of a complication due to a tracheostomy - the subject is not able to communicate without any help. He achieved an accuracy of 80%, hence the speller could be a very helpful device for him. S4 had strong artifacts caused by muscle activation in his EEG signal which influenced the accuracy negatively. For this patient further investigation such as the implementation of an automatic removal of artifacts [6] is required. For S6, who stayed in bed throughout measurements, the monitor needs to be mounted to face the patients head from above.

Two subjects suffering LIS were not able to control the speller with the predefined setting. However, changing the settings to a slower spelling rate resulted in at least one correctly spelled character for each patient.

A new study that takes into account the considerations made above is currently being designed. The aim of this work will be to find optimized settings of the speller and the testing environment for each participant.

Acknowledgment. The research leading to these results has received funding from the European Community's, Seventh Framework Programme FP7/2007-2013 under BrainAble project, grant agreement n° 247447. The authors further gratefully acknowledge the funding by the European Commission under contract FP7-ICT-2009-247935 (Brain-Neural Computer Interaction for Evaluation and Testing of Physical Therapies in Stroke Rehabilitation of Gait Disorders). The work is partly supported by the EU grant FP7-224332 "SM4ALL" project.

References

1. Sellers, E.W., Krusienski, D.J., McFarland, D.J., Vaughan, T.M., Wolpaw, J.R.: A P300 event-related potential brain-computer interface (BCI): the effects of matrix size and inter stimulus interval on performance. Biol. Psychol. 73(3), 242–252 (2006)
2. Zhang, H., Guan, C., Wang, C.: Asynchronous P300-based brain-computer interfaces: a computational approach with statistical models. IEEE Trans. Biomed. Eng. 55(6), 1754–1763 (2008)
3. Aloise, F., Schettini, F., Arico, P., Leotta, F., Salinari, S., Mattia, D., Babiloni, F., Cincotti, F.: P300-based brain–computer interface for environmental control: an Asynchronous approach. J. Neural Eng. 8, 025025 doi: 10.1088/1741-2560/8/2/025025
4. Aloise, F., Schettini, F., Aricò, P., Salinari, S., Guger, C., Rinsma, J., Aiello, M., Mattia, D., Cincotti, F.: Asynchronous P300-based brain computer interface to control a virtual environment: initial tests on end users. Clin. EEG Neurosci. 42(3), 219–224 (2011)
5. Guger, C., Daban, S., Sellers, E., Holzner, C., Krausz, G., Carabalona, R., et al.: How many people are able to control a P300-based brain-computer interface (BCI)? Neurosci. Lett. 462(1), 94–98 (2009)
6. Fatourechi, M., Bashashati, A., Ward, R.K., Birch, G. E.: EMG and EOG artifacts in brain computer interface systems: a survey. Clin. Neurophysiol. 118(3), 480–494 (2007)

Application of Robot Suit HAL to Gait Rehabilitation of Stroke Patients: A Case Study

Kanako Yamawaki, Ryohei Ariyasu, Shigeki Kubota,
Hiroaki Kawamoto, Yoshio Nakata, Kiyotaka Kamibayashi,
Yoshiyuki Sankai, Kiyoshi Eguchi, and Naoyuki Ochiai

University of Tsukuba, 1-1-1 Tenodai, Tsukuba, Japan
{yamawaki.kanako.ge@u,ryohei.ariyasu.fw@u,s1130428@u,
kawamoto@iit,kamibayashi@iit,nakata@md,
sankai@kz,kyeguchi@md,nochiai@md}.tsukuba.ac.jp
http://www.ccr.tsukuba.ac.jp/english/index.html

Abstract. We have developed the Robot Suit HAL (Hybrid Assistive Limb) to actively support and enhance human motor functions. The HAL provides physical support according to the wearer's motion intention. In this paper, we present a case study of the application of the HAL to gait rehabilitation of a stroke patient. We applied the HAL to a male patient who suffered a stroke due to cerebral infarction three years previously. The patient was given walking training with the HAL twice a week for eight weeks. We evaluated his walking speed (10 m walking test) and balance ability (using a functional balance scale) before and after the 8-week rehabilitation with the HAL. The results show an improvement in the gait and balance ability of a patient with chronic paralysis after gait training with the HAL, which is a voluntarily controlled rehabilitation device.

Keywords: Robot Suit, HAL, Rehabilitation, Locomotor training, Hemiplegia.

1 Introduction

It is important to rehabilitate the walking ability of those that have suffered a stroke to restore and maintain their everyday activities and quality of life. Locomotor training performed on a treadmill with the manual assistance of therapists has been suggested for gait rehabilitation based on motor training. Repeating a stepping motion on a treadmill promotes motion learning and improves walking ability. However, this training approach places a heavy burden on the therapists as they need to swing the patient's paralyzed legs manually.

To avoid this problem, robot technologies have been applied to locomotor training. Gait motion support is provided by the actuated joints of the robots instead of the therapists. These robots apply a predefined motion to the patient's limbs regardless of the patient's intention to step. The effect of this kind of passive locomotor training has been investigated [1].

K. Miesenberger et al. (Eds.): ICCHP 2012, Part II, LNCS 7383, pp. 184–187, 2012.

As opposed to passive drive robots, we have developed the robot suit HAL (Hybrid Assistive Limb), a wearable robot that supports the wearer's motion [2]. This motion support is provided according to the wearer's intention to move by using bioelectrical signals from muscle activity. The wearer operates the HAL voluntarily and receives its force as support.

However, little is known about the effect of long-duration locomotor training with voluntary motion support using the HAL on stroke patients. To investigate the effectiveness in a large-scale controlled study, a preliminary evaluation of the effect of rehabilitation with the HAL must first be conducted in the form of a case study.

The purpose of this research is to evaluate the efficacy of HAL locomotor training for a chronic stroke patient.

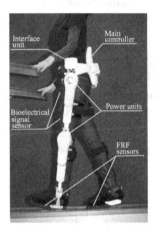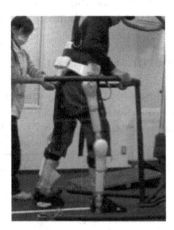

Fig. 1. The HAL suit for well-being (left side) and a stroke patient wearing the HAL (right side)

2   Methods

The HAL is an anthropomorphic structure designed to support the lower limb functions, and consists of a frame and active joints (Fig. 1). Each of the active joints of the exoskeleton (hips and knees) has one degree of freedom in the sagittal plane, and generates assistive torque for walking assistance. Control of the HAL system rests with the main controller, the purpose of which is to control and supervise the power units, monitor the batteries, and communicate with the system operator.

The HAL can be controlled using the Voluntary Control method [3]. Voluntary control provides physical support according to the wearer's voluntary muscle activity, which can be detected with the use of electrodes as electrical signals on the skin surface over the muscle. The electrodes are positioned directly above the muscles to estimate the voluntary flexion and extension torque. The electrical signals are then processed by the HAL's main controller. This signal processing allows the HAL to estimate the assistive torque that each active joint should generate to assist the wearer's leg motion.

We applied the HAL to a 74 year old male patient with hemiplegia on the left side due to a cerebral infarction that occurred three years previously (Fig. 1). The patient could walk with a cane under supervision. Although he had received rehabilitation for the past three years, improvement in his walking ability had reached a plateau. He was therefore, given locomotor training with the HAL twice a week for eight weeks. The duration of each training session was around 20 minutes. We compared the mean angles of the left hip joint with and without the HAL for a gait cycle, calculated as the average of ten gait cycles. The angle was set to 0 deg in the standing posture and considered positive during flexion. We evaluated the patient's walking ability (by means of a 10 m walking test, 10MWT) and balance ability (using a functional balance scale, FBS) before and after the eight week rehabilitation period with the HAL.

3   Experimental Results

Figure 2 illustrates the time-normalized hip joint angle starting at the left foot contact during one cycle with and without the HAL. Wearing the HAL increases the motion range of the left impaired hip joint. Figure 3(a-c) shows the change

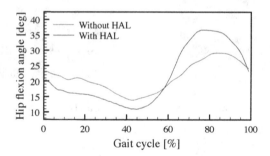

Fig. 2. Left hip joint angles with and without the HAL during walking

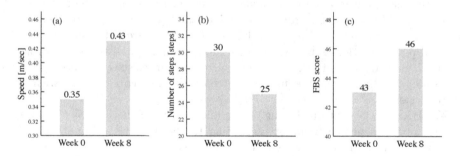

Fig. 3. Change in walking speed (a) and number of steps (b) for 10MWT, and FBS score (c) before and after the 8-weeks locomotor training period with HAL

in walking speed and the number of steps during 10MWT, and the total FBS score, respectively, before and after the 8-week training period. An increase in gait speed of 0.08 m/s and a decrease in the number of steps of 5 steps were observed. An increased FBS score was also observed with improvements of 3 points.

4   Discussion

The purpose of this research was to evaluate the efficacy of HAL locomotor training for a chronic stroke patient. Gait speed and number of steps showed improvement after the HAL training (Fig. 3(a) and (b)). The results of this rehabilitation indicate that HAL locomotor training can induce improvement in walking ability. The HAL's motion assistance in conjunction with the patient's volitional motion increased the range of hip joint motion (Fig. 2), and the patient was able to walk with improved strides during locomotor training with the HAL. This locomotor training also led to an increase in balance ability (Fig. 3(c)). Consequently, this effect would contribute to improved walking ability.

5   Conclusion

In this research, we investigated the effect of locomotor training with the Robot Suit HAL, which provides walking assistance according to the wearer's intention to move. We confirmed an improvement in the walking ability of a chronic stroke patient. As the next step, a controlled trial will be conducted to investigate the significance of the effect on stroke patients.

Acknowledgments. This study was supported by the "Funding Program for World-Leading Innovative R&D on Science and Technology (FIRST Program)".

References

1. Tefertiller, C., Pharo, B., Evans, N.: Efficacy of rehabilitation robotics for walking training in neurological disorders: a review. Journal of Rehabilitation Research and Development 48(4), 387–416 (2011)
2. Kawamoto, H., Taal, S., Niniss, H., Hayashi, T., Kamibayashi, K., Eguchi, K., Sankai, Y.: Voluntary motion support control of Robot Suit HAL triggered by bio-electrical signal for hemiplegia. In: 32nd Annual International Conference of the IEEE Engineering in Medicine and Biology Society, pp. 462–466 (2001)
3. Kawamoto, H., Sankai, Y.: Power Assist System HAL-3 for Gait Disorder Person. In: Miesenberger, K., Klaus, J., Zagler, W.L. (eds.) ICCHP 2002. LNCS, vol. 2398, pp. 196–203. Springer, Heidelberg (2002)

Sign 2.0: ICT for Sign Language Users: Information Sharing, Interoperability, User-Centered Design and Collaboration

Introduction to the Special Thematic Session

Liesbeth Pyfers

Pragma, Hoensbroek, The Netherlands
lpyfers@pragmaprojecten.nl
www.pragmaprojecten.nl

Abstract. Deaf people have always been early adopters of everything ICT has to offer. Many barriers however remain, that make it difficult for Deaf sign language users to use their preferred, and for some: only accessible language, when and where they want. In this session, some of the current R&D efforts for sign language users are presented, with the objective to promote information sharing and collaboration, so that recent threats can be dealt with productively and converted into opportunities.

Keywords: Deaf, sign language, accessibility.

1 Introduction

When the first computers appeared on the scene, deaf people were quick to see the potential. Deaf people, and people working in the deaf field, have always been 'early adopters'. The first educational computer programs for deaf children used Laser discs, then CD-I. Since then, every new technological development was quickly taken advantage of, to improve deaf people's access to information, and to enable them to participate more fully in our predominantly hearing society. Better graphics, colour, then video, enabled the storage, sharing and analysis of video of sign languages, the preferred languages of many deaf people. The internet, e-mail and cell-phones gave them worldwide access to information and communication. First in text, then – thanks to faster internet and better video codecs - in sign language, too.

2 So All is Well?

Yes and no. In the 'deaf world', the word Deaf with a capital D was usually used to indicate people who were born deaf, who consider themselves members of the Deaf community, and who use a sign language as their preferred mode of communication. Deaf with a small d (deaf) was then used to indicate people who have lost their

K. Miesenberger et al. (Eds.): ICCHP 2012, Part II, LNCS 7383, pp. 188–191, 2012.

hearing later in life and/or who prefer to communicate in spoken and/or written language. But technology has changed that. Now, the majority of children who are born deaf, receive cochlear implants (in the early days, we called them 'bionic ears') that give them access to spoken language. As a result, most deaf children (or their parents) now prefer to use a spoken language. At the moment, it is estimated that there are more hearing sign language users in the EU, then Deaf sign language users.

3   Problem Solved?

Yes and no. Cochlear Implants and other technological innovations enable some deaf people to participate more, and more fully in hearing society. But only some. A large number of deaf people, the Deaf with a capital D, prefer to use a sign language as their first, and maybe only fully accessible language. Many of them still live marginalized lives, because they depend on others for communication outside of the deaf community and for reading and writing [1].

The majority of hearing people do not know sign language, so Deaf sign language users need assistance to communicate with hearing people, and vice versa. Sign language interpreters are expensive, and not available in all countries [2].

There is no generally accepted 'alphabet' for writing sign languages, so Deaf people cannot read and write in their first language. Deaf education still has not solved the problem of how to teach reading and writing a spoken language to children who can't hear. As a result, the majority of adult Deaf sign language users are 'functionally illiterate'. They cannot read and write their first language, a sign language, and have limited skills in reading and writing the spoken language of their country; only a very few learn to read and write a second language [3].

Technology can now give given some deaf people sufficient access to auditory information, to enable them to function in the hearing world. It has however failed so far, to provide Deaf sign language users with the same opportunities. This Sign 2.0 STS is a good (or: bad) example. The majority of the research presented here focuses on making spoken and written language accessible for Deaf sign language users, and vice versa. Almost all papers however, are presented by hearing people. Deaf sign language users may have participated in the research and development activities as 'guinea pigs' to test products that were being developed for them, but not with or by them.

Many barriers remain, that make it difficult for Deaf sign language users to participate on an equal basis. For the Sign 2.0 session, invitations were sent out – in written English. Deaf people then had to go to the ICCHP website, to find information about the conference, by reading English. They had to submit abstracts and papers. In English. Only a very few managed to overcome all of these barriers and can now present their research in their preferred language, a sign language.

4   Solutions?

The presentations in the Sign 2.0 STS show, what researchers are doing to enable sign language users, whether deaf, hard-of-hearing or hearing, to use the language they want, when and where they want.

The projects presented here are only a few the research projects that that are currently ongoing. We hope that this STS will on the one hand make information about these projects accessible to sign language users, and on the other hand: will launch future cooperation. At the moment, the research field resembles confetti: many colourful 'niche' projects, overlap in objectives, little or no co-operation between projects.

In many countries, online sign language dictionaries have been developed or are being developed (for a list, see: www.opensign.org). For mobile devices, sign language apps have been and are being developed. But only for some sign languages. All sign language dictionary makers develop their own software. Users who are interested in more than one sign language, have to learn to use new software and learn to read a new foreign language, for every new sign language dictionary that they want to consult. New dictionary-makers start from scratch and have to learn from their own mistakes, instead of those made by their predecessors.

A more profitable approach was taken by the Communication Centre for Deaf and Hard of Hearing in Iceland (SHH). They developed SignWiki (www.signwiki.org), a collaborative web and mobile platform which enables collection, dissemination and analysis of sign language resources and knowledge. It uses open source software, including MediaWiki (the software behind Wikipedia) and jQuery Mobile. From the start, the principal aim was to develop a low-cost and easy-to-use tool for the dissemination of sign languages, which could be utilized by organizations involved in deaf education in different countries. Of particular interest were developing countries where great efforts are required to work towards equal access for deaf people in society. With SignWiki, a dedicated domain can be set-up on the server for each sign language. See for instance http://na.signwiki.org for Namibia.

In contrast, many of the 'dedicated' tools that have been and are being developed for sign language users, never actually reach the target group. If they do: they reach only a very small part of the target group, and because of recent threats: possibly only for a short period.

5   Threats, or Opportunities?

The objective of several projects presented in this STS was to develop tools that will translate spoken and written texts into sign language, and vice versa. To recognize signs, many projects developed dedicated video-based sign recognition systems. An example is the DictaSign prototype. It captures signs made by a signer, and then uses an avatar to sign the phrases back to the signer. The original plan was to capture signs with a webcam and video-recognition software. Instead, the Xbox Kinect™ is used. The mainstream Xbox Kinect™ may well be the end of a long line of research activities aimed at the development of dedicated video-recognition systems for sign languages [4]. On the other hand: Kinect™ may finally enable sign recognition applications to reach real users in real life settings, instead of only test-subjects in laboratories.

In spite of many years of research, machine translation of text into sign language is not (yet?) possible [5]. Many websites however now include – mostly human, sometimes avatar based - video in sign language. On some websites sign language is used as the main or only language, on other websites sign language translations are added to give Deaf people access to written texts. Examples are SignTube (www.signtube.com), a video sharing website that is dedicated to videos that are of interest to the Deaf community and the Sign Library Project (www.signlibrary.eu). We now have sign language friendly e-learning platforms, like SignAssess (www.signassess.org/), Vibelle (www.vibelle.de), and vELAP (Video-based E-Lectures for All Participants, this STS). We have dedicated online training programmes such as SignMedia (www.signmedia.eu) and Signs2Go (www.signs2go.eu), where a sign language is used as the language of instruction.

All of these 'sign language friendly' products, however, use Flash. And all of these are now threatened by the fact that Flash will no longer be supported on mobile devices, and may not be supported at all in the long term. The end of Flash poses a major threat for the long term existence of many of the products presented in this STS.

Let's hope that in the short term, it will be prove to be an opportunity as well: for more co-operation, for better and earlier involvement of the target groups, and for the developments of products that will enable deaf, hard-of-hearing and hearing sign language users to choose the language they want to use, when and where they want. Sign language users: early adopters, long-term survivors?

References

1. Wheatley, M., Pabsch, A.: Sign Language Legislation in the European Union. EUD, Brussels (2010)
2. Jokinen, M.: The Linguistic Human Rights of Sign Language Users. In: Phillipson, R. (ed.) Rights to Language: Equity, Power and Education. Lawrence Erlbaum Associates, New York (2000)
3. Trezek, B.J., Paul, P.V., Wang, Y.: Reading and Deafness: Theory, Research, and Practice. Delmar Learning, Andover (2010)
4. Dreuw, P., Ney, H., Martinez, G., Crasborn, O., Piater, J., Miguel Moya, J., Wheatley, M.: The SignSpeak project - bridging the gap between signers and speakers. In: International Conference on Language Resources and Evaluation, Valletta, Malta (2010)
5. Parton, B.S.: Sign Language Recognition and Translation: A Multidisciplined Approach From the Field of Artificial Intelligence. J. Deaf Stud. Deaf Educ. 11(1), 94–101 (2006)

Toward Developing a Very Big Sign Language Parallel Corpus

Achraf Othman, Zouhour Tmar, and Mohamed Jemni

Research Laboratory LaTICE, University of Tunis
5, Av. Taha Hussein, B.P. 56, Bab Mnara, 1008 Tunis, Tunisia
achraf.othman@ieee.org
zouhour.tmar@gmail.com
mohamed.jemni@fst.rnu.tn

Abstract. The Community for researchers in the field of sign language is facing a serious problem which is the absence of a large parallel corpus for signs language. The ASLG-PC12 project, conducted in our laboratory, proposes a rule-based approach for building big parallel corpus between English written texts and American Sign Language Gloss. In this paper, we present a new algorithm to transform a part of English-speech sentence to ASL gloss. This project was started in the beginning of 2011 and it offers today a corpus containing more than one hundred million pairs of sentences between English and ASL gloss. It is available online for free in order to develop and design new algorithms and theories for Sign Language processing, for instance, statistical machine translation and any related fields. We present, in particular, the tasks for generating ASL sentences from the corpus Gutenberg Project that contains only English written texts.

Keywords: American Sign Language, Parallel Corpora, Sign Language.

1 Introduction

To develop an automatic translator or any other tools that requires a learning task for sign languages, the major problem is the collection of a parallel corpus between text and Sign Language. A parallel corpus contains large and structured texts aligned between source and target languages. They are used to do statistical analysis and hypothesis testing, checking occurrences or validating linguistic rules on a specific universe. Since there is no standard and sufficient corpus [1], [2] because developing an automatic translation based on statistics, without pre-treatment prior to the execution of the process of learning requires an important volume of data. In many ways, progress in sign language research is driven by the availability of data. This is particularly true for the field of statistical machine translation or machine learning, which thrives on the emergence of large quantities of parallel text: written text paired with its translation into a sign language. For these reasons, we started to collect pairs of sentences between English and American Sign Language Gloss. And due to absence of data, especially in ASL, and in other side there exists a huge data of English written text; we have developed a corpus based on a collaborative approach

K. Miesenberger et al. (Eds.): ICCHP 2012, Part II, LNCS 7383, pp. 192–199, 2012.

where experts can contribute in the collection and in correction of bilingual corpus and also in validation of the automatic translation. This project [3] was started in 2010, as a part of the project WebSign [4], [5] that carries on developing tools able to make information over the web accessible for deaf. The main goal of our project Wesbsign is to develop a Web-based interpreter of Sign Language (SL). This tool would enable people who do not know Sign Language to communicate with deaf individuals. Therefore, contribute in reducing the language barrier between deaf and hearing people. Our secondary objective is to distribute this tool on a non-profit basis to educators, students, users, and researchers, and to disseminate a call for contribution to support this project mainly in its exploitation step and to encourage its wide use by different communities. In this paper, we review our experiences with constructing one such large annotated parallel corpus between English written text and American Sign Language Gloss –the ASLG-PC12, a corpus consisting of over one hundred million pairs of sentences. The paper is organized as follow. Section 2 presents methods and pre-processing tasks for collecting data from the Gutenberg Project [6]. We present two stages of pre-processing, in which each sentences had been extracted and tokenized. Section 3 presents our method and algorithms for constructing the second part of the corpus in American Sign Language Gloss. Constructed texts were generated automatically by transformation rules and then corrected by human experts in ASL. We describe also the composition and the size of the corpus. Discussions and conclusion are drawn in section 5.

2   Parallel Corpus Collection

2.1   Collecting Data from Gutenberg

Acquisition of a parallel corpus for the use in a statistical analysis typically takes several pre-processing steps. In our case, there isn't enough data between English

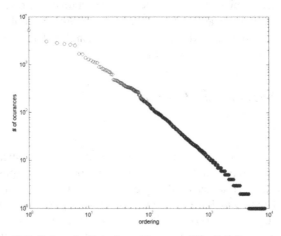

Fig. 1. Occurrence of Zipf's Law in Gutenberg Corpora of English Texts, the top ten words are (the, I, and, to, of, a, in, that, was, it)

texts and American Sign Language. We start collecting only English data from Gutenberg Project toward transform it to ASL gloss. Gutenberg Project [6] offers over 38K free ebooks and more than 100K ebook through their partners. Collecting task is made in five steps:

- Obtain the raw data (by crawling all files in the FTP directory).
- Extract only English texts, because there exist ebook in others languages than English like German, Spanish. We found also files containing AND sequences.
- Break the text into sentences (sentence splitting task).
- Prepare the corpora (normalization, tokenization).

In the following, we will describe in detail the acquisition of the Gutenberg corpus from FTP directory. Figure 1 shows the occurrence of Zipf's Law in Gutenberg Corpora of English Texts. We found that words like (the, I, and, to, of, a, in, that, was, it) are the top ten used words in corpora. Also this metrics determines which words are frequently used in English. Also, a huge work was made to remove non-English texts.

2.2   Sentence Splitting, Tokenization, Chunking and Parsing

Sentence splitting and tokenization require specialized tools for English texts. One problem of sentence splitting is the ambiguity of the period "." as either an end of sentence marker, or as a marker for an abbreviation. For English, we semi-automatically created a list of known abbreviations that are typically followed by a period. Issues with tokenization include the English merging of words such as in "can't" (which we transform to "can not"), or the separation of possessive markers ("the man's" becomes "the man 's"). We use also an available tool for splitting called Splitta [7]. The models are trained from Wall Street Journal news combined with the Brown Corpus which is intended to be widely representative of written English. Error rates on test news data are near 0.25%. Also, we use CoreNLP tool [8]. It is a set of natural language analysis tools which can take raw English language text input and give the base forms of words, their parts of speech.

3   English-ASL Parallel Corpus

3.1   Problematic

The main problem to process American Sign Language for statistical analysis like statistical machine translation is the absence of data (corpora or corpus), especially in Gloss format. In Sign Language, there exist many transcription form of Sign Language. Several notations have emerged, the most popular and are used: Stokoe [9], HamNoSys [10] and SignWriting [11]. These three systems also annotate the phonological aspect of the sign in order to understand how to interpret. Several projects have been developed using these systems to facilitate the signing avatars. However, a significant number of works using the "glosses" as a semantic representation of sign language [12]. [13]. By convention, the meaning of a sign is written correspondence to the language talking to avoid the complexity of understanding. For example, the phrase "Do you like learning sign language?" is glossed as "LEARN SIGN YOU LIKE?". Here, the word "you" is replaced by the gloss "YOU" and the word "learning" is rated "LEARN".

3.2   Ascertainment and Approach

Generally, in research on statistical analysis of sign language, the corpus is annotated video sequences. In our case, we only need a bilingual corpus, the source language is English and the language is American Sign Language glosses transcribed. In this study, we started from 880 words (English and ASL glosses) coupled with transformation rules. From these rules, we generated a bilingual corpus containing 800 million words. In this corpus, it is not interested in semantics or types of verbs used in sign language verbs such as "agreement" or "non-agreement". Figure 2-a shows an example of transformation between written English text and its generated sentence in ASL. The input is "What did Bobby buy yesterday ?" and the target sentence is "BOBBY BUY WHAT YESTERDAY ?". In this example, we save the word "YESTERDAY" and we can found in some reference "PAST" which indicates the past tense and the action was made in the past. Also, for the symbol "?" it can be replaced by a facial animation with "WHAT". For us, we are based on lemmatization of words. We keep the maximum of information in the sentence toward developing more approaches in these corpora. Statistics of corpora are shown in Table 1. The number of sentences and tokens is huge and building corpus takes many days.

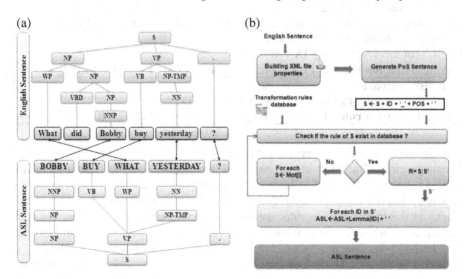

Fig. 2. (a) An example of transformation: English input (b) Steps for building ASL corpora

All parts are available to download online for free [3]. Using transformation rule in table 3, we build the ASL corpora following steps shown in figure 2-b. The input of the system is English sentences and the output is the ASL transcription in gloss. In table 2, only simple rules are shown, we can define complex rule starting from these simple rules. We can define a part-of-speech sentence for the two languages. According to figure 3, when we check if the rule of S exists in database, the algorithm will return true, in this case, we apply directly the transformation. Of course, all complex rules must be done by experts in ASL. Table 2 shows some transformation from English sentence to American Sign Language. We present the transformation rule made by an expert in linguistics.

Table 1. Size of the American Sign Language Gloss Parallel Corpus 2012 (ASLG-PC12)

	Corpus size English		Corpus size ASL Gloss	
	tokens	sentences	tokens	sentences
GUTENBERG 1	280 170 490	13 627 591	280 170 490	13 627 591
GUTENBERG 2	323 240 648	16 180 308	323 240 648	16 180 308
GUTENBERG 3	549 346 414	27 632 925	549 346 414	27 632 925
GUTENBERG 4	292 146 954	14 541 844	292 146 954	14 541 844
GUTENBERG 5	150 675 152	7 628 865	150 675 152	7 628 865

Table 2. Example of full sentences transformation rules

English sentence: what is your name ?   **ASL sentence:** IX-PRO2 NAME , WHAT ?   **Transformation rule**: 1_VBP 2_PRP 3_JJ 4_. → 2_PRP 0_DESC- 3_JJ 4_.
English sentence: Are you deaf ?   **ASL sentence:** IX-PRO2 DESC-DEAF ?   **Transformation rule**: 1_VBP 2_PRP 3_DT 4_NN 5_. → 4_NN 2_PRP 5_.
English sentence: are you a student ?   **ASL sentence:** STUDENT IX-PRO2 ?   **Transformation rule**: 1_VBP 2_PRP 3_DT 4_NN 5_. → 4_NN 2_PRP 5_.
English sentence: do you understand him ?   **ASL sentence:** IX-PRO2 UNDERSTAND IX-PRO3 ?   **Transformation rule**: 1_VB 2_PRP 3_VB 4_PRP → 2_PRP 3_VB 4_PRP

In figure 3, we describe steps to transform an English sentence into American Sign Language gloss. The input of the system is the English sentence. Using CoreNLP tool, we generate an XML file containing morphological information about the sentence after tokenization task. Then, we build the part-of-speech sentence and thanks to the transformation rules database, we try to transform the input for each lemma. In some case, we can found that the part-of-speech sentence doesn't exist in the database, so, we transform each lemma. Transformation rule for lemma is presented in table 3. In the last step, we add an uppercase script to transform the output. The transformation rule is not a direct transformation for each lemma, it can an alignment of words and can ignore some English words like (the, in, a, an, …).

Table 3. Transformation rules from English Part-of-Speech to American Sign Language Gloss

English Part-of-Speech	Transformation rule	Example
CC : Coordinating Conjunction	CC	And → AND
CD : Cardinal Number	CD	Tow → TOW
DT : Determiner	DT	This → THIS
EX : Existential there	EX	There → THERE
FW : Foreign word	FW	i → I
IN : Preposition	IN	In→ IN
JJ :Adjective	DESC- JJ	Yellow→ DESC-YELLOW
JJR :Adjective, comparative	DESC- JJR	Bigger→ DESC-BIGGER
JJS :Adjective, superlative	DESC- JJS	Wildest → DESC-WILDEST
LS :List item marker	LS	2 →2
MD :Modal	MD	Can→ CAN
NN : Noun, singular or mass	NN	Appel → APPEL
NNS :Noun, plural	NNS	Appels → APPEL
NNP :Proper noun, singular	NNP	IBM →IBM
NNPS :Proper noun, plural	NNPS	Carolinas→ CAROLINAS
PDT :Predeterminer	PDT	All → ALL
POS :Possessive ending	X-POSS	's → X-POSS
PRP :Personal pronoun	PRP	I → IX-PRO1
PRP$:Possessive pronoun	PRP$	Your → IX-PRO2
RB :Adverb	DESC- RB	Never→ DESC-NEVER
RBR :Adverb, comparative	RBR	Faster → FASTER
RBS :Adverb, superlative	RBS	Fastest → FASTEST
RP :Particle	RP	Off → OFF
SYM :Symbol	SYM	&→&
TO :To	TO	To → TO
VB : Verb, base form	VB	Eat → EAT
VBD :Verb, past tense	VB	Ate→ EAT
VBG :Verb, gerund or present participle	VB	Eating→EAT
VBN :Verb, past participle	VB	Eaten→EAT
VBP :Verb, non-3rd person singular present	VB	Eat → EAT
VBZ :Verb, 3rd person singular present	VB	Eats → EAT
WDT :Wh-determiner	WDT	Which → WHICH
WP :Wh-pronoun	WP	What → WHAT
WP$:Possessive wh-pronoun	WP$	Whose → WHOSE
WRB :Wh-adverb	WRB	Where → WHERE

3.3   Transformation Rules

Not all transformation rules used to transform English data was verified by experts in linguistics. We validate only 800 rules and transformation rules for lemma. We cannot validate all rules because there exist an infinite number of rules. For this reason, we developed an application that offer to experts to enter their rules from an English sentence, without coding. The application is just a simple user interface which contain lemma transformation rule, and the expert will compose lemma. After that, he save the result and rebuild the corpora. The built corpus is a made by a collaborative approach and validated by experts.

3.4   Releases of the English-ASL Corpus

The initial release of this corpus consisted of data up to September 2011. The second release added data up to January 2012, increasing the size from just over 800 sentences to up to 800 million words in English. A forthcoming third release will include data up to early 2013 and will have better tokenization and more words in American Sign Language. For more details, please check the website [3]. This corpus can be very useful to develop Statistical Machine Translation [14] or Sign Language Courses for Deaf children [15].

4   Discussions and Conclusion

We described in this paper the construction of the English-American Sign Language corpus. We illustrated a new method for transforming an English written text to American Sign Language gloss. We presented also the first corpus for ASL gloss that exceeds one hundred million of sentences and that we would make it available for all researches and linguistics. During the next phase of the ASLG-PC12 project, we expect to provide both a richer analysis of the existing corpus and others parallel corpus (like French Sign Language, Arabic Sign Language, etc.). This will be done by first enriching the rules by experts. This enrichment will be achieved by automatically transforming the current transformation rules database, and then validating the results by hand.

References

1. Morrissey, S., Way, A.: Joining hands: Developing a sign language machine translation system with and for the deaf community. In: Proceeding CVHI Conference, Workshop Assistive Technol. People with Vision and Hearing Impairments, Granada, Spain (2007)
2. Morrissey, S.: Assistive technology for deaf people: Translating into and animating Irish sign language. In: Proceeding Young Researchers Consortium, ICCHP, Linz, Austria (2008)
3. American Sign Language Gloss Parallel Corpus 2012 (ASLG-PC 2012) (2012), http://www.achrafothman.net/aslsmt/

 4. Jemni, M., Elghoul, O.: Towards Web-Based automatic interpretation of written text to Sign Language. In: First International Conference on ICT & Accessibility, Hammamet, Tunisia (2008)
 5. Jemni, M., Elghoul, O.: An avatar based approach for automatic interpretation of text to Sign language. In: 9th European Conference for the Advancement of the Assistive Technologies in Europe, San Sebastian, Spain (2007)
 6. Gutenberg Project (2012), http://www.gutenberg.org/
 7. Gillick, D.: Sentence boundary detection and the problem with the U.S. In: Proceedings of Human Language Technologies: The 2009 Annual Conference of the North American Chapter of the Association for Computational Linguistics, Companion Volume: Short Papers, Boulder, Colorado (2009)
 8. Toutanova, K., Manning, C.D.: Enriching the Knowledge Sources Used in a Maximum Entropy Part-of-Speech Tagger. In: Proceedings of the Joint SIGDAT Conference on Empirical Methods in Natural Language Processing and Very Large Corpora, EMNLP/VLC 2000 (2000)
 9. Stokoe, W.: Sign Language Structure: An Outline of the Visual Communication Systems of the American Deaf. Linstok Press, SilverSpring (1960)
10. Prillwitz, S., Zienert, H.: Hamburg notation system for sign language: Development of a sign writing with computer application. International Studies on Sign Language and Communication of the Deaf, Hamburg, Germany (1990)
11. Sutton, V., Gleaves, R.: SignWriter—the world's first sign language processor. Deaf Action Committee for SignWriting, La Jolla, CA (1995)
12. Huenerfauth, M., Zhou, L., Gu, E., Allbeck, J.: Evaluation of American sign language generation by native ASL signers. ACM Transaction Accessible Computing (2008)
13. Marshall, I., Sáfár, E.: Sign language generation using HPSG. In: Proceeding 9th International Conference Theoretical Methodological Issues Machine Translation (TMI 2002), Keihanna, Japan (2002)
14. Othman, A., Jemni, M.: Statistical Sign Language Machine Translation: from English written text to American Sign Language Gloss. IJCSI International Journal of Computer Science Issues 8(5(3)) (2011)
15. Jemni, M., Elghoul, O., Makhlouf, S.: A Web-Based Tool to Create Online Courses for Deaf Pupils. In: International Conference on Interactive Mobile and Computer Aided Learning, Amman, Jordan (2007)

Czech Sign Language – Czech Dictionary and Thesaurus On-Line

Jan Fikejs and Tomáš Sklenák

Support Center for Students with Special Needs, Masaryk University, Brno, Czech Republic

Abstract. The paper deals with a monolingual (explanatory) and bilingual dictionary of the spoken and sign language, which in each of the languages provides grammatical, stylistic and semantic characteristics, contextual quotes, information about hyponyms and hypernyms, transcription, and audio/video recording (front-facing and sideview captures). The dictionary also serves as a basic didactic aid for teaching deaf and hearing users and their specialized work with academic texts at Masaryk University (MU) and for this reason it also, besides the basic vocabulary, includes specialized terminology of study programs provided at MU in the Czech sign language. Another aim of this dictionary is to build a centralized on-line dictionary of newly created terminology and the existing vocabulary.

1 Introduction

Support Centre for Students with Special Needs is one of the central bodies of Masaryk University in Brno. The mission of the Centre is to grant accessibility to students with sensory and other disabilities to all study programmes and subjects accredited at the University. The Centre provides interpreting services for deaf and hard of hearing students of all Masaryk University faculties. Since deaf and hard of hearing students did not have any possibility to study a university during the communist period, there is a lack of technical terms in sign language in several fields taught at universities. In these cases we have to face the lack of professionally trained interpreters, insufficient terminology of Czech sign language in given fields and teachers' unwillingness to work with an interpreter. Therefore, we have to support creation and stabilization of Czech sign language vocabulary and enable further education of sign language interpreters working at universities in given fields. Most of this barriers to interpreting for the hearing impaired students lead to establishing a Dictionary of technical terms.

Czech and Czech sign language dictionary and thesaurus are parts of widely focused project ComIn (Universal Learning Design: Innovation in Interpreting and Communication Service) which focuses on minimizing barriers in tertiary education of the deaf and hard of hearing students. These barriers include the lack of well educated and trained (sign language) interpreters, teachers who do not cooperate with interpreters, lack of technical terms in Czech sign language in current fields. It is necessary to create missing technical terms in Czech sign language and to spread

K. Miesenberger et al. (Eds.): ICCHP 2012, Part II, LNCS 7383, pp. 200–204, 2012.

these terms to students and interpreters and make further training accessible for all sign language interpreters. This project was created with partners: Institute of Special Education Studies - Faculty of Education - Palacký University Olomouc and The Section of Artificial Intelligence at the Department of Cybernetics of the Faculty of Applied Sciences - University of West Bohemia in Pilsen.

2   Online Dictionary Features

During last decade, several online an offline (DVD based) dictionaries were produced, gathering existing and recently created terms in Czech sign language from several topics. But none of these dictionaries offer expected features e.g., searching - not only by text, but also by other options - sign language specific criteria as well, completeness of lexicographical data covering most of the language, not only limited topics, being up-to-date. That is why we needed to create a state-of-the-art sign language dictionary which supports all the mentioned features, which is both a translation and explanatory dictionary that makes all existing terms accessible to all students and interpreters and which extends and elaborates on existing technical terms in given field .

3   Components of Dictionary Entries

Every lemma compounds formal part of lemma (shape of lexical unit), front and side video record or conventional grammar, transcription by SignWriting or HamNoSys or Alternative grammar, pronunciation and phonetic transcription, grammatical information (specific sign, classifier, etc.) or grammatical information (word class, way of flection, etc.), semantic part of lemma (meaning of lexical unit), stylistic characteristic of lemma, etymological information, invariant component (primary meaning), examples of use in primary meaning, multi-word namings based on primary meaning and their meaning, synonyms, antonyms, hyponymys, heteronyms in relation to primary meaning, variant component (secondary meanings), examples of use in secondary meaning, multi-word namings based on secondary meaning and their meaning, synonyms, antonyms, hyponymys, heteronyms in relation to secondary meaning and derivatives and composites of lemma

4   Data Aquisition

Acquisition of existing signs of Czech sign language can be done in three different forms.

First acquisition method using sign language without any support of spoken language (nor written form) can be done in four ways: In the first way, meaning of lexeme is explained to the (deaf) consultants without using mentioned sign. Once they understand the meaning well, it will give us answer including mentioned sign. In the second way, more than one sing representing current lexeme are shown to the consultants to pick up the right one. In the third way, the mentioned lexeme is explained to the consultants using pictures or graphs (e.g. linear function). Consultants have to answer appropriate sign based on these pictures. The last way for this data acquisition is to record spontaneous discussion of deaf consultants about certain topic.

Second acquisition method using spoken and sign language can be done in three ways. Only lexeme itself is explained in sign language but with support of spoken language. A consultant can see written presentation that is explained by an hearing expert and interpreted into sign language. This way is the most used currently.

Third method uses only written form of spoken language without any support of sign language. Consultants are given lists of lexemes with contexts and they give an equivalent sign of sign language. This method requires good competences in mainstream language.

4.1 Creation of the List of Entries

New technical terms in sign language have to be created systematically therefore frequency analysis of written texts of certain topics, which help to extract most used terms, are made. Later on, terms without any existing equivalent in Czech sing language can be selected. Third step that will make creation of new terms in sign language more effective, is tuning-up of the list of entries by nominative representativeness, collocations of lexemes, etc.

4.2 Creation of New Signs of Sign Language

Created list of entries is a basement for further work. It requires establishment of a group of hearing-impaired consultants, acquisition of the corpus, creation of the list of

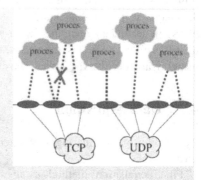

How do you identify transmitter–receiver at multiplexing and demultiplexing?

- Transitional points will be created between the transport and application layers.
- In TCP/IP, transitional points are called ports.
- A port is static, thus easier to identify.

Fig. 1. Example of presentation

entries that will be discussed, compilation of a presentation for explication, giving explication to consultants, elicitation or creation of signs. In some cases, it is possible to extend existing meaning of sign language signs or to use existing sign of foreign sign language. If new sign is created, sometimes it is also possible to make more regional varieties. At the moment, the signs which are being create have to be recorded and transcribed to notation system (SignWriting) later on. At last, all processed data are fed into the online dictionary.

Group of consultants consists of deaf experts, native sign language users, teachers, linguists, a deaf speaker who prepares explication, another person who makes text support for reader, an interpreter, a teacher or an expert making content supervision of signed explications and contexts and a native sign language user making language supervision of signed explications and contexts.

4.3   Representing Sign Language Data

Every lemma in sign language should include similar data as lemma in spoken language. Since there is no generally used written form of sign language, every lemma is represented by data recorded in several forms. Lemma itself is represented by two video records (front and both sides view), a transcription to SignWriting and HamNoSys notation and an interactive 3D avatar for detailed view. Both, signed explication and contexts, are represented by one video records and transcription to SignWriting notation. Other descriptions are stored in written language.

5   Content Management

Online dictionary contains tools for content management including several levels of user accounts with different rights. Low level accounts can access and edit only "low level data" and higher levels accounts can manage data from their level and also from lower level. The lowest level account is designed for guests. Guest can access only public level data and can not edit any item. Guests can comment any public data thou. Higher level account is designed for common user who can manage their own user interface and also comment any public data. More higher account is designed for editors of lexemes items of current field. Editors can also create new entries. Almost at the top of the levels stand supervisor accounts for people who authorise whole lemmas entries and can publish finished lemmas. Top level account - administrator - can manage every item and also whole structure of database.

6   User Interface (Preview)

In the end, we can present you an user side interface that offers many ways of searching and view to current data.

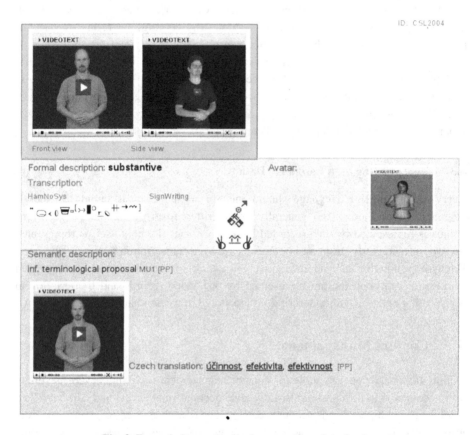

Fig. 2. Example lemma in sign language (user interface)

The Dicta-Sign Wiki: Enabling Web Communication for the Deaf

Eleni Efthimiou[1], Stavroula-Evita Fotinea[1], Thomas Hanke[2], John Glauert[3],
Richard Bowden[4], Annelies Braffort[5], Christophe Collet[6],
Petros Maragos[7], and François Lefebvre-Albaret[8]

[1] Institute for Language and Speech Processing/ATHENA RC, Ahens, Greece
{eleni_e,evita}@ilsp.gr
[2] Universität Hamburg, Hambourg Germany
thomas.hanke@sign-lang.uni-hamburg.de
[3] University of East Anglia, Norwich, United Kingdom
J.Glauert@uea.ac.uk
[4] University of Surrey, Surrey, United Kingdom
R.Bowden@surrey.ac.uk
[5] LIMSI/CNRS, Orsey, France
annelies.braffort@limsi.fr
[6] Université Paul Sabatier, Toulouse, France
collet@irit.fr
[7] National Technical University of Athens, Ahens, Greece
maragos@cs.ntua.gr
[8] WebSourd, Toulouse, France
francois.lefebvre-albaret@websourd.org

Abstract. The paper provides a report on the user-centred showcase prototypes
of the DICTA-SIGN project (http://www.dictasign.eu/), an FP7-ICT project
which ended in January 2012. DICTA-SIGN researched ways to enable
communication between Deaf individuals through the development of human-
computer interfaces (HCI) for Deaf users, by means of Sign Language. Emphasis is placed on the Sign-Wiki prototype that demonstrates the potential of sign
languages to participate in contemporary Web 2.0 applications where user contributions are editable by an entire community and sign language users can
benefit from collaborative editing facilities.

Keywords: Sign language technologies, sign-Wiki, multilingual sign language
resources, Deaf communication, Deaf user-centred HCI.

1   Research Rational

The idea driving research in DICTA-SIGN was that development of Web 2.0 technologies have made the WWW a place where people constantly interact with each other by
posting information (e.g. blogs, discussion forums), modifying and enhancing other
people's contributions (e.g. Wikipedia), and sharing information (e.g. Facebook, social

K. Miesenberger et al. (Eds.): ICCHP 2012, Part II, LNCS 7383, pp. 205–212, 2012.

news sites). However, these technologies are not friendly to sign language users, because they require the use of written language. Sign language (SL) videos cannot fulfil the same role as written text in these new technologies, given, first, that they are not anonymous and, second, that people cannot easily edit and add to a video which someone else has produced. Under this light, DICTA-SIGN's goal was to develop the necessary technologies that make Web 2.0 interactions in sign language possible. To fulfil its goals, DICTA-SIGN dealt with four sign languages: British Sign Language (BSL), German Sign Language (DGS), Greek Sign Language (GSL) and French Sign Language (LSF). The project involved research from several scientific domains in order to develop technologies for sign recognition and generation, exploiting significant knowledge of the structure, grammar and lexicon of the project Sign Languages.

2   Technological Advancements and Systems Integration

DICTA-SIGN contributed new knowledge in the domain of SL resources acquisition and corpus construction but also in the front of SL technologies, advancing research in image processing, computer vision, the statistical methods for continuous sign recognition with multimodal fusion and adaptation, as well as in virtual human technology. Another significant contribution, beyond advances in related technologies, is the user-centred interface design of the project's prototypes, which derived from systematic involvement of end-users in evaluation procedures accompanying development phases. All technologies and resources developed during the project were integrated in a sign language wiki, which enabled not only to showcase the project's outcomes, but also allowed for extensive evaluation and actual use by end-users. The prototype is based on the initially set scenario, where the user signs to a webcam providing as input isolated signs or continuous signing. The computer recognizes the signed phrases, converts them into an internal representation of sign language, and then has an animated avatar sign them back to the user. Content on the Web is then contributed and disseminated via the signing avatar.

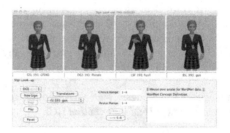

Fig. 1. Sign Look-up Tool results

The required linguistic knowledge was acquired on the basis of creation and annotation of a specially designed parallel corpus [1] and a related multilingual lexical database. The project language resources were primarily used in order to extract generalised lexical and grammar SL models, to support sign language recognition [2-6] and animation technologies [7]. The same resources were also exploited in order to allow for the application of a simple sign-to-sign translation service, integrated into the project's Sign-Wiki.

As expected, a major effort has been placed on systems' integration linking recognition technology to synthesis and animation, both supported by adequately annotated SL resources [8]. An initial Search-by-Example interface [9] to the DICTA-SIGN lexical database has been enhanced to produce a Sign Look-up Tool (Fig. 1) that provides users with a simple sign-level translation tool for exploring corresponding signs in the four project sign languages.

The Sign Look-up Tool enables a Deaf user to perform a sign and see the corresponding signs in the four project languages. The system uses an Xbox Kinect™ device to recognise signs. The sign look-up tool plays back the recognised sign, or the closest matches, to the user using an avatar. The user can then see the corresponding sign in all four languages.

Fig. 2. Tracking of (a) corpus data and (b) facial features

A practical use for this tool is where a sign language user sees a sign in an unfamiliar language on a video or when travelling to another country. Successful implementation of the Sign Look-up Tool led to integration plans for the sign language Wiki. With significant enhancement of the sign recognition technologies (Fig. 2a, 2b, 3) the sign language Wiki prototype was identified as the most useful demonstration of DICTA-SIGN technologies for Deaf people.

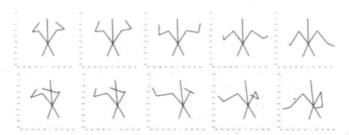

Fig. 3. Demonstration of co-articulation-relocation of signs for the continuous sign recognition framework: In the example, each row corresponds to an articulation instance of the sign TABLE which are articulated in continuous mode and located in different positions. Results are shown via the Skeleton data captured with the Kinect.

3   A Sign Language Wiki

A major requirement of contemporary Web 2.0 applications is that user contributions are editable by an entire community. The oldest, and most popular, application of this type is a Wiki, where any contribution can be edited and refined, anonymously if so wished, by someone else. As the success of Wikipedia and related sites show, this type of community collaboration results in a rapid amassing of knowledge.

There is no doubt that sign language users could benefit similarly from collaborative editing. With this in mind, a server was developed to provide the same service as a traditional Wiki, but using sign language. Instead of using text as the output medium, a signing avatar presents information (fig. 4). The use of an avatar preserves the anonymity of the user, and facilitates modification and reuse of information present on the site.

A typical Sign-Wiki page is divided in two sections, a Content Structure panel on the left to accommodate content and a Content Presentation panel on the right, where the signing avatar appears.

The Content Structure panel presents a structured view of the page content to the user allowing for navigation within the page and selection of units for presentation by the virtual human signer.

The global level of detail at which the content page structure is displayed can be controlled by the user by appropriate selection/deselection of the nodes in a tree structure which may correspond to individual signs or sign phrases, while each individual sign is labelled with its spoken language gloss name.

Fig. 4. Standard Sign-Wiki page layout

To view the page content, or any structural unit within the page using the virtual human signer, the user simply selects by clicking on the required node, so as the virtual human signer initiates presentation of the selected sequence sign by sign. As each individual sign is presented, its entry in the tree structure on the left is highlighted in blue, thus providing visual feedback to the user, also allowing for verification of the structural organisation of the content.

For any given Sign-Wiki content page, a switch from Viewing mode to Edit/Input mode is achieved by simple clicking of the relevant icon. In Edit/Input mode the user may execute the following actions:

- Save updates to the page at any stage during editing.
- Search the lexical resources of the DICTA-SIGN lexicon for a sign or signs to be added to the content of the page under editing (Fig. 7).
- Interact with the system to directly input signs, via a Kinect tracking device.

In Edit/Input mode the Content Structure panel gains the ability to act as a Drag-and-Drop based structure editor. The user can select any node within the content tree structure and move it to a new position in the tree by dragging it there, while it is possible to view any unit within the structure as often as the user desires while editing proceeds.

The currently available sign or sign sequence insertion methods involve Kinect input by exploitation of Sign Recognition technologies, Search in the Dicta-Sign Lexicon to enrich the nodes in the Content Structure panel, and an individual sign building functionality. Both the first and second of these methods allow identification of signs, if already included in the Dicta-Sign lexicon. The sign building environment allows the user to create a sign definition by identifying its individual features (hand-shape, orientation, location, movement, etc.) interactively. It also allows the user to edit signs already included in the page, using the same set of interactive techniques.

Fig. 5. Sign-Wiki input reviewing environment

The system acts as a dictation machine using sign, providing recording, playback (Fig. 5), and editing (Fig. 6). As regards Sign-Wiki implementation issues, the proto-type is built using conventional Web technology, augmented with various special purpose SL processing modules. On the server side, the Sign-Wiki Web site is implemented using the Django framework, supported by a PostgreSQL database. The client-side of the Web site is implemented using HTML and Javascript, supported by the JQuery library, and several other small JQuery-related library modules. The system also integrates a dedicated Kinect Input/Recognition server.

Fig. 6. Sign-Wiki sign building environment

To use the Sign-Wiki the user needs just a conventional personal computer system and a web browser (Windows or Mac OS X, with Firefox). To do Kinect-based SL input, a Microsoft Kinect™ input device is required, attached either to the client computer itself or to another local computer, physically located close the main client system, and connected via the local network to that system. The local computer hosting the Kinect device also needs to have the special Kinect-service software, developed within the project, installed on it. Apart from this, the Sign-Wiki depends only on standard client-side Web software technology.

Innovation achieved by DICTA-SIGN in respect to communication via sign language is noticeable in relation to the pre-DICTA-SIGN state-of-the-art regarding a number of barriers causing parameters which mainly relate to the exclusive use of video to convey the signed linguistic message. For the first time technological solutions provide the conditions so that a signing user may create new SL content by either entering his/her own productions to the system by means of a Kinect device and/or using a set of sign creation tools which are also used for editing purposes. The Web user may edit previously uploaded signs or sign phrases by applying i.e. simple copy-paste procedures on pieces of SL utterances or by changing basic components of a sign, using a visual sign editor or the set of HamNoSys notations [10]. Sign-Wiki users, like any other Wiki users, may view SL information uploaded by other individuals. This may involve information in one's own sign language or may require translation support in order to be comprehended. In the latter case, the user may find support by a Sign-Look-up translation module, which currently allows search of signs in four sign languages. This facility is rather supportive in the multilingual Web environment, since multilingual correspondences of the same concept increase the possibility of its understanding. Finally, answering a demand been strongly expressed by the Deaf communities, the user may save, upload and present his/her content preserving his/her anonymity, since performance of sign language content takes place by means of a signing avatar.

Fig. 6. Sign-Wiki lexicon search results

The DICTA-SIGN prototypes have been exposed to end-user evaluation procedures that have provided comments relating to all levels of implementation, crucially emphasising on the Deaf users' preferences in respect to interaction with the systems, thus, gaining advanced human-computer interface design for Web 2.0 sign language applications, which can be best viewed in implementation of the Sign-Wiki prototype. Especially in respect to the Sign-Wiki, since the prototype is usable online, all functions were tested via internet by end-users using one of the four project sign-languages (LSF, GSL, DGS, GSL) thanks to the translation option. Gained results revealed that the Wiki is actually used equally in order to create new utterances and to modify existing utterances. While it would also be possible to use the Wiki interface key concepts in pedagogical applications or for information providing purpose in combination with other existing solutions like 3DSigner (www.3DSigner.fr), besides possible applications, the testers pointed out provided anonymity as the major strength of such an application. Detailed reporting on end-user evaluation of the DICTA-SIGN Sign-Wiki, is the subject of project deliverable *D8.2: Evaluation report of Sign-Wiki demonstrator*[1].

4   Conclusion

DICTA-SIGN has undertaken fundamental research and development in the combined use of image processing and advanced computer vision techniques, statistical methods for continuous sign recognition with multimodal fusion and adaptation, virtual human technology, sign language modelling, grammar & lexicon design and development as well as corpus construction. The DICTA-SIGN demonstrator focused on the end user's requirements as regards human-computer interaction via sign language. Under this light, the main aim here has been to underline the range of actions and interaction possibilities that are finally offered to signing users of Web 2.0, resulting from research work that exploits properly annotated language resources.

Acknowledgments. The research leading to these results has received funding from the European Community's Seventh Framework Programme (FP7/2007-2013) under grant agreement n° 231135.

References

1. Matthes, S., Hanke, T., Storz, J., Efthimiou, E., Dimiou, N., Karioris, P., Braffort, A., Choisier, A., Pelhate, J., Safar, E.: Elicitation Tasks and Materials designed for Dicta-Sign's Multi-lingual Corpus. In: Dreuw, P., Efthimiou, E., Hanke, T., Johnston, T., Martínez Ruiz, G., Schembri, A. (eds.) LREC 2010, Proc/ 4th Workshop on Representation and Processing of Sign Languages: Corpora and Sign Language Technologies, pp. 158–163 (2010)
2. Ong, E.-J., Bowden, R.: Robust Facial Feature Tracking using Shape-Constrained Multi-Resolution Selected Linear Predictors. IEEE Trans. Pattern Analysis and Machine Learning 33(9), 844–1859 (2011)
3. Cooper, H., Pugeault, N., Ong, E.-J., Bowden, R.: Sign Language Recognition using Sub-Units. J. of Machine Learning and Recognition: Gesture Recognition (to appear, 2012)

---

[1] Available at: `http://www.dictasign.eu/attach/Main/` `PubliclyAvailable ProjectDeliverables/` `DICTA-SIGN_Deliverable_D8.2.pdf`

4. Pitsikalis, V., Theodorakis, S., Vogler, C., Maragos, P.: Advances in Phonetics-based Sub-Unit Modeling for Transcription Alignment and Sign Language Recognition. In: Proc. IEEE CVPR Workshop on Gesture Recognition, Colorado Springs, USA (2011)

5. Theodorakis, S., Pitsikalis, V., Maragos, P.: Advances in Dynamic-Static Integration of Manual Cues for Sign Language Recognition. In: Proc. 9th International Gesture Workshop (GW 2011): Gesture in Embodied Communication and Human-Computer Interaction, Athens, Greece (May 2011)

6. Theodorakis, S., Pitsikalis, V., Rodomagoulakis, I., Maragos, P.: Recognition with Raw Canonical Phonetic Movement and Handshape Subunits on Videos of Continuous Sign Language. In: Proc. Int'l Conf. on Image Processing (ICIP 2012), Orlando, Florida, USA (September 2012) (submitted)

7. Jennings, V., Elliott, R., Kennaway, R., Glauert, J.: Requirements for a Signing Avatar. In: Proc. Workshop on Corpora and Sign Language Technologies (CSLT), LREC 2010, Malta, pp. 33–136 (2010)

8. Efthimiou, E., Fotinea, S.-E., Hanke, T., Glauert, J., Bowden, R., Braffort, A., Collet, C., Maragos, P., Lefebvre-Albaret, F.: Sign Language technologies and resources of the Dicta-Sign project. In: Proc. of the 5th Workshop on the Representation and Processing of Sign Languages: Interactions between Corpus and Lexicon. LREC 2012, May 23-27, Istanbul, Turkey (to appear, 2012)

9. Elliott, R., Cooper, H., Ong, E., Glauert, J., Bowden, R., Lefebvre-Albaret, F.: Search-By-Example in Multilingual Sign Language Databases. In: Proc. Sign Language Translation and Avatar Technologies Workshops (2011)

10. Hanke, T.: HamNoSys - representing sign language data in language resources and language processing contexts. In: LREC. Workshop Proceedings, Representation and Processing of Sign Languages, pp. 1–6. ELRA, Paris (2004)

Sign Language Multimedia Based Interaction
for Aurally Handicapped People

Matjaž Debevc[1], Ines Kožuh[1], Primož Kosec[1],
Milan Rotovnik[1], and Andreas Holzinger[2]

[1] University of Maribor, SI-2000 Maribor
Faculty of Electrical and Computer Engineering (FERI)
{matjaz.debevc,ines.kozuh,pkosec,milan.rotovnik}@uni-maribor.si
[2] Medical University Graz, 8036 Graz, Austria
Institute for Medical Informatics, Statistics & Documentation (IMI)
Research Unit HCI4MED
andreas.holzinger@medunigraz.at

Abstract. People with hearing disabilities still do not have a satisfactory access
to Internet services. Since sign language is the mother tongue of deaf people,
and 80% of this social group cannot successfully understand the written
content, different ways of using sign language to deliver information via the Internet should be considered. In this paper, we provide a technical overview of
solutions to this problem that we have designed and tested in recent years, along
with the evaluation results and users' experience reports. The solutions discussed prioritize sign language on the Internet for the deaf and hard of hearing
using a multimodal approach to delivering information, including video, audio
and captions.

Keywords: deaf, hard of hearing, sign language, VELAP, SLI module, sign
language glossary.

1   Introduction

With the growth of the Internet as a mass media, and its great effect on our daily lives,
it is incomprehensible that the Internet and its services are still not accessible to everybody, despite numerous disabled end-users who could benefit highly from having
access to these services. More than ten percent of our whole world population, i.e.
more than 600 million people, is disabled [1] and 71 million have some degree of
hearing loss [2]. According to the American National Organization on Disability survey, people with hearing and vision disabilities would highly appreciate being able to
use those services at home [3].

However, up to 80% of deaf people cannot successfully understand the written
content [4]. The main reason is their lack of education and a low level of literacy,
which is a main criterion to benefit from the text-based Internet. Since sign language
is the mother tongue of hearing impaired people, and written language is only their

K. Miesenberger et al. (Eds.): ICCHP 2012, Part II, LNCS 7383, pp. 213–220, 2012.
© Springer-Verlag Berlin Heidelberg 2012

second language, deaf signer users often become confused when searching for information on Web pages [5 - 7]. It is therefore essential to provide information on the Internet in sign language.

Moreover, legal documents at international, European and national levels, including the United Nation Convention on the Rights of Persons with Disabilities (2006), Riga Declaration (2006), "Disability Action Plan" of European Union (2006) and Brussels Declaration on Sign Languages in the European Union (2010), endow the deaf with the right to use sign language. Consequently, there is an urgent need for research, design and development to provide appropriate, usable and accessible information and communication technology to the deaf and hard of hearing in order to improve their reading ability and education level and prepare them for job competition.

2   Principles and Examples of Good Practices for Deaf and Hard of Hearing

Various technologies have been used to deliver online information in sign language: avatars, streaming videos of sign language interpreters and speech recognition technology. According to research findings, natural videos are currently more accepted by the end users than signing avatars and synthetic gestures [8]. Therefore, our science and engineering approach within the last years has been focused mainly on the development of ways to deliver information to deaf and hard of hearing internet users, applying the technology of sign language interpreter natural video. In this paper, we discuss the following four successful best-practice examples and our experiences with innovative approaches to ensure e-learning accessibility for deaf and hard of hearing people:

- Video-based E-Lectures for All Participants (VELAP);
- Sign Language Interpreter Web Based Video Module (SLI module);
- E-learning Portal for Deaf and Hard of Hearing "How to get a job?";
- On-line Sign Language Glossary for Deaf and Hard of Hearing.

2.1   Video-Based E-Lectures for All Participants (VELAP)

Considering accessibility, a system called Video-based E-Lectures for All Participants (VELAP) was developed. The primary goal was to provide live streaming of lectures on demand for people with disabilities. The main features were:

- Automated recording of lectures with additional materials (presentation slides, video captions, table of contents) for live and on-demand web presentations;
- Inclusion of additional media streams (supplementary video, audio, screen capturing);
- Inclusion of accessibility options for persons with disabilities:
    - a sign language video and captions for deaf and hard of hearing users,

— audio captions, text enlargements, background/foreground color corrections and JAWS compatibility for visually impaired users;
- Personal customization of the user's view;
- Interactive questions.

In order to evaluate usability and pedagogical effectiveness of the VELAP system, four studies were conducted: a) comparison tests between traditional learning and online learning with Pre-Test/Post-Test experimental control group design, running ANCOVA, b) application of Learning and Study Strategies Inventory (LASSI), which is a 10-scale, 80-item assessment of "students' use of learning and study strategies related to skill, will and self-regulation components of strategic learning", c) application of method System Usability Measurement Inventory (SUMI), d) Question-thinking protocol [9].

In this research, two experiment groups of students were involved. In the first experiment group, 39 electrical engineering students participated and the second group consisted of 36 students of media communications. While the first group participated in face-to-face lectures, the second group watched the VELAP Web-lecture. When discussing results, ANCOVA showed that there was no distinction between the groups in the first lecture in knowledge growth with regard to prior knowledge, whilst in the second a significant difference ($p < 0.05$) was noted. A SUMI test with the value 57 indicated that the usability of the system was above standard. Secondly, 13 deaf or hard of hearing and 7 blind subjects were involved in two experiments. From the results, it was evident that deaf and hard of hearing users did not prefer two different videos, streaming simultaneously (a lecturer and sign language interpreter). However, 77% of the subjects had selected the sign language interpreter video in combination with a PowerPoint presentation as the best mode for the Web lecture. The group of blind subjects was given a Braille keyboard and the JAWS application for performing the tasks. All the subjects were able to control the videos; however, they failed to select different videos.

Due to the study, we were able to conclude the following facts:

- Requirements for switching media windows are different for deaf and blind users;
- When attending the lectures, deaf users prefer one video for a sign language interpreter without the lecturer;
- Video control bar for deaf users should be above the video window.

2.2   Sign Language Interpreter Web Based Video Module (SLI Module)

Sign Language Interpreter Web based Video Module (SLI module) is a technology that enables deaf and hard of hearing people to rapidly access information in their first language – sign language, with sign language interpreter videos together with captions. They are displayed over the existing web page with a transparent background, without altering the structure of web page and disturbing the learning process (see Fig. 1).

SLI modules provide multimodal information retrieval (video, audio and captions), Timed-Text Authoring Format is used for captioning and cross browser Flash player

(SLI player) is applied. Integration of an SLI module is enabled with a hyperlink button placed at a specific location of the web page, and the web address for the video is set to the server where the video is located.

Fig. 1. Sign Language Interpreter Module

Two evaluation studies with deaf and hard of hearing users were conducted [10]. In the first group, there were 14 participants, aged from 18 to 72. In the second evaluation, 31 deaf and hard of hearing subjects, aged between 15 and 21, participated. In the first evaluation, the gestural thinking method was applied. After using the system, users had to fill out a questionnaire with three basic questions about their experience. The results revealed that 92% of the users were satisfied with the system. In the second evaluation, we conducted a pre-test questionnaire for the participant's demographic profile, a post-test questionnaire for evaluating usability with 5-point Likert scale, and an open debate to determine positive/negative or missing functionalities of the prototype. The evaluation results showed a high degree of evaluated usability metrics, such as satisfaction (80%), ease of use (77%) and comprehension (83%).

Due to the study, we were able to conclude the following facts:

- SLI module is acceptable among deaf and hard of hearing users;
- SLI module is easy to use, comprehensible and makes users satisfied.

2.3   E-Learning Portal for Deaf and Hard of Hearing "How to Get a Job?"

The E-learning portal is an e-learning system, based on a custom modified version of Moodle. The system comprises of three parts: contextual, communicative and collaborative. Users are familiarized with advice on how to look for a job. The whole content is in written form and it is translated into the Slovenian sign language in fixed videos with captions. The video that presents the interpreter is located on the left side of a screen window and the text, which is translated in the video, is on the right (see Fig. 2). The glossary of potentially unknown words is provided with a transparent SLI module, where the words are explained in sign language and supported with captions.

The video is displayed when activated by the user on the website. The communication parts of the e-learning system are videoconference communication and collaboration tool, videoforum and chat room. Videoconference provides communication among deaf: hard of hearing and sign language interpreters with live video, text messages and interactive whiteboard. Videoforum enables the posting of messages in the form of a video recording, along with text message, or just text without a video recording. In terms of collaboration, users can do exercises, quizzes and assignments.

Fig. 2. E-learning Portal for Deaf and Hard of Hearing "How to get a job?" with fixed and transparent video (SLI module)

The system was proposed as a model for the evaluation of e-learning systems for the deaf and hard of hearing and used as a basis for the development of a common evaluation method for measuring both pedagogical richness and usability (PRU method) [11]. A starting point for the development of PRU method was Sonwalkar's method for measuring pedagogical effectiveness of e-material. He proposes 16 factors within three dimensions in relation to learning styles, media used in e-material and interaction. In the PRU method, we expanded Sonwalkar's method with the integration of new interaction factors (videoconference, videoforum and chat). Additionally, captions were added among the media factor (see Table 1), so that the method is appropriate for an evaluation of e-learning systems for deaf and hard of hearing users. On the basis of the PRU method, users' response is measured with a 5-point Likert scale questionnaire. A final result of the calculation is the value of the PRU index, which varies between 0 and 1. A value greater than 0.5, signifies an e-learning system that is pedagogically rich and user friendly.

The e-learning portal was evaluated by The System Usability Scale (SUS). Two experiments measuring usability were conducted [12]. In the first experiment group, 16 participants were involved, 7 males and 9 females, aged from 24 to 57 and with the mean age of 41. The majority (11) was deaf and 5 were hard of hearing. 12 were signers and 4 had no knowledge of sign language. There were 11 with little or no Internet skills, and 5 were average Internet users. In the second experiment group, 12 males and 7 females were included. The age varied between 16 and 24 with a mean age of 19. The majority (11) was deaf, 5 were hard of hearing and 3 subjects had no hearing loss. The majority had excellent Internet skills. Both groups used the system for one hour and the results showed that the SUS score correlated with Internet usage skills.

The first group evaluated the system with the final SUS score 57, which indicated low marginal acceptability of the e-learning portal. The SUS score of the second group was 70. It indicates that the e-learning portal was acceptable.

Table 1. Factors considered in the evaluation with the PRU method. (Source: Kožuh et al., 2011)

Learning styles	Media	Interaction
incidental learning	graphics	revision
inductive learning	audio	bulletin
deductive learning	video	videoconference
discovery	animation	videoforum
	simulation	chat
	captions	

In the study the following has been concluded:

- An e-learning system, comprised of contextual (content supported by sign language), communicative (videoconference, videoforum, chat room) and collaborative part (exercises, quizzes, assignments) can serve as a model for e-learning systems for deaf and hard of hearing;
- PRU method can serve as a universal method for measuring both usability and pedagogical richness of e-learning systems for deaf and hard of hearing users.

2.4   On-Line Sign Language Glossary for Deaf and Hard of Hearing

The system presents a unified web dictionary of sign language translations with the aim of providing accessibility to the original website and an initiative as a starting point for the development of official Slovenian sign language recognition. When the user selects the text in the browser and triggers the spacebar key stroke, the selected text is sent, using JavaScript, to the SLI Flash Glossary. The Flash player loads an HTTP request with a string parameter added to the URL. On the server side, the parameter from the URL is retrieved by the website and the asp.net logic checks against the records stored in the database in order to find the denominator of the term. If the data matches, the video URL is retrieved by the server-side web application and is returned to the Flash player. The Flash player with JavaScript dynamically creates the Flash HTML container for the signed video on the original website and the transparent signed video with captions is played automatically. When the video playback ends, the signed video is automatically closed. On the other hand, if the selected text does not exist in the database, the asp.net website inserts a new record.

Due to the study, we were able to conclude the following facts:

- On-line Sign Language glossary is a unified web dictionary of sign language translations that can serve as a base for the development of official Slovenian sign language recognition.

3   Conclusion

In this paper, we provided a technical overview along with lessons learned from several systems, their evaluation results and user experience. The discussed systems present a combination of multimodal information including video, audio and captions, and offer the option of prioritizing the sign language on the Web for deaf and hard of hearing users. The interaction is mainly managed with transparent and movable videos of a sign language interpreter. The videoforum for deaf people, for example, presents an asynchronous communication tool for the exchange of ideas among students and tutors in two languages: sign language and written text. The tools presented could have a stimulating effect for the deaf and hard of hearing since they can choose their own communication model.

We are of the opinion that the systems presented will thoroughly change the method of information transmission for the deaf and hard of hearing on the Web. The systems discussed have already been accepted at a large scale national level in Slovenia and tend to be positively accepted in countries where sign language is recognized as an official language for the deaf and hard of hearing. In Slovenia, official websites are meanwhile supported with sign language translations. Moreover, a majority of television programmes and movies are captioned. Amongst the weaknesses, one cause of indignation for the deaf is the absence of captions in live television programmes and in sign language interpreter videos on the Web. Thus, our future research will be aimed at proving that the captions integrated into sign language interpreter videos are required.

With the expansion of the discussed technologies, we could contribute to literacy improvement, rising education levels and improvement of competitiveness in job market. This will also enable them to get better opportunities for easier integration into the social network and, at the same time, it will preserve their identity and self-esteem.

References

1. World Health Organization, Access to rehabilitation for the 600 million people living with disabilities (2003), http://www.who.int/mediacentre/news/notes/2003/np24/en/ (accessed March 28, 2012)
2. World Health Organization, Deafness and hearing impairment (2005), http://www.who.int/mediacentre/factsheets/fs300/en/index.html (accessed March 28, 2012)
3. Hendershot, G.: Internet use by people with disabilities grows at twice the rate of non-disabled, yet still lags significantly behind (2001), http://www.nod.org/index.cfm?fuseaction=page.viewPage7pageID=1439&nodeID=1&Feat
4. World Federation of the Deaf (WFD), Position Paper regarding the United Nations Convention on the Rights of People with Disabilities (2003), http://www.un.org/esa/socdev/enable/rights/contrib-wfd.htm (accessed March 28, 2012)

5. Debevc, M., Peljhan, Z.: The role of video technology in on-line lectures for the deaf. Disability and Rehabilitation 26, 1048–1059 (2004)
6. Fajardo, I., Canas, J.J., Salmeron, L., Abascal, J.: Improving deaf users accessibility in hypertext information retrieval: are graphical interfaces useful for them? Behaviour & Information Technology 25, 455–467 (2006)
7. Fajardo, I., Parra, E., Canas, J.J.: Do Sign Language Videos Improve Web Navigation for Deaf Signer Users? Journal of Deaf Studies and Deaf Education 15(3), 242–262 (2010)
8. Olivrin, G.J.-L.: Is Video on the Web for Sign Languages. IN:Meraka Institute, CSIR, W3C Video on the Web Workshop, San Jose, California and Brussels, Belgium (2007)
9. Kosec, P., Debevc, M., Holzinger, A.: Towards equal opportunities in computer engineering education: design, development and evaluation of videobased e-lectures. Int. J. Eng. Educ. 25(4), 763–771 (2009)
10. Debevc, M., Kosec, P., Holzinger, A.: E-Learning Accessibility for the Deaf and Hard of Hearing - Practical Examples and Experiences. In: Leitner, G., Hitz, M., Holzinger, A. (eds.) USAB 2010. LNCS, vol. 6389, pp. 203–213. Springer, Heidelberg (2010)
11. Kožuh, I., Kosec, P., Debevc, M., Holzinger, A.: Evaluation of pedagogical richness and usability of e-learning systems for the deaf and hard of hearing. In: Fernstrom, K., Tsolakidis, K. (eds.) ICICTE 2011: Proceedings of the International Conference on Information Communication Technologies in Education, Rhodes, Greece, pp. 174–182 (2011)
12. Kosec, P., Debevc, M., Kožuh, I., Rotovnik, M., Holzinger, A.: Accessible and collaborative moodle-based learning management environment for web users with varying degrees of hearing. In: Uskov, V. (ed.) Proceedings of the 14th IASTED International Conference on Computers and Advanced Technology in Education, Cambridge, UK, pp. 73–79 (2011)

Meeting Support System for the Person with Hearing Impairment Using Tablet Devices and Speech Recognition

Makoto Kobayashi[1], Hiroki Minagawa[2], Tomoyuki Nishioka[2], and Shigeki Miyoshi[2]

[1] Faculty of Health Science, Tsukuba University of Technology, Japan
koba@cs.k.tsukuba-tech.ac.jp
[2] Faculty of Industrial Technology, Tsukuba University of Technology, Japan
{minagawa,nishioka,miyoshi}@a.tsukuba-tech.ac.jp

Abstract. In this paper, we propose a support system for hearing impaired person who attends a small meeting in which other members are hearing people. In such a case, to follow a discussion is difficult for him/her. To solve the problem, the system is designed to show what members are speaking in real time. The system consists of tablet devices and a PC as a server. The PC equips speech recognition software and distributes the recognized results to tablets. The main feature of this system is a method to correct initial speech recognition results that is considered not to be perfectly recognized. The method is handwriting over the tablet device written by meeting members themselves, not by supporting staffs. Every meeting member can correct every recognized result in any time. By this means, the system has possibility to be low cost hearing aids because it does not require extra support staffs.

Keywords: hearing impaired person, meeting support system, tablet device, speech recognition, low cost hearing aids.

1   Introduction

Summary scribe service is one of the typical support methods for people with hearing impairment. It is really useful and helpful for these people, especially who cannot understand sign language. In usual case, its input method is based on keyboard devices including special one like Stenotype [1]. Using keyboard is fast enough, however, it requires special skilled staffs and it becomes a kind of expensive services as a result. Meanwhile, performance of the speech recognition is extremely improved. The recognized result is not a perfect yet, its total quality achieves really high level compare with the quality in several years before. Even without enrollment of the specific speaker, the recognized output text is practical level if the speaker was well educated with the software and had clear pronunciation. It is not so difficult to be familiar with speech recognition software. Because of such excellent quality, speech recognition software is recently applied to the field of summary scribe services, instead of keyboard input method [2]. In such a service, supporting staff re-speaks sentences produced by the real speaker to the speech recognition software at first. After that, other

K. Miesenberger et al. (Eds.): ICCHP 2012, Part II, LNCS 7383, pp. 221–224, 2012.
© Springer-Verlag Berlin Heidelberg 2012

supporting staffs correct the output text from the software to brush it up. However, the problem of the cost to manage them is still remains, since it needs to employ supporting staffs. It is possible to apply the summary scribe service with speech recognition to a large lecture, though it is impractical to use it for a small daily meeting.

Besides this background, our project aims to develop a low-cost supporting system for the hearing impaired, which focused on a daily meeting. We assumed a situation of meeting in which members are one hearing impaired person and several hearing persons. Actually, such meeting is general case in a company or a school where accepted hearing impaired person. Of course we recognized the fact that low-cost means low-quality. Therefore our project has another aspect to clear a quality level the hearing impaired person can accept.

2   System Overview

The overview of our system is shown in Fig. 1. From the viewpoint of reducing the cost, the system should be designed as it does not require extra supporting staffs. The system consists of one personal computer as a server and several tablet devices as clients. Speech recognition software was installed to the server computer in advance and every meeting member holds the tablet device in which Android OS is running. In front of each hearing members, there are microphones connected to the server computer and in front of hearing impaired member, there is a keyboard to input text. The hearing members speak to the speech recognition software directly through the microphone and the recognition result is distributed to the all tablet devices from the server computer like online chatting software. Although the quality of the result is much better than the result of several years before as mentioned above, it would not be good enough to show to the hearing impaired member directly because the system

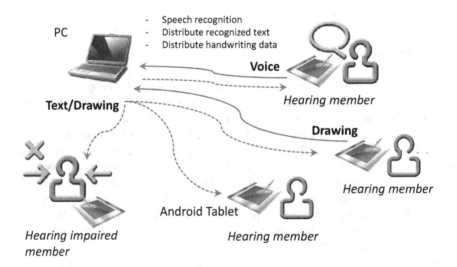

Fig. 1. An overview of our proposed system

does not utilize a re-speaker method. Needless to say, the result might have misrecognition and it needs to be corrected. The main feature of our system is its correction method, which is the handwriting via the tablet devices. It is done by hearing members themselves. This handwriting correction is basically expected to be done by the speaker himself, but it is not limited and the other members can support to correct another member's words. The correcting work does not require special skill and not take a lot of time because the work is based on the drawing, not on the keyboard typing. Additional to it, it is expected that members including hearing impaired one are able to understand the tendency of the speech recognition software by showing the correcting process. It would make speaker to change the way to speak afterwards.

3   Application Design

The software of the server computer is developed using .NET platform. It captures the output text of speech recognition software, which is named Ami Voice made by Advanced Media Inc. The captured text is distributed to Android tablets via wireless network connection.

On the other hand, client software for the Android tablet is developed using eclipse platform with Java. The client software is not only for browsing the results of speech recognition but also for correct it by handwriting. To implement the correcting function, we designed the forms of the software as landscape and make space between each line, and limit the maximum number of displayed characters in one line. As a result, drawing space is kept on screen area of right half.

Fig. 2. An appearance of client software

The appearance of the client software is shown in Fig. 2. To make a handwriting correction, the user has to touch a button with icon of finger at first. Once some member touches this button to move handwriting mode, the other members cannot access the button by exclusion control of the server to avoid mismatch drawing data. When the user touches the button again, the handwriting mode is ends and the drawing data is send to the server, then, the server distributes it to all the tablet devices. During the handwriting mode, the user can select a width and a color of pen from several choices. The software also prepares eraser button, marker pen button and undo button for basic drawing. As an additional function, stamp function of smile mark and star mark is available.

4   Summary

In this paper, we propose a low cost hearing aid system for a small meeting. The system is based on speech recognition and handwriting correction by meeting members. Of course we think high cost and high quality supporting system for the hearing impaired is important, though low cost system is as much as important in the real world.

References

1. Stenotype, http://en.wikipedia.org/wiki/Stenotype
2. Miyoshi, S., Kuroki, H., Kawano, S., Shirasawa, M., Ishihara, Y., Kobayashi, M.: Support Technique for Real-Time Captionist to Use Speech Recognition Software. In: Miesenberger, K., Klaus, J., Zagler, W., Karshmer, A. (eds.) ICCHP 2008. LNCS, vol. 5105, pp. 647–650. Springer, Heidelberg (2008)

Dubbing of Videos for Deaf People – A Sign Language Approach

Franz Niederl[1], Petra Bußwald[1], Georg Tschare[2], Jürgen Hackl[3], and Josef Philipp[3]

[1] akaryon Niederl&Bußwald OG, Grazerstraße 77, 8665 Langenwang, Austria
niederl@akaryon.com
www.barrierefreier-film.at
[2] Signtime GmbH, Schottenring 33, 1010 Wien, Austria
[3] media productions GmbH, Spittelberggasse 3/8, 1070 Wien, Austria

Abstract. Deaf people have their own language and they use the sign language to communicate. Movies are synchronized into a lot of different languages so that almost everyone is able to understand it, but sign language is always missing. This project makes a first step to close the gap by developing a "how to produce sign language based synchronization" guide for movies and a video player, which plays and shows two different movies at once. Methodical steps include modelling of sign language movie, conversion between spoken language, noise, music and sign language, development of a video player, system architecture for the distribution of the sign language movie and qualitative and quantitative examination of the approaches with an expert group.

Keywords: deaf people, sign language dubbing, accessibility, assistive technology.

1 Introduction

Deaf people are not able to conceive the content of a movie or a piece of music. Even written language is a barrier for them, because this is an abstract representation of the acoustic language, which is based on phoneme. It is almost impossible to understand the written description of the spoken text, if you have never heard any spoken language before. Therefore the current methods to make movies generally understandable for deaf people are not satisfactory for the medium. Additionally lip-reading seldom helps them to capture the story line, because many of the movies are in a foreign language and it is also almost impossible to understand complex conversations without losing information. Deaf people have their own adequate language and the usage of the sign language is necessary to communicate with them.

The goal of this project was to develop a method to synchronize a movie with sign language. Therefore a standalone movie, which only shows actors signing the spoken text, has to be produced. One part of the project was the research about how to design the sign language movies. Some of the questions have been:

K. Miesenberger et al. (Eds.): ICCHP 2012, Part II, LNCS 7383, pp. 225–228, 2012.

- Should we use different sign-language actors for different voices?
- How can we illustrate noise, music or a voice from the off?
- Where and in which size should we place the sign language video?

The second part of the project investigated the possibilities of playing back the movie together with the sign language movie. The research focused mainly on:

- How can we display two streams at the same time?
- How can we display one channel transparent?
- How can we distribute the synchronization video?

2   State of the Art

Currently the access to movies and television for deaf people is done by subtitling and visual signing[4]. A Web-based possibility are the self-contained sign language movies.

Subtitles are very important for late deafened people but for many deaf people they are not suitable. The disadvantage of this approach is that you have to read and to understand the written text. Subtitles are available for a wide variety of movies, Blu-ray discs or television programmes.

Visual signing for interpreting movies as described in the project "Digital Television for all" [1] is more complex. Beside a good understanding for deaf viewers with sign language as mother tongue, the challenges are the resistance from hearing viewers, because the often feel disturbed [2]. The amusement of watching a movie is equal regardless if it is watched by deaf people with visual signing or hearing people with an audio track; but the most significant factor to reach that equal stimulus is the quality of the visual signing [3].

The *amount of access services* provided by broadcaster depends a lot on legal regulations. In the member states of the European Broadcasting Union (EBU) the average quota for subtitling is 49,5% and for visual signing 5% [1]. In Great Britain, for example, the BBC is forced by law to provide a high percentage of its daily programme accessible for all people[2].

Self-contained sign language movies, which you can find on a lot of different websites[3], are very important to bring current news and other ongoing information to deaf people in an appropriate way. Many public institutions and non-profit associations also translate the content of their website into sign language and publish the sign language video on their site.

3   Design of the Sign Language Movie

To find out a suitable design for a sign language interpreting movie a two stage test was performed. In the first step some implementation options were presented

---

[1] http://www.psp-dtv4all.org
[2] http://www.direct.gov.uk/en/DisabledPeople/Everydaylifeandaccess/
LeisureAtHome/DG_4018341
[3] i.e.: http://signtime.tv

Fig. 1. Variants for the position of the sign language video

to an expert group of deaf people. The questions referred to the position of the sign language speaker, the size of the speaker window, the labeling of different actors in the movie posed by the same sign language speaker and the interpreting of important sounds. The options, which received the most support, were used for the production of at least three variants of three different film sequences. Figure 1 shows different options for the sign language speaker window. In the second round another two groups of deaf persons were individually interviewed after watching those different variants. The result was the base for dubbing the motion picture 'The Counterfeiters'. The closing test was the world premiere of the movie 'The Counterfeiters', which was the first movie that has been totally synchronized in sign language, at 1 Dec. 2010 in Vienna in front of an audience of deaf people.

4   Playback the Movie with Synchronized Sign Language Video

To playback a movie together with the sign language movie we can merge both movies to one and store this movie on the DVD or Blu-ray disc. The problem with this approach is, that on a DVD there is not enough space, you have to produce different discs for each sign language the movie is translated to and you need successful cooperation with all the involved organisations of the production. The second variant needs a special player, which is able to playback two different streams synchronous. The main movie comes typically from a DVD or Blu-ray and the sign language stream is fetched from the Internet or from local storage.

It was very important to select the right basic framework for the development of the player, because the player should be platform independent and it should be open source. After analysing the VLC and especially the VLC library[4] was selected as the most suitable. Some reasons besides the former mentioned have been that the VLC already supports the playback of more than one video-stream and the huge amount of supported video-codecs.

The developing of the player (figure 2) started with a subset of the original VLC player, but this did not work in the expected way. Therefore the player was developed new on the base of the VLC library. At the beginning the sign language stream was only fetched via the Internet. But some tests have shown that the Internet connections are not stable enough to provide a high transmission

---

[4] http://www.videolan.org

capacity during the whole playback. For this reason the player was extended with a pre-download functionality. A second reason for this extension was that fast forwarding and rewinding is now possible, too. The next enhancement was to isolate the signing actor by removing the background. Unfortunately the implementations of the video-codecs in the VLC-library do not support this feature. Hence a Chroma-filter in combination with a green box overtakes this task. The results of some test videos show more than sufficient quality.

Beside the player it was also necessary to develop a web service to provide the sign language movies. This web service offers a simple access to all of the stored sign language movies.

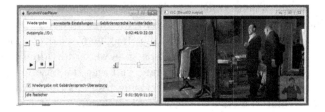

Fig. 2. Windows version of the video player

5 Summary

Currently, the accessibility provisions of subsidized films, both at EU and in the individual member states, are exacerbated without developing appropriate technologies and standards. Therefore we believe that our pioneering developments will come on the market, we see good potential for exploitation and we are convinced that a strong demand for high quality and low-cost-sign language synchronization will occur.

The results of the survey and the response after the screening of 'The Counterfeiters' give us the feedback, that we are on a good way. The next steps in our project are to refine the design model with different movie genre and to release the first version of the player on the website `www.barrierefreier-film.at`.

References

1. EBU, Access Services Study based on EBU Questionaire (2007)
2. Itagaki, T.: Digital Television For All, Final Report (2010),
   http://www.psp-dtv4all.org
3. Küng, N.: Sinnlose Unterhaltung? Das Unterhaltungserleben gehšrloser Personen vermittelt durch audiovisuelle Medien, Dissertation, Wien (2012)
4. Looms, P.O.: The case for DTV Access services (2010)

Towards a 3D Signing Avatar from SignWriting Notation

Yosra Bouzid, Maher Jbali, Oussama El Ghoul, and Mohamed Jemni

Research Laboratory of Technologies of Information and Communication & Electrical
Ingineering (LaTICE), Ecole Supérieure des Sciences et Techniques de Tunis,
5, Av. Taha Hussein, B.P. 56, Bab Mnara 1008, Tunis, Tunisia
yosrabouzid@hotmail.fr
maher.jbeli@gmail.com
oussama.elghoul@utic.rnu.tn
Mohamed.jemni@fst.rnu.tn

Abstract. Many transcription systems, like SignWriting, have been suggested in the last decades to describe sign language in a written form. But, these systems have some limitations, they are not easily understood and adopted by the members of deaf community who usually use video and avatar-based systems to access information. In this context, we present in this paper a new tool for automatically generating 3D animation sequences from SW notation. The SW notation is provided as input in an XML based format called SWML (SignWriting Markup Language). This tool aims to improve the reading and writing capabilities of a deaf person who has no special training to read and write in SL.

Keywords: Deaf, Sign Language, SignWriting, SWML, avatar, 3D signing animation.

1 Introduction

Reading and Writing are the essential tools of communication for everyone in modern society; they give us a way to express, record ideas, access information, learn new skills, enrich and expand our knowledge. This is also true for Deaf people who use signed Language. In fact, having a written form for their native language is a help to them, they could see themselves in a new positive light, outside of deafness.

Writing signed language will be a significant contribution to the development of the range of expression available to deaf community, it would mean a great deal to their daily uses where they could communicate with each other and exchange with their environment: "Literacy, being able to read and write, greatly improves the effectiveness of the controlling relations between the person and the person's environment" (McCarty, 2004). Furthermore, it might be better if novice students could learn basic educational skills from texts written in a language that is fully accessible to them. This will certainly improve their intellectual performance: "Writing in "common ordinary language" was crucial to the effective teaching of science and mathematics..." (Boststein, 1986).

Today, several notation systems for representing SL have been proposed like Stokoe [1], HamNoSys [2], Sign Front, and the famous SignWriting [5], [12]. Nonetheless, reading these notations may cause some difficulties for the deaf because of the

K. Miesenberger et al. (Eds.): ICCHP 2012, Part II, LNCS 7383, pp. 229–236, 2012.

static nature of the representation that seems to have lost the dynamicity of their gestural language. An accurate synthesis of such notation would be of major importance to those persons.

In this context, we aim to develop a new tool allowing the generation of 3D animation sequences automatically from SignWriting notation which is provided as input in an XML based format called SWML. The signs will be made automatically by the WebSign player, which is developed by the research laboratory (LaTICE) [13] in order to generate sign language using virtual avatars. The main focus of our work is the interpretation of the SWML format of a sign to produce the signing gestures that should be recognized by deaf users.

In the following, we present a state of the art of the well-known systems used to transcribe signs. Section 3 outlines the problems that can encounter deaf readers and how they can be solved. Section 4 and 5 give an overview of the SWML format and some works that use it to animate a virtual avatar. The general approach adopted to develop our tool and an example of solution, are illustrated in section 6. Finally, we present the conclusion and some perspectives.

2   Notation Systems

The need for storing and transferring the sign data makes different sign notation systems to evolve. A notation system for SL should be able to represent the manual and non-manual gestures of the signer, faithfully, as they are visually perceived. Following is brief description of the most popular examples that are actually in use.

2.1   Stokoe Notation

Stokoe system [1] is the world's first phonemic script that has been developed by the linguist William Stokoe for writing American Sign Language (ASL). The original notation contains 55 symbols, divided in three groups, each representing one of the important aspects of sign: ("tab" or sign location), ("dez" or handshape & orientation), and ("sig" or movement). These symbols, which are based on the shapes of Latin letters, punctuation, and numbers, were written in a strict tab-dez-sig order.

Stokoe research has brought to the attention of the world that sign languages, like oral ones, have an independent syntax and grammar. An example of his notation for the sign "don't know" in ASL can be seen in Figure 1.

Fig. 1. Stokoe notation for the sign "don't know" in ASL

2.2   HamNoSys Notation

The Hamburg Sign Language Notation System or HamNoSys [2] is a phonetic transcription system which has its root in the Stokoe notation. It was designed with the capacity to transcribe every natural signed language in the world. This system includes about 210 iconic characters to represent the different sign aspects. It is still being improved and extended all the time as the need arises.

An XML encoding of HamNoSys [3], SiGML(Signing Gesture Markup Language), was suggested by VisiCast project to define the notation in a form suitable for performance by a signing avatar. An example of such transcription and its translation in SiGML is given in Figure 2.

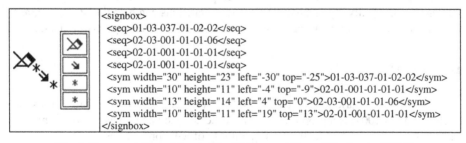	``` <sigml> <hamgestural_sign gloss="going_to_DGS"> <sign_manual both_hands="true"> <handconfig handshape="finger2" thumbpos="out"/> <handconfig extfidir="uo" palmor="l"/> <par_motion> <directedmotion curve="u" direction="o"/> <tgt_motion> <changeposture/> <handconfig extfidir="do"/> </tgt_motion> </par_motion> </sign_manual> </hamgestural_sign> </sigml> ```

Fig. 2. Representation of sign in HamNoSys and his codification in SigML

Unlike SignWriting, which was developed later by Valerie Sutton, Stokoe and HamNoSys notations have always been used for linguistic researches and analysis, rather than daily use. Its purpose is analogous to that of the International Phonetic Alphabet (API), which is used to transcribe the sounds of any given spoken language in a consistent way. In effect, the linearity of these notations and the complexity of their symbols which are too technical, make its learning a daunting task for the deaf.

2.3   SignWriting Notation

As is widely known, Sutton SignWriting system depicts a practical writing system for any variety of sign languages. It was originated from a choreographic notation system called Dance Writing. The hand shapes, palm orientation, movements, body locations, facial expressions and punctuation are all represented by a set of intuitive graphical symbols to record every sign or signed sentence [12].

	``` <signbox> <seq>01-03-037-01-02-02</seq> <seq>02-03-001-01-01-06</seq> <seq>02-01-001-01-01-01</seq> <seq>02-01-001-01-01-01</seq> <sym width="30" height="23" left="-30" top="-25">01-03-037-01-02-02</sym> <sym width="10" height="11" left="-4" top="-9">02-01-001-01-01-01</sym> <sym width="13" height="14" left="4" top="0">02-03-001-01-01-06</sym> <sym width="10" height="11" left="19" top="13">02-01-001-01-01-01</sym> </signbox> ```

Fig. 3. Representation of sign in SignWriting and his codification in SWML

Its value comes from its translation of the three dimensional signing space to an accurate two dimensional representation which can be read with no loss of understanding ; natural shapes and movements of signs can be realistically shown, and this brings a lot of advantages from the viewpoint of a writing system for SL [5].

SWML is an XML based language for encoding texts written in SignWriting system. We will describe it in detail in Section 4. An example of such transcription for the sign "prince" in ASL and its SWML translation is given in Figure 3.

3   Problematic and Objectives

The major criticisms arising around the writing systems for SL are the lack of understanding and their inability to communicate the signs effectively in a visual style. Sutton's system, for example, may cause some problems to deaf reader despite its simple graphical symbolism [6]; the signed words are created by compounding glyphs of a highly pictorial design and this can make variability across authors. For the same sign, different symbols can be used. Two different representations for the "Deaf" sign are given in Figure 4.

Fig. 4. Different representations for "Deaf" sign

In fact, the access that deaf people have to notation content could be greatly improved by the provision of sign language information in visual-gestural modality. Therefore, to offer additional support to readers, the notation should rather be presented in the form of video or virtual signing that uses avatars to perform gestures.

Thanks to its many advantages, communication systems using virtual avatar provides an attractive alternative to those based on video. Virtual signing is quicker to download than videos and does not take up lots of space on Internet servers since transcription content can be stored in XML files, which is smaller than video files. Another key advantage with virtual signing technology is the ability to control the speed of signing and change the view angle of the signer.

The objective of our work consists in developing a new tool to display SW notation content, automatically, by using a 3D signing avatar. This can help the reader to grasp and interact with the transcribing data through a more user-friendly environment.

4   SWML

The SignWriting Markup Language (SWML) [4], defined by Antonio Carlos da Rocha Costa in 2001, is a proposal format for the storage and processing of SignWriting documents, allowing thus the interoperability of SW applications.

Each sign encoded in SWML corresponds to a sign box comprising the set of symbols that together represent the notation. To identify the aspect of sign language to which it corresponds and the variation to which was subjected, each symbol is specified by a unique ID using the following fields (c–category, g–group, b–baseSymbol, v–variation, f–fill, r–rotation). The height, width and spatial coordinates of each symbol within the sign box are also denoted.

It is important to note that this encoding was not designed to computer animation purposes; it cannot provide an explicit order in which symbols are written to interpret correctly the sign, and enough information to animate automatically a virtual character in sign language. SWML describes just the original glyphs and not the relationship between them.

SignSpellings [5] are Sutton's solution which makes explicit a linear sequence of the symbols in a sign. It focuses essentially on two primary segment types: Hand and Movement. Unfortunately, this solution is not always feasible. Taking the example of the SignSpellings Sequence of the sign "prince", given in figure 3, where the movement arrow precedes the two asterisks contact, whereas it must be in the between. Moreover, the information provided by this ordering are insufficient to simulate effectively the transcribed gestures, we should add explicit details that are implicitly present in the two dimensional representation and thereby useful for the purpose of animating the avatar. For example, the SSS of the sign "prince" cannot specify exactly the parts of the body where the hand should make contact.

5   Previous Work

VSign is one of the first projects that perform animation sequences from SW notation. It is a Greek project developed by Maria Papadogiorgaki and al.[7] at the Informatics and Telematics Institute in Greece. This project has adapted the original version of SWML for the synthesis of virtual reality animations using Body Animation Parameters of the standard MPEG-4. It converts all individual symbols found in the sign box to sequences of BAPs, which are then used to animate any H-anim compliant avatar using MPEG-4 BAP player. This system can render about 3200 words, but the facial expressions, torso and shoulder movements are not implemented.

Although its effort, VSigns has failed to handle the two major limitations of the SWML format. It has interpreted the SWML file without sorting it, and this could lead to misinterpretation of the sign. Moreover, due to the lack of information provided in the sign box, some problems may occur when contacts and complex movements are involved. We can mention as example the hand-hand overlapping that could happen when the inclinations of the hand joints are not accurate enough for the exact description of the bimanual movement (Figure 5). The touch between the hands or the hand-face is also difficult to be achieved.

South African Sign Language (SASL) Project [8] at the University of the Western Cape was concerned also to render an animated avatar endowed with expressive gestures, from SW notation, using MPEG-4 BAPs. It was based on the SignSpellings sequence to find the chronological order of symbols but as we mention above, this could not complete an accurate animation. This system can produce only 8 signs.

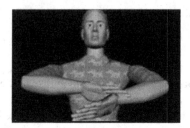

Fig. 5. An example of problem occurred due to a complex movement

6   Approach

In order to avoid the problems encountered in previous works, our tool aims to ensure a sorting process of symbols list and provide a gesture description language to describe the gestures presented within the input notation encoded in SWML.

Since SL has many more linguistic components to notate than other languages, the proposed language has to explicitly specify how sign is articulated by recording the most relevant information required to produce 3D signing animations. The sign description includes the manual features (hand shape, hand orientation, hand location), the various form of movement (forearm movement, wrist movement, finger movement) plus the non-manual features specifying facial expressions and bodily movements such as head and torso movement. To do so, we have relied on the hierarchical description of sign proposed by Olivier Losson [9].

To provide great precision, a certain amount of information will be more detailed. For example, we must identify movement properties (speed, repetition, size, muscular tense) to express subtle variations in meaning, and indicate the exact parts of the hand and body that should be in contact to improve the quality of generated animations.

6.1   General Architecture

Our proposed system architecture (Figure 6) includes the following modules: In the first one, a sorting algorithm is applied to determine the order of reading the symbols in the sign box, basing on their spatial coordinates and some preliminary rules. Next, a second module is needed to specify the missing information useful for realistic motion synthesis. After generating the description of the sign, the SML (Sign Modeling Language) [10 - 11] is then used to describe the 3D signing animation to be performed by an avatar. The animation according to SML is a set of movement or rotation of groups of joints which has a fixed time interval, during it, the rotation of every joint in the group is done. The design of the armature is compliant to the HlAnim specifications, in which each joint have a specific name and specific initial orientation. Here, the management of signing space is taken into account. Finally, the signing avatar is rendered using WebSign application.

Fig. 6. The architecture of the proposed tool

6.2   Example of Solution

As a first attempt, we have started our work by interpreting the SW notations that include symbols from two categories of IMWA [12] (The International Movement Writing Alphabet): hands and movement. To do so, we have used some preliminary rules:

- The sign always starts with a hand symbol: we cannot find a sign that begins with a movement symbol or any other type
- The movement must be preceded by a hand symbol: each movement symbol corresponds to an specified hand symbol
- The sign can be ended by a movement or hand symbol, and this can be explained by a possible articulator's change in configuration or orientation.
- The contact always occurs between two articulators: hand-face, hand-body or hand-hand.

Once symbols of the sign have been identified, we divide hand and movement symbols into two groups: the first one concerns the symbols of right hand, while the second concerns the left one. To sort the symbol list in each group, we mention their first movement symbol found in the sign box, as a referent symbol. Based on its spatial coordinates and its orientation, we can deduct those which precede it and those which follow it. Generally the symbols at the tail of the arrow are read first, followed by the symbols at the arrowhead. The initial hand symbol corresponding to the selected movement is the one that precedes it and closest to it, while its final hand symbol is the one that follows it and closest to it. (Figure 7)

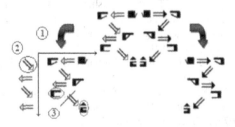

Fig. 7. The sorting algorithm applied on the 'hierarchy' sign

The same procedure is applied for all movement symbols found in this group to determine their predecessor and successor. The hand symbol, by which the sign starts, is the one that presents only a predecessor of a movement symbol. Finally, to achieve the signing animation in real time, the Sorted SWML file is converted to SML description which then interpreted with WebSign Interface.

7   Conclusion

We have presented in this paper a tool that aims to enhance the use of a written form of a sign language for deaf person. Such kind of work may well bring to light interesting problems concerning deaf accessibility to read and write from formal notations. The main challenge is to ensure the realistic animation of virtual agent in order to be recognized by deaf users. We wish adapt this tool to recover as much as possible symbols used in ISWA 2010 which fit into a set of seven categories: Hand, Movement, Dynamics & Timing, Head & Face, Body, Location and Punctuation.

References

1. Stokoe, W.: Sign Language Structure: An outline of the Visual Communication system of the American Deaf. Studies in Linguistics: Occasional Papers 8 (1960)
2. Hank, T.: HamNoSys – representing sign language data in language resources and language processing contexts. In: Strreiter, O., Vettori, C. (eds.) Fourth International Conference on Language Resources and Evaluation (LREC 2004), Lisbon, pp. 1–6 (2004)
3. Elliott, R., Glauert, J.R.W., Jennings, V., Kennaway, J.R.: An overview of the SiGML Notation and SiGML Signing Software System. In: Fourth International Conference on Language Resources and Evaluation (LREC 2004), Lisbon, pp. 98–104 (2004)
4. Costa, A.C.R., Dimuro, G.P., Freitas, J.B.: A sign matching technique to support searches in sign language texts. In: Workshop on the Representation and Processing of Sign Languages, Lisbon (2004)
5. Stuart, M.T.: A Grammar of SignWriting. Thesis in Linguistics, University of North Dakota (2011)
6. Aznar, G., Dalle, P.: Variation in the written representation of a sign in SignWriting. In: Workshop on the Representation and Processing of Sign Languages (TALN 2005), vol. 2, pp. 381–384. LIMSI, Dourdan (2005)
7. Papadogiorgaki, M., Grammalidis, N., Sarris, N.: VSigns – A Virtual Sign Synthesis Web Tool. In: Proceedings of 6th COST 276, Workshop on Information and Knowledge Management for Integrated Media Communication, Greece, pp. 25–31 (2004)
8. Moemedi, K., Connan, J.: Rendering an Animated Avatar from SignWriting Notation. University of the Westen Cape (2010)
9. Losson, O., Vannobel, J.M.: Sign language formal description and synthesis. International Journal of Virtual Reality 3(4), 27–34 (1998)
10. Jemni, M., Elghoul, O.: A System to Make Signs Using Collaborative Approach. In: Miesenberger, K., Klaus, J., Zagler, W.L., Karshmer, A.I. (eds.) ICCHP 2008. LNCS, vol. 5105, pp. 670–677. Springer, Heidelberg (2008)
11. Jemni, M., Elghoul, O.: Towards Web-Based automatic interpretation of written text to Sign Language. In: First International conference on ICT & Accessibility, Tunisia (2007)
12. Official SignWriting web site, http://www.signwriting.org
13. Research Laboratory LaTICE, http://www.latice.rnu.tn

Sign Language Computer-Aided Education: Exploiting GSL Resources and Technologies for Web Deaf Communication

Stavroula-Evita Fotinea, Eleni Efthimiou, and Athanasia-Lida Dimou

Institute for Language and Speech Processing (ILSP) / R.C. "Athena",
Artemidos 6 & Epidavrou,
GR-151 25 Maroussi, Greece
{eleni_e,evita,ndimou}@ilsp.gr

Abstract. The paper discusses the potential of exploitation of sign language (SL) monolingual or multilingual resources in combination with lately developed Web technologies in order to answer the need for creation of SL educational content. The reported use case comprises tools and methodologies for creating educational content for the teaching of Greek Sign Language (GSL), by exploiting resources, originally created and annotated in order to support sign recognition and sign synthesis technologies in the framework of the FP7 DICTA-SIGN project, along with a Wiki-like environment that makes possible creation, modification and presentation of SL content.

Keywords: Sign language resources, sign language technologies, processing of sign language data, sign language educational content, Deaf communication, HCI.

1 Introduction

Given the lack of written representation of sign languages (SLs) and the till now exclusive use of video to convey the linguistic message, we discuss how SL dedicated technologies are researching ways to deal with video data resources of natural signers, avatar based synthetic signing and SL recognition, to assist Deaf Web communication in the service of SL education mechanisms.

Since one of the major demands in creation of educational content for SL teaching is the availability of annotated SL resources, in section 2, we focus on creation and annotation of a corpus for Greek Sign Language (GSL) and an associated multilingual dictionary, which were initially intended to support development of SL technologies.

In section 3, we discuss how exploitation of these resources and technologies may contribute in setting together an advanced educational platform for SL teaching, thus recovering the currently noticed lack in respect to tools and language material in SL education. The use case reported comprises methodologies for creating educational

K. Miesenberger et al. (Eds.): ICCHP 2012, Part II, LNCS 7383, pp. 237–244, 2012.

content for the teaching of GSL, incorporating a brief discussion on the implications of sign synthesis technology in educational environments, where sign presentation is performed by a signing avatar instead of humans' video.

2   GSL Resources to Provide Educational Content

Currently available GSL resources comprise both lexical resources as well as video corpora of natural signers gathered in the framework of various research activities and annotated to serve different purposes (sign language recognition, sign language synthesis or GSL linguistic modelling).

The GSL corpus segment developed in the framework of the DICTA-SIGN project (http://dictasign.eu), is part of the parallel multilingual corpora (for GSL, DGS, LSF and BSL) that have been created and annotated to serve the project's sign recognition and sign synthesis technologies, along with requirements for the definition of a generalised sign language model. Elicitation of the DICTA-SIGN corpus applied a completely new approach to triggering as close to spontaneous signing data productions as possible. Part of the adopted elicitation methodology was the exclusion of interference from the informants' environment spoken language to the greatest possible degree [1]. The GSL DICTA-SIGN corpus segment with 5 hours and 40 minutes of fully annotated data from 16 distinguished signers, hence, significantly enhances the collection of the previously existing GSL-Corpus (GSLC) and provides a reliable source for elicitation of GSL educational content.

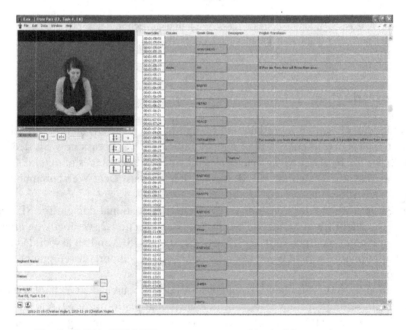

Fig. 1. DICTA-SIGN GSL segment annotated in the i-Lex environment

Annotation of the different parts of available GSL resources involves use of both ELAN (http://www.lat-mpi.eu/tools/elan) [2] for the earlier acquired parts of the corpus and i-LEX (http://www.sign-lang.uni-hamburg.de/ilex) [3] environment for the DICTA-SIGN segment (Fig.1).

Coding of lexical items makes use of HamNoSys [4] notations for the phonetic representation of manual features of signs, where non-manual feature descriptions are made available by means of a dropdown menu in the SiS-Builder tool (Fig. 2), an on-line SL lexicographic environment that provides for annotations of both HamNoSys manual and non-manual features of sign lemmas, which can directly translate to SiGML transcripts to feed avatar based sign synthesis [5].

In this context, among the available SL resources employed for the purposes of developing SL educational content, GSL makes use of both monolingual and multi-lingual resources (Fig. 3) which are currently available on-line and have increased considerably the potential of on demand SL content creation. More specifically, free access of the annotated parallel DICTA-SIGN lexical and corpora resources [6] has opened new perspectives for SL teaching methodologies regarding creation and exploitation of on demand content.

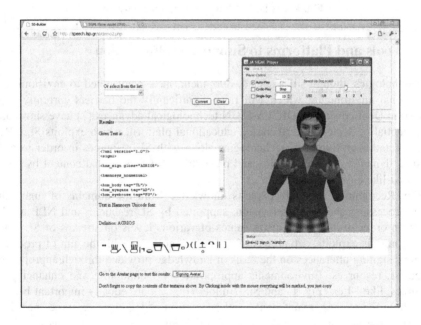

Fig. 2. SiS-Builder tool: In the screen shot coding of the GSL lexical item "WILD" with parallel presentation by the UEA avatar[1]

---

[1] http://vhg.cmp.uea.ac.uk/tech/jas/095z/SPA-framed-guiwin.html

Fig. 3. The DICTA-SIGN multilingual lexicon

3   Tools and Platforms to Support SL Education

SL technologies, though still under development, have contributed to envisioning an educational environment which will raise significantly the barriers currently experienced in Deaf education. DICTA-SIGN technological advances [7] have showcased the potential of designing a SL based educational platform which exploits Sign Recognition and Sign Synthesis technologies along with SL resources in order to make possible dynamic creation, editing and presentation of educational content by means of a Wiki-like environment.

Sign Recognition basically exploits knowledge from the domains of image and video processing and computer vision, supported by SL resources and NLP mechanisms, in order to assign linguistic values of various levels on streams of SL video. Sign Synthesis exploits virtual agent (avatar) technologies with the aim of producing dynamic signing utterances on the basis of knowledge provided through appropriately coded SL resources. Environments appropriate for maintaining and enhancing SL resources, like i-Lex (Fig. 1) and SiS-Builder (Fig. 2), are equally important because they allow for storage, maintenance and annotation of language resources necessary in developing educational content. The DICTA-SIGN Sign-Wiki prototype (Fig 4), which enabled not only to showcase the project's outcomes, but also allowed for extensive evaluation and actual use by end-users, incorporates Sign Recognition and Sign Synthesis technologies in a user centred environment, evaluation of which by end users received enthusiastic acceptance, anonymity preserved via avatar use for content presentation being one of the points to be focused by all evaluators.

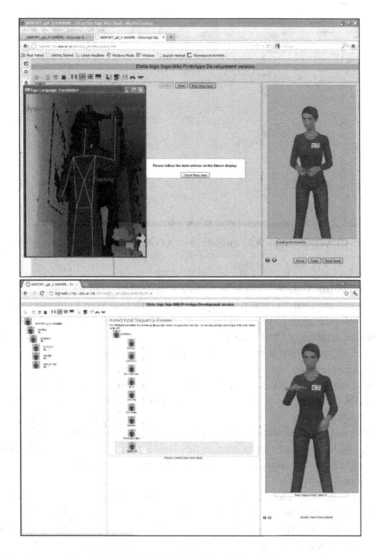

Fig. 4. Sign Recognition in the DICTA-SIGN Sign-Wiki environment: input capturing and output reviewing

The basic idea is that the user signs in front of a camera adopting dictation tempo, the system recognises the signed phrases, converts them into an internal representation of sign language, and then has an animated avatar sign them back to the user. Alternatively, the user may compose a linguistic message in his/her SL either by reusing previously created content, or by inputting content via a Kinect camera or by editing/creating/modifying his/her own content through appropriate graphical interfaces and by exploiting already available lexical resources (Fig.5).

Fig. 5. The DICTA-SIGN Sign-Wiki environment: Content creation by search in the system's lexicon

Furthermore, the Sign-Wiki incorporates a simple sign level translation tool, which is exploited for exploring corresponding signs in different sign languages and it was initially developed as an independent tool, the DICTA-SIGN Sign Look-up Tool (Fig.7), which enables a Deaf user to perform a sign and see its correspondences in four sign languages, while it plays back to the user the recognised sign or the closest matches using an avatar.

An experimental educational platform for GSL exploits both video resources and DICTA-SIGN technologies to propose a new approach to SL teaching. In this scenario video-based educational content in accordance with specific curriculum needs, may be retrieved by exploitation of the adequately annotated corpus, while tools that support the educational activity comprise SiS-Builder for creation and maintenance of SL resources, and a sign language based Wiki environment, which enables collaborative activity and information exchange.

In this setting, Web Deaf communication makes use of the DICTA-SIGN Sign-Wiki components, exploiting the system's sign recognition capabilities which enable, among other functionalities, insertion of content by a user signing in front of a Kinect camera, avatar-based sign language performance and a sign look-up tool to facilitate either retrieval from monolingual lexical resources or rough multilingual translation of sign language items, given the existence of the relevant resources in the system's multilingual database.

Initial experimentation with avatar based educational content presentation has already been reported in connection with the development of an educational platform (Fig. 6) for the teaching of GSL grammar [8], [9].

As signing avatar technologies are rapidly maturing, incorporating new features which result in more natural signing representations, it is becoming obvious that sign synthesis provides a serious option for dynamic creation of on demand SL educational content.

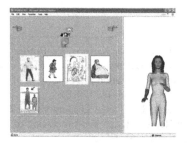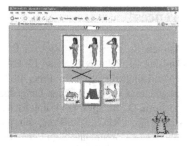

Fig. 6. Early experimental avatar use for on-line SL educational content presentation

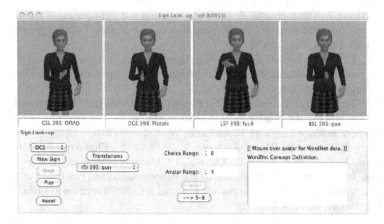

Fig. 7. Sign Look-up Tool: Avatar displaying multilingual SL information

In parallel, adequately annotated corpus resources of significant volumes allow retrieval of previously unavailable sign language content which may directly provide educational language material or support various communication needs.

Finally, the use of collaborative environments, as demonstrated with the DICTA-SIGN Sign-Wiki, which enable the use of sign language in Web information exchange, open completely new perspectives in respect to Deaf education practices.

4   Conclusion

Combined exploitation of resources and currently available technologies has opened new perspectives in designing future Deaf education paradigms. In this context SL based Web communication technologies will play a significant role, while near future tasks crucially entail end user evaluation in real use educational settings complementing the already available evaluation results on the technologies involved.

Acknowledgments. The research leading to these results has received funding from the European Community's Seventh Framework Programme (FP7/2007-2013) under grant agreement n° 231135.

References

1. Matthes, S., Hanke, T., Storz, J., Efthimiou, E., Dimiou, N., Karioris, P., Braffort, A., Choisier, A., Pelhate, J., Safar, E.: Elicitation Tasks and Materials designed for Dicta-Sign 's Multi-lingual Corpus. In: Proc. 4th Workshop on Representation and Processing of Sign Languages: Corpora and Sign Language Technologies, pp. 158–163 (2010)
2. Crasborn, O., Sloetjes, H.: Using ELAN for Annotating Sign Language Corpora in a Team Setting. In: LREC 2010, Proc, 4th Workshop on Representation and Processing of Sign Languages: Corpora and Sign Language Technologies, pp. 61–64 (2010)
3. Hanke, T., Storz, J.: iLex – A Database Tool for Integrating Sign Language Corpus Linguistics and Sign Language Lexicography. In: Crasborn, O., Hanke, T., Efthimiou, E., Zwitserlood, I., Thoutenhoofd, E. (eds.) Construction and Exploitation of Sign Language Corpora. 3rd Workshop on the Representation and Processing of Sign Languages, pp. 64–67. ELRA, Paris (2008)
4. Hanke, T.: HamNoSys - representing sign language data in language resources and language processing contexts. In: Proc. 1st Workshop on Representation and Processing of Sign Languages, pp. 1–6. ELRA, Paris (2004)
5. Goulas, T., Fotinea, S.E., Efthimiou, E., Pissaris, M.: SiS-Builder: A Sign Synthesis Support Tool. In: Proc. 4th Workshop on the Representation and Processing of Sign Languages: Corpora and Sign Language Technologies, pp. 102–105 (2010)
6. Matthes, S., Hanke, T., Regen, A., Storz, J., Worseck, S., Efthimiou, E., Dimou, A.L., Braffort, A., Glauert, J., Safar, E.: Dicta-Sign – Building a Multilingual Sign Language Corpus. In: Proc. of the 5th Workshop on the Representation and Processing of Sign Languages: Interactions between Corpus and Lexicon. Satellite Workshop to LREC 2012, Istanbul, Turkey, May 23-27 (2012)
7. Efthimiou, E., Fotinea, S.E., Hanke, T., Glauert, J., Bowden, R., Braffort, A., Collet, C., Maragos, P., Lefebvre-Albaret, F.: Sign Language technologies and resources of the Dicta-Sign project. In: Proc. 5th Workshop on the Representation and Processing of Sign Languages: Interactions between Corpus and Lexicon. Satellite Workshop to LREC 2012, Istanbul, Turkey, May 23-27 (2012)
8. Karpouzis, K., Caridakis, G., Fotinea, S.E., Efthimiou, E.: Educational Resources and Implementation of a Greek Sign Language Synthesis Architecture. International Journal Computers and Education 49(1), 54–74 (2007)
9. Efthimiou, E., Fotinea, S.E.: An Environment for Deaf Accessibility to Educational Content. In: Proc. First International Conference on Information and Communication Technology and Accessibility, Hammamet, Tunisia, April 12-14, pp. 125–130 (2007)

SignMedia

Interactive English Learning Resource for Deaf Sign Language Users Working in the Media Industry

Luzia Gansinger

Center for Sign Language and Deaf Communication, University of Klagenfurt,
Universitätsstraße 65-67, 9020 Klagenfurt, Austria
luzia.gansinger@aau.at

Abstract. An increasing number of deaf graduates and professionals enter media related careers. In the media industry it is a common practice to communicate in written English. Since English discourse can prove a barrier to sign language users, the interactive learning resource SignMedia teaches written English through national sign languages. Learners immerse in a virtual media environment where they perform tasks taken from various stages of the production process of a TV series to reinforce their English skills at intermediate level. By offering an accessible English for Specific Purposes (ESP) course for the media industry, the SignMedia learning tool supports career progression of deaf media professionals.

Keywords: sign language, e-learning, accessibility, ICT, multimedia, EFL/ESL, ESP.

1 Introduction

Film, video and broadcasting industries provide an increasing number of career opportunities for deaf graduates and professionals [1]. However, communicating in written English, which is common practice in the media business, represents a barrier to sign language users. The European project SignMedia[1] intends to overcome this language barrier by developing an innovative learning resource which is easily accessible for sign language users.

2 State of the Art and Application Idea

Most deaf sign language users' first or preferred language is their national sign language. The national written language is acquired as a second language. If they grow up outside of an English speaking country, English might be the third

---

[1] This project has been funded with support from the European Commission. This communication reflects the views only of the author, and the Commission cannot be held responsible for any use which may be made of the information contained therein.

K. Miesenberger et al. (Eds.): ICCHP 2012, Part II, LNCS 7383, pp. 245–252, 2012.
© Springer-Verlag Berlin Heidelberg 2012

language they learn. However, English literacy is becoming increasingly important. According to [2], English skills are necessary to participate in academic or other specialized discourses as well as to communicate with deaf people in other countries. Additionally, information technology and texts provided on the Internet mainly use the English language [3]. Despite the necessity of being English literate, many schools for the deaf outside of English speaking countries do not teach English as a Foreign Language (EFL). Either it is not part of the curriculum or it is viewed as less important. Due to these barriers faced in their educational career, many deaf sign language users may have a limited knowledge of English [4].

Vocational education for deaf individuals should consider the communication needs as well as the educational background of this target group [5]. Since modern language teaching involves spoken conversations, many language courses offered for hearing participants do not suit deaf learners. Even if interpreters or counselors are provided in mainstreaming courses, the needs of deaf participants can hardly be met since deaf people prefer "being taught directly through the medium of sign language" [6].

2.1   Multimedia Resources for Learning English

Some educational institutions offer in-class English courses for sign language users that teach written English through the national sign language. However, deaf learners of EFL/English as a Second Language (ESL) are a very heterogeneous group which is scattered all over a country. By offering EFL/ESL classes we may only reach few deaf learners living in the very region. In order to enhance independent learning of English, several projects have aimed at developing multimedia resources that use national sign languages as languages of instruction for teaching EFL/ESL to deaf learners. This approach respects deaf learners' culture and communication preferences. Therefore, they can easily access information without personal assistance [7].

Within the EU-project "SMILE" (1998–2001) an interactive multimedia language course for teaching European written languages was developed [8]. The findings of this innovative project then informed other projects like the electronic learning tool developed by [9]. Later, the European project "SignOn!" [2] aimed at teaching deaf adults with some knowledge of written English to use English for international online communication. For a detailed description of this project see [10]. Within the follow-up project "SignOnOne" [3] an EFL/ESL course for beginners was produced. More information on this project is provided by [7]. Also the EU-project "DEDALOS" focused on teaching English to deaf sign language users via e-Learning tools ([3] provides more information on this project.). The recent two year project "BASE" aimed at developing an e-learning

---

[2] The SignOn! online learning tool can be found at
http://www.acm5.com/signon2/index.html

[3] The SignOnOne learning resource can be accessed at
http://www.acm5.com/signonone/SignOnOne.html

tool for teaching basic English skills to deaf adults[14]. Another online English course for deaf learners can be accessed at "Vibelle", an online portal by the DESIRE-research group at the University of Aachen.[15].

The above mentioned learning resources may be used by deaf EFL/ESL learners individually or by EFL/ESL tutors for in-class teaching. This overview shows that there are already some tools for beginners or slightly advanced learners of written English available. However, none of these resources focuses on teaching ESP at intermediate or advanced level.

2.2 English for the Media Business

If e.g. German speaking professionals working in the field of broadcasting media are required to use written English, they can easily consult widely available handbooks as well as bilingual dictionaries or monolingual glossaries to gain specific terminology and grammar skills needed. They might also be given the chance to attend ESP courses which exactly meet their needs.

For deaf sign language users working in this professional field only a limited number of resources are available. Accessible tools like written English to British Sign Language (BSL) glossaries that offer BSL translations for specialized English terms[4] are rare.

This lack of learning resources for deaf ESP learners brought the SignMedia project[5] to the scene. It provides deaf graduates and professionals working in the media industry with an online resource for ESP learning.

3 The SignMedia Project

The SignMedia project (2010–2012) is funded by the Lifelong Learning Programme (Leonardo Da Vinci) of the European Commission. The involved partners are the University of Wolverhampton (coordinator) (GB), the University of Turin (I), the University of Klagenfurt (A) and the deaf led media production company Mutt&Jeff Pictures Ltd. (GB). The involvement of deaf media professionals and other deaf sign language users in the whole project enhances the quality of the learning tool and ensures its applicability.

Within this project, an interactive learning resource that teaches ESP through British, Austrian and Italian Sign Language, is developed. It primarily aims at deaf media professionals, graduates and students of media related studies with an intermediate command of written English. Furthermore, it might be used by other deaf EFL/ESL learners who gain, additionally to grammar and vocabulary, insight into media production processes. Moreover, deaf experts' hearing co-workers in the media business and sign language interpreters may use the tool for learning specialized sign language terms.

---

[4] e.g. the glossary for art and design "ArtSigns" (`http://www.artsigns.ac.uk`)

[5] Detailed information on the SignMedia project can be found at `http://www.signmedia.eu`

All learning activities resemble authentic documentation taken from the production process of a TV series. The tool enables deaf users to develop language skills that are directly transferable to their work in the media industry. The pilot of this learning tool will be ready for testing in spring 2012, the final product will be launched in autumn 2012.

4 Methodology

The SignMedia learning tool uses a bilingual approach. Written English is taught through national sign languages. By working with written texts and having delivered all necessary explanations in their first language, deaf learners easily improve their English language skills.

The online learning resource is designed for individual use. Since deaf sign language users involved in the media business form a minority which is scattered across the whole country, an online course can reach a larger number of them than in-class courses. Another advantage of individual learning is that users may determine their learning pace themselves. As the tool is permanently available, users can repeat lessons as often as they want to [10]. Being responsible for their own learning progress may also enhance their interest in learning [11].

Due to their educational experience, many deaf sign language users associate formal learning with constant communication barriers[6]. In order to increase their motivation for using the learning tool and to make them engage in the tool for a longer amount of time, a game-based approach was chosen. In a game world the users are "the most likely to stick with a problem as long as it takes, to get up after failure and try again" [12]. In contrast, when they face failure in real life, they might feel frustrated and give up quickly [12].

In the game-based learning tool, users immerse in a media environment. There, the boundaries between formal and informal learning blur. They will be able to transfer the skills gained in the immersive environment to the real world [13]. After selecting one of the three available national sign languages on the Sign-Media website (`http://www.signmedia.tv`), the users enter the learning tool and thus the world of "Sunrise Media Productions", the company responsible for broadcasting the weekly soap "Beautiful Days". For their log-in they need a personal password and a user name. This form of identification is necessary to store scores within one's account.

On entry, Crissy, their co-worker, welcomes them in their national sign language and leads them through the learning tool. Several written tasks connected to the working steps when producing a TV soap need to be completed (e.g. filling out a risk assessment form or completing a call sheet). Users find these tasks on their desktop which is shown in Fig. 1[7]. They decide on their own which task they would like to start with. However, some tasks depend on the knowledge gained in other tasks before, therefore these will only become visible when the user has completed the basic tasks first.

---

[6] For an overview of the educational situation of deaf people in Austria see e.g. [5].

[7] Figure taken from the pilot version of the SignMedia e-learning tool.

Fig. 1. The user's desktop

Each task is linked to a certain grammar topic (e.g. passive voice, articles, present tense) the users work on in the exercises. If the users need further explanations of a task, they can video-call Mark, the producer, who provides additional signed information on the English grammar involved. A click on the "phone the producer" symbol on the right of their desktop (shown in Fig. 1) opens the required video.

All tasks are divided into several exercises that require the user to either edit texts, to match pairs, to select the right words, to compile sentences by drag and drop or to choose the right answer from multiple choices. Via a virtual webcam the users contact Crissy, their co-worker, who signs the explanation of each task. Fig. 2[8] shows the user's co-worker explaining an exercise which involves text editing. Stars below a document symbolize successfully completed exercises within the respective task (shown in Fig. 1). After each completed exercise or task the users get signed feedback by their co-worker or by the executive producer. These characters either compliment them on the successful completion of the exercise/task or ask them to redo it. The more exercises and tasks they complete, the higher the bar showing the viewing figures (this bar is shown on the left in Fig. 1). For each completed task they can also win an award related to the production of a TV series. If the users' profiles are connected to their social media accounts, the won soap awards will appear e.g. on their Facebook walls.

The written text provided in the learning tool also includes links to a glossary where certain English terms are explained in and translated into the users'

---

[8] Figure taken from the pilot version of the SignMedia e-learning tool.

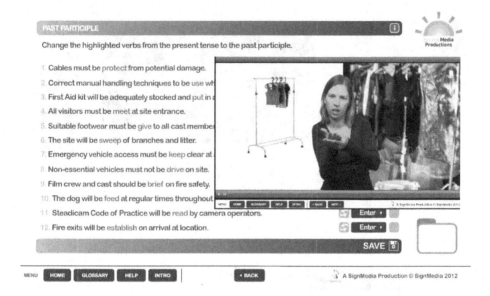

Fig. 2. Co-worker signing the explanation of an exercise

national sign language. A tutorial including explanations on how to use certain functions of the learning tool is also available. The buttons that direct the user to the required information are shown in the bottom left of Fig. 1 and Fig. 2.

All characters involved use British, Italian or Austrian Sign Language as their first language. All texts are video-taped in a professional studio and then edited using chroma key digital image manipulation for changing backgrounds before they are incorporated into the learning tool.

5   The Impact of the SignMedia Project

The final product of the SignMedia project will be an innovative learning tool for written English for the field of media designed for individual use. Sitting at their home computers, users immerse in the media environment and develop and foster their knowledge of English grammar, vocabulary and the production process of a TV series by playing and experimenting. The tool counteracts the marginalization of deaf media professionals and supports their career progression by enhancing their level of confidence. By including social media users can easily get in touch with other deaf media professionals from other countries. They can communicate using written English, which will enhance the learning process. The networking involved may also open up new career opportunities.

In addition to individual usage, elements of the learning resource may be used as part of in-class ESP courses for deaf professionals. Furthermore, the learning tool may also be used by sign language interpreters and deaf employees' hearing co-workers in the media industry. The advanced sign language literacy of these groups further enhances the career opportunities of deaf people in the media business by breaking down communication barriers.

6   Conclusion and Planned Activities

The online resource SignMedia is a first step towards accessible ESP courses for deaf graduates and professionals. The SignMedia consortium is willing to promote the re-utilization of gained knowledge and products for the generation of follow-up projects. At the end of the project, the SignMedia learning resource will be available in three national sign languages. The inclusion of other national sign languages or International Sign (IS) would be an option to make the tool accessible for a wider range of deaf users.

The resource may also be adapted to the development of ESP courses for other areas. SignMedia focuses on the needs of deaf professionals in the media business. However, other professional fields may also lack accessible ESP learning tools.

Furthermore, the SignMedia approach may be used for the development of learning resources for other national written languages. Many deaf people are marginalized because of their poor reading and writing skills which stem from barriers faced in their educational career. They could train their language skills using an interactive learning tool.

Another opportunity to further exploit the SignMedia learning resource would be the enlargement of the glossary. It then could be published as a stand-alone product. Additionally, signed multimedia manuals on film production may be produced and linked to the glossary. This would further support deaf media professionals and students of media related studies as well as their teachers.

The continuing work on projects like SignMedia will enhance deaf sign language users' quality of life by increasing the amount of accessible information. This accessibility of information also opens up a wider range of career opportunities in a variety of professional fields.

For all the plans outlined in this final section it is important to choose an empowering approach and hence to involve deaf sign language users in all stages of a project. Products intended for sign language users should rely on the expertise of deaf professionals. As potential users they are thoroughly familiar with the needs of the intended target group. This approach is liable to enhance the process and, as a consequence, the results.

References

1. Fleming, J., Hay, J.A.: Deaf and Successful, the Class of 2000. Career Destinations of Ten Deaf Students: a Summary of Case Studies and Conclusions Drawn (2006), http://www2.wlv.ac.uk/celt/events/deafandsuccessful.doc
2. Svartholm, K.: Teaching Literacy to Deaf Learners. In: Cortese, G., Duszak, A. (eds.) Identity, Community, Discourse: English in Intercultural Settings. Lang., pp. 345–358 (2005)

3. van den Bogaerde, B.: The Dedalos Project: E-learning of English as a Foreign Language for Deaf Users of Sign Language. In: Kellett Bidoli, C.J., Ochse, E. (eds.) English in International Deaf Communication. Linguistic Insights. Studies in Language and Communication, pp. 193–209. Peter Lang – Europaeischer Verlag der Wissenschaften (2008)

4. Dotter, F.: English for Deaf Sign Language Users: Still a Challenge. In: Kellett Bidoli, C.J., Ochse, E. (eds.) English in International Deaf Communication. Linguistic Insights. Studies in Language and Communication, pp. 97–122. Peter Lang – Europaeischer Verlag der Wissenschaften (2008)

5. Grbic, N., Andree, B., Gruenbichler, S.: Zeichen Setzen. Gebaerdensprache als Wissenschaftliche und Gesellschaftspolitische Herausforderung. GTS – Graz Translations Studies, vol. 8 (2004)

6. Fleming, J.: How Should We Teach Deaf Learners? In: Kellett Bidoli, C.J., Ochse, E. (eds.) English in International Deaf Communication. Linguistic Insights. Studies in Language and Communication, pp. 123–153. Peter Lang – Europaeischer Verlag der Wissenschaften (2008)

7. Hilzensauer, M.: Teaching English to Deaf Adults: "SignOnOne" – An Online Course for Beginners. In: Miesenberger, K., Klaus, J., Zagler, W., Karshmer, A. (eds.) ICCHP 2010. LNCS, vol. 6180, pp. 185–192. Springer, Heidelberg (2010)

8. Berg, C., Cavanillas, J., Coello, E., Dotter, F., Eisenwort, B., Hilzensauer, M., Holzinger, D., Krammer, K., Krocza, J., van der Kuyl, T., Montandon, L., Rank, C., Roukens, H., Schoukstra, F., Skant, A.: SMILE – A Sign Language and Multimedia Based Interactive Language Course for Deaf for the Training of European Written Languages. Preparation for the New Millennium – Directions, Developments, and Delivery. Proceedings of the 16th International Conference on Technology and Education, Edinburgh, Scotland, March 28-31, pp. 188–190. International Conferences on Technology and Education Inc. (2000)

9. Prazak, B., Kopecky, D.: ELT – Electronic Learning Tool. The Development of an Online Multimedia Tool for German Written Language for Deaf and/or Hard-of-Hearing People. In: Pruski, A., Knops, H. (eds.) Assistive Technology – From Virtuality to Reality. Proceedings of the AAATE 2005 Conference, pp. 624–628. IOS Press (2005)

10. Hilzensauer, M., Skant, A.: SignOn! – English for Deaf Sign Language Users on the Internet. In: Kellett Bidoli, C.J., Ochse, E. (eds.) English in International Deaf Communication. Linguistic Insights. Studies in Language and Communication, pp. 155–177. Peter Lang – Europaeischer Verlag der Wissenschaften (2008)

11. Schumaker, P.F.: Fishing for English: Teaching Strategic Approaches to Learning English. In: Janáková, D. (ed.) Proceedings 2000. Teaching English to Deaf and Hard-of-Hearing Students at Secondary and Tertiary Levels of Education in the Czech Republic (2nd printing), pp. 144–147. Eurolex Bohemia (2005)

12. McGonigal, J.: Gaming Can Make a Better World (2010), http://www.ted.com/talks/jane_mcgonigal_gaming_can_make_a_better_world.html; Speech at the TED Conference (February 2010)

13. de Freitas, S.: Learning in Immersive Worlds. A Review of Game-Based Learning (2007), http://www.jisc.ac.uk/media/documents/programmes/elearninginnovation/gamingreport_v3.pdf

14. BASE – Basic Skills in English for Deaf Adults, http://www.base.gva.es/

15. DESIRE-Forschungsgruppe der RWTH-Aachen, http://www.vibelle.de/elearning/englisch/

SignAssess – Online Sign Language Training Assignments via the Browser, Desktop and Mobile

Christopher John

Digital Developer, University of Bristol Centre for Deaf Studies, Bristol, UK
edxcj@bristol.ac.uk

Abstract. SignAssess is a web-based e-learning resource for online sign language training assignments simultaneously accessible to desktop and mobile applications. SignAssess was developed to meet the sign language training industry need for an e-learning standard-based online video assignment solution compatible with Course Management Systems and not reliant on local user media recording or storage resources instead to include browser-based media recording and remote storage of content streamed to users on demand.

Keywords: E-learning, Sign language, Course Management System, Sign language interpreting.

1 What Is SignAssess?

SignAssess is an e-learning resource developed by University of Bristol Centre for Deaf Studies for online sign language training assignments as part of a structured CMS (Course Management System) learning programme simultaneously accessible to desktop and mobile applications.

SignAssess communicates with a media streaming and multiuser application server to provide video/audio streaming and real-time video encoding as a service of the resource. SignAssess includes an assignment builder interface, multiple video repositories, assignment analysis tools and pre-defined assignment types to support consecutive and simultaneous sign language interpreting assignments.

2 SignAssess Origins and Early Objectives

Development of SignAssess began in 2008 from a starting point of modernisation directly influenced by:

1. **The industry need for an online video assignment solution as a replacement for offline language lab installations or hard-media use.** No longer requiring a learner to physically attend a sign language learning class to submit an assignment, likewise allowing an educator to analyse and respond to assignments remotely.

K. Miesenberger et al. (Eds.): ICCHP 2012, Part II, LNCS 7383, pp. 253–260, 2012.

2. **The industry need for an e-learning standard-based online video assignment solution.** Benefitting from existing teaching and learning infrastructures through CMS compatibility.
3. **The industry need for an online video assignment solution that includes browser - based video/audio recording and remote storage as a service of the solution and not reliant on local recording or storage resources.**

3   Technical Platform

3.1   Client-Side

SignAssess client-side has been developed to use the Adobe Flash Player browser-based runtime making it accessible to Windows, Mac OS and Linux users.

The Adobe Flash Player runtime provides SignAssess access to peripheral resources such as a web camera or microphone and can communicate with external APIs and remote streaming services.

3.2   Server-Side

SignAssess server-side has been developed using Adobe Flash Media Interactive Server. SignAssess communicates with Adobe Flash Media Interactive Server for real-time capture, encoding, remote storage and subsequent delivery of video/audio content.

Required user knowledge of the capture process is minimal, SignAssess can access local camera and microphone resources and decide optimal recording quality using bandwidth detection, video/audio is then captured through the Adobe Flash Player runtime in the web browser.

3.3   Packaging and Delivery

SignAssess has been developed to adhere to the SCORM (Shareable Content Object Reference Model) 1.2 and 2004 (4th edition) specifications and is deployed as a Package Interchange File (.zip) inside a CMS.

SCORM is an industry standard model for interoperability and reusability of e-learning content. This means that SignAssess is interoperable between different models of CMS (SCORM supporting) and functions as a trackable CMS activity able to pass information between SignAssess and the CMS.

4   Product Development and Features

SignAssess development is an evolving iterative process rooted firmly in user-centered design. The requirements of the underlying technical platform were defined by the needs of industry professionals and core-functionality and individual features are developed with the involvement of educator and learner end users.

4.1   Speed of Use

The SignAssess interface is built for speed, rendering assignment submissions as collapsible navigable video galleries.

Fig. 1. SignAssess master video gallery

The user can move quickly between all assignment submissions or focus on an individual submission, opening an additional video gallery containing analysis or feedback content.

4.2   Self-correction, Feedback and Analysis Tools

SignAssess includes tools to allow the learner to review and self-correct an assignment submission against a model answer and time-based selection of content for feedback or analysis.

Educator or learner feedback/analysis content in video or text forms can be attached to the timeline of an assignment submission or stimulus material and accessed non-linearly across an extended timeline view.

Fig. 2. SignAssess extended timeline view

4.3   Asynchronous Video Messaging and Real-Time Display Updates

At runtime all online users of an individual SignAssess assignment share a connection to each other. This connection enables asynchronous video messaging between all connected users, messaging made visible by real-time display updates.

For example, an assignment submission from a learner will be immediately visible to the educator inside the same assignment object without the need for any form of interface refresh, likewise any assignment analysis or feedback between the educator and learner will also be visible in real-time to both users, useful for online live class training scenarios.

4.4   Assignment Builder

The assignment builder allows the user to configure an individual assignment when the resource is deployed in the CMS and not need to include assignment data in the SCORM resource package, reducing administrative workload and the training needs of end users.

Fig. 3. SignAssess assignment builder interface

4.5   Simultaneous and Consecutive Interpreting Assignment Types

The assignment builder includes pre-defined assignment types to support simultaneous and consecutive sign language interpreting exercises.

Fig. 4. SignAssess interpreting exercise

When a simultaneous interpreting assignment type is chosen an automatic sync between the live recording and the interpretation target stream is saved allowing synchronous playback of the two streams later, the interpreting target stream then remaining intact as an individual stream for re-use, in contrast to an over-dub technique when the live recording would be appended to the target stream.

When a consecutive interpreting assignment type is chosen the user can make multiple recordings which are automatically turned into a single assignment submission.

4.6   Multiple Repositories

SignAssess uses multiple repositories for different resolution video content, allowing the user to move seamlessly between different quality versions of assignment content without overloading CPU or memory use during recording.

Fig. 5. SignAssess media repository

Private or shared repositories can also be created allowing individual educators to control their own resources.

SignAssess includes support for MP3, MOV, MP4, FLV, F4V video and audio files and H264, On2VP6, Sorenson video codecs. SignAssess can display content in 4:3 and 16:9 aspect ratios and HD formats (Scaled down).

4.7   Variable Video Recording Sizes

SignAssess supports video recording at 320*240 and 640*480 resolutions.

Fig. 6. SignAssess video recording at 640*480 resolution

5   Accessibility by Desktop and Mobile Devices

SignAssess server-side technology (Flash Media Interactive Server) supports connections from non-browser-based software using Adobe AIR (Adobe Integrated Runtime), a cross-platform runtime for desktop and native mobile applications.

Adobe AIR provides the tools for SignAssess application deployment on desktop and mobile platforms, taking advantage of the technological and user benefits, popularity and distribution methods of each platform whilst maintaining a single server-side application structure.

5.1   SignAssess Desktop

The SignAssess Desktop application provides the user with an alternative to browser-based navigation of a CMS.

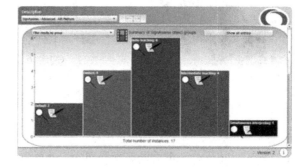

Fig. 7. SignAssess Desktop

The user can navigate seamlessly between all SignAssess assignments deployed inside a CMS without having to physically navigate the CMS using a web browser and HTTP. The alternative form of navigation enables the user to work more quickly and any updates made using SignAssess Desktop are visible in real-time in the corresponding assignments inside the CMS.

5.2   SignAssess Mobile

Using Adobe AIR native application packaging for iOS, Android and Blackberry operating systems we can provide the user with access to SignAssess content through an intelligent mobile app and not rely on a mobile device browser to render full SignAssess.

SignAssess Mobile is designed specifically for mobile devices with variable screen sizes and slower processors and supports actions such as multi-touch and gesture that are common to mobile apps.

Fig. 8. SignAssess Mobile rendering of a video gallery

6   SignAssess Future

6.1   Tighter CMS Integration

Adhering to the SCORM specification ensures interoperability between CMS models, however there is CMS database information outside of the SCORM specification that would be useful to use in SignAssess. For example obtaining the email address of the course lecturer and using it to generate email notifications. The next major version of SignAssess will include an optional module performing database inspection of the MOODLE (Modular Object-Orientated Dynamic Learning Environment) CMS.

6.2   External Repositories

YouTube is the world's largest video repository, the next major version of SignAssess will include the ability to search for and include YouTube content in assignments.

6.3   Technical Platform

The Adobe Flash Player runtime continues to offer higher PC market penetration (99%) over other runtimes [1], combined with support for Linux and Mac OS platforms, the runtime offers the best solution for widespread distribution of SignAssess for non-mobile browser-based users.

SignAssess was never developed to be reliant on Adobe Flash Player for sustainability across mobile platforms as a browser-based solution, although mobile devices supporting Flash 10.1 can use SignAssess. SignAssess Mobile development began in September 2010 using Adobe AIR to develop and package SignAssess as a native app across mobile app stores. SignAssess Mobile will continue to be developed using Adobe AIR and predates Adobe's decision to abandon its development of Flash Player for mobile platforms in favour of HTML5 and Adobe AIR [2].

References

1. Adobe Flash Platform runtimes, Millward Brown survey (July 2011), `http://www.adobe.com/products/flashplatformruntimes/statistics.html`
2. Adobe Featured Blogs, News, views and conversations, Flash to Focus on PC Browsing and Mobile Apps; Adobe to More Aggressively Contribute to HTML5, `http://blogs.adobe.com/conversations/2011/11/flash-focus.html`

Towards General Cross-Platform CCF Based Multi-modal Language Support

Mats Lundälv and Sandra Derbring

DART (Sahlgrenska Univ. Hospital), Göteborg, Sweden
Kruthusgatan 17, 411 04 Göteborg, Sweden
{mats.lundalv,sandra.derbring}@vgregion.se

Abstract. The AEGIS project aims to contribute a framework for, and building blocks for, an infrastructure for "open accessibility everywhere". One of many objectives has been to research, prototype and test freely available software services for inclusive graphical symbol support as part of mainstream ICT environments. Based on the Concept Coding Framework (CCF) technology, a "CCF-SymbolServer" has been developed. It can be installed locally on any of the major desktop platforms (GNU/Linux, MacOS X and Windows) to provide its multilingual and multi-modal representation services, or online to support many kinds of web services and networked mobile systems. The three current AEGIS applications will be presented: 1) CCF-SymbolWriter, an extension for symbol support in LibreOffice/OpenOffice Writer, 2) the new CCF supported version of Special Access to Windows (SAW6), 3) CCF-SymbolDroid, an AAC app for Android mobile devices. User evaluations and future perspectives will be discussed.

Keywords: AAC, AT, accessibility, graphical symbols, literacy, cognitive impairment, open-source.

1   Why AAC Is, and Should Be, Going Mainstream on Standard ICT Platforms

Until now, ICT support for individuals who need AAC has typically been provided in the form of dedicated software and/or devices. Although there will still be room for such, there are a growing number of reasons for a decisive move towards providing AAC functionality as part of standard mainstream ICT products:

- ICT products and services (such as smart-phones, tablets and mobile communication services) have rapidly become an integrated and often predominant part of everyday life, and acquire more general features (portability and usability combined with computing power for running full-featured multi-media apps, larger displays of excellent quality etc.) making them suitable and desirable for AAC needs. It is natural that both users and their environment expect and request that a wide range of needs, including the specific ones in the area of AAC and language support, should be well accommodated as part of these mainstream products.

K. Miesenberger et al. (Eds.): ICCHP 2012, Part II, LNCS 7383, pp. 261–268, 2012.

- Some previously special functions of Assistive Technology (AT), such as text-to-speech synthesis, are gradually becoming mainstream technology.
- A solid infrastructure of flexible multi-modal and multilingual language representation technology is needed for good AAC support. There are potentially substantial advantages of such an infrastructure going mainstream, both in terms of inclusion and participation, and in terms of cost and availability – in particular where resources are scarce. More and more parents, (pre-school) teachers and others discover that access to synthetic speech and a range of graphical symbol representations are great for most learners at some stages in early literacy development and early new language learning. This is particularly the case in multi-cultural and multilingual environments.

Some of this integration is now rapidly happening as AAC software is being developed for and/or migrated to mainstream mobile devices in the form of mobile "apps" (though generally still with more limited or specific functionality than traditional dedicated AAC applications and devices). Though this is primarily only integration on the mobile device level, the consequences are still expected to be profound by experts in the field [1]. However, AAC and symbol support within standard activities and services is still a major step to be taken. The Widgit products "Point" and "Insite" [2] are early examples of more integrated symbol support on the Web.

2   Preconditions for Inclusive AAC Support in Mainstream ICT

To allow AAC methodologies and ICT tools to go from special to mainstream, there is a need for an infrastructure for inclusive and integrated graphic symbol (and signing) representation of content and meaning in standard software environments. These infrastructural tools need to be based on open standards, be widely and freely available, and be multilingual and multi-modal so that more language representations may be added subsequently and in a distributed manner by local stake-holders. Components and tools need to be available to make it easy to provide the multi-modal support in a widening range of different services.

There are of course some more fundamental conditions and limitations that will create difficulties for AAC support in some environments and services. On the technical side, for example chat and messaging protocols are not supporting graphics. It is essential that a discussion is initiated around how such limitations may be overcome to allow future multi-modal communication also via these channels. There are different possible longer and shorter term ways to overcome these restrictions, such as: a) adding support for graphics in some of these standards, or; b) providing support for some graphic libraries packaged as private area Unicode fonts. This latter method is now successfully used in the AEGIS CCF development for LibreOffice/OpenOffice Writer (see below) [3], [6].

But the purely technical obstacles may not be the most difficult ones. We are facing major challenges in terms of attitudes, predominance of proprietary resources, and the lack of well established open standards and resources for multi-modal and multilingual vocabulary interoperability.

It will be a major task in the coming years to address these challenges in order to improve the preconditions for progress. We hope that the CCF based developments within the AEGIS project [3] may serve as a platform and inspiration for further European and international co-operation to this end. In addition to the European programs and the international standardisation bodies, it seems sensible to link such work to developing international frameworks like "Raising the Floor" and "GPII" (Global Public Inclusive Infrastructure) [4].

3   The AEGIS Project Developments

The AEGIS project's [3] overall goal is to contribute with vital elements of an infrastructure for "open accessibility everywhere". A wide range of user needs and technology platforms have been addressed. One of the many objectives has been to research, prototype and test freely available software components for inclusive graphical symbol support as part of mainstream environments to benefit people with communication, cognitive and multiple impairments. This has resulted in the development of a "graphical symbol server" based on the Concept Coding Framework (CCF) technology [5].

The "CCF-SymbolServer" is implemented in Java, and can provide multilingual and multi-modal representation services locally on any of the major desktop platforms; GNU/Linux, MacOS X and Windows. It can also run as an online webserver, to serve many kinds of web services and mobile devices (Fig. 1.).

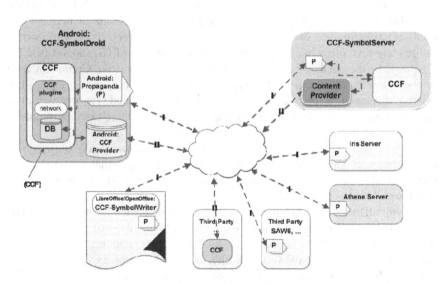

Fig. 1. The CCF-SymbolServer (top right) together with its current two major clients (CCF-SymbolWriter and CCF-SymbolDroid) and other existing (SAW 6) and potential interacting 3rd party software services.

Currently two symbol systems (Blissymbolics[6] and ARASAAC[7]) and four languages (English, Swedish, Spanish and Dutch) are supported, and the design is open to add more. A word in a given language can be sent to the CCF Server. The server will look up possible meanings or concepts in its databases, and return these as Concept IDs with available possible symbol representations. Fig. 2 below shows the Graphical User Interface (GUI) of the CCF-SymbolServer, installed and running locally on a desktop system. It is configured to support English together with Blissymbolics and ARASAAAC symbols, and has here received and looked up the word "horse". The concept information is displayed in a verbose format together with the found symbol representations. If the concept ID is known, the SymbolServer can directly return alternative representations in other languages and symbol systems.

Fig. 2. The CCF-SymbolServer's GUI window, running in a verbose configuration on a desktop system

Three applications interacting with the CCF-SymbolServer have been developed within AEGIS:

1. CCF-SymbolWriter, an extension for symbol support in LibreOffice/OpenOffice Writer[8]. It allows graphical symbol support for several kinds of needs: **a)** the needs of struggling text users to support and confirm comprehension while writing and reading text, often in combination with text-to-speech (TTS) support (see Fig. 3 below); **b)** the needs of AAC (Augmentative and Alternative Communication) symbol users to have access to full symbol representation (as far as possible) with symbols displayed on top of each word (see Fig. 4 – right nand side - below); **c)** the needs of helpers (parents, teachers, therapists etc.) to support users by preparing and presenting documents with graphic symbol support
2. A new CCF supported version of Special Access to Windows (SAW 6) [9], an advanced free and open-source on-screen-keyboard application that allows the creation of symbol selection charts for the control of any mainstream program on a Windows system
3. CCF-SymbolDroid, an AAC app for Android mobile devices, with the following functionality: **a)** Face-to-face AAC with graphic symbols, text and the system speech that is available on the device; **b)**AAC for indirect communication via messaging in several forms; **c)** Access to the full CCF vocabulary database via the online CCF-SymbolServer; **d)** Log in with user ID to access the online CCF-SymbolServer services - save, restore and share local set-ups via the server (the Iris and Ithene server services in Fig. 2. above); **e)** Integration with Tecla Access[10] for alternative input control

Here follows a somewhat more detailed presentation of these three applications.

3.1   The CCF-SymbolWriter Extension for LibreOffice Writer

CCF-SymbolWriter – is a free and open source software package for graphical symbol support in Libre/OpenOffice Writer on all its supported platforms. It consists of the locally installed CCF-SymbolServer and an extension for Writer, providing the option of graphic symbol representations of words contained in, or entered into, the document text. The key innovations of the CCF-SymbolWriter suite are; a) the application of the free and open source Concept Coding Framework technology for the provision of multilingual and multi-modal language support through graphic symbol representation in a standard and free office software environment on all major operating system platforms; and b) the underpinning CCF-SymbolServer technology allowing for future distributed application in other software, and for a growing range of languages and symbols and signs libraries to be added by different stake holders over time. Existing corresponding state of the art alternatives are all special proprietary software implementations, e.g. Widgit "SymWriter" and "Communicate: In Print" [2]. The intended uses of the CCF-SymbolWriter package are a) for users with cognitive difficulties and users who in general have problems in their interaction with text, to help with text production and text comprehension, by adding a graphic symbol representation modality (in addition to text only – and text-to-speech if available); b) for information providers who want to provide better access to text content for target users with the help of graphical symbol representation; c) for parents, teachers, assistants who need this as a tool to support users (from children to adult) in their literacy development; d) for 3rd party software and symbol library developers who want to use the CCF Symbol Server for allowing flexible graphical symbol support for a growing number of languages, symbol resources and software implementations.

More is found below about SAW 6 as a first 3rd party software implementation of the CCF symbol support done within AEGIS.

Fig. 3. LibreOffice Writer with the CCF-SymbolWriter extension in "View only" mode. The word currently in focus is looked up and displayed by the CCF-SymbolServer. Left; focus in the English, and rigth; focus in the Swedish section of a multi-language document.

Software installation downloads and preliminary end user documentation for CCF-SymbolWriter are found at:

http://dev.androtech.se/ooo/content.html.

The home of the full open source project release will be decided during the summer of 2012 – probably www.conceptcoding.org or/and at SourceForge.

3.2   SAW 6 – Special Access to Windows – with CCF Support

SAW6 – Special Access to Windows version 6 (with WindowCatcher) is a major update and merge of the two open-source applications SAW5 [9] and Window-Catcher, which provide a highly configurable and scriptable on-screen-keyboard (OSK) assistive tool for users with motor impairments, and for inspection and interaction with the UI of accessible target applications via the MSAA and UI-Automation accessibility APIs respectively.

SAW 6 is now upgraded to full compatibility with Windows 7, including the 64 bit version, and with full Unicode support. Dedicated language neutral word-prediction and abbreviation expansion has also been added, together with several other minor improvements since the SAW 5 version. SAW6 presents two key innovations:

- the integration of WindowCatcher, resulting in the to our knowledge first OSK in Windows capable of direct interaction with target applications via the MSAA and UI-Automation accessibility API:s [11]
- the added capability to interact with the CCF-SymbolServer, resulting in unique features for creating and maintaining multilingual and multi-modal symbol supported on-screen selection charts. Fig. 4 – left – below shows SAW 6 in set-up mode, interacting with the locally installed CCF-SymbolServer to look up symbols for the English word "angry". Symbol charts may later be semi-automatically translated between the supported languages and symbol representations.

This, among many other things, allows AAC symbol users to better interact with text based standard applications as well as with target applications that also make use of the CCF technology, such as LibreOffice Writer with the CCF-SymbolWriter extension.

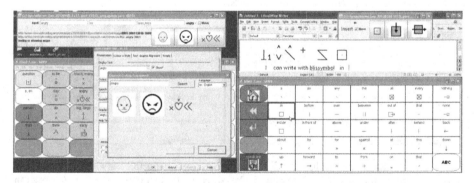

Fig. 4. These two screen captures show (left); SAW 6 in editing mode, retrieving symbol representations by word-to-concept-to-symbol lookup via the CCF-SymbolServer (shown on top), and (right); input of words from a SAW symbol selection chart into LibreOffice Writer with symbol insertion from the CCF-SymbolWriter extension in Symbol Insert mode

SAW6 will be available as free software, e.g. at www.oatsoft.org. It is expected to establish a new benchmark for free and open-source OSK solutions in general, and in some aspects for the OSK segment as a whole.

3.3   CCF-SymbolDroid – AAC App for Android Mobile Devices

CCF-SymbolDroid mobile AAC app enables the user to create symbol messages for direct person-to-person communication, or to communicate remotely via text messaging, email, and directly to other registered users via a dedicated webserver. It can make use of standard text-to-speech (TTS) installed on the device, and it will be compatible with the Tecla Access app and Tecla Shield hardware [10] for alternative input for persons with physical limitations (see example screen shots in Fig. 5 below.)

The CCF-SymbolDroid is, when this is written, a prototype version moving towards beta. A release version will be available on Android Market by summer 2012.

The key innovations of the CCF-SymbolDroid is that's it's a first mobile AAC app built on the multilingual and multi-modal CCF technology, that it's based on communication through standard communication channels such as network (TCP/IP) and SMS, and the possibility to synchronize and interact with an online CCF-SymbolServer. Features include sharing of symbol maps as well as individual settings which can be accessed via the cloud based the "CCF-SymbolCloud" services. The interchangeability between different symbol languages or natural languages is specific for the CCF technology. A section of the private Unicode range is also planned be used to map concept codes, so that they can be transmitted over any text channel.

Fig. 5. The **CCF-SymbolDroid** communicator app – 3 screens with ARASAAC and Blissymbols in runtime mode to the left, and in settings and editing mode to the right

Software installation downloads and preliminary end user documentation for CCF-SymbolDroid are found at

```
http://dev.androtech.se/ooo/content.html.
```

4   Conclusions

The longer term CCF perspectives include:

The work to integrate the CCF technology, as well as the graphic language of Blissymbolics, as part of the ISO TC 37 multi-modal terminology standards, has only been initiated within AEGIS. It will continue beyond the duration of the project.

The general maintenance of the CCF vocabulary resources is a long-term commitment to further refine of the support for the current languages and representational resources, and to subsequently add new ones.

The second pilot evaluation of the second alpha version clearly indicated that the innovative approach to provide multi-modal and multilingual language support as part of a standard office suite is fully feasible. The on-going third and final pilot testing will contribute further input for release versions of the CCF related software implementations of the AEGIS project. This will provide a new basic level support for access to text content, and a new and wider range of opportunities to communicate for people.

Acknowledgements. The development of the CCF_SymbolServer, with the CCF-SymbolWriter extension for LibreOffice/ OpenOffice Writer, the CCF symbol support in SAW 6, and the CCF-SymbolDroid AAC app on Android, have been made possible with the financial contribution of the European Commission in the context of the AEGIS project [3].

References

1. White Paper on Mobile Devices and Communication Apps from AAC-RERC (2011), http://aac-rerc.psu.edu/index.php/pages/show/id/46
2. Widgit, http://www.widgit.com/
3. AEGIS - Accessibility Everywhere: Groundwork, Infrastructure, Standards, http://www.aegis-project.eu/ co-financed by the European Commission's 7th FP
4. Raising the Floor, http://raisingthefloor.org/ and GPII, http://gpii.net/
5. Concept Coding Framework (CCF), http://www.oatsoft.org/Software/concept-coding-framework-ccf/
6. Lundälv, M., Derbring, S., Nordberg, L., Brännström, A., Farre, B.: Graphic Symbol Suppor. In: Open/LibreOffice Shaping Up - Graphic Symbol Server And Inline Symbol Font Display Based On The CCF, http://www.slideshare.net/aegisproject/conference-proceedings-2011-aegis-international-workshop-and-conference
7. Blissymbolics Communication International, http://www.blissymbolics.org/
8. ARASAAC, http://www.catedu.es/arasaac/
9. Special Access to Windows, http://www.oatsoft.org/Software/SpecialAccessToWindows
10. Tecla Access, http://scyp.idrc.ocad.ca/projects/tekla
11. Microsoft UI Automation (and MS Active Accessibility), http://en.wikipedia.org/wiki/Microsoft_UI_Automation

Developing an Augmentative Mobile Communication System

Juan Bautista Montalvá Colomer, María Fernanda Cabrera-Umpiérrez,
Silvia de los Ríos Pérez, Miguel Páramo del Castrillo,
and María Teresa Arredondo Waldmeyer

Life Supporting Technologies, Universidad Politécnica de Madrid, Av. Complutense 30,
28040 Madrid
{jmontalva,chiqui,srios,mparamo,mta}@lst.tfo.upm.es

Abstract. The widespread use of smartphones and the inclusion of new technologies as Near Field Communications (NFC) in the mobile devices offer a chance to turn the classic Augmentative and Alternative Communication (AAC) boards into Hi-Tech AAC systems with lower costs. This paper presents the development of an augmentative communication system based on Android mobile devices with NFC technology, named BOARD (Book Of Activities Regardless of Disabilities) that not only enables direct communication with voice synthesis, but also through SMS and expands the functionality of AAC systems allowing control of the smartphone and home appliances, all in a simple way just by bringing the phone next to the pictogram.

Keywords: AAC, mobile phone, NFC, assistive technology, smart home, cerebral palsy, ALS.

1   Introduction

An inquiry of the National Statistics Institute of Spain [1] shows that 74% of the Spanish population with disabilities (2,8 millions) suffers some kind of limitation performing daily basic activities (DBA), while about 1,39 million cannot perform DBA at all without the assistance of specialized personnel. In this context the most vulnerable people are those who, in addition to mobility problems, have speech and cognitive limitations. This is, for example, the case of people affected by cerebral palsy. AAC high-tech systems serve users with speech impairments to communicate their needs or even perform some of their DBA [2-3].

Nowadays, there are many high-tech augmentative and alternative communication systems to facilitate communication through the use of dedicated devices developed solely for AAC such as DynaVoxXpress [4], or non-dedicated devices such as generic computers that run additional software such as Gateway [5] or Minspeak [6].

These types of systems based on dedicated computer devices or software have several drawbacks, not because of the software solely but on the hardware requirements as well. On the one hand, these systems are hardly portable due to the requirements of

K. Miesenberger et al. (Eds.): ICCHP 2012, Part II, LNCS 7383, pp. 269–274, 2012.

using a monitor and a CPU, and cannot be carried where the user goes. They are intended to be used in the user's home. And although computers are smaller and there are screens and CPUs integrated such as a panel pc, there is the disadvantage that the batteries of these computers with built-in screen do not last more than a few hours and require power supply. One of the most important disadvantages is that these systems are also very expensive, especially when they are dedicated devices.

With the appearance in the market of smartphones and tablets, the devices size have been reduced and battery life has been improved with new possibilities for the development of augmentative and alternative communication based on these portable devices [7-8]. Also the prices have dropped for these devices as every 6 months there are new models reaching the market. Yet even today, the augmentative and alternative communication systems most used by users outside the home are the low tech communication boards due to their simplicity and ease of customization for each user [9].

2   Book of Activities Regardless of Disabilities (BOARD)

For these reasons we have developed a project combining: a low-tech communication board with a classic look which has Near Field Communication (NFC) tags [10] attached behind the pictographic symbols, and the accessible high-tech mobile software that can read the NFC tags in the communication board only approaching the mobile device [11]. The user uses the mobile as an extension of his hand to point to the different pictograms, receiving audible and visual feedback of what is happening in each moment. The mobile works like a magic wand with which the user can communicate, send messages, change the phone settings, and even control the house appliances. The project is called BOARD, Book Of Activities Regardless of Disabilities.

The BOARD system consists of two different parts:

- BOARD communication board: The BOARD communication board is a usable communication tool set of ordered cards enhanced by the attachment of formatted NFC tags matching an action. The cards are grouped by categories and each card contains a pictogram that consists on an image or symbol describing the programmed action, a text description and Braille printed etiquette. Behind every card, there is an NFC tag with an embedded action previously recorded.
- BOARD app over an NFC capable Android device: The device will act as a gateway between the actions to be performed and the BOARD communica-tion board itself. With the device, users can just read the smart tags ap-proaching the mobile to an image of the BOARD communication board and therefore, the device will trigger automatically the selected action reading aloud the action through the mobile Text To Speech engine.

Figure 1 shows an image of the actual BOARD communication board proto-type.

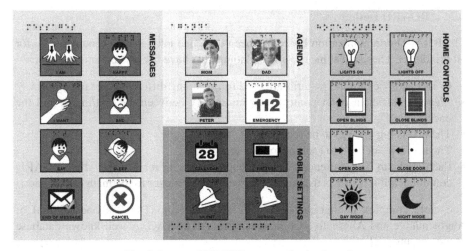

Fig. 1. Image of BOARD communication board

2.1   BOARD Functionalities

The BOARD communication board prototype is a sample of what the BOARD system and the NFC technology can do. In this case, there are four different categories as shown in Figure 1.

1. Messages category: The messages category combines the Text To Speech technology with the pictogram expression methods, allowing a user to concatenate different pictograms to form a sentence. This is the main communication area; here the users conforms his sentences. After making a sentence the user has the option to send a SMS with the sentence to a chosen destinatary on the contact category.
2. Contact category: A contact card contains a contact picture with a phone number (in normal or international format). The approach of the mobile device to one of the contacts will perform an automatic call to the specific selected person. For security reasons, this process has to be confirmed by the user just to avoid mistakes. If the previous interactions were related to pictogram and message sending, then the system will send an SMS to the target contact instead of performing a call.
3. Mobile settings: Within this category, the user can automatically perform tasks over its phone without having to know or navigate through the menus. In the prototype there were included samples of typical functionality. However, these functions can be customized to perform almost any kind of action in the device.
4. Home controls: The home controls are just another example of what the system can do. When the device has 3G or Wi-Fi connectivity, it can trigger actions over the appliances of a smart home.

2.2   BOARD Design

The BOARD communication board has been designed taking into account design for all principles. These are some recommendations that have been taken into account:

- Colors and background patterns are used for grouping different types of actions.
- There is sufficient color contrast and luminosity between the text/image and the background.
- The text is big enough to be read.
- The text is associated to each pictogram in a card.
- Each card can be substituted easily without needing to remake the whole BOARD communication board as the cards are glued with a sticker to the main card holder.

The more complex pictograms have been selected from The Aragonese Portal of Augmentative and Alternative Communication, ARASAAC. A well known database of pictograms [12].

The BOARD app has also been developed taking into account the accessibility guidelines WCAG 2.0, taking into account that it is an application for the mobile platform Android. Some of the recommendations followed are:

- All the actions performed provide visual feedback of the pictogram recognized.
- All the actions performed provide audible feedback when the TTS engine is enabled.

3   BOARD App

The BOARD application on the mobile phone, when started, shows a simple Graphical User Interface (GUI) interface. This application allows the users to record NFC

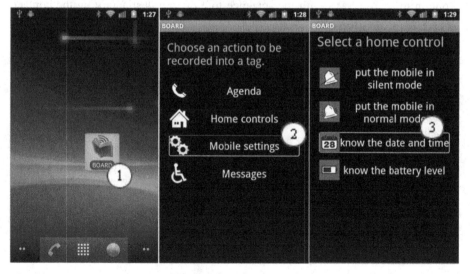

Fig. 2. BOARD app menu

tags with the desired functionality (see number 1 in Figure 2). The use is very simple. The user has to choose among the four categories (agenda, home controls, mobile settings and messages), (see number 2 in Figure 2). Once the user has decided the actions (see number 3 in Figure 2 and 4 and 5 in Figure 3), he has to click on the "Record" button and scan a tag (see number 6 in Figure 2). If the user makes a mistake, he can cancel the process or retry any step anytime. After pressing the "Record" button and scanning a tag, it will be automatically recorded and protected against second recordings. The next time the user scan it, it will perform the recorded action, without needing to open the application.

Fig. 3. BOARD app recording tags menu

4   Conclusions and Future Work

The BOARD prototype was successfully pre-tested with three different users by asking them to perform an exemplary task: composing and sending a SMS. The users; Silvia a 32 year old girl with cerebral palsy, Paco a 67 years man with Parkinson's Disease and Sergio an 18 year old with Down Syndrome were satisfied with the easiness of use of the application and the different actions that BOARD allows to perform.

The cost of each NFC tag is around 1€, depending on the amount of tags ordered. And the BOARD communication board can be easily customised and hand made. It only requires printing the pictograms and attaching to them a NFC tag, that can be recorded with a customised action using the BOARD app.

This shows that the BOARD approach is a much affordable system than the dedicated high-tech AAC system devices. This concept makes the BOARD an interactive high-tech AAC communication system fully customizable and scalable. The BOARD is a great tool and an assistive technology not only in-novative and useful for communicating purposes, but also a very easy tool for managing the mobile phone and control the house appliances.

After checking the potential of the prototype, the future work will cover two fields. 1) Expand the features and capabilities that the application BOARD can offer to the users. Increasing the number of programmable pictograms, and thus the lexicon to build messages and increasing the capabilities with which to interact with the mobile phone, for example, activate the camera. And 2) developing an evaluation with more users, where the system usability, and acceptability, among other parameters will be assessed.

References

1. Instituto Nacional de Estadística (INE): Encuesta de Discapacidad, Autonomía personal y situaciones de Dependencia (EDAD). National Institute of Statistics: Survey on Disabilities, Personal Autonomy and Dependency, Spain, November 4 (2008)
2. Reichle, J.: Evaluating Assistive Technology in the Education of Persons with Severe Disabilities. Journal of Behavioral Education, March 1 (2011) ISSN 1053-0819
3. Wadnerkar, M.B., Pirinen, T., Haines-Bazrafshan, R., Rodgers, J., James, D.: A single case study of a family-centred intervention with a young girl with cerebral palsy who is a multimodal communicator. Child: Care, Health and Development Journal 38(1), 87–97 (2012) ISSN 1365-2214
4. McAfoose, L.R.: Using AAC Device Features to Enhance Teenager's Quality of Life. Assistive Technology Outcomes and Benefits (2004) ISSN 1938-7261
5. Gateway software, http://www.gatewaytolanguageandlearning.com/AboutGateway.html (last checked March 31, 2012)
6. van der Merwe, E., Alant, E.: Associations with Minspeak™ icons. Journal of Communication Disorders 37(3), 255–274 (2004) ISSN 0021-9924
7. Higginbotham, J., Jacobs, S.: The Future of the Android Operating System for Augmentative and Alternative Communication. Perspectives on Augmentative and Alternative Communication 20(2), 52–56 (2011) ISSN 1940-7483
8. Hershberger, D.: Mobile Technology and AAC Apps From an AAC Developer's Perspective. Perspectives on Augmentative and Alternative Communication 20(1), 28–33 (2011) ISSN 1940-7483
9. Baxter, C.S., Enderby, P., Evans, P., Judge, S.: Barriers and facilitators to the use of high-technology augmentative and alternative communication devices: a systematic review and qualitative synthesis. International Journal of Language & Communication Disorders 47(2), 115–129 (2012) ISSN 1460-6984
10. Al-Ofeishat, H.A., Al Rababah, M.A.A.: Near Field Communication (NFC). IJCSNS International Journal of Computer Science and Network Security 12(2) (February 2012) ISSN 1738-7906
11. Pyykkönen, M., Riekki, J., Alakärppä, I., Sanchez, I., Cortes, M., Saukkonen, S.: Designing Tangible User Interfaces for NFC Phones. Advances in Human-Computer Interaction 2012, 12 pages (2012) ISSN 1687-5907
12. The Aragonese Portal of Augmentative and Alternative Communication, http://www.catedu.es/arasaac/ (last checked March 31, 2012)

The Korean Web-Based AAC Board Making System

Saerom Choi[1], Heeyeon Lee[2], and Ki-Hyung Hong[1]

[1] Department of Computer Science, Sungshin University, Seoul, S. Korea
{saeromi.choi,kihyung.hong}@gmail.com
[2] Center for QoLT(Quality of Life Technology), Seoul National University, Seoul, S. Korea
heeyeonlee@hotmail.com

Abstract. The purpose of this study was to develop a Korean web-based customized AAC board making system that is easily accessible and compatible across devices in Korean cultural/linguistic contexts. Potential users of this system are individuals with communication disorders and their parents/teachers. Board making users can make customized symbol boards using either built-in or customized symbols. The AAC users can access their own AAC page generated by personalized AAC page application using any devices only if they can access to a web-browser. We expect that this system plays a role for Korean AAC users to generate customized AAC boards on the web and to use the boards in meaningful environments to meet their unique communication needs.

Keywords: Accessibility, Augmentative and Alternative Communication, Board Making, Web-Based System.

1   Introduction

The users of Augmentative and Alternative Communication (AAC) devices use different types and levels of communication tools based on their current level of communication abilities [1]. At the beginning, AAC users may start with simple communication boards printed as a paper-copy. As their communication abilities using AAC have improved, they may need more complicated and dynamic AAC boards with a speech output. Using a web-based customized AAC board making system, AAC users can enhance their communication abilities by adapting and expanding their symbolic vocabularies using a variety of customized boards across settings. Many AAC devices currently used in Korea are hardware-based, so accessibility, extensibility, and portability of the devices are limited. The web-based AAC board making system makes it possible for AAC users to create communication boards using any devices, anytime anywhere only if they can access to a web-browser.

2   Related Works

One of the popular AAC board making systems is Boardmaker(Mayer-Johnson) [2]. It provides a web-based version of Boardmaker called as Print Editor, and it also

K. Miesenberger et al. (Eds.): ICCHP 2012, Part II, LNCS 7383, pp. 275–278, 2012.

provides the users an internet community called as Boardmakershare.com in order to help them to share their customized boards. However, Print Editor is not available on the mobile web-browser because it uses Adobe Flash working on the plug-in based web-browser. In addition, the primary functions of Print Editor are limited to edit, save and print published boards, and it does not support the voice output function which is an essential part of effective functional communication trainings [3]. The other popular web-based AAC board making system is AAC Cloud of Alexicom Tech [4]. After the users log in the Alexicom web system, they can manage their persona-lized boards by making and editing the boards on the web. Alexicom AAC supports twenty voices and five languages (English, Spanish, German, Italian, and French) using AT&T Natural Sounding Voices [5]. However, Alexicom AAC does not sup-port Korean, and it is complicated to search and reuse individual symbols since there is no symbol-level search feature. It is also difficult to manage users and to classify symbols in Alexicom AAC.

3   System Implementation

As the population of individuals with disabilities has been steadily increased in Korea, the characteristics of individuals with disabilities have also been varied and compli-cated. However, there has been little effort to develop Korean AAC systems in both hardware and software, and no web-based AAC system is currently available in Ko-rea. Thus, there are strong needs to develop AAC devices that are easily accessible and compatible across devices and contexts, and to develop customize AAC symbol boards with voice outputs appropriate to each AAC user's unique communication needs, disability characteristics, and cultural/linguistic environments [6, 7].

We developed a web-based customized AAC board making system to compensate the limitations of current AAC systems and it has the following advantages: (1) it is independent on the client's environment, so the users can easily access to the web-based AAC board making system using any device only if they can access to a web-browser without any extra hardware, (2) it compensates the limitations of current web-based board making systems by supporting the voice output function and by not using Adobe Flash, and (3) it provides symbols/words that are appropriate to Korean cultural/linguistic contexts. Its database contains more than 3,000 Korean symbolic vocabularies developed by Ewha Womans University in Seoul, Korea in order to meet the unique communication needs of Korean users [8].

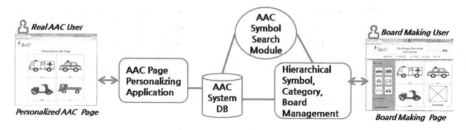

Fig. 1. Components of the Korean web-based AAC board making system

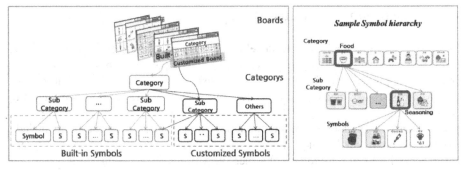

Fig. 2. AAC Symbol Data Model

We implemented the Korean AAC board making system on Tomcat (a web application container) and MySQL as a backend database system. We used a TTS (Text-to-speech) engine to generate a sound for each AAC symbol on AAC boards. Figure 1 shows the major components of the system.

- *AAC Users:* There are two types of users: board making users such as teachers and parents who make AAC boards for their students and children, and real AAC users who actually communicate using the AAC boards customized by their teachers/parents.
- *Hierarchical Symbol/Category/Board Management:* Figure 2 shows the data model for AAC symbol database of the board making system. The basic unit of AAC boards is the AAC symbol that consists of its graphical symbol or image, a text label, a tag (a keyword for searching), and a sound generated by TTS. The system provides a set of built-in symbols. Board making users can make customized symbol boards for individuals with diverse disabilities. A category is a group of related built-in and/or customized symbols. The system predefines a set of built-in categories, and board making users can create new customized categories. An AAC board is a collection of symbols that can be used as a paper-copy or as a graphic display with a voice output. Board making users can create a customized board for a specific user from the scratch or using a built-in board by editing them. They can also select a board layout and arrange the symbols on the board at their convenience. The users can save, search, and edit the customized symbol boards whenever they need through their board lists or recent board-making history.
- *AAC page personalizing application:* Real AAC users can access their own AAC page generated by personalized AAC page application. Personalized AAC pages may include a simple 2-cell board, a more complicated 16-cell board, or a multiple board according to each user's communication level.
- *AAC symbol search*: The AAC board making users can search and select symbols in the AAC symbol database. The search can be done by navigating the category hierarchy or by typing text keywords. In the AAC symbol database, we developed an index for keyword searching. In addition to all built-in symbols, the search space for a user includes his/her own customized symbols.

4   Conclusion and Future Work

The purpose of this study was to develop the Korean web-based customized AAC board making system that is easily accessible and compatible across various devices and that is appropriate to Korean cultural/linguistic contexts. We expect that the Korean web-based AAC board making system plays a role for Korean users to generate customized AAC boards on the web and to use the boards in meaningful environments to meet their unique communication needs. It is planned to include more symbolic vocabulary lists in this web-based AAC board making system to enhance accessibility and usefulness. Further study needs to be conducted to get actual users' feedback on the user interface of this system through a user-centered usability testing.

Acknowledgments. This work was supported by the R&D program [10036438, Development of Speech Synthesizer and AAC software for the visually and vocally impaired] and by the Technology Innovation Program [100036459, Development of center to support QoLT industry and infrastructures] funded by the MKE/KEIT, Korea.

References

1. Beukelman, D.R., Mirenda, P.: Augmentative and Alternative Communication: Supporting Children and Adults with Complex Communication Needs, 3rd edn. Bookes Publishing. Co. (2006)
2. Boardmaker, http://www.boardmakershare.com, (last visited on Monday, January 29, 2012)
3. Schlosser, R.W.: Roles of Speech Output in Augmentative and Alternative Communication: Narrtive Review. Augmentative and Alternative Communication 19(1), 5–27 (2003)
4. Alexicom AAC Cloud, http://www.alexicomaac.com (last visited on Monday, January 29, 2012)
5. Park, H.S.: An Overview of an Augmentative-Alternative Communication-AAC System. The Korean Journal of the Human Development 23(1), 25–46 (1995) (in Korean)
6. Kim, J.Y., Park, E.H., Kim, K.Y.: Preliminary Study regarding Voice Output Communication Content and System Development. The Journal of Special Education: Theory and Practice 11(4), 345–374 (2010) (in Korean)
7. Park, E.H., Lee, J.E.: A Study of Developing Web-based Augmentative and Alternative Communication Tool. The Journal of Special Education 35(3), 17–43 (2000) (in Korean)
8. Lim, J.H., Park, E.H.: The Effects of Tablet PC Based AAC Intervention with the Inclusive Classroom. The Journal of Special Education 46(2), 85–106 (2011) (in Korean)

SymbolChat: Picture-Based Communication Platform for Users with Intellectual Disabilities

Tuuli Keskinen[1], Tomi Heimonen[1], Markku Turunen[1],
Juha-Pekka Rajaniemi[1], and Sami Kauppinen[2]

[1] TAUCHI, University of Tampere
Kanslerinrinne 1, FI-33014 University of Tampere, Finland
firstname.surname@sis.uta.fi
[2] Laurea University of Applied Sciences
Vanha Maantie 9, FI-02650 Espoo, Finland
sami.kauppinen@laurea.fi

Abstract. We introduce a multimodal picture-based communication platform for users with intellectual disabilities, and results from our user evaluation carried out with the target user group representatives and their assistants. Our current prototype is based on touchscreen input and symbol and text-to-speech output, but supports also mouse and keyboard interaction. The prototype was evaluated in a field study with the help of nine users with varying degrees of intellectual and motor disabilities. Based on our findings, the picture-based approach and our application, SymbolChat, show great potential in providing a tool for users with intellectual disabilities to communicate with other people over the Internet, even without prior knowledge of symbols. The findings highlighted a number of potential improvements to the system, including providing even more input methods for users with physical disabilities, and functionality to support the development of younger users, who are still learning vocabulary and developing their abilities.

Keywords: symbol communication, instant messaging, accessibility.

1   Introduction

Information and communication technology (ICT) solutions offer possibilities to enhance the quality of life for people with cognitive disabilities, by activating them intellectually and physically, and by providing communication methods that help reduce social isolation [5]. Cognitive disabilities affect the capacity to think. These disabilities cover a wide spectrum from mental retardation and learning disabilities to changes in cognitive ability caused by brain injury and various neurodegenerative diseases. Cognitive disabilities pose challenges and limitations for interpersonal communication beyond speech and expressive methods such as signing because accessing textual information is difficult [4]. Often the use of graphic representation is the only possible means of written communication [7]. This symbol-based communication can take

K. Miesenberger et al. (Eds.): ICCHP 2012, Part II, LNCS 7383, pp. 279–286, 2012.
© Springer-Verlag Berlin Heidelberg 2012

many forms, from selecting pictures from picture folders to using specialized communication devices or computer software.

One of the challenges for communication is that people with intellectual disabilities currently lack accessible, real-time distance communication tools. Although there are several face-to-face communication applications available for users with special needs, most instant messaging clients are inaccessible for this user group: they are too complex and require reading and writing skills. To overcome these problems, we created an accessible tool for people with intellectual disabilities to communicate in real-time over distance that can be easily adapted for each individual user.

This paper presents SymbolChat, a software platform that supports the creation of personalized multimodal instant messaging applications over the Internet. End users and their support personnel can customize the input and output features of the application based on the user's individual needs. We report results from a field study of SymbolChat, carried out with nine users with varying degrees of intellectual disabilities. Our participants were able to express themselves in basic, day-to-day communication with the assistance of their caregivers using picture-based vocabulary, even without prior training in the use of symbol languages. Several future development issues were also identified.

The rest of the paper is organized as follows. First, we introduce the SymbolChat application, and related work. Then we describe the conducted user evaluation with target user group representatives. Finally, we present our results and discuss the findings.

2   The SymbolChat Application

The SymbolChat application was designed in close co-operation between professionals working with intellectually disabled people and researchers of interactive technology. The design is based on end users' needs, context of use and activities. Initial prototypes of SymbolChat were tested by users with intellectual disabilities and their assistants.

SymbolChat is a client-server application based on touchscreen PC computers in the client end. SymbolChat interface (Fig. 1) is organized into three main sections:

1. *The message history* view shows the sent and received messages either as symbols or text according to the selected output method, and a list of participants' names and pictures. Messages are read out loud once using text-to-speech (if enabled), and they can be replayed using the button in front of each message.
2. *The symbol input view* provides functionality for composing, previewing and sending messages. Messages can be played back before sending them. Symbols can be selected either from the symbol grid or from the message history view. If all the symbols in a category cannot fit in the symbol grid, they are distributed on several "pages" represented as folder icons. The symbols have been given a binary priority value, with higher priority symbols being listed at the start of the symbol grid.

3. *The symbol category view* shows a list of available symbol categories. Selecting a category (or subcategory) updates the symbol input view accordingly. Navigation up in the category hierarchy is possible using the Back button.

The current version of SymbolChat uses a set of about two thousand Picture Communication Symbols (PCS) . The used symbols were selected by professional speech and other therapists. The symbols are divided into a customizable Quick Menu category and seven main categories (e.g., People, Verbs and Nouns), which include up to 11 subcategories, and are distinguished also by color.

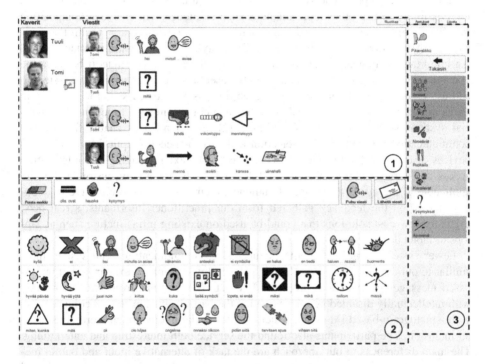

Fig. 1. The Finnish version of the SymbolChat user interface and an example discussion between two participants

The application supports several input and output methods. The current version is designed for graphical symbols and speech output, with touch input on large touchscreens. Text output, mouse interaction and keyboard input are also available for literate users. Users can customize the interaction methods depending on their preferences and abilities. Touch input was selected as the primary input modality in order to provide an interaction method as easy as possible for users with limited computer skills [3] and users who have fine motor disabilities.

The input and output methods can be changed during the usage of SymbolChat. The settings also include controls for the text-to-speech functionality (e.g. speech synthesis rate) and the size of the symbols. Being able to modify the size of the symbols helps the users with fine motor disabilities or visual impairments.

3   Related Work

Picture-based communication systems are a form of augmentative and alternative communication (AAC) technology that is based on the use of graphics, such as drawings, pictograms and symbols [7]. AAC research prototypes and commercial applications exist both for collocated and remote picture-based communication.

Image-Oriented Communication Aid [6] is a system for preliterate users with speech and motor impairments who require assistance in the form of image-based communication support. The system is used with a touchscreen tablet computer, with the possibility to use other input methods such as mouse. The message composition interface is organized as a two-dimensional canvas, intended to assist with the difficulties AAC users have with the standard linear style of concatenating syntactic units. An important finding suggested by the authors is the need for a tradeoff between the vocabulary size and cognitive demands on the user. The need for scaling the system to address changing needs and developing abilities is also discussed, for example in terms of symbol complexity, vocabulary size and communicative functions. Commercial systems such as the DynaVox family [2] are intended to enable face-to-face communication through symbol selection and text-to-speech output. More advanced devices also allow for the use of Web, email and text messaging for information access and remote communication. While such tools are highly customizable and applicable to the needs of the target audience, their cost can be prohibitive to adoption. Based on the feedback gathered from our practitioner informants, a real need exists for low-cost solutions that could be used on existing infrastructure such as laptops or tablet devices with touchscreens.

Fewer systems exist for remote picture-based communication. The system most similar to ours is the Messenger Visual [11]. It allows people to exchange pictogram-based messages in real time across the Internet. The findings from their user study with intellectually disabled people show that the participants are able to communicate with a pictogram-based IM client, which enables social interaction and promotes digital inclusion. The participants also found the service both interesting and entertaining. The main differences to our approach are the lack of alternative input and output methods (e.g., text-to-speech and touchscreen). Zlango [12] is a commercial Web and mobile service for icon-based messaging that allows users to generate icon-based messages that can be shared on the Web, email and on social media sites such as blogs. Although the main target user group of the service is not people with intellectual disabilities, it is to our knowledge one of few primarily image-based commercial Web-based communication services.

4   Evaluation

We evaluated SymbolChat with nine male participants aged 14–37 (median = 26 years) and the level of their intellectual disability varied from low to high, except for one participant who had severe speech and physical disabilities but no intellectual disability. Only two participants had prior experience on symbol languages. The evaluation consisted of four evaluation weeks, each week having a group of two to three participants communicating with each other using SymbolChat in three separate sessions. The caregivers were present throughout the evaluation to assist the participants, and the communication with the participants was also done by the familiar caregivers, so that the participants would feel as comfortable as possible.

Data from the evaluation were collected with interviews, subjective feedback questionnaires, informal walkthrough [9] and observation. In addition to the open questions, four questions concerning the participants' experiences were elicited using a modified version of the Smileyometer [8], which is an emotional Likert scale originally designed for children (see the cards in Fig. 2 for our version).

We were also interested in comparing user expectations before the use and experiences after the use. This was done by using a subjective evaluation method SUXES [10] adapted to suit these users and this context. The main difference to the typical procedure was to use the participants' caregivers as the primary informants regarding the expectations and experiences [1]. They had built rapport with the participants over time and were able to comment on what they perceived to be the participants' experiences. Additionally, they were able to provide insights into the applicability of SymbolChat for our participants' communication needs in the present and in the future.

5   Results and Discussion

Results from the participants' subjective experiences can be seen in Fig. 2. Although the users considered the communication to be quite hard (median = 2), they clearly indicated that it was fun (median = 4.5) and they would like to communicate this way again (median = 4).

As people with intellectual disabilities may easily lack motivation to communicate, it shows great potential for the symbol-based approach and SymbolChat that the participants consider it fun and would like to use it again. Although the actual speed of the communication was somewhat slow, the participants, interestingly and positively, rated communication to be fast. It is noteworthy that the median results in Fig. 2 include answers from only one participant with prior knowledge on symbols. This is very encouraging, as it shows that the approach adopted in SymbolChat was able to

Fig. 2. The smiley face cards based on Smileyometer [8] and participants' subjective experiences (median values, due to missing data n=6)

provide a positive experience to users with limited practice with and understanding of symbol communication. We believe that the reason for the stated difficulties is also linked to the lack of experience with symbol-based communication. As the users were unfamiliar with the structuring and content of the symbol set, finding appropriate symbols for message construction was time-consuming.

The results from the adapted SUXES questionnaires [10] show that the expectations were met almost on all nine statements (see Fig. 3). The use of the SymbolChat application was reported to be more natural than expected. Despite the high expectations on usefulness, the experiences met these expectations. Before the use of SymbolChat, the assistants reported that the participants would most likely want to use the application again, and also highly rated expectations were met. Even the lowest rated experiences reached at least a neutral level, which can be considered a positive sign. As with the participants' subjective experiences, these ratings related to the speed, clarity and error-free use and functioning of the interface are likely related to the symbol set and its presentation. We believe that training on symbol-based communication and the use of personalized symbol sets could overcome these difficulties.

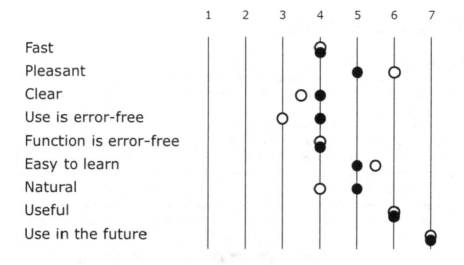

Fig. 3. Expectations and experiences: white circles represent the expectations (n=6); black circles represent experiences (n=7) (median values, due to missing data the n varies)

In general, our results show that social inclusion for people with intellectual disabilities can be improved with simple instant messaging tools that can be adapted to the individuals' personal requirements. Many of our participants had physical, visual, hearing, speech and behavioral disabilities. The results show that they can benefit from alternative input and output methods, and even more input methods should be developed for users with more severe physical and motor disabilities. Finally, since most of our test participants were not symbol users, the results suggest that people with intellectual disabilities can learn to communicate in an assisted manner with symbols even without prior formal training in their use.

A review of the evaluation sessions with AAC professionals revealed several avenues for future work. Our AAC experts noted that SymbolChat could foster the learning of more independent communication and social skills. For younger individuals, who are still on the way of developing such skills and finding the right tools for enabling this development, SymbolChat could provide, for example, cues to respond to incoming messages that facilitate the learning of turn-taking, and functionality for enlarging the symbol set based on the progress of the individual. For more settled users, whose abilities are not developing constantly anymore, SymbolChat could provide a more static tool for communicating and learning communication by having a fixed set of symbols tailored to the abilities of the individual.

Looking back, the experimental design in our research may have been a little too challenging – both from researchers' and participants' point of view. Conducting evaluations with this kind of special user group does not only concern the participants and the researchers, but also assistants and other stakeholders. Thus, recruiting participants is challenging, and considering the varying individual abilities and limitations of the few participants, finding "matching" communication parties even more difficult. People with intellectual disabilities may lack motivation to engage in such com-munication scenarios, and the variety in communication skills and vocabulary be-tween the parties most probably does not decrease this issue. Another issue may be that the conversation partner is not known well and simply does not feel like an interesting communication partner. As a conclusion, it might have been more beneficial to design the evaluation so that the participants with intellectual disabilities would have communicated with caregivers, relatives or friends who are familiar with the abilities, needs and desires of the participants. As our goal with the SymbolChat was to provide a tool for users with intellectual disabilities for communicating – not only with other people with intellectual disabilities, but with anyone they like – it is possible that this first stage evaluation would have provided more insights to the actual potential of the SymbolChat approach had the communication parties not been limited to the target user group representatives only.

6   Conclusion

We have presented a picture-based remote communication tool for users with intellectual disabilities, and findings from our user evaluation with the target user group representatives. Based on the results, it can be concluded that the SymbolChat platform forms a solid basis for further improvements and new symbol-based communication services, such as participation in social media.

At the moment we are developing an application version for tablet devices. This will enable a reasonably priced mobile option for communicating while still achieving the benefits of touch input, large screen and speech synthesis. In addition to people with intellectual impairments, symbol-based mobile communication could be used to enable affordable access to information services for illiterate users in developing countries.

Acknowledgements. This work was part of Eureka/ITEA2 programme, and it was supported by the European Commission and Tekes – the Finnish Funding Agency for Technology and Innovation in the "Do it Yourself Smart Experiences" project ("DiYSE"). We would like to thank Tuula Kotimäki, Maija Rimpiläinen and the Rinnekoti Foundation for their assistance with the design and evaluation efforts.

The PCS symbols are copyrighted and were used with permission: The Picture Communication Symbols ©1981-2011 by DynaVox Mayer-Johnson LLC. All Rights Reserved Worldwide. Used with permission.

References

1. Allen, M., Leung, R., McGrenere, J., Purves, B.: Involving Domain Experts in Assistive Technology Research. Univers. Access Inf. Soc. 7(3), 145–154 (2008)
2. DynaVox, http://www.dynavoxtech.com
3. Holzinger, A.: Finger Instead of Mouse: Touch Screens as a Means of Enhancing Universal Access. In: Carbonell, N., Stephanidis, C. (eds.) UI4ALL 2002. LNCS, vol. 2615, pp. 387–397. Springer, Heidelberg (2003)
4. Lewis, C.: HCI for people with cognitive disabilities. SIGACCESS Access. Comput. 83, 12–17 (2005)
5. Newell, A.F., Carmichael, A., Gregor, P., Alm, N.: Information technology for cognitive support. In: Jacko, J.A., Sears, A. (eds.) The Human-Computer Interaction Handbook, pp. 464–481. L. Erlbaum Associates Inc., Hillsdale (2002)
6. Patel, R., Pilato, S., Roy, D.: Beyond Linear Syntax: An Image-Oriented Communication Aid. Journal of Assistive Technology Outcomes and Benefits 1(1), 57–66 (2004)
7. Poulson, D., Nicolle, C.: Making the Internet accessible for people with cognitive and communication Impairments. Univers. Access Inf. Soc. 3(1), 48–56 (2004)
8. Read, J.C., MacFarlane, S.J., Casey, C.: Endurability, Engagement and Expectations: Measuring Children's Fun. In: Proceedings of Interaction Design and Children, Eindhoven, The Netherlands, August 28–29, pp. 189–198. Shaker Publishing (2002)
9. Riihiaho, S.: User testing when test tasks are not appropriate. In: Norros, L., Koskinen, H., Salo, L., Savioja, P. (eds.) European Conference on Cognitive Ergonomics: Designing beyond the Product — Understanding Activity and User Experience in Ubiquitous Environments (ECCE 2009), Article 21, 9 pages. VTT Technical Research Centre of Finland, Finland (2009)
10. Turunen, M., Hakulinen, J., Melto, A., Heimonen, T., Laivo, T., Hella, J.: SUXES – User Experience Evaluation Method for Spoken and Multimodal Interaction. In: Proceedings of Interspeech, Brighton, United Kingdom, September 6–10, pp. 2567–2570 (2009)
11. Tuset, P., López, J.M., Barberán, P., Janer, L., Cervelló-Pastor, C.: Designing Messenger Visual, an Instant Messaging Service for Individuals with Cognitive Disability. In: Bravo, J., Hervás, R., Villarreal, V. (eds.) IWAAL 2011. LNCS, vol. 6693, pp. 57–64. Springer, Heidelberg (2011)
12. Zlango, http://www.zlango.com

Developing AAC Message Generating Training System Based on Core Vocabulary Approach

Ming-Chung Chen[1], Cheng-Chien Chen[1], Chien-Chuan Ko[2],
Hwa-Pey Wang[3], and Shao-Wun Chen[1]

[1] Department of Special Education, National Chiayi University
300 Syuefu Rd., Chiayi, 600 Taiwan, R.O.C.
{mtchen,chcc,s0963123}@mail.ncyu.edu.tw
[2] Department of Computer Science and Information Engineering, National Chiayi University
300 Syuefu Rd., Chiayi, Taiwan
kocc@mail.ncyu.edu.tw
[3] Graduate Institute of Rehabilitation Counseling, National Taiwan Normal University
162, Sec. 1 Hoping East Rd., Taipei, Taiwan
hpwang@mail.aide.gov.tw

Abstract. Alphabetical-based message generating method is one of the essential features for an augmentative and alternative communication (AAC) system, although it is not the most efficient method. For the Mandarin Chinese AAC users, Chinese text entry is very important if they are expected to say what they want to say. However, a user is required to assemble specific keys to generate a Chinese character. Users need to learn a specific text entry method before they could generate any Chinese character. This study aims to develop a web-based training system which comprises the core Chinese characters to assist the individual with disabilities to learn to generate Mandarin Chinese message more efficiently. This study conducted a usability evaluation to exam the system. In addition this paper also recruited children with learning disabilities and mental retardation to test the training system.

Keywords: augmentative and alternative communication, Mandarin Chinese, core vocabulary.

1   Introduction

Augmentative and alternative communication (AAC) is to provide interventions that will optimize expressive communication, both spoken and written, for individuals with complex communication needs [1]. The ability "to say what you want to as fast as possible" or to generate rapid, spontaneous, novel utterances is valued by individuals who rely on AAC [2]. Single-meaning picture, alphabetic, and sematic compaction are three major methods to generate message for AAC devices [2]. Each abovementioned method has his contribution to assist the persons with severe communication disorders to express their thought. When the single-meaning picture and sematic compaction methods could generate message more rapidly, the alphabetic method is

K. Miesenberger et al. (Eds.): ICCHP 2012, Part II, LNCS 7383, pp. 287–294, 2012.

the only method to produce whatever the persons with severe communication disorder want to say because of its small number of symbols and the capability to generate endless messages.

With the rapid development of information technology, more and more AAC devices are computerized. Not only increasing the message storage, the computerized AAC devices also embed various keyboarding systems to allow the AAC users to generate whatever they want to say. Some devices comprise different keyboarding layouts, from traditional QWERTY keyboard layout to alphabetic order layout, and word prediction methods.

In addition to oral expression, communication on the Internet through text message also has become more important in the digital society. Computerized AAC device also built-in WiFi capabilities and word processor, such as Essence PRO (http://store.prentrom.com/). Therefore, keyboarding becomes one of the essential methods to generate messages for both oral and text communication.

Different from the spelling system, Chinese text entry system requires combining some keys to generate a Chinese charter. It also could be regarded as a kind of coding system. A user should learn a specific method to generate a Chinese character based on a specific rule. These methods can be grouped into two types [3]. One is phonetic-coding input; and another is pattern-coding input. Phonetic-coding input requires a typist to press Zhyinor Hanyuphonitic symbols to generate homonyms, while the pattern-coding input a typist input codes of disassembled basic character patterns, such as the Changjay or Dayi pattern coding, to produce a corresponding Chinese character.

Many kinds of Chinese text entry methods are built in Windows system already. However, the issue is how to be familiar with a kind of text entry method. Chinese text entry system, as abovementioned, is similar with coding system in English. Morse code, for example, requires a user to learn the codes for each English character before he/she could generate a character correctly even he/she know a character very well.

Therefore, an AAC user or potential user must learn a specific text entry method. Without a text entry method, he/she could not be a real communicator even an advanced AAC device is equipped. There are two issues an AAC clinical professionals will face when teaching an AAC user or potential user to learn a specific text entry method. One is which method should be taught because of so many text entry methods available; the other one is what characters should be learned, because there are thousands of Chinese characters used for communication. Some studies explored the effect of teaching the students with disabilities to learn a kind of the text entry methods (e.g. [3],[4]). The studies demonstrated the positive effectiveness of learning text entry, but no training material was developed systematically. For example, Chen and his colleagues (2002) only used 120 Chinese characters which were developed for a specific text entry method as training material [3]. Therefore, the AAC clinical professionals need a proper text entry learning system to train the AAC users or potential users to learn a kind of text entry method that serves as a message generating method in AAC system.

As a good message generator, a person should be familiar with the codes to assemble Chinese characters. But what should be learned at first if a person starts to learn the codes? Core vocabulary should be a good approach to initiate the first set of Chinese character for a novice learner.

The core vocabulary comprises of only a small number of word (approximately 250-400 words), but make up 80%-85% of the total words used in the participants' language sample. In addition, the core vocabulary does not change across environments, topics, situations, activities or between individuals [5], [6]. Individuals who rely on AAC access to the core words not only for communicating effectively but also for developing language competence.

Although selecting core vocabulary to develop communication vocabulary set for AAC user is not a new issue in AAC field, it has not been explored in Chinese users. Due to the huge number of Chinese vocabulary used in communication, learning the most frequent Chinese words or characters at the initial stage might be a more efficient and systematic way. Therefore, core vocabulary list should be also considered when developing Chinese text entry training system. Accordingly, this study aims to develop a Chinese character entry training system based on the core vocabulary approach and evaluate its usability.

2 System

This Mandarin Chinese Characters Entry Training system (MCChEn system) is a web-based training system which is implemented through a three-tier model (client/application server/database server). The system comprises training module and testing module as well. Based on the task analysis of a Chinese character generating process, as shown in Figure 1, three steps are required for generating a Chinese character. The first step is to be familiar with the codes of a Chinese character for a specific method. The following second step is to assemble the codes base on a specific order. This stage will create one or many corresponding characters that are assembled by the same codes. Therefore, selecting the correct character from a list is required in the third step.

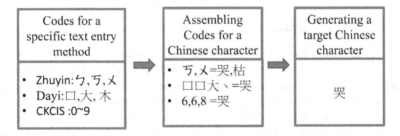

Fig. 1. The process for generating a Chinese character with different text entry method

2.1   System Framework

The major framework of the MCChEn system is shown in Figure 2.According to the above process, both training module and testing module comprise three major text entry tasks. They are codes matching, codes assembling, and character generating.

Codes Matching. This task requires a learner to find out the specific code for a text entry method. A learner should press the target key on the keyboard which matches the code displays on the screen.

Codes Assembling. A learner should assemble the corresponding codes for a Chinese character without selecting the correct character in this task. The major purpose of this task focuses on gathering the codes of a character in a specific text entry method.

Character Generating. This task requires a learner to generate a precise Chinese character by whatever text entry method he/she is familiar with. A learner should generate the target character shown on the screen by assembling the correct codes and selecting the correct character for a list.

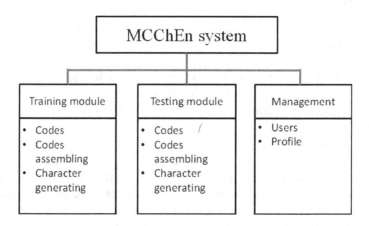

Fig. 2. The framework of the MCChEn System

2.2   Material for Training

The Chinese character used for text entry training included two groups, first groups is core vocabulary, and the second one is extended vocabulary. The characters were collected from the text books for Chinese Art in the school. The text books, published by three major text book providers, were collected from grade one to grade nine. The text of each book was separated into Chinese characters at first. Then the characters generated from each book were grouped into six levels, two grades for each level in elementary school, one grade for a level in junior high school. The frequency of each character was calculated for each level. The characters those comprise the 90% of the text were regarded as the core characters; meanwhile, the last characters were regarded as the extended characters.

2.3   The Feature of the System

Core Vocabulary Based. The Chinese characters used for learning in this system were sorted by each character's frequency which display in the textbooks of Mandarin Chinese from first grade to ninth grade. The higher frequency the higher priority to learn. The learner would learn to generate the Chinese character based on the frequency of the characters.

Embedded Prompting Strategy. A good training text entry system should prompt the learner how to generate a Chinese character correctly, because it is impossible to expect a learner who did not know the codes of a character to type the codes by himself/herself. This system provides the correct codes after three incorrect trials. The screens of displaying prompts are shown in Figure 3.

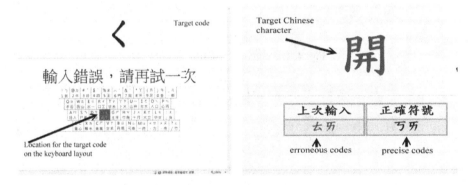

Fig. 3. Two snapshots of the prompting feature, left one provides location cue for code on the QWERTY keyboard layout; right one shows the corresponding codes for the target Chinese character

Individual Learning Pace and Content. The characters were grouped into six levels based on the grades of the text books belonged, level one for grade one and two; level two for grade three and four; level three for grade five and six; level four to six for grade seven, eight, and nine. The learner could select a proper level based on his/her grade or his/her cognitive ability. In addition, based on the master learning theory, a character would display in the practice until the learner could generate it correctly.

Providing Learner Profile. Learner profile could allow the learner's teacher or instructor to manage the content for learning, to monitor the progress, and to find out some characters with high error rate. This system allows a teacher/instructor to manage his/her responded learners. An authorized teacher could assign the proper learning procedure for the learner and could monitor the progress of the learners as well. The examples of the information provided by the system are show in Figure 4 and 5. As the Figure 4 illustrated, in addition to the accuracy rate, the outcome of each test reports time spent, number of keystroke, and erroneous codes for each character. The Figure 5 provides the amount for each practice section, the total number of the characters have been generated precisely, the counts for a character been generated erroneously.

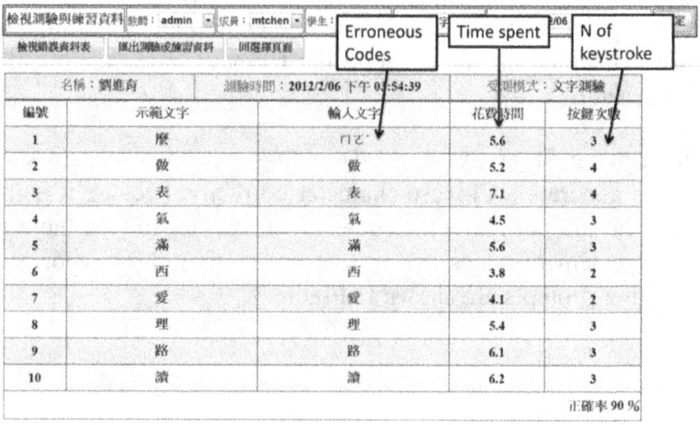

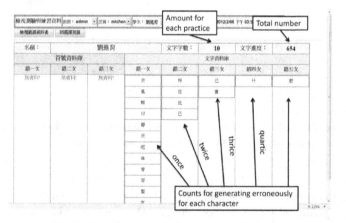

Fig. 4. The outcome report for a test

Fig. 5. The error analysis for a learner after a test

3   Usability Evaluation

A preliminary usability evaluation was conducted to explore the usability of MCChEn system. Thirteen special education teachers participated in the evaluation voluntarily. They attended a three hour workshop to learn how to use the MCChEn system at first, then they recruited one of their students at least touse the system to learn Chinese characters generation before they completed a questionnaire. The 5-point Likert scale questionnaire for usability evaluation was developed. The participants rated from very disagreement to very agreement.

The results of evaluation are shown on table 1. As the result indicated, except 2 items, the other six items were rated higher than 4 points. The results of evaluation reveal that the special education teachers agreed that the design of the MCChEn system is clear and consist, the training material is efficiency, the pace of learning is individualized, and the error analysis is clear.

Table 1. The results of usability evaluation for MCChEn system

Items	Mean	SD	Items	Mean	SD
Clarity of operation	4.31	0.75	Individualized training load	4.77	0.44
Consistence of interface	4.69	0.48	Efficiency of content	4.77	0.44
Difficulty of learning	4.85	0.38	Prompt for learning correctly	3.85	1.28
Errorless of operation	3.77	0.93	Error analysis for mistake correcting	4.58	0.90

4   Pilot Study

A 5th grade student with intellectual disabilities (Allan) and a 6th grade student with learning disabilities (Kay) were invited to participate in the pilot study. Because the purpose of this pilot study was to explore the usability of the MCChEn system in the schools, this experiment only use the top 100 core Chinese charters as content. Each session comprised 20 characters that were not learned or not typed correctly in the previous session.

A pre-test was conducted before the training session. Five training sessions were provided. In each session, a participant practiced every single character at first. During the practice, the system will provide prompts if the participant could not assemble the codes correctly. The participant took a typing test after practice all 20 characters. Accuracy and characters per-minute (CPM) were adopted to represent the performance.

The performance of accuracy was not improved because of the high accurate rate in the pre-test(95%) for Allan. But the CPM was doubled for him (pre-test=3.04, pro-test=6.5). For Kay, on contract, the accurate rate raised from 76% in pre-test to 98% in protest. However, the CPM did not improved (pre-test=3.44, pro-test=3.77).

5   Discussion

Alphabetical based message generating method ensures AAC user to say exactly what he/she wants to say. In order to help the Mandarin Chinese AAC user to learn a specific text entry method, thisMCChEn system was developed based on the core vocabulary approach which could provide the learners with systematic text entry learning process and contend. The results of a preliminary usability evaluation demonstrated that the design and content of MCChEn system is good, but the effect of purposed prompting strategy should be improved. In addition, the results of pilot experiment also indicated that students with different disabilities could benefit from this system.

Therefore, the MCChEn system might be a proper training system for speech therapists or special educators to adopt to train their AAC users to learn Chinese message generating systematically and efficiently. However, the prompting strategy used in the training module should be improved by providing dynamic and clear prompts in the next version of MCChEn system.

Besides, in order to demonstrate the effect of MCChen system on assisting a AAC user or potential user to learn text message generating skill, a training program should be conducted to explore the learning procedure and learning performance for students with various capabilities and limitations.

Acknowledgments. The authors would like to thank the National Science Council of the Republic of China for financially supporting this research under Contract No. NSC 98-2511-S-415-011-MY3.

References

1. American Speech-Language-Hearing Association.:Preferred Practice Patterns for the Profession of Speech-Language Pathology (PreferredPractice Patterns) (2004),
   http://www.asha.org/docs/html/PP2004-00191.html
2. Hill, K., Baker, B., Romich, B.: Augmentative and Alternative Communication (AAC) Technology. In: Cooper, R., Ohnabe, H., Hobson, D. (eds.) Introduction to Rehabilitation Engineering, pp. 355–384. Institute of Physics Publishing, London (2007)
3. Chen, M.C., Wang, H.P., Li, T.Y.: Teaching Adolescents with Disabilities to Learn Chinese Keyboarding by Using Multimedia Computer Assisted Input Method Learning System. In: Miesenberger, K., Klaus, J., Zagler, W. (eds.) ICCHP 2002. LNCS, vol. 2398, pp. 271–272. Springer, Heidelberg (2002)
4. Chen, M.C., Hill, K.: Redesign of a keyboard layout for enhancing the proficiency of text-entry for single digit Mandarin Chinese Users. Post at Clinical AAC Research Conference. Charlottesvill, VA, USA (September 2008)
5. Balandin, S., Iacono, T.: Crews, Wusses, and whoppas: Core and fringe vocabularies of Australian meal-break conversations in the workplace. Augmentative and Alternative Communication 15, 95–109 (1999)
6. Stuart, S., Beukelman, D.R., King, J.: Vocabulary use during extendedconversations by two cohorts of older adults. Augmentative and Alternative Communication 13, 40–47 (1997)

New Features in the VoxAid Communication Aid
for Speech Impaired People

Bálint Tóth, Péter Nagy, and Géza Németh

Department of Telecommunications and Media Informatics (TMIT),
Budapest University of Technology and Economics (BME),
1117 Budapest, Magyar Tudósok krt. 2., Hungary
{toth.b,nagyp,nemeth}@tmit.bme.hu

Abstract. For speech impaired persons even daily communication may cause problems. In many common situations, where speech ability would be necessary, they are not able to hold on. An application that uses Text-To-Speech (TTS) conversion is usable not only in daily routine, but in treatment of speech impaired persons as a therapeutic application as well. The VoxAid framework from BME-TMIT gives solutions for these scenarios. This paper introduces the latest improvements of the Voxaid framework, including user tests and evaluation.

1   Introduction

With the latest mobile devices we are able to make phone calls, write text messages, gain access to the Internet, use the devices for multimedia purposes. Complex, resource-demanding applications can be run.

A long list of available functionalities and services are provided in these systems, but just a few services can be found that have been developed directly for disabled people. For speech impaired people voice communication over mobile networks is not possible without a dedicated solution. Mobile devices are important for speech impaired persons in both everyday life and in emergency situations as well.

The number of severely speech impaired persons is about two million, and the number of moderately speech impaired persons is about three million in the European Union[1]. One can lose the ability to speak because of birth defect, external impacts (e.g. accidents, surgery) or illness.

The aim of this study is to investigate the existing methods and devices along with the needs of speech impaired people, and to introduce the design and development work and the results of a new communication aid platform.

2   Problem Statement

In the following chapter the possible user groups and application area are introduced, followed by the evaluation of present assistive solutions.

---

[1] http://www.tiresias.org/phoneability/telephones/
user_numbers.htm

K. Miesenberger et al. (Eds.): ICCHP 2012, Part II, LNCS 7383, pp. 295–302, 2012.

2.1   User Groups and Application Area

The VoxAid framework [5-7] has been designed directly for speech impaired persons. The everyday activities that are natural for people with speech ability can lead to difficulties in case of speech impaired persons. The obstructed voice based communication can cause inhibitions regarding social contact establishment. This may be the source of problems both in private life and in work. The loss of speech can cause different mental disorders (e.g. depression, continuous anxiety) [1], however speaking aids may influence these problems in a positive way.

A well designed application with speech output can serve as a communication aid for speech impaired people and it is also suitable for therapeutic purposes. In some cases (e.g. people with aphasia) speech and language therapy should be a solution for speech ability improvement [2]. Although therapy rarely solves all problems, repeated practice under supervision of a trained language or speech therapist can enhance the speech ability. If the application is capable of producing appropriate voice feedback, it may contribute to provide individualized therapy. The speech therapist defines the vocabulary, which can be practiced by the patient without his/her presence [3].

2.2   Present Solutions

Regarding the chosen carrier device we have to distinguish solutions designed for everyday use, and solutions for therapeutic use. For daily use a lightweight, small device is optimal, with a relatively large display. Smartphones are ideal devices for this purpose, because of their high computing power, low weight and moderate screen size. For therapeutic use the chosen hardware is personal computers, as the text input on the keyboard is easier than on a smartphone, they have bigger screens, and loudspeakers can be easily connected.

There are some existing solutions for speech impaired people. These solutions can be divided into two main categories: dedicated hardware solutions; software solutions for PCs or smartphones.

Usually dedicated devices consist of a keyboard for text input and from an integrated speaker for speech output (e.g. TextSpeak[2]). In some cases the device has a screen, memory for text storage and word prediction functionality (e.g. Allora[3]). Software solutions can operate on Palmtop [4], on Windows Mobile 5 powered personal digital assistants (PDAs) [6] or on Android devices (SpeakingPad, Talk Now[4]).

The problem with dedicated devices is that the user has to carry an additional device. In addition some of these devices cannot be operated by one hand. Software solutions do not offer extensive services (e.g. multiple text input methods), or the used carrier device may be based on an obsolete technology, and replacement parts are often not available. All this implies the need for a new solution regarding communication aids for speech impaired users.

---

[2] http://www.digac.com/talktype.htm

[3] http://www.zygo-usa.com/usa/index.php?option=com_virtuemart
&page=shop.browse&category_id=65&Itemid=11

[4] http://newburygraphics.com/talknow/talknow.html

3   System Design

The new generation of the VoxAid framework works on multiple platforms: personal computers, Android and Windows Mobile 6 smartphones. A well designed, intuitive and common user interface is highly important among all solutions; because speech impaired users have to be able to operate them as fast as possible. It is also important that platform switching does not require a long learning process. On any platform the system should be able to convert Text-To-Speech (TTS).

3.1   Application Concept

There are three applications implemented inside the new VoxAid framework based on our decade-long experience [5-7]. They are called SayIt, SayItDesktop and SayItAndroid.

Each application offers three different ways for text input: free text input; fixed text input and partly-fixed text input. The free text input is basically a text editor, where the user gets the opportunity to enter text without any restrictions. The application may read the provided content, or a part of this content (e.g. sentence, selection). In the fixed text input mode the application uses a pre-stored collection of sentences. These sentences are ordered into different unique categories to allow fast and efficient search between the sentences. The applications do not have any restriction regarding the number of categories and sentences used. In this input method the user does not have the opportunity to modify these sentences and categories directly, only the stored sentences can be used. The partly-fixed text input method is similar to the fixed text input, but with this method after sentence selection the user gets the opportunity to edit parts of the sentence. For example if we have the sentence "Please pick me up at <place>", the <place> field can be replaced by the user. Each sentence may contain multiple editable parts. The only restriction is that these parts cannot be encapsulated in each other. The predefined sentences and categories are stored in an XML (eXtensible Markup Language) file, and these files are compatible among all elements of the VoxAid framework.

In this paper only SayItDesktop and SayItAndroid will be introduced. SayIt operates on Windows Mobile smartphones. It was previously discussed in detail [6], [8].

3.2   SayItAndroid

Nowadays the most widespread operating system among smartphones is Android[5]. These devices are very heterogeneous regarding the operating system version and hardware capabilities. A great amount of different distributions are employed, and their performance, available memory, screen size and screen resolutions are different. So the application should be highly optimized to be able to work on many different devices.

---

[5] http://www.gartner.com/it/page.jsp?id=1924314

SayItAndroid is usable on Android 2.2 (or above) powered smartphones for everyday usage. It is a newer version of SayIt [6][8]. The application employs all three previously mentioned input methods. A redesign was necessary regarding the graphical user interface, furthermore additional functions was implemented.

Fig. 1. Graphical user interface of SayItAndroid. Left: free text, middle: category list of fixed text, right: sentence editor of partly fixed text

Nowadays smartphones use capacitive touchscreens instead of resistive ones. The main difference is that resistive touchscreens can be controlled by a special pen (stylo), but capacitive screens are manageable by the users' fingers. The redesigned user interface is depicted on Fig 1.

The user interface provides a view divided into three tabs for the different input methods. Smartphones have a relatively small screen with virtual keyboard, the text input can be still fast, thanks to the built in word prediction functionality provided by the Android operating system.

The different categories and sentences for the fixed and partly fixed text can be modified. For modification the application has a different view that can be accessed under the settings menu item. The user can modify and delete items, and has the possibility of adding new ones.

3.3   SayItDesktop

SayItDesktop operates on personal computers powered by Windows XP (or above) operating system. This version was designed for therapeutic use. The bigger screen size, the easier text input, and more accurate pointing device give the possibility to create an application that can be used during treatment sessions.

All the three input methods are also available in this application. The user interface is tabbed as the smartphone versions. For fast usage the application can be controlled with just the keyboard, without using any pointing device. There is no separated interface to modify fixed and partly fixed items. The application allows the modification and amendment of these substances, and to create new ones. The software offers the opportunity to use multiple different substances, and to switch these files in run-time.

In addition these substances can be exported under arbitrary names and locations. This solution is necessary to ensure for the speech therapist the option that they can handle these substances for each patient separately, and to be able to construct personalized vocabularies. With this capability the application can be used as an administrative extension for the other two versions of SayIt as well. Thus the applied changes can be exported directly to the smartphone, and without any further settings these can be used there. Furthermore the application is able to store multiple texts that were constructed with the free text input method. In this way speech therapists may pre-create practice sessions, and they can reuse them with multiple patients.

Regarding personalization of the user interface, the application may change text size, and adjust settings of the TTS engine (volume, speed and pitch). For therapeutic purposes the application ensures the possibility for word by word reading, where the TTS engine takes a break before each word. The length of this break can be specified by the user. With this reading method it is possible to read out the sentences with preserving accentuation or with rejecting it. With accentuation preservation emphasis in the sentence is not changed, only pauses are inserted between the words. If the reject accentuation option is active each word is pronounced as a separate sentence.

4   Evaluation Results

The VoxAid framework has been continuously tested by potential users during the whole development process. We started different real-life user tests with all the three new applications nearly half a year ago with speech therapists and also with speech impaired persons. The evaluation method is to hold regular interviews, where the users tell their impressions about the applications. They also tell their comments, which are taken into consideration. Based on the user feedbacks and proposals new features have been implemented in the desktop version.

In this paper the results of a comprehensive assessment are presented, where the evaluation was based on a questionnaire regarding the Android and the desktop versions. The assessments were performed by 13 participants. Six of them used the desktop version, and seven subjects used the Android version of the application. From the total number of 13 participants, six male and seven female volunteers took part in the assessment. The age of participants covered the 17-58 range, with a mean value of 34. In the final assessment the evaluation results from an 86 year-old participant wasn't taken into consideration, because he never used a computer before, thus he evaluated both the device and the software and not just the application.

The evaluation was divided into three phases. In the first phase everybody received 20 minutes to get familiar with the application and its functionalities. In order to measure the ease of use of the application, no detailed description was provided for the test persons, just some brief information about the basic functionalities. They were aware that the application is able to convert text-to-speech, and it has three different text input methods, and they had knowledge about how these methods work. In the second phase every participant had three tasks to perform:

a.)   Find the given sentence and make the application read it up.

b.)   Change the text size used by the application to a specific value.

c.)   Create a new fixed text category and add a new sentence to it.

In the final phase the participants were asked to fill out a questionnaire, where they had to evaluate the application by multiple criteria on a scale of five.

Table 1. Task completion time results (mean ± variance)

Task completion time	SayItAndroid (sec)	SayItDesktop (sec)
Task a.)	27 ± 11	15 ± 4
Task b.)	31 ± 21	20 ± 7
Task c.)	74 ± 37	58 ± 24

All participants were able to operate the application and complete the given tasks. The average task completion time was shorter with the desktop version of the application (Table 1.). This implies that the desktop version is easier to control, and also that higher text input speed is reachable on the keyboard. All participants who evaluated the desktop version used a computer before, but from the smartphone testers 2 participants have never used a smartphone before.

The results of the questionnaire based evaluation can be found in Table 2. In the first row the difficulty of the three tasks is evaluated. On average, users who tested the desktop version of the application gave higher marks. It may be caused by the previously mentioned issues: pointing and typing can be faster and easier on a computer as it is on a smartphone, but for both applications the mean values are high.

For simplicity the smartphone version received higher marks compared to the desktop version, but not sharply. This implies that both of the applications are easy to use, and easy to handle. All participants were able to handle the application correctly, and neither of them reported incorrect or unwanted behavior.

The third row depicts the results regarding how logical the application structure is. Here the smartphone version received lower marks, mostly because of the modification view, where the users can modify the used fixed and partly-fixed categories and sentences, is a hidden function. This means that this view is not reachable directly from the main screen, it is on the second page of the settings menu.

Table 2. Evaluation results (mean ± variance)

Criteria	SayItAndroid	SayItDesktop
	Value*	Value*
Task simplicity	4,71 ± 0,24	4,83 ± 0,17
Handling simplicity	4,71 ± 0,24	4,67 ± 0,27
Logical structure	4,71 ± 0,24	4,83 ± 0,17
Application speed	5 ± 0	4,83 ± 0,17
Function access	4,14 ± 0,14	4,5 ± 0,3
Usability	4,85 ± 0,14	4,5 ± 0,7

*On a scale of five, where 1 is the worst and 5 is the best

For application speed both versions reached a high value. The applications were designed to consume as few resources as possible, in order to assure high speed.

In the function access row the respondents evaluated the minimum time that is necessary to gain access to specific functions (e.g: modification interface, settings). SayItAndroid received lower marks compared to the desktop version. This is because the limited screen size of the smartphones forced us to distribute the application functions into more views, thus some functions only reachable with more touches on the screen.

The majority considered the applications usable solutions for speech impaired people. The smartphone version was preferred, due to its portability, and ease of use. Also its simpler user interface is a great advantage regarding participants' opinion.

5 Future Plans

Besides the above mentioned cooperation with speech impaired persons and speech therapists we are looking for further partners for cooperation. Based on their opinion and preferences, the user interface will be adapted and new features may also be introduced.

Our current solutions support the Hungarian language only. We used standard Android and Windows speech interfaces, thus it is easy to switch between TTS engines and we have the potential to create multilingual versions. A cloud-based storage system [9] is also under investigation, where users may store all their preferences, fixed/partly-fixed messages in a cloud. This could assure rapid change between devices and platforms without the risk of data loss, and without the inconvenience of manual data transport.

For the time being the applications are ready to use on multiple platforms. The number of speech impaired people cannot be neglected, and they need a solution to replace their lost speaking ability, even if this is a partial solution only. Our goal is to create applications on prevalent platforms for this purpose. We hope our system can serve as a useful communication aid for many people, and with continuous support and development we can assure an elevated standard of living for them. We are also looking for the possibility to route TTS output to the phone line during phone calls on Android. For the time being the developers of Android deny this feature for developers.

Acknowledgements. This research was partly supported by BelAmi ALAP2-00004/2005, TÁMOP 4.2.2-08/1/KMR-2008-2007 and the TÁMOP-4.2.1/B-09/1/KMR-2010-0002 projects.

References

1. Public Foundation for Equal Opportunities of Persons with Disabilities - Summary of the study, SZ25/12 Speech therapy of speech impaired adults in a pilot program, Budapest, pp. 20–36 (2005) (in Hungarian)

2. Kitzing, P., Ahlsén, E., Jönsson, B.: Communication aids for people with aphasia. Logopedics Phoniatrics Vocology 30, 41–46 (2005)
3. Hawley, M.S., Green, P., Enderby, P., Cunningham, S., Moore, R.K.: Speech Technology for e-Inclusion of People with Physical Disabilities and Disordered Speech. In: 9th European Conference on Speech Communication and Technology, Interspeech 2005, pp. 445–448 (2005)
4. Van De Sandt-Koenderman, M., Wiegers, J., Hardy, P.: A computerized communication aid for people with aphasia. Disability and Rehabilitation 27(9), 529–533 (2005)
5. Olaszy, G., Németh, G.: VOXAID: An Interactive Speaking Communication Aid Software for the Speech Impaired. In: Proceedings of Eurospeech 1993, Berlin Germany, pp. 1821–1824 (September 1993)
6. Tóth, B., Németh, G., Kiss, G.: Mobile Devices Converted into a Speaking Communication Aid. In: 9th International Conference on Computer Helping People with Special Needs, Paris, France, July 5-9, pp. 1016–1023 (2004)
7. Tóth, B., Németh, G.: VoxAid 2006: Telephone Communication for Hearing and/or Vocally Impaired People. In: Miesenberger, K., Klaus, J., Zagler, W.L., Karshmer, A.I. (eds.) ICCHP 2006. LNCS, vol. 4061, pp. 651–658. Springer, Heidelberg (2006) ISSN 0302-9743
8. Nagy, P.: Communication aid application on PDA devices, BME-VIK, Budapest, Thesis, pp. 23–45 (2010) (in Hungarian)
9. Katzan Jr., H.: Cloud Software Service: Concepts, Technology, Economics. Service Science 1(4), 256–269 (2009)

AAC Vocabulary Standardisation and Harmonisation

The CCF and BCI Experiences

Mats Lundälv and Sandra Derbring

DART (Sahlgrenska Univ. Hospital), Göteborg, Sweden,
Kruthusgatan 17, 411 04 Göteborg, Sweden
{mats.lundalv,sandra.derbring}@vgregion.se

Abstract. The Concept Coding Framework (CCF) effort, started in the European WWAAC project and now continued in the European AEGIS project, as well as the current vocabulary efforts within BCI (Blissymbolics Communication International), highlight that issues of AAC vocabulary content, management and interoperability are central. This paper outlines some stages of this work so far, including the important role of the Authorised Blissymbol Vocabulary (BCI-AV) and its relation to resources like the Princeton WordNet lexical database and the ARASAAC symbol library. The work initiated to link Blissymbolics and other AAC symbol vocabularies, as well as the CCF concept ontologies, to the ISO Concept Database (ISO/CDB) and the work of ISO Technical Committee 37 (ISO TC 37), will be discussed. In this context the long-term ambition to establish an ISO standardised Unicode font for Blissymbolics will also be brought to the fore. We'll stress the importance of clarified and, when possible, harmonised licensing conditions.

Keywords: AAC, graphic symbols, vocabulary, multilingual, multi-modal, speech impairment, language impairment, cognitive impairment, language learning.

1 Background

1.1 The Concept Coding Framework

The Concept Coding Framework (CCF) [1] technology was defined as part of the European World Wide AAC (WWAAC) project [2] 2001-2004. The CCF has slowly developed through several phases, and now with increased pace in the current more substantial CCF efforts as part of the European AEGIS project [3].

The CCF was created as a means to break down the isolation and barriers between different AAC symbol vocabularies by defining an open technology for connecting these vocabularies to each others and to standard lexical resources. This means that it was also developed to break the isolation between the AAC field in general and the rapidly developing and more widely adopted standard language technologies. Thus the CCF was largely based on the free lexical resources of the Princeton WordNet [8],

K. Miesenberger et al. (Eds.): ICCHP 2012, Part II, LNCS 7383, pp. 303–310, 2012.

and on technologies of the Semantic Web, like RDF and OWL. For details, see Deliverable 10 of the WWAAC project, "Code of Practice" [1].

To this common foundation of free language technologies, dedicated free CCF technology, and mainstream web/internet technologies, both free and proprietary AAC Assistive Ontology resources may then be connected and allowed to interact, as indicated in Fig. 1 below.

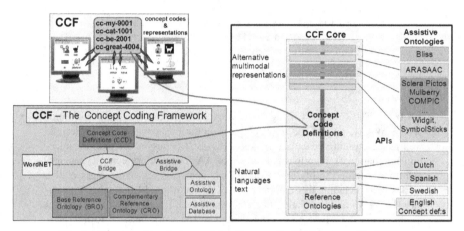

Fig. 1. Three combined views of the Concept Coding Framework (CCF)

1.2   The Blissymbolics Vocabulary

During the period of 2007-2011, Blissymbolics Communication International (BCI) has invested much work to make its BCI Authorised Vocabulary (BCI-AV) [4] available in more secure and effective data formats suitable for modern ICT based applications. For example, the format of the English gloss (used in the file names of the Blissymbols in the graphics libraries) has been revised and made consistent.

The licensing policy has also been updated to suit both the need for free language resources and the need to efficiently support commercial providers of AAC software and services. It has become natural to cooperate closely between the CCF and BCI parallel efforts due to the special qualities of Blissymbolics.

Blissymbolics is an interesting and valuable resource in the general vocabulary standardisation and interoperability work, as it was initially developed as an artificial semantic graphical language, inspired by Chinese writing, and later adopted and applied for AAC use. Thus Blissymbolics is a thoroughly semantically defined lexical resource, in particular compared to other AAC symbol libraries. It is unusually concise and well structured, and bridges in some ways the space between traditional ideographic and phonological writing systems and concurrent graphic libraries for AAC.

New Bliss-words may continuously be created from the existing library of Bliss-characters according to the detailed specifications of the BCI "Blissymbolics Fundamental Rules" document [4]. This may be done as needed by local Blissymbol users in the form of "private Blissymbols", or officially by the BCI Panel as amendments to the BCI-AV [4]. On rare occasions the BCI Panel may also amend new Bliss-characters to the BCI-AV, but the policy for this is gradually becoming more restrictive as the Blissymbol vocabulary matures, and the number Bliss-characters increases. A few examples from the Blissymbol vocabulary are shown in Table 1 below:

Table 1. Example Blissymbols with English gloss and "derivations"

Blissymbol	Gloss (en)	"Derivation" (description)	Our comments
	name, label, term, title	(pen + mouth: something that can be spoken or written)	A Bliss-character constructed from two overlaid previously existing ones. A rather wide concept definition compared to e.g. WordNet concepts
	address	(name + place + house) Use appropriate specifier.	Bliss-word with three Bliss-characters. Note suggestion to make other kinds of addresses by replacing 'house' specifier
	letter, mail, post	(pictograph: symbol suggests an envelope)	A pictograph Bliss-character, like the symbol for house in address above
	e-mail, email	(letter + digital)	... where "digital" is represented by the digits 1 and 0
	e-mail address, email address	(name + place + e-mail)	... and here we have another kind of address as suggested above

These qualities, together with current and earlier ambitions to certify the Blissymbol vocabulary as part of international standards [5], have made it natural for representatives of ISO TC 37 [6] and the ISO Concept Database [7] to approach BCI for renewed inclusion of Blissymbolics in these on-going standardisation efforts.

In connection to the above discussed ambitions, the since long pending ambition of BCI to establish am ISO standardised Unicode font for Blissymbolics[13] has again become a working item on the forefront of the agenda. This is not just a plain matter of drawing a Unicode font typeface. It is deeply tied to the basic structure of the language and writing of Blissymbolics as built from Bliss-characters and Bliss-words. It will require a major joint effort of the Blissymbolics community and Unicode experts we know who are eager to help, and it will be a work of value for the general objective of AAC vocabulary standardisation and harmonisation.

2   Experiences of Early Standardisation and Harmonisation Efforts

The work of aligning mainstream natural language lexical resources like WordNet [8] with Blissymbolics, ARASAAC [9] and other AAC symbol libraries, and supporting multiple languages, is a far from straight-forward task. It is in fact and in principle a never-ending one that will ask for on-going iterations for better and wider coverage.

There are many difficulties in mapping and harmonising the above mentioned resources against each other, and against subsequently more natural language translations. Concepts and meanings are not congruent between natural languages, neither between graphical languages themselves,   and of course not between these two categories.

Fig. 2 below may give an impression of the complications involved in mapping symbol vocabularies via concept codes to a lexical ontology resource like WordNet.

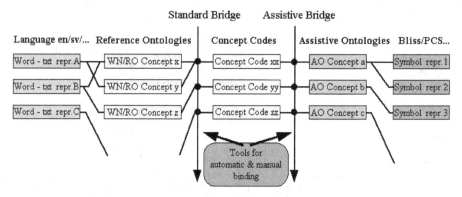

Fig. 2. Possible relations between words (e.g. English), WordNet and CCF Reference Ontology concepts - to the left, CCF Concept Codes - in the middle, and so called Assistive Ontologies with words mapped to symbol representations - to the right

In Fig. 1 we can see that a written word may represent several concepts with different meaning (homonyms). Several different words may represent the same concept (synonyms). Some Concept Codes we may also link to more than one WN/RO concept. This is because WN concepts are often split up in very fine-grained definitions. For the "inter-lingua" layer of Concept Codes we typically don't want that level of detail, but want a wider and more "generous" coverage of meaning. On the Assistive Ontology side the situation is a bit more diverse between different symbol systems:

Blissymbolics is concise with no symbol homonyms and few synonyms. Pictorial systems like ARASAAC may contain numerous homonyms (e.g. one symbol representing both a noun and a related verb) and often plenty of synonyms (due to the concrete representations making generalised use difficult). This causes rather complex preconditions for consistent mapping.

2.1   Populating the CCF Database

Two sets of symbols are currently used to populate the database, Blissymbolics and ARASAAC, consisting of around 5,000 symbols each. Princeton's lexical database WordNet is used to extract lemma as well as part of speech and a dictionary definition for a majority of these symbols.

In WordNet, words sharing the same concept are grouped together in synonym sets. Each synonym set is linked to other sets via lexical and semantic relations. Each sense of a concept has a frequency score and is categorized by part of speech. Over 150,000 words combined in over 117,000 synsets make WordNet a large ontology resource for natural language processing, as an alternative to standard lexicons.

An application has been developed (in Python) that uses a stripping algorithm to transform the symbol's file name to a string that will be searchable. Since WordNet stores single words or collocations as entries, the file names of the symbols are adjusted to create the best matches possible. This means that there are several algorithms operating to ensure that crucial information is not being left out while extracting the simplest searchable string possible.

It is important to be able to present the possible symbols to the end-users according to likeliness. There is a ranking algorithm to decide this. This selection is mainly based on the frequency with which each lemma occurs in corpora, but also on the occurrence of related words in the definitions. For each return of a WordNet match, there are algorithms for extracting Swedish, Spanish and Dutch translations, using manually translated lists. These translations are also inflected according to their part of speech.

This extraction of lexical information is done for each symbol set, and the resulting output is all found entries in the WordNet database for each given symbol in a set. This is produced as text files with all this information lined up, one for each symbol set.

These are, in a next step, merged via the WordNet index number, which is the common attribute between the outputs. Entering such a large data set into the database is very time-consuming, and thus this output, a text file with information from both symbol sets, is divided into smaller sets of 100 words. A final script is used to populate the database with these sets. The populated database is then used by CCF aware applications like the CCF-SymbolWriter extension to LibreOffice/OpenOffice Writer, or the CCF-SymbolDroid AAC app for Android mobile devices, both developed for the AEGIS project [3], to support end-users with the look-up of concepts and symbols for words.

Problems Encountered. The work has, and still is, presenting numerous problems, many of which have only been partially solved, and some still waiting to be solved. These include:

— Words are not in the lexicon (including many common function words not present in WordNet, added and handled in a partly ad hoc manner)
— Fewer symbols than expected found (partly due to ad hoc handling of versions of data resources)
— More symbols than expected found (incorrect cross-linking in database population – major clean-up needed)
— Major improvements needed in handling of ranking information (concepts and symbols are not presented in an optimal order for the user)
— Inconsistencies in the handling of inflected forms (varying between languages)
— Natural language translation lexicons used need improvements
— ARASAAC symbol resource needs to be switched form ad hoc to a more consistent one (now available, but not yet used)

Solutions. To solve problems like these on a short-term solution, we have been reviewing and updating the data and improved algorithms when needed as we go. Even though this has been necessary to keep the process going, it requires too much time and deters too much to temporary fixes to be a long-term solution. Instead, we need to find a qualitative approach. One way of doing that would be to rebuild the database from scratch in a controlled manner. Instead of entering 5,000 symbols at once, trusting a system to process them completely accordingly, we need to enter smaller sets and use a system to manually review and accept or decline the proposed entries.

Conclusions. The CCF work has highlighted that freely available resources for more reliable automatic mapping between semantically corresponding terms in a growing number of languages would be immensely helpful. The unfortunate fact that the EuroWordnet effort in the 1990s [10] resulted in proprietary resources is still having destructive effects, even though later work has resulted in free WordNet resources [11]. Current attempts aiming for free resources are encouraging, such as the "Open linguistic infrastructure" (CIP-ICT-PSP.2010.6.1) network projects [12]. So far, and until resources are more thoroughly established and available, the semi-automatic methods used to map up the different representation ontologies require a lot of manual checking and correction to end up with reasonably accurate and reliable resources.

3   Licensing Issues

The AAC field is facing an in some ways absurd situation in terms of property rights claims and licensing policies. Individuals who are not capable of communicating via spoken or conventionally written language are offered alternative means of communication via graphical symbol vocabularies. Using these resources however, these persons are often made dependent on proprietary owned and managed language resources, which are provided under restrictive commercial licensing conditions. Increasingly often this brings about the natural question: Shouldn't language resources be free, as in free speech, also for AAC users? This is becoming an increasingly awkward situation in our age of expanding ICT based interactive online communication.

There is a range of more freely available AAC alternatives such as Blissymbolics, ARASAAC, Straight-Street Mulberry Symbols [14] and Sclera Pictograms [15]. However, here as well we have problems with conflicting and/or unclear licensing policies that cause problems for integrating or mixing these resources with other free material or software. A joint effort to promote a common straight licensing policy for free resources without other limitations than the protection of their continued freedom would be of great value. Licences compatible with the main-stream of free software and other free resources, licenses such as GPL, LGPL [16], and CreativeCommons-BY-SA [17], should be encouraged. Additional incompatible unnecessary and counter-productive restrictions (such as Non-Commercial) should be discouraged.

This should not exclude parallel licensing alternatives for use in non-free proprietary commercial products. This is, and will be, the policy applied by both the CCF and Blissymbolics communities. Others will be encouraged to follow the same track. A more concrete discussion on these issues will be encouraged. On the other hand; co-operation with proprietary and otherwise licensed resources for interoperability based on open standards should in any case be initiated and continued.

4   Future Perspectives

The work for establishing a standardised foundation for interoperability between multi-modal and multilingual AAC vocabulary resources has just started. To succeed, his work will require decisive and enduring efforts in close co-operation between AAC resource maintainers, relevant mainstream language technology developments, and with the involved standardisation bodies. We want to strongly encourage all involved stake-holders to join forces in the gradual building of a common free infrastructure of multilingual and multi-modal language ontology resources, including a growing range of AAC graphic symbol and sign language representations. This will not only be of major benefit for the minorities of people in need of AAC support, but also for a much wider area of Special Educational Needs, and all the way to mainstream education in early literacy and second language learning.

Acknowledgement. The CCF technology has been developed with the financial contribution of the European Commission in the context of the WWAAC [2] and AEGIS [3] projects, and from the Nordic Council in the context of the SYMBERED project []. Thanks also to Princeton University and WordNet [8], to Blissymbolics Communication International (BCI) [4], and to Centre of Technologies for the Education (CATEDU - under the authority of the Department of Education, University, Culture and Sports of the Aragonese Government) [9], for their contributions of the free lexical and symbol vocabulary resources that the CCF is being built around.

References

1. Concept Coding Framework (CCF), http://www.oatsoft.org/Software/concept-coding-framework-ccf/ and the original CCF definition document "Code of Practice,
    http://www.wwaac.eu/products/Docs/D10_v10%20CoP.pdf
2. The WWAAC (World-Wide AAC) project, http://www.wwaac.eu/
3. AEGIS - Accessibility Everywhere: Groundwork, Infrastructure, Standards, http://www.aegis-project.eu/
4. Blissymbolics Communication International (BCI), http://www.blissymbolics.org/
5. In 1993 Blissymbolics was registered as an encoded character set for use in ISO/IEC 2022, in the ISO-IR international registry of coded character sets. The Blissymbolic language is approved as an encoded language, with code zbl, into the ISO 639-2 and ISO 639-3 standards
6. Galinski, C.: Semantic Interoperability and Language Resources- New aspects of global semantic interoperability, http://www.iim.fh-koeln.de/IWKolloquien/GalinskiSemO.pdf
7. The ISO Concept Database, http://www.iso.org/iso/concept_database_cdb.htm
8. WordNet, Princeton University, http://wordnet.princeton.edu/
9. ARASAAC, http://www.catedu.es/arasaac/
10. EuroWordnet, http://www.illc.uva.nl/EuroWordNet/
11. BalkaNet, http://cordis.europa.eu/ictresults/index.cfm?section=news&tpl=article&ID=73737 and DanNet, http://wordnet.dk/dannet/lang
12. Information Society Projects in Open linguistic infrastructure (CIP-ICT-PSP.2010.6.1), http://ec.europa.eu/information_society/apps/projects/index.cfm?obj_id=CIP-ICT-PSP.2010.6.1&menu=secondary
13. Encoding Blissymbolics in Plane 1 of the UCS, http://std.dkuug.dk/JTC1/SC2/WG2/docs/n1866.pdf
14. Straight-Street Mulberry Symbols, http://straight-street.com/
15. Sclera Pictograms, http://www.sclera.be/index.php?taal=ENG
16. GNU Licenses, http://www.gnu.org/licenses/
17. Creative Commons - Attribution-ShareAlike (CreativeCommons-BY-SA) license, http://creativecommons.org/licenses/by-sa/3.0/us/

Speaking and Understanding Morse Language, Speech Technology and Autism

András Arató[1], Norbert Markus[1], and Zoltan Juhasz[2]

[1] Wigner RCP, Laboratory of Speech Technology for Rehabilitation
[2] University of Pannonia, Electrical Engineering and Information Systems

Abstract. The language nature of morse is discussed, showing similarities and differences with spoken language. The radio amateur club working at the Laboratory of Speech Technology for Rehabilitation was used to educate and investigate behavior of a stuttering autistic boy. Morse codes' (phonemes') perception accuracy was measured changing the speed of the phonemes. A hypothesis is described that the language elements have to be fixed at different speeds for quick recognition. Experiments with a non-speaking autistic girl using tablet PC are also described.

1   Is Morse a Language? Yes!

Morse can be seen as a specific language [1]. If you compare the sonograms of the morse and the spoken speech you can see the main differences.   Spoken language can be characterized with three main parameters, the rhythm, energy and frequency. Morse is a marginal case having only rhythm, if we do not consider the fading and the frequency difference of the sine waves because of the beat oscillator. Morse characters' sound are actually the phonemes of the language.

One can think that morse is only a code system serving ciphering and deciphering a text. This was not true even when morse was used mainly by the army. This old USA Army didactic film underlines the necessity to learn the rhythm of words and phrases as a whole unit: http://www.youtube.com/watch?v=Li8Hiwbc664 &feature=youtube_gdata_player.

Nowadays only radio amateurs use morse. Language elements are special abbreviations, English and national characters, words, phrases and sentences.

The phonemes of morse are not redundant, which is an extra burden to the learner, but the main learning process is very similar to that of the spoken language. If the only morse language parameter, the length of the short (dit) or long (dash) or the pause are distorted, it is very difficult to recognise the morse phoneme properly. The three parameters of the "normal" speech are overlapped in diads and triads of the phonemes, which add extra redundancy.

There is another difference: we speak morse with our fingers. It is especially true when we use the so called straight key:

(http://en.wikipedia.org/wiki/Telegraph_key).

K. Miesenberger et al. (Eds.): ICCHP 2012, Part II, LNCS 7383, pp. 311–314, 2012.

A Hungarian doctor of laryngology Laszlo Pataki played two sounding parts of white noise for autistic children [3]. He found that they could distinguish less these parts than healthy children. Pataki supposed that autistic children hear these sound longer. Pataki did not use sinusoidal sounds because different children are sensitive to different frequencies. This test encouraged me to experiment with morse.

2   The Rehabilitation with Speech Technology Radio Club (HA5RST)

For more than two years there has been a radio amateur club working in the Laboratory of Speech Technology for Rehabilitation. The club has the callsign HA5RST, which stands for (R)ehabilitation with (S)peech (T)echnology, but RST is also the abbreviation of the so called report (R)eadability (S)ignal-strength and (T)one which is used during morse contacts.

The main goal of creating the club was to investigate behavior of a stuttering autistic boy. The morse language has the very important similarity to other languages existing in a specific societies (nations). Amateur club is like a family, where members speak the same language and they teach new members the common morse language.

One says that autism is a social type of disorder "social blindness". I must contradict. I have experience with several people having different level of autism. The "social blindness" is not the nature of autism, but is a side effect of it - in my opinion. All the autistic people who I know are very empathic. The HA5RST club gives me a good environment for observation and education.

3   Learning Morse Language with an Autistic Boy

The subject of this article is a stuttering boy, who was diagnosed with autism in his early childhood. He was 16 year old (now he is 18), when he with his mother appeared in the radio club. It was his decision to become a radio amateur. He had several strange eye-catching manners at the beginning. He refused handshaking, he avoided eye contact, and he was running up and down, but he was also persistent to listen to and observe radio amateur activity.

He does not speak much, because he is stuttering. He has kink not only in his speech, but also in his arms from time to time. Two years ago, when I got acquainted with him, I explained my goals to teach him to become a radio amateur. He agreed to learn morse language and also to investigate his behavior during learning. Other radio club members also took him into the club, so he felt himself comfortably.

We taught the boy how to construct small electronic circuits, wind coils. Winding was a difficulty for him because of sudden arm jerking. I gave him training tasks to insert many 16 pinned IC sockets into printed circuit board holes, and also to solder them properly. At the same time we started to learn morse phonemes.

I suggested him to use the G4FON self-learning morse trainer program (http://www.g4fon.net), and agreed with him to set Farnsworth timing – http://www.justlearnmorsecode.com/farnsworth.html, which means fast character speed with long spaces in between. He even turned character speed faster then I suggested and used a similar on-line trainer program LCWO (http://lcwo.net/) instead of G4FON. When he reported me that he had learned all the 26 letters and 10 digits, we organised a test.

We set the following values in G4FON for our testing:

Actual Character Speed 30 WPM, Effective Code Speed, 3 WPM, 26 letters only, 113 randomly generated letters. He did 5 mistakes. After this test I set the following values with CW_player to be able to set the same effective speed (http://www.southgatearc.org/articles/morsetutor.htm):

Actual Character Speed 3 WPM, Effective Code Speed 3 WPM, 26 letters only, 113 randomly generated letters.

His number of mistakes increased to 10! I made similar tests with persons without autism and had similar results, with the increase of mistakes. The reason for this increase in my opinion is that people learn morse patterns at a given speed, and when they hear the same pattern with very different speed, they are not able to match the sound. There is no time to convert the sound pattern even to a lower speed, during mental load of the test. People have to learn morse (and probably spoken speech) patterns at different speeds.

I found this myself during my long morse learning process, that it was no joy to copy morse texts character by character. I started to enjoy morse language communication, only when I was able to understand not different characters, but whole words and phrases as one patterns, and also learned all the speeds and fists ("dialects") too. We say in morse instead of dialect: "the operator has a nice fist".

My autistic pupil produced very interesting results. When I asked him to read the characters by phonetic spelling (Alpha, Bravo, Charlie etc.) he never stopped in his speech. He learned both the English and Hungarian spelling. He does not stutter in spelling with either language. His English language knowledge is rather good. He can understand and speak with our native English speaking club mate. My assumption was that his newly learned morse and spelling helped him stop stuttering. We tested his morse conversation without using radios. He was sure of himself and never stopped his morse sending. Later we repeated this test with real partners and in real radio contacts. The results were good, he "stuttered" in morse sending only rarely.

Other interesting results were produced, when he started phone mode contacts with spoken language. He became confident in it too. He is still stuttering when he speaks with us, but when he is in a radio contact, he stops stuttering. It seems when he presses the Push-to-Talk button of the microphone, he switches off his stuttering.

Similar progress happened in his arm jerking. I ordered a small transceiver kit KX1 (www.elecraft.com) and let him solder all the parts alone following the very detailed English descriptions. He assembled the two band transceiver almost without any help and completed the very first morse contact with it. Parents and school teachers also mentioned the remarkable advance in his behavior over the last two years. The latest news is that he passed the highest international radio amateur exam plus optional morse code test.

4   Talking Tablet Experiments with a Non-speaking Autistic Girl (TalkPad)

We had another attempt to help autistic child. She was 12 year old when we first met. She is now 16 and can "speak" with the help of her mother using the facilitated communication tool. It is a piece of paper containing the Hungarian alphabet. She is pointing with her finger, but her mother had to keep her finger in her hand. Now her mother holds her elbow only to facilitate communication.

We created a talking program using a Personal Data Assistant and a tablet PC (she does not want to see the screen). The name of the program is TalkPad. She accepted our help, but later she was negative. She did not like the quality of the speech program. Later we changed to a better text-to-speech, which she accepted, and said, that it is almost as good as her mother's speech. Later she told that she wants to speak alone, with her own voice. She wants to break out from autism. She belongs also to the quarter of autistic people with high IQ. She learned German language alone from books found at her home.

The last two years she became less negative to the computers, but she is still struggling with the slowness of the facilitated communication method. Sometimes she speaks understandable sentences, especially when she is very excited. We intend to follow working with her and her mother using Android tablets. We have to find the way how she will accept other persons to facilitate her communication.

The TalkPad program has several levels of logging (see the first level above the number pads). These logs helped our research. Speech echo has also more levels. The first one done by recorded speech for the highest quality. Word and sentence level is produced be different text-to-speech systems. It is similar to our MObile SlateTalker (MOST) [2] developed for blind people.

5   Conclusions

It is not easy to develop devices and programs for people with autism. Nevertheless we have to find (sometimes even unusual ways) how to help children to break out from autism. We must try to receive them into the society. Autistic people have no "social blindness"! They are empathic people. They are only hyper sensitive and that is why they become sometimes aggressive.

References

1. András Arató Beszéd- és morze-érthetőség valamint azok zavarai RádióTechnika Évkönyv 2000 (Speech and Morse Understanding and its Difficulties)
2. Juhasz, Z., Arato, A., Bognar, G., Buday, L., Eberhardt, G., Markus, N., Mogor, E., Nagy, Z., Vaspori, T.: Usability Evaluation of the MOST Mobile Assistant (SlatTalker). In: Miesenberger, K., Klaus, J., Zagler, W.L., Karshmer, A.I. (eds.) ICCHP 2006. LNCS, vol. 4061, pp. 1055–1062. Springer, Heidelberg (2006)
3. Laszlo Pataki Logopedia and Autism Presentation at the Gusztav Barczi Special Education faculty of ELTE University, March 10 (2012)

Reverse-Engineering Scanning Keyboards

Foad Hamidi and Melanie Baljko

Department of Computer Science and Engineering, York University
4700 Keele St., Toronto, Ontario, Canada, M3J 1P3
{fhamidi,mb}@cse.yorku.ca

Abstract. *Scanning* or *soft keyboards* are alternatives to physical computer keyboards that allow users with motor disabilities to compose text and control the computer using a small number of input actions. In this paper, we present the *reverse Huffman algorithm* (RHA), a novel Information Theoretic method that extracts a *representative latent probability distribution* from a given scanning keyboard design. By calculating the *Jensen-Shannon Divergence* (JSD) between the extracted probability distribution and the probability distribution that represents the body of text that will be composed by the scanning keyboard, the efficiency of the design can be predicted and designs can be compared with each other. Thus, using RHS provides a novel *a priori* context-aware method for reverse-engineering scanning keyboards.

Keywords: Scanning Keyboards, Information Theory, Huffman Algorithm.

1 Introduction and Background

For many people with disabilities, using conventional keyboards is a challenge due to the fine motor skills required. Using *scanning* or *soft keyboards* is a popular alternative indirect text entry technique that allows users to compose text using as little as one or two reliable input actions [8] (see figure 1, left). In this approach, an arrangement of alphanumeric symbols and system commands, referred to as *selectables*, is displayed on a screen and highlighted or put in focus in some order (hence, the use of the term scanning). The user selects a highlighted selectable by performing an *input action*, ranging from single button presses to the use of puff switches and EMG signals [3]. *Focus advancement*, the movement of focus over the hierarchy, can either be triggered by a separate input action (i.e., *active*) or automatic (i.e., *passive*). While active focus advancement requires more effort, it provides more control over the pace of the interaction and is preferred by some users.

The selectables are often grouped. In order to select a selectable, the user has to select its group by performing the input action when it is in focus. This action will select the group, after which only its subgroups, one of which contains the desired selectable, will be highlighted. The user has to keep selecting subgroups that contain the desired selectable until it is highlighted by itself, at which point an input action would add it to the created text. Scanning keyboards are often speeded up by various techniques, such as text completion or text prediction and have been effectively used by

K. Miesenberger et al. (Eds.): ICCHP 2012, Part II, LNCS 7383, pp. 315–322, 2012.

people with disabilities in various contexts, especially as part of *voice output commu-nication aids* (VOCAs) that synthesize created text into speech using a *text-to-speech* (TTS) module [1, 6] and are used by individuals with little or no functional speech, writing or gesture (the so-called *communication disorders*). The scanning keyboards examined here can also be used in other contexts, such as mobile computing, in which small keyboard size and number of input actions is desirable [8, 9].

Fig. 1. A scanning keyboard with selectables highlighted in rows and columns (left) and the corresponding encoding tree (right)

Among the different factors affecting the performance of scanning keyboards, the layout of the keyboard (i.e., the ordering and placement of the selectable) is an impor-tant design aspect that affects the performance directly [3]. In this work, we focus on analyzing this aspect of scanning keyboard design. Many variations of scanning key-board layout design exist [13, 14]. In *linear* design, selectables are not divided into subgroups and are presented to the user one after the other in some order. For exam-ple, in an alphabetical linear design, the user moves among selectables one after the other in alphabetical order. The shortcoming of this approach is that to make a selec-tion, all the selectables that are placed before the desired selectable have to be tra-versed. In other words, a shortcut to the selectable does not exist. This method is often improved by placing the most frequent letters of the alphabet at the beginning of the list so that fewer focus advancements are required to reach them. Another popular approach, the *row-column* design, groups the selectables into categories as mentioned above. There are many possible variations on the row-column design that aim to im-prove the performance by having subgroups within groups or arranging selectables according to the occurrence probability of their corresponding symbols or commands. Scanning keyboards can either have a *static* or a *dynamic layout*. Static layouts, which we focus on in this work, remain the same during the interaction but dynamic layouts might change after each selection, usually rearranging themselves so that the next most likely selectable is easier to select [8]. There is a tradeoff between the speedup that dynamic layouts can provide and the disorientation users might experience due to selectable rearrangements.

We present an *a priori* method (i.e., a method that can precede human participant experiments) for the analysis and comparison of scanning keyboard designs. This method is context-aware, in the sense that information about context of use is incorporated in the evaluation, and can be used to make predictions about the efficiency of a particular design prior to conducting user experiments, thus decreasing cost and effort considerably.

2   Models of Scanning Keyboards

Different descriptive and predictive models have been developed for the evaluation and design of indirect text entry methods for both assistive technology [1] and mobile computing [9]. The goals of work in this vein include the development of tools for the prediction of outcome (in terms of text entry rate and other efficiency measures) and for the principled design of novel and improved entry techniques. One popular model is the *keystroke-level model* (KLM) [2] that predicts expert error-free task completion times by breaking down a task into sub-tasks and summing up the sub-task times and the additional required overhead. When applied in a priori analysis, the metrics essentially boil down to *mean encoding length* (MEL): the mean number of input actions per character (or the mean amount of time required per character, depending on how "encoding" is characterized). MEL is sometimes normalized in terms of words per minute (wpm).

In prior work, we recognized the similarity of indirect text entry to a code transmission task [1]. In the popular variant of scanning keyboards that uses automatic focus advancement - the encoding alphabet ($\sum$) corresponds to actions that consist of a mix of *dwell periods* (i.e., time it takes for focus to traverse from one element to the next) and input actions. In this context, MEL is a more apt and generalizable evaluation metric than KSPC [7] since it does not assume an equal-cost encoding alphabet and takes into account the time required for focus advancement, if any. It followed from our observation that Information Theoretic source and channel coding techniques could be applied [1]. The behavior of the scanning keyboard can be expressed using an encoding tree and the focus advancement rules, if any. The *encoding tree* is a directed acyclic graph in which each leaf node corresponds to a single selectable in W and each internal node corresponds to a group of selectables that are highlighted during interaction with the system (see figure 1, right). The dynamic behavior of the system is captured by the notion of *focus*. At any given point in time a single node in the graph is in focus. The focus moves in the tree corresponding to the movement of highlighting on the interface of the scanning keyboard. In order to select a selectable, the user has to traverse the focus on the tree from the root to the leaf with the corresponding selectable.

For each selectable, the path from the root of to the corresponding leaf is unique and expresses a prefix-free encoding. Given an encoding tree, MEL can be calculated by weighing the length of each of these encodings by the empirically occurring probability of the symbol corresponding to the selectable in extant text.

3   Reverse-Engineering Scanning Keyboards

We present the *reverse-Huffman algorithm* (RHA), a novel method for *a priori* evaluation of indirect text entry designs. RHA is developed with the view that even extant interfaces are formulable as solutions to the source coding problem and any indirect text entry technique can be seen as an optimal solution for some set of parameters. It aims to extract these parameters and compare them with ones relevant to a target user population.

We hypothesize that there is a hierarchy, often latent, in every scanning keyboard design. This hierarchy expresses the relative importance of the selectables in terms of their occurrence frequency and can also be characterized using a probability distribution. While the existence and ordering of this hierarchy is clear in linear layouts where the selectables are ordered by their frequency or alphabetic occurrence, it is less apparent in more complex layouts that use groups and subgroups. Even in designs where other considerations, such as the user's familiarity with popular layouts such as the alphabetical or QWERTY layouts, inform the layout design, there is still a latent hierarchy that expresses the relative ease of selection for each selectable. In the design of scanning keyboards, it is desirable to make the more frequent selectables easier to select (in terms of time and input actions needed), thus an important design goal is to require a smaller number of input actions to select a more frequent selectable. This is the principle behind using MEL and other related metrics [8]. Thus, this hierarchy would capture the design rational behind a specific layout and recovering it would allow us to compare different designs with each other.

Our method extracts this probability distribution and measures its proximity to extant empirically occurring probability distributions. The result of this comparison predicts the efficiency of the design. This method is a tool for designers to analyze and compare their various designs before conducting experiments with human participants that is a necessary complement to our method and helps paint an accurate picture of what the interaction would eventually look like.

3.1   The Reverse-Huffman Algorithm (RHA)

The Huffman encoding or algorithm is a well-known method for generating efficient encodings [5]. Given a set of *selectables* (W), a probability distribution over W and an *encoding alphabet* ($\sum$), the Huffman algorithm produces an encoding tree with the smallest MEL for each symbol. The *outdegree* of the tree (k), which is the maximum number of children internal nodes can have, is another factor affecting its structure.

We have developed a *reverse Huffman algorithm* (RHA) that views any given encoding tree as the output of the Huffman algorithm for some input probability distribution. Given W, $\sum$ and an encoding tree, RHA extracts a *representative latent probability distribution* from the design. RHA answers the question of what probability distribution best describes the text that a given scanning keyboard can most efficiently create.

We describe the steps of the algorithm: Given a scanning keyboard design variant, we create its corresponding encoding tree. As mentioned before, this tree expresses the ordering of focus advancement over the selectables during interaction. We then transform the given tree into a new encoding tree in which every internal node has the same number of children or outdegree by adding *ghost leafs,* simple place holders that cannot be selected during interaction, to them.

Next, we generate a set of linear constraints on the relationships between the probabilities associated with the selectables that describes the hierarchy of the tree. For a given tree, the constraints describe the infinite set of latent probability distributions that can create the tree if input to the Huffman algorithm.

The constraints are defined as follows. First, the sum of all probabilities must be 1. Second, the probability of each internal node is set to the sum of the probabilities of its immediate children. Next, the selectables are ordered by performing a breadth-first traversal of the tree that visits leaf-nodes in decreasing order of probability. Constraints are created expressing this relationship; the probability of each selectable is more than the probability of the selectable following it. These linear constraints identify the aforementioned set of latent probability distributions. Inputting any member of this set into the Huffman algorithm would result in the modified encoding tree.

Next, a single representative latent probability distribution is identified by using an empirically occurring probability distribution. The empirically occurring probability distribution is derived from extant text corpora and can capture a context in which the design will be used. For example, in our experiments we have used two empirically occurring probability distributions: PCw, derived from a corpus of chat logs and PFw, derived from a corpus of formal English. The differences between the two distributions reflect and express the difference between the texts (due to factors such as different topics of discussion, spelling conventions or degree of language formality among others) created in each context in probabilistic terms. Their incorporation makes our method *context-aware*. Previous research has stressed the importance of incorporating such information about the context in which text will be created [4].

Given an empirically occurring probability distribution, we choose from the set of latent probability distributions, the probability distribution with the minimum sum of absolute differences between its corresponding probability values and the values of the empirically occurring distribution as the representative latent probability distribution. This allows the design rational to be expressed as a single probability distribution that is comparable with other designs, once the same input parameters are applied to them. As will be shown next, the representative distribution is used to measure the efficiency of a design with respect to extant text.

3.2 The Jensen-Shannon Divergence (JSD) as a Measure of Efficiency

The *Jensen-Shannon Divergence* (JSD) is a well-known measure for calculating the distance between two probability distributions [7]. We hypothesized that the JSD value between a representative latent probability distribution and an empirically occurring probability distribution measures the efficiency of the given design for the creation of text similar to the empirically occurring text. To test this hypothesis, we conducted an experiment in which we performed RHA on 36 scanning keyboard design variants. The designs included of 15 variants described by Venkatagiri [11]. These included both row-column variants and linear variants. The row-column variants included the familiar QWERTY layout, as well as, designs informed by symbol occurrence probabilities. The linear designs also included the alphabetical layout, as well as, designs informed by symbol occurrence probabilities. The designs also included 21 variants created automatically by the Huffman algorithm using varying input probability distributions and outdegree values. Together, these design variants formed a diverse set that included both manually and automatically designed layouts. We calculated MEL and JSD values using two, previously described, empirically occurring probability distributions: PCw and PFw.

Next, for each variant, we calculated the normalized ratio of JSD to MEL, calculated as the JSD value over the percentage of improvement of MEL over the worst-case MEL. To clarify the analysis, we grouped the design variants based on their outdegrees and compared two groups of variants: the first group consisted of variants with outdegree 4 and the other group consisted of designs with outdegrees of 6, 6.25 and 7. Figure 2 shows the results.

A correlation analysis of the results showed that the two metrics are positively correlated and a correlation coefficient test showed that the correlation is significant for both PCw and PFw. The results were the same for both design variant groups. The design variants with outdegrees of 4 showed a significant positive correlation for both PCw ($\beta = 7.21$, $t(3) = 22.3$, $p < .005$) and PFw ($\beta = 7.26$, $t(3) = 16.6$, $p < .005$). Also, the design variants with outdegrees of 6, 6.25 and 7 showed a significant positive correlation for both PCw ($\beta = 2.91$, $t(4) = 5.54$, $p < .005$) and PFw ($\beta = 3.13$, $t(4) = 4.15$, $p < .005$).

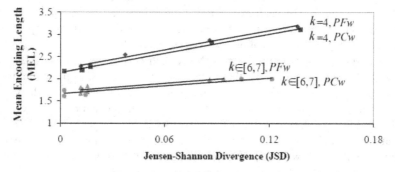

Fig. 2. Relationship between JSD and MEL for designs with outdegrees, k, of 4, 6, 6.25 or 7

Further ANOVA analysis revealed that the correlation between MEL and JSD is not affected by other independent variables. In these tests, the dependant variable was the normalized ratio of JSD to MEL and the independent variables were (1) derivation technique, with two levels indicating whether the design variant was generated using the Huffman algorithm or manually-derived; (2) probability distribution input to RHA, with two levels indicating whether or not the probability distribution used to generate the design variant and the probability distribution used as input to the RHA are the same; and (3) outdegree size, with two levels: large (values larger than 6) and small (values smaller or equal to 6). If JSD is reflective of MEL, we would expect that none of the independent variables will have a significant effect on our dependent variable. ANOVA analysis showed that the effect of all the independent variables is insignificant.

That JSD is positively correlated with MEL confirms our hypothesis that JSD can be an alternative to MEL. Our conjecture has been that JSD effectively measures the divergence of a layout's latent probability distribution and the one that occurs empirically and that this divergence is a fundamental factor in scanning keyboard evaluation. Thus, both MEL and JSD are essentially capturing the "optimality" of the design, but are doing so from different perspectives.

JSD provides several benefits. Firstly, it is easier to interpret than MEL; it has a lower bound of zero and tends to infinity. Moreover, it is valid to compare JSD values of designs that differ from each other in terms of factors such as encoding structure and keyboard layout. In order to analyze design choices, the researcher can build up a distribution of JSD values and develop an intuition about how to interpret particular JSD values prior to implementation. For instance, in our data analysis, the range of JSD values encountered was [0.002, 0.322]; since our data set included design variants that are known to be highly inefficient (e.g., linear QWERTY designs), we know that JSD values around the 0.3 threshold are indeed indicators of very poor designs. A corollary of this finding is that a design is doomed (in terms of its optimality), no matter how clever its underlying design principles, if its representative latent probability distribution diverges by around 0.3 from the empirically occurring probability distribution. A divergence of zero means that the a priori probability distribution is the same as the probability distribution that occurs empirically — that is, the design variant is perfectly matched to the application domain. In sum, a non-zero JSD value means that there will be a difference between how the scanning keyboard is designed and how it actually gets used in its domain. The larger the JSD, the more the actual application domain differs from how the design was envisioned to be used.

The interpretation of MEL, on the other hand, is more complex. Given a particular MEL value, how can one know whether it indicates a reasonably efficient design? It is difficult to know the lower and upper bounds in advance — they depend on the empirically observed probability distribution used to derive MEL. Two cases must be identified. In the first case the evaluation probability distribution is precisely the same as the one used to generate the layout and in the second case it differs. For the first case, the worst-case MEL, for any outdegree size, occurs when the codewords are equiprobable, where MEL will be equal to $\log_{|\Sigma|}(|W|)$, where $|W|$ is the size of the set of selectables and $|\Sigma|$ is the size of the encoding alphabet. The best-case MEL is 1, but this occurs only for boundary cases — for encoding alphabets of size equal to the number of source symbols and for probability distributions so skewed that one source symbol is many times more likely to occur than any other (the precise factor depends on the size of the encoding alphabet). For the second case: the worst- and best-case MELs actually depend on the nature of the divergence between the two probability distributions. So, in sum, given a particular MEL value, it is difficult to ascertain whether it is a "good" or "bad" value — doing so requires an analysis that needs to take into account the size of the encoding alphabet, the shape of the empirically occurring probability distribution, and the divergence between the two probability distributions used for the design and the evaluation of the scanning keyboard design. The lower bound for MEL values differs according to each combination of these three parameters.

4   Conclusion

Our work is built upon the observation that a set of probability distributions that expresses the design rational in terms of the relative importance of the selectables is latent in a given scanning keyboard layout design. We presented the *reverse-Huffman algorithm* (RHA), an Information Theoretic reverse engineering method that extracts a representative latent probability distribution from a given scanning keyboard design variant.

We postulated that the *Jensen-Shannon Divergence* (JSD) between the extracted probability distribution and an empirically occurring probability distribution is a useful metric for the *a priori* evaluation and comparison of design variants. We applied RHA to 36 design variants, extracted their representative latent probability distributions and calculated JSD values using two different empirically occurring probability distributions. We showed that JSD is positively correlated with *mean encoding length* (MEL) and that it is more straightforward to interpret its values. Thus, we established the usefulness of JSD as a metric in this context and have shown that both JSD and MEL are alternative ways of looking at a given design from different perspectives.

References

1. Baljko, M., Tam, A.: Indirect text entry using one or two keys. In: Proceedings of ASSETS 2006, pp. 18–25 (2006)
2. Card, S.K., Nordmann, R.: The keystroke-level model for user performance time with interactive systems. Communications of the ACM 23, 396–410 (1980)
3. Felzer, T., Nordmann, R.: How to operate a PC without using the hands. In: Proc. of ASSETS 2005, pp. 198–199 (2005)
4. Grinter, R.E., Eldridge, M.A.: y do tngrs luv 2 txt msg? In: Prinz, W., Jarke, M., Rogers, Y., Schmidt, K., Wulf, V. (eds.) Proc. of ECSCW 2001, pp. 219–238 (2001)
5. Huffman, D.A.: A method for the construction of minimum-redundancy codes. Proc. of the Institute for Radio Engineers 40(9), 1098–1102 (1952)
6. Kullback, S., Leibler, R.A.: On information and sufficiency. Annals of Mathematical Statistics 22, 79–86 (1951)
7. Lin, J.: Divergence measures based on the Shannon entropy. IEEE Transactions on Information Theory 37(1), 145–151 (1991)
8. MacKenzie, I.S.: The one-key challenge: Searching for a fast one-key text entry method. In: Proc. of ASSETS 2009, pp. 91–98 (2009)
9. MacKenzie, I.S., Soukoreff, R.W.: Text entry for mobile computing: Models and methods, theory and practice. Human-Computer Interaction 17, 147–198 (2002)
10. Majtey, A.P., Lamberti, P.W., Martin, M.T., Plastino, A.: Wootters' distance revisited: a new distinguishability criterium. European Physics Journal D 32, 413–419 (2005)
11. Venkatarigi, H.S.: Efficient keyboard Layouts for sequential access in augmentative and alternative communication. Augmentative and Alternative Communication 15(2), 126–134 (1998)

A Communication System on Smart Phones and Tablets for Non-verbal Children with Autism

Harini Sampath, Bipin Indurkhya, and Jayanthi Sivaswamy

International Institute of Information Technology,
Hyderabad, India
harini@research.iiit.ac.in, {bipin,jsivaswamy}@iiit.ac.in

Abstract. We designed, developed and evaluated an Augmentative and Alternative Communication (AAC) system, *AutVisComm,* for children with autism that can run on smart phones and tablets. An iterative design and development process was followed, where the prototypes were developed in close collaboration with the user group, and the usability testing was gradually expanded to larger groups. In the last evaluation stage described here, twenty-four children with autism used *AutVisComm* to learn to request the desired object. We measured their learning rates and correlated them with their behavior traits (as observed by their teachers) like joint attention, symbolic processing and imitation. We found that their ability for symbolic processing did not correlate with the learning rate, but their ability for joint attention did. This suggests that this system (and this class of AACs) helps to compensate for a lack of symbolic processing, but not for a lack of joint-attention mechanism.

1 Introduction

Autism is a developmental disorder characterized by impairments in social interaction, impairments in verbal and non-verbal communication, and presence of repetitive behaviors. Many children on the autism spectrum lack sufficient speech to meet their communication needs. Augmentative and alternative communication (AAC) systems are designed to fill this void and help these children communicate.

The most prevalent AAC technique used is Picture Exchange Communication System (PECS). PECS uses picture cards and a systematic training approach to help children with autism communicate. PECS training proceeds through six stages in a strict sequence. The first stage is *requesting,* where, using physical and verbal prompts, the child is led to learn to exchange a picture card with the communication partner in order to obtain a desired object. Subsequent stages involve helping the child to learn to make a choice, to combine pictures and make phrases, and so on. The success of PECS with children with autism has been widely reported in literature[1]. But picture cards suffer from a lack of portability and require access to pre-arranged picture cards. Attempts to improve on these two fronts led to the development of electronic communication

K. Miesenberger et al. (Eds.): ICCHP 2012, Part II, LNCS 7383, pp. 323–330, 2012.

aids. These, however, have traditionally been dedicated, custom-built systems for individuals with specific communication difficulties. Some of the commercially available dedicated AAC devices include Dynavox [2] and Vantage Lite [3]. These are picture-based speech generating devices where the child presses a picture on the device's display to playback an appropriate speech message. These speech messages could be either pre-recorded or synthesized using a text-to-speech conversion module.

Recent research on AAC systems has concentrated on improving the speed and richness of the messages constructed by users. BLISS2003 [4] is a communication software that allows users to construct messages using *blissymbols*, which is a graphical language that represents concepts by geometric shapes that are not necessarily iconic. BLISS2003 also features a prediction assistant that can aid faster message construction and the ability to translate bliss messages into natural language. Sibyl [5] is a text-based AAC system, which features letter prediction, word prediction and word completion to improve the speed of message construction. *How was school today?* [6] aims at helping users communicate in terms of conversational narratives. This tool uses sensors to collect data of children's activities, and uses Natural Language Generation to help them in creating narratives based on this data.

The recent proliferation of mobile touchscreen devices like smart phones and tablets offers a new platform to build AAC applications as well as new directions of research. Such devices are more affordable and easily available than the dedicated AAC systems. They are also more socially acceptable as they do not stigmatize the user and adhere to the *Design for Social Acceptance* [7] strategy to develop assistive technology. Currently available AAC applications on mainstream devices include Proloquo2Go [8] and iAugComm [9]. Though there is some anecdotal evidence available that these applications are usable, no formal evaluations have been carried out to assess their efficiency.

Our goal in this research is to design and evaluate an AAC system on a commonly available device that is effective, inexpensive, accessible, and inconspicuous. Light *et al* [10] have proposed a model in which they argue that an individual's ability to effectively use an AAC device depends on three factors: the individual's skills (motor skills, sensory issues, cognitive skills), the device architecture (display organization, selection technique etc.,) and the demands of the communication task (one-on-one communication vs group interaction). Children with autism are a heterogeneous group in terms of their skills and hence it is a challenge to design an application that would ideally suit the need for all. In order to understand the right set of features that would be appropriate for the children and their parents, we opted for a participatory design process. Other recent participatory design approaches to developing assistive systems for children with autism include vSked [11], which is a visual scheduler for classrooms containing students with mild to moderate autism; and the ECHOES project, which aims to teach social skills to children with autism through virtual agents [12].

2   Preference for AAC Platforms - A Survey

In order to find out the users' preferences for AAC platforms we started with a paper-based survey with the parents of children with autism. Twenty parents participated in this survey. Parents were given a form with two questions. The first question was which platform they would prefer for an AAC. They were provided with three options: a laptop, a tablet, a smart phone. In the second question, they were asked to give reasons for their choice. Eighteen responses were collected and analyzed. Seventy-two percent of the parents preferred using a smart phone or tablet as the communication device. The reasons provided by them were: ease of use (the touch screen), portability, cost and interest of the child. Some sample responses from the parents are:

A communication device on a tablet. Touchscreen is easier than keyboard and is portable. It is small in size and he won't attract attention using it.

I think my son can manage a touch screen. If it is a smart phone or tablet, I can carry it wherever I go.

I would prefer a communication device on a laptop. He is very interested in his father's laptop. He watches with interest what is being displayed on the screen.

Since the parents equally preferred a smart phone and a tablet, we chose to build our first prototype on a smart phone as it is more portable and affordable. In the next section, we describe the experiences we had with this prototype with a child with autism and his mother.

3   Participatory Design: Experience with Initial Prototypes

We developed several prototypes in close collaboration with a child with autism and his mother. The child was an eight-year old boy, who was non-verbal and attended a school for children with autism. He had difficulties with fine motor control, and though he had a general affinity for gadgets, he had not used any AAC device before. His mother was a college graduate and had a reasonable exposure to technology: she used a smart phone and a laptop for day-to-day communication and browsing. When we met the child and his family, the parents were trying to teach the child how to use gestures to communicate. Since the child was non-verbal, his mother acted as the proxy and provided us feedback on the prototypes of the design.

We chose to call our system *AutVisComm*. The first prototype was developed on a smart phone with a 3.2" capacitive touchscreen running Google's Android ^{TM}operating system. The vocabulary for the system contained the child's favorite food items. The mother used *AutVisComm* with the child to ask him what he wanted for breakfast that day. However the child had difficulty in choosing the target picture accurately with this form factor. Hence, in the second iteration, we ported the application to a tablet form-factor device. With a tablet, the child was able to choose the images without errors.

The mother felt that a dynamic display, where she could choose the items to be displayed on-the-fly on the screen, would help her to contextualize the AAC better. For instance, if breakfast on a day had apples and bread, she would like to present only those two choices. She felt that the presence of multiple irrelevant items on the screen distracted the child from understanding the ongoing communication. Consequently, we redesigned the application where she could construct *AutVisComm*'s display on-the-fly by choosing images from the device's camera, from the web or from the existing images in the device's memory card. Interestingly, we found that the device's camera was used only rarely. The mother's explanation was that when using the in-built camera, there were always other background items along with the object of interest, and this seemed to distract the child. So we disabled this option in the final prototype. The final prototype is as shown in Figure 1. Once the user opens the application, all the pictures available to them are displayed. Users can choose the pictures they need to construct the display. We used this prototype for further usability evaluation.

4   Usability Study with a Larger Group

At this point we expanded our user group to four children with autism. Three boys and one girl (Mean Age: 8 years; SD: 7 months), and their teacher participated in this usability study. All four children were recruited from a special school for children with autism. Informed consent was obtained from the parents. The teacher and the children used the device for one month. The teacher was initially explained how to use *AutVisComm* and configure the display. The device was used to offer choices like whether the child would like to play in the pool or in the playground.

All activities made with *AutVisComm* like configuring the display, choosing a picture etc. were logged with time-stamp. We found that the configuration time (duration between opening the application to finishing the display configuration) decreased significantly during initial sessions, and from there on remained relatively constant. This shows that teachers could learn to configure *AutVisComm* in very few sessions. Many touchscreen devices provide a tactile feedback when touching a screen element. One child had an aversion to this vibration, and hence this feature was turned off. This apart, no significant usability issues were reported from children. Also the teacher felt that it was easier for her to use *AutVisComm* than to prepare laminated picture cards for each child and keeping track of them.

Our learnings from the participatory design and usability study process are summarized below

- None of the children in the group we worked with found the texture of the device or the touch screen aversive.
- AAC with dynamic display allows caregivers to configure the same device for different children and for different contexts.
- Some children might be aversive to the vibratory feedback available in these devices
- The size of the device to use depends on the fine motor skills of the child.

5 Learning to Communicate Using *AutVisComm*

To help children learn to communicate using *AutVisComm*, we conducted training sessions for all the non-verbal children from a local school for children with autism. The inclusion criteria were the children had no functional speech or speech consisting of less than five words or word approximations. Twenty-four children took part in these sessions and informed consent was obtained from their parents. Each child had two one-on-one sessions per week. Each session lasted for about 15-20 minutes. The goal of these sessions was similar to the *requesting* stage of PECS - to help the child to learn to request his or her desired object using *AutVisComm*.

The session setup is shown in Figure 1. It involved the child, an adult communication partner (teacher), the child's preferred snack item and *AutVisComm*. The food item was beyond the reach of the child, close to the teacher. To receive the food item, the child had to request using *AutVisComm*, i.e. press the appropriate picture on the touch screen device. A single session consisted of five trials. The desired food item remained the same across all trials. In each trial, the teacher asked the child, "What do you want?" If the child responded spontaneously by touching the picture, this was considered an *independent response (IN)*. If the child did not respond spontaneously, the teacher verbally prompted the child, "Press the picture here." If the child responded to this prompt, it was considered a *verbally prompted (VP)* response. If the child did not respond even after the verbal prompt, the teacher held the child's hand and pressed the picture. This was considered *physically assisted (PA)* response.

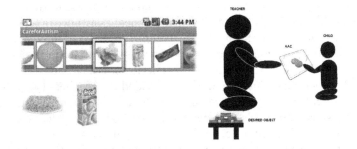

Fig. 1. Final prototype of AutVisComm (left); communication training setup (right)

5.1 Communication Performance

The type of the child's response in each trial (IN, VP or PA) was noted. Then the numbers of IN, VP and PA responses for each child in a session were tabulated, averaged across children, and the mean PA, VP and IN responses per session were computed. Figure 2 shows the data for the first ten sessions. The graph shows that in the first session most children had to be physically assisted: the

328   H. Sampath, B. Indurkhya, and J. Sivaswamy

mean PA response is close to 5. As sessions progressed, the need for physical
assistance became less frequent and most children started responding to the
verbal prompts as indicated by the peak in mean VP response at around session
4. Further into the sessions, the need for verbal prompts also became less frequent
and the children started responding spontaneously as indicated by the increasing
trend of mean IN response.

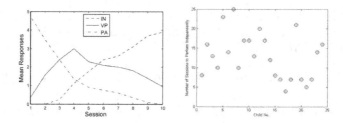

Fig. 2. Communication Performance (left). PA - child pressed the picture with physical
assistance, VP - child pressed the picture after verbal prompt IN - child spontaneously
pressed the picture . Individual differences in learning (right). Each dot denotes the
number of sessions required by the child to achieve at least three IN response trials in
a session. There are 24 dots in all one for each child.

5.2 Individual Differences in Performance

The goal of the training process was to help the children to learn to request the
desired object independently. We consider the child to have learnt this when they
request spontaneously (IN) without verbal or physical assistance in at least three
of the five trials and this performance is sustained in at least three consecutive
trials. In our analysis, we found that there was a large variance in the number of
sessions required for each child to attain this performance as shown in Figure 2.

In order to understand this variance, we provided the teachers (who were not
involved in the children's training sessions with AutVisComm) of the children
a checklist as shown in Table 1. Two teachers rated the students using this
checklist. This was a one-time rating collected at the end of the intervention.
The items in the checklist were drawn from the Autism Behavior Checklist [13].
These items measure for various cognitive capacities of the children like joint
attention, imitation, social skills, symbolic processing etc. The teachers were
asked to rank the children on the 1–5 scale, where 1 indicates that the child
always exhibits the behavior and 5 that the child never exhibits the behavior.
We analyzed the correlation between the ratings provided by the teachers and
the number of sessions required by the child to request independently (IN) with
AutVisComm. The correlations and their associated significance values are also
shown in Table 1. Requesting an object by gesturing (pointing) requires the child
to share attention with the care giver and shift attention between the care giver
and the object of interest and hence considered a measure of joint attention [14].

Toy play indicates that children can use toys to represent objects in reality and hence considered a measure of symbolic thinking [15]. The results indicate that the measure of joint attention was significantly correlated with the performance of the children ($r = 0.526$, $p = 0.01$), while measures related to their symbolic processing and imitation ($r = 0.06$, $p = 0.7$) were not correlated.

Table 1. Performance analysis checklist. Statistically significant ($p < 0.05$) correlations shown in bold text.

No.	Checklist Item	Relates To	Correlation(r)
1	**Gets desired objects by gesturing**	**Joint Attention [14]**	**0.526**
2	**Not responsive to other peoples facial expressions**	**Theory of Mind [16]**	**0.477**
3	Has sensory issues	Sensory Issues	0.324
4	Often frightened or very anxious	Sensory Issues	0.144
5	Does not follow simple commands	Receptive Language	0.138
6	Actively avoids eye contact	Eye Contact	0.114
7	Strong reactions to minor changes in routine	Repetitive Behavior	0.102
8	Does not use toys appropriately	Symbolic Processing [15]	0.067
9	Has special abilities in one area	Rules out mental retardation	0.032
10	Has motor control issues	Motor Issues	0.030
11	Rocks self for long periods of time	Repetitive Behavior	0.028
12	Has not developed any friendships	Social overture	0.020
13	Does not imitate other children at play	Imitation	-0.153
14	Prefers to be occupied with inanimate objects	Repetitive Behavior	-0.298

6 Discussion

Two major deficit areas are considered as contributing to the socio-communication difficulties in children with autism - a) deficits in *joint attention,* that is, the capacity to coordinate attention between people and objects; and b) deficits in *symbolic thinking,* that is, the ability to think in terms of representations rather than actual objects, and understanding the concepts of shared meaning. Both these factors are crucial to language development [14]. Using concrete pictorial representations, which are lesser abstract than language, compensates for the deficit in symbolic thinking. This is suggested from our results where the symbol processing ability of the children does not correlate significantly with performance. However, a picture-based communication system cannot compensate for difficulties in joint attention, and hence this correlates with the children's performance.

7 Future Work

We plan to supplement the analysis presented here with the psychophysical studies with the children with autism to see how psychophysical parameters correlate with behavioral parameters. We also plan to measure the progress in the communication capacity in these children with respect to their ability to combine pictures and communicate in pictorial sentences.

References

1. Charlop-Christy, M.H., Carpenter, M., Le, L., LeBlanc, L.A., Kellet, K.: Using the picture exchange communication system (pecs) with children with autism: assessment of pecs acquisition, speech, social-communicative behavior, and problem behavior. Journal of Applied Behavior Analysis 35(3), 213–221 (2002)

2. Dynavox, http://www.dynavoxtech.com/products/maestro/ (last accessed January 24, 2012)
3. VantageLite, http://www.prentrom.com/vantagelite (last accessed January 24, 2012)
4. Gatti, N., Matteucci, M., Sbattella, L.: An Adaptive and Predictive Environment to Support Augmentative and Alternative Communication. In: Miesenberger, K., Klaus, J., Zagler, W.L., Burger, D. (eds.) ICCHP 2004. LNCS, vol. 3118, pp. 983–990. Springer, Heidelberg (2004)
5. Schadle, I.: Sibyl: AAC System Using NLP Techniques. In: Miesenberger, K., Klaus, J., Zagler, W.L., Burger, D. (eds.) ICCHP 2004. LNCS, vol. 3118, pp. 1009–1015. Springer, Heidelberg (2004)
6. Black, R., Reddington, J., Reiter, E., Tintarev, N., Waller, A.: Using nlg and sensors to support personal narrative for children with complex communication needs. In: Proceedings of the NAACL HLT 2010 Workshop on Speech and Language Processing for Assistive Technologies, SLPAT 2010 (2010)
7. Shinohara, K., Wobbrock, J.O.: In the shadow of misperception: assistive technology use and social interactions. In: Proceedings of the 2011 Annual Conference on Human Factors in Computing Systems, CHI 2011 (2011)
8. Sennott, S., Bowker, A.: Autism, aac, and proloquo2go. Perspectives on Augmentative and Alternative Communication 18(4), 137–145 (2009)
9. iAugComm, http://www.apps4android.org/?p=186 (last accessed January 24, 2012)
10. Light, J., Wilkinson, K., Drager, K.: Designing effective aac systems:research evidence and implications for practice. In: ASHA 2008 (2008)
11. Hirano, S.H., Yeganyan, M.T., Marcu, G., Nguyen, D.H., Boyd, L.A., Hayes, G.R.: vsked: evaluation of a system to support classroom activities for children with autism. In: Proceedings of the 28th International Conference on Human Factors in Computing Systems, CHI 2010, pp. 1633–1642 (2010)
12. Alcorn, A., Pain, H., Rajendran, G., Smith, T., Lemon, O., Porayska-Pomsta, K., Foster, M.E., Avramides, K., Frauenberger, C., Bernardini, S.: Social Communication between Virtual Characters and Children with Autism. In: Biswas, G., Bull, S., Kay, J., Mitrovic, A. (eds.) AIED 2011. LNCS, vol. 6738, pp. 7–14. Springer, Heidelberg (2011)
13. Volkmar, F., Cicchetti, D., Dykens, E., Sparrow, S., Leckman, J., Cohen, D.: An evaluation of the autism behavior checklist. Journal of Autism and Developmental Disorders 18(1), 81–97 (1988)
14. Toth, K., Munson, J., Meltzoff, A., Dawson, G.: Early predictors of communication development in young children with autism spectrum disorder: Joint attention, imitation, and toy play. Journal of Autism and Developmental Disorders 36(8) (2006)
15. Piaget, J.: Play, dreams, and imitation in childhood. Norton, New York (1962)
16. Baron-Cohen, S., Leslie, A.M., Frith, U.: Does the autistic child have a theory of mind. Cognition 21(1), 37–46 (1985)

Assessment of Biosignals for Managing a Virtual Keyboard

Manuel Merino[1], Isabel Gómez[1], Alberto J. Molina[1], and Kevin Guzman[2]

[1] Electronic Technology Department, University of Seville
Avd. Reina Mercedes s/n, 41012, Seville, Spain
manmermon@dte.us.es
{igomez,almolina}@us.es
http://matrix.dte.us.es/grupotais/
[2] Guadaltel S.A. Pastor y Landero, 19, 41001, Seville, Spain
kevinguzman@guadaltel.es

Abstract. In this paper we propose an assessment of biosignals for handling an application based on virtual keyboard and automatic scanning. The aim of this work is to measure the effect of using such application, through different interfaces based on electromyography and electrooculography, on cardiac and electrodermal activities. Five people without disabilities have been tested. Each subject wrote twice the same text using an electromyography interface in first test and electrooculography in the second one. Each test was divided into four parts: instruction, initial relax, writing and final relax. The results of the tests show important differences in the electrocardiogram and electrodermal activity among the parts of tests.

Keywords: affective interfaces, biosignals, control system, disability.

1 Introduction

According to the Eurostat [1], the total population in Europe was 362 million in 1996 which 14.8% of the population between 6 and 64 years old have physical, psychological or sensory disabilities. Therefore, assistive and adapted systems have to be developed. The aim of these ones is to help users in their diary tasks, letting them to live in a more comfortable way.

Focus on software, in general, it can be claimed that these applications have a high degree of flexibility and customizable, but their throughput strongly depends on the adapted device or interface the user needs to interact with it. The aforementioned throughput might also be dramatically reduced for people who suffer from severe disability. Another lack of these software programs is that they cannot be automatically adapted when they are running and self-adjusting to user requirements.

The goal of developing a method for matching parameters that could be modified in an adaptative row-column scanning to each individual user is discussed in [2], but, in that paper contextual information of the application is considered instead of physiological signals. Nowadays there are several researches focus on in incorporate the

K. Miesenberger et al. (Eds.): ICCHP 2012, Part II, LNCS 7383, pp. 331–337, 2012.
© Springer-Verlag Berlin Heidelberg 2012

feature of self-adaptation in different systems or applications. So, based on this concept there are papers whose aim is modify the environment to adapt to the user needs/preferences (Ambient Intelligence) or use biosignals to adjust an application automatically (Physiological Computation [3]).

This paper describes how the use of virtual keyboard (VK) affects different physiological signals and how these ones could be used to incorporate automatic adaptation of functioning parameters in this VK application.

2   Related Work

Disable people need interfaces to be adapted to their physical and cognitive skills. Whatever the user's type of disability, the interface needs to detect user's will in order to select the highlighted row or column on the virtual keyboard. In most cases, user is able to move some muscles and press a special switch, or control a mouse pointer on computer screen through an accelerometer [4]. But sometimes user's ability is constrained to move the eyes; therefore an eye-tracker is required. Electric biosignals can be used instead of those systems. For instance, an electromyography (EMG) system can record muscle activity and substitute the switch, and also electrodes placed around the eyes can be used to detect gaze [5, 6]. Moreover, interfaces based on Brain Computer Interface (BCI) don't require   user movements [7] because this one is based on electroencephalogram (EEG).

Biosignals can be also used as a source of information when user emotional state must be determined. Electrodermal activity (EDA) [8] and electrocardiogram (ECG) are two of the biosignals most used in this area. EDA has been used in several researches about stress and cognitive load [8-10]. It has been shown EDA is a good method to detect different emotional states. A typical experiment to measure the stress [9] is to make a subject calculate several arithmetic operations of different level of difficult in 4 minutes and 3 phases. From phase to phase the level of stress goes up by increasing the operation difficulty. Significance changes in EDA among phases have been reported, such that the cognitive load was evaluated correctly in 82.8% of studied cases.

It has also reported in several papers that the cardiac activity is also affected by the kind of task. In [10] the authors have used biosignals as objective indicators of state of users, where EDA, ECG, EMG and breath frequency were recorded while the subjects played a game.

3   Methodology

3.1   Application

The tests were developed using a customizable VK [6] shown in figure 1. Among other things the VK allows: keys personalization, using different control interfaces based on events and generating a list of predicted words. An extended VK distributed by rows of six characters each is selected. High frequency characters in Spanish language are placed on first rows. A row/column scanning method was used to select a letter or a word on a prediction list. The minimum number of selected characters used to turn on prediction engine was set to 3. The scan time or dwell time was established in 1.6s for EMG control interface and 1.8s for EOG control interface based on 0.65 rule [11].

						antes
OK	e	o	r	c	b	ante
a	s	i	t	q	f	antonio
n	l	u	v	h	ñ	anterior
d	p	g	j	x	w	animales
m	y	z	k	<-	Exit	análisis
						anteriores

Fig. 1. Extended Letter VK

3.2   Signal Acquisition

Three different biosignals were simultaneously recorded during the tests. One of them was used to manage a VK application (EMG or EOG), and the others were registered to determine the stress/fatigue of the user induced by the control interface (ECG, EDA) [8-10].

The assembly used to record the different biosignal is shown in the figure 2. A monopolar assembly was employed to record the ECG signal (figure 2.a). The EDA assembly was placed on the wrist (figure 2.b) [12]. Three electrodes on the arm were used for the EMG signal (figure 2.c). Finally, to pick EOG signal up two electrodes by direction (figure 2.d) where placed around the eye [13] and the ground and reference sensors were placed respectively in the right and left ears.

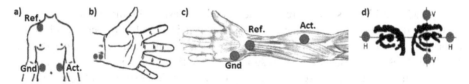

Fig. 2. Electrode positions. a) ECG. b) EDA. c) EMG. d) EOG.

Ag/AgCl electrodes with self-adhesive/conductive gel were used to record the biosignals. Two bioamplifiers were employed: g.USBamp and g.MOBILab of gTec. The first of them registered the control biosignals with a sample frequency of 512Hz for EMG and 128Hz for EOG. A notch filter in (48, 52)Hz was implemented to eliminate the power electric noisy, and a bandpass filter in (5, 200)Hz for EMG and (0.1, 30)Hz for EOG. Also, the version 2.0 of the BCI2000 software was employed [7] to send the event to the VK through a socket. The other bioamplifier recorded the ECG signal with a frequency of 256Hz, a notch filter in (48, 52)Hz and a bandpass filter in (0.5, 100)Hz.

The EDA signal employed a different system: QSensor [12]. This one is a wearable system that wears in the wrist and uses Ag/AgCl electrodes. Different sample frequency can be employed and the data are stored in the internal memory. 32Hz of sample frequency was setting.

The version 7.6.0.324 of Matlab application was utilized to offline analysis of the recorded data.

3.3   Procedure

Trials are focused on text input function of the VK. EMG and EOG signal are considered like control interfaces. Five users without disabilities between 26 and 45 years old participated in these trials (mean 31.2, sd. 7.79); only one of them had used the application before.

The temporal line of the experiment is splitted into four parts:

1. Task explanation and electrode setting. Users are instructed about the task they are going to do. Then electrodes to record EDA, ECG, EOG and EMG signal are placed.
2. Ten minutes of relax. During this time user is reading a magazine.
3. Main activity. Users input a predefined text using virtual keyboard. Command to control the application is based on biosignals. Duration of the trial is user dependent, this is, there is no time to finish it.
4. Rest time. 10 minutes to recover, reading a magazine.

The main task consists in writing a text of 43 words (209 characters). The application is operated by a single event which, in turn, is generated in two different ways: Muscle activity by EMG signal processing or Horizontal Eye Movement by EOG analysis. A wrong character had to be corrected. However, the mistakes made by selecting an incorrect word from the prediction list had to be ignored, so the user had to write the next word.

The ECG and EDA signals are recorded in all phases, excluding phase 1 where the users are instructed. By measuring these signals, it is possible to acquire objective information about the user emotional state. Two State-Trait Anxiety Inventory (STAI) questionnaires were also provided to subjects. They filled them in at the beginning of the relax phases (phases 2 and 4). So, a subjective measure of stress is also achieved.

4   Work and Results

Different parameters of affective signals have been researched. The heart rate variability (HRV) has been the main extracted feature from ECG. Each HRV vector element shows the time between two neighbor heartbeats. The extracted data are classified in two groups: information based on temporal analysis or based on frequency analysis. The standard deviation of beat-to-beat or NN intervals (SDNN), the square root of the mean squared difference of successive NN intervals (RMSSD), the proportion of NN intervals that differ by more than 50 ms (pNN50), the width of the minimum square difference triangular interpolation of the highest peak of the histogram of all NN intervals (TINN), and the entropy of HRV are the parameters of the first group. The other group is based on calculate the power spectrum density (PSD) of the HRV. The PSD is divided in 4 parts: frequency from DC to 0.003Hz (Ultra Low Frequency - ULF), from 0.003 to 0.04Hz (Very Low Frequency - VLF), from 0.04 to 0.15Hz (Low Frequency) and from 0.15 to 4Hz (High Frequency - HF). One additional parameter is the ratio between HF and LF (HF/LF). The influence of each band about the PSD was calculated as the sum of PSD of the band divided by overall PSD sum. In all parameters, a slide window of 5 minutes of width with a shift of 1 heartbeat was applied.

Five parameters were extracted from EDA signal: tendency, average amplitude, mean of derivative, average increase in periods of rising, and time ratio increase. A slide window of 5 minutes of width with a shift of 1 sample was applied.

The extracted information was analyzed through an analysis of variance (ANOVA) for each single subject with a threshold of 1% (alpha parameter - $p < 0.01$). Four analyses for each subject were realized: relax phase 1 vs. main task, main task vs. relax phase 2, relax phase 1 vs. relax phase 2, and relax phase 1 vs. main task vs. relax phase 2. Difference between using EMG or EOG interfaces was the goal of the next ANOVA analysis: relax phase 1 of EMG control vs. relax phase 1 of EOG, main task of EMG vs. main task of EOG, and relax phase 2 of EMG vs. relax phase 2 of EOG. The expected results were the relax phases weren't affected ($p > 0.01$) and the main activities showed significative difference between EMG and EOG ($p < 0.01$). However, the ANOVA results of majorities of subjects in relax phases showed an important influence of unknown variable ($p < 0.01$). So, variations in ECG and EDA signals due to doing main task with EMG or EOG interfaces are not conclude, in despite of the expected results for main tasks were obtained.

Table 1. STAI test results for control interfaces

Phase	User 1		User 2		User 3		User 4		User 5	
	EMG	EOG	EMG	EOG	EMG	EOG	EMG	EOG	EMG	EOG
Relax 1	40	46	43	38	43	47	52	50	43	44
Relax 2	44	45	44	35	41	36	46	45	38	37

The EMG and EOG control interfaces showed the kind of phase affects directly all EDA parameters ($p < 0.00045$). Also, SDNN, RMSSD, pNN50 ($p < 0.0007$) and the bands ULF and VLF ($p < 0.0085$) of ECG parameters showed significative changes when using the EMG interface, while SDNN, pNN50 ($p < 0.0004$) and all frequency bands ($p = 0$) were affected for EOG control . On the other hand, the table 1 with the STAI result showed that the different phases affected to stress state of the subjects, such that the subjective stress level of two of them was higher in the end of the main task than in the begging of test for EMG. The others were a stress level higher in the begging of the test than in the end of main task. Also, the variance (var.) of the modulus of the difference between phases in STAI test was bigger in EOG (var. 8) than EMG (var. 3.44).

5   Conclusion and Planned Lines of Research

This paper presents how the biosignals can be used to manage an application from two points of view: the voluntary control actions and self-adaptation based on the measure of emotion. EMG and EOG are used to control and EDA and ECG to measure emotion.

To sum up, it have done EMG and EOG test and it has been determined by ANOVA analysis what are the parameters of EDA and ECG signals that are affected in different phases of trial. Significant changes were observed in these parameters. So, important differences were found between relax phases and main task. However, it was not possible determinate ECG and EDA changes between EMG or EOG interface, because an unknown variable affected the relaxed periods.

In the future, the aim will be develop an intelligent agent to incorporate to the VK application. This one will adapt automatically the software depending on emotional state of the user to do easier the use of system. So, it is necessary to determine exactly what the causes are which produce the changes in the biosignals, tired or stressed, and how these states affect to the measured parameters.

Acknowledgements. This project has been carried out within the framework of a research program: (p08-TIC-3631) – Multimodal Wireless interface funded by the Regional Government of Andalusia.

References

1. Eurostat. Heath Statistics. Luxembrourg: Office for Official Publications of the European communuties (2002), http://epp.eurostat.ec.europa.eu ISBN: 92-894-3730-8 (retrieved on January 2012)
2. Simpson, R.C., Koester, H.H.: Adaptive One-Switch Row-Column Scanning. IEEE Transactions on Rehabilitation Engineering 7(4), 464–473 (1999)
3. Fairclough, S.H.: Fundamentals of Physiological Computing. Interacting with computers 21(1-2), 133–145 (2009)
4. Gómez, I., Anaya, P., Cabrera, R., Molina, A.J., Rivera, O., Merino, M.: Augmented and Alternative Communication System Based on Dasher Application and an Accelerometer. In: Miesenberger, K., Klaus, J., Zagler, W., Karshmer, A. (eds.) ICCHP 2010. LNCS, vol. 6180, pp. 98–103. Springer, Heidelberg (2010)
5. Dhillon, H.S., Singla, R., Rekhi, N.S., Rameshwar, J.: EOG and EMG Based Virtual Keyboard: A Brain-Computer Interface. In: 2nd IEEE International Conference on Computer Science and Information Technology (2009)
6. Merino, M., Gómez, I., Rivera, O., Molina, A.J.: Customizable Software Interface for Monitoring Applications. In: Miesenberger, K., Klaus, J., Zagler, W., Karshmer, A. (eds.) ICCHP 2010, Part I. LNCS, vol. 6179, pp. 147–153. Springer, Heidelberg (2010)
7. Schalk, G., McFarland, D.J., Hinterberger, T., Birbaumer, N., Wolpaw, J.R.: BCI 2000: A General-Purpose Brain-Computer Interface (BCI) System. IEEE Transactions on Biomedical Engineering 51(6), 1034–1043 (2004)
8. Boucsein, W.: Electrodermal Activity, 1st edn. Springer (1992)

9. Setz, C., Arnrich, B., Schumm, J., La Marca, R.: Discriminating Stress from Cognitive Load Using a Wareable EDA Device. IEEE Transactions on Information Technology in Biomedicine 14(2), 410–417 (2010)

10. Mandryk, R.L., Inkpen, K.M., Calvert, T.W.: Using Psychophysiological Technique to Measure User Experience with Entertainment Technologies. Behavior & Information Technology 25(2), 141–158 (2006)

11. Simpson, R., Koester, H.H., Lopresti, E.F.: Selecting an appropriate scan rate: the rule. 65. Assistive Technology 19(2), 51–58 (2007)

12. Poh, M.-Z., Swenson, N.C., Picard, R.W.: A Wearable Sensor for Unobtrusive, Long-Term Assessment of Electrodermal Activity. IEEE Transactions on Biomedical Engineering 57(5), 1243–1251

13. Merino, M., Rivera, O., Gómez, I., Molina, A., Dorronzoro, E.: A Method of EOG Signal Processing to Detect the Direction of Eye Movements. In: SensorDevices 2010, pp. 100–105 (2010)

Applying the Principles of Experience-Dependent Neural Plasticity: Building up Language Abilities with ELA®-Computerized Language Modules

Jacqueline Stark[1,2], Christiane Pons[1,2], Ronald Bruckner[1], Beate Fessl[1], Rebecca Janker[1], Verena Leitner[1], Karin Mittermann[1], and Michaela Rausch[1]

[1] ELA® Photo Series Vienna, Austria
[2] Austrian Academy of Sciences, Vienna, Austria

Abstract. In this paper, a computerized language therapy program that aims at supplying the required dose of practice for PWAs will be presented, namely the ELA®-Language Modules. The rationale and underlying principles for each linguistic level and the linguistic structure of the language tasks for the word, sentence and text level and for dialogues will be explained and how the components of the ELA®-Language Modules adhere to the principles of experience-dependent neural plasticity. First pilot applications of the ELA®-Language Modules with PWAs are discussed in terms of the principles of experience-dependent neural plasticity and usability.

Keywords: Aphasia, computerized language training, neural plasticity.

1   Introduction

Providing language therapy face-to-face, on a one-to-one basis, to persons with an acquired language disorder ('aphasia') is a dynamic and complex process. In recent years leading clinicians have stressed the necessity of identifying the crucial parameters of the language therapy process and of making this intricate process more explicit (Byng, 1995; Byng & Black, 1995). In this context, Byng's discussion of 'what aphasia therapy is' and 'what constitutes a language therapy session' is basic to any analysis of aphasia therapy conceived for improving the verbal communicative abilities of persons with aphasia (hence PWAs). Within the impairment based approach to aphasia therapy, the focus of therapy refers to the decision made by the therapist in collaboration with the PWA as to how to address his/her language deficits. Optimally, according to an overall therapy schedule based on the individual needs of the PWA, two possible methods are available:

1. Reorganization of the residual language functions by directly working on improving impaired language skills using well thought out therapy protocols, which are based on an analysis of the PWA's impairment(s), or

K. Miesenberger et al. (Eds.): ICCHP 2012, Part II, LNCS 7383, pp. 338–345, 2012.
© Springer-Verlag Berlin Heidelberg 2012

2. Compensating for impaired language functions by circumventing the specific deficit(s) through training (a) particular linguistic unit(s) in a different way to obtain a goal, or
3. A combination of a) and b).

Irrespective of the approach, the structure of each session and the overall therapy protocol as well as the content of every task constituting a session are important. With regard to the structure of the therapy, the emphasis lies on providing specific, linguistically-based therapy protocols that encompass a sequence of steps or tasks, which are conceptualized according to linguistic and psycholinguistic parameters. The term content of the therapy has a twofold meaning. On the one hand, this term refers to the overall structure of the therapy protocol. On the other hand, it relates to the semantic content of the materials used in each therapy session/language task. Every therapy protocol should be based on information, topics, themes which are relevant for the PWA in carrying out his/her daily routines.

Two important variables related to the decision making process for the provision of language therapy are the intensity and the duration of the language therapy. The real-world situation regarding these two variables differs greatly in countries around the world. In light of the increasing financial cutbacks in the health sector, the provision of therapy is becoming increasingly limited in intensity and duration.

In light of this development the ELA®-Language Modules were conceptualized and developed as a supplement to face-to-face therapy on an individual basis and/or as the only option for language rehabilitation for longstanding chronic PWAs when individual therapy is no longer available. By adopting computerized language programs for PWAs the scope of aphasia therapy can be broadened to meet the actual needs of PWAs. In this process, the principles of experience-dependent neural plasticity can be brought to bear and govern the adequate use of computerized language tasks by allowing a PWA to receive the required amount of input to obtain significant gains in his/her language performance.

2   Methods

Language production and comprehension tasks were conceptualized based on multimedia principles, psycholinguistic parameters, and variables relevant for each linguistic level: word, sentence, text and pragmatic (dialogue) as well as for cognitive, non-verbal tasks addressing memory and other higher cortical functions. To date, with partial funding from the Zentrum für Information und Technologie (ZIT – FemPower Call 2007), three language tasks for the processing of language stimuli for each of the aforementioned linguistic levels have been developed in German and programmed (JAVA 1.6, Java Script) for the auditory and visual modalities. Three levels of complexity were developed for each task to enable persons of varying degrees of severity to use the program. Selected tasks were administered to PWAs (n=8) according to their language processing difficulties and applied and discussed in a group setting (i.e. Aphasie-Club (n= 15)).

3   ELA® - Language Modules

Based on the successful applications of the analogue version of the Everyday Life Activities ('ELA®') Photo Series (Stark, 1992 to 2003) administered on a one-to-one basis as well as in group sessions with PWAs, the next logical step was to develop a computerized version of language tasks for rehabilitating the specific language defi-cits of PWAs. The premise of basing the language tasks on everyday life activities was maintained for the computer version keeping the content of the tasks relevant and salient for each PWA. The psycholinguistic and linguistic variables selected for the tasks on each level encompassed basic parameters for the specific level in question (e.g., frequency, length, structure, complexity factors for each linguistic level). An overview of the language tasks developed to date is provided in Table 1.

Table 1. Overview of the tasks in the ELA®-Language Modules software (to date)

Linguistic Level	Task	Nr. of items for auditory/ visual task	Modality of presentation
Word	Object naming according to semantic categories	225 / 225	Auditory/visual
	Object naming of simple and compound nouns	90 / 90	Auditory/visual
	Judging rhyme words	120 / 120	Auditory/visual
	Comprehending minimal pairs	380	Auditory/visual
Sentence	Sentence production	90 / 90	Auditory/visual
	Sentence comprehension	90 / 90	Auditory/visual
	Yes/No sentence judgment	90 / 90	Auditory/visual
Text	Constructing a story	120 / 120	Auditory/visual
	Selecting a title	120 / 120	Auditory/visual
Pragmatic (Dialogue)	Producing a dialogue to themes	200 / 200	Auditory/visual
	Judging politeness	120 / 120	Auditory/visual
	Understanding a dialogue	60 / 60	Auditory/visual
Cognitive	Constructing a picture story	30	Visual (pictures)
	Finding pairs of objects	180	Visual (pictures)
Basic Vocabulary	(Re-) Building a vocabulary	3100 / 3100	Auditory/visual

3.1   Word Level Tasks

The word-level tasks encompassed oral and written naming of picture stimuli and the comprehension of single words presented auditorily and visually, auditory discrimination of minimal pairs and judgment of rhyming of single words. The variables included the structure of the words, the semantic categories, the frequency of the words according to an objective rating (Wortschatz Universität Leipzig, http://wortschatz.uni-leipzig.de) and also a subjective rating by ten persons. For the rhyme judgements and the comprehension of minimal pairs, the levels of complexity for the auditory and written modalities varied according the number of items presented sequentially from two to four words.

3.2   Sentence Level Tasks

The developed sentence-level tasks trained the oral and written sentence production and comprehension of auditorily and visually presented sentences in a multiple choice task design (n=4 picture stimuli), as well as a judgment task requiring the PWA to affirm or negate (Yes-No) that a sentence corresponds to the activity depicted. The three levels of complexity were based on a combination of the variables verb-argument structure, semantic reversibility, sentence structure and length. For the sentence comprehension task, three distractors were chosen based on the variables selected for the sentence level.

For remediating word and sentence level language processing difficulties several computer programs are available. However, computer programs with systematically, well structured language tasks for text and pragmatic level (dialogue) abilities are lacking. For both the text level and the pragmatic (dialogue) tasks, the context in which a test item is embedded is important. For this reason, the context is given in the form of a heading for each item for several of the tasks.

3.3   Text Level Tasks

For the text/discourse level, the developed tasks include producing or constructing a text from auditorily presented or visually presented, i.e. written stimuli, finding a title for a story and comprehension of auditorily and visually presented texts. The complexity of the texts presented in the task "finding a title" is based on the length of the texts. The texts varied from ~ 35 words for level 1, ~52 for level 2, to ~71 for level three. Complexity was also built into the number of titles to choose from. Two, three or four titles were provided for level 1, level 2 and level 3, respectively.   For the task text production/construction, the number of sentences varied for the three levels of complexity from three sentences for level 1, four for level 2 to five sentences for level 3 presented in auditory or written form to be put in the correct order to form a 'story'.

3.4   Pragmatic (Dialogue) Level Tasks

The pragmatic level is represented in the ELA® - Language Modules in the form of tasks requiring the production of a dialogue on numerous themes that encompass various semantic categories reflecting daily routines in everyday life, judging the politeness of utterances in specific contexts and judging or comprehending auditorily or visually presented dialogues, by determining which picture stimulus reflects the presented dialogue. For the task of producing a dialogue, the complexity of the dialogues ranges from one turn-taking for level 1, to one turn-taking plus a response for level 2, to two turn-takings for level 3. The same parameters hold for the length of the dialogue for the three levels of complexity for the task of judging which picture stimulus reflects the content of a dialogue. In this task the context is provided by picture stimuli. Upon hearing or reading a dialogue, which is based on a set phrase, the PWA is expected to select the picture that matches the dialogue. For level one the selection is from two picture stimuli and for level three from three picture stimuli, whereby the distractors are selected according to linguistic variables.

For the pragmatic level task of judging the politeness of utterances in a specific con-text, the complexity was governed by the number of responses to choose from, e.g. for level 1, one response out of three is polite and for levels 2 and 3, two out of four responses are polite. The third level of complexity makes added use of intona-tion, whereby one of the auditorily presented items is spoken in an ironic manner.

In particular, the text and pragmatic level tasks allow for the remediation of the language processing deficits revealed by high level aphasics, i.e. PWAs who have minimal language impairments. For these PWAs adequate, more complex language stimuli covering relevant semantic categories are required, whereas the tasks com-posed of linguistically less complex stimuli are essential for more severely impaired PWAs, i.e. word and sentence level tasks. For these severely impaired PWAs, the level 1 of the word and sentence level tasks are necessary and proved to be more ade-quate in the pilot applications.

3.5   ELA® -Basic Vocabulary

An additional software package developed in conjunction with the ELA® - Language Modules is the ELA® - Basic Vocabulary program. It is conceived primarily as a program for (re-) learning vocabulary, in this case the names of over 3000 depicted objects can be repeatedly practiced in a structured manner. The words can be selected based on their semantic categories, frequency and the number of main forms (with and without determiners/articles) to be presented for a single item, e.g.: 'Mensch' – 'ein Mensch' – 'der Mensch' – 'Menschen' – 'die Menschen'. An auditory and a visual/written version are the two options for administering the program.

Examples for the sentence level, text level, pragmatic level (dialogue) and for the basic vocabulary are shown in Figures 1a and b and 2a and b, respectively.

Fig. 1. a and b. Examples of items for the task written sentence and text production, respec-tively

Fig. 2. a and b. Examples of items for the task producing a dialogue in written language and for the auditory version of the ELA® Basic Vocabulary, respectively

4   Application of the Principles of Experience-Dependent Neural Plasticity

The tasks included in the ELA® - Language Modules are linguistically structured. The question arises as to how the tasks and the overall modules are in accordance with the principles of experience-dependent neural plasticity. In consideration of the amount of linguistic input and practice that is required for (re-)learning language following brain damage, it is comprehensible that providing sufficient opportunity to learn is a major challenge. Equally important, however, is what is to be learned. The structure and the content of the ELA® -Language Modules fulfill the principles 1 to 7 put forward by Kleim and Jones (2008). These principles are summarized in Table 2.

Table 2. Principles of experience-dependent plasticity (from Kleim and Jones, 2008)

1. Use It or Lose It	Failure to drive specific brain functions can lead to functional degradation.
2. Use It and Improve It	Training that drives a specific brain function can lead to an enhancement of that function.
3. Specificity	The nature of the training experience dictates the nature of the plasticity.
4. Repetition Matters	Induction of plasticity requires sufficient repetition.
5. Intensity Matters	Induction of plasticity requires sufficient training intensity.
6. Time Matters	Different forms of plasticity occur at different times during training.
7. Salience Matters	The training experience must be sufficiently salient to induce plasticity.
8. Age Matters	Training-induced plasticity occurs more readily in younger brains.
9. Transference	Plasticity in response to one training experience can enhance the acquisition of similar behaviors.
10. Interference	Plasticity in response to one experience can interfere with the acquisition of other behaviors.

With each application of the program and by repeated use of the software, Principles 1 and 2 are implemented. The user-friendly format of the modules and the randomization of the items each time a task is started will motivate the PWA to go through the tasks repeatedly to improve his/her language performance and practice at a self-prescribed pace without becoming bored.

Principle 3 is directly addressed by the systematic and linguistic structure of the overall program. Each task is based on psycholinguistic and linguistic variables relevant for the specific units to be practiced. Specificity of each task is a feature of the overall concept of the ELA®-programs. Another very individualized aspect of the structure of the tasks is that a PWA determines the pace of progressing through the exercises. After responding to each item, he/she can listen to the stimulus and/or correct a response as often as he/she feels the necessity to do so. The program does not automatically proceed to the next item after a response has been given to each item. This allows each PWA to work through the tasks at his/her own speed. The breakdown in three levels of complexity and in auditory and written modalities permits a structured build-up, which is particularly important for more severely impaired PWAs and for obtaining a transfer from one modality to another (Principle 9). Tasks are available for a range of difficulties.

Inherent in computerized language software are Principle 4 and Principle 5: Repeat to remember and remember to repeat. These principles stress the necessity of allowing the PWA to receive sufficient repetition and intensity. A high dosage can be achieved by repeated applications throughout the day. In connection with the repetition of language stimuli, intensity and duration are two principles crucial for achieving improvement in language performance and for obtaining a transfer to other items, tasks, etc.

As it is not known which forms of plasticity come into play at specific times in the recovery process, being able to practice for a long period of time will make it more possible to apply the programs at the appropriate times for learning.

The relevance of the themes and topics for all of the items in the program make the tasks sufficiently salient (Principle 7). Since basic everyday life activities constitute the organizing principle, salient task items are guaranteed. The further breakdown according to the frequency of single items into three groups - frequently used, less frequently used and least frequently used words/terms - allows a structured build up.

According to the principles of experience-dependent neural plasticity an enormous amount of repetition is necessary. This high dosage is achievable by means of com-puterized language programs. The pilot applications with the individual PWAs result-ed in repetition of those tasks which were accomplishable and also allowed a step-by-step build up from less to more complex. Overall in the pilot applications, the option to listen to and repeat the items several times before going on to the next item, was utilized on a regular basis. This demonstrates the need for a great deal of repetition to strengthen and enhance performance. With regard to enhanced performance, it is assumed that with extended use of the program, Principle 9, i.e. a transfer to other items, tasks or modalities will be observed. Continued use of the software will also demonstrate transference from one modality and/or from one level of complexity to another. The pilot applications cannot address this issue. Only extended use of the program will allow the clinician to document the progress made by each PWA. In order to document the evolution of a PWA's progression and changes in language performance accurately, a statistics program must be built into the software program. The next step in the development of the ELA® - Language Modules is the programming of such a procedure.

5   Summary

On average, the amount of therapy a PWA receives does not comply with what would be necessary to bring about significant changes in verbal communicative abilities. In order to fill the gap, additional practice can be provided by computerized language therapy programs. As previously stressed, the content of what is to be learned is a crucial variable. The structure and the content of the tasks constituting the ELA® - Language Modules comply with the principles put forward by Kleim and Jones (2008). It is this synthesis of linguistic structure, specificity and the repeated applicability that makes this program suitable for PWAs of varying degrees of severity of their language impairments. The ELA®- Language Modules allow the PWA the necessary repeated applications, which inevitably enhance the process of (re-) learning of language on the word to text level and within each linguistic level for the three levels of complexity.

In summary, the first applications demonstrate the value of selecting adequate linguistic parameters for the language tasks on all linguistic levels and also for the breakdown according to three levels of complexity. The combined adherence to psycholinguistic and linguistic variables and the principles of experience-dependent neural plasticity provide a conducive environment for (re-) learning and, thus, are more likely to facilitate transfer to everyday use of language in various contexts.

References

1. Byng, S.: What is Aphasia Therapy? In: Code, C., Muller, D. (eds.) The Treatment of Aphasia, pp. 1–17. Whurr, London (1995)
2. Byng, S., Black, M.: What Makes a Therapy? Some Parameters of Therapeutic Intervention in Aphasia. Europ. Journal of Disorders of Comm. 30, 303–316 (1995)
3. Kleim, J., Jones, T.: Principles of Experience-Dependent Neural Plasticity: Implications for Rehabilitation after Brain Damage. Journal of Speech, Language, and Hearing Research 51, S225–S239 (2008)
4. Raymer, A., et al.: Translational Research in Aphasia: From Neuroscience to Neurorehabilitation. Journal of Speech, Language, and Hearing Res. 51, S259–S275 (2008)
5. Robertson, I.H., Murre, J.M.J.: Rehabilitation of brain Damage: Brain plasticity and Principles of Guided Recovery. Psychological Bulletin 125, 544–575 (1999)
6. Stark, J.: Everyday Life Activities Photo Series. Jentzsch, Vienna (1992, 1995, 1997, 2003)

Assistive Technology: Writing Tool
to Support Students with Learning Disabilities

Onintra Poobrasert and Alongkorn Wongteeratana

NECTEC, Pathumthani, Thailand
{onintra.poobrasert,alongkorn.wongteeratana}@nectec.or.th

Abstract. Previous studies show that assistive technology has a significant impact on helping students with disabilities achieve their academic goals. Assistive technology is hardware, devices and software equipment that help students with disabilities by giving them the same access to perform certain tasks that would otherwise have been challenging. Selecting an appropriate AT tool for a student requires parents, educators, and other professionals take a comprehensive view, carefully analyzing the interaction between the student, the technology, the tasks to be performed, and the settings where it will be used. Therefore, this study was conducted in order to confirm the effective use of assistive technology such as Thai Word Search. The results reflected an improvement in student achievement and appeared to make a greater contribution toward student in this study when using assistive technology to support writing.

Keywords: Assistive technology, Dysgraphia, Learning disabilities, Single subject design, Writing tool.

1 Introduction

Most physicians state that people usually has a learning disability from birth or sometimes from early childhood. Although it is a permanent condition, people with a learning disability can and do learn and develop with the right sorts of support from other people [1]. In addition, Horowitz [2] informs that people with learning disabilities fall into one of two categories which are nonverbal and verbal. People with nonverbal learning disabilities may have difficulty processing what they see. They cannot understand the visual details like numbers on a book or the blackboard. Nonverbal learning disability may confuse the plus sign with the sign for division. They also have problem with abstract concepts like fractions which may be difficult to master for them. People with verbal learning disabilities have difficulty with words, both spoken and written. Verbal learning disabilities such as disabilities in basic writing affect the learner's ability to write words with correct spelling, appropriate word choice, and basic mechanics such as letter formation, grammar, and punctuation [3]. People with learning disabilities in basic writing may not understand the relationship between letters and the sounds they represent and often cannot distinguish the correct written word from the incorrect word. Learning disabilities in basic writing are also sometimes referred to as Dysgraphia [4]. Learning disabilities in writing may be genetic, caused by differences in brain development, brain

K. Miesenberger et al. (Eds.): ICCHP 2012, Part II, LNCS 7383, pp. 346–352, 2012.

injury, or stroke. They are not solely the result of problems with expressive or receptive language, visual or hearing problems, or hand-eye coordination, but they can be complicated by these conditions [5].

Moreover, writing and reading process are related to each other. Students with learning disabilities in reading also have problems in spelling as well. Spelling difficulties can be endured in individuals with reading difficulties, sometimes even after reading has been successfully remediated. Addressing spelling difficulties is important, because poor spelling can hamper writing and can convey a negative impression even when the content of the writing is excellent [6]. Therefore learning methods of students with learning problems are different from other students. The techniques used are also different as well as the technologies. Although some students with learning disabilities will be able to study with normal students, they require special processes or methods of teaching to draw out their expertise and unique talents in order to replace or remove their weaknesses [7].

2   Methodology

In this study *single subject research design* (a single-case experimental design) was applied into our experiment. We use this method when the sample size is one or when a number of individuals are considered as one group. These designs are typically used to study the behavioral change an individual exhibits as a result of some treatment [8]. In single-subject design, each participant serves as his or her own control.

2.1   Subject Selection

- The instructor of grade 6th at the school in Bangkok gave advice on selection of student to finally get one student named Pete (Pseudo name).
- Pete is a student with severe learning difficulties who struggle with writing. He was selected to participate in the experiment.
- Pete's writing ability was tested on the specific vocabulary where each of which was allocated about 12 minutes to finish the test (25 words). This is to confirm that he has learning difficulties in writing and is willing to participate in this study.

2.2   Material and Equipment Used in the Study

The number of children with learning disabilities is increasing whereas the use of assistive technology is still limited in Thailand. Moreover, students with learning disabilities still have to learn the same way as normal students because the use of assistive technology in the country is still limited [9]. Though in the market, there are various types of assistive technology for students with learning disabilities, those tools are not suitable for Thai students. Most of them are designed and developed for English speakers. The prices of those assistive technology tools are also expensive. Hence, we have to design and develop our own assistive technology for students with learning disabilities in Thailand. Previous researches on assistive technology and disabilities stated that assistive technology will help increase the ability or adjusting proficiency of students with learning disabilities to learn effectively. Therefore Thai Word Search Program is designed and developed in order to confirm previous researches.

The Thai Word Search program assists the students with learning disabilities when they want to write any vocabulary that he or she cannot spell it correctly, the student will just type part of word according to pronunciation or as guessed, the program will then check and demonstrate the words for selection that most likely matches the one desired by the student including their pronunciation. The program will provide assistance in searching for vocabulary either in the mode of Homophony or Soundex   or Word Approximation (words with a similar depiction; probably be misspelled or wrong tone) [10].

In this study we applied Vaja-TTS (Thai text to speech) as one of its components aimed to read text and convert it to voice for the user. Pronunciation of vocabulary by Vaja-TTS can help students with learning disabilities to hear and select the desired vocabulary correctly [11]. We also applied the Thai Query Correction or Thai Q Cor (a service rendered in the pattern of web server with an ability to verify vocabulary wrongly written by the user, by presenting in, for instance, homophony or related written word due to wrong word writing or spelling) [12] into our program.

Additionally, interface design and the component of Thai Word Search Program will demonstrate in figure 1. Figure 1 shows the interface design and the components of Thai Word Search Program. The Component of Thai Word Search Program consists of 4 parts (1) Menu Button, (2) Keyboard Parameter Display, (3) Vocabulary List, and (4) Page Selection.

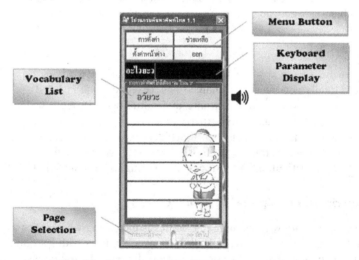

Fig. 1. The Component of Thai Word Search Program

3   Experiment

3.1   Activity A:

- The subject was required to write 25 vocabularies with pen or pencil on paper.
- The subject was required to type instead of writing the same vocabularies using a word processor with the assist of assistive technology program Thai Word Search.

3.2   Activity B:

- The subject was required to summarize the lesson learned in Science class.
- The subject was required to write on favorite activity during the holidays.

Figure 2 demonstrates Pete's handwriting on paper and displays Pete's typing in a word processor. He also uses assistive technology *Thai Word Search Program* to assist him in his writing. This figure also shows his personal log file.

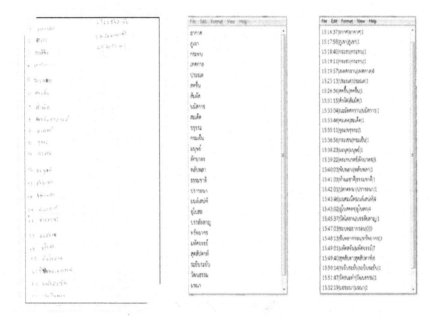

Fig. 2. Pete's handwriting and Pete's typing with Word Processor and log file

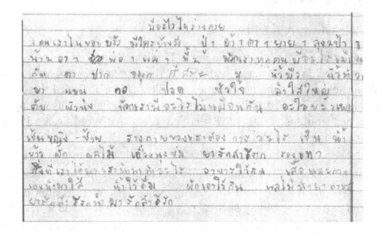

Fig. 3. Pete's handwriting on the title: Anatomy of Our Body

After the Science class, Pete was required to summarize the lesson he learned. He was required to accomplish two tasks (i) writing down with a pen or pencil on his workbook and (ii) typing with Word Processor using Thai Word Search program. Figure 3 presents Pete's handwriting on the title: Anatomy of Our Body. Figure 4 shows Pete's personal log files when he used Word Processor with Thai Word Search.

Fig. 4. Personal log file

4   Analysis and Results

Analysis of the Activity A as follows:

1. When Pete wrote 25 vocabularies, he made 23 misspelling words.
2. When Pete typed 25 vocabularies with Word Processor and use assistive technology Thai Word Search program, he made a 1 mistake. This is indicated that Pete made less mistakes while he used assistive technology to support him in his writing.
3. We examined from his personal log file, Pete used Thai Word Search Program as assistive technology to help him select the right word. However, he made a mistake of word สะเด็ด   [sa-ded] since he selected สะเด็ด instead of เสด็จ [sa-dej]. The pronunciation of สะเด็ด and เสด็จ are quite similar but both have different meaning.
4. From the personal log file, Pete was trying to use Thai Word Search in assisting him to find correct vocabulary such as word ทรัพยากร. He repeated 2 trials because the first round his typing did not match with Soundex or approximation process used within the program. He tried again and this time Soundex was working.

Then he finally found the correct word ทรัพยากร, which was attempted to be in the third place on the list.

5. With the assist of assistive technology, Thai Word Search Program, Pete can be able to select correct vocabularies more than without the assist of assistive technology (88%).

Figure 5 shows the comparison of Pete's scores between using assistive technology and without using assistive technology.

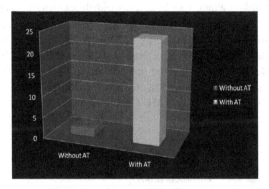

Fig. 5. Comparison of Pete's scores

Analysis of the Activity B as follows:

1. Pete has a strong intention to practice and use assistive technology program on his writing.
2. As mentioned from his teachers and shows on Figures 2, and 3 Pete has a severe learning disability in writing however, with the assist of Thai Word Search Program, Pete can perform his writing skill better.
3. His writing on the title: Anatomy of Our Body, Pete used assistive technology program Thai Word Search to assist him to choose correct vocabularies. Pete did not make any mistake in his typing therefore he can type correctly 100%.
4. His writing on the title: Makha Bucha Day, Pete used assistive technology program Thai Word Search to assist him to choose correct vocabularies. He made a few mistakes. In this topic, Pete can type correctly 91.67%.
5. The pronunciations of some vocabularies are similar, hence Pete made a few mistakes because the meanings of those vocabularies are different.

5   Conclusion

In conclusion, Pete was in agreement with the advantages of the assistive technology; Thai Word Search which could help him in his spelling and search words well and fast. Pete also mentioned that the program assisted him to be able to choose vocabulary and print the work correctly.

In addition, he agreed that Thai Word Search was simple, and not complicated. The program also helps him to know how each word is spelled as it provides pronunciation for each word. Although the pronunciation by the program for some word was deviated, Pete admitted that the program could help him to be able to pronounce vocabulary better than without using the program. Moreover, in the near future, Thai Word Search features can be applied to work in combination with programs such as Thai Spell Checker for LD, Thai Word Prediction for LD, and Thai Word Processor for LD in order to enhance students with learning disabilities in their learning as well as to optimize their accurate writing.

Acknowledgements. We would like to convey our thanks and acknowledge the assistance of the Human Language Technology Lab (HLT), National Electronics and Computer Technology Center (NECTEC). Our thanks also extend to the Cluster and Program Management Office (CPMO), National Science and Technology Development Agency (NSTDA) for funding the project. Additionally, we would like to give our special thanks to Ms. Wantanee Phantachat, Dr. Putthachart Pothibal, Dr. Somporn Warnset, Ms. Kuanjai Poyu, and Ms. Chadanit Sripanit.

References

1. Lyness, D'Arcy: Learning Disorders (2007),
   http://kidshealth.org/teen/diseases_conditions/learning/lear
   ning_disabilities.html
2. Horowitz, S.: Learning Disabilities Explained (2008), http://www.ncld.org/ld-
   basics/ld-explained/basic-facts/learning-
   disabilitiesexplained-again
3. The Learning Disabilities Association Canada. Learning Disabilities (2005),
   http://www.ldactaac.ca/defined/defined_new-e.asp
4. Kemp, G., Smith, M., Segal, J.: Learning Disabilities in Children (2011),
   http://www.helpguide.org/mental/learning_disabilities.htm
5. Logsdon, A.: Basic Writing Disabilities and Learning Disabilities (2012),
   http://learningdisabilities.about.com/od/learningdisabilityb
   asics/p/ldbasicwriting.htm
6. Spear-Swerling, L.: Spelling and Students with Learning Disabilities (2005),
   http://www.ldonline.org/article/5587
7. Gersten, R., Fuchs, L., Williams, J., Baker, S.: Teaching Reading Comprehension Strategies to Students with Learning Disabilities: A Review of Research. Review of Educational Research Summer 71(2), 279–320 (2001), doi: 10.3102/00346543071002279
8. Gay, L.R., Airasian, P.: Educational Research: Competencies for Analysis and Applications. Merrill Prentice Hall, Columbus (2003)
9. Poobrasert, O., et al.: Technology-enhanced Learning for Students with Learning Disabilities (2011),
   http://doi.ieeecomputersociety.org/10.1109/ICALT.2011.154
10. Wren, S.: Phoneme Awareness (2004),
    http://www.balancedreading.com/phonemeawareness.html
11. Human Language Technology Lab: HLT-VAJA (2009),
    http://www.hlt.nectec.or.th/products/vaja.php
12. Haruechaiyasak, C., et al.: A Comparative Study on Thai Word Segmentation Approaches. In: Proceeding of ECTI-CON (2008)

Communication Access for a Student with Multiple Disabilities: An Interdisciplinary Collaborative Approach

Frances Layman[1], Cathryn Crowle[2], and John Ravenscroft[3]

[1] Cerebral Palsy Alliance
NSW Australia
flayman@cerebralpalsy.org.au
[2] Children's Hospital Westmead,
NSW Australia
cathryn.crowle@health.nsw.gov.au
[3] Moray House School of Education
The University of Edinburgh
United Kingdom
john.ravenscroft@ed.ac.uk

Abstract. This case study highlights the challenges and outcomes of implementing assistive technology for a 17 year old school student with a profound hearing loss, and significant physical disabilities. It demonstrates the importance of a collaborative team approach and the benefits for the student of using assistive technology with regards to the development of self determination and social relationships. This article is of benefit for inter-professional teams working in special education, particularly with students with multiple disabilities.

Keywords: Accessibility, Assistive Technology, Augmented and Alternative Communication (AAC), Design for All, and User Involvement.

1   Introduction

We know the significant effect of secondary disabilities, including multisensory impairments, on the participation and independence of people with cerebral palsy (CP) [13]. While cerebral lesions associated with CP can affect cognitive functioning, conversely, restrictions in social participation resulting from CP can also result in delays to cognitive development. This implies that opportunities for participation and social interaction are vital for maximising cognitive potential [4].

Young adults with disabilities, including those who use augmentative and alternative communication (AAC), may have reduced social networks and are at risk of experiencing loneliness due to limited access to social interactions. This can make it difficult to form and maintain friendships and other relationships [5].

Technology has been shown to improve the quality of life, academic achievements, access to education and independence of people with disabilities [3]. More specifically, the benefits of assistive technology for students with multiple disabilities are well documented. Assistive technology has improved access and participation for children

K. Miesenberger et al. (Eds.): ICCHP 2012, Part II, LNCS 7383, pp. 353–360, 2012.

with multiple disabilities in their school & home environments, and has been described as a means of enabling mastery or control over the environment [6]. Some of the benefits of assistive technology include the ability to make choices with the use of augmented or alternative communication [20], enhanced social interactions; [9], [1], and increased motivation and self-esteem [18]; [19].

1.1   The Collaborative Team Approach

Collaboration appears to have no single definition, as models of teamwork vary according to the disciplines involved and the structure of the organisation in question. The interchangeable terms joined-up services, co-ordinated approaches and interdisciplinary working, have all appeared under the umbrella term "integrated services delivery" [14]. In any setting, collaboration implies critical co-operation towards a mutually agreed outcome; in this case supporting a young adult with multiple disabilities through the assistive technology process. According to Gilbert and Bainbridge [11], effective collaboration requires open boundaries and an effective means of sharing resources between disciplines.

1.2   Collaborative Working in Action

In order to successfully meet assistive technology goals for students with multiple disabilities, a collaborative model for assessment and planning is needed [6].

Each member of the educational team has a significant role to play in AT assessment and implementation. The literature describes the role of teachers as being responsible for technology integration into the curriculum and providing opportunities for students to practice using their technology for functional tasks. Conversely, paraprofessionals are described as being more involved with the set up of equipment and general support to the student [3]. While these role descriptions are valid, successful AT assessment and implementation only occurs when these roles are carried out collaboratively. Within the school setting, constant evaluation of AT implementation and sharing of ideas occurs through regular informal discussion and more formally as part of the student's Individual Education Plan [IEP] which is developed with input from teachers, therapists and the students' family.

One of the occupational therapist's responsibilities is to determine ways for the student to interface effectively with technology [6]. In this case study, the process of deciding on suitable switches and appropriate switch sites was lengthy, and involved many trials. Importantly, it involved significant liaison with the student's family and classroom staff. Integral to this was continual monitoring and modifications to the student's seating in his wheelchair to ensure optimal postural support and alignment.

A Speech Pathologist's role in the assistive technology team is to recognise the impact of the students' physical, sensory and intellectual limitations on functional communication and to assist in sourcing and implementing appropriate hardware and software that promotes the expressive and receptive language skills, and interaction opportunities, of the student [12]; [8]. This is not done in isolation, relying on collaboration with the Occupational Therapist regarding alternative access methods, and external agencies who can provide equipment trials and up-to-date information about advances in software and switching devices.

Many other professionals played vital roles in the long term implementation of the Assistive Technology system outlined in this case study. The Psychologist's role included early assessment of the student's intellectual ability, and a specific interest in his ability to demonstrate new skills as his independent functioning increased with the implementation of his AT, as this contributed to the team's understanding of his cognitive ability. The Orthoptist's involvement increased once regular use of the AT equipment began, as regular use of a computer monitor created some visual discomfort for the student. The Physiotherapist was involved in maintaining general postural alignment and health to support the use of AT, and worked jointly with the OT to achieve the optimum seating for function.

1.3   Process of Assessment

There are several examples in the literature of structured AT assessments. Copley & Ziviani [7] describe the Lifespace Access Profile and Lifespace Access Profile Upper Extension. The types of information collected in these assessments include general health, vision, hearing and sensation, postural control, muscle tone, coordination, mobility support, range of motion, and body sites for switch access. These assessments also consider cognition, receptive and expressive communication, understanding of switch functions, and methods of choice-making. Information is also gathered on which position the student is best able to access technology and the body parts used, including ways of facilitating or stabilising the student.

A Lifespace Access Profile was completed for our student at the age of 7 years, 9 months. However, factors such as his health, motivation, availability of technology, staffing changes and the process of trialing numerous access methods and devices meant that it was nearly a decade later that his current assistive technology system was implemented for computer access, voice output communication and independent mobility in his power chair. This indicates that while the information gathered in the LAP is essential for AT assessment and prescription, a single discrete assessment event will not always lead to a prompt and final AT prescription. For this student, ongoing assessment and a flexible approach to implementation was needed. In a school program there is the advantage of having ongoing involvement with the student and their family over a number of years, which allows this flexibility and the potential to continually review outcomes as a team, in response to collaborative goal setting and student needs.

2   Case Study

The subject of this case study is Nick[1] a 17 year old male student who attends a special school in Sydney, Australia. Nick has a diagnosis of dystonic Cerebral Palsy with

---

[1] Nick's name has been changed to ensure confidentiality.

spastic quadriplegia (GMFCS level V) [16], and a profound hearing loss, for which he is unaided due to a perceived lack of benefit from hearing aids fitted when he was younger. He is non-verbal and communicates expressively using an alphabet board facilitated by a communication partner who finger scans through the letters until Nick indicates that they have reached the correct letter. He has a clear and consistent "yes"/"no" response and uses natural communication modes such as vocalisations, eye gaze and facial expression to communicate his mood, needs and interests. Nick's communication partners use signs (in combination with gesture, facial expression, reference to real objects, and handwriting) to convey messages to him. Nick's inability to speak, and lack of independence in daily living activities makes it difficult to reliably assess his level of intellectual functioning. During his most recent cognitive assessment Nick's scores in different subtests varied within the "extremely delayed" to "average" range. As a result of this variance and due to the modifications required to present test items to Nick (e.g. signing instead of speaking the instructions) and the fact that some subtests couldn't be administered due to Nick's lack of manual control, the assessing psychologist was unable to definitively state Nick's level of cognitive functioning. However, his progress in his literacy and communication, ability to learn new skills and develop independent computer proficiency since implementing his assistive technology are indicative of an effective memory and an ability to perform tasks he was not able to demonstrate before, when his independence was facilitated with appropriate AT.

Using a collaborative working approach that has been engendered, the extended team consists of Teachers, teacher's aides, Physiotherapists, Occupational Therapists, Speech Pathologists, Orthoptists, a School Psychologist and an Audiologist. The team operates in an interdisciplinary, collaborative manner [15]. Staff generate their own goals related to their specific area of focus (e.g. communication, fine motor skill development, positioning), but work with other team members to develop joint goals, share information and responsibilities, and train others in relevant techniques. The team, with family and carers regularly discuss priorities for each student and goals are documented in the students' Individualised Education Plans.

3   Outcomes

Finding a viable access method for computer control was a breakthrough for Nick allowing him to access a variety of computer applications, including synthetic speech, independently for the first time. This could not have been achieved without consistent involvement from the interdisciplinary team including Nick's family. The collaboration of team members with different priorities, ideas and areas of expertise has also meant that the benefits for the student have been varied and have impacted on many aspects of his life and development. In his own words…

> *My name is Nick–age sixteen.*
> *I like that I can get to the Internet, email, number work,*
> *Science and PDHPE with Grid 2.*
> *I use the "puff and sip" switch to get to Grid 2..*
> *I like using Grid 2 to find Face Book.*

Before the implementation of AT, a message of this kind would have needed to be dictated letter-by-letter using his alphabet board for a communication partner to record, so Nick was unable to express himself in connected sentences as in the example above. Other functional gains of AT are discussed in the following themes:

Academic. Nick now uses the internet for independent research on curriculum topics, and uses Microsoft Word to document his findings. This allowed for more formal teaching of syntax (especially grammar) and different text types, as teachers could provide feedback on his written work. Independence in communication, writing and research allowed for clearer assessment of Nick's level of intellectual and academic functioning.

Nick's ability to type independently impacted on his narrative and literacy development as he can now generate a variety of texts such as recounts, reports and letters. An example of this was,

> *Hi Jacqui*
> *how are you. Next month i am go to dentist operation [...].*
> *This morning i am go to meet people about gas i am lovely post school options this year [...]*

Communication. While Nick has always been interested in his friends and the people working with him, the time-consuming task of using his alphabet board meant that Nick predominantly needed to express his own needs, interests and questions as succinctly as possible, in order to keep his communication partner's attention. Being able to construct messages in his own time to e-mail, rather than always needing to meet the pace demands of a face-to-face conversation have meant that he was more able to maintain topics of conversation over several turns. This included responding to questions and requests for clarification from other people, and asking questions about other people's activities and discussing mutual interests as seen in table 1.

Table 1. Communication functions used in Nick's e-mail communication

Communication function	Example from Nick's written communication using AT
Sharing news	*I feel excited because about tomorrow my dad [...] is go to pet shop buy a new puppy. i am go to see donkey.*
Requesting information	*when graduation dinner?*
Making jokes	*i tell police coming to pick up you*
Expressing feelings	*i am angry with power box bad* *i am feel sick sore tummy*
Commenting	*My birthday same your birthday on december*
Sharing interests	*i like toy story 3 woody and buzz*
Requesting	*Do you want to buy a postcard to me*

Social Relationships. For the first time, Nick was able to independently maintain interpersonal contact and social relationships with people outside of his home and school environments via web-based email and social networking such as Facebook, including making and informing people of social arrangements.

Mobility. Nick's accuracy in using the "sip and puff" switch to select a desired target in a scanning display has meant that his team has also been able to use it as a means to control his power wheelchair. He did this by using a scanning display to select which direction he would like to move in allowing him to explore his environment, and approach people or locations of interest.

Self Determination. Access to e-mail has allowed Nick to contact members of his team directly to request assistance when his AT is not functioning properly, or with ideas to improve aspects of his communication system (e.g. adding numbers to his alphabet board.) He has also been able to play a role in researching his technology prior to implementation (e.g. searching for laptop brands). Nick commented,

> *i am no work the percentage key on grid. you fix a the percentage on the grid. please can you I want you is make a new window live to grid*
> *I like that head switch better.*

4   Discussion and Conclusion

The International Classification of Functioning, Disability and Health (ICF) [21] has described the use of assistive devices as one intervention to address activity limitations and participation restrictions in people with disabilities. For this particular student with severe-profound cerebral palsy, significant hearing impairment and additional disabilities, the collaboration process to implement AT for communication and computer access has had a significant and positive impact. Nick's participation in his environment has profoundly changed, with increased communication skills, leisure options, functional mobility, and ability to actively direct his educational and therapy team to meet his needs. These positive gains were evidenced by an AT system that is now in daily use, and that is supported by a team of family members and carers with the skills and knowledge to operate and troubleshoot problems. Furthermore, use of the AT system has quickly become Nick's preferred activity, both at home and in his post-school program.

In this setting, the benefits of interdisciplinary collaboration have included a functional communication system, the creative exchange of ideas, sharing of goals and priorities, and a shared understanding and ongoing exchange of information about the student's needs across a range of domains including his physical and sensory status, communication and academic progress and have facilitated the continuity of service delivery when members of the team changed.

The process of setting up the AT system described in this article was ongoing throughout the majority of Nick's time at school, due to a variety of factors and challenges outlined in this article. There was not a 'one-size-fits-all' approach to AT assessment and implementation [10], as consideration for the individual user's unique physical, cognitive and sensory abilities was required [7]. Other important issues that that had to be considered was to ensure that the collaborative team did not to fall into the trap of not considering carer preferences and family dynamics when implementing AT solutions, for this can lead to mismatch, delay in acceptance of the device or abandonment [2]; [17]. The team also considered the availability of funding, the availability of appropriate hardware and software, family support and motivation, technological support, as well as organisational support for collaboration between interdisciplinary team members. This case study was shared in order to document a process which has continued over a decade, and to particularly highlight the need for a collaborative team effort between the individual, the family, therapists, educators, rehabilitation and AT specialists, to achieve a successful outcome.

It is important, however, to recognise that the successful implementation of an AT system is not an end in itself but rather a starting point for new avenues for learning and development for the student and the team. It will continue to be necessary to develop strategies for ongoing increased functionality of the AT system as improvements in technology become available, the ideas and creativity of new people involved in the AT team arise, and ongoing collaboration occurs between the AT user, the family, therapists, carers and educators.

References

1. Angelo, D.H.: Impact of Augmentative and Alternative Communication Devices on Families. Aug. and Alter. Comm. 16, 37–47 (2000)
2. Ball, L.J., Beukelman, D.R., Pattee, G.L.: Acceptance of Augmentative and Alternative Communication Technology by Persons with Amyotrophic Lateral Sclerosis. Aug. and Alter. Comm. 20(2), 113–122 (2004)
3. Bausch, M.E., Ault, M.J., Evmenova, A.S., Behrmann, M.M.: Going Beyond AT Devices: Are AT Services Being Considered? J. Spec. Ed. Tech. 23(2), 1–16 (2008)
4. Bottcher, L.: Children With Spastic Cerebral Palsy, Their Cognitive Functioning, and Social Participation: A review. Child Neuropsych. 16, 209–228 (2010)
5. Cooper, L., Balandin, S., Trembath, D.: The Loneliness Ex-periences of Young Adults With Cerebral Palsy Who Use Al-ternative and Augmentative Communication. Aug. and Alter. Comm. 25(3), 154–164 (2009)
6. Copley, J., Ziviani, J.: Barriers to the Use of Assistive Tech-nology for Children With Multiple Disabilities. Occ. Therapy Intern. 11(4), 229–243 (2004)
7. Copley, J., Ziviani, J.: Use of a Team-Based Approach to As-sistive Technology Assessment and Planning for Children With Multiple Disabilities: A Pilot Study. Ass. Tech. 19, 109–125 (2007)
8. Dell, A.G., Newton, D.A., Petroff, J.G.: Assistive Technol-ogy in the Classroom. Pearson Education, New Jersey (2008)
9. Derer, K., Polsgrove, L., Reith, H.: A Survey of Assistive Technology Applications in Schools and Recommendations for Practice. J. Spec. Ed. Tech. XIII(2), 62–80 (1996)
10. Enders, A., Hall, H. (eds.): Assistive Technology Source-book. RESNA Press, Washington (1990)

11. Gilbert, J., Bainbridge, L.: Canada- Interprofessional Educa-tion and Collaboration: Theoretical Challenges, Practical Solutions. In: Leathard, A. (ed.) Interprofessional Collaboration: From Policy to Practice in Health and Social Care, pp. 280–296. Brunner-Routledge, Hove (2003)

12. Hemsley, B., Balandin, S.: Working With People Who Have Cerebral Palsy: A Speech Pathology Perspective. Acquiring Knowl. in Speech, Lang. and Hearing 5(1), 25–27 (2003)

13. Koritsas, S., Iacono, T.: Limitations in Life Participation and Independence Due to Secondary Conditions. Am. Assoc. on Intell. and Dev. Dis. 114(6), 437–448 (2009)

14. Lloyd, G., Stead, J., Kendrick, A.: Inter-agency Working to Prevent School Exclusion, http://www.jrf.org.uk/publications/inter-agency-working-prevent-school-exclusion2

15. Orelove, F.P., Sobsey, D.: Educating Children with Multiple Disabilities: A Transdisciplinary Approach. P.H. Brookes Publishing Co., Baltimore (1996)

16. Palisano, R., Rosenbaum, P., Walter, S., Russell, D., Wood, E., Galuppi, B.: Development and Reliability of a System to Classify Gross Motor Function in Children with Cerebral Palsy. Dev. Med. & Child Neuro. 89, 214–223 (1997)

17. Parette, H.P., Brotherson, M.J.: Family-Centred and Cultur-ally Responsive Assistive Technology Decision Making. Inf. and Young Children. 17(4), 355–367 (2004)

18. Reed, B.G., Kanny, E.M.: The Use of Computers in School System Practice by Occupational Therapists. Phys. and Occup. Therapy in Ped. 13(4), 37–55 (1993)

19. Swinth, Y., Case-Smith, J.: Assistive Technology in Early In-tervention: Theory and Practice. In: Case-Smith, J. (ed.) Occupational Therapy and Early Intervention, pp. 342–368. But-terworth Heinemann, Boston (1993)

20. Todis, B., Walker, H.M.: User Perspectives on Assistive Technology in Educational Settings. Focus on Except. Children 26(3), 1–16 (1993)

21. World Health Organization: Towards a Common Language for Functioning, Disability and Health, ICF (The International Classification of Functioning, Disability and Health), http://www.who.int/classification/icf

Multimedia Advocacy

A New Way of Self Expression and Communication for People with Intellectual Disabilities

Gosia Kwiatkowska[1], Thomas Tröbinger[2], Karl Bäck[2], and Peter Williams[3]

[1] Rix Centre, University East London, United Kingdom
G.M.Kwiatkowska@uel.ac.uk
[2] atempo Betriebsgesellschaft mbH, Graz, Austria
{thomas.troebinger,karl.baeck}@atempo.at
[3] Department of Information Studies, University College London, United Kingdom
peter.williams@ucl.ac.uk

Abstract. The paper describes the early stages of one strand of an international project entitled Web 2.0 for People with Intellectual Disabilities (W2ID). The project team reports on a project pilot that involves five countries, 400 learners with Intellectual Disabilities (ID) (13 to adulthood), their teachers and supporters, developing rich media web content using Multimedia Self Advocacy Approach and the specially designed 'Klik in' platform.

The 'Klik in' Web2.0 platform was designed to enable people with ID to express their views and preferences using pictures, videos, sounds and text and to share these with their peers and supporters. Easy-to-use learning materials and a standardised pedagogic approach were also developed to assist learners and supporters throughout the project. The project is being monitored and evaluated using mostly quantitative instruments, although some qualitative data is also being collected and will inform final findings. The early results indicate that learners with ID are motivated to work with rich media content and the web 2.0 'Klik in' platform and are able to express their right to self advocacy.

Keywords: self advocacy, multimedia, digital inclusion, intellectual disability, web 2.0, klik in, website, internet, rich media content.

1   Introduction

The concept of Multimedia Advocacy was developed by researchers at The Rix Centre, based at the University of East London in the UK through their work with people with ID (Intellectual Disabilities).

The Rix Centre is a research and development organisation committed to realising the benefits of new media technologies to transform the lives of people who have ID. It combines expertise in practical development of products and services for this population, with academic evaluative research reflecting on its own activities for both self-improvement and as a contribution to a wider pedagogical debate on using accessible information technology.

K. Miesenberger et al. (Eds.): ICCHP 2012, Part II, LNCS 7383, pp. 361–368, 2012.

The Centre's research involves the interplay between 'development activity' and 'research activity', weaving a path between the two streams of research and development. For example, web developers will take time out to reflect on their learning from the production process and a research project will incorporate practical development work to generate data and evidence. Thus, the research agenda is developed through a dialogue between developers, researchers and communities of existing and potential users, including people with ID themselves.

Multimedia advocacy or more accurately 'multimedia self-advocacy' is an approach employed by the Rix Centre whereby information technology is used with people with ID enabling them to self advocate. It mobilises people around specific topic and methods, which lend themselves to research practice. This is because in the gathering and imparting of the expertise required in multimedia production, the ICT itself – in the form of digital cameras, microphones and recording equipment etc. – facilitate research because they stimulate activity.

2   Self Advocacy

Self-advocacy is facilitated in three key areas: enabling people to express themselves in various situations; helping to promote self satisfaction, pride and confidence; enabling people to better understand information.

The term has been defined as an individual's ability to communicate effectively, convey, negotiate or assert one's own interests, desires, needs, and rights. It involves making informed decisions and taking responsibility for those decisions (VanReusen et al., 1994). The aims of research promoting self-advocacy include empowerment (e.g. Oliver, 1992), inclusivity (e.g. Walmsley, 2001), and self-reflection (Porter and Lacey, 2005). As Test (2005: p43) points out, 'Literature in both disability and educational research has identified the development of self-advocacy skills as crucial to the successful transition of students with disabilities into adult life'. Of course, self-advocacy skills do not come naturally – people need instruction in acquiring them (Test, 2005; Lehman, et al, 2000).

David Test and colleagues at the University of North Carolina at Charlotte (Test et al, 2005) reviewed the literature on self-advocacy, from which they constructed a 'conceptual framework' of self-advocacy for students with disabilities. The framework includes four components: knowledge of self, knowledge of rights, communication, and leadership. It is worth quoting the framework description at length, as it mirrors the views of the Rix Centre.

'Knowledge of self and knowledge of rights are viewed as the foundations of self-advocacy, because it is necessary for individuals to understand and know themselves before they can tell others what they want. … The next component … is communication of one's knowledge of self and rights. Learning how to communicate information effectively with others through negotiation, assertiveness, and problem solving … is critical to self-advocacy. The final component, leadership, enables a person to move from individual self-advocacy to advocating for others as a group of individuals with common concerns' (Ibid: p45).

All these components of the framework devised by Test et al (2005) fit the work of the Rix Centre, with a central theme of its work encouraging participants to self-reflect, to learn about rights and services, and to communicate that knowledge. The final component, 'leadership' is of particular importance, as the Rix Centre is a strong advocate of peer support and sees this as a key aspect of self-advocacy. As found in Rix's own research (Minnion et al, 2008, 2006; Williams, 2008), people with learning disabilities have difficulty in putting themselves in the position of others, although there is some evidence that technology can help individuals do this (Williams, 2008).

3   The W2ID Project (Web 2.0 for People with Intellectual Disabilities)

In this EU funded project organisations from Portugal, Latvia, Finland, UK and Austria work together for 2 years. The primary aim of the W2ID project is to enhance employability skills and active citizenship of people with ID by developing and adapting an existing prototype Web 2.0 platform called "Klik in".

Fig. 1. Screenshot of the Web 2.0 platform Klik in; Pilotplan (www.klikin.eu/pilotplan)

The platform is designed to give people with ID a virtual space for creating knowledge and sharing their experiences and views of the work and life with others. Content identified as having most impact amongst people with ID is rich media content created by the users themselves via Web 2.0 technologies that share individual experiences. Hence the online platform consists of an accessible, easy-to-use content management system in the back-end, that enables people with ID to upload, organise and finally publish rich-media content within a given framework and a standardised front-end in form of a mind map-looking website for presenting, publishing and 'consuming' rich-media content produced by themselves.

In each country the project will culminate in the publication of a set of self-made multimedia websites that provide personal stories, information and guidance produced by people with intellectual disabilities. This peer support and learning resource will be accessed from a single national portal.

The W2ID Project focuses on three different target groups: school aged learners 13-18, adults aged 24+ who have an ID and 18-24 year olds with ID not in formal education, employment or training (NEET).

At the core of the project is to pilot the web 2.0 platform and its accompanying pedagogic approach within 5 European countries, evaluate and report on personal level outcomes and impacts among the pilot group of end users with ID.

4   End-User Pilot and Its Curriculum

This chapter briefly describes an extract of the standardised session plans, as it is an essential part of the accompanying pedagogy and evaluation design.

4.1   Session 1: Getting Started

Working with 'Klik in' starts with a brief introductory session for learners on the project itself and its goals. This is followed by the baseline analysis process, designed to find out about the pilot learners' present knowledge, confidence and skills in each of the four areas that the pilot intends to cover: Active Citizenship, Employability, Web & ICT and Communication.

Learners are introduced to the 'About Us' website in this first session and get an opportunity to experience how the 'Klik in' easy-build system works and how easy it is to use. The 'About Us' website is password protected, so it cannot be seen publicly on the Web.

4.2   Session 2: About Us

This session focuses on the class as a group as well as aiming to give website building experience to each individual, introducing and developing the activity of making multimedia by using photos, videos, audio and text to present yourself and talk about your life. There is a lot to learn in this session e.g. communicating in pictures, using cameras, recording video and sound. Adding titles and captions to pictures and how this can shape and change what they mean. Planning together using pen & paper or a whiteboard. Team-working skills etc. – plus of course 'How to make a 'Klik in' website!'

4.3   Session 3: Thinking Pictures

The primary aim of this session is a focus and practical examination of how to take effective pictures. What is a good picture? How can I express something with an image/picture? How do I want to present myself in public? What experiences do I have of publishing pictures on the Internet (e.g. on a social network like Facebook). These are some examples of questions that should be raised in this session. The aim is that learners learn to plan and take pictures in a more conscious and thoughtful way and then review them to make selections of the best images to use.

Fig. 2. Screenshot of the Web 2.0 platform Klik in; About us (www.klikin.eu/aboutus)

4.4   Session 4: Going Out

This session is about active participation in society. Out of many possibilities, we have elected to start with the general activity of "Going out" as a true-to-life example of how to actively participate in society. We talk about going out with friends or family, going to the movies, etc. It could be any "going-out activity" that learners suggest. In this session learners go out to public places of their choice and take pictures, record video and audio clips to represent places that are significant to them and share them with others. Their work is structured and guided by questions like: Why is it worthwhile to go there? What do you like about that place/activity? Etc.

4.5   Session 5: Jobs and Activities

The focus of this session is the learners' personal experiences of work, jobs or everyday activities (e.g. supported employment, activities within a day center). School-aged participants or people without any job experiences can alternatively talk about their dream job or their ideas and wishes about work, volunteering or other activities that contribute to the community. The aim of the session is to share some of these experiences and wishes with others and find out more about learners' skills and abilities.

4.6   Session 6: Sharing

The last pilot session aims to give users the opportunity to visit the national portals to see what websites others have created. Viewing and experiencing the different multimedia outputs of other people with ID is a crucial part of Klik in. It enables pilot users to have additional learning experience, as they see what others have done and draw on their experience to evaluate the usefulness and quality of the material. They are taking a significant further step as they share their multimedia online via the national portal. This also provides opportunity for learning about risks and responsibilities as you publish content online. They review what they have learned and experienced during the pilot. At the end the learners finalise this reflective process by evaluating the pilot by completing questionnaires and feeding back their points of view.

5   Evaluation Design and Methodology

The evaluation is still in its early stages. It follows an explorative research design and therefore makes use of a multi-perspective approach to capture different points of view. It puts the main emphasis on the user's perspective, but also asks for the supporter's perception of the pilot and its impacts on people with ID as well as an analysis of the generated content output in form of created multimedia websites.

The methodology employed for the data collection and analysis is quantitative as it will provide good standardised, comparable data and results. We will also collect some qualitative data by asking open ended questions to address more difficult topics, such as changes in personality, self-perception or satisfaction.

5.1   Users Perspective

The users view will be captured at two different points in time: prior to the pilot workshops and at the end of the pilot delivery. The first survey will measure the pilot users existing knowledge, confidence, self advocacy and skills in areas such as employment, active citizenship and communication/ICT, providing a baseline for impact evaluation. The designed questionnaire is written in easy-to-read language and mostly easy answer categories are used (e.g. 4-point frequency scales).

This survey will also be used for setting individual goals. People are asked to say what they want to learn. The possible aims are partly predefined and orientated on the content of the standardised sessions – they reflect possible learning impacts and help users to focus on their goals for the pilot.

Within the impact survey in the last pilot session supporters repeat the set goals and ask the learners to assess if they have achieved the aims or not.

5.2   Supporters' Perspective

Supporters and teachers will trial the pedagogic approaches and the learning materials. Their experiences and perceptions during the pilot are essential components of the further development of 'Klik in' and the learning materials. Their perspective is a key resource for getting a richer picture of users' learning impacts and developments. The supporters' point of view will also be captured by a specially designed questionnaire that will cover the following: Learning impact of users (concerning the core themes, confidence, and motivation); Training of supporters (scope, contents); Learning materials; Conduct of pilot sessions; Challenges & lessons learned; Recommendations and improvements.

5.3   Analysis of Website Output

Another source of information on the pilot is the final output of the websites produced by participants.

According to the aims of the end-user pilot delivery a minimum of 8 websites per country should be produced (involving 80 learners). Partly the thematic orientation of these Websites is determined by the standardisation of the pilot (due to the general session plans), but there is still a lot of space for personal interests and individual priorities. Furthermore, the final focus and realisation of the content-output depends on the learners themselves and how the supporters lead the workshops.

5.4   Sample and Data Collection

The aim of the End-User Pilot is to implement and evaluate 'Klik in' with 400 Users with ID from the 3 target groups. This means that every partner organization is expected to involve 80 users. Because of different levels of learning disabilities and capacities it is improbable, that all participating users can also participate in the evaluation. Nevertheless, we aim for a total population survey, expecting as many users as possible to participate in the survey. The expected participation rate should be at least 50%, which means 40 users per country.

The expected distribution of participating learners is at least 30% school aged and 30% adults.

6   Outlook and Early Findings

The pilot was still continuing at the submission date of this paper in April 2012. Therefore it is not possible to present any empirical evaluation results. At the ICCHP statistical results as well as some case studies will be presented focusing on personal level impacts of users and possible fields of application of multimedia advocacy.

Within the Austrian Pilot an interim meeting took place, where the participating organisations reported their first experiences. In Austria, over 11 different organisations participate in the pilot. Most of them have a focus on digital inclusion and education. Some of these reflections conclude this paper.

In General learners were motivated to work with rich-media and the web 2.0 platform. They showed willingness and enthusiasm to actively participate in the sessions, take pictures of themselves and their colleagues and finally build their own websites.

All organizations unanimously assessed 'Klik in' as very user-friendly and reported that learners very fast found themselves able to use it independently and also felt confident in using it. Some of them experienced challenges in using the tool due to a lack of ICT knowledge and confidence in working with computers and multimedia.

Difficulties were reported concerning independent work and the responsibility to take one´s own decisions (e.g. in selecting pictures or movies). Different pedagogic approaches were used. Some supporters provided more guidance and structure, but others preferred to hand over the projects lead to learners themselves and let them manage the pilot sessions with a lot of room to maneuver. One supporter reported an interesting development which leaves us with a lot of questions for the analysis of the evaluation data: "For our clients it was a totally new experience to be in control of a project, to realise, that it´s their project and that they can decide what to do. At the beginning they were confused and overtaxed. But very fast the whole process gained momentum and they started to take the wheel".

References

1. Lehman, J.P., Davies, T.G., Laurin, K.M.: Listening to student voices about postsecondary education. Teaching Exceptional Children 32(5), 60–65 (2000)
2. Minnion, A., Staples, P., Singh, R., Williams, P.: Beyond the Road Ahead London: University of East London Report submitted to the Social Care Institute of Excellence (2008)
3. Minnion, A., Williams, P., Kennedy, H., Bunning, K.: Project @pple: e-learning and the World Wide Web Report submitted to the ESRC PACCIT Programme. University of East London, London (2006)
4. Oliver, M.: Changing the Social Relations of Research Production. Disability Handicap & Society 7(2), 101–115 (1992)
5. Porter, J.M., Lacey, P.J.: Researching Learning Difficulties. Paul Chapman, London (2005)
6. Test, D.W., Fowler, C.H., Wood, W.M., Brewer, D.M., Eddy, S.: A conceptual framework of self-advocacy for students with disabilities. Remedial and Special Education 26(1), 43–54 (2005)
7. VanReusen, A.K., Bos, C.S., Schumaker, J.B., Deshler, D.D.: The self-advocacy strategy for education and transition planning. Edge Enterprises, Lawrence (1994)
8. Walmsley, J.: Normalisation, Emancipatory Research and Learning Disability. Disability and Society 16(2), 187–205 (2001)
9. Williams, P.: Transition and people with learning disabilities: reflections on the quality of content that emerges from the process of involving service-users in information provision Aslib Proceedings 60(5), 474–492 (2008)

How Long Is a Short Sentence? –
A Linguistic Approach to Definition
and Validation of Rules
for Easy-to-Read Material

Annika Nietzio, Birgit Scheer, and Christian Bühler

Forschungsinstitut Technologie und Behinderung (FTB),
der Evangelischen Stiftung Volmarstein,
Grundschötteler Str. 40, 58300 Wetter (Ruhr), Germany
kontakt@di-ji.de
http://www.ftb-esv.de

Abstract. This paper presents a new approach to empirical validation
and verification of guidelines for easy-to-read material. The goal of our
approach is twofold. One the one hand, the linguistic analysis investigates
if the well-known rules are really applied consistently throughout the
published easy-to-read material. The findings from this study can help
define new rules and refine existing rules.

One the other hand, we show how the software developed for
the linguistic analysis can also be used as a tool to support authors
in the production of easy-to-read material. The tool applies the rules to
the new text and highlights any passages that do not meet those rules,
so that the author can go back and improve the text.

1 Introduction

One of the main aspects of access to information for people with intellectual
or learning disabilities is the accessibility of the content – especially of written
information. In recent years the need to provide information in easy-to-read format has become widely recognised. For instance the German legislation requires
easy-to-read content on national public web sites [4]. At international level the
topic is promoted among others by the European initiative Inclusion Europe [5]
and the W3C Research and Development Working Group (RDWG) [9].

However, most of the easy-to-read material is produced by small organisations
and businesses, using a variety of guidelines, rules, and approaches. For the
German language there exist several different sets of easy-to-read guidelines.
The project *Digital informiert – im Job integriert (Di-Ji)* compiled an overview
of the available guidelines [3].

In the majority of cases it is not documented how the rules were derived.
Presumably, most rules are based on the expertise of the authors. Through several years of involvement of people with cognitive and learning disabilities the

K. Miesenberger et al. (Eds.): ICCHP 2012, Part II, LNCS 7383, pp. 369–376, 2012.

translated texts – and thus implicitly the rules – were validated by the target audience of easy-to-read material.

In this paper we present a new approach to empirical validation and verification. We use linguistic analysis to find out if the proposed rules are really applied consistently throughout the easy-to-read material. We also show how this approach can help define new rules and refine existing rules. Linguistic analysis of easy-to-read texts captures the implicit knowledge of the experts and can thus help to clarify rules that inexperienced authors may find too unspecific.

Furthermore, the software that was developed for the linguistic analysis can also be used as a tool that supports authors in the production of easy-to-read material. The tool applies the rules to the new text and highlights any passages that don't meet those rules, so that the author can improve the text.

The next section provides some background information on the idea of easy-to-read and on grammar checking. In section 3 we describe the implementation of the author support tool and explain the concept of the linguistic analysis. Section 4 presents the result of the analysis. The experiments described in this article address the rules for length and complexity of sentences in easy-to-read material. The analysis was carried out on German language texts but the methodology can be applied to other languages as well. Finally, section 5 concludes the paper with some prospects for further development.

2 Background

2.1 Easy-to-Read

The terms "people with learning disabilities" or "people with intellectual disabilities" describe a wide spectrum of different persons with varying skills and abilities, ranging from persons who only have minor problems with understanding complex texts to persons who cannot read at all. The goal of easy-to-read material is to convey the information to as many people as possible. It is accepted that there will still be some people who can not understand the texts.[1]

Easy-to-read guidelines include requirements and recommendations for different aspects of a document:

Words: Use words that are easy to understand. Avoid foreign words and metaphors.

Phrases and sentences: Use short sentences and address the reader directly. Avoid negative sentences and passive voice.

Structure and consistency of text: Use the same words to describe the same thing. Order to information so that it is easy to follow. Repeat important information.

---

[1] There are also other groups who benefit from easy-to-read material: Persons with low literacy, persons with another native language, or elderly people with reduced visual and cognitive ability. Some of the diverse requirements of those user groups might not be covered by the guidelines analysed in this paper.

Formatting and layout: Start each sentence in a new line. Choose a font and font size that are easy to read. Ensure good contrast between text and background.

Presentation: Include images to support the understanding of the text.

Our approach focuses on the first two of these aspects because layout and presentation aspects usually depend on the text format and software application used to process the text. The checking of the consistency of texts can not be addressed either because it would require linguistic analysis of longer runs of text beyond the level of individual sentences.

The implementation presented in this paper is based on the European *Information for all guidelines* [5] which are currently the most widely recognised standard for easy-to-read material in Europe. The *Information for all guidelines* are available in several languages, which will simplify the application of our approach to other languages in the future.

2.2   Grammar and Style Checking

Style and grammar checkers for word processing software were first introduced in the 1970s. Initially the tools could carry out checks of punctuation and highlight commonly misused words and phrases. The advancement of natural language processing software lead to new capabilities including sophisticated grammar checks and assertion of controlled language. The term controlled language refers to a natural language with restricted grammar and vocabulary. The purpose of controlled language is the reduction of complexity and ambiguity for example in instruction manuals or other written documentation. O'Brien [8] presents a (theoretical) linguistic comparison of eight different controlled language rulesets.

The implementation presented in this paper is based on LanguageTool [6,7], the grammar checker extension for OpenOffice.org/Libre Office. We chose this software package for several reasons:

- The software is made available under a free and open source licenses.
- It can be easily extended with user-defined grammatical rules.
- It provides basic linguistic analysis for multiple languages.
- The checker can be used as part of OpenOffice.org/Libre Office but also with a stand-alone user interface and as a web service.

3   Methodology

3.1   Implementation of Rules for Easy-to-Read

The linguistic rules in LanguageTool are implemented in a special XML-format. It can check conditions on words and on part-of-speech (i. e. on the grammatical form of a word such as verb, noun, singular, plural, pronoun, or conjunction). It supports not only exact matches but also regular expressions.

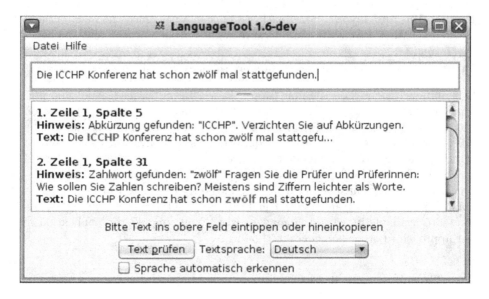

Fig. 1. Screenshot showing the application of rules to a German sentence

For Example: The linguistic analysis assigns the part-of-speech tag ZAL to numbers written as words. The rule below matches words with the part-of-tag ZAL and gives the recommendation to use digits instead.

```
<rule id="easy-to-read:numbers">
    <pattern>
        <token postag="ZAL"/>
    </pattern>
    <message>Write numbers as digits, not as words.</message>
</rule>
```

In the current prototype, thirty rules to check grammatical aspects of easy-to-read material could be implemented, including rules to check the use of numbers (numbers written as words, Roman numeral, dates, high numbers, percentage values), the use of abbreviations and acronyms, and the use of passive voice and subjunctive mood.

Figure 1 shows the LanguageTool stand-alone user interface. Users enter the text in the text field. The bottom part presents the potential problems and hints how to improve the text.

3.2   The Corpus

Our experiments are based on the assumption that quality-assured easy-to-read material can serve as source of implicit knowledge about the linguistic structure of easy-to-read texts and the underlying rules.

We collected easy-to-read material from several sources, making sure to include only material that was written by experts and tested by people with intellectual or learning disabilities. The corpus contains German language texts from Austria and Germany. In a preprocessing step the documents were converted into plain texts and split into sentences, resulting in a corpus of almost 3000 sentences (approximately 22 000 words).[2]

3.3   Validation of Rules

Besides recommendations for words and phrases, easy-to-read guidelines contain also recommendations for sentences. In the easy-to-read guidelines for the German language, these recommendations differ in level of strictness as well as in level of detail.

The Information for all guidelines recommend "short sentences with only one idea per sentence". The German legislation (BITV 2.0) requires "short sentences with clear structure". Sentences with a single dependent clause are allowed but the use of further nested sentences is discouraged [2]. Other guidelines like the Austrian *Capito-Leicht Lesen Quality Standards* [1] include more detailed rules about the use of subordinating conjunctions (such as German "obwohl" which means "although").

The requirement for short sentences is a typical example of an unspecific rule. Especially less experienced authors might ask: **"How long is a short sentence?"**

4   Results

4.1   Sentence Length

In Figure 2 we present the results of sentence length analysis in our test corpus. The data is distributed according to the Poisson distribution. The mean sentence length is approximately eight words. The majority of sentences has less than 13 words.

In the proposed author support tool, this result could be used in the following way: The author is warned if the sentence length of the new text deviates from this distribution, i.e. if sentences are too long in general. Moreover, specific sentences that are longer than the others are highlighted so that the author can revise them.

4.2   Sentence Complexity

The analysis uses two indicators of sentence complexity. Both indicators can be related to the easy-to-read guidelines described in section 3.3.

First, we suggest to measure the complexity of sentences and the number of ideas presented in a single sentence by counting the number of dependent

---

[2] The corpus was collected as proof of concept. We are aware that more data are needed to confirm the findings presented in this paper.

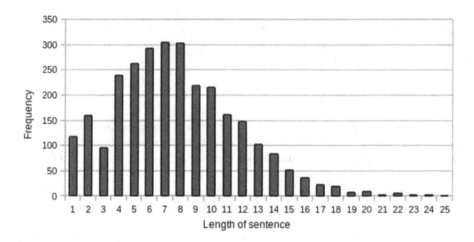

Fig. 2. Distribution of sentence length in the easy-to-read corpus (3000 sentences)

sentences. Table 1 shows to relative frequencies of the four types of sentences identified in the test corpus.

Overall, almost 80% of the sentences in the corpus consist only of a main clause and have no dependent sentences. About 20% of the sentences have one dependent clause. Only a few sentences (less than 2%) have a more complex structure (i.e. two dependent sentences or a nested relative clause). It can be assumed that those more complex sentences slipped in unintentionally and might have been avoided if the authors had used a language checking tool to identify those cases.

Moreover, Table 1 also allows a comparison among the texts. It can be seen that text A on average has a simpler sentence structure. However, we can draw no conclusions if this is caused by the individual style of the author or if a different set of easy-to-read guidelines has been applied.

The second indicator is the type of conjunction use in the texts. Frequently occurring are "wenn" (Eng. *if*), "dass" (Eng. *that*), "und" (Eng. *and*), "oder" (Eng. *or*), "aber" (Eng. *but*), and "weil" (Eng. *because* used as subordinating conjunction). Our conclusion is that sentences using these conjunction meet the easy-to-read quality standards.

Only few occurrences were encountered for "denn" (Eng. *because* used as coordinating conjunction), "als" (Eng. *when*), "sondern" (Eng. *but instead*), and "obwohl" (Eng. *although*). Some of the conjunctions in the second group are even described as to be avoided in the easy-to-read guidelines. The proposed author support tool could flag the use of these more difficult conjunctions and ask the author to find alternatives or split the complex sentence into two simpler ones.

This experiment shows how the empirical results of a linguistic analysis can be used to refine and clarify existing easy-to-read guidelines resulting in rules that are specific enough to be checked by software applications such as the proposed author support tool.

Table 1. Analysis of sentence structure: Relative frequency of different types

	Text A	Text B	Text C	complete corpus
only main clause	86.7%	73.6%	76.4%	78.9%
one dependent sentence	12.7%	25.9%	21.0%	19.9%
two dependent sentences	0.3%	0.4%	2.2%	0.9%
nested relative clause	0.3%	0.1%	0.4%	0.3%
	100.0%	100.0%	100.0%	100.0%

4.3 Further Findings

The test corpus was also checked with the LanguageTool easy-to-read implementation. We found that the quality-assured easy-to-read material generally meets the rules quite well. There were no validations of the "avoid subjunctive mood" rule. There were a few occurrences of the genitive case, which might even have been caught if the authors had had a style checker at their disposal. Other rules are not followed consistently. For instance we found many occurrences of passive voice and negations. This might be an indication that these rules need to be refined.

5   Conclusion and Future Work

This paper demonstrated how linguistic analysis can provide new insights in the structure of easy-to-read language. The approach can be used to validate and refine existing rules. Our experiments show that quality-assured easy-to-read material generally meets the easy-to-read standards but we also found some rules that need further refinement. We also found an indication of systematic differences between easy-to-read texts. Further research in this direction, could help to harmonise the currently existing guidelines.

The grammar and style checker is not only useful for empirical studies. It is also a helpful tool to support (less experienced) authors of easy-to-read material.

In the future we plan to extend the tool with more rules and carry out further linguistic experiments which could lead to the discovery of currently unknown easy-to-read rules.

Acknowledgements. The project Di-Ji is based on the outcome of the conference Digitally informed – integrated at work which was held by AbI. AbI is the German Alliance for barrier free Information technology. The project Di-Ji is funded by the German Federal Ministry of Labour and Social Affairs.

References

1. Capito: Barrierefreie Information - Qualittsstandard (2012),
   http://www.capito.eu/ (retrieved January 27, 2012)
2. Di-Ji Project: Begründung zur BITV 2.0 Anlage 2, Teil 2 – Leichte Sprache (2012),
   http://www.di-ji.de/r/bitv2a2t2 (retrieved April 19, 2012)

3. Di-Ji Project: Leitfaden zur erstellung von online-informationen in leichter sprache (2012), `http://www.di-ji.de/r/rls` (retrieved April 19, 2012)
4. German Federal Ministry of Labour and Social Affairs: Verordnung zur Schaffung barrierefreier Informationstechnik nach dem Behindertengleichstellungsgesetz, BITV (2011), `http://www.gesetze-im-internet.de/bitv_2_0/index.html` (retrieved February 01, 2012)
5. Inclusion Europe: Information for all - European standards for making information easy to read and understand. (Available in English, German, and several other languages) (2009), `http://www.inclusion-europe.org/LLL/documents/` (retrieved January 31, 2012)
6. LanguageTool: Style and Grammar Checker (2012), `http://www.languagetool.org/` (retrieved February 01, 2012)
7. Naber, D.: A Rule-Based Style and Grammar Checker. Master's thesis, Universität Bielefeld (2003)
8. O'Brien, S.: Controlling Controlled English - An Analysis of Several Controlled Language Rule Sets. In: Proceedings of EAMT-CLAW (2003)
9. World Wide Web Consortium (W3C): Web Accessibility Initiative Research and Development Working Group, RDWG (2012), `http://www.w3.org/WAI/RD/` (retrieved January 27, 2012)

CAPKOM – Innovative Graphical User Interface Supporting People with Cognitive Disabilities

Andrea Petz[1], Nicoleta Radu[1], and Markus Lassnig[2]

[1] Institute Integriert Studieren, JKU Linz, Austria
{andrea.petz,nicoleta-ioana.radu}@jku.at
[2] Salzburg Research Forschungsgesellschaft mbH, Salzburg, Austria
markus.lassnig@salzburgresearch.at

Abstract. Most research activities on web accessibility focus on people with physical or sensory disabilities, while potential users with cognitive disabilities still lack adequate solutions to overcome barriers resulting from their disability. The innovative graphical user interface to be developed within the project CAPKOM intends to change this. In a novel approach, this user interface shall be instantly adaptable to the very different demands of people with cognitive disabilities. Iterative user tests will feed results into practical software development, first exemplified by a community art portal for people with cognitive disability.

Keywords: Accessibility, Webdesign, Graphical User Interface, Cognitive Disability.

1 Background / State of the Art

There is an extensive set of rules and guidelines for designing, implementing and publishing barrier free websites and software concerning general, technical accessibility (e.g. WAI-W3C, WCAG etc.) from the perspective of different groups involved in providing content and information via the internet. Those rules guarantee that a broad scope of users with and without disabilities is able to access and use the web as information and communication facility also comprising users with motor and/or manipulation disability, blind and partially sighted users, deaf and hard of hearing users and older adults.

People with cognitive disabilities face a different (if not even a reverse) situation as conventional navigation and "pure" textual description build up insurmountable obstacles (in getting information or using mainstream ICT) [2]. An example of a contradictory situation might be a flash-video explaining a website before use. This can be superfluous or even annoying for mainstream users but very helpful if not necessary for the target group. The same applies to the so called "mouse-over function", that might be helpful to understand the meaning / function of a word / link or the use of specific colors to explain contextual relations, what contradicts to wai-w3c regulations when used on its own but is highly beneficial when used to enrich the given information and eases perception (e.g. red ("be careful") / green ("proceed" / "clear").

K. Miesenberger et al. (Eds.): ICCHP 2012, Part II, LNCS 7383, pp. 377–384, 2012.

In recent years, a number of experts raised awareness on challenges in making internet accessible for people with cognitive disabilities [10], [11]. Most experts judge that accessibility for users with cognitive disabilities can be a far greater challenge than for those with other types of disabilities [3]. The individual needs of people with cognitive disabilities vary widely depending on grade and form of the disability. Experience shows that despite the complexity of the problem, there is evidence that users with cognitive disabilities could use internet if an appropriate and customized user interface was provided. Preferably this should be a graphical user interface (GUI). The development of such an innovative graphical user interface instantly adaptable to the needs of people with different types of cognitive disabilities is one of the aims of the project CAPKOM.

Some existing solutions for web accessibility translate mainstream websites into symbols or read them aloud [12], yet the meaning of the text still remains inaccessible for users with respective impairments. Further criticism arises as some experts claim that even sites serving the cognitively disabled population often are not accessible to the cognitively disabled. In many cases they appear to be designed for parents and caregivers instead of the intended target group, the users with cognitive disabilities [3]. The adaptability of the planned graphical user interface in the context of the CAPKOM project clearly targets users with cognitive disabilities themselves. As part of the user testing, we will try to monitor to what extent people with cognitive disabilities are able to gain independence from their caregivers in using information and communication technologies and identify the necessary prerequisites.

One of the big assets of the CAPKOM interface is its technological platform independence. This fact is highly important, especially as the market for assistive technologies is changing quickly. A number of experts assess that new mainstream hardware technologies like tablets – if equipped with dedicated software – contain the potential to disrupt the market for assistive technologies. Often-quoted example is the iPad with Proloquo2Go or a similar communication app [6]. The planned graphical user interface will run on PC/laptop environments with different operating systems and will also be easily transferable to other devices like tablets or smartphones.

2   Methodology

The terms "people with cognitive disabilities" / "people with learning disabilities" or "people with intellectual disabilities" describe a wide spectrum of people with most diverse levels of abilities and competences ranging from mixing up single letters or numbers to not being able to read or write at all and using symbols instead.

Within the project CAPKOM, we aim at implementing measures and activities to guide people with cognitive disabilities towards the use of new media applications and in the same time adapt structures to include people with cognitive disabilities in the digital world and prevent them from further discrimination. With an initial survey amongst institutions and carers for people with cognitive disabilities we analyzed the problems and the internet surfing behavior of the target group. 31 guardians answered the different questions for altogether 491 clients and the most important result was that people with cognitive disabilities face biggest difficulties through high text complexity (19 %), confusing advertisements (18 %), inconsistent menu as well as navigation structures (16 %) and overloaded pages / websites (12 %). Concerning the surfing behavior, we found out, that 46 % use the internet without help and 39 % need personal assistance. The relatively high figure of 46% is partly due to the fact that a number of clients were surveyed who had participated in dedicated IT workshops before.

The survey gave an overview on the most hindering issues for our target group discussed later on. Following the results, we for example pay special attention to text complexity. Besides the use of basic "easy2read" rules and guidelines, symbols will support and enrich navigation and content. An experimental pilot study by Bernasconi [1] on technical conditions and participatory impact of people with cognitive disabilities showed the importance of such supporting symbols. According to this study the target group preferred to click on icons in the menu instead of using text links (buttons with text). Following Bernasconi [1], the use of well introduced and known icons and symbols facilitates navigation, understanding and use of a website.

As next step, we evaluated the current situation with regard to barriers and difficulties, browsing behavior and IT skills of our target group and started to categorize our panel in three gradations (self-dependent with minor adaptations, self-dependent with major adaptations, depending on personal assistance) using a draft field manual:

- group description, "cross section"
  − description of disability in terms of grade, form and typical constraints
- physical description, "individual persona"
  − use of and experience with technology
- scenario
  − typical application environment (e.g. private, leisure time, for work)
  − usage (e.g. self dependent use, AT usage, needed personal assistance,…)
  − target application (e.g. does the respective person surf the internet; if yes, with which devices (PC, Smartphone, Tablet, with/without AT)

Experiences in (accessible) web-design show that intuitively useable, clearly (what does not necessarily mean plainly) designed and consistently structured websites serve all (intended and unintended) users comprising users with mobile devices, elderly people, non-native speakers as well as blind people and of course people with cognitive disabilities. Besides this, our aim is to introduce the target group to the internet and give them the opportunity to use CAPKOM as a supporting platform. Some outstanding products following the "Design for All" concept show that many inventions initially targeted to people with disabilities or elderly pay off and are a major benefit for all − independent from knowledge, age or disability. The remote control, originally developed to assist people with mobility constraints is nowadays an integral part of most households. Like the remote control, CAPKOM should pave the way for imaginative new services with target-group-oriented websites and software applications.

3   R & D Idea

People with or without disabilities that are not able to read or write at all are at the risk of being left behind as even basic tasks like entering a username or password puts them in the situation of needing assistance. As this target group in most cases depends on personal assistance in using new media, one of our main goals is to build up an engaging yet barrier free web application (supported by symbols) to spark their interest in the internet and its possibilities, raising their competence in using these offers and provide facilities to include them.

From a technical perspective, our targets are:

- Design and development of a software-framework for the creation of user interfaces for people with cognitive disabilities
- Implementation of this framework using the example of:
  - A community art portal [4]
  - An application for smartphones
  - A communication software suite [already sketched and in development by PLATUS, a project partner and company working in the area of Augmented and Alternative communication (AAC)] [5]
- Based on the findings and results from intensive user testing (our panel comprises around 400 individuals with a very diverse set of abilities and competences), we will develop mobile applications for smartphones and software solutions for Augmented and Alternative Communication (AAC)
- Last but not least we plan to develop a wizard to easily adapt the user interface to the needs of the respective user with cognitive disabilities.

This requires a special methodology:

- Research and development of a knowledge model adapted to people with cognitive disabilities,
- Development of a symbol based communication system adapted for the specific needs of people with cognitive disabilities,
- Provision of an adequate user interface adapted to the project framework,
- Experience-prototyping for iterative software development and evaluation routines.

4   First Results

We designed different mock ups with symbols and navigation structure and implemented them within a user interface and a website (a community art portal) for people with cognitive disabilities seen on Fig. 1. below, containing some pages for uploading, showing and discussing self-made pieces of art with:

- An easy to use, color indicated navigation scheme.
- Symbols additionally to textual indicators
- Simplified text

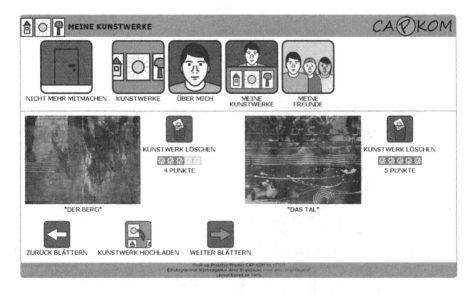

Fig. 1. Screenshot showing a page out of the community art portal for people with cognitive disabilities (mock-up) before CAPKOM user tests and expert feedback

With the mockup shown in Fig. 1 we went into testing (people with cognitive disabilities, their caregivers and communication experts) and adapted the first idea following the feedback. Furthermore, we gained useful information on the preparation of an action plan following focused discussions with experts and caregivers for people with cognitive disabilities:

- A separate database should give the opportunity to upload a user's own icons or pictures.
- The portal should provide the possibility to learn a certain structure of websites, which supports the target group by giving them tools, methods, community experiences and training actions for other internet sites and platforms.
- Possibility to easily implement own (known) and restore default symbols.
- Undo-function, acting as safety net mechanism.
- AAC: icons with text, speech output, mouse-over-function.
- Clear distinction between website content and navigation area.
- Search-function placed in the upper right part of the site.
- Navigation placed on the left side, with pointed out buttons and control elements enriched by big icons, leading to a better overview and orientation.
- A short introduction of the platform is necessary, especially in making settings and adjustments.

As displayed in Fig. 2., the color based navigation disappeared. Additionally, we took all texts on this portal and translated them into an easier language version following the "European standards in easy to read and use information" [7] and last but not least, we adapted the whole structure of the page to a better overview and usability.

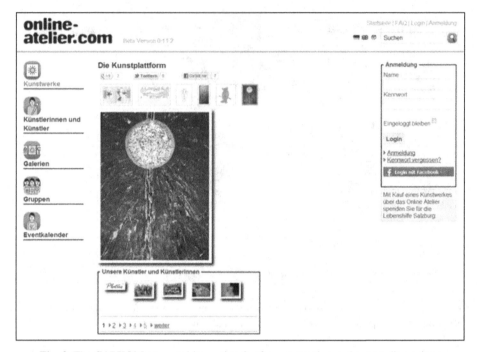

Fig. 2. The CAPKOM art portal in version 2, after user testing and expert discussions

In a next step, we will go into further user testing and develop and implement the wizard for adapting the user interface to the individual needs of users. Results will be a newly adapted user interface and the art portal with symbol support and easier language adaptable to at least 3 different grades of complexity:

- "Mainstream users" – self-dependent with no or only minor adaptations or audio output (as we do not want to build up another "ghetto application" but give people with and without disability the equal chance to display, discuss and possibly sell their masterpieces) and with all the navigation items available (including building up own galleries and groups with different artists, entering events etc.);
- "Easier language without symbols" – to facilitate self-dependent people with a higher level of language proficiency, giving them easier language and also the chance to toggle between audio on and off to get support (speech output) with most of the navigation items available,
- "Easier language with symbols" – the most simple version, including audio output and with only some of the navigation items facilitating basic tasks within the art portal (the exact set of possibilities and items are subject to upcoming user tests).

5   Conclusion

With the CAPKOM project and all related applications, we aim at two primary goals:

- Ethical goal: To include as many people as possible in innovative applications of information and communication technologies and bring them together (e.g. in a community art portal where they can express themselves and discuss their works) without barriers. In this context, the community art portal can be regarded as an easy and reliable starting point, which gives users the opportunity to learn how to realize the different possibilities provided by the internet.
- Practical goal: By using our example applications, we show how modern ICT and AT is best implemented and adapted to the needs of a very diverse user group and how this knowledge can also provide commercial benefit. There is a great demand for ICT for people with disabilities but still, the offer is very limited. Concerning the commercial benefit, ever more people are getting access to the internet and the wired disability community continues to grow at incredible rates. Ultimately, there is a new market to be opened up [9].

Acknowledgements. The project CAPKOM is funded by the Austrian Research Promotion Agency (FFG), proposal number 830867 / CAPKOM, COIN program. Project partners involved:

- Institute Integriert Studieren, JKU Linz: http://www.jku.at/iis
- Salzburg Research: http://www.salzburgresearch.at
- UTILO KG: http://www.utilo.eu
- Platus Learning Systems GmbH: http://www.platus.at
- Lebenshilfe Salzburg: http://www.lebenshilfe-salzburg.at

References

1. Bernasconi, T.: Barrierefreies Internet für Menschen mit geistiger Behinderung. Eine Experimentelle Pilotstudie zu Technischen Voraussetzungen und Partizipativen Auswirkungen. BIS-Verlag der Carl von Ossietzky Universität Oldenburg, Oldenburg (2007)
2. Bohman, P.: Cognitive disabilities Part 2: Conceptualizing Design Considerations. WebAIM, http://webaim.org/articles/cognitive/conceptualize/ (last lookup January 2012)
3. Gregg, D.: Cognitive Accessibility Online (2010), http://yaccessibilityblog.com/wp/cognitive-accessibility-online.html#more-1745 (last lookup April 2012)
4. http://www.online-atelier.com (last lookup January 2012)
5. http://www.platus.at/en/platus.html (last lookup January 2012)
6. Hyatt, G.W.: The iPad: Cheap and Disruptive AAC? (2010), http://yaccessibilityblog.com/wp/ipad-cheap-and-disruptive-aac.html#more-1774 (last lookup April 2012)

7. Inclusion Europe: European Standards on how to make information easy to read and understand for people with intellectual disabilities (2009), `http://inclusion-europe.org/images/stories/documents/Project_Pathways1/Information_for_all.pdf` (last lookup April 2012)

8. online-atelier.com: Die Kunstplattform für Galerien, Künstler und Kunstinteressierte `http://www.online-atelier.com/OnlineAtelier/` (last lookup April 2012)

9. Paciello, M.G.: Web Accessibility for People with Disabilities, p. 11. CMP Books, Kansas (2000)

10. Poulson, D., Nicolle, C.: Making the Internet accessible for people with cognitive and communication impairments. Universal Access in the Information Society 3(1), 48–56 (2004)

11. Pouncey, I.: Web accessibility for cognitive disabilities and learning difficulties (2010), `http://dev.opera.com/articles/view/cognitive-disability-learning-difficulty/`

12. Roe, P.R.W.: Towards an inclusive future. Impact and wider potential of information and communication technologies. COST, Brussels (2007)

13. Schlick, A.: Feldtests und Evaluierung (2009), `http://capkom.utilo.eu/joomla/images/downloads/ Deliverable_D3.2_V05.pdf` (last lookup April 2012)

A Real-Time Sound Recognition System
in an Assisted Environment

Héctor Lozano[1], Inmaculada Hernáez[2], Javier Camarena[1], Ibai Díez[1], and Eva Navas[2]

[1] Tecnalia, Health and Quality of Life Unit, Parque Tecnológico, Edificio 202. E-48170
Zamudio (Bizkaia), Spain
{hector.lozano,javier.camarena,ibai.diez}@tecnalia.com
[2] University of the Basque Country, Department of Electronics and Telecommunications,
E-48013 Bilbao (Bizkaia), Spain
{inma.hernaez,eva.navas}@ehu.es

Abstract. This article focuses on the development of detection and classification system of environmental sounds in real-time in a typical home for persons with disabilities. Based on the extraction of acoustic characteristics (Mel Frequency Cepstral Coefficients, Zero Crossing Rate, Roll Off Point and Spectral Centroid) and using a probabilistic classifier (Gaussian Mixture Model), preliminary results show an accuracy rate greater than 93% in the detection and 98% in the classification task

1 Introduction

The research presented in this article broaden previous studies by the authors [1], [2] focus on finding solutions which allow the detection and classification of household sounds with two clearly defined objectives:

1. Helping people with hearing impairment to cope with daily situations in which they are presented with meaningful sounds, such as warnings/alarms, doorbells or telephones ringing, alarm clocks, etc.
2. To collect information from the environment which may be used to track the behaviour pattern of an individual. With this, daily activity can be later analyzed in order to detect and prevent habits which may lead to illness or physical/cognitive deterioration.

Various solutions or devices for the hearing impaired, aimed at detecting and identifying sounds can be found. However, most of them are based only on the detection of any sound over a particular pre-set intensity threshold and/or duration. In scientific literature different publications describe the search of acoustic characteristics [3] that define environmental events and the algorithms that help in their discrimination [4]. Nevertheless, the number of such research projects is very limited and most of them focus on the surveillance field [5], [6].

K. Miesenberger et al. (Eds.): ICCHP 2012, Part II, LNCS 7383, pp. 385–391, 2012.
© Springer-Verlag Berlin Heidelberg 2012

This article presents the implementation and evaluation of a final environmental sound recognition system at home working in real time. The system has been installed and tested in a Homelab with pre-recorded typical sounds.

2   Sound Recognition System

The work presented in this article is explained in detail in the next sections. These sections define the methodology used for this research.

2.1   Techniques Selection for the Detection and Classification

Before writing this article several studies were carried out by the authors using commercial databases of "non-speech" sounds [1], [2]. These experiments were aimed to determine the acoustic parameters and the most appropriate classification models in the field of environmental sound recognition. The techniques used in developing the described system are the result of this analysis.

Acoustic Parameters. Having obtained the audio signal to be analysed, it is divided into pieces of small duration. From them, acoustic information representative of the different kinds of sounds to be evaluated is obtained.

In our work the audio signals were divided into frames of 60 milliseconds and the acoustic characteristics extracted were the first 13 Mel Frequency Cepstral Coefficients (typically used in the speech recognition field), Zero Crossing Rate, Spectral Centroid and Roll Off Point (more frequent in the music recognition field) [2]. At the same time the first and second differences - delta and delta-delta coefficients - were obtained from all parameters.

Mel Frequency Cepstral Coefficients. This is a perception parameter based on the FFT. After calculating the logarithm for the FFT magnitude of the signal, the bins (minimum units in the spectral domain) group together and soften in line with the Mel Frequency scale which is defined mathematically in formula 1:

$$Mel\ (f) = 2595\ \log_{10}\left(1 + \frac{f}{700}\right) \tag{1}$$

Lastly, a DCT (Discrete Cosign Transform) is performed in order to decorrelate the vector of the resulting parameters. The function defining this process is as follows:

$$c_q^{(p)} = \sum_{n=1}^{k=20} \log m_n^{(p)} \cos \frac{\pi q(2n+1)}{2K} \tag{2}$$

Zero Crossing Rate. This is the number of zero crossings which occur in the analysis frame. In the signal spectrum, high (or low) frequencies imply high (or low) zero crossing rates. As such, the number of zero crossings is an indicator of the signal's high frequency content. The mathematical definition is shown in equation 3:

$$Z_t = \frac{\frac{1}{2} \sum_{n=1}^{N} \left| sign\ (x[n]) - sign\ (x[n-1]) \right|}{t} \tag{3}$$

where t is the frame length.

Spectral Centroid. This parameter measures how strong a sound is. The centre of gravity is assessed based on the information obtained from the Fourier Transform. It is defined as:

$$C_t = \frac{\sum_{k=1}^{N} |X_t[k]| \cdot k}{\sum_{k=1}^{N} |X_t[k]|} \tag{4}$$

where $X_t[n]$ represents the nth sample of the Fourier Transform for the *t* frame.

Roll Off Point (RF). This parameter represents the frequencies below which 85% of the energy in the audio spectrum resides. It is commonly used to identify sounds from musical instruments. In this context, the percussive sounds and note attacks usually have more energy, which is why this is a measure of the existence of abrupt signal changes. Equation 5 defines this characteristic, $M[f]$ being the energy of the signal in frequency bands higher than f. The maximum value of f is delimited by the size and the sample ratio of the acoustical band.

$$RF : \sum_{f=1}^{RF} M[f] = 0.85 * \sum_{f=1}^{N} M[f] \tag{5}$$

Delta and Delta-delta Coefficients. At the same time the first and second differences - delta and delta-delta coefficients - were obtained from all parameters.

Classification Model. Not all classifiers offer the same performance in non-speech sounds recognitions [7]. The chosen classifier, Gaussian Mixture Model (GMM) [6], is a simple model which can be described as a Hidden Markov Model (HMM) of a single state. Impulsive sounds which are difficult to separate into states are classified by observing the distribution followed by the extracted parameters. Its implementation cost is low and it offers good properties for identifying short and impulsive events. Equation 6 defines the model.

$$gm(x) = \sum_{k=1}^{K} w_k \cdot g(\mu_k, \Sigma_k)(x) \tag{6}$$

$$\sum_{i=1}^{k} w_i = 1 \quad \forall \quad i \in \{1, \ldots, K\} \quad : w_i \geq 0$$

K is the number of gaussians or order of the model. Adjusting the number of Gaussians to optimize the performance of the system is not trivial. If a very high number is chosen the model can overfit the extracted data. Otherwise, a small K can lead to a too general model not sufficiently different from other models, and the sound will not be adequately recognized. After some preliminary tests carried out in the Homelab, a value of K=60 was used in the experiments.

2.2   Environment and Sound Selection

Recording and Evaluation Environment. In the evaluation of the different techniques for environmental sound recognition with commercial databases, it is important to see how they behave in real environments. The developed system has been tested with sounds produced in a functional Homelab of over $30m^2$ with a bedroom, a living-room, a kitchen area, a bathroom, and a corridor.

The Homelab was provided with a PC equipped with a multichannel audio card connected to 6 microphones located on the ceiling of the different areas / rooms. Additionally, a tablet-pc and a mobile phone were used as user interfaces which displayed the recognized events (see figure 1 and 2).

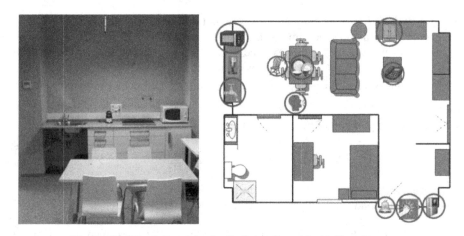

Fig. 1. The Homelab and the Audio Sources used in the Experiment

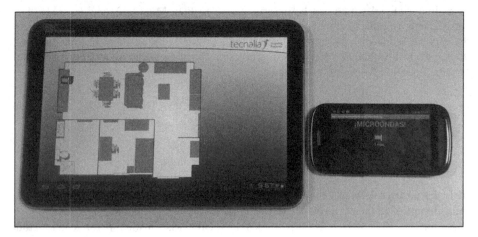

Fig. 2. Tablet PC and mobile phone showing a detected event

Sounds Selection and Recording. In order to train and validate the sound recognition system, it is essential to have a sound database with representative data both in quality and quantity.

Taking into account the different sound sources available in the Homelab, there was a selection of interesting sounds based on the aims discussed above (to help deaf people and to track behavioral patterns). The set of acoustic events that form the corpus has 12 sounds: doorbell, intercom, knocking on the door, telephone, opening cupboards, cutlery, chairs noise, open/closed microwave, microwave working, microwave final whistle, tap water and speech.

For the training of the models, samples were recorded of about 2 minutes for each class of event. Subsequently a manual removal of the silences found in each audio track was performed.

3   Experiments Performed

The experiments described here were carried out using just the microphone located in the kitchen area. This would allow us to test the possibilities offered by a single microphone and at the same time minimizes the cost in a future commercial development. The locations of the audio sources are shown in Figure 1.

As a preliminary test to determine the accuracy and reliability of the classifier, the recordings of two minutes were evaluated at the frame level (60 milliseconds). To avoid overtraining of the models, the obtained frames were separated into two sets: one for training (60% of the frames) and one for the test (40% of the frames).

Subsequently, with the system running in real time, the evaluation was performed at event level. Accordingly, during a period of approximately one hour, each sound source was triggered 25 times and the system's ability to recognize them was analyzed. Due to the short duration of the frames a smoothing was applied to avoid false positives.

4   Results

In order to provide a measure capable of combining precision and recall, results of the experiments were given based on the formula of the F_1-score. This is a classic measure used by the statistical classification community. It is a combination of precision and recall in a single metric through the harmonic mean of the two values. that can be more concise when presenting and comparing results.. Expression 7 defines this measure.

$$F_1 Score = 2 * \frac{(Precision * Recall)}{(Precision + Recall)} \qquad (7)$$

At frame level we obtain a F1-score of 88%. At sound level, during the evaluation of the real-time system, 93% of the sounds were detected. The remaining 7% correspond to no detected events and false positives. From the properly-detected ones, 98% were correctly classified.

In Figures 3 and 4 confusion matrices show the precision and recall for the evaluation at frame and at sound level.

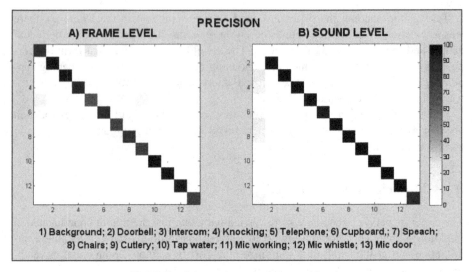

Fig. 3. Precision at frame and at sound level

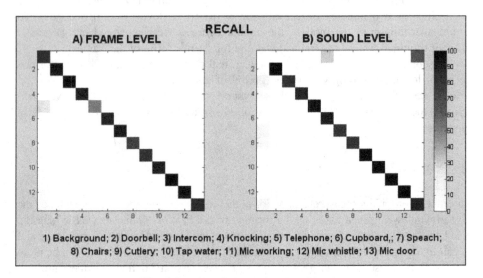

Fig. 4. Recall at frame and at sound level

5   Conclusions and Future Lines

This work shows a real implementation of an environmental sounds recognition system designed to promote independence and quality of life for the elderly or hearing impaired. The results obtained in the evaluation of the application demonstrate how recognition techniques applied offer high accuracy and reliability using training signals of only 2 minutes and a single microphone.

Future areas of work include the use of the information provided by the additional microphones to increase the robustness of the system taking into account that most of the sounds produced in a home environment are located in a specific area (kitchen, bedroom,...). This will also allow adaptation of the recognizer to adverse noise situations that may cause false positives that are not preventable with the use of a single microphone. Finally the evaluation of the system with end users which can test and assess it for its improvement and sophistication, will be of great interest.

In the frame of the RUBICON Project, the sound recognition system will be evaluated and used for the detection and classification of daily live activities in an AAL environment. Information extracted from sounds together with data collected from autonomous wireless networks of sensors and actuators will be processed allowing higher classification level and an improvement in the accuracy and reliability.

Acknowledgements. The technologies and developments presented in this paper are partially supported by the European Union (7th Frame Programme ICT, project RUBICON, contract N. 269914, www.fp7rubicon.eu) and by the Basque Government through the grant IT537-10

References

1. Lozano, H., Hernáez, I., Picón, A., Camarena, J., Navas, E.: Audio Classification Techniques in Home Environments for Elderly/Dependant People. In: Miesenberger, K., Klaus, J., Zagler, W., Karshmer, A. (eds.) ICCHP 2010. LNCS, vol. 6179, pp. 320–323. Springer, Heidelberg (2010)
2. Lozano, H., Hernáez, I., Navas, E., et al.: Non-Speech Sounds Classification for People with Hearing Disabilities. In: AAATE, pp. 276–280 (2007)
3. Cowling, M.: Non-Speech Environmental Sound Classification System for Autonomous Surveillance. Phd Thesis. Griffith University (2004)
4. Temko, A.: Acoustic Event Detection and Classification. Phd Thesis. Universitat Politècnica de Catalunya (2007)
5. Clavel, C., Ehrette, T., Richard, G.: Events Detection for an Audio-Based Surveillance System. In: Proc. of the IEEE Int. Conf. on Multimedia and Expo., ICME, pp. 1306–1309 (2005)
6. Atrey, K., Maddage, C., Kankanhalli, S.: Audio Based Event Detection for Multimedia Surveillance. In: IEEE International Conference ICCASP, pp. 813–816 (2006)
7. Vacher, M., Istrate, D., Besacier, L., Serignat, J.F.: Life Sounds Extraction and Classification in Noisy Environment. In: IASTED'SIP, Honolulu, Hawaii, USA (2003)

Gestures Used by Intelligent Wheelchair Users

Dimitra Anastasiou[1] and Christoph Stahl[2]

[1] Computer Science/Languages Science, University of Bremen, Germany
anastasiou@uni-bremen.de
[2] German Research Center for Artificial Intelligence (DFKI), Bremen, Germany
christoph.stahl@dfki.de

Abstract. This paper is concerned with the modality of gestures in communication between an intelligent wheelchair and a human user. Gestures can enable and facilitate human-robot interaction (HRI) and go beyond familiar pointing gestures considering also context-related, subtle, implicit gestural and vocal instructions that can enable a service. Some findings of a user study related to gestures are presented in this paper; the study took place at the Bremen Ambient Assisted Living Lab, a 60m² apartment suitable for the elderly and people with physical or cognitive impairments.

Keywords: assisted living, gestures, intelligent wheelchair, smart home.

1 Introduction

According to the International Society for Gesture Studies, gesture studies is a rich and old interdisciplinary field, broadly concerned with examining the use of the hands and other parts of the body for communicative purposes. Gesture researchers work in diverse academic and creative disciplines including anthropology, linguistics, psychology, history, neuroscience, communication, art history, performance studies, computer science, music, theater, and dance. Gesture is a necessary modality for people with speech disorders, but also in general, in situations where hand interaction is not feasible.

This paper is laid out as follows: in section 2 we present taxonomies of gestures based on a linguistic and computational point of view, and stress the importance of gestures in smart homes. Our research study and its findings are presented in section 3 and a conclusion and future prospects follow in section 4.

2 Gestures in Theory and Practice

Gesture is an already established scientific research field in verbal and particularly non-verbal communication, both from theoretical and practical points of view. Before the 1980s gesture was part of non-verbal communication research; only after the 1980s, gesture was closely tied with speech in creating meaning.

McNeill (1992 [1]), based on Kendon (1982) [2], laid the philological foundations about gestures and mind, and classified gestures into gesticulation, pantomime,

K. Miesenberger et al. (Eds.): ICCHP 2012, Part II, LNCS 7383, pp. 392–398, 2012.

emblem, and sign language. Various dimensions were assigned to these types of gestures, namely i) degree of speech accompaniment (reducing from gesticulation to sign language), ii) degree of linguistic properties (ascending from gesticulation to sign language), iii) conventionality (also ascending), and iv) semiotic differences (gesticulation is global/synthetic, pantomime segmented/synthetic, emblem global/ analytic, and sign language segmented/analytic).

Within the context of Human-Computer Interaction (HCI), there is a taxonomy of gestures developed by Quek (1994) [3]; based on this taxonomy, meaningful gestures are differentiated from unintentional movements. Meaningful gestures are classified into communicative and manipulative gestures. The former are used to act on objects in an environment and the latter have an inherent communicational purpose. Manipulative gestures can occur both on the desktop in a 2-D interaction using a direct manipulation device (mouse, stylus), as a 3-D interaction involving empty handed movements to mimic manipulations of physical objects (virtual reality interfaces), or by manipulating actual physical objects that map onto a virtual object in tangible interfaces. Wexelblatt (1998) [4] provided an overview of the primary classifications referred to in some computing literature too.

2.1   Gestures in Smart Homes

Ambient Assisted Living (AAL) has been the research topic of many scholars of the last decade. AAL is a research domain supported by national programmes (such as the German BMBF and the European Ambient Assisted Living Joint Programme) which promotes intelligent assistant systems for a better, healthier, and safer life in the preferred living environments through the use of Information and Communication Technologies (ICT). AAL technologies and applications are used in domotics, as the motivation for AAL research is to improve the lifestyle of the seniors in their domestic environments. The homes where such AAL technologies are applied to are called smart homes.

In smart homes multimodal applications are necessary to compensate specific limitations of physically challenged people. For example, people with motor disabilities would prefer or need speech interaction, while people with speech impairments prefer gestural interaction; more information on why gestures are needed in AAL can be found in Anastasiou (2011) [5]. Nazemi et al. (2011) [6] stated that gestural interaction is more natural and simpler for seniors, as they often have problems with precise movements to open applications through clicking on programme symbols at interfaces. Besides, it is difficult for them to use the common TV remote control, because the buttons as well as the text written on them are too small. Moreover, in situations where the hands are employed, such as cooking in the kitchen or talking to the phone, where verbal communication is impossible or constricted, gestural interaction is helpful.

As for intelligent wheelchairs/personal assistants in AAL, traditional electric-powered wheelchairs are normally controlled by users via joysticks, which cannot satisfy the needs of elderly and disabled users who have restricted limb movements caused by some diseases, such as Parkinson and quadriplegics (Jia et al., 2007 [7]). Generally speaking, unlike existing techniques, gesture-based interaction as a mode of explicit interaction is more natural and appealing to people while accessing various services (Chen et al., 2010 [8]).

As far as gesture recognition techniques applied in AAL is concerned, Jaimes & Sebe (2007) [9] stated that recognizing gestures and integrating them to access ambient services has been under-researched due to the lack of accuracy, limited set of gestures, extensive learning efforts, overall robustness of the particular gesture recognition techniques, and their special setup requirements and operating constraints. Many initiatives have been undertaken in AAL by applying three dimensional acceleration sensor information of the *WiiMote*, e.g. Nazemi et al. (2011) [6] and Neßelrath et al. (2011) [10].

3   User Study

A pilot user study[1] in BAALL took place in November-December 2011 and included a real-life everyday scenario of a human user using a wheelchair to navigate in their environment by means of speech and gesture. Both HRI and home device control are available in BAALL (see Krieg-Brückner et al. 2010 [11]) at the German Research Center for Artificial Intelligence. BAALL is an apartment suitable for the elderly and people with disabilities. It has an area of $60m^2$ and contains all standard living areas, i.e. kitchen, bathroom, bedroom, and living room. In BAALL the autonomous wheelchair/robot *Rolland*, offers mobility assistance being equipped with two laser range-sensors, wheel encoders, and an onboard computer; *Rolland* has a spoken dialogue interface that allows the user to choose destinations and control devices in BAALL; control with smart phone or tablet PC is also possible. The intelligent wheelchair *Rolland* and a participant pointing to a landmark are depicted in Figure 1.

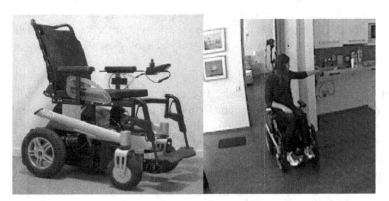

Fig. 1. Rolland and a participant pointing to the kitchen in BAALL

The goal of the study was to observe whether people would gesture and how, and what they would say, if they used a wheelchair in their smart home to carry out daily activities. One of the hypotheses was whether the participants would gesture more in case their addressees can see them. Indeed speakers gesture more in this situation than

[1] Acknowledgments to Daniel Vale, Bernd Gersdorf, Thora Tenbrink, and Carsten Gendorf.

when their addresses cannot see them (Cohen, 1977 [12]; Alibali & Don, 2001 [13]). Moreover, Rimé & Schiaratura (1991) [14] said that gestures' type and density change in relation to the referent, the recipient, and the communication mean. 20 German student participants took part in the study (mean age 26) and were asked to act as if they were dependent on the wheelchair, so that the scenario is close to reality. The participants had to perform the following activities in this order:

- Rinse your mouth with water.
- Take something to eat or drink.
- Wash your hands.
- Take a book.
- Read the book on the sofa while Rolland recharges.
- Open the door when someone knocks.

The user study was Wizard-of-Oz (WoZ) controlled, i.e. an experimenter A was in an office observing by live audio and video streaming what was going on in BAALL in order to remotely set *Rolland's* navigational goal. An experimenter B was inside BAALL giving instructions to the participants and following them during the task execution. There were three cameras in total which recorded the subjects' activities: two cameras placed in BAALL and one placed on *Rolland's* back, so that *Rolland* could see and 'supposedly' recognize their gestures. The verbal instructions included introduction of the lab and *Rolland,* and instruction of the tasks that the participants should perform. The written instructions included the 6 tasks presented above and were also put as a note on *Rolland's* armrest; they were not given as handouts, so that participants have their hands free to gesture. In the verbal and written instructions we did not refer to the landmarks, i.e. 'living room', 'bathroom', etc., but to the activities instead, e.g. "Read a book on the sofa" instead of "Go to the living room". This decision was made because one of the goals in this study, apart from observing gestural frequency and gesture types, was to collect empirical data of natural dialogue in HRI. There were tasks where the user is sitting on *Rolland*, but also when *Rolland* drives autonomously without the user (part of task 5), as differences in gesture may change based on the recipient. In the end of each session, a retrospective protocol approach was followed (Dorst & Dijkhuis, 1995) [15]; the participants were asked to go through the tasks that they just performed and say what they were thinking. They were also asked to recommend future improvements of the HRI. An example answer from the retrospective protocol was that one female participant expected *Rolland* to have a female voice (see Crowell et al. 2009 [16]). Most of the participants said that *Rolland* "parked" too far and a person with disabilities would not have been able to reach it.

As for the findings of the study in relation to gestures, in 7 sessions out of total (35%) participants employed at least one gesture during a session (6 sessions with deictic gestures, 1 with iconic). In 2 of the 7 sessions participants gestured more than once, while in the remaining 5 sessions, people gestured once. The deictic gestures were pointing at a place where *Rolland* should go to, as *Rolland* was too far from the landmark that the participants wanted to go. The iconic gesture by one participant was 'hand rubbing' under the tap to represent a state of washing her hands. In general, the study has shown that participants gestured mostly when something happened out of order, e.g. *Rolland* drove to a wrong destination point or stopped too far from the participant or was close to hit a wall or door. When everything went well, i.e. *Rolland* drove the participant where he/she wanted to, participants did not gesture. An exception was one female participant who gestured during all the tasks. This situation can be explained by personal influences, e.g. the user's personality (see Rehm et al., 2008) [17]. From the study also the attitude and expectations of the participants against the robot have been evaluated. The style, the volume of the utterance, the waiting time for *Rolland* to react as well as the content of the lexical content of the utterance itself have shown that humans' perception of robots vary and can significantly change during a study. For example, a participant waited firstly for 9 seconds for *Rolland* to react, then for 3 seconds, until finally she uttered the context-sensitive spatial instruction "come here": "Rolland, <break 9 sec> Rolland, <break 3 sec> komm her (*Rolland, Rolland, come here*)". It is worth noting that one female participant characteristically expected *Rolland* to have female voice. A video recording showing some of the scenes where participants employed gestures is available[2].

In order to make an analysis of gestures in the multimodal grammar, we follow the model by Hahn & Rieser (2010) [18]. Figure 2 represents an example of the speech-gesture alignment of the phrase *Dreh dich hierhin (Turn over here)* in the dialogue part. The arrows outside the pictures pointing towards the lexicon definition indicate that gesture content operates on lexical content.

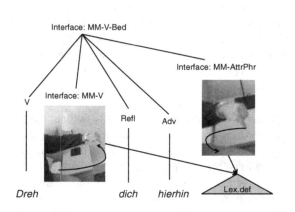

V: **Verb**
Adv: **Adverb**
AttrPhr: **Attribute phrase**
Lex.def: **Lexicon definition**
MM: **multi-modal**
Refl: **reflexive pronoun**

Fig. 2. Interface of speech-gesture in HRI (adapted from Hahn & Rieser, 2010)

4   Conclusion and Future Prospects

In this paper we introduced a philological and computational taxonomy of gestures. We are interested in contact-free, touch less gestures, i.e. *gesticulation* according to

---

[2] The video is available at http://ai.cs.uni-sb.de/~stahl/d-anastasiou/ DiaSpace/Resources/

the philological taxonomy and *meaningful gestures* according to the computational taxonomy. Then a user study with the goal to collect empirical speech-gesture data was presented. The findings have shown that only in situations where *Rolland* parked too far and generally when something went out of order, participants gestured. In the future we plan to have participants coming from different countries to see whether cultural differences in pointing gestures in AAL domain exist (see Kita [19]). In addition, more user studies with specific constraints, e.g. participants are prohibited to speak, and/or ambiguous situations ("Bring me to the sofa", having many sofas in BAALL) etc. are planned for the near future in order to focus more on gesture generation. Gesture recognition will follow after we have established a theoretical framework about a set of natural and intuitive gestures used in a smart home.

Acknowledgments. We gratefully acknowledge the support of the Deutsche Forschungsgemeinschaft (DFG) through the Collaborative Research Center SFB/TR 8 Spatial Cognition.

References

1. McNeill, D.: Hand and Mind: What Gestures reveal about Thought. University of Chicago Press (1992)
2. Kendon, A.: The study of gesture: some observations on its history. Recherches Semiotique/Semiotic Inquiry 2(1), 25–62 (1982)
3. Quek, F.: Toward a vision-based hand gesture interface. In: Proceedings of the Virtual Reality System Technology Conference, pp. 17–29 (1994)
4. Wexelblat, A.: Research Challenges in Gesture: Open Issues and Unsolved Problems. In: Wachsmuth, I., Fröhlich, M. (eds.) GW 1997. LNCS (LNAI), vol. 1371, pp. 1–11. Springer, Heidelberg (1998)
5. Anastasiou, D.: Gestures in assisted living environments. In: Proceedings of the 9th International Gesture Workshop (2011)
6. Nazemi, K., Burkhardt, D., Stab, C., Breyer, M., Wichert, R., Fellner, D.W.: Natural gesture interaction with accelerometer-based devices in ambient assisted environments. In: 4. AAL-Kongress, pp. 75–84 (2011)
7. Jia, P., Hu, H., Lu, T., Yuan, K.: Head gesture recognition for hands-free control of an intelligent wheelchair. Industrial Robot: An International Journal 34(1), 60–68 (2007)
8. Chen, K.Y., Chien, C.C., Chang, W.L., Teng, J.T.: An integrated color and hand gesture recognition approach for an autonomous mobile robot. In: Proceedings of the 3rd International Congress on Image and Signal Processing (2010)
9. Jaimes, A., Sebe, N.: Multimodal human–computer interaction: A survey. Computer Vision and Image Understanding 108(1-2), 116–134 (2007)
10. Neßelrath, R., Lu, C., Schulz, C.H., Frey, J., Alexandersson, J.: A Gesture Based System for Context – Sensitive Interaction with Smart Homes. In: Wichert, R., Eberhardt, B. (eds.) Ambient Assisted Living, vol. 63, pp. 209–219. Springer, Heidelberg (2011)
11. Krieg-Brückner, B., Röfer, T., Shi, H., Gersdorf, B.: Mobility Assistance in the Bremen Ambient Assisted Living Lab. GeroPsych: The Journal of Gerontopsychology and Geriatric Psychiatry 23(2), 121–130 (2010)
12. Cohen, A.: The communicative functions of hand illustrators. Journal of Communication 27, 54–63 (1977)

13. Alibali, M.W., Don, L.S.: Children's gestures are meant to be seen. Gesture 1, 113–127 (2001)
14. Rimé, B., Schiaratura, L.: Gesture and speech. Fundamentals of nonverbal behavior. In: Studies in Emotion & Social Interaction, pp. 239–281 (1991)
15. Dorst, K., Dijkhuis, J.: Comparing paradigms for describing design activity. Design Studies 16, 261–274 (1995)
16. Crowell, C.R., Scheutz, M., Schermerhorn, P., Villano, M.: Gendered voice and robot entities: perceptions and reactions of male and female subjects. In: Proceedings of the 2009 IEEE/RSJ Intl. Conference on Intelligent Robots and Systems, IROS (2009)
17. Rehm, M., Bee, N., André, E.: Wave like an Egyptian: accelerometer based gesture recognition for culture specific interactions. In: Proceedings of the 2nd British HCI Group Annual Conference on People and Computers: Culture, Creativity, Interaction, vol. 1, pp. 13–22 (2008)
18. Hahn, F., Rieser, H.: Explaining Speech Gesture Alignment in MM Dialogue Using Gesture Typology. In: Proceedings of the 11th Annual SIGdial Meeting on Discourse and Dialogue (2010)
19. Kita, S.: Cross-cultural variation of speech-accompanying gesture: A review. Language and Cognitive Processes 24(2), 145–167 (2009)

Augmented Reality Based Environment Design Support System for Home Renovation

Yoshiyuki Takahashi and Hiroko Mizumura

Toyo University, Department of Human Environment Design, Faculty of Human Life Design,
Oka 48-1, Asaka-shi, Saitama, 351-8510 Japan
y-takahashi@toyo.ac.jp

Abstract. To improve the living environment for elderly persons, home renovation is performed. A part of home renovations cost is supported by long-term care insurance in Japan and several tens of problems related to renovation constructions are reported. They are caused by lack of communication and knowledge of constructions. We have developed an Augmented Reality environment design support system for home modifications. Especially it is designed for the persons that need long-term care. The preliminary experiment has been carried out and confirmed the functionality of the system.

Keywords: Home renovation, Augmented reality, Image processing.

1 Introduction

To improve the living environment for elderly persons, home renovation is performed. A part of home renovations cost is supported by long-term care insurance in Japan. Japanese local governments provide this insurance system and all insured persons can be supported for home renovation. Maximum of 200,000 Japanese Yen of renovation cost is supported by the insurance. Following 6 renovation items are applicable,

- Installing handrails
- Eliminating level differences
- Changing materials of floors for anti-skid and easy moving
- Replacing hinged doors to sliding doors
- Squat toilet to sitting toilet
- Reinforcing structural components according to modifications.

However, several tens of problems related to renovation constructions are reported in each year by national consumer affairs center of Japan. The problems are categorized by the following reasons,

- Lack of confirmation for the construction between an insured, a care manager and a constructor.
- Constructors lack of knowledge in home renovation for elderly people.

K. Miesenberger et al. (Eds.): ICCHP 2012, Part II, LNCS 7383, pp. 399–406, 2012.

To apply for the long-term care insurance, following documents are required,

- An application
- An estimate and a detailed list of estimated expenses
- A written statement of reason detailing the necessity of home renovations (must be drawn up by the care manager)
- A picture prior to renovations
- An image of the completed home renovations
- A copy of written consent for home renovations.

Persons related to the insurance application, such as a care manager, are mostly non professional about architecture. Therefore, they have difficulties to understand drawings for renovation. Usually, design of housing is shown in a plan view and development chart. Details of renovation e.g. installation position of handrails will be explain on the drawing. Furthermore, for insured persons and families may not be easy to understand the modification plan and can be difficult to imagine the result of modification. In case of the constructor, some of them lack knowledge of insurance system and ADL of elderly persons. Then, some construction was done before finishing the applying process to the governmental office or arbitrary and non required construction was proceeded in some case [1].

To solve these problems, we tried to design an augmented reality based environment design support system for home renovation. This system is based on augmented reality system which displays virtual components for home renovation e.g. the virtual handrails mixed to the real environment. For the user will be easy to understand how the home will be reconstructed by seeing real environment combined virtual components. The system is aimed to design an intuitive user interface for environmental design. We have carried out preliminary experiments to confirm the functionality of this system and its possibility.

2   Augmented Reality and Applications for Architecture

Augmented Reality (AR) is a variation of Virtual Reality (VR). VR provides a complete virtual environment and a user is immersed in the virtual environment. On the other hand, AR provides real environment and a superimposed virtual component or environment. Therefore, the virtual and the real objects are coexisting in the same view. AR system has the following characteristics [2],

- Combines real and virtual.
- Interactive in real time
- Registered in 3-D.

VR is widely applied for simulation and visualization systems. For example, visualizing evacuation simulation [3], driving simulators [4] and so on. AR is used for see-through display system e.g. head up display (HUD), information tools e.g. Sekai Camera which is a software application for the camera phone. By holding camera phone up and looking through the camera view, we can access information that are relevant to that place and time, shown as an overlay on the real world [5].

There are several researches for applying AR to the architectural design. For example, interior simulator can display virtual furniture in the real room and realized to examine in real scale environment [6]. Application of appearance simulation of building modifications and 3D virtual model of architecture exist. However, the research about AR based environment designs support system for home renovation, especially for the person need long-term care, has not been done yet.

3   System Design

3.1   System Structure

Fig. 1. shows the system structure of our developed system. The system consists of a head mounted display (HMD), a video signal converter, a PC and a Web camera. Web camera is mounted on the eyeglass frame and it takes the images which the user is looking at. If the virtual components generator detects the markers in the captured images, virtual components are generated and mixed to the captured image.

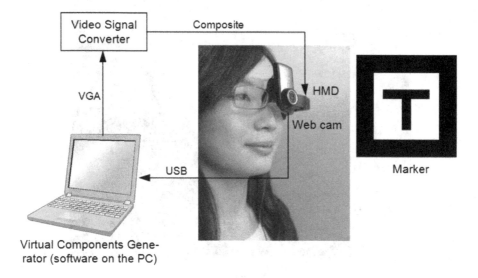

Fig. 1. System architecture

Video signal converter changes the video signal format from the VGA signal to the composite video signal in way to display the image on the HMD. The HMD displays captured image and mixed virtual images to the user. Virtual components generator is based on ARToolKit and OpenGL [7].

3.2   User Interface

Each virtual component corresponds to an individual marker. The markers for virtual component e.g. hand rail are prepared. The user looks around wearing glass with Web camera and HMD; if the markers are perceived, the type of marker is recognized and the virtual components corresponding to the markers will be displayed on the images. A shape, a position and an attitude of the virtual components are registered in the data file of the markers together with surface materials and lighting data. Three different markers and virtual components were prepared for the experiments.

To provide an interactive interface, vision based hand gesture interface is prepared (Fig. 2.). It is used to change the dimensions of the virtual components without any program source code changing and recompiling. When a bare hand appears in front of the Web camera, a main menu appears in the camera captured image. The menu is shown as a billboard. Therefore, the menu is always facing the camera. The user can select and set the desired parameters on the menu e.g. a length and a height. To select the menu item, the hand should be in front of the menu. Detected hand image area is extracted from the camera captured image and overlaid on the menu and the virtual components. An image processing is based on OpenCV.

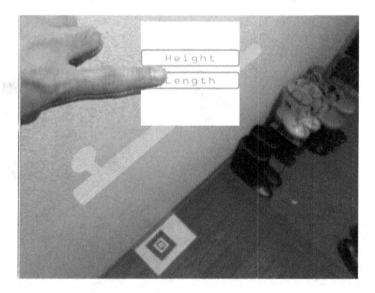

Fig. 2. User interface

4   Markers Detection Experiments

4.1   Markers

The maker in this system is according to the ARToolkit system specifications. The marker is square plate. A frame and symbols are printed on the surface. Original size of the marker is 80 mm square. This size is adequate for desktop experiments. To use the markers for everywhere in a house, several different size and pattern markers were prepared and tested. Fig. 3. shows the example of the markers. (a) Alphabetic character, (b) Japanese character and (c) Chinese character were used for a pattern of the markers. The markers with known characters could be easy to understand a related virtual object more than geometrical patterns.

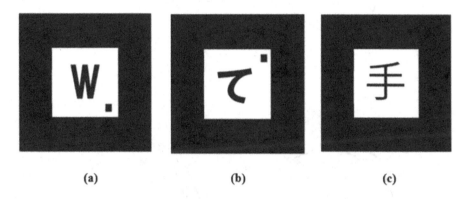

(a)   (b)   (c)

Fig. 3. Example of markers

4.2   Methods

The marker was put on a slider with a turntable on the floor. The marker was rotated each 45 deg, moving away from the Web camera and virtual object visible distance from the Web camera was recorded. Web camera was set to the eye position at 1600 mm height from the floor level. Three different patterns and four different sizes (80 mm, 120 mm, 140 mm and 180 mm square) , totally 12 markers, were tested.

4.3   Results

Virtual objects visible distances were plotted on the radar charts in Fig. 4. Markers (a), (b) and (c) correspond to the markers in Fig. 3. There are significant differences between the 180 mm x 180 mm size marker and other small size markers ($p < 0.05$). The visible distance was in accord to the size of the maker and the average of visible distance was 3.25m. Thus, 180 mm x 180 mm size marker can be used in Japanese houses that are based on the old Japanese unit and module.

The results of the marker (b) and (c) were not equal in each direction, especially in case of marker (c). The reason of that can be explained by the fact that these characters contain a curvature line. And also, the line of the marker (c) was thinner than the other characters. The character with thick lines and which consists of straight lines will be appropriate for the marker.

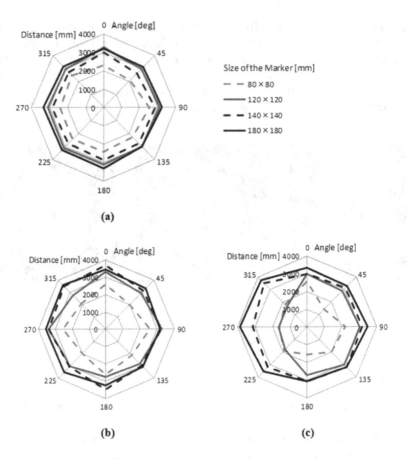

Fig. 4. Marker visible distances of each rotation angle

5   Preliminary Experiment in Real Environment

To confirm the functionality of the whole system, preliminary experiment has been carried out in the laboratory and inside a house. Single and multi markers are used to show the home renovation items. We have developed different types of handrails and slopes, different for shape and length.

Fig. 5. shows the example images for the experiment in real environment. The items were placed on the floor. It was confirmed that the virtual objects were placed as designed, also the size of them. However, sometimes missing markers and wrong detection have been occurred. They might be caused by setting parameter of threshold for marker detection. The reasons of that are that the luminance conditions were different on each location. Then, the binarization of the image might not work well and could not recognize the shape of the markers.

We had interviews to therapists who are familiar with home renovation for elderly persons. Positive impressions were feedbacked.

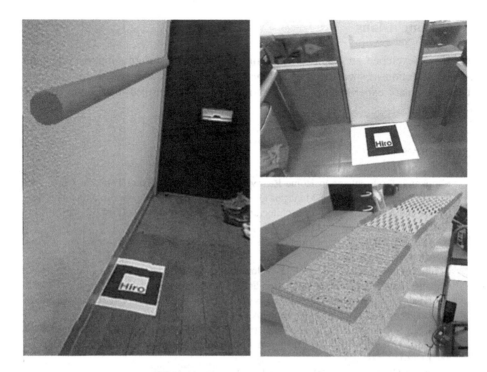

Fig. 5. Virtual components in the real environment

It was confirmed that the virtual objects were projected and mixed in the real image. However, we cannot touch these objects. That is the most important problem in this system. For example, to decide the height of the handrail for rise up, the user need to grasp and pull down the handrail and check it is in the appropriate position or not. Currently, our developed system is only effective to check the appearance. However, this system will be used to check not only the appearance but also to check the dimension of renovated parts visually e.g. width of the corridor after installing the handrail and so on.

6   Discussions

The user can see virtual components in appropriate positions and the functionality of the system has been confirmed. It may be possible to use the developed system for prior examination of home renovation. However, a marker was not detected even if it is in the captured image. It is necessary to consider changing threshold of marker detection dynamically and using a camera with auto iris function. In a next step, other components should be prepared and tested. And also, interviews and experiments with the care managers and the constructors.

7   Conclusions

We have developed an Augmented Reality environment design support system for home renovations. Especially it is designed for the persons who need long-term care. The preliminary experiment has been carried out and confirmed the functionality of the system.

References

1. Murakami, Y.: Problems in Home Renovation System Using Long-Term Care Insurance from the Viewpoint of Care-Manager: Questionnaires to Care-Manager in Kumamoto Prefecture and Kitakyusyu City 2. Architectural Institute of Japan (42) 20030301, pp.145–148 (2003) (in Japanese)
2. Azuma, R.T.: Survey of Augmented Reality. Presence: Teleoperators and Virtual Environments 6(4), 355–385 (1997)
3. Honma, M., Watanabe, M., et al.: Development of VR simulator for Fire of underground markets : Part2 : Evacuation simulation and System of VR simulator. Summaries of technical papers of Annual Meeting Architectural Institute of Japan F-1, Urban planning, building economics and housing problems, pp.397–398, (2000) (in Japanese)
4. Suda, Y., Shladover, S.E., et al.: Validation of the Interactive Traffic Simulation for the Universal Driving Simulator. The Japan Society of Mechanical Engineers 2006(5), 479–480 (2006)
5. Tonchidot Corporation (2009), http://sekaicamera.com/
6. Yamada, Y., Kado, K., et al.: Interior Simulator by Augmented/Mixed Reality. Summaries of technical papers of Annual Meeting Architectural Institute of Japan A-2, Fire Safety, Off-shore Engineering and Architecture, Information Systems Technology, pp.505–506 (2008) (in Japanese)
7. Kato, H., Billinghurst, M.: Marker Tracking and HMD Calibration for a Video-Based Augmented Reality Conferencing System. In: Proceedings of the 2nd IEEE and ACM International Workshop on Augmented Reality, pp. 85–94 (1999)

Fall Detection on Embedded Platform Using Kinect and Wireless Accelerometer

Michal Kepski* and Bogdan Kwolek

Rzeszów University of Technology, 35-959 Rzeszów, Poland
bkwolek@prz.edu.pl

Abstract. In this paper we demonstrate how to accomplish reliable fall detection on a low-cost embedded platform. The detection is achieved by a fuzzy inference system using Kinect and a wearable motion-sensing device that consists of accelerometer and gyroscope. The foreground objects are detected using depth images obtained by Kinect, which is able to extract such images in a room that is dark to our eyes. The system has been implemented on the PandaBoard ES and runs in real-time. It permits unobtrusive fall detection as well as preserves privacy of the user. The experimental results indicate high effectiveness of fall detection.

1 Introduction

Special needs and daily living assistance are often associated with seniors, disabled, the overweight and obese, etc. The special needs of the elderly may differ from that of an obese person or an overweight individual, but they all have special needs and often require some assistance to perform their daily routines. Assistive technology or adaptive technology (AT) is an umbrella term that encompasses assistive, adaptive, and rehabilitative devices for people with special needs [3]. Assistive technology for ageing-at-home has become a hot research topic since it has big social and commercial value. One important aim of assistive technology is to allow elderly people to stay as long as possible in their home or familiar environment without changing their living style. Even though physical activity is essential in the prevention of disease and enhancing the quality of life, falls frequently happen during walking and various forms of physical activity.

Falls are major causes of mortality and morbidity in the elderly. Many research findings show that high percentage of injury-related hospitalizations for seniors are the results of falls [6]. Thus, fall detection has become one of hot research problems in assistive technology as it can contribute toward independent living of the elderly. The goal of fall detection technology is to detect the fall occurrence as soon as possible and to generate an alert. Many efforts have been undertaken to develop technology permitting human fall detection [10]. They were inspired by the large demand and the considerable value of the fall detection market. However, despite many efforts undertaken to achieve reliable fall detection, the

---

* Currently a student, doing his MSc thesis on fall detection.

K. Miesenberger et al. (Eds.): ICCHP 2012, Part II, LNCS 7383, pp. 407–414, 2012.

existing technology does not meet the requirements of the users with special needs [13].

Most proposed systems to fall detection are based on a wearable device that monitor the movements of an individual, recognize a fall and trigger an alarm. Prevalent methods only utilize accelerometers or both accelerometers and gyroscopes to separate fall from activities of daily living (ADLs) [10]. As a result, it is not easy to distinguish real falls from fall-like activities [2][7]. Several ADLs like fast sitting have similar kinematic motion patterns with real falls and in consequence such methods might trigger many false alarms. Moreover, in [5] the authors point out that the common fall detectors, which are usually attached to a belt around the hip, are inadequate to be worn during the sleep and this results in the lack of ability of such detectors to monitor the critical phase of getting up from the bed. In general, the solutions mentioned above are somehow intrusive for people as they require wearing continuously at least one device or smart sensor.

There have been several attempts to attain reliable human fall detection using single CCD camera [1][11], multiple cameras [4] or specialized omni-directional ones [9]. The currently offered CCD-camera based solutions require time for installation, camera calibration and they are not generally cheap. Typically, they require a PC computer or a notebook for image processing. The existing video-based devices for fall detection cannot work in nightlight or low light conditions. In addition, in most of such solutions the privacy is not preserved adequately. Video cameras offer several advantages in fall detection, among others the ability to detect various activities. Additional advantage is low intrusiveness and the possibility of remote verification of fall events. However, the lack of depth information may lead to many false alarms.

2   Primary Challenges and Proposed Solution

The existing technology permits reaching quite high performance of fall detection. However, as mentioned above it does not meet the requirements of the users with special needs. Our literature survey show that most of the approaches offers incremental improvements that can not lead to technology breakthrough, and which have insufficient potential for cutting edge scientific breakthroughs to make the life of people with special needs more fulfilling. Our work brings new insight into fall detection by the use of a wireless wearable device and Kinect, which is a central component of our system for fall detection.

The Kinect is a revolutionary motion-sensing technology that allows tracking a person in real-time without having to carry sensors. Unlike 2D cameras, Kinect allows tracking the body movements in 3D. It is the world's first system that combines an RGB camera and depth sensor. In order to achieve reliable and unobtrusive fall detection, our system employs both the Kinect and a wearable motion-sensing device, which complement each other. The fall detection is done by a fuzzy inference system using low-cost Kinect and the wearable motion-sensing device consisting of an accelerometer and a gyroscope. The fuzzy inference system is a central ingredient of our fall detection prototype, and it is based on expert knowledge and demonstrates high generalization abilities [8]. We show that the low-cost Kinect contributes toward reliable fall detections. Using both devices, our system can reliably distinguish the falls from activities of daily living, and thus the number of false alarms is reduced. In context of fall detection the disadvantage of Kinect is that it only can monitor restricted areas. In the areas where the depth images are not available we utilized only a wearable motion-sensing device consisting of an accelerometer and a gyroscope. On the other hand, in some ADLs during which the use of this wearable sensor might not be comfortable, for instance during changing clothes, wash, etc., the system relies on Kinect camera only. An advantage of Kinect is that it can be put in selected places according to the user requirements. Moreover, the system operates on depth images and thus preserves privacy for people being monitored. In this context, it is worth noting that Kinect uses infrared light and therefore it is able to extract depth images in a room that is dark to our eyes. The system runs in real-time and has been implemented on the PandaBoard ES, which is a low-power, low-cost single-board computer development platform.

3   The System for Fall Detection

This section is devoted to presentation of the main modules of the embedded system for fall detection. At the beginning the system architecture will be outlined. The wearable device will be presented later. Then, the usefulness of the Kinect for fall detection is discussed in detail. Afterwards, the extraction of the object of interest in depth images on the computer board with limited computational resources is presented.

3.1   Main Modules of the Embedded System

Our fall detection system uses both data from Kinect and motion data from a wearable smart device containing accelerometer and gyroscope sensors. Data from the smart device (Sony PlayStation Move) are transmitted wirelessly via Bluetooth to the PandaBoard on which the signal processing is done, whereas Kinect is connected via USB, see Fig. 1. The system runs under Linux operating system. Linux provides various flexible inter-process communication methods, among others message queues. Message queues provide asynchronous communication that is managed by Linux kernel. Message queues are appropriate choice for well structured data. Our application consists of three concurrent processes that communicate via message queues, see Fig. 1. The first process is responsible for acquiring data from the wearable device, the second process acquires depth data from the Kinect, whereas the third one is responsible for processing data and triggering the alarm.

The algorithm runs on PandaBoard ES, which is a mobile development platform and features a dual-core 1 GHz ARM Cortex-A9 MPCore CPU with Symmetric Multiprocessing (SMP), a 304 MHz PowerVR SGX540 integrated 3D

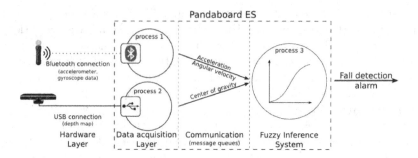

Fig. 1. The architecture of the system for fall detection

graphics accelerator, a programmable C64x DSP, and 1 GB of DDR2 SDRAM. The board includes wired 10/100 Ethernet as well as wireless Ethernet and Bluetooth connectivity.

3.2   The Wearable Device

The wearable device contains one tri-axial accelerometer and a tri-axial gyroscope that consists of a dual-axis gyroscope and a Z-axis gyroscope. The first sensor measures acceleration, the rate of change in velocity across time, whereas the second one measures the rate of rotation. The acceleration is measured in units of "g", where 1 g corresponds to the vertical acceleration force due to gravity. The smart sensor delivers the measurements along three axes together with the corresponding time stamps. The sampling rate of both sensors is equal to 60 Hz. The measured acceleration signals were median filtered with a window length of three samples to suppress the noise and then used to calculate the acceleration's vector length. Figure 2 depicts the plots of acceleration and angular velocities readings vs. time for simulated falling and sitting down. As illustrated on Fig. 2, the acceleration and the angular velocity are rapidly changed when people fall. As can bee seen, the motion patterns of falling and sitting down are quite similar. Therefore, in order to reduce the false positives we employ a fuzzy inference system using both data from the wearable device and the Kinect. The depicted plots were obtained for the device that was worn near the pelvis region. It is worth noting that the attachment of the wearable sensor near the pelvis region or lower back is recommended because such body parts represent the major component of body mass and move with most activities [7].

3.3   Depth Images

The Kinect sensor simultaneously captures depth and color images at a frame rate of about 30 fps. The Kinect sensor consists of an infrared laser-based IR emitter, an infrared camera and an RGB camera. The IR camera and the IR projector form a stereo pair with a baseline of approximately 75 mm. Kinect's field of view is fifty-seven degrees horizontally and forty-three degrees vertically.

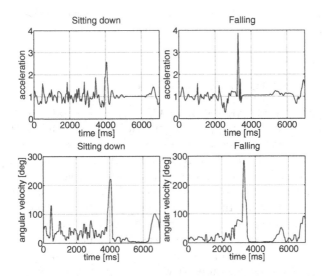

Fig. 2. Acceleration (top row) and angular velocity (bottom row) for sitting down and real fall

The minimum range for the Kinect is about 0.6 m and the maximum range is somewhere between 4-5 m. The device projects a speckle pattern onto the scene and infers depth from the deformation of that pattern. In order to determine the depth it combines such a structured light technique with two classic computer vision techniques, namely depth from focus and depth from stereo. Pixels in the provided depth images indicate calibrated depth in the scene. The depth resolution is about 1 cm at 2 m distance. The depth map is supplied in VGA resolution (640 × 480 pixels) on 11 bits (2048 levels of sensitivity). Figure 3 depicts sample color and the corresponding depth images, which were shot by Kinect in various lighting conditions, ranging from the day to late evening. As

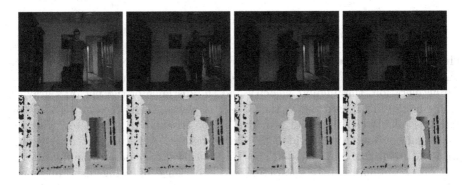

Fig. 3. Color images (top row) and the corresponding depth images (bottom row) shot by Kinect in various lighting conditions, ranging from the day to late evening

we can observe, owing to the ability of Kinect to extract the depth images in unlit or dark rooms the fall detection can be done in the late evening or even in the night.

3.4 Extraction of the Object of Interest

The depth images ware acquired using OpenNI (Open Natural Interaction) library [1]. OpenNI framework supplies an application programming interface (API) as well as it provides the interface for physical devices and for middleware components. In order to extract the foreground object a mean depth map was extracted in advance. It was extracted on the basis of several consecutive depth images without the subject to be monitored and then it was stored for the later use in the detection mode. In the detection mode the foreground objects ware extracted through differencing the current image from such a reference depth map. Afterwards, the foreground object was determined through extracting the largest connected component in the thresholded difference map. Finally, the center of gravity of the object of interest was calculated. The reference map-based extraction of the foreground object has been selected due to reduced computer computational resources of the PandaBoard. The code profiler reported about 50% CPU usage by the module responsible for detection of the foreground object. Figure 4 illustrates the extraction of the object of interest in the depth image.

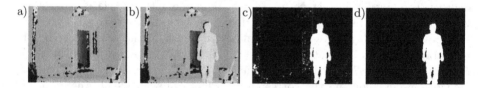

Fig. 4. Extraction of the object of interest. Reference depth image a), depth image with a person b), difference of the images c), extracted object of interest d).

3.5 Fuzzy Inference Engine

The fall alarm is triggered by a fuzzy inference engine based on expert knowledge, which is declared explicitly by fuzzy rules and sets. As inputs the engine takes the acceleration, the angular velocity and the distance of the person's gravity center to the altitude at which the Kinect is placed. The acceleration's vector length is calculated using data provided by the tri-axial accelerometer, whereas the angular velocity is provided by the gyroscope. A fuzzy inference system proposed by Takagi and Sugeno (TS) [12] is utilized to generate the fall alarm. It expresses human expert knowledge and experience by using fuzzy inference rules represented in $if - then$ statements. In such an inference system the linear

---

[1] Available at: http://www.openni.org/

submodels associated with TS rules are combined to describe the global behavior of the nonlinear system. The inference is done by the TS fuzzy system consisting of 27 rules [8]. The filtered data from the accelerometer and the gyroscope were interpolated and decimated as well as synchronized with the data from Kinect, i.e. the center of gravity of the moving person.

4 Experimental Results

Five volunteers with age over 26 years attended in evaluation of our developed algorithm and the system. Intentional falls were performed in home by four persons towards a carpet with thickness of 2 cm and in a gym, see Fig. 5, towards mattress with thickness of 10 cm. The accelerometer was worn near the pelvis. Each individual performed three types of falls, namely forward, backward and lateral at least three times. Each individual performed also ADLs like walking, sitting, crouching down, leaning down/picking up objects from the floor, lying on a bed. All intentional falls performed in home towards the carpet were detected correctly. In particular, sitting down fast, which is not easily distinguishable from a typical fall when only an accelerometer or even an accelerometer and a gyroscope are used, was detected quite reliably by our system, see results in Tab. 1. The system correctly detected seventeen falls of the eighteen falls in the gym towards the mattress. Slightly smaller detection rate is due to larger thickness of the mattress than the carpet.

Fig. 5. Images with activities of daily living: walking, crouching down, leaning down/picking up objects from the floor and sitting down, which were shot by Kinect

Table 1. The effectiveness of the fall detection

fall	sitting down	crouching down	walking	lying in a bed	picking up objects
12/12	23/25	23/25	25/25	12/12	25/25

5 Conclusions

In this paper we demonstrated how to achieve reliable fall detection on an embedded platform. The detection was done by fuzzy inference system using Kinect, accelerometer and gyroscope. The system runs on low-cost PandaBoard ES.

It permits unobtrusive fall detection as well as preserves privacy of the user. The results show that a single accelerometer with gyroscope and Kinect are completely sufficient to implement low-cost system for reliable fall detection.

Acknowledgments. This work has been supported by the National Science Centre (NCN) within the project N N516 483240.

References

1. Anderson, D., Keller, J., Skubic, M., Chen, X., He, Z.: Recognizing falls from silhouettes. In: Annual Int. Conf. of the Engineering in Medicine and Biology Society, pp. 6388–6391 (2006)
2. Bourke, A., O'Brien, J., Lyons, G.: Evaluation of a threshold-based tri-axial accelerometer fall detection algorithm. Gait & Posture 26(2), 194–199 (2007)
3. Cook, A., Hussey, S.: Assistive Technologies — Principles and Practice, Mosby, 2nd edn. (2002)
4. Cucchiara, R., Prati, A., Vezzani, R.: A multi-camera vision system for fall detection and alarm generation. Expert Systems 24(5), 334–345 (2007)
5. Degen, T., Jaeckel, H., Rufer, M., Wyss, S.: Speedy: A fall detector in a wrist watch. In: Proc. of IEEE Int. Symp. on Wearable Computers, pp. 184–187 (2003)
6. Heinrich, S., Rapp, K., Rissmann, U., Becker, C., König, H.H.: Cost of falls in old age: a systematic review. Osteoporosis International 21, 891–902 (2010)
7. Kangas, M., Konttila, A., Lindgren, P., Winblad, I., Jamsa, T.: Comparison of low-complexity fall detection algorithms for body attached accelerometers. Gait & Posture 28(2), 285–291 (2008)
8. Kepski, M., Kwolek, B., Austvoll, I.: Fuzzy Inference-Based Reliable Fall Detection Using Kinect and Accelerometer. In: Rutkowski, L., Korytkowski, M., Scherer, R., Tadeusiewicz, R., Zadeh, L.A., Zurada, J.M. (eds.) ICAISC 2012, Part I. LNCS, vol. 7267, pp. 266–273. Springer, Heidelberg (2012)
9. Miaou, S.-G., Sung, P.-H., Huang, C.-Y.: A customized human fall detection system using omni-camera images and personal information. In: Distributed Diagnosis and Home Healthcare, pp. 39–42 (2006)
10. Noury, N., Fleury, A., Rumeau, P., Bourke, A., Laighin, G., Rialle, V., Lundy, J.: Fall detection - principles and methods. In: Annual Int. Conf. of the IEEE Engineering in Medicine and Biology Society, pp. 1663–1666 (2007)
11. Rougier, C., Meunier, J., St-Arnaud, A., Rousseau, J.: Monocular 3D head tracking to detect falls of elderly people. In: Annual Int. Conf. of the IEEE Engineering in Medicine and Biology Society, pp. 6384–6387 (2006)
12. Takagi, T., Sugeno, M.: Fuzzy Identification of Systems and its Applications to Modeling and Control. IEEE Trans. on SMC 15(1), 116–132 (1985)
13. Yu, X.: Approaches and principles of fall detection for elderly and patient. In: 10th Int. Conf. on e-health Networking, Applications and Services, pp. 42–47 (2008)

Controlled Natural Language Sentence Building as a Model for Designing User Interfaces for Rule Editing in Assisted Living Systems – A User Study

Henrike Gappa, Gaby Nordbrock, Yehya Mohamad, Jaroslav Pullmann,
and Carlos A. Velasco

Fraunhofer FIT, Sankt Augustin, Germany
{henrike.gappa,gaby.nordbrock,yehya.mohamad,
jaroslav.pullmann,carlos.velasco}@fit.fraunhofer.de

Abstract. As part of the web-based services developed within the WebDA-project the Action Planner was implemented to allow care givers of people with dementia to support them in accomplishing activities of daily living and counteract restlessness amongst others. In order to define rules that include a description of situations indicating e.g. restlessness as well as an action that should be undertaken in such situations, a user interface was designed enabling care givers to express these rules in a controlled natural language setting. Here, rule expressions were offered in preformulated natural sentences that could be manipulated by changing (pre)selected notions as "daily" in pop-up menus embedded in the sentences. A user study was conducted with 24 test participants (12 < 65 years; 12 > 65 years) proofing that this approach can be understood as intuitive and well usable also for test participants beyond 65 years of age.

Keywords: User interface design, elderly, ambient assisted living, monitoring systems, natural language usage.

1   Introduction

In order to support elderly people to live at home independently as long as possible IT-based assisted living systems aim at becoming successful assistants in compensating for declining skills, e.g. in everyday life management. Beyond this the health condition of elderly people usually deteriorates critically at some point, so they will become dependent on help from care givers often being the spouse or another family member. For care givers it is not easy to take on this task while still coping with their own life, so quite often care givers feel overburdened. Services capable of balancing this situation need to offer powerful technical functionality causing in return complex user interfaces for control. End users of such services are often elderly people with less computer expertise, so designing easily useable user interfaces is challenging. Allowing for natural language usage appears to fulfil this requirement best as it matches with the user's background [1], [3]. Thus modelling natural sentence building was chosen as a suitable approach for the user interface of the Action Planner, a

K. Miesenberger et al. (Eds.): ICCHP 2012, Part II, LNCS 7383, pp. 415–418, 2012.

web-based reminder and alarm service developed within the WebDA-Project (Web-based Services for Elderly People and Care Givers).

2   Rule Editing in the WebDA-Action Planner

The Action Planner allows care givers to support their relative with mild up to moderate dementia to carry out activities of daily living, counteract restlessness and monitor threatening situations like leaving the house or not getting up in the morning. The service includes an RFID-based tracking system to locate a person in his or her home environment [2], [5], thus allowing for runtime evaluation of time- and location-aware rules with the goal of triggering events, e.g. a reminder to drink, only when appropriate which might mean, only if a person is located near the living-room table where the glass of water is standing.   Due to the personal situation of a person with dementia, the variety of possible rules is unforeseeable thus demanding for a very rich and flexible user interface.

It was considered to be most intuitive for the user to define a rule in complete sentences as this reflects how a rule would be expressed in natural language. The approach of striving for natural language usage also implied that definition of rules needed to be possible without having to use technical terms or anglicisms. Beyond this the user should not be forced to formulate rules in propositional logic-like manner, e.g. in when…if…then…conditions. This method prevails often in programmable environments also in the AAL-context [4]. It may allow for high flexibility but causes usability issues, because users encounter difficulties when translating envisioned rules in such concepts besides facing the challenge to combine logic operators adequately. However since it was expected to be a nearly unaccomplishable task for users to formulate a concept of a rule in non-ambiguous terms considering all side effects even in natural language, it was decided to present prestructured sentences for rule building. These sentences included pop-up menus to manipulate the meaning (see Fig. 1.) and adjusted dynamically in accordance to the user's choices.

Fig. 1. User interface of the WebDA-Action Planner

Sentence building happened therefore in a controlled manner to ensure efficient use. As immediate feedback on the impact of a user's choice a rule summary was always provided at the bottom of the rule editor displaying the entire content of a rule as in effect of now. A rule summary could be for instance: The intended action of the rule is a notification "Mom, please drink some water," which will be displayed and read aloud. The rule applies daily from 10:00 am up to 9:00 pm and will be activated every two hours. The notification will only occur in case the person is located at the chair at the living-room table. A rule of the Action Planner consisted of the components action, time and location. Editing these components was split in 4 tabs (see Fig. 1) to avoid visual clutter and to keep sentences as simple as possible.

3   The User Study

The user study conducted to evaluate the aforementioned design of the user interface consisted of a standardized test environment comprising a typical usage scenario, session protocols and structured questionnaires for data collection. The questionnaire investigating usability issues was composed of 19 statements to be rated on a Likert scale (1 (most positive rating) and 7 (most negative rating)) and 3 open questions. The test items were clustered in regard to the usability criteria information presentation and suitability for the task. 24 test participants (tps) took part in the user study, 12 being above the age of 65 and 12 being below the age of 65. All test participants had closer contact to a person with dementia.

Test results showed that overall the design of the user interface was considered appropriate by the test participants as it scored well in regard to the cluster information presentation (on a scale 1-7: tps age < 65 => median 1,8; tps age > 65 => median 2,4) and suitability for the task (on a scale 1-7: tps age < 65 => median 2,3; tps age > 65 => median 2,2). All test participants considered editing a rule with controlled sentence building as an appropriate and intuitive approach. Also, providing a rule summary that updates dynamically according to the selected choices was understood as very helpful in the rule editing process. When comparing evaluation results of both test groups it became apparent that it posed a problem for both groups to bear in mind the content hidden in the pop-up menus. For test participants above age 65 this was of bigger impact, so this user group would have appreciated some guidance as to what comes next. In consequence of this test result a wizard is now under development that provides step-by-step guidance through the rule editing process always providing an example in natural language to demonstrate the meaning of an option. Besides this the user interface of the Action Planner will be redesigned accounting for the requirement to convey the content of pop-up menus.

4   Conclusion

As the evaluation of the Action Planner's user interface has shown it is a user-friendly approach to support the definition process for complex rules by controlled natural sentence building. Assisted living systems require often rules as input for control and query their data via complex forms. For particularly less experienced computer users this is often not practicable. Designing user interfaces as suggested could be a feasible alternative in such cases. Also, as it could be seen in the user study providing a dynamically adjusting summary of what the users choices have been so far can serve as a successful support mechanism for accomplishing complex tasks like rule editing particularly for less computer experienced users.

References

1. Holzinger, A., Searle, G., Auinger, A., Ziefle, M.: Informatics as Semiotics Engineering: Lessons Learned from Design, Development and Evaluation of Ambient Assisted Living Applications for Elderly People. In: Stephanidis, C. (ed.) HCII 2011 and UAHCI 2011, Part III. LNCS, vol. 6767, pp. 183–192. Springer, Heidelberg (2011)
2. Mohamad, Y., Gappa, H., Pullmann, J., Nordbrock, G., Velasco, C., Handte, M., Wagner, S., Schweda, M.: Context-aware Support for People with Dementia and their Families. In: Deutscher AAL-Kongress 2012 (Technik für ein selbstbe-stimmtes Leben). VDI/VDI IT, Berlin (2012)
3. Mészáros, T., Dobrowiecki, T.: Controlled Natural Languages for Interface Agents. In: 8th International Conference on Autonomous Agents and Multiagent Systems (AAMAS 2009), Richland SC, vol. 2, pp. 1173–1174 (2009)
4. Rex, A.: Design of a Caregiver Programmable Assistive Intelligent Environment. Master Thesis Aalto University School of Engineering, Aalto (2011)
5. Wagner, S., Handte, M., Zuniga, M., Marrón, P.J.: On Optimal Tag Placement for Indoor Localization. In: IEEE International Conference on Pervasive Computing and Communications (PerCom 2012). IEEE Press, New York (2012)

MonAMI Platform in Elderly Household Environment

Architecture, Installation, Implementation, Trials and Results

Dušan Šimšík[1], Alena Galajdová[1], Daniel Siman[1], Juraj Bujňák[1],
Marianna Andrášová[1], and Marek Novák[2]

[1] Department of Automation, Control and Human Machine Interactions,
Technical University of Košice,
Letná 9, 042 00 Košice, Slovakia
[2] Department of Computers and Informatics, Technical University of Košice,
Letná 9, 042 00 Košice, Slovakia
{dusan.simsik,alena.galajdova,daniel.siman,
juraj.bujnak,marianna.andrasova,marek.novak}@tuke.sk
http://www.sjf.tuke.sk/karakr/

Abstract. Paper describes how ambient technology platform MonAMI and related ICT services were adapted into society of Slovakia. MonAMI is European project focusing on ambient assisted living based on software, human machine interfaces and hardware. Main aim was to increase autonomy, enhance ICT services for monitoring purposes for carers and support safety of vulnerable people living alone. Broader description of architecture, devices, process of installation and implementation follow.

Keywords: ambient technology, interface, open architecture.

1 Introduction

The changes in the demographic trends in Slovakia incline to develop appropriate social services for the growing population of seniors with an emphasis on improving their quality of life, security, autonomy and supporting their daily activities. The international research project Mainstreaming on Ambient Intelligence - MonAMI is one of several projects devoted to improvement of independent life and well-being of elderly and disabled people supported by the European Commission. The project has been focused on building new services using mainstream systems [1].

Our objective was to demonstrate that such system is acceptable by elderly and supportive in their daily activities in the specific Slovak environment. We have successfully tested services in households of 20 seniors.

Thanks to the open platform OSGi4AMI [1] of MonAMI system, we have developed new interfaces for different platforms as Android, iOS, plug-in into multimedia center software operable on a TV and new user centered interface for ASUS touch screen. Thus we have supported more commonly used an affordable devices.

K. Miesenberger et al. (Eds.): ICCHP 2012, Part II, LNCS 7383, pp. 419–422, 2012.

2   Technology and Methods MonAMI Platform

MonAMI technology platform is a three level architecture comprising of sensors, logic and external services and interfaces [3]. The idea of MonAMI platform was to construct technology platform which is derived from subsistent standard technologies. The platform is assigned to deliver services, which integrate reliable wireless (ZigBee technology) SON networks, wired networks (1-wire technology), user friendly interaction technology, wearable devices and components for health monitoring. [6]

The main interconnecting abstraction of the system is a set of interfaces OS-Gi4AMI [1] currently accessible as an open source project [4]. They define precisely functions and operations of all devices, actuators on various platforms as well as services – OSGi components [5]. Therefore new devices, either wired or wireless, may be easily added to the system. Central component of the installation in household is a Residential Gateway (RG) - a computer with touchscreen, where 1-Wire and ZigBee sensors or actuators are connected. The UI could be supported by other devices as smart phones, tablets or a TV [9]. The HTML based User Interface consist of 3 different UIs with specific dedication to beneficiaries, carers and developers. All of these user interfaces are user friendly and can be reached by ICT devices with common web browser. [6, 8]

MonAMI system is build from three pre-defined packages, local or remote monitoring of temperature, luminance, connected electrical appliances, etc.; remote control of various actuators as switchers, actuators and electric appliances, which are automatically based on individual predefined thresholds; notification of risky situations, where the responsible person (carer, medical staff and family) is informed through online messages about current status of environment or user.

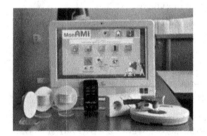 

Fig. 1. Equipment used in study and User Interface, MonAMI 2012

2.1   OSGi4AMI

OSGi4AMI represents a reference point for all developers of the MonAMI system. It is a common interface framework developed as an open source technology [1, 2, 3, 7], which enables through provided ontology the interaction between MonAMI Framework modules. This ontology defines the concepts used by MonAMI software modules of RG.

As the devices are the common representations of the physical devices virtually connected to the RG, they encapsulate the real device operation, and expose members related to its functionalities. As mentioned above, devices are basically divided into devices able to sense physical magnitudes e.g. temperature, presence, humidity, etc.(sensors) and devices able to change status of physical simple apparatus e.g. switching on/off, open binds, etc. (actuators). Any of new devices added requires module for implementation into system structure. Using of mounted devices will need structural bundle created in OSGi4AMI. All the changes in base platform will immediately have visible output at web interface for both kinds of users (carers – users). [6]

2.2 Architecture of Provided ICT Services

The goal of the OSGi4AMI interfaces is to define a common set of interfaces for each category of MonAMI devices and functions. The OSGi4AMI interface defines Java interfaces for common needs and can be extended as soon as a new feature is needed. The service object implementing this interface is owned by, and runs within, a bundle. This bundle registers the service object with the OSGi framework service registry so that the ser-vice's functionality is available to other bundles under control of the Framework [6]. All services are configurable to the users' needs.

The services used in MonAMI platform can be modified and upgraded easily because of OS-Gi4AMI modularity so they are fully adaptable. They operate above devices' layer, recruit existing ones, combine each other and provide high level information to the RG [6, 7, 8]. Main tested services were:

- SURE services (gas, smoke) – monitoring level of gas or smoke; if it has been detected, alert is sent,
- 1-Wire gas and smoke sensor – enable monitoring of living space and alert in case of higher concentrate of gas or smoke,
- App SURE – if the user has forgotten to switch off an electric device and this device is in usage for more than a predefined time or energy spent, device is switched off,
- Temp SURE – sends an alert if temperature is lower or higher than a predefined threshold for a longer time,
- Zone SURE – if the system recognizes (or do not recognizes) a user activity during a pre-defined time in predefined area and it should not be (should be) recognized, responsible person is informed about situation.

3   Results

The whole system was tested in 20 real households during a period of three months. The users and their carers provided useful and effective feedback to researchers and developers in the content of user experience and usability. Among the most positively evaluated services is Zone SURE, which recognizes that people enters a room/area when they are not allowed to or even that people haven't entered a room/area when they have to. In such a case the service can send an alarm to someone by e-mail, sms or the user interface. Another highly appreciated service is Connect SURE, which connects the user to carer through CareIP, who could remotely check how dangerous the sit-uation is. Project MonAMI offers an alternative for common platform for AAL solutions looking in large scale implementation of new services [9].

4   Conclusion

What we found as a positive response, is that with the usage of the provided technol-ogies, seniors became more interested in using the computer and internet due to the possibilities of contacting the family members abroad, playing internet games or read-ing online news, then increasing of safety, self-confidence and autonomy.

Acknowledgment. The research leading to these results has received funding from the European Community's 6th Framework Program (FP7/2007-2013) under grant agreement IST-5-0535147 MonAMI - „Mainstreaming on Ambient Intelligence "and Slovak grant agency VEGA „1/1162/11 – "Theoretical principles, methods and tools for diagnostics and rehabilitation of seniors mobility".

References

1. Fagerberg, G.: Mainstream Services for Elderly and Disabled People at Home. In: Proc. of Int. Conf.: 10th Euro-pean Conference AAATE, Florence, Italy, Assistive Technology From Adapted Equipment to Inclusive Environments. Assistive Technology Research Se-ries, vol. 25, pp. 287–291 (2009), doi:10.3233/978.1.60750.042-1.287.
2. Marco, A., Casas, R., Bauer, G., Blasco, R., Asensio, A., Jean-Bart, B., Ibane, M.: Com-mon OSGi Interface for Ambient Assisted Living Scenarios. Ambient Intelligence and Smart Environments 3, 336–357 (2009)
3. Kung, A., Jean-Bart, B.: Making AAL Platforms a Reality. In: de Ruyter, B., Wichert, R., Keyson, D.V., Markopoulos, P., Streitz, N., Divitini, M., Georgantas, N., Mana Gomez, A. (eds.) AmI 2010. LNCS, vol. 6439, pp. 187–196. Springer, Heidelberg (2010)
4. OSGi4AMI, Sourceforge, http://sourceforge.net/projects/osgi4ami/
5. OSGi Service Platform Core Specification, rel.4, http://www.osgi.org/download/r4v41/r4.core.pdf
6. Kung, A., Jean-bart, B.: Making AAL Platforms a Reality. In: de Ruyter, B., Wichert, R., Keyson, D.V., Markopoulos, P., Streitz, N., Divitini, M., Georgantas, N., Mana Gomez, A. (eds.) AmI 2010. LNCS, vol. 6439, pp. 187–196. Springer, Heidelberg (2010)
7. OSGi Alliance: About the OSGi Service Platform (June 2007), http://www.osgi.org/wiki/uploads/Links/ OSGiTechnicalWhitePaper.pdf (accessed: November 2011)
8. Simsik, D., et al.: First experience of implementation of social services based on ICT in Slovakia. - (CD-ROM). European Journal of Physical and Rehabilitation Medicine 47-suppl.1(2), 33–34 (2011) ISBN 1973-9087
9. Fagerberg, G., Kung, A., Wichert, R., Tazari, M.-R., Jean-Bart, B., Bauer, G., Zimmermann, G., Furfari, F., Potortì, F., Chessa, S., Hellenschmidt, M., Gorman, J., Alex-andersson, J., Bund, J., Carrasco, E., Epelde, G., Klima, M., Urdaneta, E., Vanderheiden, G., Zinnikus, I.: Platforms for AAL Applications. In: Lukowicz, P., Kunze, K., Kortuem, G. (eds.) EuroSSC 2010. LNCS, vol. 6446, pp. 177–201. Springer, Heidelberg (2010)

Modeling Text Input for Single-Switch Scanning

I. Scott MacKenzie

Dept. of Computer Science and Engineering,
York Univeristy,
Toronto Ontario Canada M3J 1P3
mack@cse.yorku.ca

Abstract. A method and algorithm for modeling single-switch scanning for text input is presented. The algorithm uses the layout of a scanning keyboard and a corpus in the form of a word-frequency list to generate codes representing the scan steps for entering words. Scan steps per character (*SPC*) is computed as a weighted average over the entire corpus. *SPC* is an absolute measure, thus facilitating comparisons of keyboards. It is revealed that *SPC* is sensitive to the corpus if a keyboard includes word prediction. A recommendation for other research using *SPC* is to disclose both the algorithm and the corpus.

Keywords: Single-switch scanning, text input, models of interaction, scan steps per character.

1   Introduction

One enduring method of accessible text entry is single-switch scanning using a virtual keyboard. Keys are highlighted in sequence ("scanned") with selections made with a single input switch when the key bearing the desired character is highlighted. To speed-up entry, a two-tier scanning pattern is often used, such as row-column scanning. Scanning thus proceeds row by row. When the row bearing the desired character is highlighted, it is selected. Scanning proceeds within the row until the key bearing the desired character is highlighted. A selection adds the character to the text message, with scanning restarted at the top row.

To further speed-up entry, the keyboard is often arranged with high-frequency letters (e.g., *e*, *a*, or *t*, for English) near the beginning of the scanning sequence. This reduces the required number of scan steps to reach letters. To speed-up entry even further, word prediction techniques are often added. This allows a word to be selected after only part of the word is entered.

It is apparent from the points above that text entry using single-switch scanning can be modeled analytically. The rate of entry will depend on the scanning interval and the number of scan steps to enter letters or words. The physical demand on users will depend on the required number of switch activations to enter letters or words. Techniques to optimize aim to lower the number of scan steps or the number of switch activations. Comparing the computed numbers can assess alternate designs.

This paper is on modeling text entry using single-switch scanning. The goal is to both review existing modeling techniques in the literature and to suggest improvements to these techniques. The most serious deficiency in existing models is the use

K. Miesenberger et al. (Eds.): ICCHP 2012, Part II, LNCS 7383, pp. 423–430, 2012.

of relative metrics. Relative metrics reveal the percent drop in scan steps when a design is optimized in some way. While relevant for variations on a design, relative metrics cannot be used to compare designs across publications, because the baseline design is different, not precisely known, or inherently dissimilar. Because of this, the body of research on text entry using single-switch scanning is a collection of distinct publications that cannot be compared. The work does not form a unified coherent body of research. One goal here is to correct this.

2   Relative versus Absolute Metrics

As noted above, the efficiency of text entry using single-switch scanning can be improved using a variety of techniques. Research on this spans several decades [1-7], [13-16]. The problem alluded to above is apparent in Lesher et al.'s review [7] where comparisons of alternate designs are expressed in relative terms. As an example, row-column scanning using an alphabetic letter arrangement is contrasted with an optimized letter-arrangement. See Fig.1.a and Fig.1.b. It is noted that the optimized arrangement is "more efficient" [7, p. 83], but no statistics are given. For other comparisons, statistics are given, but only in relative terms, for example, "incorporation of a word list provides a 24% savings in switch counts" [7, p. 84]. (Note: a "switch count", as used here, is the same as a "scan step"). The full details of the baseline design are not given, nor are any absolute measures provided. The alluded-to 24% savings is meaningful only within the cited publication. In another paper, we learn of "keystroke savings … in the range of 37-47%" [4]; but, again, the baseline design is insufficiently detailed and no absolute measures are given.

The examples above are not unique. Despite a considerable body of work, it is difficult, arguably impossible, to compare designs from one publication to the next. Mankowski echoes this sentiment: "unfortunately, they only report the relative savings, not the actual number of scan steps" [11, p, 103].

This limitation is easily rectified, drawing upon text entry modeling from mobile computing. The efficiency of text entry on phone keypads and their variants is aptly reflected in keystrokes per character (*KSPC*) [8], [10]. *KSPC* is the average number of keystrokes required to produce each character of text on a given keyboard, in a given language, using a given entry method. The statistic is an absolute measure. The equivalent for scanning keyboards is scan-steps per character (*SPC*). *SPC* is calculated a similar way except using the average number of scanning intervals to produce a character of text.[1] *SPC* is computed as a weighted average for a language and requires a letter-frequency list or word-frequency list derived from a corpus.

To illustrate the utility of *SPC*, Fig.1. shows 12 scanning keyboards from 7 sources. For this analysis, only the core letters (*a-z*) and *space* (_) are shown. Letters are in lowercase. Where word prediction is used, *Word* appears. Additional columns on the right or rows at the bottom, if present, are not shown, as these do not impact the calculation of *SPC* (assuming top-to-bottom, left-to-right scanning).

---

[1]   A related statistic is selections per scan-step, *SPS*, which reflects the motor demand of entry. *SPS* is not elaborated in this paper.

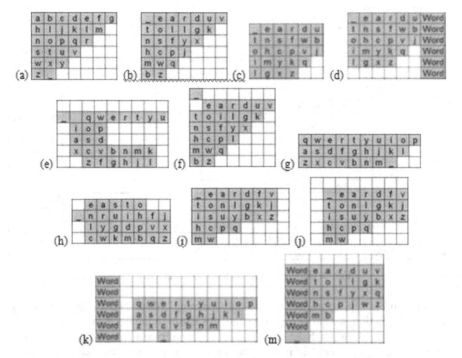

Fig. 1. Twelve scanning keyboards. See Fig. 2 for further details.

The layouts in Fig.1. are diverse, suggesting vastly different objectives in each design. Scan-steps per character (SPC) is useful because it enables comparing designs from different sources.

3   Coding Examples and Calculation of *SPC*

To calculate SPC, the keyboard geometry and operation are embedded in an algorithm implemented in software. A corpus in the form of a word-frequency list is also required. The algorithm processes each word to determine the scan steps required to enter the word. Some scan steps are passive (no selection) while others require a switch activation. A space is assumed to follow each word. Creating a graphical representation of the scan steps is important both for debugging and for examining and demonstrating the keyboard's operation. See Fig.2. For this demonstration, the optimized keyboard by Koester and Levine [6] was used (see Fig. 1c and 1d). Three variations are included along with scan steps for some example words. The words are the, of, and, weapons, spot, and slow. The word rankings are from the BNC-1 corpus (discussed below). The scan steps include the entry of a terminating space.

Passive scan steps are coded as periods. The methods in Fig.2a and Fig.2b use conventional row-column scanning. A row selection appears as an uppercase R. Switch activations generating characters appear as the corresponding lowercase letter. For word prediction, a selection in the word list appears as uppercase W.

Keyboard	Rank	Word	Freq.	Scan steps	Notes
(a) Fig. 1c	1	the	5,776,384	.Rt..R.hR.eR_	Optimized (row-column scanning)
	2	of	2,789,403	..Ro.R...fR_	
	3	and	2,421,302	R..a.R.nR....dR_	
	2000	weapons	3,861	.R....wR.eR..a..R...p..Ro.R.n.R..sR_	
	2001	spot	3,859	.R..s..R...p..Ro.RtR_	
	2002	slow	3,855	.R..s....R1..Ro.R....wR_	
(b) Fig. 1d	1	the	5,776,384	R......W	Optimized + word prediction (row-column scanning)
	2	of	2,789,403	.R......W	
	3	and	2,421,302	..R......W	
	2000	weapons	3,861	R......wR.eR..a..R......W	
	2001	spot	3,859	.R..s..R...p..Ro...R......W	
	2002	slow	3,855	.R..s....R1..R......W	
(c) Fig. 1d	1	the	5,776,384	.HW	Optimized + word prediction (half & half scanning)
	2	of	2,789,403	.H.W	
	3	and	2,421,302	.H..W	
	2000	weapons	3,861	HR......wHR.eHR..a.H..W	
	2001	spot	3,859	H.R..sH..R...pH..Ro.H...W	
	2002	slow	3,855	H.R..sH....R1.H..W	

Fig. 2. Coding examples. See text for discussion.

The method in Fig.2.c uses "half-and-half scanning" [6, p. 44]. To speed-up entry with word prediction, scanning initially alternates between the letter-half (left) and the word-half (right) of the keyboard (see Fig.1.d). The user first selects the desired half (*H* in Fig.2.c), then selects within the letter or word half of the keyboard. Within the letter region, conventional row-column scanning is used.

Word prediction allows a word to be selected before all letters are entered. The algorithm assumes the word is selected at the earliest opportunity. This will depend on the corpus and the size of the word list. The keyboard in Fig. 1d includes a word list with six entries. The list appears before the first letter of a word is entered and is updated during entry according to the current word stem. At the beginning of a word, the list is simply the six most-frequent words in the corpus. These words can be entered by selecting the word half of the keyboard (.H), then selecting the word, for example, W for *the*, .W for *of*, or ..W for *and*. See Fig.2.c.

Less common words must be partially or fully entered before word selection is possible. As seen in the last row in Fig.2., *slow* was entered after the input of *sl*. After *s*, the list contained *she*, *said*, *some*, *so*, *should*, and *such* – the six most frequent words beginning with *s*. After *sl*, the list contained *slightly*, *slowly*, *slow*, *sleep*, *slight*, and *slipped*. *Slow* is the third entry. The user selects the word half of the keyboard (.H), then selects *slow* (..W). See Fig. 4c, last row.

With software to generate the scan step codes, as in Fig.2., scan steps per character (*SPC*) is calculated as a weighted average over the entire corpus:

$$SPC = \frac{\sum (S_W \times F_W)}{\sum (C_W \times F_W)} \qquad (1)$$

where SW is the number of scan steps to enter a word, FW is the frequency of the word, and CW is the number of characters in the word. SW and CW are adjusted to include a terminating space after each word.

The *SPCs* for the 12 layouts in Fig.1. are given in Fig.3. Values are given for four corpora (discussed below). The values range from a low of *SPC* = 2.45 for Fig.1.m to a high of *SPC* = 7.45 for Fig.1.g.

Fig. 1	Source (1st author, year, reference)	SPC (by Corpus)				Spread (%)	Notes
		BNC-1	BNC-2	Brown	Phrases		
a	Lesher, 1998, [7, Fig. 1b]	5.78	5.79	5.77	5.88	1.9%	alphabetic
b	Lesher, 1998, [7, Fig. 1c]	4.27	4.30	4.31	4.34	1.6%	optimized
c	Koester, 1994, [6, Fig. 2]	4.28	4.32	4.32	4.36	1.8%	optimized
d	Koester, 1994, [6, Fig. 3]	3.35	3.44	4.34	3.20	26.3%	optimized + word pred. (row/col scanning)
d	Koester, 1994, [6, Fig. 3]	2.73	2.87	2.89	2.55	11.8%	optimized + word pred. (half & half scanning)
e	Steriadis, 2003, [14, Fig. 29]	7.40	7.42	7.44	7.38	0.8%	qwerty
f	Steriadis, 2003, [14, Fig. 30]	5.08	5.12	5.13	5.16	1.6%	optimized
g	Bhattacharya, 2008, [1, Fig. 1]	7.43	7.41	7.40	7.45	0.7%	qwerty
h	Szeto, 1993, [15, Fig. 1]	5.35	5.36	5.37	5.37	0.4%	optimized
i	Mankowski, 2009, [11, p. 105]	4.28	4.31	4.32	4.34	1.4%	optimized
j	Mankowski, 2009, [11, p. 105]	6.28	6.31	6.32	6.34	0.9%	optimized with row/col delay
k	http://wivik.com/	3.80	4.08	4.17	3.49	16.3%	qwerty + word pred.
m	http://wivik.com/	2.64	2.80	2.84	2.45	13.7%	optimized + word pred.

Fig. 3. Scan-steps per character (*SPC*) for the 12 keyboards in Fig.1., computed using the BNC-1, BNC-2, Brown, and Phrases corpora. See text for discussion

The benefit of using an absolute metric like SPC to model scanning keyboards is apparent in Fig.3.. Using SPC, comparisons are possible both for designs from the same source and for designs from different sources. For example, the first two rows in Fig.3. are for the alphabetic and optimized layouts in Lesher et al. [7]. The optimized layout is more efficient since it can produce text with about (5.78 – 4.27) / 5.78 × 100 = 26.1% fewer scan steps per character. Although the difference is expressed as a percentage, the calculation requires SPC, an absolute metric. Provided SPC is reported, comparisons are possible for keyboards in different publications. For example, consider the Koester-Levine keyboard in Fig.1.d and the Wivik keyboard in Fig.1.m. Both are optimized keyboards using word prediction. The Koester-Levine keyboard places the word list on the right but uses half-and-half scanning to speed-up entry. The Wivik keyboard places the word list on the left and uses conventional row-column scanning. Evidently, the Wivik keyboard is slightly more efficient, since it requires about (2.73 – 2.64) / 2.73 × 100 = 3.3% fewer scan steps per character of text. Although given in relative terms, the comparison is only possible because of the availability of SPC, an absolute metric.

4   Corpus Effect

The calculation of SPC is sensitive to the linguistic structure of the corpus. To test for a possible "corpus effect", SPC values were computed for four corpora: the British

National Corpus (BNC-1, BNC-2) [12], the Brown Corpus (see Wikipedia), and Phrases [9]. Each corpus was reduced to a word-frequency list for computing SPC. The Phrases list was built from a phrase set commonly used to evaluate text entry methods. It is only included here to test the effect of using a very small corpus on the calculation of SPC. The linguistic structure of the four corpora is given in Fig.4.

Corpus	Unique Words	Total Words
BNC-1	9,022	67,962,112
BNC-2	64,588	90,563,847
Brown	41,532	997,552
Phrases	1,163	2,712

Fig. 4. Characteristics of corpora used for calculations of *SPC* in Fig. 3

The spread of SPC values by corpus in Fig.3. is less than 2% for all designs not using word prediction. So, in the absence of word prediction, SPC is relatively insensitive to the corpus. However, the spread varies from 11.8% to 26.3% for the four designs using word prediction. In general, larger dictionaries yield higher SPC values. The wide spread for designs using word prediction is a problem. Comparisons of keyboards from different publications will be compromised, perhaps wrong, unless the SPC calculations use the same algorithm and the same corpus.

To illustrate the problem, let's revisit the comparison above – between the Koester-Levine keyboard (Fig.1.d) and the *Wivik* keyboard (Fig.1.m). The observation that the *Wivik* keyboard is about 3.3% more efficient was based on the *SPCs* calculated using the BNC-1 corpus. What if the comparison used *SPCs* calculated using a different corpus for each keyboard? This question is explored in Fig.5. which provides a cross-corpus comparison of *SPCs* for the two keyboards. The 3.3% figure just cited is in the top-left cell. Provided the *SPCs* are calculated from the same corpus (diagonal entries), the conclusion is consistent: The *Wivik* keyboard is slightly more efficient. However, if the comparison is based on *SPCs* calculated using a different corpus for each keyboard, the effect is dramatic. See Fig.5.. One comparison gives the *Wivik* keyboard a 15.2% advantage; another comparison gives it an 11.4% disadvantage! Clearly, research on scanning keyboards using *SPC* as an indicator of keyboard efficiency should disclose both the algorithm and the corpus.[2]

			SPCs for Koester-Levine keyboard (Fig. 1d)			
			BNC-1	BNC-2	Brown	Phrases
			2.73	2.87	2.89	2.55
SPCs for	BNC-1	2.64	3.3%	8.0%	8.7%	-3.5%
Wivik	BNC-2	2.80	-2.6%	2.4%	3.1%	-9.8%
keyboard	Brown	2.84	-4.0%	1.0%	1.7%	-11.4%
(Fig. 1m)	Phrases	2.45	10.3%	14.6%	15.2%	3.9%

Fig. 5. Cross-corpus comparison of *SPCs* for two scanning keyboards

---

[2] The software and word-frequency lists used to generate the *SPC* statistics herein are available at http://www.yorku.ca/mack/ScanningKeyboardSPC.zip

5   Discussion

If scan-steps per character (SPC) is calculated only using the core symbols (a-z, space), the result is robust but does not generalize to the broader text entry experience. To improve external validity, the model must include punctuation and other symbols. The first step is to position the added symbols in the layout. A revised corpus is also required – to include the added symbols. There is a problem, however. While common symbols, such as periods and commas, are relatively stable within corpora, many other symbols are not. Consider the variety of symbols on a conventional keyboard (e.g., ~, #, &, ^). Corpora that include these are likely to do so erratically. The symbols will be rare in some text samples, more frequent in others. SPC, so calculated, will address a broader context (high external validity), but will be unstable (low internal validity), thus weakening comparisons between designs from different sources.

The calculation of SPC does not factor in the human element. The statistic is purely a measure of inherent efficiency. Of course, assuming perfect behaviour for the operator (i.e., no errors, no selections missed), text entry throughput can be calculated from the scanning interval and SPC. Additional behaviours must be accounted for, however. Many scanning keyboards include a row delay, timer restart, or other adjustments to the scanning pattern to aid the user. Text entry throughput can be calculated if these properties are included along with SPC and the scanning interval. The calculation is a "best case". User efficiency can thereafter be measured as the ratio of the observed throughput to the best-case throughput.

6   Conclusion

Scan steps per character (SPC) was demonstrated as metric for modeling scanning keyboards. Since SPC is an absolute metric, designs from different sources can be compared. Where word prediction is used, comparisons are strengthened if SPC is calculated using the same corpus (word-frequency list).

References

1. Bhattacharya, S., Samanta, D., Basu, A.: Performance models for automatic evaluation of virtual scanning keyboards. IEEE Transactions on Neural Systems and Rehabilitation Engineering 16, 510–519 (2008)
2. Damper, R.I.: Text composition by the physically disabled: A rate prediction model for scanning input. Applied Ergonomics 15, 289–296 (1984)
3. Foulds, R., Baletsa, G., Crochetiere, W.: The effectiveness of language redundancy in non-verbal communication. In: Proceedings of the Conference on Devices and Systems for the Disabled, pp. 82–86. Krushen Center for Research and Engineering, Philadelphia (1975)
4. Higginbotham, D.J.: Evaluation of keystroke savings across five assistive communication technologies. Augmentative and Alternative Communications 8, 258–272 (1992)

5. Jones, P.E.: Virtual keyboard with scanning and augmented by prediction. In: Proceedings of the 2nd European Conference on Disability, Virtual Reality and Associated Technologies, pp. 45–51. University of Reading, UK (1998)
6. Koester, H.H., Levine, S.P.: Learning and performance of able-bodied individuals using scanning systems with and without word prediction. Assistive Technology 6, 42–53 (1994)
7. Lesher, G., Moulton, B., Higginbotham, D.J.: Techniques for augmenting scanning communication. Augmentative and Alternative Communication (AAC) 14, 81–101 (1998)
8. MacKenzie, I.S.: KSPC (Keystrokes per Character) as a Characteristic of Text Entry Techniques. In: Paternó, F. (ed.) Mobile HCI 2002. LNCS, vol. 2411, pp. 195–210. Springer, Heidelberg (2002)
9. MacKenzie, I.S., Soukoreff, R.W.: Phrase sets for evaluating text entry techniques. In: Extended Abstracts of the ACM SIGCHI Conference on Human Factors in Computing Systems - CHI 2003, pp. 754–755. ACM, New York (2003)
10. MacKenzie, I.S., Tanaka-Ishii, K.: Text entry with a small number of buttons. In: MacKenzie, I.S., Tanaka-Ishii, K. (eds.) Text Entry Systems: Mobility, Accessibility, Universality, pp. 105–121. Morgan Kaufmann (2007)
11. Mankowski, R.E.: Predicting communication rates: Efficacy of a scanning model, MSc Thesis, Univeristy of Pittsburg (2009)
12. Silfverberg, M., MacKenzie, I.S., Korhonen, P.: Predicting text entry speed on mobile phones. In: Proceedings of the ACM SIGCHI Conference on Human Factors in Computing Systems, CHI 2000, pp. 9–16. ACM, New York (2000)
13. Simpson, R.C., Koester, H.H.: Adaptive one-switch row-column scanning. IEEE Transactions on Rehabilitation Engineering 7, 464–473 (1999)
14. Steriadis, C.E., Constantinou, P.: Designing human-computer interfaces for quadriplegic people. ACM Transactions on Computer-Human Interaction (TOCHI) 10, 87–118 (2003)
15. Szeto, A.Y.J., Allen, E.J., Littrell, M.C.: Comparison of speed and accuracy for selected electronic communication devices and input methods. Augmentative and Alternative Communication 9, 229 (1993)
16. Venkatagiri, H.S.: Efficient keyboard layouts for sequential access in augmentative and alternative communication. Augmentative and Alternative Communication (AAC) 15, 126–134 (1999)

DualScribe: A Keyboard Replacement for Those with Friedreich's Ataxia and Related Diseases

Torsten Felzer[1], I. Scott MacKenzie[2], and Stephan Rinderknecht[1]

[1] Institute for Mechatronic Systems, Technische Universität Darmstadt,
Darmstadt, Germany
[2] Department of Computer Science and Engineering, York University,
Toronto, Canada M3J 1P3
{felzer,rinderknecht}@ims.tu-darmstadt.de, mack@cse.yorku.ca

Abstract. An alternative text composition method is introduced, comprising a small special-purpose keyboard as an input device and software to make text entry fast and easy. The work was inspired by an FA (Friedreich's Ataxia) patient who asked us to develop a viable computer interaction solution – taking into account the specific symptoms induced by his disease. The outcome makes text entry easier than with the standard keyboard without being slower. It is likely that the system has general use for anyone with a similar condition, and also for able-bodied users looking for a small-size keyboard. We present a usability study with four participants showing the method's effectiveness.

Keywords: Human-computer interaction, special-purpose keyboard, word prediction, ambiguous keyboards, neuromuscular diseases, Friedreich's Ataxia.

1 Introduction

John is 41 years old and was diagnosed 20 years ago with the inherited neuromuscular disease Friedreich's Ataxia (FA). He has considerable motor problems, worsened by secondary neurological symptoms affecting his sight and speech. He depends on a computer for everyday work, in particular to compose text documents. Lacking viable alternatives, John still uses a standard manual keyboard for text entry. However, this requires substantial time and effort. The entry rate is very low, sometimes only 2–3 wpm, and is decreasing as the disease progresses.

Our work sought to make John's life easier by developing an efficient, effortless, and practical alternative to the standard keyboard. The alternative is tailored to his needs which are a direct consequence of his disease. The resulting solution fully utilizes what someone with FA can do, while compensating for what such a person cannot do. The system is therefore not only usable by John, but by anyone with similar conditions.

The work is significant since the estimated prevalence of inherited neuromuscular disorders is one person in 3,000 [1]. In the USA, for example, that translates

K. Miesenberger et al. (Eds.): ICCHP 2012, Part II, LNCS 7383, pp. 431–438, 2012.

into more than 100,000 people. The work is also important to text entry in general. In addition to use in the workplace, using a computer for e-mail, Internet chat, texting, etc., is unthinkable without a quick and efficient means to enter text.

In the next section, we examine common alternatives for persons with disabilities and evaluate them in view of someone with a neuromuscular disease. After that, we describe the newest version of our text composition application: *DualScribe*, which is tailored to the needs of that particular user group. This is followed by the description of a usability study with four participants, including John and three able-bodied computer users. The paper is concluded with a short summary and some thoughts on future work.

(a)   (b)

Fig. 1. *DualPad*: Special-purpose keyboard used as replacement for the standard keyboard. It consists of four rows and five columns and has 18 active keys (not $4 \times 5 = 20$), because the rightmost key in row 1 is a double-width key and the leftmost key in row 4 is deactivated. Columns 1 and 2 are operated with the left thumb, while the right thumb is responsible for columns 3-5. (a) With hands. (b) Without hands.

2   Literature Review

There are many ways to assist persons with motor disabilities to enter text. These may be categorized by looking at the targeted input device. First, there are standard techniques, such as word prediction, which aims to save keystrokes. After each character, a list of extensions of the string is presented, and the user can select among those candidates. This reduces the physical load on the user, but looking through the list to find the desired word increases the cognitive load; so, word completion is not always faster [2]. Since someone with FA usually has motor problems leading to unsteady movement, utilizing a full-size keyboard may be problematic due to key-to-key "travel" distances.

Dasher [3] is an assistive tool for a variety of pointing devices, in the simplest form a standard mouse. It allows the user to enter text quickly (normally!) by moving the mouse pointer into areas on the screen associated with characters. Because of missing fine motor control and reduced hand-eye coordination, this tool is not a suitable alternative for FA patients.

The second group of text entry methods focuses on switch-like devices. Input relies on a small number of signals with the help of a scanning scheme [4]. Instead of using a full keyboard, the user confirms suggestions made by the computer, for example, by actuating a key or switch. One example is a row-column scanning keyboard where the computer suggests first the row, and then the column within the row, of a character in a two-dimensional matrix. These systems (e.g., [5,6]) typically do not make full use of the physical capabilities of an FA patient (who can employ both hands, for example). So, input is unnecessarily cumbersome, resulting in a very low input rate. Editing tasks, such as rearranging a sentence, are particularly difficult.

The third approach involves contact-free devices. For those who cannot use their hands or arms, automatic speech recognition (ASR) is an efficient alternative (e.g., [7]). As the voice of an FA patient is usually subject to dysarthria, the recognition algorithm may falter due to speech variations. Non-verbal voice interaction (NVVI) – involving humming or whistling – might be an answer (e.g., [8]), but the vocal problems are often too overwhelming.

Another method for hands-free text entry is eye tracking, where the user's eyes can move a mouse cursor, for example, to select characters displayed on an on-screen keyboard (e.g., [9]). Since FA is often accompanied by pathological nystagmus, eye tracking is often impossible. An idea quite similar to eye tracking is the camera mouse [10], which tracks a freely selectable spot on the user's face with the help of a standard webcam. However, that may also be too difficult if the user's head movements are unsteady or uncontrollable.

Hamidi et al. [11] present an interesting text entry approach. It is also based on speech recognition, but in contrast to allowing arbitrary words, the system merely discriminates between a limited number of user-definable keywords which are translated into emulated keystrokes. In other words, instead of typing on a standard manual keyboard, the user can define, for example, "Marc" as "M" or "Tom" as "T", and the system only has to distinguish the keywords. This could be the starting point for an adequate contact-free alternative.

In our approach, we combine some of the ideas above and convert them to a text composition application called *DualScribe*, which is characterized by the special-purpose keyboard shown in fig. 1. This input device was chosen because of anecdotal evidence: John (who usually uses the middle fingers of both hands) likes to type the leftmost keys on the keyboard (like "A", "Q", "Tab", or left "Shift"), since he then can use his left thumb for typing while handling the left edge of the keyboard as a guide.

3   *DualScribe* – System Description

It is beyond the scope of this paper to detail every feature of *DualScribe*, so we focus only on the main concepts. In short, the software emulates virtual keystrokes in response to the physical keystrokes of the user on the 18 keys of the *DualPad*. The keys of the *DualPad* are not only associated with direct keystroke emulation, but also with changes in the program state of *DualScribe*.

The program offers a small number of modes with the mappings from keys to functionality depending on the currently active mode. Each key's function is similar in every mode (although not always identical).

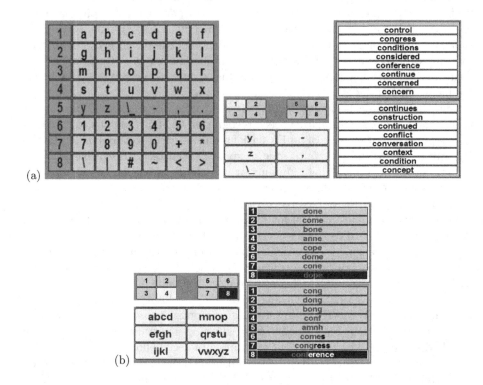

Fig. 2. Input ideas. (a) *Dual mode* with eight-by-six selection grid and a word prediction list after entering "con", which requires pressing the keys "↑", then "3", "←", "3", "←", and finally "2" on the *DualPad*. (b) *Ambiguous mode* where each character key stands for four or five characters with candidate list after entering the sequence "1442".

The default entry of a character (also called *dual mode*) involves two keystrokes (leading to the program's name). The selectable characters are arranged in eight rows and six columns (as depicted in fig. 2a for lower-case letters). The user selects the row of a character with the help of the four arrow keys located on the *DualPad* and the column with the six character keys. In *single keystroke mode*, the arrow keys of the *DualPad* do the same as the arrow keys on the standard keyboard – that is the reason for their labeling. In *dual mode*, they could as well be labeled A, B, C, D, as they are simply four keys to directly select rows 1-4 – or 5-8 if pressed twice – of the 8 × 6 grid.

The *KSPC* (keystrokes per character) for the input method is 2.0; however, word prediction using a 100k-item dictionary (compiled from Ref. [12]) reduces *KSPC*. Considering all 100,000 words and always taking the shortest path to enter a word [13] yields a *KSPC* of 1.1159. This is close to the inherent *KSPC* = 1.0 for a regular QWERTY keyboard.

There is also an *ambiguous mode* which is T9-like except only using six keys. As the user enters the characters "1"–"6", *DualScribe* looks for matches in the same dictionary as is used for word prediction. A frequency-ordered list of up to 16 candidates (including extensions, but with priority given to *exact* matches) is suggested to the user (as two lists with eight entries each) who then selects the desired word in a manner similar to the row in *dual mode*. The implementation is analogous to MacKenzie and Felzer's definition of a *scanning ambiguous keyboard* [14], except with direct selection instead of scanning.

Since the dictionary is large, almost every word (including some proper names) is known and can thus be entered without switching to *dual mode*. Moreover, the user can easily extend the dictionary, i.e., make arbitrary expressions known to the system. On the other hand, a large dictionary also implies a high ambiguity, which means that the candidate list may contain many matches and only few extended suggestions (as depicted in fig. 2b). In any event, this method leads to a low *KSPC* of 0.8807.

The user is not restricted to the 48 symbols shown in fig. 2a. Various mechanisms, such as a "SHIFT" key or a *menu mode*, let the user produce any character or symbol that is found on a standard keyboard. Besides, *DualScribe* has its own editor window and offers features that integrate with any regular text composition software, including a movable cursor, copy/paste, find/replace, undo/redo.

4 Empirical Data

A pilot study revealed that entering text in *ambiguous mode* is faster and more comfortable than in *dual mode* (which is not really surprising, given the lower *KSPC*). Therefore, *ambiguous mode* was chosen for a first field test using the German language version of the program. During an exhibition at the local university, visitors were given the opportunity to measure their text entry rate with *DualScribe* in comparison to the standard QWERTY keyboard.

The participants' task was to transcribe – as fast and as accurately as possible – nine German phrases randomly drawn from a list of 56 phrases with lengths varying between 31 and 81 characters. All phrases contained upper- and lower-case letters and punctuation, and it was made sure that every single word was in the dictionary (based on the DeReWo [15] in the German version), so that all text could be entered in *ambiguous mode*.

The nine runs were divided into three blocks with three runs each. Participants were instructed to employ the *DualPad* in the first and third blocks and the standard keyboard in the second block. Correcting typing errors (e.g., by using backspace) was allowed, but not required, and the number of correction operations used in each run was noted.

In addition to John (for whom the system was originally developed), three able-bodied participants, one 26-year-old female participant, and two male participants (aged 45 and 27, respectively) completed the entire procedure. For the study, the four participants – all frequent computer users – were coded P0 (for John), P1, P2, and P3. The resulting entry rates are depicted in fig. 3 for the *ambiguous mode* in *DualScribe* and in fig. 4 for the standard keyboard.

The most striking result is that John's entry rate with *DualScribe* appears comparable to that of the able-bodied participants. Of course, the comparison is

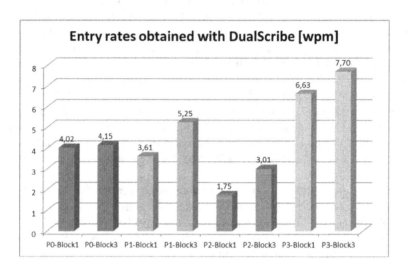

Fig. 3. Average text entry rates obtained in the four-participant usability study. Results for two blocks with three phrases each while the participants were using the *DualPad*.

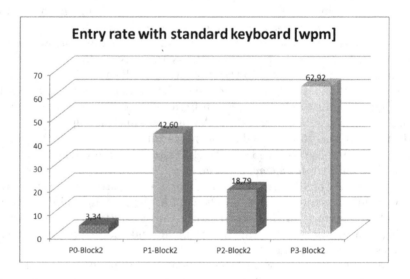

Fig. 4. Average text entry rates for one block while using the standard keyboard

a little unfair, since John was already familiar with the input method, while the visitors to the exhibition only practiced for a few minutes prior to the test (P1 for 2 minutes, P2 only for 1 minute, but P3 for at least 20 minutes). Anyway, his performance using *DualScribe* is not "that far off" as with the standard keyboard (with up to 20 times slower entry rate).

The practice time is also the main reason for the difference in blocks 1 and 3. John (P0) has a lot of experience with *DualScribe*, and a few more sentences can hardly improve his entry rate. However, this amount of practice is enough for the other participants to considerably improve their performance. Even though it seems likely that their learning curves will continue the upward trend, it has to be said that the built-in acceleration techniques cannot compensate for a full keyboard, if it can be operated fast. So *DualScribe* is a viable alternative for persons with certain disabilities, but for able-bodied users, it is only adequate in specific situations.

5   Conclusion

A text entry tool optimized for a small keypad which can replace a full-size keyboard has been introduced. The pad is held with both hands and operated with the thumbs only. The tool – an advancement of a simpler system involving a game controller [16] – is therefore ideal for someone with FA. A usability study justified that assumption. It was shown that it is possible for an FA patient to achieve text entry rates with the system that are somehow on par with those achieved by able-bodied computer users.

The fact that a first prototype is already in use currently (by a particular individual with FA, for composing private e-mails) also shows its usefulness. For the future, it is planned to extend the idea to computer operation in general (not just text composition). This requires directing virtual keystrokes to any active application (instead of a dedicated editor window), as well as adding a mouse mode.

Acknowledgments. This work is partially supported by DFG grant FE 936/6-1 "EFFENDI – EFficient and Fast text ENtry for persons with motor Disabilities of neuromuscular orIgin".

References

1. Lecky, B.R.F.: Neuromuscular disorders: Clinical and molecular genetics. Brain 122(4), 1–790 (1999)
2. Koester, H.H., Levine, S.P.: Modeling the speed of text entry with a word prediction interface. IEEE Trans. Rehab. Eng. 2(3), 177–187 (1994)
3. Ward, D.J., Blackwell, A.F., MacKay, D.J.C.: Dasher - a data entry interface using continuous gestures and language models. In: Proc. UIST 2000, pp. 129–137. ACM Press (2000)
4. Baljko, M., Tam, A.: Motor input assistance: Indirect text entry using one or two keys. In: Proc. ASSETS 2006, pp. 18–25. ACM Press (2006)

5. Wandmacher, T., Antoine, J.Y., Poirier, F., Départe, J.P.: Sibylle, an assistive communication system adapting to the context and its user. ACM Trans. Access. Comput. 1(1), 1–30 (2008)
6. Felzer, T., MacKenzie, I.S., Beckerle, P., Rinderknecht, S.: Qanti: A Software Tool for Quick Ambiguous Non-standard Text Input. In: Miesenberger, K., Klaus, J., Zagler, W., Karshmer, A. (eds.) ICCHP 2010, Part II. LNCS, vol. 6180, pp. 128–135. Springer, Heidelberg (2010)
7. Zhang, W., Duffy, V.G., Linn, R., Luximon, A.: Voice recognition based human-computer interface design. Computers & Industrial Engineering 37, 305–308 (1999)
8. Sporka, A.J., Felzer, T., Kurniawan, S.H., Poláček, O., Haiduk, P., MacKenzie, I.S.: Chanti: Predictive text entry using non-verbal vocal input. In: Proc. CHI 2011, pp. 2463–2472. ACM Press (2011)
9. Kumar, M., Paepcke, A., Winograd, T.: EyePoint: Practical pointing and selection using gaze and keyboard. In: Proc. CHI 2007, pp. 421–430. ACM Press (2007)
10. Gips, J., Betke, M., Fleming, P.: The camera mouse: Preliminary investigation of automated visual tracking for computer access. In: Proc. RESNA 2000, pp. 98–100. RESNA Press (2000)
11. Hamidi, F., Baljko, M., Livingston, N., Spalteholz, L.: CanSpeak: A Customizable Speech Interface for People with Dysarthric Speech. In: Miesenberger, K., Klaus, J., Zagler, W., Karshmer, A. (eds.) ICCHP 2010, Part I. LNCS, vol. 6179, pp. 605–612. Springer, Heidelberg (2010)
12. Davies, M.: Word frequency data from the Corpus of Contemporary American English (COCA), http://www.wordfrequency.info (January 27, 2011)
13. MacKenzie, I.S.: KSPC (Keystrokes per Character) as a Characteristic of Text Entry Techniques. In: Paternó, F. (ed.) Mobile HCI 2002. LNCS, vol. 2411, pp. 195–210. Springer, Heidelberg (2002)
14. MacKenzie, I.S., Felzer, T.: SAK: Scanning Ambiguous Keyboard for Efficient One-Key Text Entry. ACM Transactions on Computer-Human Interaction (TOCHI) 17(3), 11:1–11:39 (2010)
15. Institut für Deutsche Sprache: Korpusbasierte Wortformenliste DeReWo, v-100000t-2009-04-30-0.1, mit Benutzerdokumentation. Programmbereich Korpuslinguistik, Mannheim, Deutschland (2009), http://www.ids-mannheim.de/kl/derewo/
16. Felzer, T., Rinderknecht, S.: Using a game controller for text entry to address abilities and disabilities specific to persons with neuromuscular diseases. In: Proc. ASSETS 2011, pp. 299–300. ACM Press (2011)

Easier Mobile Phone Input Using the JusFone Keyboard

Oystein Dale and Trenton Schulz

Norsk Regnesentral, P.O. Box 114 Blindern, 0314 Oslo, Norway
{oystein.dale,trenton.schulz}@nr.no

Abstract. We present an alternate mobile phone keyboard for inputting text, the JusFone Keyboard. This keyboard allows people to enter characters by resting their finger on a the desired key, and rocking to select a specific character. We ran user tests of the keyboard with 12 seniors comparing it against a touch-screen keyboard, a phone with large buttons, and an on-screen PC keyboard. The users found several things to like about the JusFone Keyboard, including comfort and size of keys and having direct access to characters. Users also had several suggestions about how to make the keyboard better such as making the text on the keys bigger and adjusting the spacing between keys. We also conducted a diary study of a user with reduced hand function who used the JusFone keyboard on his PC. The results indicate that the keyboard may be of assistance to persons with reduced hand function.

Keywords: User testing, mobile phones, keyboards, input methods.

1 Introduction

As smartphones and apps are increasingly adopted, there is an increasing demand for inputting text, numbers, and other characters on mobile phones. The trend in smartphones has been the widespread use of touch interaction through on-screen keyboards with no physical keyboard. This is not always desirable or suitable for everyone. There are still many people that prefer a physical keyboard on their mobile phone. We introduce the JusFone keyboard that is an attempt to simplify text input and input in general on mobiles phones and other electronic devices. The keyboard is meant to make it easier for certain groups, e.g., persons with reduced hand function, to operate their mobile devices.

The paper is based on work conducted in the project "JusFone – a smartphone for everyone". It was conducted from 2010 to 2011 with support from the Norwegian Research Council. The main goal of the project was to conduct user testing of the concept phone JusFone on seniors to generate feedback to be used in further product development, as well as contribute to the general development of accessible mobile phones. The main activities in the project were to produce a prototype of the JusFone keyboard, to conduct user testing of the keyboard on seniors, and to conduct a survey on seniors and their mobile phone use. Here we present the JusFone keyboard and report on the findings from the user testing of the keyboard.

K. Miesenberger et al. (Eds.): ICCHP 2012, Part II, LNCS 7383, pp. 439–446, 2012.

Richard Chan developed the JusFone keyboard and manufactured three prototypes for the purpose of user testing. The keyboard prototypes have a keypad shape, and the finished product will be built into mobile phones. The keys are the size of a regular keyboard key, but are concave with four directional rocker keys (see Fig 1). The main idea is to rest the finger in the middle of the key, which will input nothing, and then rock the key in any of the four directions. This will result in a character being input on the phone based on the direction. An advantage of this approach is that one can easily anchor a finger in the middle of a key and input characters even if one has poor precision (e.g., one has a very shaky hand or one is wearing bulky gloves). People with vision impairment could also benefit from using the keyboard given the tactile support it provides.

The keys provide easy and direct access to all characters, and there are dedicated keys for shortcuts and phone control. The physical form and mechanical characteristics of the keyboard is intended to improve accessibility for several user groups. A variant of the keyboard with an USB-interface can be a standalone device connected to a computer or a tablet to provide an alternative input method. A photo of a JusFone prototype is provided in Fig. 2.

The purpose of the user testing was to try out the JusFone keyboard with seniors, and to use the experiences gathered in further development of the keyboard. We also compared the JusFone keyboard with other relevant input methods. These were: 1) a basic standard mobile keypad with large keys and large numbers/letters, 2) an on-screen keyboard on a mobile device – iOS on an iPod Touch, and 3) an on-screen keyboard on a Windows tablet PC.

Fig. 1. Close up of a JusFone key (Source: Richard Chan)

Fig. 2. A prototype of the JusFone keyboard (Source: NR)

2   State of the Art

Research in alternate input methods is continuing and many products exist. Starting at the desktop, there have been many keyboards that aim at being more ergonomic or efficient [1]. Beyond the keyboard we have methods like speech or Dasher [2], a way of "driving" to letters based on the probability that they will be next in a word. Dasher has even been extended to be steered by the brain [3] or combined with speech [4] to speed writing. If we turn to the mobile world, we can see that speech recognition is starting to become a popular choice, but keyboards are preferred in many circumstances. Other keyboards researched in the mobile space include the Twiddler [5]: a chording keyboard for inputting text with one hand, BigKey [6]: a virtual keyboard that attempts to make the key for next letter in a word larger, and BrailleTouch [7]: an eye's free way of inputting text using a touchscreen. The EasyWrite [8] prototype is another virtual keyboard that targets people with motor coordination problems, though it tries to tackle the problem in a much different way than JusFone.

3   Methodology

The test persons were recruited from members of Seniornett – an organisation providing ICT training for seniors. The test persons were from 65 up to 80 years of age, and the gender balance was even. Their self-assessed computing skills were medium to high levels of experience. 13 user tests were conducted. These were done with three different set ups:

1. Seven seniors with no disclosed disabilities conducted user tests with the JusFone keyboard connected to a PC completing various tasks, and conducted the same tasks on a Windows tablet PC using an on-screen keyboard.
2. Five seniors with no disclosed disabilities conducted user tests with the JusFone keyboard connected to a PC completing various tasks. They conducted the same tasks with a Doro mobile phone with a basic standard mobile keypad with large keys and large numbers/letters, and an on-screen keyboard on a mobile device (iOS on an iPod Touch).
3. One person with reduced hand function used the JusFone keyboard instead of his normal PC keyboard over several days, and kept a "diary" detailing the experiences with the keyboard.

The seniors in Groups 1 and 2 were videotaped, and the usability software Morae was used for screen and audio capture. In Group 1 a researcher conducted the testing, while in Group 2 two researchers conducted the testing (one interviewer and one observer). The set up is shown in Fig. 3.

Fig. 3. Set up using video capture and the Morae usability software (Source: NR)

In Groups 1 and 2 the participants solved different tasks and answered concrete questions from a test protocol. The protocol was adjusted based on the experiences in Group 1 and to accommodate the different comparisons between input methods conducted in Group 2. The tasks consisted of writing text, numbers, symbols, and punctuation marks with the different input methods. The participants were encouraged to think aloud, ask questions, and to make comments.

By using the Morae usability software, a qualitative analysis was conducted by the researchers on all the material collected (video, audio and electronic and handwritten notes). For Groups 1 and 2 the observations made and the participants' comments were categorized and summarised. A summary was made of the diary notes taken down by the participant with reduced hand function.

4   Results

The results are divided by the device that was evaluated.

4.1   JusFone Keyboard

The keys on the JusFone keyboard are concave; to ease usage, the users can place and rest their fingers in the middle of the concave surface and rock in four different directions to depress the desired key, e.g. letter 'a' at nine o'clock, letter 'b' at six o'clock, or 'c' at three o'clock. One thing that was noticeable was that the informants did not use this rocking method, but rather pressed directly on the letters on the edges of each key in a pecking manner. When asked to try the rocking method some found it easier, but most quickly reverted back to the pecking method. Several pointed out that the concave design could be of benefit to persons with hand tremors or other hand impediments, because one could use the "well" as a finger guide and resting place. Some felt that the keys were firm and comfortable to press.

The seniors were positive about having direct access to all letters and numbers and that all characters, symbols, and punctuation marks are visible. Many mobile keyboards have these hidden in sub-menus and require prior knowledge to their position or multiple key presses to access. Several mentioned that the visibility and ease of direct access was especially important during the more intricate writing tasks. The alphabetical layout was beneficial according to some.

The test users mentioned that it was easy to edit text with the JusFone keyboard. It was pointed out that it was easier to move the cursor using the JusFone keyboard compared to touch screens. They highlighted that one of the advantages with the JusFone keyboard is that it is bigger than conventional mobile keypads, and that one gets direct access to all letters. It appeared that seniors who were dissatisfied with the input method on their own mobile phones were somewhat more positive to the JusFone keyboard. This was especially the case for the ones who had touch phones.

The majority said it was easy to use the JusFone keyboard. They expressed that it was easy and intuitive to understand how to use it, but that it would still be useful with some instructions and a manual for beginners. The use of multiple characters per key was not a problem, and it was an advantage that different colours were used to separate different types of characters.

Some of the test persons mentioned that they initially had to do a bit of searching for symbols and punctuation marks since they were not familiar with their placement. They said, however, that this is something one gets used to. It was pointed out that the keyboard was large and bulky. It was also brought to our attention that one of the symbols was impossible to access as it was placed on the same key and opposite to the Shift function. As its use relied on depressing Shift it was impossible to access it without having activated the Sticky keys function, which we unfortunately turned off during the user trials.

There were some suggestions from the seniors on how to improve the keyboard. These include:

- Slightly bigger and more readable letters, especially symbols and punctuation marks.
- Slightly more space between the keys.
- A Delete button in addition to the Backspace when editing.
- Native terms on keys, e.g. the Norwegian "mellomrom" instead of "space" on the Space key.
- Should be lighter, smaller, and more aesthetically pleasing (this was the first prototype).

Our impression is that, by and large, the JusFone keyboard was well received by the seniors, but that there are some aspects that need improvement.

4.2 Doro Large Key Keypad

The Doro device has large keys and large numbers. In addition to the keypad it has a scrolling wheel and some other keys required for its operation. It is targeted as a "senior phone", meant to cater to the needs of elderly persons. We wanted the informants to try it, as a comparison to the JusFone keyboard. The experiences are summarized below:

- The keys were considered large and comfortable.
- It was considered especially suited for writing short texts and for dialling numbers.
- The seniors mentioned that it was difficult to tell if you were in letter or number mode, as the indicator for this was small.

The fact that the informants found it very cumbersome to access certain symbols that were hidden in sub-menus and requiring many key presses or use of the scrolling wheel, appeared to impact negatively on the overall impression.

Table 1. A comparison between the JusFone keyboard, the Doro mobile phone, the iOS on-screen keyboard and PC on-screen keyboard

Feature/activity	JusFone keyboard	Doro	iPod Touch	Tablet on-screen keyboard
Key and character size	Adequate sized keys; letters somewhat small	Large keys and letters	Small keyboard and letters	Adequate sized keys
Ease of access to characters	Direct access to all letters & numbers. Some symbols and punctuation marks require two key presses	Some symbols in sub-menus – cumbersome to access	Some symbols in sub-menus – cumbersome to access	Gap between spacebar and bottom of the screen made it very easy to miss key. Reflective screen also caused problems.
Editing	Easy to edit	No particular comment.	Editing can be difficult	Editing was difficult, one gave up
Writing	Well liked – especially for longer texts and complicated writing combining letters, numbers, symbols and punctuation marks	Well liked – especially for shorter texts and to dial numbers. Cumbersome access to certain symbols in sub-menus	Easy to make mistakes due to small characters positioned close together	Missing the spacebar resulted in many errors. Many times discovered after other words were written.

4.3   iPod Touch On-Screen Keyboard

The informants also tested a second-generation iPod Touch running the most recent version of iOS for this device at the time. This represents the identical on-screen keyboard found on the iPhone, and similar to many other popular touch based smart phones. Here follows a summary of the informant's use of the iPod Touch:

- The seniors found the keyboard to be small – it was referred to as "Lilliputian" – and it was easy to accidentally press neighbouring characters.
- It was easy to make typing errors, and editing was challenging for some.
- It was difficult to access certain symbols as they were placed in sub-menus.
- The keyboard displays capital letters despite being in lower case mode.
- Some informants tried to use their fingernails to improve accuracy, but, as the screen was capacitive, this did not work.

4.4   On-Screen Tablet Keyboard

The seniors also tried an on-screen touch keyboard on a Windows Tablet PC. This worked reasonably well, and there were not many comments besides the Spacebar being somewhat difficult to access. A comparison between the four input modalties is given in Table 1.

4.5   Diary Data

To examine how the JusFone keyboard performs for a person with reduced hand function, one informant who suffers from hand tremor used the keyboard instead of his standard PC keyboard for a couple of days. The informant recorded his comments using a tape recorder.

From the outset he noticed that the bulkiness of the keyboard resulted in an awkward writing angle. He used a book to change the angle, but the awkward angle still caused some problems throughout the trial. He said, "It is very different from using a standard keyboard on a PC... I suppose you have to use it and get used to finding your way around".

He noticed he had to look down at the keyboard while writing, and he noticed increased fatigue and shaking in his right hand after one hour of use. After a few days use he said, "It is quite easy to place your finger in the right place ... I believe that if you use it a great deal it will become easier. If you have problems with your hands or arms it is easier to use [than a standard keyboard]. I find it a lot easier to use than a touch screen. I cannot use touch screens".

Despite the testing being unstructured and anecdotal documentation, the trial did show promise that the keyboard can be used with niche populations, such as persons with reduced hand function.

5   Impact or Contributions to the Field

The work described in this paper detailing the initial user testing of the JusFone keyboard shows that the JusFone keyboard can be a possible alternative to touch based on-screen keyboards and existing physical mobile phone keyboards. As a standalone unit, it may also be used as an input method for other electronic devices such as tablets, smart-TVs, etc. Its innovative rocker keys may provide easier input for persons with reduced hand function. It may also be of use for persons who rely on tactile input such as persons with vision impairment.

6   Conclusion and Planned Activities

The relatively low number of user test performed and certain methodological issues means that one needs to be cautious in the conclusions drawn. That aside, the user testing revealed many positive attributes of the JusFone keyboard. Direct access to characters, ease of editing, alphabetical layout, intuitive to use, and the visible display of all characters were among some of the positive feedback provided by the informants. There was also some room for improvement, such as more spaced out keys and slightly larger letters. Further development and refining is needed for the device to be released as a commercial product, but these initial user tests show a great deal of promise. Mr. Chan is working on further developments of the keyboard.

Acknowledgements. We would like to thank the Norwegian Research Council for providing funding for the project; our project partners Richard Chan and Seniornett; and of course – many thanks, to all the informants who generously gave their time to take part.

References

1. Anderson, A.M., Mirka, G.A., Joines, S.M.B., Kaber, D.B.: Analysis of alternative keyboards using learning curves. Human Factors 51, 35–45 (2009)
2. Mackay, D.: Dasher - an Efficient Keyboard Alternative. ACNR 3, 24 (2003)
3. Van Vliet, M.: Text-input using a brain-computer interface: introducing Dasher. Twente Student Review (2007)
4. Vertanen, K., MacKay, D.J.C.: Speech Dasher: Fast Writing using Speech and Gaze. Writing, pp. 595–598 (2010)
5. Lyons, K., Starner, T., Gane, B.: Experimental evaluations of the Twiddler One-Handed Chording Mobile Keyboard. Human-Computer Interaction 21, 343–392 (2006)
6. Al Faraj, K., Mojahid, M., Vigouroux, N.: BigKey: A Virtual Keyboard for Mobile Devices. In: Jacko, J.A. (ed.) Human-Computer Interaction, Part III, HCII 2009. LNCS, vol. 5612, pp. 3–10. Springer, Heidelberg (2009)
7. Romero, M.: BrailleTouch: Designing a Mobile Eyes- Free Soft Keyboard. In: Proc. MobileHCI 2010, pp. 707–709 (2010)
8. Condado, P.A., Godinho, R., Zacarias, M., Lobo, F.G.: EasyWrite : A touch-based entry method for mobile devices. Proceedings of the 13th IFIP TC13 International Conference on Human-Computer Interaction (INTERACT 2011), Workshop on Mobile Accessibility (MOBACC 2011), Lisbon, Portugal, pp. 1–8 (2011)

Automatic Assessment of Dysarthric Speech Intelligibility Based on Selected Phonetic Quality Features

Myung Jong Kim and Hoirin Kim

Department of Electrical Engineering, Korea Advanced Institute of Science and Technology
myungjong@kaist.ac.kr, hrkim@ee.kaist.ac.kr

Abstract. This paper addresses the problem of assessing the speech intelligibility of patients with dysarthria, which is a motor speech disorder. Dysarthric speech produces spectral distortion caused by poor articulation. To characterize the distorted spectral information, several features related to phonetic quality are extracted. Then, we find the best feature set which not only produces a small prediction error but also keeps their mutual dependency low. Finally, the selected features are linearly combined using a multiple regression model. Evaluation of the proposed method on a database of 94 patients with dysarthria proves the effectiveness in predicting subjectively rated scores.

Keywords: Dysarthria, phonetic quality, speech intelligibility assessment.

1   Introduction

A speech intelligibility test for patients with dysarthria, which is a motor speech disorder, is conducted to diagnose and treat the articulatory disorder through utterance-based subjective perceptual evaluation by experts or naïve listeners [1]. In general, such an intelligibility test is costly, laborious, and subject to listener bias. Hence, an automated method (i.e. objective measurement) of the intelligibility test that is highly correlated with the expert's score (i.e. subjective grade) will be very useful in diagnosis area or dysarthric speech processing.

An important issue on developing a reliable objective assessment method, which may replace the expert with a computational algorithm, is how to extract and select proper speech features that show distinct characteristics depending on severity of disorders. However, in most cases, the existing methods rely on intuition and empirical comparison without any systematic selection strategy during feature extraction and selection process [2]. In this paper, we focus on the selection of a phonetic quality feature set to effectively represent the characteristics depending on severity of disorders in aspect of spectral distortion. Phonetic quality is mainly related to a spectral envelope determining phone identity. To this end, several phonetic quality features are extracted and then a proper feature set among them is selected using a new feature selection strategy. Finally, the selected features are linearly combined using a multiple regression model.

K. Miesenberger et al. (Eds.): ICCHP 2012, Part II, LNCS 7383, pp. 447–450, 2012.
© Springer-Verlag Berlin Heidelberg 2012

2   Feature Extraction

In this section, several model-based and model-free phonetic quality features are introduced to effectively characterize the spectral distortion of dysarthric speech. Model-based features make use of acoustic models, which are hidden Markov models (HMMs) in this work, trained by normal speech, while model-free ones do not need to use any acoustic models. Model-based features include word recognition rate (*WR*), state-level log-likelihood ratios (*SLLRs*), and log-likelihoods (*LLs*). In *SLLRs*, dysarthric speech and the corresponding normal speech are compared using log-likelihood ratios in the states of the normal reference HMMs. Model-free features include zero-crossing rate (*ZCR*), spectral centroid (*SC*), spectral bandwidth, spectral flatness (*SF*), spectral tilt (*ST*), spectral roll-off (*SRoll*), spectral flux, second-order spectral flux, ratio of *SF* and *SC* (*RSS*), and ratio of *ST* and *SRoll*.

Basically, the log-likelihoods and model-free features are extracted on frame-level. Since the characteristics of speech disorder cannot be observed within a short-time region, frame-level features need to be transformed into long-time features. Thus, the mean (E), variance (σ^2), skewness (Sk), and kurtosis (K) of the frame-level features are computed in an utterance. Each statistic feature is averaged for all utterances of each speaker and then the averaged features are used for the final speaker feature set.

3   Feature Selection and Intelligibility Prediction

3.1   Feature Selection

In this section, we introduce a new feature selection strategy to choose a proper feature set, which predicts accurately subjective intelligibility scores, from a number of features described in Section 2. The proposed selection criterion is in the form of penalty-based objective function with its associated weighting parameter for the purpose of selecting proper features which not only produce a small prediction error but also keep their mutual dependency low.

In the method, we find the best feature set by iteratively selecting one feature satisfying the feature selection criterion. To this end, the prediction error of m-th feature at t-th round is calculated based on the 0-1 step loss function defined by

$$\varepsilon_{t,m} = 2/\left\{1 + \exp\left(-\alpha \cdot \gamma_{t,m}\right)\right\} - 1, \quad \alpha > 0 \tag{1}$$

where

$$\gamma_{t,m} = \left\{\sum\nolimits_n \left(y_n - \hat{y}_{m,n}\right)^2 / N\right\}^{1/2}, \tag{2}$$

N is the number of training speakers, y_n is the intelligibility score of n-th dysarthric speaker, $\hat{y}_{m,n}$ is the predicted score of n-th dysarthric speaker based on a multiple linear regression model using both already selected features at the previous round and m-th feature to be selected at current t-th round.

To quantify mutual dependence, one natural choice is to compute mutual information between features. This method requires accurate estimation of joint distributions over the features, but in dysarthric speech it is very difficult due to their data sparseness. To cope with this, a simple but effective alternative way, which is a kind of correlation, has been proposed as

$$\pi_{t,m} = \sum\nolimits_{h_{t-1} \in \mathbf{H}_{t-1}} \left| r(h_{t-1}, x_m) \right| / N_{\mathbf{H}_{t-1}} \tag{3}$$

where

$$r(h_t, x_m) = \sum\nolimits_{n=1}^{N} (h_{t,n} - \bar{h}_t)(x_{m,n} - \bar{x}_m) / \sqrt{\sum\nolimits_{n=1}^{N} (h_{t,n} - \bar{h}_t)^2 \sum\nolimits_{n=1}^{N} (x_{m,n} - \bar{x}_m)^2}, \tag{4}$$

h_{t-1} denotes a feature from already selected feature pool $\mathbf{H}_{t-1}$, x_m denotes the m-th feature to be selected, and $N_{\mathbf{H}_{t-1}}$ is the number of already selected features. Also, $\bar{h}$ and $\bar{x}$ are the average feature values of training speakers. The mutual dependence is not considered at the first round.

Using (1) and (3), the best feature at the t-th round is determined as follows:

$$\hat{h}_t = \arg\min_{x_m} J_{t,m}, \qquad J_{t,m} = \varepsilon_{t,m} + \lambda \cdot \pi_{t,m} \tag{5}$$

where $0 \le \lambda < 1$. Note that in (5), the objective function value $J_{t,m}$ of each x_m has a penalty term $\pi_{t,m}$ and a weighting parameter λ that controls the trade-off between $\varepsilon_{t,m}$ and $\pi_{t,m}$ in order to enforce low mutual dependence between selected features. Considering performance in our experiments, a good compromise has been found by setting λ in the range of [0.3, 0.5]. At t-th round, the corresponding best feature $\hat{h}_t$ is then added to $\mathbf{H}_t$. After terminating the feature selection, T features contained in final $\mathbf{H}_T$ are used to predict the intelligibility score.

3.2 Intelligibility Prediction

All selected speaker-level features need to be converted into an objective intelligibility score for a speaker. Intelligibility can be successfully expressed as a linear combination of the selected features. As such, we use a linear regression model learned by means of least square approximation.

4 Experimental Results

To evaluate the proposed method, we used 37 Korean Assessment-of-Phonology-and-Articulation-for-Children (APAC) word set from 94 dysarthric speakers including 75 high, 15 mid, 2 low, and 2 very low subjects diagnosed by a subjective intelligibility test from five naïve listeners. To train a referential acoustic model, 37 APAC words and 150 Korean Phonetically Balanced Words (PBW) from 23 normal speakers (16 males and 7 females) were used. To obtain referential likelihoods used in SLLRs, 37 APAC words from 5 normal speakers (3 males and 2 females) were used.

The features selected among the possible features introduced in Section 2 were combined for predicting the subjective scores. Since the speakers are limited, all experiments were performed in a leave-one-out cross validation (LOOCV). The prediction accuracy was evaluated in terms of an root mean square error (RMSE) between the predicted scores and the subjectively rated scores.

When $\lambda=0.5$ in (5), a combination of model-based and model-free features achieved an RMSE of 10.2 in the range of 0 to 100 even with selecting only 5 features, corresponding to relative improvements of 8.1% and 32.0% over those of the model-based and model-free features, respectively. Here, the best 5 features averaged ranked during training consist of WR, $\sigma^2(SRoll)$, $K(LL)$, $K(RSS)$, and $Sk(ZCR)$. Thus, model-based and model-free features complement each other effectively. For $\lambda=0$, which means that the prediction error defined in (1) is only taken into account during feature selection process, an RMSE of 10.8 was obtained. This result ensures that considering both mutual dependence and prediction errors by using λ for feature selection allows achieving better performance. Also, the proposed feature selection method improved relatively 5.6% over the existing forward feature selection method [3]. Therefore, the proposed method clearly verifies the effectiveness in predicting the subjective scores.

5   Conclusion

We proposed a new method to automatically assess the disordered speech intelligibility. First, phonetic quality features were extracted to capture the spectral distortion of disordered speech. Then, a best feature set was selected by using a new feature selection method which the selected features produce small prediction errors as well as low mutual dependency among them. Finally, the selected features were linearly combined using a multiple regression model. In the experimental results, the proposed method obviously shows the effectiveness of our approach.

Acknowledgements. This work was supported by the R&D program of MKE/KEIT. [10036461, Development of an embedded key-word spotting speech recognition system individually customized for disabled persons with dysarthria]

References

1. Kent, R.D., Weismer, G., Kent, J.F., Rosenbek, J.C.: Toward Phonetic Intelligibility Testing in Dysarthria. J. Speech Hearing Disorders 54(4), 482–499 (1989)
2. Falk, T.H., Hummel, R., Chan, W.-Y.: Quantifying Perturbations in Temporal Dynamics for Automated Assessment of Spastic Dysarthric Speech Intelligibility. In: Proc. IEEE ICASSP, pp. 4480–4483 (May 2011)
3. Middag, C., Martens, J.-P., Nuffelen, G.V., De Bodt, M.: Automated Intelligibility Assessment of Pathological Speech Using Phonological Features. EURASIP J. Advances Signal Process. 2009, 9 pages (2009)

Adaptation of AAC to the Context Communication: A Real Improvement for the User Illustration through the VITIPI Word Completion

Philippe Boissière, Nadine Vigouroux, Mustapha Mojahid, and Frédéric Vella

Université Paul Sabatier, Institut de Recherche en Informatique de Toulouse,
UMR CNRS 5505, 118, Route de Narbonne
F-31062 Toulouse Cedex 9, France
{boissier,vigourou,mojahid,vella}@irit.fr

Abstract. This paper describes the performance of the VITIPI word completion system through a text input simulation. The aim of this simulation is to estimate the impact of the linguistic knowledge base size through two metrics: the Key-Stroke Ratio (KSR) and the KeyStroke Per Character (KPC). Our study shows that the performance of a word completion is depending of the % of words not available and the size of the lexicon.

Keywords: AAC Word completion system, KSR and KSPC metric, AAC.

1 Introduction

Many researches on text entry on the area of assistive and augmentative communication have been conducted (for an overview, see [6]). Text prediction systems were initially designed to help people with a low text composition rate. This includes people with severe speech and motor disabilities (cerebrally and physically disabled persons, Locked-in syndrome, cerebral palsy, etc.). The main aim of a predictor system is both to reduce the effort required and the message composition time. To reduce the effort, it is necessary to decrease the number of keystrokes needed for composing a message by anticipating the next block of characters (letters, syllables, words, sentences, according to the predictor system nature).

To facilitate the text entry, many solutions consisting in displaying a candidate word list have been designed and tested. The scientific community has clearly identified some theoretical improvements brought by the prediction system (for instance, the low keystroke number and the accelerated speed rate), while the use studies shows that the prediction system are rarely actually used.

This paper will present the new VITIPI version, a word completion component of Augmentative and Alternative Communication system designed in the framework of the PALLIACOM project: recherche.telecom-bretagne.eu/palliacom.

After our review of related works, we will introduce the principles of word completion algorithm. Then, we will describe our experiment to demonstrate the impact of

K. Miesenberger et al. (Eds.): ICCHP 2012, Part II, LNCS 7383, pp. 451–458, 2012.

size corpora on completion system's performance trough the KSR and KSPC parameters. Finally, results will be presented and discussed.

2   State of the Art

Most Augmentative Alternative Communication (AAC) systems include method to speed up communication by trying to save the number of keystrokes needed for the composition of a message. There are two main methods: word completion and word prediction. Both are basic technologies for text entry as well as an important component in augmentative language technology tools. Their main aim is to reduce the number of keystrokes typed during text entry and, consequently the tiredness of the person. We will illustrate through an example the differences between then.

Suppose that the lexicon contains the following list of French words:

— directeur
— direction
— directrice
— égalisateur
— égalisation
— égalisatrice

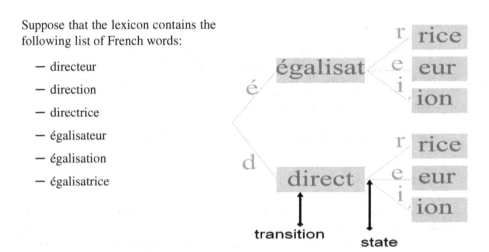

Fig. 1. Linguistic representation through a transducer

2.1   Principles of Completion Mode

When the user has typed the letter "*d*", the system automatically displays "*irect*" until there is no ambiguity for the generation process; then the user can enter another letter ("*e*" "*i*", "*r*") and the system completes by the appropriate sequence of letters "*eur*", "*ion*", "*rice*" according the linguistic representation (Fig. 1). In this mode no word list was presented to the user.

The completion system has only added the letters that could be completed automatically. However the user can refute them if they do not suit it. The most popular system is the T9, used on the standard 12-key keypad on the majority of mobile phones [10].

2.2   Principles of Prediction Mode

When the user has typed the letter "*d*", the prediction system proposes the list of words beginning with this letter: "*directrice*", "*directeur*", "*direction*" for the example. The word list can be ordered by decreasing probability or alphabetically according the system characteristics [6]. This list may be truncated to the first n elements (generally between 5 and 7).

2.3   Background Studies

These two modes were investigated through numerous studies to improve text entry: A list of words is provided: for instance, Dasher [15], [2], FASTY [12], SIBYLLE [14], etc. A survey of text prediction systems can be found in [6]. These studies reported encouraging user experiences.

However [14] mentioned that some users did not select the intended word even though it is clearly present in the prediction list. [5], [9], [8] explained that user's cognitive load is due to more attention and visual efforts. In fact they have to continuously look between the word list, the keyboard and the text entry focus. [1] has proposed a new distribution of the keyboard around a word list to avoid this problem.

A possible solution to reduce the cognitive load could be to implement direct "word completion" [3], [13] by proposing the most probable termination of the current word immediately after the latest typed letter by the writer.

3   Principles of the VITIPI Completion System

The VITIPI system principles consist of completing (automatically typing by the computer) the word, in part or in whole, while the user is inputting it. After each character typed by the user, the VITIPI system proposes a string (which may be empty), which extends or completes the word. The VITIPI linguistic kernel is based on a transducer [3] without probability (Fig. 1). VITIPI models the previous context through a N-gram model like.

4   Experiment

The aim of this experiment is to estimate the evolution of VITIPI performance by taking into account different representations of linguistic structures (words, sentences) through the transducer by means of a simulation system.

4.1   Simulation Principles

To value from a theoretical point of view the text entry performance a simulation program was developed. The text that the writer could have written is given to the simulation system: each character is entered one after one without orthographic fault. At each character typing step, the completion system is trying to propose, as soon as possible, a completion string. Then a comparison string algorithm compares the completion string to the word part string expected. Two assessment states are possible:

— Strings are identical: the completion is counted as right; the completion string is automatically inserted ; then a new character is entering;
— Strings are not identical: the completion is counted as false; the completion string is removed from the string; then the current character is entering.

The process is iterative until the end of word. A log program captures the following data to compute the letter number to be entered, the letter number proposed by the simulation system and the number of false completion list.

4.2   Corpora

The topic of the corpora is weather forecast. We have chosen to evaluate the VITIPI system on the field of meteorology because its lexical coverage is relatively small (see description below). This choice relies on the following hypothesis: the word completion must be adapted to the application field (for instance, personal mail, written communication topic, etc.); then the word completion is more efficient; in consequence this treatment reduces the subject's fatigue for long text entry [2].

Each sub corpus (coded from 1 to 33) corresponds to the text of a daily weather. The set of the 33 sub corpora is composed of 457 sentences including 8 436 words. The lexicon size corresponds to 948 words. The context size retained for the VITIPI system is 3-gram.

4.3   Simulation Task of Typing Text

The test has consisted to simulate the text entry of the sub corpus (daily j) with the transducer which models the set of the (j-1) sub corpora. Two serials of test were run according two modes: chronological and randomly mode for the construction of the transducer.

4.4   The Metrics

Two metrics were used as evaluation parameters:

— The Keystroke Saving Rate (KSR) [4] which is an estimation of the percentage of letters typed by the user. The KSR estimates the percentage of letters automatically written by the system.

$$KSR = \left(1 - \frac{Nb\_char\_typed + Nb\_function\_keys}{Length\_of\_text}\right) * 100 \qquad (1)$$

where:

- *Nb_char_typed* is the number of characters typed by the user to write his/her text,

- *Nb_function_keys*, the number of function keys used by him/her to correct erroneous word completion;
- and *Length_of_text* is the text length to be typed.
- The KSPC (KeyStroke Per Character) generally used by the text entry community [11] to compare the performance between prediction systems.

4.5   Results

We have measured the effect of the transducer enrichment, daily corpus by daily corpus, by means of the KSR parameter. Two measure sets have been done according the two modes of the transducer construction.

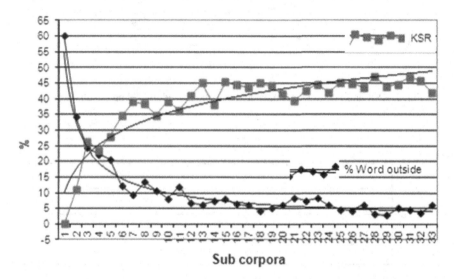

Fig. 2. KSR and rate of words outside the lexicon (chronological adding of sub corpora)

Firstly, the figures (Fig. 2 & Fig. 3) show that there is no effect of the adding mode of the sub corpora in the KSR performance. Secondly, we note that for the sub corpus 1 (Fig. 2) and for the sub corpus 23 (Fig. 3) the KSR is respectively null and negative (-0.85) because the transducer has still no representation of words. These two figures demonstrate also the great importance of the learning phase to update the lexicon and the linguistic representation with the sentence structure. KSR is increasing very quickly and then move around 45.75% for the transducer modeling the set of 15 sub corpora (Fig. 2).The adding of new sub corpora (from 16 until 33) has quite no effect on the KSR. The same effect is observed on the (Fig. 3) (after the consideration of 16 sub-corpora the KSR is around 44,5).

The figures (Fig. 2 & Fig. 3) demonstrate also that for a percentage of words not available in the lexicon lower than 5% the KSR is quite stable. This suggests us to formulate the hypothesis that for a lexicon of 1 000 words, it would be possible to obtain a stable KSR average around 45.

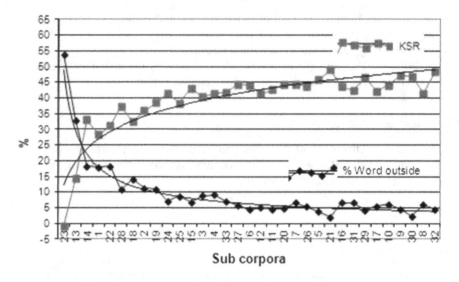

Fig. 3. KSR and rate of words outside the lexicon (random adding of sub corpora)

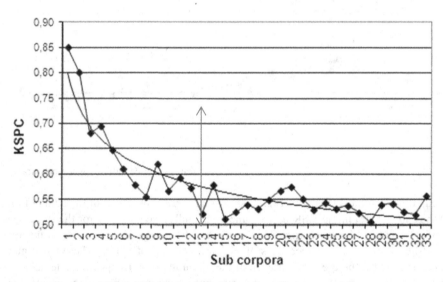

Fig. 4. KSPC (chronological adding of sub corpora)

The KSPC parameter has an opposite variation to the KSR parameter (Fig. 4 & Fig. 5). It strongly decreases until a set of 13 (Fig. 4) or of 10 (Fig. 5) sub corpora are taken into account in the transducer representation. Then it is in the range [0.50, 0.57] with few little variations.

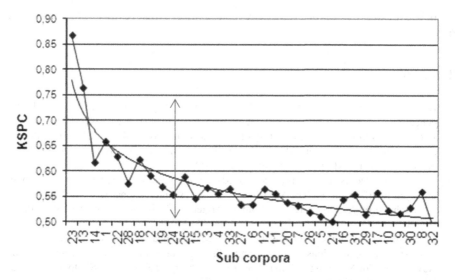

Fig. 5. KSPC (randomly adding of sub corpora)

4.6   Discussion

When the KSR is compared to the percentage of new words from the lexicon size (Fig. 2 & Fig. 3), we observe that these two curve variations are antagonist: growth corresponds to a decline of the other and vice versa. The experiment reports that the highest is the number of entries in the lexicon, the lesser the VITIPI system completes the user's current input. And vice versa, the more the lexicon will be reduced, the more the VITIPI system will perform

New words is also strongly penalizing for the KSR. When the word is unknown of the VITIPI linguistic representation, the writer has to type all letters. Moreover for the weather domains, the new words of the lexicon are often proper nouns: Consequently, it is impossible to use inference process of the VITIPI system. These results postulate that it extremely important to built quickly representative transducer.

To validate the robustness of these results it is necessary to study the correlation between the KSPC and KSR parameter for more hug corpora including words which are not specific of the domain.

5   Conclusion and Perspectives

We have demonstrated the variation in performance of a word completion system. This change is depending of the % of words not available and the size of the lexicon. This result demonstrates that "finalized" corpora might be defined according to the language register of the user. These results are extremely encouraging to adapt AAC to the user. However, these results must be consolidated on longer simulation trials and other topics (daily communication for instance).

Acknowledgement. This work is partially funded by the ANR TECSAN (PALLIACOM Project).

References

1. Badr, G., Raynal, M.L.: CentraList, AAATE'2011, Everyday Technology for Independence and Care. In: Gelderblom, G.J., et al. (eds.), pp. 944–951. IOS Press (2011)
2. Bérard, C., Neimeijer, D.: Evaluating effort reduction through different word prediction systems. In: Proceedings of the IEEE International Conference on Systems, Man and Cybernetics, La Haye NL, vol. 3, pp. 2658–2663 (2004)
3. Boissière, P., Dours, D.: From a specialized writing interface created for disabled, to an universal interface for all: The VITIPI System. In: 1st International UAHCI 2001 Conference (Universal Access for Human Computer Interfaces), News-Orleans, August 5-10, pp. 895–899 (2001)
4. Boissière, P., Schadle, I., Antoine, J.-Y.: A methodological framework for writing assistance systems: applications to Sibylle and VITIPI systems. Edited by Association for the Advancement of Modeling & Simulation Techniques in Enterprise, AMSE-Journals, Modeling C 67 (supp. Handicap 2006), 167–176 (2006)
5. Dubus, N.: Evaluation de l'interface intelligente d'aide à la saisie informatique, VITIPI au ly-cée Le Parc Saint-Agne. Journal d'Ergothérapie, 95–100 (Mars 1996)
6. Garay-Vitoria, N., Abascal, J.: Text prediction systems: a survey. International Journal on Universal Access in the Information Society 4(3), 88–103 (2006)
7. Garay-Vitoria, N., Abascal, J.: Modelling text prediction systems in low- and high-inflected languages. Computer Speech and Language 24, 117–135 (2010)
8. Goodman, J., Venolia, G., Steury, K., Parker, C.: Language modeling for soft keyboards. In: IUI 2002: Proceedings of the 7th International Conference on Intelligent User Interfaces, pp. 194–195. ACM, New York (2002)
9. Koester, H.H., Simon, P., Levine, S.P.: Modeling the Speed of Text Entry with a Word Prediction Interface. IEEE Transactions on Rehabilitation Engineering
10. MacKenzie, I.S., Kober, H., Smith, D., Jones, T., Skepner, E.: LetterWise: Pre_x-Based Disambiguation For Mobile Text Input. In: UIST 2001: Proceedings of the 14th Annual ACM Symposium on User Interface Software and Technology, pp. 111–120. ACM, New York (2001)
11. Soukoreff, R.W., MacKenzie, S.I.: Metrics for text entry research: an evaluation of MSD and KSPC, and a new unified error metric. In: Proceedings of the SIGCHI Conference on Human Factors in Computing Systems (2003), pp. 113–120 (2003)
12. Trost, H., Matiasek, J., Baroni, M.: The Language Component of the FASTY Text Prediction System. Applied Artificial Intelligence 19(8), 743–781 (2005)
13. van den Bosch, A.: Effects of Context and Recency in Scaled Word Completion. Computational Linguistics in the Netherlands Journal 1, 79–94 (2011)
14. Wandmacher, T., Antoine, J.-Y., Poirier, F., Departe, J.-P.: SIBYLLE, an Assistive Commu-nication System Adapting to the Context and its User. ACM Transactions on Accessible Computing 1(1), Article 6, p. 6.1-6.30 (2008)
15. Ward, D., Blackwell, A., Mckay, D.: Dasher: A Data Entry Interface Using Continuous Gestures and Language Models. In: Proceedings of the 13th Annual ACM Symposium on User Interface Software and Technology, UIST 2002, San Diego, CA, pp. 129-137 (2000)

Tackling the Acceptability of Freely Optimized Keyboard Layout

Bruno Merlin[1], Mathieu Raynal[2], and Heleno Fülber[1]

[1] Universidade Federal do Pará, FACE, Cametá, Brazil
{brunomerlin,fulber}@ufpa.br
[2] Institut de recherche en Informatique de Toulouse, Toulouse, France
raynal@irit.fr

Abstract. Reorganization of a keyboard layout based on linguistic characteristics would be an efficient way to improve text input speed. However, a new character layout imposes a learning period that often discourages users. The Quasi-QWERTY Keyboard aimed at easing a new layout acceptance by limiting the changes. But this strategy prejudices the long term performance. Instead, we propose a solution based on the multilayer interface paradigm. The Multilayer Keyboard enables to progressively converge through a freely optimized layout. It transform the learning period into a transition period. During this transition period, user's performance never regresses and progressively improves.

Keywords: Input text, multilayer interface, layout, soft keyboard.

1 Introduction

Several experiments demonstrated the lack of efficiency of the mini-QWERTY soft keyboard [3], [9], [12], [16] and suggested solutions improving significantly the performances at long term. But, as assistive technology for text entry, the mini-QWERTY remains the standard soft-keyboard deployed on exploration systems. These innovations fail to reach a large population of the assistive technology users.

Based on the same observation, several researches [1], [9] concluded on the relativity of the concept of performances: in a non-controlled context, reaching performances at long term implicates that users use the software at long term and do not abandoned it during the learning period. Thus, to be efficient, a keyboard should not only enable to reach good performances in the long term but it should satisfy users in the short term and encourage them to adopt the new artifact.

Among the solutions traditionally explored, the reorganization of keyboard layout as a function of linguistic characteristics should be a very efficient way to improve the performances of soft keyboard in the long term [3], [12], [16]. The reorganization of the layout reduces the distance between frequently paired characters and then the global distance covered by the pointing device during the input. As a consequence of the overall distance reduction, the reorganization should provide a time gain and

K. Miesenberger et al. (Eds.): ICCHP 2012, Part II, LNCS 7383, pp. 459–466, 2012.
© Springer-Verlag Berlin Heidelberg 2012

reduce the fatigue induced by the keyboard usage. However, a new layout disorients a user well accustomed to a previous one. The user is turned back into a beginner and the majority of them is reluctant to make the effort to learn the new layout.

In order to reduce this problem, Bi [1] proposed a compromise between obtaining performances at long term and maintaining the user's references during initial use: the quasi-QWERTY keyboard. The quasi-QWERTY keyboard optimizes the layout toward linguistic properties but allows only permutations of neighboring characters are allowed. Thus, because the characters remain located in the same closed space, this new keyboard eases the character visual search for a mini-QWERTY user. During the first usages, Bi demonstrates better performances than performances obtained with a layout freely reorganized, whereas the user still remains less efficient with the quasi-QWERTY than with the mini-QWERTY.

We are convicted that this strategy of smoothing the transition between the QWERTY layout to another layout is promising, we propose and studied the concept of Multilayer Keyboard. Inspired by the concept of multilayer interface used to smooth the transition between two versions of a system [7], the multilayer keyboard enables to progressively improve the layout by proceeding casual permutations converging through an optimal freely reorganized layout.

In a first section, we will detail the related work referring to the layout reorganization and the concept of multilayer interface. Then, in a second section, we detail the idea of Multilayer Keyboard. Section 3, we present a first evaluation of the keyboard investigating how users react to the casual permutations. Finally, we will discuss the constraints and perspectives for the Multilayer Keyboard.

2   Related Works

2.1   Keyboard Reorganization

The reorganization of the keyboard layout improves input speed from a motor aspect toward the Fitts' law [3]. Fitts showed that a movement cannot be both precise and fast. The reorganizations of keyboard layout are based on linguistic properties and consist in bringing together the characters frequently paired in a language. Consequently, it reduces the distance between the pointing, turns them easier, and then speeds up the input.

Several techniques were proposed to elaborate the new layouts. Fitaly [15] and OPTI [6] proposed empirical optimizations based on keyboard and language observations. Metropolis [16] used an algorithm based on thermodynamic laws, and GAG [12] used a genetic algorithm to automatically create optimal layouts toward language benchmarks. The evaluation of those solutions shows that they should be able to improve the input speed by about 40% in comparison with the QWERTY and to reduce the distance covered by the pointing device in the same proportions.

But, these new layouts need a learning period to reach performances equivalent to the performances reached with the standard QWERTY soft keyboard [6] (for a user well accustomed to input text with it). This learning period frequently discourages the use of the new layouts.

2.2   Multilayer Interface

The concept of multi-layer interface [13], [2], [5] was initially proposed to promote a universal access to software. It enables heterogeneous users with different skills (beginner, casual user, expert, etc.) and goals (amatory or professional objectives for instance) to use the same application efficiently. The interface is divided in gradual layers progressively increasing their complexity. For each layer, the number of accessible functionalities, their parameters and the ways to interact with the interface are adapted to a typical user expertise level and goal.

Merlin & al. [7], [8] revisited the concept of interface multilayer and exploited it to ease the transition between two versions of an interactive system (particularly when this evolution of the software is confronted to the user's reluctance). They applied it to ease the evolution of working methods in the air traffic control field. This time, a homogeneous population of air traffic controllers was supposed to adopt a new tool and to adapt their working method toward new collaboration paradigms. To smooth the transition and turn it easier to accept, the new software was divided in several layers: several steps between the former and the future system. The first layer reproduced the original working method. The other layers accompany the users in the transition toward new ones. Every layer brings attractive new functionalities encouraging the user to adopt it.

This strategy enabled to ease the acceptation of the new software because the more reluctant users could at least maintain their former working method. So, they easily accepted the first layer and then had the possibility to discover progressively the new layers. Motivated by the new features provided by the other layers, they quickly adopted them.

3   Multilayer Keyboard

3.1   Concept

The Multilayer Keyboard is based on this concept of multilayer interface. The principal goals of the keyboard are:

- Maintaining the users complete efficiency with the keyboard during the whole time (no learning period must be needed);
- Making the keyboard and the users evolving progressively during a transition period;
- Stimulating the user to require the further evolutions.

Specifically, the concept implementation is based on the following observation. With a physical keyboard and some experience, a user can easily perform text input without looking at the keyboard. So, the permutation of two characters gets an important impact on the input. However, to input text with a soft keyboard a visual retro-control is needed. Thus, switching only two neighbored keys should not have a deep impact on text input.

Based on the same observation, Bi [1] proposed the Quasi-QWERTY Keyboard. To obtain the final keyboard, he performed one round with several simultaneous permutations. As a consequence, the resulting keyboard layout:

- Does not enable to reach the performances obtained with a keyboard layout freely reorganized;
- The cost for a beginner is lower than the cost with a layout freely organized, but it remains significant due to the multiplication of the permutations performed simultaneously.

With the Multilayer Keyboard, we proposed to perform the permutations one by one and spaced in the time. The permutations enable to progressively improve the performances by reducing the distances between the characters frequently enchained in the language. When a user has completely absorbed the consequences of one permutation, the next one is performed. Thus, the user must learn one permutation at a time that should not have a significant impact on the character search. Moreover, permutation after permutation, we can progressively reach the configuration of a freely organized layout and then beneficing of optimal performances.

The transition period between the initial layout (QWERTY) and the final layout may be long. However, during this period, the user is supposed to:

- Have a permanent domination of the current layout;
- To have no regression of his performance;
- And to progressively see improvement through the distance reduction consequences of the permutations.

Finally, the expectation is that the user perceives the progressive gain and begins to be involved in the evolution process by soliciting himself the further permutations.

3.2   Implementation

There is not a unique and absolute implementation of the Multilayer Keyboard. Many different optimized layouts can be reached by many different permutations sequences.

In a first time, our aim was not to discuss the best layout and the best permutation sequence but to evaluate quickly the concept of multilayer, and then to verify if users would accept the sequential permutations spaced in the time better than several simultaneous permutations. We proposed a sequence of 30 permutations elaborated as a function of the following strategies: at every step we perform the permutation that provides the best gain in speed toward the upper-bound[1] calculus [14]. The sequence[2]

---

[1] It consists in calculating the maximal input speed by considering only the mechanical time required for the input. The upper-bound sums the pointing time between every key K1-K2 pondered by the frequency of the digraph K1K2 in the language considered. The pointing time is calculated by the Fitts law [2].

[2] (A;S) (A;D) (A;F) (D;F) (S;F) (Y;U) (Y;I) (Y;O) (Y;P) (O;K) (J;O) (K;P) (H;O) (G;O) (B;N) (B;M) (A;O) (V;N) (V;M) (A;N) (Q;W) (J;L) (I;H) (H;P) (G;I) (U;P) (T;P) (R;P) (G;L) (H;G) (H;B) (Z;X) (N;I) (I;A) (C;I) (K;J).

obtained enables to reach theoretically a maximal text entry speed from 27wpm (words per minute [4]) at the beginning, to 38wpm after the 30 permutation for Portuguese language (language used during the experimentation).

4   Evaluation

We performed a first evaluation of the multilayer keyboard. It aimed at testing if the users were able to assimilate the permutations without prejudicing their performance, if they were understanding the benefit of the permutations, and if they began to take part of the mutation process by soliciting further permutations.

4.1   Participants

We recruited 6 volunteer participants (4 men and 2 women) ranged in age from 19 to 34. The learning and acceptance problematics do not tackle specifically motor impaired users, consequently we recruited valid users for this first experimentation because of an easier access to them.

4.2   Apparatus

The experiment has been performed with the EAssist-II platform [11], [12] accessed through a web browser. The Multilayer keyboard has been designed in KeySpec [12]: XML language provided by the platform.

We created manually a phrase set to be entered [10]. The phrase set contains 30 phrases in the user's native language (Portuguese). The sentences respect the character and bigram frequencies of the language with a high level of correlation (96% for the character frequency and 90% for the bigram).

4.3   Design

The users were involved in 80 sessions at a rhythm of 5 sessions per day. During every session, each user had to copy 10 short sentences. The sentences were the same during every session. The session duration was about 8 minutes at the beginning of the experimentation. The time per session decreased during the experimentation according to the user's performances growth.

The sentences to copy and the input text were presented in two strips. The input errors were not displayed, but the users had to input the correct character and the input strip did not changed until that. The user was warned that an error occurred by a visual and a sonorous feedback.

The 10 first sessions were performed with the QWERTY keyboard in order to enable the user to reach an expert level with the QWERTY keyboard and to learn the sentences. For the 11th session, a first permutation has been performed. 30 successive permutations were planned. During the further sessions, the user chose when to perform the next permutations. They were not forced to do it.

The 10 sessions training period enabled to stabilize the user's performances with the QWERTY keyboard. As a consequence, after the 10th session the performance raise or decline should be related to the permutation effects.

4.4   Results

We analyzed individually and statistically the results. The individual results were presented as illustrated figure 1: the red curve shows the input speed evolution, the blue one shows the errors rate evolution (**with values multiplied by 4** on the graphics to improve the graphics readability), the green bars identify the sessions when a permutation where performed, the gray and white bars identify the day alternations.

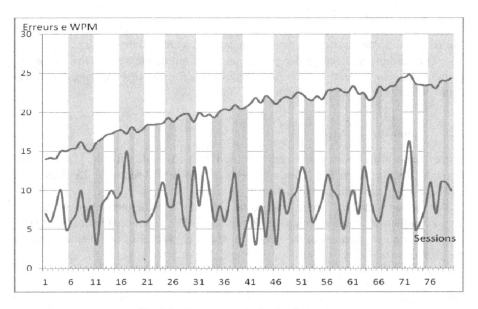

Fig. 1. Individual results for the first user

The error analysis did not highlight any significant information. The error rate remained unchanged during the 10 first sessions (with the QWERTY keyboard) and during the next 70 sessions.

During the 80 sessions, every user performed the 30 planned permutations. As forecasted, between the 10th (beginning of the permutations) and the 80th session, they increased their input speed by 40% without the feeling to loose their complete domination of the keyboard at any time. No regression of the performances was noticed. The major criticism of the system was that, some time, the users would have performed the permutations in a different order. It proved their implication in the process and the perception of the permutation interest.

5   Discussion and Conclusion

The quasi-QWERTY Keyboard [1] and the Multilayer Keyboard reintroduced the interest for optimized layouts. However, they do not only target the performances improvement. The quasi-QWERTY keyboard mainly focuses the problematic on acceptability at short term and sacrifices long term performance. The Multilayer Keyboard conciliates the both aspects enabling to reach an optimized layout preserving the user's performances during the transition process.

The evaluations performed on the Multilayer Keyboard were done in a context favorable for the keyboard: a relative intensive usage (between 30 and 20 minutes per day at the end of the experimentation). To be significant for a large population using cell phone with touch screen, they should be completed by other experiences where the keyboard would have to compete with the QWERTY keyboard during a long period. Nevertheless, they showed that the multilayer keyboard enables to break the QWERTY paradigm and to raise the enthusiasm for other layouts.

Moreover, the usage explored during the experimentation fits with the usage of soft keyboard as assistive technology (usage by motor impaired users for instance). Indeed, these users daily work with soft keyboards and then the transition period should be shortened for them.

To conclude, if we are able to demonstrate that users are able to assimilate one permutation every 6 months, by performing one permutation every 6 months simultaneously on every soft keyboard, the whole population would improve its performances by 40% after 10 years without a real cost for anyone.

References

1. Bi, X., Smith, B.A., Zhai, S.: Quasi-qwerty soft keyboard optimization. In: Proceedings of CHI 2010, pp. 283–286. ACM, New York (2010)
2. Clark, B., Matthews, J.: Deciding Layers: Adaptive Composition of Layers in a Multi-Layer User Interface. In: Proceedings of 11th International Conference on Human-Computer Interaction, vol. 7 (July 2005)
3. Fitts, P.M.: The information capacity of the human motor system in controlling the amplitude of movement. Journal of Experimental Psychology (1954)
4. Gentner, D.R., Grudin, J.T., Larochelle, S., Norman, D.A., Rumelhart, D.E.: A glossary of terms including classification of typing errors. In: Cooper, W.E. (ed.) Cognitive Aspects of Skilled Typewriting, pp. 39–43. Springer, New York (1983)
5. Kang, H., Plaisant, C., Shneiderman, B.: New approaches to help users get started with visual interfaces: multi-layered interfaces and integrated initial guidance. In: Proceedings of the 2003 Annual National Conference on Digital Government Research, Boston, MA, May 18-21, pp. 1–6 (2003)
6. MacKenzie, I.S., Zhang, S.Z.: The design and evaluation of a high performance soft keyboard. In: Proc. CHI 1999, pp. 25–31. ACM Press (1999)
7. Merlin, B., Benhacène, R., Kapp, V.: Interface multi-layer et processus d'évolution des systèmes interactifs en activité critique. In: Proceedings of the 19th International Conference of the Association Francophone d'Interaction Homme-Machine (IHM 2007), pp. 191–198. ACM, New York (2007)

8. Merlin, B., Hurter, C., Benhacène, R.: A solution to interface evolution issues: the multi-layer interface. In: Proceedings of CHI 2008 (2008)
9. Merlin, B., Raynal, M.: Soft Keyboard evaluations: Integrating user's background in predictive models. In: IADIS IHCI, Freiburg, Germany, July 28 - 30 (2010)
10. Merlin, B., Raynal, M.: Evaluation of SpreadKey System with Motor Impaired Users. In: Miesenberger, K., Klaus, J., Zagler, W., Karshmer, A. (eds.) ICCHP 2010. LNCS, vol. 6180, pp. 112–119. Springer, Heidelberg (2010)
11. Merlin, B.: Méthodologie et instrumentalisation pour la conception et l'évaluation des claviers logiciels. Phd Thesis (2011)
12. Merlin, B., Raynal, M., Fülber, H.: E-Assist II: a platform to design and evaluate soft-keyboards. In: CHI 2012, Workshop Designing and Evaluating Text Entry Methods Austin. Extended Proceedings of Conference on Human Factors in Computing Systems. ACM Press, New York (2012)
13. Raynal, M., Vigouroux, N.: Genetic algorithm to generate optimized soft keyboard. In: Proc. CHI EA, pp. 1729-1732. ACM Press (2005)
14. Shneiderman, B.: Promoting universal usability with multi-layer interface design. In: Proceedings of the 2003 Conference on Universal Usability, Vancouver, Canada, November 10-11, pp. 1–8 (2003)
15. Soukoreff, R.W., MacKenzie, I.S.: Theoretical upper and lower bounds on typing speeds using a stylus and soft keyboard. Behaviour & Information Technology 14, 370–379 (1995)
16. http://www.fitaly.com/fitaly/fitaly.htm
17. Zhai, S., Hunter, M., Smith, B.A.: The metropolis keyboard - an exploration of quantitative techniques for virtual keyboard design. In: Proc. UIST 2000, pp. 119–128 (2000)

Measuring Performance of a Predictive Keyboard Operated by Humming

Ondřej Poláček, Adam J. Sporka, and Zdeněk Míkovec

Faculty of Electrical Engineering, Czech Technical University in Prague, Karlovo nam. 13, 12135 Prague 2, Czech Republic
{polacond,sporkaa,xmikovec}@fel.cvut.cz

Abstract. A number of text entry methods use a predictive completion based on letter-level n-gram model. In this paper, we investigate on an optimal length of n-grams stored in such model for a predictive keyboard operated by humming. In order to find the length, we analyze six different corpora, from which a model is built by counting number of primitive operations needed to enter a text. Based on these operations, we provide a formula for estimation of words per minute (WPM) rate. The model and the analysis results are verified in an experiment with three experienced users of the keyboard.

Keywords: Text Entry Methods, N-Gram Model, Measuring Performance, Non-Verbal Vocal Interaction.

1 Introduction

Many virtual keyboards, which has been designed for users with severe motor impairments, employ a text completion technique. They suggest possible continuations of an already written text (further referred to as context). The continuations are extracted from a language model and sorted according to their probability in the context. After entering a completion, the virtual keyboard offers a different set of completions with respect to the updated text. The question arises what is the optimal size of the language model in terms of efficiency of the text entry.

In our previous work, we described a novel text entry method called Humsher [1]. The method is operated by non-verbal vocal interaction (NVVI) [2]. The NVVI can be described as an interaction modality in which sounds other than speech are produced, for example humming [3] or vowels [4]. The Humsher utilizes an adaptive language model for text prediction and is based on selecting letters or longer completions from a list sorted by the probability of their occurrence in the text being entered. We measured the performance of the Humsher in a user study with 17 participants. We explored four interface designs which differed in the organization of the suggestions list (layout, size, etc.) and the navigation in it. We also performed an evaluation of the method

K. Miesenberger et al. (Eds.): ICCHP 2012, Part II, LNCS 7383, pp. 467–474, 2012.

with people with motor and speech disability, and found Humsher suitable for them.

2   Related Work

There is a wide range of text entry methods targeting the motor-impaired users, however, several common principles of text entry can be identified in the literature – predictive completion, scanning, and ambiguous keyboards. These principles are often combined to gain a better performance. A text entry method can be accelerated by prediction when a list of possible completions is updated with each entered letter or word. This reduces the number of keystrokes per character. The letters or words already entered are very often used to improve the prediction accuracy. An example of this is a predictive system called Dasher [5] which is based on a continuously updated display and an adaptive letter-level language model. In ambiguous keyboards, the alphabet is divided into several groups of characters. Each group is then assigned to one of the keys. The user enters the desired characters by selecting corresponding keys and is requested to perform a dictionary-assisted disambiguation. The ambiguous keyboards were designed for physically impaired people [6]. Scanning keyboards are often used when the number of distinct signals, which can be issued by the user, is limited to only one or two. Scanning is often combined with ambiguous keyboards [7].

The non-verbal vocal interaction (NVVI) has also been used for keyboard emulation. Sporka et al. [3] describe a humming-based method of keyboard emulation. Each vocal gesture is assigned a specific key on the keyboard. When a sound is produced a corresponding key is emulated. Another keyboard operated by humming is CHANTI [8] which is based on scanning ambiguous keyboard QANTI [7] but the scanning is replaced by direct selection of a key by the humming. The humming input and the PPM language model [9] is combined in Humsher [1]. Both CHANTI and Humsher were evaluated with motor-impaired users.

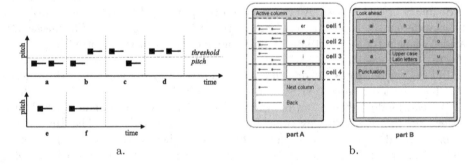

a.   b.

Fig. 1. a. Vocal gestures used for interaction. b. Humsher interface. Part A – active column, part B – look ahead matrix.

3   Overview of the Humsher

Our virtual keyboard Humsher utilizes an n-gram language model on letter level based on prediction by partial matching (PPM) algorithm [9]. An n-gram is a sequence of n characters. The n-grams with length equal to one, two, and three character are being called unigrams, bigrams, and trigrams respectively. The language model contains n-grams together with their probabilities. The *order of the model* further refers to the longest n-gram contained in the language model. The model is initialized from a small text corpus, but it adapts as the user types. Possible completions extracted from the language model are offered to the user sorted according to their probability. The probability is predetermined by the context of given length. For kth-order language model the maximal length of the context is equal to k-1. It stands for a reason that the order of the model has an effect on efficiency of both the model and the method itself. For example, the first-order model stores unigrams therefore only static probability of letters can be used for prediction. In case of second-order model, the model stores probabilities of bigrams and one letter context can be used to improve the prediction.

Once the language model is initialized, the keyboard starts offering possible completions sorted according to their probability. The completions can be both letters and strings. After entering a completion, the context is updated and probabilities of following completions are recounted and the layout is displayed accordingly. The length of a completion is not limited, only probability matters. The completions to display are chosen according to the following steps:

1. Add all unigrams to the list L that will be displayed.
2. For each n-gram in the list L compute probability of all $(n+1)$-grams using the language model and add them to the list L if their probability is higher than a threshold.
3. Repeat step 2 until no n-gram can be added.
4. Sort the list L according to probability of each n-gram.

The original paper on the Humsher [1] discusses and evaluates four different keyboard interfaces. For our experiment, we chose the Direct interface as it was the fastest one relatively well accepted by the users. The keyboard interface utilizes six vocal gestures as depicted in Fig. 1a. The vocal gestures are explicitly identified by its length (short/long) or by its pitch (low/high). In order to distinguish low and high tones a threshold pitch needs to be adjusted for each user - e.g. the difference between male and female voice is as much as one or two octaves. The keyboard (see Fig. 1b) allows users to directly choose from four cells (labeled cell 1 to 4) in the Active column (part A). These cells contain strings that have been determined as the most probable following letters of the context. Cells can be directly selected by vocal gestures depicted in Fig. 1a (gesture a: two consequent low tones - cell 1, b: a low tone followed by a high tone - cell 2, c: a high tone followed by a low tone - cell 3, d: two consequent high tones - cell 4). If there is no cell in the Active column that contains the desired letter, the user has to move the leftmost column in the Look ahead (part B) to the Active column by producing a single short tone (see Fig. 1b, gesture e), and keep repeating it until the desired n-gram appears in one of the cells in Active column. The written text can be erased by producing a long tone (see Fig. 1b, gesture f). The longer the user keeps producing the tone the faster are the letters erased.

4 Analysis

The main aim of the analysis was to explore how the order of the language model affects efficiency of the Humsher. The other question was how the ideal length of the n-grams differed for various text corpora and languages. We used four publicly available text corpora and three languages:

1. *Dasher.* The corpus is available as a training text for the Dasher[1]. Corpora for various languages is provided – we used English, German and Czech.
2. *AacText.* A crowdsourced corpus of augmentative and alternative communication (AAC) collected by Vertanen and Kristensson [10].
3. *EnronMobile.* A subset of sentences written by Enron employees on Black-Berry mobile devices published by Vertanen and Kristensson [11].
4. *SmsCorpus.* This public research corpus contains SMS messages collected by National University of Singapore[2].

All text corpora were split to training and test data sets. The training data set was used to train the language model and the test data set was used for text entry simulation. Detailed information about corpora is shown in the Table 1.

We used the *gestures per character* (GPC) measure [12] to express a performance of the text entry method. As a gesture is regarded as an atomic operation, and in our case (the humming input) vocal gestures are treated as atomic operations. The GPC rate is defined by the Eq. 1 where CM is a number of column movements that corresponds to finding the desired column by linear scanning, DS is a number of direct selections that corresponds to selection of desired cell by one of four vocal gestures, and $|T|$ is a length of the test data set. The sum of CM and DS corresponds to total number of vocal gestures in an input stream.

$$GPC = \frac{CM + DS}{|T|} \tag{1}$$

The GPC rate is a characteristic measure that is similar to *keystrokes per character* (KSPC) measure and can be used for capturing initial performance of a text entry method [13]. The theoretical text entry speed in terms of *words per minute* (WPM) can be estimated from the CM and DS variables according to the Eq. 2. The constants a and b represent an average time needed for the column movement and the direct selection respectively. These constants are measured in an subsequent experiment with users described in the Section 5.

$$WPM = \frac{|T|}{5} \times \frac{60}{aCM + bDS} \tag{2}$$

---

[1] http://www.inference.phy.cam.ac.uk/dasher/Download.html
[2] http://wing.comp.nus.edu.sg:8080/SMSCorpus/history.jsp; version 2011.12.30

We analyzed theoretical GPC for each corpus, while changing the order of the language model (i.e. size of n-grams stored in the model) from 1 to 16. As the user actions were simulated by computer, no human errors were taken into account. The resulting dependence of GPC on the order of the language model is depicted in Fig. 2 The effect is significant for 1st-order to 5th-order model. The difference for higher order models is negligible. Minimal GPC values and corresponding order of the language model are shown in the Table 2. Nevertheless, using 6th-order model is sufficient for each corpus as the difference of 6th-order GPC value and the minimal GPC value is always less than 2%.

Table 1. Minimal theoretical GPC and corresponding order of the language model

Corpus	Training part size	Words	Unique words	Sentences	Test part size
Dasher (English)	289 KB	51 064	8 676	2 568	30 KB
Dasher (German)	884 KB	122 130	21 951	7 051	53 KB
Dasher (Czech)	419 KB	59 179	21 131	6 148	33 KB
AacText	127 KB	25 125	2 206	3 646	14 KB
EnronMobile	97 KB	18 472	3 041	2 050	10 KB
SmsCorpus	2 748 KB	536 029	27 905	81 836	80 KB

Table 2. Minimal theoretical GPC and corresponding order of the language model

Corpus	Dasher (English)	Dasher (German)	Dasher (Czech)	AacText	EnronMobile	SmsCorpus
Min. GPC	1.23	1.17	1.55	1.11	1.27	1.42
Order	7	11	5	8	6	11

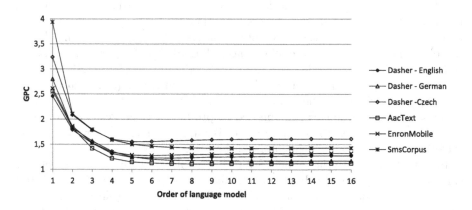

Fig. 2. Dependence of Humsher text input efficiency in terms of GPC on the order of language model

5   Experiment

The aim of the experiment was to validate results from the aforementioned analysis and to find out the *a* and *b* values for the WPM estimation (see Eq. 2). In the experiment 3 able-bodied participants (all men, aged 29–36) took part. They had previous experience with the Humsher as they already participated in an experiment described in [1].

The task in the experiment was to copy two sentences. The independent variables were a corpus and an order of the language model. We used all six corpora and following orders of the language model: 1, 3, 6, and 12. The sentences were unique for each corpus and they were chosen from the test part of each corpora. The experiment was conducted in two trials, in each trial the participant had to copy the two sentences under all conditions (4 orders × 6 corpora = 24 conditions). Each participant had to copy 96 sentences in the experiment (2 trials × 2 sentences × 24 conditions). The experiment took approximately 4 hours per participant. The sequence of corpora the order of the model was randomized for each participant to compensate for learning effects.

Results. Two-factor ANOVA showed a significant interaction between the order and the corpus for GPC ($F(15,264) = 21.3$, $p<.001$) and WPM ($F(15,264) = 6.45$, $p<.001$) values. Therefore, we evaluated the effect of order on both values separately for each corpus. The Table 3 shows significantly different pairs in the GPC and WPM rates denoted by *less than* ($<$) sign. The differences were considered significant on $p<.05$ level.

Two-factor ANOVA for the *a* and *b* values showed no interaction between order and corpus, nor significant main effect for the corpus factor. However, significant main effect for the context was found for both values (*a*: ($F(3,264) = 40.5$, $p<.001$); *b*: ($F(3,264) = 15.2$, $p<.001$)). Subsequent ANOVA and post-hoc pairwise comparisons on the order of the model revealed that both values *a* ($F(3,254) = 33.1$, $p<.001$) and *b* ($F(3,254) = 14.1$, $p<.001$)) are significantly lower for the 1st-order model. The explanation is simple. Using the 1st-order model ($a=1.3s$; $b=1.25s$), the layout of characters is static regardless the already written context. The letter are offered according to their frequency in a corpus. In case of higher-order models ($a=1.58s$; $b=1.56s$), on the other hand, a context is used for prediction and it causes different layout of letters (or *n*-grams) as the user types. Therefore, higher effort is needed to visually locate desired letters, which is reflected in longer time needed to produce a vocal gesture. Note that the difference between the *a* and *b* values is minimal. Therefore, we can merge them into one variable, which simplifies the Eq. 2.

In order to evaluate the model of WPM estimation (see Eq. 2), a correlation calculation was performed between estimated and measured WPM for all test conditions. Correlation coefficients of the WPM rate for the three participants were .91, .88, and .93 respectively. As correlations above .90 are considered very high in experiments with users [14], this result indicates validity of the model for WPM estimation (see Eq. 2). However, the correlation can be even improved

Table 3. Significant differences of the four orders of language model (1,3,6, and 11) in GPC and WPM rates for each corpus

Corpus	GPC	WPM
Dasher (English)	1 < 3,6,12	1 < 3,6,12
Dasher (German)	1 < 3,6,12	1 < 3 < 6,12
Dasher (Czech)	1 < 3,6,12	1 < 3,6,12
AacText	1 < 3 < 6,12	1 < 3 < 6,12
EnronMobile	< 3,6,12	1 < 3 < 6,12
SmsCorpus	1 < 3 < 6,12	1 < 3 < 6,12

by incorporating corrections. The number of correction per character rate was .03, .12, and .10 for each participant respectively. The GPC correlation was even higher (.98, .97, and 0.98) confirming the correctness of the corpora analysis.

6 Conclusion

In this paper we analyzed dependence of gesture per character (GPC) rate on order of language model when using Humsher – a predictive keyboard operated by humming. For the analysis purposes, we used six publicly available text corpora with three languages variants. The analysis results were verified in an experiment with three experienced users. We defined and verified a relation for estimating WPM rate from number of primitive operations. In the experiment, we found that producing vocal gestures was faster when no prediction was used and the layout of characters was statically arranged (1st-order language models). However, the prediction used with higher-order models helps to achieve significantly better GPC and WPM rates. We also found that the 6th-order model is adequate for the optimal performance of the keyboard. It is significantly faster than 1st- and 3rd-order model, but is not significantly faster than the 12th-order model. In some cases the 12th-order model even decreases the performance of typing.

The number of corrections influences the WPM rate. However, this fact is not incorporated in the model for WPM estimation. Therefore, in the future work we would like to focus on improvement of the WPM estimation formula by incorporating the error rate or the number of corrections.

Acknowledgments. This research has been supported by the Veritas project (IST-247765).

References

1. Polacek, O., Mikovec, Z., Sporka, A.J., Slavik, P.: Humsher: A Predictive Keyboard Operated by Humming. In: 13th International ACM SIGACCESS Conference on Computers and Accessibility, ASSETS 2011, pp. 75–82. ACM, New York (2011)

2. Igarashi, T., Hughes, J.F.: Voice as sound: using non-verbal voice input for interactive control. In: 14th Annual ACM Symposium on User Interface Software and Technology, UIST 2001, pp. 155–156. ACM, New York (2001)
3. Sporka, A.J., Kurniawan, S.H., Slavík, P.: Non-speech operated emulation of keyboard. In: Clarkson, J., Langdon, P., Robinson, P. (eds.) Designing Accessible Technology, pp. 145–154. Springer, London (2006)
4. Harada, S., Landay, J.A., Malkin, J., Li, X., Bilmes, J.A.: The Vocal Joystick: Evaluation of voice-based cursor control techniques. In: 8th International ACM SIGACCESS Conference on Computers and Accessibility, ASSETS 2006, pp. 197–204. ACM, New York (2006)
5. Ward, D.J., Blackwell, A.F., MacKay, D.J.C.: Dasher – a data entry interface using continuous gestures and language models. In: 13th ACM Symp. on User Interface Software and Technology, UIST 2000, pp. 129–137. ACM, New York (2000)
6. Kushler, C.: AAC: Using a Reduced Keyboard. Technical report (1998)
7. Felzer, T., MacKenzie, I., Beckerle, P., Rinderknecht, S.: Qanti: A Software Tool for Quick Ambiguous Non-standard Text Input. In: Miesenberger, K., Klaus, J., Zagler, W., Karshmer, A. (eds.) ICCHP 2010. LNCS, vol. 6180, pp. 128–135. Springer, Heidelberg (2010)
8. Sporka, A.J., Felzer, T., Kurniawan, S.H., Polacek, O., Haiduk, P., MacKenzie, I.S.: CHANTI: Predictive Text Entry Using Non-verbal Vocal Input. In: 2011 Annual Conference on Human Factors in Computing Systems, CHI 2011, pp. 2463–2472. ACM, New York (2011)
9. Teahan, W.: Probability estimation for PPM. In: New Zealand Research Students' Conference (1995)
10. Vertanen, K., Kristensson, P.O.: The Imagination of Crowds: Conversational AAC Language Modeling using Crowdsourcing and Large Data Sources. In: Conference on Empirical Methods in Natural Language Processing, EMNLP 2011, pp. 700–711. Association for Computational Linguistics (2011)
11. Vertanen, K., Kristensson, P.O.: A versatile dataset for text entry evaluations based on genuine mobile emails. In: 13th Int. Conf. on Human Computer Interaction with Mobile Devices and Services, MobileHCI 2011, pp. 198–295. ACM, New York (2011)
12. Wobbrock, J.O.: Measures of text entry performance. In: MacKenzie, I.S., Tanaka-Ishii, K. (eds.) Text Entry Systems: Mobility, Accessibility, Universality, pp. 47–74. Morgan Kaufmann (2007)
13. MacKenzie, I.S.: KSPC (Keystrokes per Character) as a Characteristic of Text Entry Techniques. In: Paternó, F. (ed.) Mobile HCI 2002. LNCS, vol. 2411, pp. 195–210. Springer, Heidelberg (2002)
14. MacKenzie, I.S.: Movement time prediction in human-computer interfaces. In: Graphics Interface 1992, Toronto, pp. 140–150. Canadian Information Processing Society (1992)

Dysarthric Speech Recognition Error Correction Using Weighted Finite State Transducers Based on Context–Dependent Pronunciation Variation

Woo Kyeong Seong, Ji Hun Park, and Hong Kook Kim

School of Information and Communications
Gwangju Institute of Science and Technology (GIST)
1 Oryong–dong, Buk–gu, Gwangju 500–712, Korea
{wkseong,jh_park,hongkook}@gist.ac.kr

Abstract. In this paper, we propose a dysarthric speech recognition error correction method based on weighted finite state transducers (WFSTs). First, the proposed method constructs a context–dependent (CD) confusion matrix by aligning a recognized word sequence with the corresponding reference sequence at a phoneme level. However, because the dysarthric speech database is too insufficient to reflect all combinations of context–dependent phonemes, the CD confusion matrix can be underestimated. To mitigate this underestimation problem, the CD confusion matrix is interpolated with a context–independent (CI) confusion matrix. Finally, WFSTs based on the interpolated CD confusion matrix are built and integrated with a dictionary and language model transducers in order to correct speech recognition errors. The effectiveness of the proposed method is demonstrated by performing speech recognition using the proposed error correction method incorporated with the CD confusion matrix. It is shown from the speech recognition experiment that the average word error rate (WER) of a speech recognition system employing the proposed error correction method with the CD confusion matrix is relatively reduced by 13.68% and 5.93%, compared to those of the baseline speech recognition system and the error correction method with the CI confusion matrix, respectively.

Keywords: context–dependent pronunciation variation modeling, dysarthric speech recognition, weighted finite state transducers, error correction.

1 Introduction

Dysarthria is comprised of a family of motor speech disorders that arise due to the damage to the central or peripheral nervous system, and it is characterized by poor articulation [1]. Individuals with speech–motor disorders also have physical disabilities caused by neuromotor impairment [2]. Thus, it may be a significant challenge for them to use typical text entry interfaces, including a keyboard, a mouse, and so on [3]. As an alternative, an automatic speech recognition (ASR) system can be a very useful and practical text entry interface for dysarthric speakers so that they can interact with machines such as computers and mobile devices [4].

K. Miesenberger et al. (Eds.): ICCHP 2012, Part II, LNCS 7383, pp. 475–482, 2012.
© Springer-Verlag Berlin Heidelberg 2012

Unfortunately, ASR performance for dysarthric speech degrades dramatically due to the particular characteristics of dysarthric speech, e.g., the distortion, insertion, and deletion of phonemes [5]–[7]. Some research works on error correction approaches have investigated to improve ASR performance for dysarthric speech [8]–[10]. For example, Hosem et al. proposed a user–interactive dysarthric ASR error correction method [8]. The proposed method in [8] initially provided the n–best words. After that, users chose another candidate word among the n–best word list if the most probable word was not matched with their spoken word. In contrast to [8], Rudzicz incorporated the articulatory data into an ASR error correction method in order to choose the most probable word systematically [9]. In other words, the n–best words were rearranged in accordance with the likelihoods derived from the models that were trained by relating the acoustic data to the articulatory data. While these methods were based on the assumption that a corrected word should be one of candidates in an n–best word list, they caused unsatisfactory performance of an error correction system due to an erroneous n–best list. On the other hand, Morales et al. built an error correction system that refined incorrectly recognized words by using the whole word lists included in a dictionary [10]. In particular, an error in an ASR system was corrected to the most probable word among all possible words by employing weighted finite state transducers (WFSTs) with pronunciation variation models. However, erroneous corrections in ASR results still existed because the pronunciation variations were assumed to be independent for each phoneme, regardless of its context. Thus, to reflect the fact that phoneme pronunciations have different variations in different contexts, it is necessary to utilize context–dependent (CD) pronunciation variation modeling.

In this paper, we propose a dysarthric speech recognition error correction method using WFSTs based on CD pronunciation variations. To this end, two different confusion matrices are constructed according to the CD and context–independent (CI) pronunciation variations. The CD confusion matrix is then combined with the CI confusion matrix to mitigate an underestimation problem that arises from the insufficiency of the dysarthric speech database. Finally, a CD confusion matrix transducer is transformed from the interpolated CD confusion matrix and is integrated with a dictionary and language model transducers in order to construct a WFST–based error correction system.

2   Baseline ASR System

This section describes how to construct the baseline ASR system. As a training database for the ASR system, the British English database WSJCAM0 [11] was used, which was composed of 10,000 sentences spoken by 92 non–dysarthric speakers. In addition, the ASR system was adapted and evaluated by using the Nemours database [12] composed of ten sets of 74 nonsense sentences, which corresponded to 740 sentences in total. Each set was spoken by ten different dysarthric speakers with different

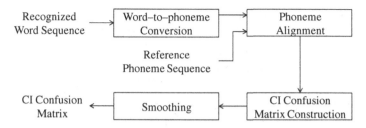

Fig. 1. Block diagram of the conventional pronunciation variation modeling method

degree of dysarthria. In particular, 34 sentences out of the 74 sentences in each set were used to adapt the baseline ASR system for dysarthric speech and to construct pronunciation variation models. The remaining 40 sentences from each set were utilized to evaluate the ASR system with the proposed error correction method.

As a feature vector used to construct the baseline ASR system, 12 mel–frequency cepstral coefficients (MFCCs) were extracted with a logarithmic energy and they were concatenated with their first and second derivatives by using the ETSI standard distributed speech recognition (DSR) front–end [13]. The cepstral mean normalization and energy normalization were then applied to the feature vectors. In addition, the acoustic models were 45 monophones represented by 3–state left–to–right hidden Markov models (HMMs) with a mixture of 8 Gaussians using diagonal covariance matrices, which were trained by using the WSJCAM0 database. The acoustic models were then adapted for each dysarthric speaker with a maximum likelihood linear regression (MLLR) method [14]. As a result, ten sets of acoustic models adapted depending on different dysarthric speakers were obtained. Consequently, the average word error rate (WER) of the baseline ASR system was reduced from 52.87% to 39.42% through the speaker dependent adaptation.

3   Proposed Context–Dependent Pronunciation Variation Modeling

In this section, we propose a CD pronunciation variation modeling method and describe how much the proposed method is different from the conventional method. Fig. 1 shows a block diagram of the conventional pronunciation variation modeling method proposed in [10]. As shown in the figure, a CI confusion matrix is first constructed by aligning the word sequence recognized from the baseline ASR system with the corresponding reference sequence at the phonemic level. The constructed CI confusion matrix is then interpolated with the value estimated from the pre–defined rules [10]. However, erroneous corrections in ASR results still exist because the pronunciation variations are assumed to be independent for each phoneme, regardless of its context. Thus, to reflect the fact that phoneme pronunciations have different variations according to the contexts, it is necessary to handle context–dependent (CD) pronunciation variation.

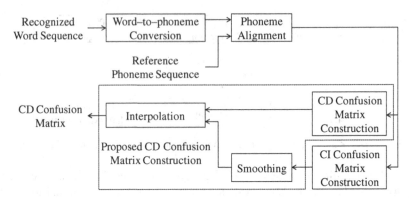

Fig. 2. Block diagram of the proposed CD pronunciation variation modeling method by interpolating the CD confusion matrix with the CI confusion matrix

Fig. 2 shows a block diagram of the proposed CD pronunciation variation modeling method. As shown in the figure, the word sequence recognized from the baseline ASR system is initially aligned with the reference sequence obtained by manual transcription at the phonemic level. From the phoneme alignment results, CI and CD confusion matrices are obtained. In other words, the CI confusion matrix is built from the pronunciation variation probability, $Pr_{CI}(P'_C|P_C)$, which represents the probability that phoneme $/P_C/$ is recognized as $/P'_C/$ and is computed context–independently. On the other hand, the CD confusion matrix is constructed by using the pronunciation variation probability estimated in a context–dependent manner, $Pr_{CD}(P'_C|P_L - P_C + P_R)$, where $/P_L/$ and $/P_R/$ as its left and right contexts of $/P_C/$.

In general, because the speech database could not cover all phonemes, there are some unseen elements in the confusion matrices, resulting in erroneous corrections. Thus, both of the CI and CD confusion matrices should be interpolated to mitigate the problem caused by unseen elements. First, in order to estimate the unseen elements in the CI confusion matrix, the overall average probability of correctness, p, for each dysarthric speaker is assigned to the unseen diagonal elements, while the rest of the probability, $(1 - p)$, is uniformly distributed along the non–diagonal elements. For the CD confusion matrix, we can simply apply the same interpolation algorithm as for the CI confusion matrix. However, this approach results in very noisy elements because the CD confusion matrix is extremely underestimated as compared to the CI confusion matrix. Thus, the interpolated CI confusion matrix is used to estimate the unseen elements and the smooth noisy seen elements of the CD confusion matrix as follows:

$$Pr'_{CD}(P'_C|P_L - P_C + P_R) = \lambda Pr_{CD}(P'_C|P_L - P_C + P_R) + (1 - \lambda)Pr_{CI}(P'_C|P_C) \quad (1)$$

where $Pr'_{CD}(P'_C|P_L - P_C + P_R)$ represents the interpolated CD pronunciation variation probability by interpolating the CI pronunciation variation probability with the CD pronunciation variation probability. In addition, λ indicates an interpolation factor and is set to 0.3 by the exhaustive search.

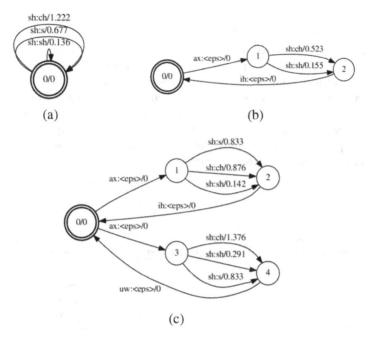

Fig. 3. Examples of (a) the CI confusion matrix transducer, (b) the underestimated CD confusion matrix transducer, and (c) the CD confusion matrix transducer interpolating (a) with (b) for the phoneme /sh/

In order to apply to a WFST–based error correction system, further described in Section 4, the CD confusion matrix should be transformed into the corresponding transducer. Fig. 3 illustrates an example of a part of the CD confusion matrix transducer resulted by the interpolation of an underestimated CD confusion matrix and a CI confusion matrix. As shown in Fig. 3(a), the CI confusion matrix transducer models the pronunciation variations of a phoneme, /sh/, regardless of its contexts. The underestimated CD confusion matrix transducer in Fig. 3(b) models the CD pronunciation variation of a phoneme, /sh/, with /ax/ and /ih/ as its left and right contexts, which can compensate for the defect of the CI confusion matrix transducer. However, due to the insufficiency of the data, it has a number of unseen CD pronunciation variations by noise–likely models. In contrast with the underestimated CD confusion matrix transducer, the interpolated CD confusion matrix transducer in Fig. 3(c) estimates the unseen CD pronunciation variations, which cannot be modeled in the CD confusion matrix transducer as shown in Fig. 3(b), i.e., the pronunciation variations of a phoneme /sh/ with /ax/ and /uw/ as its left and right contexts.

4   WFST–Based Error Correction System

Fig. 4 shows a block diagram of a WFST–based error correction system incorporated with the proposed CD pronunciation variation model. As illustrated in the figure, errors in the recognition results obtained from the baseline ASR system can be corrected by employing the composition of WFSTs. In other words, the recognized word sequence is first transformed to the corresponding phoneme sequence transducer by using the British English BEEP pronouncing dictionary [15]. The phoneme sequence transducer is then composed with the CD confusion matrix transducer. The composed transducer is additionally integrated with a dictionary and language model transducers, which allows the mapping of phonemes to words being matched to pronunciations in the dictionary transducer but restricts the words to the language model. Finally, the most probable word sequence that has the lowest weight in the entire integrated transducer is selected as a corrected word sequence.

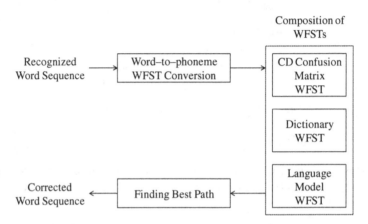

Fig. 4. Block diagram of a WFST–based error correction system incorporated with the proposed CD pronunciation variation models

5   Performance Evaluation

In order to evaluate the performance of the proposed method, we constructed the baseline ASR system described in Section 2 and two WFST–based error correction systems: an error correction system with CI pronunciation variations [10] and another with the proposed CD pronunciation variations. To construct these two error correction systems, CI and CD pronunciation variations were first modeled by using 34 sentences from each of the ten dysarthric speakers that were used for the adaptation of the baseline ASR system described in Section 2. From the pronunciation variations models, all transducers, such as the confusion matrix, dictionary, and language model transducers, were constructed and composed by employing the finite state machine (FSM) library [16].

For testing, 40 sentences from each of the ten dysarthric speakers, which were different from the 34 sentences used in modeling pronunciation variations, were used. Table 1 shows the average word error rates (WERs) of the different error correction systems. For simplicity, the WFST–based error correction systems with the CI pronunciation variation model and with the proposed CD pronunciation variation model were denoted as WFST–CI and WFST–CD, respectively. As shown in the table, WFST–CD provided the lowest WER. Specifically, WFST–CD achieved a relative average word error rate (WER) reduction of 13.68% and 5.93%, as compared to the WERs of a baseline ASR system and WFST–CI, respectively. Therefore, it could be concluded here that the proposed CD pronunciation variation model provided a more effective reflection of the pronunciation variations for dysarthric speech than the conventional CI pronunciation variation model.

Table 1. Comparison of average word error rates (%) of the baseline ASR system (Baseline), WFST–based error correction systems using CI pronunciation variations (WFST–CI) and proposed CD pronunciation variations (WFST–CD)

System	Baseline	WFST–CI	WFST–CD
Word error rate (%)	39.42	36.17	34.03

6   Conclusion

In this paper, we proposed a dysarthric speech recognition error correction system using WFSTs incorporated with CD pronunciation variation models to improve the performance of a dysarthric ASR system. The proposed method constructed a CD confusion matrix by interpolating with an underestimated CD confusion matrix to mitigate the underestimation problem due to the insufficiency of the database. The WFST–based error correction system was then built by employing the constructed CD confusion matrix. Subsequently, the performance of the proposed method was evaluated in terms of the ASR performance and compared with that of the error correction with the CI pronunciation variation model. It was shown from the ASR experiment that the proposed error correction system with the CD pronunciation variation model achieved relative WER reductions of 13.68% and 5.93%, compared with the baseline ASR system and the conventional error correction system with the CI pronunciation variation model, respectively.

Acknowledgments. This work was supported by the R&D Program of MKE/KEIT [10036461, Development of an embedded key–word spotting speech recognition system individually customized for disabled persons with dysarthria].

References

1. Haines, D.: Neuroanatomy: an Atlas of Structures, Sections, and Systems. Lippingcott Williams and Wilkins, Hagerstown (2004)
2. Hasegawa–Johnson, M., Gunderson, J., Perlman, A., Huang, T.: HMM–based and SVM–based recognition of the speech of talkers with spastic dysarthria. In: Proceedings of IEEE International Conference on Acoustic, Speech, and Signal Processing (ICASSP), Toulouse, France, pp. 1060–1063 (2006)

3. Rudzicz, F.: Towards a noisy–channel model of dysarthria in speech recognition. In: Proceedings of the NAACL HLT 2010 Workshop on Speech and Language Processing for Assistive Technologies (SLPAT), Los Angeles, CA, pp. 80–88 (2010)
4. Poock, G.K., Lee Jr., W.C., Blackstone, S.W.: Dysarthric speech input to expert systems, electronic mail, and daily job activities. In: Proceedings of the American Voice Input/Output Society Conference, Alexandria, VA, pp. 33–43 (1987)
5. Kotler, A.L., Tam, C.: Effectiveness of using discrete utterance speech recognition software. Augmentative and Alternative Communication 18(3), 137–146 (2002)
6. Rosen, K., Yampolsky, S.: Automatic speech recognition and a review of its functioning with dysarthric speech. Augmentative and Alternative Communication 16(1), 48–60 (2000)
7. Polur, P.D., Miller, G.E.: Effect of high–frequency spectral components in computer recognition of dysarthric speech based on a Mel–cepstral stochastic model. Journal of Rehabilitation Research and Development 42(3), 363–371 (2005)
8. Hosem, J.P., Jakobs, T., Baker, A., Fager, S.: Automatic speech recognition for assistive writing in speech supplemented word prediction. In: The 11th Annual Conference of the International Speech Communication Association, Makuhari, Japan, pp. 2674–2677 (2010)
9. Rudzicz, F.: Correcting error in speech recognition with articulatory dynamics. In: The 48th Annual Meeting of the Association for Computational Linguistics, Uppsala, Sweden, pp. 60–68 (2010)
10. Morales, S.O.C., Cox, S.J.: Modeling errors in automatic speech recognition for dysarthric speakers. EURASIP Journal on Advances in Signal Processing, Article ID 308340, 14 pages (2009)
11. Fransen, T.J., Pye, D., Foote, J., Renals, S.: WSJCAM0: a British English speech corpus for large vocabulary continuous speech recognition. In: Proceedings of IEEE International Conference on Acoustic, Speech, and Signal Processing, Detroit, MI, pp. 81–84 (1995)
12. Menendez–Pidal, X., Polikoff, J.B., Peters, S.M., Leonzio, J.E., Bunnell, H.T.: The Nemours database of dysarthric speech. In: Proceedings of International Conference on Spoken Language Processing, Philadelphia, PA, pp. 1962–1965 (1996)
13. ETSI Standard Document ES 201 108.: Speech Processing, Transmission and Quality Aspects (STQ); Distributed Speech Recognition; Front–end Feature Extraction Algorithm; Compression Algorithms (2000)
14. Leggetter, C.J., Woodland, P.C.: Maximum likelihood linear regression for speaker adaptation of continuous density hidden Markov models. Computer Speech and Language 9(2), 171–185 (1995)
15. Robinson, T.: British English Example Pronunciation Dictionary (BEEP). Cambridge University, Cambridge (1997)
16. Mohri, M., Pereira, F., Riley, M.: Weighted finite–state transducers in speech recognition. Computer Speech and Language 16(1), 69–88 (2002)

Text Entry Competency for Students with Learning Disabilities in Grade 5 to 6

Ting-Fang Wu[1] and Ming-Chung Chen[2]

[1] Graduate Institute of Rehabilitation Counseling, National Taiwan Normal University,
162, Sec. 1 Hoping East Rd., Taipei, Taiwan, R.O.C.
tfwu@ntnu.edu.tw
[2] Department of Special Education, National Chiayi University
300, Syuefu Rd., Chiayi, 600 Taiwan, R.O.C.
mtchen@mail.ncyu.edu.tw

Abstract. This study intended to understand the computer text entry skills for students with learning disabilities in grade 5 to 6. 35 students with learning disabilities, who received special education services in resource room at school, and 35 non-disabled students participated in our study. "Mandarin Chinese Character Entry Training system (MCChEn system)" was used to measure the students' text entry skills. SPSS19.0 was used to compare the difference in text entry skills between children with and without learning disabilities. In addition, the correlations between the abilities of recognition in Chinese characters, and text entry skills were also explored. The results indicated that children with learning disabilities perform significantly poorer than children without disabilities in recognizing Chinese characters orally and in computer text entry skills. Chinese characters recognition is an important factor affecting Chinese Character entry skills in children with learning disabilities. The tool, "Mandarin Chinese Character Entry Training system (MCChEn system)", we utilized is able to discriminate the computer text entry skills between children with and without learning disabilities. The results of this study can provide educators important information about text entry skills of children with learning disabilities, in order to develop further training programs.

Keywords: text entry competency, learning disabilities.

1 Introduction

With the blending of information communication technology (ICT) into our daily life, so came the wide exploration of ICT in education (e.g. [1-3]). Due to the impact of ICT on learning, both developed and developing countries enact educational technology policies to integrate ICT in educational environment [4]. Taiwanese government is no different; Taiwan has invested lots of effort in creating a high quality e-learning environment for students by attempting to place a computer in each classroom that is Internet accessible and connected to an interactive whiteboard. Use of technology also can support students with disabilities to learn in regular school environment.

K. Miesenberger et al. (Eds.): ICCHP 2012, Part II, LNCS 7383, pp. 483–489, 2012.

School-aged children with learning disabilities (LD) represent 3%-5% of students [5]. LD are a group of disorders that affect the ability to acquire or use listening, speaking, concentrating, reading, writing, reasoning or math skills [5]. Previous research has support that use technology can support students with LD reading and writing [6-7]. For example, the students with reading difficulties could comprehend the content of the e-text books when the computer read aloud for them [8-9], or provide cognitive supports [10]. Therefore, learning with ICT is essential for the students with LD.

Text entry competency is a basic skill for ICT, selecting an input method is an important issue for typists who use Chinese [11]. Different from the spelling system, Chinese typists usually need to learn a specific method to type Chinese characters in computers. These methods can be grouped into two categories, one is phonetic-coding input and the other is pattern-coding input. For typists using phonetic-coding input methods, they need to press Tzu-Yin or Han-Yu phonetic symbols on the keyboards, and the computer will display the homonyms. When using pattern-coding input methods, typists decode Chinese character into several basic character patterns, such as the Chang-Jay or Da-Yi pattern coding, and the computer will display a corresponding Chinese character. In this study, we select Tzu-Yin phonetic spelling input method because all the primary students in Taiwan have to learn Tzu-Yin phonetic symbols in Grade 1. When use this method to type Chinese in computer, users have to type Tzu-Yin phonetic symbol codes, and assemble several phonetic symbol codes, then the computer will show the Chinese characters.

The purposes of this study were to compare the computer text entry skills based on Tzu-Yin phonetic input method between students with and without LD. The specific research questions were

1. Is there any difference between students with and without LD in the abilities of recognition in Chinese characters?
2. Is there any difference between students with and without LD in the abilities of typing Tzu-Yin phonetic symbols?
3. Is there any difference between students with and without LD in the abilities of typing Chinese characters based on Tzu-Yin phonetic input method?
4. Is there correlation between the abilities of recognition in Chinese characters, text entry skills in students with and without LD?
5. What is the possible predictor of typing Chinese characters in students with LD?

2   Methods

2.1   Participants

35 students (22 males and 13 females) with LD and 35 students without LD (22 males and 13 females) from 5th grade to 6th grade participated in this study with their parental consents. All the participants were recruited from elementary schools in Taipei Metropolitan area. They all were placed in the regular class. None of them was

reported in neurological deficits, intellectual delay or physical impairments. Students with LD were identified by the local education agent in Taiwan, and receive special education services in resource room.

2.2   Instrument

A self-developed system "Mandarin Chinese Character Entry Training system" was used to measure the students' computer text entry skills. In this study, two text entry tests were administrated. The first test was "Phonetic symbols typing test". Participants were asked to match the Tzu-Yin phonetic symbols on the Chinese keyboard when the screen showed it. 10 Phonetic symbols were selected to test. Figure 1 show the screen of the "Phonetic symbols typing test".

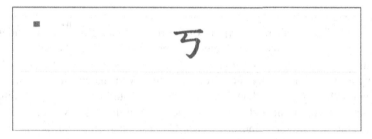

Fig. 1. The screen display of the "Phonetic symbols typing test"

The second test was "Chinese character typing test". Participants were asked to type the Chinese characters by assembling Tzu-Yin phonetic symbols. 80 Chinese characters were used to test. Figure 2 show the screen of the "Chinese character typing test".

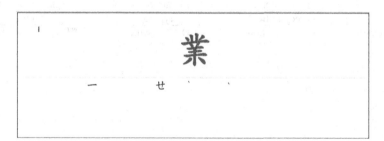

Fig. 2. The screen display of the "Chinese character typing test"

2.3   Procedure

All the participants were tested in a quiet room individually. In addition to the above two typing tests, participants were asked to pronounce the 80 Chinese characters, same as 'Chinese character typing test", orally to make sure they recognize those characters before the typing tests. Follow by the Chinese recognition test, the phonetic symbols typing test and Chinese character typing test were administered. The accuracy rate of Chinese recognition, and two typing tests were calculated.

2.4   Data Analysis

An independent samples *t*-test was used to explore if the abilities of recognition in Chinese characters, typing Tzu-Yin phonetic symbols and typing Chinese character were statistically different between children with and without LD. Pearson correlation procedures were used to determine the relationships between recognition in Chinese characters, typing Tzu-Yin phonetic symbols and typing Chinese character. Multiple stepwise linear regression analysis was performed to characterize the relationship of typing Chinese characters with related variables. A p-value < 0.05 was considered as statistically significant.

3   Results

Table 1 indicated the accuracy rate of Chinese characters recognition, phonetic symbol typing and Chinese character typing of the participants. Most of the students are able to recognize the Chinese character and pronounce those characters orally no matter with or without LD. The high accuracy rate was also found in the phonetic symbol typing test, which only measured the abilities to match the symbol codes in the keyboard. Most of the students with LD demonstrated difficulties in typing Chinese characters which indicated lower accuracy rate in this test. We can find participant might able to recognize and pronounce Chinese characters, but not able to type them correctly, especially for students with LD. Typing Chinese characters may need more skills than just recognizing those characters

Table 1. The accuracy rate of Chinese characters recognition, phonetic symbol typing and Chinese character typing

Accuracy	Chinese characters recognition		Phonetic symbol typing		Chinese character typing	
	LD	without LD	LD	without LD	LD	without LD
0-60%	1	0	1	1	9	1
61-80%	0	0	1	2	4	5
81-90%	0	0	8	5	11	16
91-99%	20	8	0	0	11	13
100%	14	27	25	27	0	0

When converted the accuracy rate into scores in those tests, table 2 showed the scores of three tests between students with and without LD. There were no significant difference found between students with and without LD in Chinese characters recognition test and Phonetic symbol typing test. The only significant difference was found in Chinese character typing test. Students with LD performed poorer than those without LD. Students with LD can pronounce those characters and able to match the phonetic symbol on the keyboard, but are not able to assemble phonetic symbol codes into Chinese characters.

Table 2. The scores of Chinese characters recognition, phonetic symbol typing and Chinese character typing

Variables	LD	without LD	p
Chinese characters recognition	97.25(±1.79)	99.57(±1.00)	0.034[*]
Phonetic symbol typing	94.29(±17.20)	96.29(±8.43)	0.379
Chinese character typing	73.97(±24.21)	85.89(±9.11)	<.001[**]

*P<0.05   **P<.001

Correlation analysis showed that the score of recognition in Chinese characters was no correlated with the scores of phonetic symbol typing test and Chinese character typing test in children without LD (table 3). However, for children with LD, the score of recognition in Chinese characters was significantly correlated with the scores of Chinese character typing test (r=0.48). In addition, the result of regression analysis (table 4) indicated that Chinese characters recognition is an important factor affecting of Chinese character typing in children with LD.

Table 3. Results of the correlation between Chinese characters recognition and Chinese character typing in children with and without learning disabilities

	Phonetic symbol typing		Chinese character typing	
	LD	without LD	LD	without LD
Chinese characters Recognition	0.24	-0.13	0.48[**]	-0.19
Phonetic symbol typing			0.24	0.19

Table 4. Results of the regression analysis, focused on Chinese characters recognition and Chinese character typing in children with learning disabilities

Dependent Value	Independent Value	B	95%CI Lower	95% CI Upper	Adjusted R^2	p
Chinese character typing	Constant	-142.76	-238.84	-46.69		
	Chinese characters recognition	2.23	1.24	3.21	0.37	<.001

4   Discussion

The results indicated that students with LD perform significantly poorer in typing Chinese characters than those without LD. Although the students with LD had no difficulty in matching the Tzu-Yin phonetic symbols on the Chinese keyboard, but typing the Chinese characters by assembling Tzu-Yin phonetic symbols is difficult for students with LD. In addition, the results indicated that ability of recognition in Chinese characters was correlated with the ability of typing Chinese character in students with LD.

Based on past research, no significant difference in the opportunities to access computers at home or school was found for children with and without LD [13]. The difficulties in typing Chinese character for children with LD should not due to the lack of access opportunities. The possible reasons may root from that the children with LD had difficulty in phonetic awareness [14]. In our study, we asked the children to type Chinese character by using Tzu-Yin phonetic input method, which is most popular Chinese input method in Taiwan. However, children with LD may have difficult in using it.

In further study, we might explore the possibility in using pattern-coding input method for children with LD. The results of this study can provide educators important information about text entry competency of children with LD, in order to develop further training programs. The tool, "Chinese input training system", that we utilized are able to discriminate the text entry competency between students with and without LD.

Acknowledgments. The authors would like to thank the National Science Council of the Republic of China for financially supporting this research under Contract No. NSC98-2511-S-003-MY3.

References

1. de Jong, T., Specht, M., Koper, R.: A study of contextualised mobile information delivery for language learning. Educational Technology & Society 13(3), 110–125 (2010)
2. Huang, C.J., Liu, M.C., Chang, K.E., Sung, Y.T., Huang, T.H., Chen, C.H., Shen, H.Y., Huang, K.L., Liao, J.-J., Hu, K.-W., Luo, Y.-C., Chang, T.-Y.: A learning assistance tool for enhancing ICT literacy of elementary school students. Educational Technology & Society 13(3), 126–138 (2010)
3. Tosun, N., Baris, M.F.: Using information and communication technologies in school improvement. The Turkish Online Journal of Educational Technology 10(1), 223–231 (2011)
4. European Commission ICT research.: The policy perspective, e-government and e-participation, http://ec.europa.eu/information_society/eeurope/i2010/docs/digital_literacy/digital_literacy_review.pdf
5. Hallahan, D.P., Lloyd, J.W., Kauffman, J.M., Weiss, M.P., Martinez, E.A.: Learning disabilities: Foundations, characteristics, and effective teaching. Allan & Bacon, Boston (2004)
6. Berkeley, S., Lindstrom, J.H.: Technology for the struggling reader: Free and easily accessible resources. Teaching Exceptional Children 43(4), 48–55 (2011)
7. MacArthur, C.A.: Reflections on research on writing and technology for struggling writers. Learning Disabilities Research & Practice 24(2), 93–103 (2009)
8. Raskind, M.H., Higgins, E.L.: The effects of speech synthesis on proofreading efficiency of postsecondary students with learning disabilities. Learning Disabilities Quarterly 18, 141–158 (1995)

9. Wetzel, K.: Speech-recognizing computers: A written-communication tool for students with learning disabilities? Journal of Learning Disabilities 29(4), 371–380 (1996)
10. Ko, C.C., Chiang, C.H., Lin, Y.L., Chen, M.C.: An individualized e-reading system developed based on multi-representations approach. Educational Technology & Society 14(4), 88–98 (2011)
11. Chen, M.C.: The study of teaching individuals with mental retardation to learn Da-Yi input method. Bulletin of Special Education 19, 195–214 (2000)
12. Joel, K., Alit, E., Michal, Z., Nira, G., Tamar, I.: An assistive computerized learning environment for distance learning students with learning disabilities. Open Learning 21(1), 19–32 (2006)
13. Wu, T.F., Wang, H.P., Chang, C.H.S., Chen, M.C.: Digital divide goes beyond access to technology: A survey of children with learning disabilities in grade 3 to grade 9 in Taiwan. Oral presents at Asia-Pacific Conference on Technology Enhanced Learning, Xi'an, China (2011)
14. Catts, H.W., Gillispie, M., Leonard, L.B., Kail, R.V., Miller, C.A.: The role of speed of processing, rapid naming, and phonological awareness in reading achievement. Journal of Learning Disabilities 6, 509–524 (2002)

Vision SenS

Berenice Machuca Bautista, José Alfredo Padilla Medina,
and Francisco Javier Sánchez Marín

CIO. Centro de Investigaciones en Óptica,
A.C. Loma del Bosque #115. Col. Lomas del Campestre C.P. 37150
yanber55@hotmail.com

Abstract. The electronic prototype for vision developed in this paper intends to show that it is possible to build an inexpensive and functional device which serves to partly compensate the sense of sight for visually impaired individuals through sensory substitution, by replacing some functions the sense of sight with functions of the sense of touch, with the proposed prototype, blind users receive electrical signals in the tips of their fingers generated from the capture of images objects with a camera and processed on a laptop to extract visual information.

Keywords. Blind people, touch image, perceive objects, camera for touch, visionsens, sense of sight.

1   Introduction

VisiónSenS is an electronic prototype for vision. VisionSenS helps blind people to interact with their environment. The base of the investigation came from the question "Do you need eyes to see?" We know that the eyes work with electrical signals, displaying these signals became our objective. Through sensory substitution, we can replace the sense of sight with the   sense of touch and we can send electrical signals to the brain; through the hand. Our principal objective is developing a product with high technology and, with the sense of touch, blind people can see objects at distance more quickly than Braille system.

2   Antecedents

The beginning of the Twentieth Century began with the design of prototypes for blind people, based on sensory substitution. In 1920, in England, Fournier d'Albe designed a reading machine for the blind called "Optophone" [Otlet, 1996].

During the decade of the 60's, Dr. Paul Bach y Rita [2] began working in the sensory substitution developing different devices that converted visual signals in tactile stimulation, "I see with the brain and not with the eyes" [3] was the basis of his work, that brain plasticity is such that no matter the source of the electrical impulses received if they represent a properly coded image.

K. Miesenberger et al. (Eds.): ICCHP 2012, Part II, LNCS 7383, pp. 490–496, 2012.
© Springer-Verlag Berlin Heidelberg 2012

In 1966 LinVill-Bliss [4] developed a photo-cells system.

In 1970 [5] created a mechanic stimulation system, under the direction of Carter C. Collins and Smith Kettlewell.

In 1971 Starkiewicz, Kuprianowics and Petruczenko [6] presented a tactile image on the front of the person. In the same year Smith-Kettlewell [7] developed a portable electrical stimulator.

In 1998, Bach y Rita, Kaczmarek KA, Tyler ME and García-Lara J, developed a perception form, to be used as a stimulator in 49 points of the tongue [8]. The percentage of recognition of language to these stimuli was at least of 79.8% [9].

In the beginning of the XXI century, was developed a "Forehead Electro-tactile display for vision substitution" system [10].

In 2004 the Dr. Bach and Rita made a study of tactile sensors leveraging plasticity of the brain, for this test he used a TV camera, accelerometer for people with vestibular lost and a microphone [11]. Two years after Dr. Bach y Rita and Danilov YP, Tyler ME y Skinner KL, observed that patients with lateral vestibular lost experimented a lot of problems with the balance. Vestibular dysfunction of central or peripheral origin may significantly affect the balance, posture and walking, so it conduces to a study on the effectiveness of electrotactil vestibular substitution in patients with bilateral vestibular loss and central balance. The study used the device "Brainport balance" that transmits information via the electro-tactile stimulation of the guidance, and should provide the vestibular system on its position.

They tested the effectiveness of training using this device with 40 people, 18 of which showed positive effects that remained even after they stop using the prototype.

In recent years research to provide visual information to blind people, using the skin as receiver of visual information, have continued to advance. Here are some prototypes of interest.

Development of a wearable prosthesis for the blind. [12]. This prototype is formed with a stereo camera to perceive depth in the image. Vibratory mechanisms are put in the back of the person; the software used can generate a range of disparity maps at a speed close to one frame per second. The sensor is formed by 64 DC motors in a 8x8 matrix using pulses with modulation and a microcontroller that communicates to the computer via serial port. Its great disadvantage is that the components are very expensive.

A Navigation Aid for the Blind Using Tactile-Visual Sensory Substitution [13] Is a compact apparatus with different sensor modalities which produces the perception of distant objects in the users. The prototype sensor was designed to be settled on the abdomen or any other flat region of the body. It consists of two web cams, a laptop, 14 servo motors and a control plate with 14 vibrating motors that are located in a plastic tube. The control board is placed in a box and kept in a backpack with a laptop which processes the visual information.

The objective of using this prototype is that the user can walk without problems, detecting in real time the location of objects with the vibrations produced by the device.

Vision system for providing the blind with 3D color perception of the environment. [14].This prototype is a visual sensory substitution system that captures the profile of objects in three dimensions and the surrounding colors just with the sensations of a touch. The device allows the user to detect obstacles and recognize places of interest in color and shape. Communication with the person is via electro-neuronal pulses applied on the fingers, where the distance of the pulses is directly proportional to the distance in the region corresponding a depth map.

The frequency of the pulses is determined by the predominant color in the region. In the process for converting the first image; tactile information is taken with a video camera where depth information is obtained and is sent to a laptop where take place some calculations whose results are transformed into electrical pulses that can be captured through the skin.

Forehead Electro-tactile Display for Vision Substitution [10]. The frequency of the pulses is determined by the predominant color in the region. The process to convert the first image tactile information, starts with a video camera where depth information is obtained, which is sent to a laptop where take place some calculations whose results are transformed into electrical pulses that can be captured through the skin.

3   Justification

The sense of the sight is the most important sense to obtain information from the environment around us, the lack of this sense markedly affects the quality of life of people with this condition.

In Mexico, there have been few scientific and technological developments that support people with disabilities, specially blind people. It is expected that the prototype designed and constructed (the matter of this paper) got improved and built just to contribute to improve the quality of life for blind and, at the same time, encourage the scientists and technicians to develop such applications.

The electronic prototype has the following features:

- Detection of objects at a distance.
- Stimulation of the sense of touch is performed by electrical currents that can be regulated by the user.
- Feeding the information of the environment to the computer is done via USB port, giving it the flexibility and speed of that port.
- It's portable.
- It's a non expensive device.

4   Development

The electronic prototype for vision shows that it is possible to build an affordable and functional device, which serves to compensate part of visual impairment, of individuals who are blind, through sensory substitution replacing some functions of the sense of sight with the sense of touch. The proposed prototype sends electrical signals to the tips in the fingers of a blind user, generated from the capture of images of objects with a camera and further, processing the visual information to electric currents. Images are captured by a video camera and processed on a laptop computer to extract useful visual information. The camera of this prototype is connected to the laptop through a USB port interface in such a way that the information extracted from the image is processed, by a microcontroller, to be perceived by the person by stimulating array that generates enough current to tingle, so that the brain can interpret the information, originally visual, by the sense of touch.

4.1   Electrical Stimulator Matrix

The electrical stimulator matrix was built with different materials, we used safety pins (iron wire), nails (stainless steel) and conventional pins (copper material) see Fig.1.

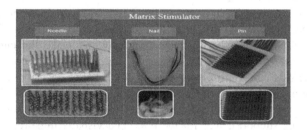

Fig. 1. Electrical Stimulation Matrix with different materials

The operation of the stimulator array is similar to driving a LED array. To display the information sent in the first tests we used an array of LEDs. The information is transferred from the first column which turns on the rows that have more information and, after a few microseconds, turns off to put the information in the second column and so on, to cover the entire array. It is therefore necessary, that the shift in the columns gets fast, less than the decay time of the first led in the first column. This stimulation is show in Fig. 2.

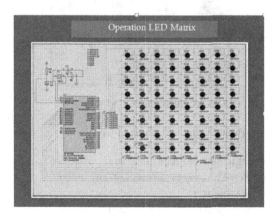

Fig. 2. Simulation of the array of leds

5   Results and Discussions

The first array consists of two pixels each, consisting of two terminals, one terminal from the circuit (Vcc) and the other is the ground so that our skin, in contact with the two terminals, acts as a resistor with values in the order of millions of Ohms. The electrical resistance of the skin depends on each individual variable and in the moisture. As mentioned to make contact with the skin, a circuit with two terminals is closed and the current begins to flow through it, where the skin was stimulated with a resistance of 2.2 M Ω by which flows a current of 2.27 µA with an input voltage of 5V. As the skin is a continuous matter there would be an intermediate resistance every two pixels (R1), but the current passing between the pixels is very small (0.01nA) so it can be considered 0.

The resistance of the skin in a person involves many variables and may even depend on their feeling's sensitivity, humidity, diseases, etc. There must be a pressure, also, to make good contact between the terminals and make the current flowing, which could become annoying to the user, so it was determined to use a current regulator so that the user can control by it himself. It included a security system to isolate the power to prevent the harm of the skin or other parts of the body. The electronic prototype tests were performed with the help of two young blind persons from Cydevi Institute (Learning support center for the blind and visually impaired) in the City of Leon. One of the assistants was born blind and the other, a woman, was visually impaired (she perceives light and shadows).

As in any new system, this device is unfamiliar to the user and demands previous training, and the tingling sensation to feel the intensity becomes normal and comfortable as shown in Fig. 3.

Fig. 3. Sensitivity test of the material

The conditions under which they were tested were:

- Distance to the object to see and feel in meters.
- Artificial lighting (lamps).
- Current, controlled by the user.
- Objects to be observed (point, line and square).

The tests consisted in detecting a point, a line and a square in different parts of the array. The cover locates your position, the difference between the figures and get familiar with the material.

6   Conclusions and Future Outlook

The human eye processes at least 16 frames per second in order to perceive a single image, but also sees a flicker between them [Martinez Sierra. 2000], compared with the prototype vision that sends 2.52 frames per second. It covers only 15.75% of the human eye, taking in account that the image is reduced to 16 x 16 pixels (feature that increases the processing time). It would increase 84.25% the processing speed to meet the minimum speed of operation of the eye.

The user intended to try the device elsewhere in the body in order to observe the reaction, not only in the hand but also on the forehead, which offers a flat surface where the stimulator can be placed. The user discarded the idea to use the hand on the forehead because it was more uncomfortable. Once the person got familiar to the device, he was stimulated with an array of 4 x 2 pixels to feel the tingling and choose the intensity of their preference, as shown in Fig. 4.

Fig. 4. Proof of current

After adjusting the intensity there was another test in which the user placed the hand on a matrix of 8 x 2 pixels, this case was presented the tingling in different places in a line of two pixels in length.

The test was conducted with two people, who distinguished the figure of a line and its position in the array.

The following test was with a square that was turned in two positions, left and right in the matrix, it took longer to distinguish the shape of the square but the difference between a line and a square was felt obtaining a result of 100% in all the tests. The next phase of the test, was the implementation of the 16 x 16-pin matrix with a design of a star, because by this time the users were accustomed to the tickling sensation. The electronic prototype proposed had a wide acceptance among the blind and visually impaired who have tried it. It is the purpose to obtain a better resolution, in order to increase the processing speed and make the recognition software independent of Matlab, which seems to be a serious problem. These points are the goals that you, developers, have for future works. So far as this paper demonstrates that the material used met the goals settled for initial stimulation, and could be affordable to many people, even considering the socioeconomic level of these populations.

References

1. Paul, O.: El tratado de documentación, Ediciones Mundaneum Palais Mondial, Bruselas, 1st edn. (1996)
2. Bach-y-Rita, P.: Mecanismos Cerebrales de la sustitución sensorial, 1st edn., Ed. Trillas. México DF (1979)
3. Bach-y-Rita, P., Tyler, M.E., Kaczmarek, K.A.: Seeing with the Brain. International Journal on Human-Computer Interaction. Special Edition on Mediated Reality, 285–296 (2003)
4. William, S., Emerson, F.: Tactual perception: a sourcebook, 1ª Edición. Cambridge University Press, Cambridge (1982)
5. Collins, C.C., O'Meara, D., Scott, A.B.: Muscle tension during unrestrained humane eye movements, New York (1974)
6. Bach-y-Rita, P.: Tactile sensory substitution studies. Annals of New York Academic Sciences 1013, 83–91 (2004)
7. Ruperto, P.L.: Revista sobre ceguera y deficiencia visual. Redacción C/Prado, 24-2. Publicación No. 6. Madrid (1990)
8. Bach-y-Rita, P., Kaczmarek, K.A., Tyler, M.E., García-Lara, J.: Form perception with a 49-point electrotactile stimulus array on the tongue. J. of Reab. Research and Dvelop. 35, 430–472 (1998)
9. Bach-y-Rita, P., Tyler, M.E.: Tongue man-machine interface. Medicine Meets Virtual Reality, Amsterdam (2000)
10. Hiroyuki, K.: Forehead Electro-tactile Display for Vision Substitution, Tachi Laboratory, The University of Tokyo, Tokio (2008)
11. Danilov, Y.P., Tyler, M.E., Skinner, K.L., Bach-y-Rita, P.: Efficacy of electrotactile vestibular substitution in patients with bilateral vestibular and central balance loss. In: EMBS Meeting, New York, vol. 17, pp. 119–130 (2006)
12. Gonda, M.: Tactile Vision - Development of a Wearable Prosthesis for the Blind. In: ACRA 2000, Monash University, Melbourne (2000)
13. Johnson, L.A., Higgins, C.M.: A Navigation Aid for the Blind Using Tactile-Visual Sensory Substitution. The University of Arizona (2006)
14. Simon, M., Koren, W.: A visión system for providing the blind people with 3D color perception of the environment, School of IT and Computer Science, University of Wollongong, Wollongong (2004)
15. Bach-y-Rita, P., Tyler, M.E., Kaczmarek, K.A.: Seeing with the Brain. International Journal on Human-Computer Interaction. Special Edition on Mediated Reality, 285–296 (2003)

Computer-Aided Design of Tactile Models
Taxonomy and Case Studies

Andreas Reichinger[1], Moritz Neumüller, Florian Rist,
Stefan Maierhofer[1], and Werner Purgathofer[1]

[1] VRVis Forschungs-GmbH, Donau-City-Str. 1, 1220 Wien, Austria
reichinger@vrvis.at

Abstract. Computer-aided tools offer great potential for the design and production of tactile models. While many publications focus on the design of essentially two-dimensional media like raised line drawings or the reproduction of three-dimensional objects, we intend to broaden this view by introducing a taxonomy that classifies the full range of conversion possibilities based on dimensionality. We present an overview of current methods, discuss specific advantages and difficulties, identify suitable programs and algorithms and discuss personal experiences from case studies performed in cooperation with two museums.

Keywords: accessibility, design for all, blind people, visually impaired people, tactile graphics, tactile models, CAD, CAM, 3D scanning.

1 Introduction

Tactile models are an important tool for blind and visually impaired people to perceive images and objects that otherwise are incomprehensible for them. Of course, verbal description or use of residual sight are always favorable, but may often be greatly complemented by the sense of touch. While touching the original objects would be best, this is not always feasible due to inappropriate scale, lack of tangible features or conservatory and safety concerns. For a long time, tactile models have mostly been created manually by skilled people (e.g. [2,5]). Today, the availability of digital scanning and production tools opens possibilities for automation—shifting from a manual to a computer-aided design process. In order to open its full potential for faster, easier and more accurate creation we investigate the optimization of digital workflows (i.e. the conversion and adaption from scanned input to data required by rapid prototyping tools).

To date many publications [8,9,15] deal with the creation of raised line drawings or tactile diagrams from images or the reproduction of 3D objects [14]. In the present work we specifically include cross-dimensional conversions in a common taxonomy embedded in the continuum of spatial dimensions.

2 Continuum of Dimensions

Our taxonomy is based on spatial dimensionality, which has the largest impact on the required workflow. We categorize *objects to be converted* (input) and

K. Miesenberger et al. (Eds.): ICCHP 2012, Part II, LNCS 7383, pp. 497–504, 2012.

generated tactile media (output) based on the dimensionality they can express. The continuum ranges from two-dimensional (2D) objects such as paintings to full three-dimensional (3D) objects like sculptures. In between we can find the limited three-dimensional spaces: 2.5D and 2.1D—a terminology borrowed from visual computing. 2.5D denotes height fields, surfaces that can be represented by a function $z = f(x, y)$, giving every point above a plane a single height value. 2.1D representations pose a further limitation on 2.5D, in that only a correct ordering of depth-layers is imposed, but no actual height values are given.

2.1 2D Objects

The 2D *input* category is formed by paintings, drawings, maps, photographs and so forth. They have in common that they are inherently flat with no elevation that would give meaningful tactile input. The optical channel is the only source of information and has to be interpreted and transformed into adequate tactile sensations. Despite being physically two-dimensional, the depicted content can have higher dimensions encoded in various visual cues that can be decoded by the human brain [1]. For instance, occlusion cues induce a depth-ordering of depicted objects, creating a 2.1D impression. Additional cues like shading, shadows, focus or haze, can lift the content to 2.5D. These circumstances may influence the choice about the optimal output medium for a particular image.

Strictly speaking, there are no 2D tactile *output* media. However, we categorize media like *swell paper* and embossed paper [5] as 2D, because they are mainly limited to display 2D-lines, curves and shapes, although their output is strictly speaking 2.1D. Several companies offer hardware and printing services, making 2D tactile media the easiest and cheapest to produce. However, due to limited expressiveness and resolution, careful design is required [2].

2.2 2.1D Objects

2.1D input objects hardly occur in nature, but are rather a visual phenomenon. Artists, however, often use layering techniques, e.g. in image processing software, in animations or physically as dioramas or paper-on-paper build-up cards.

Build-up techniques using various materials (paper, plastic, fabric) are often used as 2.1D tactile media [5]. To simplify the production, computer-aided tools like vinyl- or laser-cutters can be used to cut the individual layers [11]. Some Braille embossers can also produce 2.1D output by varying embossing strength.

2.3 2.5D Objects

Typical examples are reliefs, embossings on coins, terrain models or building façades. In contrast to full 3D, a 2.5D object only works from a limited set of views. Since only a single height value per position is stored, 3D features like undercuts or backsides cannot be represented. From the technical point of view it has several advantages in acquisition, storage, computation and production.

In fact many 3D scanners generate 2.5D depth images as intermediate results. Stereo photography is also a 2.5D medium, since it captures not only an image but also the depth of a scene. Several algorithms [12] and software (e.g. *Stereo-Scan*, `www.agisoft.ru`) can decode the depth in the image pairs, as long as the depicted objects feature sufficient non-similar texture and have diffuse surfaces.

2.5D reliefs of appropriate size can be very helpful touch tools, adding a perception of depth while being comparably flat and easier to handle than full 3D sculptures. Since no undercuts are possible, reliefs are more robust and easier to mount because of their flat backside. This fact also makes production easier: simple 3-axis CNC-milling machines can be directly used, there is no need for artificial support structures in additive production methods, and thermoform or similar embossing techniques may be used to create low-cost copies.

2.4   3D Objects

All kinds of objects, sculptures, architecture and so on can be acquired in full 3D by a wide range of 3D scanners. Recent low-cost alternatives [10] or photogrammetric multi-view reconstruction algorithms [13] and software (e.g. *123D Catch*, `www.123dapp.com` or *PhotoScan*, `www.agisoft.ru`) open scanning to the general public. The latter require no special hardware but only a number of photos to create a 3D model of a static scene provided the objects are suitably textured.

Production is more complicated than in the 2.5D case. Subtractive methods like milling are possible depending on the complexity of the object, but require more expensive (polyaxial) machines and careful path-planning or splitting into multiple parts. Additive 3D printing methods do not have these restrictions [7]. Many kinds of professional and DIY printers for different material types of various strengths and several printing services are available. However, 3D printers often have limited build size, less durable materials, high costs, long printing times and/or unwanted printing artifacts. For larger, moderately complex models, (semi)manual model building might still be the most efficient way.

3   Conversion Workflows

In this section we discuss the steps necessary to get from the data of an input class to the data required by an output class. Table 1 summarizes the main challenges for each conversion and rates them based on the automation potential.

In general, not changing the dimensionality is technically less demanding, but correction of scanning errors, and increasing the expressiveness and robustness for touch may still be necessary. Similarly, reduction of dimensionality is easier than increasing it. While in the first case information is omitted, recreation of missing information (e.g. depth, . . .) in the second case can get very difficult.

2D output may therefore be generated from all inputs, since rendering a 2D image is always possible using 3D computer graphics. However, in many cases designing 2D tactile media is not trivial, because of their limited expressiveness and often limited resolution. Abstraction of the content is important [5].

Table 1. Challenges and automation potential in conversion workflows

from \ to	2D output	2.1D/2.5D output	3D output
2D input	Abstraction, find semantically important lines.	Needs interpretation of depth and surface.	Needs interpretation of depth, surface and invisible parts.
2.5D input	Like above, but depth may help finding boundaries.	Compress depth.	Needs interpretation of invisible parts.
3D input	Like above. Multiple views possible.	Like above. Multiple views possible.	Directly useable in appropriate scale.
	Automation possible to a large extent.		
	User interaction necessary for abstraction / depth generation.		
	Often difficult. Requires user interaction for content creation ("hallucination" of invisible parts). Exception: multi-view input.		

Although specialized design programs [3,8,9,15] exist, support for abstraction (e.g. tracing semantically important lines, emphasizing essential parts) is rarely available. Higher-dimensional input may help finding important edges in the depth data. From 3D input, generation of multiple 2D views might be beneficial.

Creation of higher dimensional output from 2D input is often desirable (cf. Sect. 2.1), but the missing depth has to be re-created. The computer vision community has proposed algorithms that generate depth based on user input [4,11,17] or directly from extracted depth cues (e.g. [1]), but full automation is still very error prone and limited.

In most cases, creation of full 3D models from lower-dimensional input is very difficult, because backsides and hidden parts are not present in the input and have to be completed or "hallucinated". Only in some cases (e.g. technical drawings, floor plans) and especially when additional knowledge or multiple views are available, the conversion may be easier.

3D-3D conversion is typically straightforward (e.g. [14]); scaling and reinforcing fragile parts may be considered. Scanners are mostly bundled with software (e.g. *Geomagic*) to process scanning data into printable formats. For more complex corrections, digital sculpting programs (e.g. *ZBrush*) can be useful.

2.5D data can be generated from 3D data by rendering the object from a desired view into a depth-buffer [16]. Compression of depth from 2.5D data may be necessary, a technique perfected by relief artists. Several algorithms (e.g. [16]) have been developed that mimic this step and potentially enhance readability.

In general, correction and manipulation of 2.5D data is easier than 3D data. A 2.5D depth map can be exported as a gray-scale image encoding the height at each location and can therefore easily be shared between applications. Such depth maps may be retouched in image editing software. Better alternatives are special relief-editing programs (e.g. *Delcam ArtCAM*), although their set of editing tools is still rather limited. It is also possible to use manipulation techniques of 3D modeling software, a technique we used in some of our case studies

(Sect. 4.2). We created a 3D mesh representation from the height map, manipulated it in the 3D software, and converted it back to the 2.5D representation by orthographic rendering of a depth map.

4   Case Studies

In order to cover the technically most challenging conversion possibilities according to Table 1, and to gain hands-on experience in the different fields, we performed two projects in co-operation with local museums.

Fig. 1. Tactile paintings [11] of Raffael's *Madonna of the Meadow*. From left to right: a) original 2D painting, ©Kunsthistorisches Museum, b) 2.1D layered depth diagram, c) 2.5D textured relief.

4.1   Tactile Paintings (2D-2.1D, 2D-2.5D)

Together with *Kunsthistorisches Museum* (KHM) in Vienna we developed a workflow [11] for converting figural paintings to higher-dimensional output:

2D-2.1D. *Layered depth diagrams* are a layer-by-layer buildup technique (cf. Fig. 1b). We developed a semi-manual design program that quickly allows defining layers on segmented regions and directly outputs data suitable for laser-cutters. After manual assembly a diorama-like image enables visually impaired visitors to quickly get the shape of individual scene elements, and their spatial three-dimensional relation, which is missing in purely two-dimensional media.

2D-2.5D. *Textured reliefs* are an extension of layered depth diagrams (cf. Fig. 1c). We extract texture information from the image and create tactile sensations from it. The design software gives a 3D preview and allows the generation of more complex surfaces. Textured reliefs were produced using milling machines and a subsequent casting process. In addition to layered depth diagrams, blind test persons could also perceive curved surfaces like faces, and painted texture. According to one of the test persons it "opens blind people a new perspective of perceiving images, especially to get a three-dimensional impression".

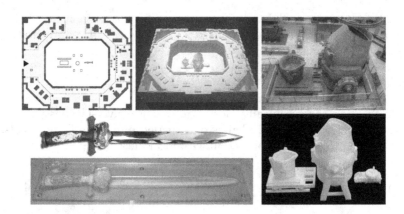

Fig. 2. Top f. l. t. r.: a) exhibition floor plan, b) 1:50 tactile model, c) LD-converter; Bottom f. l. t. r.: d) hunting dagger and its relief, e) 1:50 3D print of LD-converter

4.2   Tactile Exhibits (2D-2.1D, 2D-2.5D, 2D-3D, 3D-2.5D, 3D-3D)

A temporary exhibition at *Technisches Museum* in Vienna was adapted according to a design-for-all philosophy. Besides preparing an audio guide, a tactile guiding system, embossed diagrams (2D-2.1D) and adapting some exhibits for a multi-sensorial experience, we created several kinds of tactile models as detailed below. A preliminary evaluation was performed with 5 visually impaired experts (4 completely blind) by use of structured interviews after a 2 hour guided tour.

2D-2.5D. A stylized 1:50 model ($81 \times 66 \times 17$ cm) of the whole exhibition space including the view to the lower floor in the center of the model was created based on 2D floor plans (Figs. 2a & b). We conceived a tactile language based on simple forms and height that allows easy differentiation of walls (30 mm high), pillars (30 mm, cylindrical), windows (24 mm), exhibits (12 mm polygonal), chairs (9 mm cylindrical) and doors (0 mm), as confirmed by test persons. Since the lower floor is also included in the model, it can even be seen as a simple form of **2D-3D** conversion. Indeed, all test persons reported to have gained a three-dimensional impression of the architecture, and that it was very helpful to get an overview of the exhibition space. The elements were cut from white Hi-Macs boards and hand assembled, resulting in a very durable model.

3D-3D. 1:50 miniatures of large exhibits on the lower floor—which are important in the exhibition context—were included in the 1:50 exhibition model (Figs. 2c & e). We reconstructed each object with photogrammetric methods from a total of 167 photos, taken from all floors all around the objects during normal opening hours. In order to manage the strong brightness contrast, high-dynamic-range imaging was used by fusing 3 bracketed images each and performing local adaptive compression using *HDRsoft's Photomatix*. Photogrammetric reconstruction was performed using *Agisoft's PhotoScan*. *Geomagic* was used to correct large errors and for hole filling of invisible parts, before using the sculpting program *3D Coat* for further corrections, smoothing and feature enhancement. The resulting models (up to 16 cm high) were augmented with support-structures to increase robustness, printed on a *Dimension BST 768* 3D printer with dense filling for stability and manually sanded to remove printing artifacts. The 3D models were highly appreciated by the test persons. Having the same scale as the rest of the exhibition model helped to get a reference of size, but a standalone touch model could be larger to feel even more details.

3D-2.5D. We produced 2.5D reliefs of three different types of knives (Fig. 2d). The original knives are presented in glass cases for conservation reasons. Therefore, we chose to reproduce them in a 1:1 scale, and to mount them on the showcase in front of the actual exhibit. For reasons of stability we created 2.5D reliefs of one side of the knives, corresponding to the visual presentation of the objects on display. Scanning was performed with a *Nikon ModelMaker MMD50* 3D scanner. Although theoretically straightforward, scanning the knives composed from various shiny materials was very difficult, requiring extensive post-processing. This was performed in 2D, 2.5D and 3D programs (cf. Sect. 3) exploiting the advantages of each representation. The final models were milled out of transparent acrylic glass in correspondence to the exhibition design. Test persons understood the limited 2.5D presentation very well, being "the next best alternative to touching the originals". One design element (a dog at the end of a handle) was difficult to understand in its original orientation and was supplemented by a separate upright copy to improve comprehension (Fig. 2d top left).

In general, our test persons pointed out, that verbal description is still most important in order to get the context, background information and guidance while touching. The chosen plastic materials were reported as pleasant to the touch but sterile, which is however necessary in terms of hygiene. Having different materials than the original objects is no problem, since the true material could be imagined from verbal description or by feeling reachable parts of the original objects. Persons with residual sight would benefit from colored models.

5 Conclusions and Future Work

We gave an overview and introduced a new taxonomy for touch tool creation and tested many possibilities in our case studies. General digital tools are already available, making the production of tactile models easier. However, some issues specifically targeted to touch tool design are not covered, such as increasing emphasis on more important parts or automatically making improvements for stability without strongly affecting the content. During our case studies, we started to create some specific tools addressing these issues, but many fields are open for improvement. A further direction of research would be to directly incorporate haptic feedback during the design process using digital force feedback devices, although the usefulness of current devices seems to be limited [6].

504   A. Reichinger et al.

Acknowledgements. Special thanks to Kunsthistorisches Museum (esp. Rotraut Krall), Technisches Museum (esp. Ingrid Prucha), Institute of Arts and Design, Vienna University of Technology (esp. Florian Rist, Raimund Krenmüller, Nora Pucher) and Design for All-Foundation Barcelona.

References

1. Assa, J., Wolf, L.: Diorama Construction from a Single Image. Comput. Graph. Forum 26(3), 599–608 (2007)
2. Axel, E.S., Levent, N.S. (eds.): Art Beyond Sight: A Resource Guide to Art, Creativity, and Visual Impairment. AFB Press (2003)
3. Breider, J.: TactileView (April 2012), http://www.tactileview.com/
4. Criminisi, A., Reid, I., Zisserman, A.: Single View Metrology. Int. J. Comput. Vision 40, 123–148 (2000)
5. Edman, P.K.: Tactile graphics. American Foundation for the Blind (1992)
6. Evans, M., Wallace, D., Cheshire, D., Sener, B.: An evaluation of haptic feedback modelling during industrial design practice. Design Studies 26(5), 487–508 (2005)
7. Gibson, I., Rosen, D.W., Stucker, B.: Additive Manufacturing Technologies: Rapid Prototyping to Direct Digital Manufacturing, 1st edn. Springer, Heidelberg (2009)
8. Hernandez, S.E., Barner, K.E.: Tactile imaging using watershed-based image segmentation. In: Proc. of 4th Int. ACM Conference on Assistive Technologies, Assets 2000, pp. 26–33. ACM, New York (2000)
9. Jayant, C., Renzelmann, M., Wen, D., Krisnandi, S., Ladner, R., Comden, D.: Automated tactile graphics translation: in the field. In: Proc. of 9th Int. ACM SIGACCESS Conf. on Computers and Accessibility, pp. 75–82. ACM, New York (2007)
10. Newcombe, R.A., Davison, A.J., Izadi, S., Kohli, P., Hilliges, O., Shotton, J., Molyneaux, D., Hodges, S., Kim, D., Fitzgibbon, A.: Kinectfusion: Real-time dense surface mapping and tracking. In: 10th IEEE International Symposium on Mixed and Augmented Reality, pp. 127–136 (October 2011)
11. Reichinger, A., Maierhofer, S., Purgathofer, W.: High-Quality Tactile Paintings. J. Comput. Cult. Herit. 4(2), 5:1–5:13 (2011)
12. Scharstein, D., Szeliski, R.: A taxonomy and evaluation of dense two-frame stereo correspondence algorithms. Int. J. Comput. Vision 47(1-3), 7–42 (2002)
13. Seitz, S.M., Curless, B., Diebel, J., Scharstein, D., Szeliski, R.: A comparison and evaluation of multi-view stereo reconstruction algorithms. In: Proceedings of the 2006 IEEE Computer Society Conference on Computer Vision and Pattern Recognition, vol. 1, pp. 519–528. IEEE Computer Society, Washington (2006)
14. Teshima, Y., Matsuoka, A., Fujiyoshi, M., Ikegami, Y., Kaneko, T., Oouchi, S., Watanabe, Y., Yamazawa, K.: Enlarged Skeleton Models of Plankton for Tactile Teaching. In: Miesenberger, K., Klaus, J., Zagler, W., Karshmer, A. (eds.) ICCHP 2010. LNCS, vol. 6180, pp. 523–526. Springer, Heidelberg (2010)
15. Wang, Z., Li, B., Hedgpeth, T., Haven, T.: Instant tactile-audio map: enabling access to digital maps for people with visual impairment. In: Proc. of 11th Int. ACM SIGACCESS Conf. on Computers and Accessibility, pp. 43–50. ACM, New York (2009)
16. Weyrich, T., Deng, J., Barnes, C., Rusinkiewicz, S., Finkelstein, A.: Digital bas-relief from 3D scenes. ACM Trans. Graph. 26 (July 2007)
17. Zhang, L., Samson, J.S., Seitz, S.M.: Single View Modeling of Free-Form Scenes. In: IEEE Conference on Computer Vision and Pattern Recognition, pp. 990–997 (2001)

Three-Dimensional Model Fabricated by Layered Manufacturing for Visually Handicapped Persons to Trace Heart Shape

Kenji Yamazawa[1], Yoshinori Teshima[2], Yasunari Watanabe[2], Yuji Ikegami[1], Mamoru Fujiyoshi[3], Susumu Oouchi[4], and Takeshi Kaneko[4]

[1] Advanced Manufacturing Team, RIKEN Advanced Science Institute, 2-1 Hirosawa, Wako, Saitama 351-0198, Japan
{kyama,yikegami}@riken.jp
[2] Department of Mechanical Science and Engineering, Chiba Institute of Technology, 2-17-1 Tsudanuma, Narashino, Chiba 275-0016, Japan
yoshinori.teshima@it-chiba.ac.jp, wistajp@yahoo.co.jp
[3] National Center for University Entrance Examinations 2-19-23 Komaba, Meguro, Tokyo, 153-8501 Japan
fujiyoshi@rd.dnc.ac.jp
[4] National Institute of Special Needs Education, 5-1-1 Nobi, Yokosuka, Kanagawa 239-8585, Japan
{oouchi,kaneko}@nise.go.jp

Abstract. In this study, we fabricated three-dimensional models of the human heart by stereolithography and powder-layered manufacturing; using these models, visually handicapped persons could trace the shape of a heart by touching. Further, we assessed the level of understanding of the visually handicapped persons about the external structure of the heart and the position of blood vessels. Experimental results suggest that the heart shape models developed in this study by layered manufacturing were useful for teaching anatomy to visually handicapped persons.

Keywords: three-dimensional model, layered manufacturing, visually handicapped persons, heart shape.

1   Introduction

The heart pumps and circulates blood in the human body, and it is an indispensable organ to life support. Understanding the shape of the heart is necessary to fully understand its function and mechanism, especially for visually handicapped persons [1], [2]. However, the shape of the heart is complex. A three-dimensional model of the human heart has been developed. However, it has not been designed for use by visually handicapped persons to trace the heart shape correctly. Moreover, it is difficult to process it to the shape that the user intended.

K. Miesenberger et al. (Eds.): ICCHP 2012, Part II, LNCS 7383, pp. 505–508, 2012.

On the other hand, layered manufacturing techniques have been used for modelling complex shapes from three-dimensional data acquired using a computer. In layered manufacturing, first, cross-section data is obtained from a three-dimensional CAD (computer aided design) data [3]. The material used in layered manufacturing is deposited such that each layer according to the cross-section data; thus, a target three-dimensional shape is automatically generated. This technique is called rapid prototyping, i.e. rapidly developing a prototype of an industrial product with a complex shape.

In this study, we generated three-dimensional models of the human heart by layered manufacturing; using these models, visually handicapped persons could trace the shape of a heart by touching. Further, we assessed the level of understanding of the visually handicapped persons about the external structure of the heart and the position of blood vessels.

2   Experimental Methods

Recently, various layered manufacturing techniques have been developed. We used stereolithography and powder-layered manufacturing to generate three-dimensional models of the heart. The specifications of the models used in the experiment are shown in Table 1, and Figure 1-2 show the outer shape of a model. The thickness of each layer in the models was 0.1 mm. The three-dimensional data of the heart was obtained using a CAD system (CoCreate Solid Designer).

10 visually handicapped persons (totally blind, 8 boys and 2 girls), current and former students of a school for the blind in Japan, were chosen as subjects. We explained the shape of the heart to each subject at the beginning of the experiment. Next, the subjects were asked to trace the shape of the heart by touching the three-dimensional models using both their hands. The subjects were assessed for:

- their ability to experience a sense of learning about the heart,
- their level of understanding the shape by touching the models, and
- concerning three dimensional model of heart made by using layered manufacturing.

The subjects indicated the various parts of the heart by touching with a finger. The duration of the experiment was about 20 min per subject.

Table 1. Specifications of models

Model No.	Manufacturing technique	Outer dimensions (W×D×H: mm)	Weight (g)	Material
Model-1	Stereolithography	120×87×140	225	Photocurable resin
Model-2	Stereolithography	90×65×105	114	Photocurable resin
Model-3	Powder-layered manufacturing	90×65×105	226	Gypsum

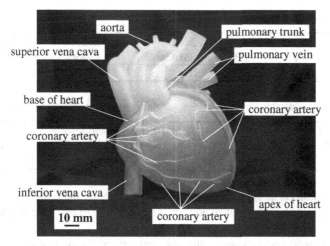

Fig. 1. Outer shape and identified parts of Model-1

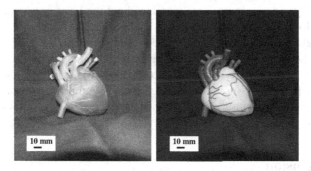

Fig. 2. Outer shape (left) Model-2, (right) Model-3

3   Results and Discussion

Tables 2-4 show the main results of the experiment.

Table 2. Level of understanding of outer shape of heart after touching (Number of subjects)

Question (Use: Model-1)	Correct	Error
Apex of heart and base of heart	10	0
Aorta	10	0
Superior vena cava	10	0
Inferior vena cava	10	0
Pulmonary trunk	10	0
Pulmonary vein	10	0
Coronary artery	10	0

Table 3. Level of tactually feeling of material (Number of subjects)

Question (Use: Model-2 and Model-3)	Model-2 > Model-3	Model-3 > Model-2	Model-2 = Model-3
Level of tactually feeling	4	5	1

Table 4. Level of understanding by touching according to size of model (Number of subjects)

Question (Use: Model-1 and Model-2)	Model-1 > Model-2	Model-2 > Model-1	Model-1 = Model-2
Level of understanding	8	1	1

9 out of 10 subjects could experience a sense of learning about the heart, which is a chief organ in living beings. However, only 4 subjects could trace the shape by touching a three-dimensional model.

The experimental results suggest that the outer shape of the heart was understood correctly by the subjects using the models built by layered manufacturing regardless of whether they experienced a sense learning about the heart or whether they touched the model. Moreover, it was found that, to understand the shape of heart vessels, the size of Model-1 was suitable, and, to understand the shape of the heart, the size of Model-2 and Model-3 was suitable. The level of understanding of each subject varied with the material used in layered manufacturing. However, it was concluded that the models developed in this study by stereolithography and powder-layered manufacturing were unquestionably useful to visually handicapped persons in tracing the shape of the heart by touching.

4   Conclusion

Experimental results suggest that the heart shape models developed in this study by layered manufacturing were useful for teaching anatomy to visually handicapped persons.

Acknowledgements. This work was partially supported by Grant-in-Aid for Scientific Research (A) (18200049) of Japan Society for the Promotion of Science(JSPS).

References

1. Takei, Y.: Touching observation of cock's and pig's heart. JASEB News Letter. Bulletin of Japanese Association of Science Education for the Blind (20), 5–9 (2001) (in Japanese)
2. Teshima, Y., Matsuoka, A., Fujiyoshi, M., Ikegami, Y., Kaneko, T., Oouchi, S., Watanabe, Y., Yamazawa, K.: Enlarged Skeleton Models of Plankton for Tactile Teaching. In: Miesenberger, K., Klaus, J., Zagler, W., Karshmer, A. (eds.) ICCHP 2010, Part II. LNCS, vol. 6180, pp. 523–526. Springer, Heidelberg (2010)
3. Nakagawa, T., Marutani, Y.: Sekisou-zoukei sisutemu (Layered Manufacturing System), pp. 65–94. Kogyo Cyosakai, Japan (1996) (in Japanese)

Viable Haptic UML for Blind People

Claudia Loitsch and Gerhard Weber

Human Computer Interaction Research Group, Technical University of Dresden
Nöthnitzer Straße 46, 01187 Dresden, Germany
{claudia.loitsch,gerhard.weber}@tu-dresden.de

Abstract. We investigate tactile representations and haptic interaction that may enable blind people to utilize UML diagrams by using an industry standard editor. In this paper we present a new approach to present tactile UML diagrams by preserving spatial information on a touch-sensitive tactile display. Furthermore we present the results of a fundamental evaluation showing that blind people retain orientation during exploration of tactile diagrams and which problems are associated with the usage of ideographs. We compared our new developed representation with the common method blind people utilize sequence diagrams: non-visually through verbalization. We indicate problems for both representations.

Keywords: accessibility, blind, tactile graphics, UML diagrams, tactile graphics display, Braille display, screen reader.

1 Introduction

Electrical circuit diagrams, architectural drawings, chemical formulas, and graphical notations such as the Unified Modeling Language (UML) allow the modeling of technical systems by ideographic writing [13]. UML capitalizes on visual characteristics and facilitates education and management tasks for sighted programmers. Traditional text based source code is accessible to blind people using assistive technology (i.e. screen readers). But the emerging rich visual presentation within software engineering causes many barriers. Blind people cannot communicate with sighted people while referring to schematic information in the process where UML is used during development. Editing of the content as well as autonomous and quick access of different diagram types is needed and expected. Using non-visual access to UML-diagrams through a verbalized substitute allows editing by regular text editors but hampers communication in the collaborative software development process together with sighted colleagues. Verbal and visual presentations are incoherent.

We investigate tactile representations and haptic interaction that may enable blind people to utilize ideographs by using an industry standard UML editor. Currently our investigation focuses on UML sequence diagrams. In this paper we present the results of a fundamental evaluation with blind people, whether haptic interaction can build an understanding when exploring tactile UML sequence diagrams. Furthermore we investigated if blind people retain orientation during exploration of tactile diagrams and

K. Miesenberger et al. (Eds.): ICCHP 2012, Part II, LNCS 7383, pp. 509–516, 2012.

which problems are associated with the usage of ideographs. The investigation is based on the research of the HyperBraille project [12] in which a new touch-sensitive tactile display was developed. The refreshable device allows a representation of tactile graphical information with 120 by 60 pins as well as direct manipulation via touch input [8]. By extending screen reader technology a modular audio-tactile screen explorer (called HyperReader) was developed providing blind people access to information displayed on the screen [14]. Specifically graphical information as well as spatial proximity in geometric shapes for example graphical notations for math, technical drawings or diagrams can be perceived by blind people using this technology. For our investigation we developed a screen explorer for UML diagrams by extending this screen reader technology.

We investigate in the following, if blind computer scientists can build an understanding of tactile sequence diagrams by comparing different modalities. Both a tactile representation and a verbalized variation were developed. Beyond that we measured the associated workload for both representation techniques. The results revealed that blind computer scientists can explore tactile UML sequence diagrams by navigating on a planar display, although we detected problems that occurred while navigation.

2   Related Work

Access to UML diagrams is mainly effected by using either verbal descriptions or tactile diagrams [4]. Currently no unitary solution for transcribing UML diagrams in a useful textual representation exists. Different isolated applications have been developed in practical use [6] [9]. A current initiative, BLINDUML, works at solutions for making UML diagrams more accessible by using textual representations.

Developing viable tactile reliefs for blind people requires considerable knowledge of designing textures and labelling spots and areas. The design of educational materials, children books, calendars, maps or even scientific graphs using plastic foils, swell paper or Braille printing is a manual process. Recent progress in the production of software using OCR and other editing features has shown that it may take about 6-10 min for a sighted person to transform a figure of math and astronomy text books [5] into embossed tactile printout. Tactile diagrams may be grasped through an audio-haptic approach by touching tactile printouts placed on a touch tablet [9]. Spatial cognition when exploring textures and tactile markings is more closely coupled with verbal spoken output of labels in this non-visual multimodal approach. If an author provides all data necessary to generate the tactile graphics, the process can be automatically performed with 'negligible intervention' as has been demonstrated by the publishers of the American Physical Society Journals [2] in order to publish also the data associated with the graphs used in articles for all readers.

While tactile graphics preserves the spatial layout, interaction techniques may express spatial relationship through hyperlinks. This may provide cost-effective speech-only access to graphics and can include several methods: Navigating a hierarchical structure through a joystick [4], navigating a spatially motivated structure with a tangible user interface [7] or navigate along connecting lines through keyboard commands and spoken output describing the semantics of graphical elements and their relationship [1].

3   Screen Explorer for UML

We developed a screen explorer for UML which preserves the layout information and textual labels of diagrams. It allows reading of UML-diagrams both by blind and sighted people in a software system consisting of a standard UML editor and assistive technology while ensuring coherence. Currently we use Microsoft Visio 2007 as visual editor for UML diagrams. We developed a filter and a renderer for Visio and integrated both in the HyperReader that enables browsing of UML on the planar display as well as synchronizing it with mouse-based interaction by sighted people. The technical details of this technology are described in [8].

The notation of the UML elements is basically maintained but the layout is affected by the size of Braille and the size of the haptic display. The resolution of 120 x 60 pins limits the representation and requires scrolling by the user. Figure 1 shows a sequence diagram and the maximal area that can be rendered on the display. The user explores the diagram through panning performed by gesture or navigation bar. More information about different interaction techniques can be obtained in [11]. All tactile positions of shapes and Braille elements refer to the original Visio shapes on the screen.

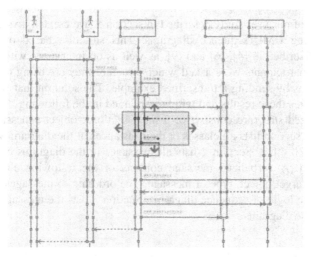

Fig. 1. A tactile diagram and the current area rendered on the tactile display. The arrows illustrate the exploration of the diagram through panning.

The central UML element is a 'lifeline' which is represented by a vertical line and a rectangle that symbolizes the active time slots of an object (Figure 2.a). The sequences of messages are made up from horizontal tactile lines and arrows (Figure 2.b).

These tactile notations are similar to the visual ones. Textual labels and methods are rendered as Braille. Long methods containing different parameters are collapsed by a space saving tactile 'plus'-sign (Figure 2.c). When the user clicks on the sign, the entire Braille label is read aloud by integrated speech output. Further elements in Figure 3 are so called 'connection points' that are specific for Visio and necessary for the subsequent editing (Figure 2.d). Scroll bars help the user to keep the orientation while he navigates (Figure 2.e).

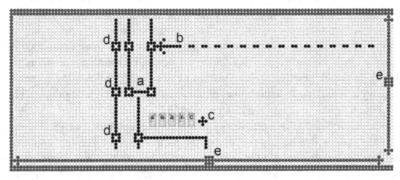

Fig. 2. The current area rendered on the tactile display. a) lifeline with activation; b) message; c) shortened method; d) connection points; e) scroll bars.

4   Verbal Description of UML Sequence Diagrams

In preparation of our user study described in section 5, we created a verbalized structure representing UML sequence diagrams. This structure based on existing approaches as described in [4], [6] and [9], as well as on interviews with stakeholders. Therefore, all participants were asked which structure they are using to verbalize sequence diagrams by sending a transcribed example. The solution that we used in our study summarizes these results and will be explained in the following.

The verbalized structure consists of 3 main sections: objects, messages and time order. The first section lists all classes or their instances of the diagram with name and type among each other. Section 2 lists all messages in the diagrams chronologically for each object. A verbalized message consists of the following elements: name, source object, target object, type of message. The ordering of messages by horizontal lines depicts the logic of sequence diagrams. Section 3 lists the messages in the logic time order of the diagrams.

5   User Study

The new haptic representation of UML sequence diagrams was evaluated in an experimental user test. We were interested whether blind people are able to understand sequence diagrams presented on the planar display. Furthermore we have measured the workload associated with reading graphical sequence diagrams on the planar display in comparison to a verbalized representation. The user test was completed by 7 blind people between 20 and 40 years. All participants were computer scientists and therefore familiar with UML. Furthermore good knowledge in reading Braille was preconditioned. In their normal working or study environment, all participants read verbalized UML diagrams with a simple text editor.

We formulated different types of questions (Q1, Q2, and Q3) that referred to a specific level of understanding UML and analyzed the answers provided by blind subjects. A question of type Q1 referred to the number of objects and required a low level of understanding. A question of type Q2 referred to the number of messages that were sent and received by one object and required a middle level of understanding. A type Q3 question referred to the chronological order of a message sequence and required a high level of understanding. Furthermore we used the weighted NASA task load index (TLX) [3] to measure the workload that is associated with reading graphical sequence diagrams on the planar display in comparison to a linear representation.

The test consisted of 2 single tasks. Both were successfully completed by each participant. The tasks basically differed in the kind of presentation. In task 1 the subject explored the newly designed haptic notation on the planar display. In task 2 the subject read a linear representation as a tactile print-out. In both tasks the participants had to answer various substantive questions while reading a diagram. To eliminate the learning effect we randomized the order of diagrams as well as the presentation technique. After completing one task the weighted TLX was applied to measure the workload that is associated with the presentation technique. The whole test was grouped into the following parts:

1. Preparation phase: reply the pre-questionnaire.
2. Training phase: teaching the concept of the planar display; teaching the graphical notation of sequence diagrams as well as the verbal description described in section 4.
3. Familiarization phase: independently practicing the concepts of sequence diagrams.
4. Execution of task 1: reading one of the two diagrams with one of the two presentation techniques. Answering substantive questions and reply the post-questionnaire.
5. Execution of task 2: reading the other diagram with the other presentation technique. Answering substantive questions and reply the post-questionnaire.

After the preparation and familiarization phase the subjects began with task 1. The type of presentation for the first diagram depended on the random assignment. Before the subject started the task all subjective questions were read aloud. After that the first question was read again, the subject began reading the diagram and tried to answer the question. This procedure was repeated for all questions and both tasks.

6   Results

The user evaluation revealed that all subjects were able to answer most of the formulated questions. Table 1 summarizes the total count of errors indicating the misunderstanding of particular fragments of the represented sequence diagrams. Table 2 presents the mean weighted workload for each representation technique. A two sided paired-sample t-test suggests that there is no significant difference in the workload between task completion where the graphical representation on our planar display was used and the tasks completion where the linear presentation of sequence diagrams was used ($t(6) = 0.460$; $p < 0.05$; $t = 2.45$).

Table 1. Total count of errors according to the presentation technique. Q1, Q2 and Q3 are the formalized types of questions related to a specific level of understanding (LoU). Q1=low LoU; Q2=middel LoU, Q3=LoU

Representation	Q1	Q2	Q3
Graphical	2	1	1
Linear	0	5	2

Table 2. Mean Weighted Workload with standard deviation according to the presentation technique

Representation	Mean Weighted Workload	Standard deviation
graphical	61.9	15,4
Linear	57.0	21.9

7   Discussion

Although the small number of participants the study provides important findings that will be briefly discussed in the following. In general the experiment has shown that all users were able to work on the task and developed an understanding of the sequence diagrams used. All subjects were able to answer substantial questions. As presented in Table 1 participants made some errors while editing both tasks: Working with the linear representation, all subjects answered questions of type Q1 successfully (Table 1). In the linear representation objects were arranged among each other making it simple to count them. In contrast, in the graphical representation errors were made (Table 1). Due to the small size, the tactile display contents had to be scrolled several times for counting the number of objects. All participants commented it would be helpful to have more overview presentation as well as audio-haptic feedback. For example helpful information such as the count of objects could be presented as audio feedback when the diagram is opened. Questions of type Q2 were solved more successfully in the graphical representation (Table 1). We observed that all subjects made the same mistake using the linear representation. They overlooked important details of the UML notation while using the linear representation. These included self-calls, the type of message and the message direction. Self-calls are objects calling methods on themselves. For a better understanding Figure 3 shows the typical graphical notation of this UML element (Figure 3.a). Figure 3.b illustrates our tactile representation and Figure 3.c shows the linear representation of a self-call. The subjects had to recognize that the events e1 and e2 belong to one message.

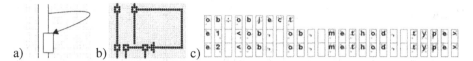

Fig. 3. Representation of a self-call. a) visual; b) tactile; c) linear.

Furthermore, referring to a question of type Q2, participants needed considerable time solving the task to count all messages along a lifeline. The reason for this is the same problem that we observed in questions of type Q1. Subjects commented they needed more overview presentations. The count of scrolling and panning operations should be reduced in further developments. Questions of the type Q3 that referred to the timing sequence could be answered at test time. Only one of the subjects made a mistake while exploring the graphical presentation. Two of the seven participants made a mistake while exploring the linear presentation. Re-occurring problems were the same for questions of type Q1 and Q2: missing overview presentation and missing audio-haptic feedback for the graphical representation and missing understanding of details of the UML notation when reading the linear representation.

The average workload during the processing of the tasks was very high for both representations (Table 2). Particularly the mean mental demand was very high (graphical: M=72.14, SD=14.68; linear: M=63.57, SD=23.93). Although all subjects solved the tasks with both representations, they needed considerable time and needed more support while exploring a diagram. An improvement might be obtained by extended concepts for orientation as well as audio-haptic feedback. The linear representation was evaluated as slightly less demanding. Reasons for this difference appear to be caused by the low knowledge of the UML notation and the lack of experience in exploring such diagrams.

8   Conclusion and Future Work

The screen explorer for UML diagrams enables blind computer scientists understanding UML diagrams created by an industry standard UML editor in a graphical manner. The user test has shown that the developed representations are useful and evince the meaning for further developments in haptic interaction as well as developing appropriate usability measures. We conclude a combined representation of UML diagrams with graphical elements as well as linear elements is meaningful, particularly in order to obtain information quickly for specific tasks. Due to the small resolution of the planar display, orientation is of special relevance. New interaction techniques and audio-haptic feedback are a further important issue in this context. The approach presented preserves layout information to support the collaborative work between sighted and blind people by using the same UML editor. Future investigations in this field will be enabling the editing of diagrams as well. In [8] is demonstrated how selecting and editing will become possible using the HyperReader through mouse-routing. Further developments supporting the work and the education of blind people are important to reduce barriers within the software development with UML.

References

1. Esmaeili, S.: Transcoder and User Agent for acessible UML diagrams. Diploma thesis, TU Dresden, Dept. Computer Science, Institute for Applied Computer Science (2007) (in German)
2. Gardner, J., Bulatov, V., Kelly, R.: Making Journals Accessible to the Visually-Impaired – The Future is Near. Learned Publishing 22(4), 314–319 (2009)
3. Human Performance Research Group: NASA TLX, http://human-factors.arc.nasa.gov/groups/TLX/
4. Horstmann, M., Lorenz, M., Watkowski, A., Ioannidis, G., Herzog, O., King, A., Evans, D.G., Hagen, C., Schlieder, C., Burn, A.-M., King, N., Petrie, H., Dijkstra, S., Crombie, D.: Automated interpretation and accessible presentation of technical diagrams for blind people. New Review of Hypermedia and Multimedia 10(2), 141–163 (2004)
5. Jayant, C., Renzelmann, M., Wen, D., Krisnandi, S., Ladner, R., Comden, D.: Automated tactile graphics translation: in the field. In: Proc ASSETS 2007, pp. 75–82. ACM Press (2007)
6. Kalina, U.: Verbalized UML Diagrams (2006) (in German), http://sonderpaedagogik.bildung.hessen.de/unterstuetzung/bli nd_sehbehindert/informatik/material/Vuml.doc
7. King, A., Blenkhorn, P., Crombie, D., Dijkstra, S., Evans, G., Wood, J.: Presenting UML Software Engineering Diagrams to Blind People. In: Miesenberger, K., Klaus, J., Zagler, W.L., Burger, D. (eds.) ICCHP 2004. LNCS, vol. 3118, pp. 522–529. Springer, Heidelberg (2004)
8. Kraus, M., Völkel, T., Weber, G.: An Off-Screen Model for Tactile Graphical User Interfaces. In: Miesenberger, K., Klaus, J., Zagler, W.L., Karshmer, A.I. (eds.) ICCHP 2008. LNCS, vol. 5105, pp. 865–872. Springer, Heidelberg (2008)
9. Müller, K.: How to Make Unified Modeling Language Diagrams Accessible for Blind Students. In: Miesenberger, K., et al. (eds.) ICCHP 2012, Part I. LNCS, vol. 7382. Springer, Heidelberg (2012)
10. Parkes, D.: Nomad: An audio-tactile tool for the aquisition, use and management of spatially distributed information by visually impaired people. In: Proc. Second International Symposium on Maps and Graphics for Visually Handicapped People, pp. 24–29. A.F & Dodds, London (1988)
11. Prescher, D., Weber, G., Spindler, M.: A Tactile Windowing System for Blind Users. In: Proc. Assets 2010, pp. 91–98. ACM Press (2010)
12. HyperBraille - The graphics-enabled display for blind computer users, http://www.hyperbraille.de
13. Rational Software, e.t.al.: UML Summary. OMG document ad/97-08-03 (1997)
14. Spindler, M., Kraus, M., Weber, G.: A Graphical Tactile Screen-Explorer. In: Miesenberger, K., Klaus, J., Zagler, W., Karshmer, A. (eds.) ICCHP 2010. LNCS, vol. 6180, pp. 474–481. Springer, Heidelberg (2010)

Non-visual Presentation of Graphs
Using the Novint Falcon

Reham Alabbadi, Peter Blanchfield, and Maria Petridou

School of Computer Science, University of Nottingham, Nottingham, NG8 1BB, U.K.
{rua,pxb,mzp}@cs.nott.ac.uk

Abstract. Several technological advances have contributed to providing non-visual access to information by individuals who have sight impairments. Screen readers and Braille displays, however, are not the means of choice for conveying pictorial data such as graphs, maps, and charts. This paper thus proposes the "Falcon Graph" interface which has been developed to enable visually impaired individuals to access computer-based visualisation techniques: mainly pie charts, bar charts, and line graphs. In addition to its interaction with Microsoft Excel, the interface uses the Novint Falcon as the main force feedback media to navigate the haptic virtual environment. Initial findings gathered from testing the interface are also presented.

Keywords: Haptic Technology, Force Feedback, Accessible Graphs, Novint Falcon, Visual Impairment.

1   Introduction

Diagrammatic mapping of information is an abstract representation of complex real-world ideas, used extensively in educational contexts as an assistive tool to solve problems. While some people can use graphs to grasp trends and important features among a large set of data in a matter of seconds, others can be deprived from accessing such methods primarily due to some type of visual impairment especially with representations that have a strong dependency on high resolution graphics.

There are a variety of alternative formats available to present information contained in diagrams and graphs to visually impaired individuals. Diagrams can be generated by converting them into textual descriptions, tactile drawings, or audio sounds. While these methods can be adapted separately or combined together to a great extent they come with associated complications. Many researchers have thus undertaken another approach of using haptics to provide a non-visual output of graphs.

There are currently a number of haptic force feedback displays in which the human sense of touch is being stimulated. They are force reflecting devices that enable the user to physically interact with simulated objects in a virtual world, some of them also enable accessibility to graphs and charts stored on web pages. Most of the studies regarding haptics for people who have visual impairment tend to focus on the PHAN-ToM family of devices. One of the notable projects aiming to provide a multi-modal interface to output different types of graphs for visually impaired computer users

K. Miesenberger et al. (Eds.): ICCHP 2012, Part II, LNCS 7383, pp. 517–520, 2012.

through the PHANToM display is the MultiVis Project by Glasgow University [1]. There is also a set of algorithms that have been developed at the University of Delaware for haptic visualisation of scientific data sets including graphs [2]. The PHANToM was also used in their study.

2   Implementation

The implementation of the proposed interface consists of two main components: Windows dialogue boxes in which Microsoft Excel can be accessed and the haptic virtual environment where the actual graph will be represented. The goal was to provide a flexible system which can help the visually impaired explore graphs using haptic force feedback media within the familiar context of Microsoft Excel. The user can open an Excel file and enter the data set required to be mapped in a chart, and then the system draws a representation of the chart in a virtual environment for haptic exploration.

The Novint Falcon force feedback device was chosen for haptic interaction mainly due to its reasonable price. It was very important to use affordable technology so that it can be obtained by organisations, schools, or even individuals. The Novint Falcon is a game console interface developed by Novint Technologies, Inc. as their first three-dimensional touch controller where the user can feel the texture, weight, and shape of game components.

The methods used to render the different types of graph which are used in this project (pie charts, bar charts, and line graphs) are all OpenGL based implementations using the CHAI3D haptic library. The technical characteristics applied for haptic rendering (e.g. stiffness, vibration, and surface effects) are derived from previous stage experimentation on the perception of basic models such as cubes, spheres, and pyramids [3].

For the bar chart, two different types of bars have been considered during the development: cubic and cylindrical bars. Both types were designed using a triangular mesh with a vibration effect. Due to the limited workspace of the Novint Falcon, no more than 15 bars can be presented on the screen at once. Pie charts, however, were designed as a wide cylinder using a triangular mesh. Vibration is a very important factor as it is the only way that was found during the development of this prototype to haptically differentiate between the different portions within the chart. Every portion of the pie chart was mapped to a vibrating effect with different frequency depending on the size of that portion (the bigger the size the higher the vibration frequency).

3   Testing

Five visually impaired individuals took part in testing the "Falcon Graph" interface. Four of them were students of whom three were congenitally blind (they had also participated in previous experiments using the Novint Falcon as reported in [3]), and one had low vision. All four student participants are at school level and considered to have a high level of understanding of mathematical concepts as it is compulsory for the schools to include students with disabilities in all the same classes as their sighted peers. The participants also attend special classes for the blind in the afternoon for additional support on a variety of topics including computer science, thus they are considered well-skilled in terms of interaction with technologies. The fifth participant, however, was an adult who had suffered progressive sight loss over a number of years and had become completely blind by the summer of 2011during an accident. This participant also had a good background in mathematics and in the use of technologies including the use of Microsoft Excel, as did the school students.

Each participant was asked to perform a series of tasks regarding the exploration of the system including constructing their own graphs using the Excel interface. In terms of haptically exploring the charts, in addition to finding the charts and identifying their shape, the main interest of the research was whether the vibrations would lead to correct identification of the portions in the pie chart, bars of the bar chart and lines in the line graph. Participants were briefed about the procedures to be used. The participants who were using the Falcon for the first time (the adult participant and the student with low vision) were allowed to explore the device and the virtual environment for up to twenty minutes before using the graph interface. During all the sessions the NVDA (Non Visual Desktop Access) screen reader was also used.

4   Results

During the research the perception of three types of graphs (pie charts, bar charts, and line graphs) was tested and evaluated. Generally locating and identifying the graphs was less accurate than the perception of basic models (e.g. cube, sphere, and pyramid). During the initial exploration of the pie chart all participants needed assistance at first but repeating the same task a few time resulted in a better overall performance. This shows the importance of training and prior knowledge in coping with haptic object discrimination.

Identifying how many bars were on the screen was the most difficult task. None of the participants was able to count them without help. It was concluded that this was for the following reasons:

- The size of the bars was smaller than all the other objects used throughout the rest of the research.
- There was also no vibration effect or audio sounds to distinguish between the different values of the bars. The vibration effect was used only to locate the bars (i.e. all the bars had the same vibration frequency).
- It was also noted that the gap between the bars made it difficult to navigate through the whole chart. Thus, it is recommended to render the chart with all the bars together with no gap in between, but with different levels of vibration or audio output to distinguish between the bars.
- Cubic bar charts in general were better than cylindrical ones.

Regarding the line graph, although all of the participants were able to say whether the lines were increasing or decreasing and count how many lines were on the screen accurately, the issue of the single point contact was clearly noticed. The small graphical features of the line graph could not easily be traced as the Falcon's grip often slipped off these features. However, rendering the lines using both sides of the triangular mesh is haptically detectable and can be effective in improving this situation as it forces the Falcon's grip to stick inside the cylindrical lines. Finally, identifying components of intersecting line graphs was a very difficult task; none of the participants understood what exactly was being represented. More investigation is needed regarding this as only the idea of blind persons' ability to recognise that there were two intersecting lines was examined.

Regarding the surface effects of the virtual objects that were used, a "magnetic" effect had no great value to the participants for locating or identifying the objects. Vibration, on the other hand, though sometime a little confusing and not very helpful for identifying the objects more accurately definitely had a great effect on the process of locating the objects within the virtual environment. Vibration was also found to be effective when used to represent different information about the portions of the pie chart. Every portion of the pie chart was mapped to a vibrating effect with different frequency depending on the size of that portion (the bigger the size the higher the vibration frequency). Thus, the process of counting the number of pieces in the chart can easily be conducted.

5   Conclusion and Future Direction

The "Falcon Graph" is a convenient interface that connects a virtual environment presentation to a well known commercially available spreadsheet system as Microsoft Excel in which graphical output has been provided haptically using a low cost commercial haptic display. This makes graphic representation useful to visually impaired persons at an acceptable price for individuals as well as institutions.

The outcome of the research is very encouraging but further work is needed in developing the interface to deal with issues identified during testing, particularly related to line graph representation. Future work can also focus on integrating audio media into the system in which synthetic speech and auditory landmarks can be used to aid the navigation process throughout the haptic virtual environment.

References

1. Yu, W., Ramloll, R., Brewster, S.A.: Haptic Graphs for Blind Computer Users. In: Brewster, S., Murray-Smith, R. (eds.) 1st International Workshop on Haptic Human-Computer Interaction, Glasgow, UK, pp. 41–51 (2000)
2. Fritz, J.P., Way, T.P., Barner, K.E.: Haptic Representation of Scientific Data for Visually Impaired or Blind Persons. In: Technology and Persons With Disabilities Conference (1996)
3. Petridou, M., Blanchfield, P., Alabbadi, R.: The Development of Educational Interactive Virtual Environments for Children with Low or No Vision: The First Evaluation. Submitted to the Interactive Technologies and Games: Education, Health and Disability Conference, Nottingham, UK (October 2011)

Towards a Geographic Information System Facilitating Navigation of Visually Impaired Users

Slim Kammoun, Marc J.-M. Macé, Bernard Oriola, and Christophe Jouffrais

IRIT, CNRS & University of Toulouse, Toulouse, France
{kammoun,mace,oriola,jouffrais}@irit.fr

Abstract. In this paper, we propose some adaptation to Geographical Information System (GIS) components used in GPS based navigation system. In our design process, we adopted a user-centered design approach in collaboration with final users and Orientation and Mobility (O&M) instructors. A database scheme is presented to integrate the principal classes proposed by users and O&M instructors. In addition, some analytical tools are also implemented and integrated in the GIS. This adapted GIS can improve the guidance process of existing and future EOAs. A first implementation of an adapted guidance process allowing a better representation of the surroundings is provided as an illustration of this adapted GIS. This work is part of the NAVIG system (Navigation Assisted by Artificial VIsion and GNSS), an assistive device, whose aim is to improve the Quality of Life of Visually Impaired (VI) persons via increased orientation and mobility capabilities.

Keywords: Geographical Information System, Electronic Orientation Aids, Participatory design, Assistive technology.

1 Introduction

GPS-based personal guidance systems are assistive devices designed to increase the autonomy of Visually Impaired (VI) travelers. In 1998, Golledge et al. [1] raised three main issues to be solved in order to render these devices readily usable. Firstly, the hardware was expensive, but it was also too cumbersome and heavy, and all these factors prevented the adoption of these devices by VI users. Secondly, because of software limitations in 1998, the designers were forced to exclude potential functionalities to comply with limitations on data storage and processing power. Finally, it was necessary to have a better understanding of spatial cognition in the absence of vision to design a usable guidance device.

Improvements in electronic hardware – including computer systems, GPS receivers, sensors, Inertial Measurement Units, etc. – associated to price reductions have contributed to address the first two issues. Regarding the last issue, several studies have been done in order to understand spatial cognition in the absence of vision. It has been shown that mental mapping of spaces and of the possible paths to navigate within these spaces is essential for the development of efficient orientation and mobility (O&M) skills [3]. These skills are taught during O&M training sessions in specialized

K. Miesenberger et al. (Eds.): ICCHP 2012, Part II, LNCS 7383, pp. 521–528, 2012.

centers. Mobility depends on skillfully coordinated actions in order to detect paths and avoid obstacles in the immediate environment. Spatial orientation requires locating oneself and the desired destination, as well as the path linking these two points, in a global mental representation of space. Therefore, whether they are mental, printed on paper, or in an electronic format, maps are essential in order to navigate. Jacobson and Kitchin [4] suggested that an adapted GIS could provide VI people with access to detailed spatial information that would promote spatial learning, orientation, and appropriate decision making. Then, one challenge for assistive technology research consists in improving the transfer of spatial information from an adapted Geographical Information System (GIS) to cognitive maps.

Many research projects addressed this challenge and lead to navigation systems tailored to the needs of visually impaired (see e.g. MoBIC [5] and Drishti [6]). However, evaluations have shown that such systems are primarily limited by the lack of details in the GIS database and the insufficiency of maps in relation to the specificity of navigation without sight. Even commercialized devices such as Trekker (Humanware, Inc) or Kapten (Kapsys, Inc) are based on commercial GIS that are designed for vehicles navigation and are not suitable for pedestrians.

In this context, we have designed and implemented the NAVIG assistive device, which relies on a GIS adapted to guidance and spatial cognition of VI users (see [7] [8] for details). The primary purpose of the current article is to present the GIS component used in NAVIG. Through a participatory design framework with the visually impaired and O&M instructors, we focused on the adaptation of the geographical database and the guidance to VI pedestrian in navigation tasks. We then suggest a set of GIS analytical tools to ensure the construction of a proper cognitive map when using an electronic orientation aid. Finally we propose a first guidance process based on the adapted GIS that will assist VI users in building a better mental representation of the environment.

2   GIS and Assisted Navigation for the Blind

The GIS is one of the major components in a GPS-based personal guidance system. It is composed of a database and software that selects routes, provides guidance and tracks the traveler's itinerary. However, the guidance system must rely on accurate positioning (around one meter precision in real time) to determine if the user is on the right or the left sidewalk, if he is in front of a pedestrian crossing or if he has already started to cross the street, etc. The GIS database may be used to improve positioning through map matching methods that align a sequence of estimated positions with the road or sidewalk networks on the digital map. The GIS database may also be a valuable source of information to indicate the location of close or remote environmental features (e.g. landmarks) that are useful for orientation and spatial learning of the surroundings. It is known that landmarks are essential in order to provide a better sense of the environment [9]. These different GIS functions are not available without improving the resolution of the map and adding appropriate information into the database (e.g. the presence of walking pathway such as sidewalks and pedestrian crossing).

2.1   Data Collection

When compared to car navigation, this is obvious that pedestrian navigation, especially with visually impaired travelers, imposes additional requirements upon geographical data collection. For visually impaired pedestrians, completeness and accuracy of geographical data are critical in order to safely reach destination. As it appears that systematic collection and update of geographical data is very expensive and difficult, interesting complementary approaches have been proposed. For example, social cooperation (crowdsourcing) is a promising approach based on collection, sharing and multimodal annotation of geographical data within a community of users [10]. Another interesting proposition by Elias [11] relies on the development of different methods to automatically derive maps adapted to the needs of pedestrians from available geographical databases.

2.2   Data Extraction

Data extraction is a very relevant issue in the context of VI pedestrian guidance. Indeed, the device tracks the displacement of the traveler, selects the optimal pathway, provides guidance along the selected route and may extract relevant information to be displayed through a non-visual interface. This information may be used by VI users to build a cognitive map of the surroundings; but it is important to determine what geographical information to extract, from which distance relative to the user location, when to present it and with which frequency. A proposition to answer the last two questions was presented in a previous work [12]. In response to "what" and "where", [1] proposed a buffering method to select data from the GIS database of the space immediately around the traveler (the current position being estimated by the GPS). However, when selecting data corresponding to an area in a large database, all the stored features in this area are extracted. If these features are all instantaneously displayed to the user, this can hinder the process of cognitive mapping. Sub-selection and sorting must be performed, but these processes require time and resources that are scarce in a mobile device.

Another important functionality assumed by the GIS component is the route selection. It is the procedure of choosing an optimal pathway between an origin and a destination. Traditionally, path selection for pedestrians is assumed to be the result of minimizing procedures such as selecting the shortest or the quickest path. For the visually impaired, a longer route that avoid difficulties and includes known or preferred landmarks can be more convenient than a shorter route. When based on commercial GIS (with inadequate database and functions), route selection cannot be adapted to VI pedestrian guidance.

3   The NAVIG GIS Component

The NAVIG system [8] is an assistive device whose aim is to improve mobility and orientation of visually impaired pedestrians when navigating in unknown environments. The prototype architecture is divided into several functional elements structured around a multi-agent framework employing a communication protocol based on the IVY middleware. In this prototype, user position is estimated from fusion of artificial vision and GPS signals [13]. The GIS module, presented in this paper, consists of an adapted digital map including walking areas (e.g. sidewalks, zebra crossing) and environmental features (landmarks, points of interest, etc.). The user interface is based on speech and/or sound interaction using a 3D rendering engine (LSE from the LIMSI, see [8] for details).

3.1   Participant and Design Process

In the NAVIG project, we have adopted a long-term user-centered design approach in collaboration with the Institute of Young Blinds (CESDV-IJA, Toulouse). We interviewed 19 users to define more precisely their needs as well as their degree of autonomy and technological knowledge. The target population comprised 7 females and 12 males with a mean age of 37. For daily mobility, 5 of them use a guide dog and 10 use the white cane. The last 4 prefer to have a person to guide them. All of them are legally blind and expressed their motivation and agreement to participate in this project. We had three meeting with four different O&M instructors from the CESDV-IJA. They precisely described the different steps and techniques that they teach to VI persons during O&M training. We also analyzed (videos and a posterior interviews) the O&M behavior of two VI users (one with a white cane and one with a guide-dog). We finally performed three brainstorming sessions with at least 4 VI users in which we focused on issues related to GIS used in electronic orientation aids.

3.2   The NAVIG GIS Database Scheme

The guidance process relies on the estimate of the location of a pedestrian relative to the expected trajectory. Guidance then provides her/him with the appropriate direction instructions, and/or with pertinent information about the surroundings. This definition clarifies the role of the GIS component in the context of assisted navigation. Four classes of objects were added and properly tagged in the GIS database. 1/ Walking Areas (WA) represent all the possible pedestrian paths (e.g., sidewalks, and pedestrian crossings). 2/ Landmarks (LM) are places or objects that can be detected by the user in order to make a decision or confirm his own position along the itinerary (e.g. changes in texture of the ground, telephone poles, or traffic lights). 3/ Points of Interest (POI) are potential destinations for a pedestrian (e.g. public buildings, shops, metro station, etc.). 4/ Difficult Points (DP) are not tagged in the database but are dynamically extracted (e.g. street crossing with the number and layout of the different streets). In the NAVIG device, the different classes of objects are displayed with different sounds that are virtually localized on the real object via binaural synthesis (see [8] for details). In figure 1 we present the class diagram of the NAVIG database.

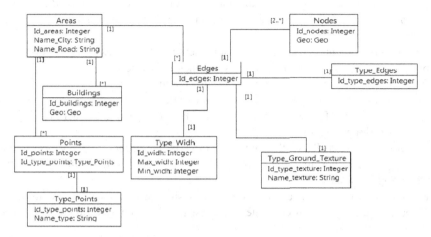

Fig. 1. Database scheme diagram

Each walking area is identified as an edge, having at least two nodes. Each edge has a specific type (sidewalk, crossing, staircase, pedestrian path) and width that can be used when selecting a path according to user preference. Five different widths have been considered: very narrow (less than 1m), narrow (between 1m and 2m), average (between 2m and 4m), wide (between 4m and 8m) and very wide (more than 8m). Each edge also includes a specific ground texture, which may be used as a landmark. In addition, the "Points" class defines specific points that are potential tactile (e.g. tactile guide paths), auditory (e.g. fountains) or olfactory (e.g. bakery) landmarks. The "Buildings" class is generally used to extract information about nearby services (office, post-office, etc.), which could be explicitly required by the user or used to map the environment.

3.3   The NAVIG GIS Software Design

In addition to the GIS database specification, several analytic functions have been proposed after brainstorming sessions. For pedestrian navigation and in the absence of vision, the GIS must integrate a set of functions similar to visual and cognitive (e.g. estimation of distance and direction) functions used by sighted travelers when they explore a new environment [1]. A list of the functions that we proposed in the GIS is presented here:

- List of Points in a Disc (LPD): this primitive extracts the list of tagged points around the user. The input is the distance of detection defined by the user or the system. The center of the disc is the current user location. This function is currently used when the user requests a survey of his surroundings.

- List of Points around a Line (LPL): this primitive extracts the list of tagged points around a segment (street, walking area, etc.). The input is the distance defined by the user or the system, and the name of the segment. It is generally used by the system to extract relevant points (Landmarks or Points of Interest) around a sec-tion. It may also be used by the user to get an overview of relevant points along a section.
- List of POlygons in a Disc (LPOD) is identical to LPD but extracts polygons (e.g. buildings) only. This primitive allows a general overview of the section and informs the user about the buildings in the surroundings.
- List of POlygons around a Line (LPOL) is identical to LPL, but extracts polygons only. As LPL, this function is generally used by the system to extract buildings information along a section.
- Position to address (P2A): this function converts the current GPS position into an address (i.e. number and street name). It also provides the user with his position when asking "where am I?"
- Route Selection (RS): The procedure of choosing an optimal itinerary, using the proposed classification. It computes the most suitable path according to user needs and preferences [7].

Additional functions to compute distance between different points were also added. These functions can be used by the system itself or by the user when asking for additional information such as the nearest bank for instance. To interact with the system, a vocal menu has been implemented.

3.4   Cognitive Mapping via Adapted GIS

When selecting a route between two points, a list of geolocalized Itinerary Points (IP) is generated. The selected path is composed of several sections; each section being defined by two successive IPs. For each section, lists of geolocalized landmarks, difficult points and points of interest are produced by the GIS component. Using IPs, the system then generates turn-by-turn instructions based on the traveler position and direction provided by the positioning component. Landmarks, difficult points and points of interest are displayed to provide the user with information about the travel and the surroundings. Verbosity can be adjusted according to ongoing task and/or user preference.

To track the user location, a simple algorithm based on activation fields was used. To trigger the display of information, a radius was defined according to each type of point (see Fig. 2). The radiuses of the different activation fields were determined during preliminary tests that were conducted with the positioning module. We chose a radius of five meters for both IPs, difficult points and landmarks, and a radius of 30 meters for POIs. When the user was closer than five meters from the current IP, the next one in the roadmap was displayed via a virtual 3D sound. TTS and 3D TTS were used to describe and/or localize landmarks, difficult points, and points of interest when the user reached the corresponding activation fields.

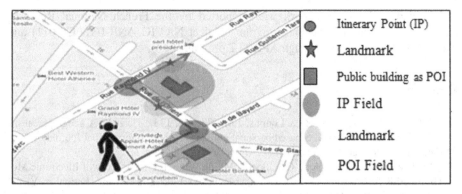

Fig. 2. Part of a selected route with Itinerary Points (IP - small circle), Points of Interest (POIs - squared shapes) and landmarks (stars) is represented. The activation field of IPs, POIs and landmarks are respectively figured in gray, red and green.

4   Conclusions and Discussion

In this paper, we examined how GIS technology may assist visually impaired persons during the different processes of a navigation task. Based on several brainstorming with VI users and O&M instructors, we designed a GIS adapted to VI needs and suitable for electronic orientation assistance. We proposed to improve both data collection (adding relevant information) and data extraction (defining new functions to extract and display spatial information). We specifically suggested that data collection should include environmental features especially useful for VI pedestrians such as pedestrian paths, difficult points, non-visual landmarks, and POIs. Of course, we implemented specific functions that extract and display these different types of points. We suggest that these functions may improve guidance as well as cognitive mapping. In addition to a putative enhancement of cognitive mapping, the GIS may be used to increase positioning accuracy. Indeed, when the estimated user location (GPS position) and the map are very accurate, map-matching techniques proved to be very efficient.

In the context of VI pedestrian navigation, it is critical to improve the display of spatial information to the traveler, especially with the objective of enhancing cognitive mapping. Using an adapted GIS, route selection and guidance may be greatly improved. However, the experimental testing of different guidance algorithms for VI users is really difficult and dangerous in real environments. Many research groups have shown that navigation in virtual environments may assist VI people in learning Orientation and Mobility skills (see e.g. [3]). Instead of representing abstract places, virtual environments may be based on the GIS of a city. We have designed a virtual environment based on a real – representing part of the Toulouse city – but adapted GIS [14]. In future work, we will systematically evaluate different algorithms according to usability of guidance and resultant cognitive mapping.

Acknowledgements. This work was supported by the French National Research Agency (ANR) through TecSan program (project NAVIG ANR-08TECS-011) and the Midi-Pyrénées region through APRRTT program.

References

1. Golledge, R.G., Klatzky, R.L., Loomis, J.M., Speigle, J.M., Tietz, J.: A geographical information system for a GPS based personal guidance system. International Journal of Geographical Information Science 12, 727–749 (1998)
2. Roentgen, U.R., Gelderblom, G.J., Soede, M., de Witte, L.P.: Inventory of Electronic Mobility Aids for Persons with Visual Impairments: A Literature Review. Journal of Visual Impairment & Blindness 102, 702–724 (2008)
3. Lahav, O., Mioduser, D.: Haptic-feedback support for cognitive mapping of unknown spaces by people who are blind. International Journal of Human-Computer Studies 66, 23–35 (2008)
4. Jacobson, R.D.A.N., Kitchin, R.M.: GIS and people with visual impairments or blindness: Exploring the potential for education, orientation, and navigation. Transaction in Geographic Information Systems 2, 315–332 (1997)
5. Petrie, H., Johnson, V., Strothotte, T., Raab, A., Fritz, S., Michel, R.: MoBIC: Designing a travel aid for blind and elderly people. Journal of Navigation 49, 45–52 (1996)
6. Helal, A., Moore, S.E., Ramachandran, B.: Drishti: an integrated navigation system for visually impaired and disabled. In: Fifth International Symposium on Wearable Computers, pp. 149-156. IEEE (2001)
7. Kammoun, S., Dramas, F., Oriola, B., Jouffrais, C.: Route selection algorithm for Blind pedestrian. In: International Conference on Control Automation and Systems (ICCAS), pp. 2223–2228. IEEE (2010)
8. Kammoun, S., Parseihian, G., Gutierrez, O., Brilhault, A., Serpa, A., Raynal, M., Oriola, B., Macé, M.J.-M., Auvray, M., Denis, M., Thorpe, S.J., Truillet, P., Katz, B.F.G., Jouffrais, C.: Navigation and space perception assistance for the Visually Impaired: The NAVIG project. BioMedical Engineering and Research 33, 182–189 (2012)
9. Loomis, J.M., Klatzky, R.L., Golledge, R.G.: Navigating without vision: basic and applied research. Optometry and vision science 78, 282–289 (2001)
10. Völkel, T., Kühn, R.: Mobility impaired pedestrians are not cars: Requirements for the annotation of geographical data. In: International Conference on Computers Helping People with Special, pp. 1085–1092 (2008)
11. Elias, B.: Pedestrian Navigation-Creating a tailored geodatabase for routing. In: 4th Workshop on Positioning, Navigation and Communication, WPNC 2007, pp. 41–47 (2007)
12. Kammoun, S., Macé, M.J.-M., Oriola, B., Jouffrais, C.: Toward a Better Guidance in Wearable Electronic Orientation Aids. In: Campos, P., Graham, N., Jorge, J., Nunes, N., Palanque, P., Winckler, M. (eds.) INTERACT 2011, Part IV. LNCS, vol. 6949, pp. 624–627. Springer, Heidelberg (2011)
13. Brilhault, A., Kammoun, S., Gutierrez, O., Truillet, P., Jouffrais, C.: Fusion of Artificial Vision and GPS to Improve Blind Pedestrian Positioning. In: International Conference on New Technologies, Mobility and Security. pp. 1–5. IEEE (2011)
14. Kammoun, S., Macé, M.J.-M., Oriola, B., Jouffrais, C.: Designing a Virtual Environment Framework for improving guidance for the Visually Impaired. In: Langdon, P., Clarkson, J., Robinson, P., Lazar, J., Heylighen, A. (eds.) Designing Inclusive Systems (CWUAAT), pp. 217–226. Springer, Heidelberg (2012)

Combination of Map-Supported Particle Filters with Activity Recognition for Blind Navigation

Bernhard Schmitz, Attila Györkös, and Thomas Ertl

Institute for Visualization and Interactive Systems, Universität Stuttgart
{Bernhard.Schmitz,gyoerkaa,Thomas.Ertl}@vis.uni-stuttgart.de

Abstract. By implementing a combination of an activity recognition with a map-supported particle filter we were able to significantly improve the positioning of our navigation system for blind people. The activity recognition recognizes walking forward or backward, or ascending or descending stairs. This knowledge is combined with knowledge from the maps, i.e. the location of stairs. Different implementations of the particle filter were evaluated regarding their ability to compensate for sensor drift.

Keywords: Pedestrian Navigation, Indoor Navigation, Activity Recognition, Particle Filter.

1 Introduction

Exact positioning is still a problem in blind navigation, especially indoors and without pre-installed infrastructure. However, exact maps of indoor facilities are sometimes available, such as on our University campus (Universität Stuttgart) and will become more widely available with applications such as Google indoor maps. Previous work has shown that combining maps with probabilistic approaches such as particle filters, can significantly improve positioning [11]. In the context of map-based positioning, each particle represents a possible position, annotated with a certain probability, depending on the measurement that has been carried out. In the simplest case, the probabilities are evenly distributed across all particles, except for those that have passed through walls and are therefore set to zero. The concrete position is then computed from these particles.

Unfortunately, according to our experience the performance of gyroscopes can be quite unstable, introducing a significant drift in the collected data. Additionally, our navigation system automatically switches between floors when the user crosses a so-called hypergate, which is normally located on steps. Missing or wrongly crossing such a hypergate will therefore result in the system displaying an incorrect floor map, which calls for improved accuracy near the hypergates. We have therefore evaluated different implementations of a particle filter in order to test their ability to correct directional drift. Additionally the particle filter is combined with an activity recognition that detects steps and can therefore be used to improve accuracy near stairways and therefore hypergates.

K. Miesenberger et al. (Eds.): ICCHP 2012, Part II, LNCS 7383, pp. 529–535, 2012.

2   Related Work

Monte-Carlo based particle filters have first been used in positioning systems for robot navigation [4]. Later, they have also been successfully employed for pedestrian navigation, mostly with a foot-mounted inertial sensor [2,7,11].

Activity Recognition with inertial sensors has been a widely researched topic in recent years. Many systems have been built that use a single sensor [6,8], or several sensors placed on different parts of the body [1,10]. The former show that a single sensor can be used to detect simple activities like walking or ascending stairs, and an activity detection can therefore be used in our navigation system, which is fitted with a single sensor.

3   System Overview

Our system consists of an Ultra-Mobile PC that is attached to a strap worn around the neck. An Xsens Mtx measurement unit, which combines an accelerometer, a magnetic field sensor and a gyroscope is attached to this strap [9], as seen in figure 1. Compared to attaching it to a foot, this has the disadvantage of not having zero crossings in forward acceleration. However, it is easier to wear, the sensor data is not influenced by additional foot movements and (excepting pitch) the device coordinate system corresponds to the body coordinate system.

Fig. 1. Our navigation system. The combined accelerometer, magnetic field sensor and gyroscope can be seen on the strap.

At first, a step detection, step width estimation and activity recognition is performed on the accelerometer data. The results of the step width estimation together with the direction given by the sensor's combined gyroscope and magnetic field sensor is used as an input to the particle filter.

3.1   Step Detection and Width Estimation

A lowpass filter is applied to the accelerometer data, and list of zero crossings and extrema is generated from the mean adjusted resulting data. Steps are then detected by applying a deterministic finite automaton accepting the regular expression zc min* zc* max* zc to this list, where zc stands for a zero crossing and min and max for minimum and maximum respectively.

For each step the walking velocity v is estimated based on the simple formula

$$v = (max - min) * s_{factor} + s_{offset} \ , \tag{1}$$

where max and min are the maximum and minimum values for the observed step. The parameters s_{factor} and s_{offset} are different for each person and are negative, if the activity walking backwards is recognized (see section 3.2). As the sampling rate of the sensor data is given, the duration of one step is also known and therefore the step width can be calculated.

3.2   Activity Recognition

To recognize activities, a plain decision tree algorithm was implemented. Our algorithm detects four different activity types: walking, walking backwards, ascending stairs and descending stairs. In order to train the decision tree, a total of 1.5h of acceleration data was collected.

Buildings do not have continuous steps but a level area on each floor (and often in between floors). Therefore, the data for ascending and descending stairs had to be manually edited to remove the steps on those areas as well as the first and the last step of each staircase, which have distinct acceleration patterns. Because of this only about 45% of the data originally collected could be used for ascending and descending stairs. Furthermore stairs with different slope angles must be taken into consideration.

As feature points, the mean value and the standard deviation are extracted for each axis from the data in addition to the minimum and maximum values of the vertical acceleration. With this data, the decision tree is trained, using a CART (Classification and Regression Tree) algorithm [3]. Ten-fold cross validation was used to evaluate the decision tree, i.e. the data is divided into ten disjoint subsets, nine of which are used for training, while the tenth is used as a test data set. This is repeated ten times, so that each data set is used as a test set once. The recognition rates of the resulting decision tree obtained by computing the mean rates of all ten test data runs can be found in table 1.

4   Particle Filter

Particle Filters are an intuitive probabilistic approach to handling inertial positioning: Instead of tracing a single location, a number of possible locations, each with an associated probability, are being traced. A possible position together with its probability is called a particle. All particles represent a subset of

Table 1. Confusion matrix of recognition rates. Rows indicate activities as they were recorded, columns show the recognized activities.

	Recognized As			
Activity	Walking	Backwards	Ascending	Descending
Walking	**94.69**	0.21	5.30	0.00
Backwards	18.52	**81.48**	0.00	0.00
Ascending	0.00	0.00	**90.91**	9.09
Descending	0.00	0.00	9.52	**90.48**

all possible locations and are used to compute the most probable location. The details of how particles are distributed and probabilities are assigned can vary. For particle distribution, we implemented two different models, a direct and an indirect one. In the direct model, two normally distributed random variables are used. One is added to the direction, the other to the step length. This is the more intuitive implementation, as errors made in the detection and computation of direction and step length are independent. The indirect model uses three normally distributed random variables. One is added to the direction, the other two to the x and y position respectively, after the position has been computed.

In both models, probabilities are directly affected by two factors: Walls and activity type. It is not possible for a person to move through a wall, and the maps are considered accurate. Therefore all particles that passed through a wall are assigned a probability of 0, i.e. there is no uncertainty involved regarding collisions with walls.

If no collisions are found, the activity type is taken into account. The activity types that are used for the correction are *walking*, *ascending stairs* and *descending stairs*. The recognized activity is compared with the expected activity based on the particle position. If they match, the probability for this particle should theoretically be 1.0, otherwise 0.0. However, the activity recognition does not work perfectly. The recognition rates are known for each possible combination of activity and detection (see Table 1), and these rates can be used to determine the uncertainty for the measurement. Before being used to compute the approximated position of the user, the probabilities of the particles have to be normalized.

The use of elevators is currently not a supported activity. This decision was based on two reasons: Previous work shows that recognition rates for elevator usage are not very good [1], and even if an elevator usage would be recognized, it would not give the number of the floor in which the elevator stops. Currently our system can optionally be fitted with an RFID reader that recognizes tags which can be fixed at the elevator entrances. Upon reading a tag, the system automatically switches to the correct floor [5]. However, because of the reader's high energy consumption, the short reading distance, and the need for added infrastructure (tags), this is not an ideal solution.

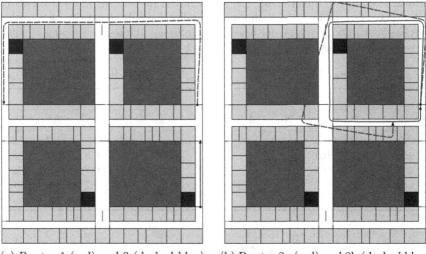

(a) Routes 1 (red) and 3 (dashed blue)   (b) Routes 2a (red) and 2b (dashed blue)

Fig. 2. Plan of the University building together with the recorded routes. Route 2b does not show the real route (which is the same as 2a), but the route that would result without collision detection and particle filter.

5   Results

Data from three different routes were collected in order to test the developed algorithm (figure 2). One route was collected twice, once with a sensor that had a drift of up to 40° (Route 2b).

All Routes have been evaluated with the direct and indirect model, using normally distributed random variables with a standard deviation ranging from 5° to 30° (in 5° steps) for directional variables and from 0.2m to 1.0m (in 0.2m steps) for position and length variables. The best results have been achieved with a standard deviation of 5° or 10° and 0.2m or 0.4m, respectively.

Table 2 shows the accuracy obtained with the direct and the indirect model. For this table the best results from the experiments with differing random variables have been selected, in order not to discriminate against a model. If no distance is given, the estimated location did not end up anywhere near the real location, due to getting stuck in a room somewhere along the way. As can be seen, the direct model achieves better results throughout, but is not able to cope with the highly drifting sensor, where the indirect model is still able to compute a result.

Figure 3 shows the average accuracy over routes 1, 2a, and 3 for the direct and indirect model, and average and maximum runtime of one step using between 50 and 1000 particles. The performance measurements have been executed on a Laptop with an Intel Core i5 2410M Processor with 6 GB of RAM. While the performance continually deteriorates, the accuracy does not improve significantly

Table 2. Accuracy in meter, using the direct model (a) and the indirect model (b). The last line, given as a reference, shows the result using only step estimation, without a particle filter. The direct model has better accuracy, the indirect model is able to cope with a drifting sensor (route 2b).

<table>
<tr><td colspan="5" align="center">(a) Direct Model</td><td colspan="5" align="center">(b) Indirect Model</td></tr>
<tr><td></td><td colspan="4" align="center">Route</td><td></td><td colspan="4" align="center">Route</td></tr>
<tr><td>Particles</td><td>1</td><td>2a</td><td>2b</td><td>3</td><td>Particles</td><td>1</td><td>2a</td><td>2b</td><td>3</td></tr>
<tr><td>50</td><td>0.3</td><td>0.5</td><td>-</td><td>1.3</td><td>50</td><td>0.5</td><td>0.8</td><td>11.7</td><td>11.7</td></tr>
<tr><td>100</td><td>0.1</td><td>0.3</td><td>-</td><td>1.3</td><td>100</td><td>0.5</td><td>0.8</td><td>9.8</td><td>10.8</td></tr>
<tr><td>250</td><td>0.3</td><td>0.3</td><td>-</td><td>1.2</td><td>250</td><td>0.5</td><td>0.7</td><td>9.2</td><td>3.2</td></tr>
<tr><td>500</td><td>0.2</td><td>0.3</td><td>-</td><td>1.3</td><td>500</td><td>0.6</td><td>0.7</td><td>9.1</td><td>2.0</td></tr>
<tr><td>none</td><td>0.2</td><td>-</td><td>-</td><td>-</td><td>none</td><td>0.2</td><td>-</td><td>-</td><td>-</td></tr>
</table>

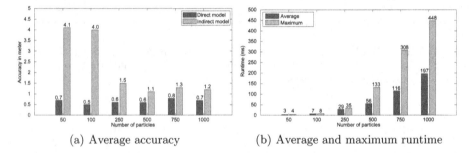

(a) Average accuracy   (b) Average and maximum runtime

Fig. 3. Accuracy and runtime, using between 50 and 1000 particles

with more than 250 particles with both models. This surprising result that shows that the number of particles should be tested and not automatically be set to max out the hardware that is used. The maximum runtime can be more than twice as high if a resampling occurs, i.e. new particles have to be generated.

6   Future Work

Unfortunately, the effectiveness of combining activity detection with the particle filter could not be reasonably determined. In our building staircases are entered through doors, whereby particles not entering the staircase are automatically assigned a probability of 0, as they would pass through a wall. Other buildings with openly accessible stairs (e.g. in a lobby) are currently being mapped, making a future evaluation possible.

Due to the architecture of the system, it should be easy to integrate further sensors like a GPS receiver for outdoor environments. Additionally, different probabilities for the particles could be chosen based on surface properties, e.g. lower probabilities for walking on grass. Because the direct model is more accurate, but not as robust against drift as the indirect model, a possible automatic detection of drift that allows switching between models or possibly correcting drift could further improve the system. Furthermore it is planned to implement a user-supported mapping function for areas where exact maps are not available.

Acknowledgements. This work was funded by the Deutsche Forschungsgemeinschaft (DFG).

References

1. Bao, L., Intille, S.S.: Activity Recognition from User-Annotated Acceleration Data. In: Ferscha, A., Mattern, F. (eds.) PERVASIVE 2004. LNCS, vol. 3001, pp. 1–17. Springer, Heidelberg (2004)
2. Beauregard, S., Widyawan, Klepal, M.: Indoor pdr performance enhancement using minimal map information and particle filters. In: 2008 IEEE/ION Position, Location and Navigation Symposium, pp. 141–147 (May 2008)
3. Breiman, L., Friedman, J.H., Olshen, R.A., Stone, C.J.: Classification and Regression Trees. Wadsworth and Brooks, Monterey (1984)
4. Fox, D., Burgard, W., Dellaert, F., Thrun, S.: Monte carlo localization: Efficient position estimation for mobile robots. In: Proceedings of the National Conference on Artificial Intelligence, pp. 343–349 (1999)
5. Hub, A., Schmitz, B.: Addition of RFID-based initialization and object recognition to the navigation system TANIA. In: Proceedings of the California State University, Northridge Center on Disabilities 24th Annual International Technology and Persons with Disabilities Conference (CSUN 2009), Los Angeles, CA, USA (2009)
6. Karantonis, D., Narayanan, M., Mathie, M., Lovell, N., Celler, B.: Implementation of a real-time human movement classifier using a triaxial accelerometer for ambulatory monitoring. IEEE Transactions on Information Technology in Biomedicine 10(1), 156–167 (2006)
7. Krach, B., Robertson, P.: Cascaded estimation architecture for integration of foot-mounted inertial sensors. In: 2008 IEEE/ION Position, Location and Navigation Symposium, pp. 112–119 (May 2008)
8. Najafi, B., Aminian, K., Paraschiv-Ionescu, A., Loew, F., Bula, C., Robert, P.: Ambulatory system for human motion analysis using a kinematic sensor: monitoring of daily physical activity in the elderly. IEEE Transactions on Biomedical Engineering 50(6), 711–723 (2003)
9. Schmitz, B., Becker, S., Blessing, A., Großmann, M.: Acquisition and presentation of diverse spatial context data for blind navigation. In: 2011 12th International Conference on Mobile Data Management (MDM), pp. 276–284 (2011)
10. Slyper, R., Hodgins, J.K.: Action capture with accelerometers. In: Proceedings of the 2008 ACM SIGGRAPH/Eurographics Symposium on Computer Animation, SCA 2008, pp. 193–199. Eurographics Association, Aire-la-Ville, Switzerland, Switzerland (2008)
11. Woodman, O., Harle, R.: Pedestrian localisation for indoor environments. In: UbiComp 2008: Proceedings of the 10th International Conference on Ubiquitous Computing, pp. 114–123. ACM, New York (2008)

AccessibleMap

Web-Based City Maps for Blind and Visually Impaired

Klaus Höckner[1], Daniele Marano[1], Julia Neuschmid[2], Manfred Schrenk[2],
and Wolfgang Wasserburger[2]

[1] Hilfsgemeinschaft der Blinden und Sehschwachen Österreichs, Jägerstrasse 36, 1200 Wien
{hoeckner,marano}@hilfsgemeinschaft.at
http://www.hilfsgemeinschaft.at
[2] CEIT ALANOVA – Institute of Urbanism, Transport, Environment and Information
{j.neuschmid,m.schrenk,w.wasserburger}@ceit.at

Abstract. Today cities can be discovered easily with the help of web-based maps. They assist to discover streets, squares and districts by supporting orientation, mobility and feeling of safety. Nevertheless do online maps still belong to those elements of the web which are hardly or even not accessible for partially sighted people. Therefore the main objective of the AccessibleMap project is to develop methods to design web-based city maps in a way that they can be better used by people affected with limited sight or blindness in several application areas of daily life.

Keywords: Accessible Maps, Semantic description of maps, Web Map Services, Styled Layer Description.

1 Towards Accessibility of Maps

1.1 Background

Web-based city maps are crucial means in terms of helping people to orientate themselves in physical space. Their purpose is to assist users with discovery of new cities, mobility, orientation, and can therefore support the overall feeling of safety. Further they are a supportive tool to get a better overall image of the city or a district, or to discover streets, squares and crossings in detail by receiving information about existing points of interest, street types (e. g. pedestrian area, bicycle lane, main road), lengths of street, type of crossings (e. g. X-crossing, T-crossing, etc.), footprint of building blocks, street names and house numbers, tactile systems, acoustic traffic lights, and many more data and attributes. Fig. 1 shows an extract from a web-based map as an example for the great variety and amount of map content.

So far comprehensive research and development activities exist in the field of navigation for blind people. Several visual aids have been developed such as Electronic Travel Aids and Personal Guidance Systems [2], [5] often in combination with tactile, haptic, sound components [4]. Example projects working on the development of navigation or guidance systems for visually impaired pedestrians are Ways4all, Nav4blind, Loadstone, Poptis and Argus. [14], [9], [7], [11], [1]

K. Miesenberger et al. (Eds.): ICCHP 2012, Part II, LNCS 7383, pp. 536–543, 2012.
© Springer-Verlag Berlin Heidelberg 2012

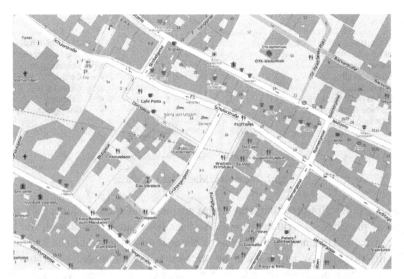

Fig. 1. Example of broad web-map content. Source: OpenStreetMap.

However, even though different types of assistive technology and visual aids (e. g. screen reader, Braille display, text to speech technology) as well as guidelines and standards of accessible web design (e.g. WCAG – Web Content Accessibility Guidelines, [15]) have been developed, it is currently difficult or even impossible for people with vision deficiency to fully discover web-based city maps.

1.2   The AccessibleMap Project

The aim of the AccessibleMap project – funded by the Federal Ministry for Transport, Innovation and Technology in the benefit programme – is to develop methods which can make web-based maps accessible for visually impaired people. The target group is specified into detail and divided into three sub-groups. These are (1) visually impaired (caused by different eye disorders), (2) colour blind and (3) blind persons, and are characterised and analysed with methods from empirical social research and statistic procedures. An online survey tool was developed and distributed in autumn 2011 for the definition of the requirements of the target group, the determination of their mobility and orientation patterns as well the specification of preferred representation modes of visual information.

Based on the user requirements analysis methods are developed to (1) automatically generate a textual description of a web-based map (map in words) as well as (2) an optimised cartographic design/layout. Hence, the AccessibleMap user interface is developed as a multi-sensory interface. As presented in Fig. 2 it contains the map component with an optimised cartographic design (visual user interface) and the voice output of the textual description (acoustic user interface).

Acoustic user interface
Text information about
* Street Name
* Street length
* Street type
* Points of Interest
* Surface texture
* Crossing streets
* ...

Visual user interface
Optimised cartographic design, according to
* Colour
* Object size
* Labeling
* Cartographic symbol
* ...

Fig. 2. AccessibleMap User Interfaces

The textual description of the map relates attribute and geometric (spatial) information and is provided in written form to the user who can access it with the help of existing visual aid technology that supports accessibility of text, such as screenreaders and Braille displays. What needs to be stressed is the automatic generation of the spatial description out of vector data so that a large area can be covered. The automatic approach reduces costs as there is no need for extensive manual and time consuming updates. Furthermore, this method makes the accessible map flexible so that it can be easily applied in different cities and regions.

The second aspect that is tackled is how to optimise cartographic design (choice of colours, object size, etc.) according to the needs of visually impaired. Different eye diseases like colour blindness, retinitis pigmentosa, macula degeneration just to mention some, require that the representation of visual information of web-based maps must be adapted to the needs of different users. It is therefore necessary to investigate the needs of the user group according to the specific eye conditions.

Functionalities are implemented which allow (1) to configure, i. e. select the cartographic design depending on user abilities and preferences, (2) to access verbal descriptions (text and speech output), and (3) to perform basic map operations such as search, zoom, and pan. The result will be a prototype of the web-based map which will be tested intensively by the target group.

1.3   Semantic Description of Space

The basic geographic data is open data, i.e. open government data and OpenStreetMap (OSM) data. The latter has been created by its community, is free to download, contains a great variety of attributes and is kept up-to-date in a satisfying way. Besides the use of OSM data, the AccessibleMap geodatabase is prepared to add additional data, for example data provided by the local community governments. As a first sample the City of Vienna provides data for a test region. These data is published under the Creative Commons license which targets at promoting open and shared data access and use via web services for the public. Due to the great variety of data and their attributes, the described data sources provide a wide range of information, which meets data demanded by the target group. Therefore, most general information (street names etc.), tactile information (surface of roads), useful landmarks, etc. is available for the users.

Description of maps in words and provision of meaningful information to the user require a lot of efforts on semantics. Data, i.e. spatial database content, need to be related and linked to each other in a meaningful way to create information, knowledge, and therefore better understanding of (urban) space (Fig. 3).

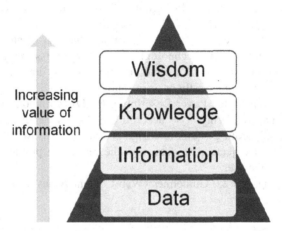

Fig. 3. From data to better understanding of space. Source: based on Laurini 1991 [6].

The following gives an example for the semantic description of crossroads. Mathematically a crossroad consists of two or more intersecting lines and a specific angle in between. Nevertheless do most users prefer a semantic description Instead of receiving figures of angles users prefer a more semantic description of crossroads using hour system instead of receiving angular dimensions (e. g. [12]). Hence, the verbal description of the directions of a street or crossroad could be designed as follows (Fig. 4): „Street B diverges at 1 o'clock (respectively 20 degree); street A at 11 o'clock (respectively 340 degree) from street C." In other words the shape of the crossroad can be described as a "Y-crossroad" or a "triple-trace crossroad".

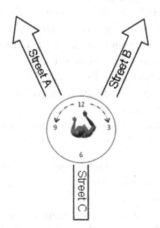

Fig. 4. Description of crossroad based on hour system, Sánchez & Torre 2010 [12]

2   Technical Implementation

The AccessibleMap prototype is developed to be used either with PC or by mobile devices (e. g. smartphone, tablet PC, etc.). The software architecture is made up of open source technology, i.e. a PostgreSQL/PostGIS database, Geoserver, Open Layers and PHP Application Server. The accessible map is based on geographic information systems (GIS) extended with algorithms that can create semantic spatial descriptions automatically. The technologies chosen to access the textual output are screenreaders or Braille displays for blind and high visually impaired people. Screenreaders are available commercially or open source.

For the map layout Styled Layer Description (SLD) technology is used. SLD allows creating a map rendering style according to the user requirements which includes e. g. the configuration of colour design and labelling as well as colour contrast between the different objects. The data, i. e. the maps, are provided via Web Map Services (WMS) to the user.

In this context WCAG 2.0 Guidelines (Web Content Accessibility Guidelines) are of high importance.

3   Analysis and Specification of User Requirements

Within the AccessibleMap project constructive co-operations between users and target group experts as well as developers are principally seen as a fundamental precondition for and a central aspect of the application development process.

The project analysis and specification of user requirement is based on a literature review as well as on a user survey, focusing on the above outlined target user groups. Therefore an online questionnaire was designed using the internet survey tool SurveyMonkey according to the principles of empirical social research. The survey was developed in close co-operation between the different project partners (ICT-experts, GI-experts, target user group experts).

The questionnaire design is based on the results of the comprehensive literature review which covers literature from e. g. Web Cartography, Modern Cartography, Special Needs Cartography, and Cybercartography [3]. From reviewing the literature available on the topic, it became obvious that detailed information on design and implementation of web map applications for visually impaired is mostly missing. Thus the questionnaire was particularly designed to get response on open questions regarding user interface design and functionalities, map design, and map content.

The questionnaire consisted of 55 open and closed questions addressing the different types of visual impairment. The questions referred to:

1. Demographic issues (sex, age, education, profession, place of residence etc.);
2. Aspects regarding the visual impairment of the participants (type, extent and timing of the visual impairment etc.);
3. General characterization of internet user behavior (extent of internet use, use of digital devices, use of assistive technology and visual aids etc.);

4. General characterization of web map user behavior (extent of use, problems, purposes etc.);
5. User needs on map content (user group specific information, supplementary links, etc.);
6. User preferences on the graphical and non-graphical user interface design (access and use) including functionalities;
7. User preferences on the (carto-)graphical and non-(carto-)graphical map design (cartographic means of design, use of additional information media like photos, audio signals, verbal description etc.).

The AccessibleMap user survey resulted in 199 returned and 158 valid questionnaires. The valid questionnaires are grouped under three subgroups of target users as follows:

- people with reduced and limited vision: 59 %,
- colour blind: 4 %, and
- blind: 37 %.

Even though the interviewed persons show a high level of internet usage, only 56 % point out to use web maps. Respondents mentioned different reasons therefore:

1. Web map applications are not (easily) operable, i. e. not (easily) usable.
2. Web map applications do not provide verbal descriptions of their content.
3. Web map applications cannot be interpreted by screen reader, Braille display or voice output.
4. Users lack knowledge on the existence of web-based maps.
5. Users make use of voice-operated navigation devices instead of web map applications.

Hence, the provision of voice output and textual, i. e. readable descriptions is a fundamental requirement to enable usage of computer applications including web map applications to these users.

4   Accessible Map in Practice

AccessibleMaps aims to make web-based maps accessible to blind people. A direct advantage for the target group could result in its increased mobility.

Anyone who has ever had to find its way around in unfamiliar surroundings will know just how valuable a good orientation system can be. If a blind person does not know where the next bus stop is, how many intersections need to be crossed before reaching the side street she/he is looking for, or she/he has not a clue about how to get to the desired destination, it is essential to provide a save guiding system. This type of situation is very challenging and stressful for people with impaired vision.

Improving the accessibility of maps will therefore not only enable blind and partially sighted people to access them but also enable their use within other way finding and orientation solutions that rely on the availability and accessibility of maps.

In this respect it is worth to mention a few examples of possible integration of AccessibleMap within existing way finding projects.

POPTIS (Pre–On–Post–Trip–Information–System) is an acoustic orientation system offered by the transport operator "Wiener Linien" in the underground network of Vienna. All possible footpaths in stations of the underground are explained to visually impaired people. POPTIS is used among others to support the trip preparation.

AccessibleMap could support a blind person in the preparation of his/her journey through the availability of accessible maps that can be explored also in terms of spatial relations to determine for example the position of a bus or metro station.

As a further development of POPTIS the project Ways4All envisages the conception of a barrier-free total system for orientation and movement in public space for people with special needs. The concept includes components which allow for navigation both indoors and outdoors, communication with public transport and public infrastructure to ensure a safe travel. With navigation system persons with special needs should have access to up-to-date traffic information.

Ways4All strives to integrate various components in the mobility chain of a blind persons (visual, tactile guidance systems, POPTIS, electronic passenger information, barrier-free internet pages). The availability of accessible maps is pivotal for the achievement of an integrated approach in the mobility chain of visually impaired persons. AccessibleMap will therefore be essential in the environment and mobility discovery of urban settings.

Mobile services Quando and Scotty respectively of the Vienna Public Transport and the Austrian Federal Railways offer besides timetables also informations about delays, public traffic interruptions, different kinds of online service and a route planner. The use of maps is an integral part of these and similar mobile applications that at the current stage can not be accessed by visually impaired persons.

The accessibility of web-based maps is a very important factor for the mobility and orientation of visually impaired persons and must be viewed as a necessary component to be considered in the development of different guiding systems.

5   Outlook

The presented methodology to make easier the access to web-based maps for visually and blind people can be integrated into other existing web-based maps and web-mapping technologies. Further the automatic textual description, with focus on semantics, can be an added-value for pedestrian navigation. Instead of navigating the user in a linear way from A to B (e.g. "turn right after 300 meters"), as it is the case for most traditional navigation systems, another option is to describe the route with the help of landmarks (e.g. "turn right after the second street, in front of the park").

References

1. ARGUS, http://projectargus.eu/participants.asp (accessed on March 14, 2012)
2. Golledge, R.G., Rice, M., Jacobson, R.D.: Multimodal Interfaces for Representing and Accessing Geospatial Information. In: Rana, S., Sharma, J. (eds.) Frontiers of Geographic Information Technology, pp. 181–208. Springer, Berlin & New York (2006)

3. Hennig, S., Zobl, F.: Ergebnisse der Literaturrecherche zu Nutzeranforderungen von (Teil-) Zielgruppen AccessibleMap, Projektbericht, Salzburg, pp. 1–20 (2011)
4. Horstmann, M., Heuten, W., Miene, A., Boll, S.: Automatic Annotation of Geographic Maps. In: Miesenberger, K., Kemper, J., H.-G., Mehanna, W., Unger, C. (eds.) Business Intelligence – Grundlagen und praktische Anwendungen. Vieweg (2006)
5. Jacobson, R.D.: Navigation for the visually handicapped: Going beyond tactile cartography. Swansea Geographer 31, 53–59 (1994)
6. Laurini, R.: Modelling Geographic Data and Knowledge, Odense (1991)
7. LOADSTONE, http://WWW.LOADSTONE-GPS.COM/ (accessed on April 04, 2012)
8. Lynch, K.: The Image of the City, Cambridge (1960)
9. NAV4BLIND, http://www.nav4blind.de/ (accessed on April 04, 2012)
10. OPENSTREETMAP, http://www.openstreetmap.org (accessed on April 12, 2012)
11. POPTIS: System of the Vienna Transportation System (Wiener Linien), http://www.wL-barrierefrei.at/index.php?id=8034 (accessed on April 12, 2012)
12. Sanchez, J., Torre, N.: Autonomous navigation through the city for the blind. In: ASSETS 2010, pp. 195–202 (2010)
13. Tolman, E.C.: Cognitive Maps in Rats and Men. Psychological Review 55, 189–208 (1948)
14. WAYS4ALL, http://www.ways4all.at/index.php?lang=de (accessed on March 12, 2012)
15. WCAG (Web Content Accessiblity Guidelines):
http://www.w3.org/TR/WCAG20/ (accessed on March 11 2012)

Design and User Satisfaction of Interactive Maps for Visually Impaired People

Anke Brock[1], Philippe Truillet[1], Bernard Oriola[1], Delphine Picard[2], and Christophe Jouffrais[1]

[1] IRIT-UMR5505, Université de Toulouse & CNRS, Toulouse, France
{brock,truillet,oriola,jouffrais}@irit.fr
[2] Octogone, Université de Toulouse, France & Institut Universitaire de France
delphine.picard@univ-tlse2.fr

Abstract. Multimodal interactive maps are a solution for presenting spatial information to visually impaired people. In this paper, we present an interactive multimodal map prototype that is based on a tactile paper map, a multi-touch screen and audio output. We first describe the different steps for designing an interactive map: drawing and printing the tactile paper map, choice of multi-touch technology, interaction technologies and the software architecture. Then we describe the method used to assess user satisfaction. We provide data showing that an interactive map – although based on a unique, elementary, double tap interaction – has been met with a high level of user satisfaction. Interestingly, satisfaction is independent of a user's age, previous visual experience or Braille experience. This prototype will be used as a platform to design advanced interactions for spatial learning.

Keywords: blind, visual impairment, accessibility, interactive map, tactile map, multi-touch, satisfaction, SUS, usability.

1 Introduction

Human navigation is a very complex behavior that mainly relies on vision. Indeed, vision provides the pedestrian with static and dynamic cues that are essential for position and orientation updating, estimation of distance, etc. Hence, for a visually impaired person, navigating in familiar environment is not obvious, and becomes especially complicated in unknown environments. The major problem is a lack of information concerning the environment which leads to deficits in orientation and mobility. These problems often mean that the visually impaired travel less, which influences their personal and professional life and can lead to exclusion from society. With 285 million people being visually impaired around the world [1], it is therefore a very important task to make spatial information accessible to the visually impaired.

Accessible geographic maps represent valuable assistance for journey preparation and can thus help to overcome the fear and stress related to traveling. Maps are projective two-dimensional symbolic representations of a real-space in smaller scale [2]. They can represent spaces of different dimensions (going from a room up to the

K. Miesenberger et al. (Eds.): ICCHP 2012, Part II, LNCS 7383, pp. 544–551, 2012.
© Springer-Verlag Berlin Heidelberg 2012

whole world). Maps allow the absolute and relative localization of objects as streets or buildings, the estimation of distances and directions, as well as finding an itinerary between two points. As stated by Hatwell et al [2] this information is only accessible if the user possesses the necessary perceptual and cognitive skills allowing access to the symbolic codes of the maps. Conversely, the map must be designed so that a person with visual impairments can access the information.

Traditionally, raised-line paper maps are used to present geographic information to visually impaired people. However, Jacobson [3] mentioned that raised-line paper maps have numerous limitations. Most importantly, the map content needs to be simplified as the fingertip's resolution is less than the eye's. Furthermore, Braille is used for giving textual information, which requires a lot of space. Therefore tactile maps tend to be overloaded and thus unreadable. Besides, not every visually impaired person can read Braille. Finally, the content of such a map cannot be adapted dynamically. Multimodal interactive maps undoubtedly represent a solution to overcome these problems.

There are different concepts for interactive maps, some with auditory only, some with auditory and haptic feedback. An auditory map was proposed by Jacobson [3]. The user navigates in a model of the environment with a touchpad and receives auditory feedback. Buzzi et al proposed a similar system based on data gathered from the web [4]. Rice et al [5] added haptic feedback to an auditory map by using a force-feedback mouse. Different studies [6, 7] proposed a combination of audio and tactile output based on a matrix of refreshable pins. The 3D-Finger system [8] used image recognition to follow a user's finger during map exploration. The finger position was associated to the content of the underlying tactile paper map in order to determine the corresponding audio output. Finally, several map projects were based on a combination of touch screens and raised-line paper maps [9–12]. The user could retrieve tactile information by exploring the raised-line map. The systems gave additional audio information (e.g. street names) when the user touched the screen.

Several advantages and disadvantages exist for the different types of interactive maps. We chose to place a raised-line map on top of a touch-screen for the following reasons: First of all, most blind users are used to explore raised-line maps. The usage of the prototype is then easy to learn and relies on acquired skills. Second, Rice et al [5] proposed combining tactile and audio modalities because they may both represent spatial information but have complementary functions. For example, Braille labels can be avoided when using speech output. The map can then be designed without overcrowding, including essential tactile information only. Furthermore, when using a raised-line map, it is easy to use tactile cues (e.g. outlines of the map) for keeping mental orientation. Besides, the usage of both hands allows the user to keep fixed reference points while exploring with the other hand. On the contrary, when using a pointing device (e.g. a force-feedback mouse with a single moving cursor), it is much more difficult to keep the reference frame in mind [5]. The last argument in favor of research on an embossed paper map placed on a multi-touch table is that touch screens and raised-line printers are nowadays relatively cheap. They may actually be used by visually impaired people in associations and schools. Even more convincing is that the improvement of haptic refreshable touch screens (as for example the

Surfpad [13]) will promote the design of interactive maps, without having to superimpose raised-line paper maps.

2   Designing an Interactive Map for Visually Impaired People

The following paragraphs describe the different steps for designing an interactive map based on the combination of paper map, touch-screen and audio output which consist in drawing and printing the raised-line paper map, choice of multi-touch technology, interaction methods and software architecture.

2.1   Step 1: Drawing and Printing a Tactile Map

The design of a raised-line paper map includes two aspects: the layout of the map as well as the method for printing the map.

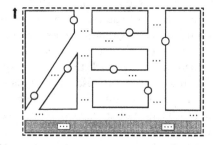

Fig. 1. Drawing of the tactile map used for our prototype

There are no conventions for designing tactile maps, which means that each map uses different symbols and textures. Nevertheless, there are several guidelines that rely on the specificities of the tactile modality. It is important to note that tactile resolution is inferior to visual resolution [14]. In addition, tactile perception is rather serial, whereas vision is synoptic. In contrast to audio description, tactile exploration does not follow an imposed order. Yet, as stated by Hatwell [15], this does not imply that touch is not adapted for perceiving spatial information. Tatham [14] identified a set of symbols with their minimum and maximum perceptible dimensions. Recently, Paladugu et al [16] evaluated different tactile patterns, proposing a set of symbols for tactile maps. We based our map design on these existing guidelines, and chose a set of tactile symbols that were clearly distinguishable.

For map design, we used the Inkscape editor and SVG file format. SVG is used in many different map projects (see e.g. [10]). It is based on the extensible markup language (XML) which is specified by the World Wide Web Consortium (W3C). It allows both visual and textual views, which is very convenient for adding names and description tags to geographic elements.

For this study, we designed a simple fictive map with 6 streets, 6 points of interests and one river (Fig. 1). Names of streets and points of interests were chosen according to the number of syllables and the frequency of usage as mentioned in the

French-speaking database Lexique [17]. Before any experimentation, pre-tests with a blind user confirmed that the map elements were all fully accessible.

The two main methods used for printing raised-line maps are vacuum forming and microcapsule paper. Perkins [18] showed that both techniques are efficient for presenting spatial information. We chose microcapsule paper maps because it is easier to use as production material, and also because the paper used in this case is slimmer, which is advantageous to detect inputs on the touch table through the map.

2.2   Step 2: Selecting the Multi-touch Screen

The multi-touch market is rapidly evolving, introducing a great number of new models and technologies. We identified requirements in order to select an adapted technology for designing an interactive map prototype (see [19] for details). Briefly, we tested different devices and we finally chose the 3M Inc. multi-touch screen (model M2256PW) relying on the projected capacitive multi-touch technology. At the time of purchase it was the only multi-touch screen functioning with a paper map placed on top of it. In addition, the size of the table was adapted for displaying various geographic maps.

2.3   Step 3: Interaction Technologies

The choice of input and output modalities is an important aspect of interactive map design. The relief of the tactile map was the first available sensory cue. We added the Realspeak SAPI 4.0 French text-to-speech synthesis (voice "Sophie") which possesses a good intelligibility and user appreciation [20].

Most interactive maps use simple touch events for input (see e.g. [10]). Kane et al [21] studied gesture interaction for blind people. They found that simple and double taps were easily usable. We chose a simple tap as a basic interaction method in order to validate the map layout and interactivity. Once again, we made pre-tests with two legally blind subjects who were both experienced map users. Interestingly, one of them had explored another interactive map beforehand. Although the simple tap worked fine with sighted users, it did not work with blind users. We observed that, contrary to sighted subjects, the visually impaired users explore tactile maps with several fingers. When multiple fingers were simultaneously applied on the display, many sound outputs were produced. The two blind users who tested the system were then not able to comprehend which finger caused sound outputs. This problem appeared to be specific to an interactive map based on a multi-touch surface (to our knowledge all other projects relied on mono-touch tables). We therefore implemented a double-tap as input interaction, which proved to be efficient to interact with the prototype.

2.4   Step 4: Software Architecture

There exist multiple application programming interfaces for multi-touch devices. As we needed to directly access the touch events, we used the touch-screen low level driver. For each touch event, we obtained an ID (automatically reused when free), the (x; y) coordinates and a timestamp. These data were used for online interaction and logged in a data file for offline analysis. The software architecture of the prototype was made of different software modules connected via the Ivy middleware [22] (see [19] for details). This architecture is very versatile as it allows replacing software modules. The prototype can then easily be adapted with different hardware, maps or experimental requirements.

3   Testing User Satisfaction for the Interactive Map

3.1   Experimental Protocol

In our study, we assessed the user satisfaction concerning the interactive map with the SUS questionnaire [23] translated into French. As proposed by Bangor et al [24] we replaced the usage of the word "cumbersome" by "awkward" to make question 8 of the SUS easier to understand. In an earlier study we had observed negative reactions to the question 7 "I would imagine that most people would learn to use this product very quickly". Users remarked that "most people" would not use a product for visually impaired people. Therefore, we proposed "I think that most visually impaired people would learn to use this product very quickly".

Twelve legally blind users (6 men, 6 women) were involved in the experiment. All users possessed prior experience with regular tactile paper maps and were Braille readers. Each user attended an individual session with one experimenter. The session started with a familiarization phase during which the user explored a map similar to the one used for testing. The experimenter checked that the user was used to the double-tap interaction technique. Next, the experimenter interviewed the user on personal characteristics (chronological age, Braille experience and age at onset of blindness; see Table 1). Then, the instruction was to explore and learn the interactive map as quickly and accurately as possible. The user finally completed the SUS questionnaire and was asked to describe the aspects that he particularly enjoyed or disliked during exploration.

3.2   Results

SUS scores were calculated according to Brooke [23]. Results (see Table 1) provided evidence for a high user satisfaction concerning the interactive map. The mean value of the scores was 87.3 (SD = 15.1). Bangor et al [24] considered scores above 85 as "excellent". The maximum score obtained was 97.5. All scores were superior to 75 points (thus at least "good" [24]) with exception for one subject whose score was 45. Users' characteristics varied significantly according to age (from 21 to 64 years), age at onset of blindness (congenitally blind, late-blind including a user who only lost sight some years ago), and Braille reading experience (from 5 to 58 years). However, we did not observe any correlation between the SUS scores and at least one of these characteristics.

Most users quickly learned the double-tap, whereas the user who gave a SUS score of 45 encountered problems using the double-tap. This user (female, aged 64) possessed prior experience with paper maps with Braille legends and almost 60 years of experience in Braille reading. She mentioned that she enjoys reading Braille and that she had been 'surprised' with the usage of an interactive map.

We asked users for the aspect that they most enjoyed or disliked about the interactive map prototype. As positive aspects they stated that it did not require reading Braille or that they generally prefer speech output (3 users), that there was no need to read a legend (1 user), that it was easy to memorize (1 user), that it was easy to use (1 user) and that usage was ludic (1 user). Aspects they did not like concerned interaction problems with the map (1 user) or that they could more easily memorize written information (1 user).

In addition to this user group, we met a very interesting case: a participant aged 84 years who lost sight at the age of 66. Hence, he learnt Braille lately and had limited reading skills. A standard raised-line map with Braille text was not accessible for him, unless we printed the Braille with large spacing between letters. Contrary, he could immediately use the interactive map and gave an excellent score of 87.5 points in the SUS questionnaire. The interactive map provided him with access to spatial information that he could not have obtained with a regular paper map.

Table 1. Personal characteristics and SUS scores for each user

User	1	2	3	4	5	6	7	8	9	10	11	12
Gender	F	F	M	M	F	M	M	F	F	F	M	M
Age	31	58	25	21	33	53	31	54	38	64	48	59
Onset of blindness (age)	2	15	0	14	26	19	5	0	0	10	25	0
Braille experience (years)	25	46	19	6	5	35	25	48	26	58	22	49
SUS score	90	97,5	95	95	80	90	97,5	95	97,5	45	75	90

Note: Age at onset of blindness corresponds to the age of legal blindness and not to the first occurrence of visual impairment.

4   Conclusion and Future Work

In this article we presented the design and we evaluated the satisfaction related to an interactive map prototype based on a double-tap interaction. It appears that the prototype is very versatile and is an ideal platform to design more advanced interactions. In addition, despite important inter-individual differences, SUS scores provided evidence for a general high satisfaction. First we may note that the interactive map is satisfactory independently of chronological age (range from 21 to 64 years old), which is counterintuitive as one might think that the older are more refractory to technologies. Interestingly, the satisfaction was also excellent independently of the age at onset of blindness. This is important as we know that the age at onset of blindness has important outcomes in terms of adaptation to blindness (general operation, mental imagery, etc.). Finally, the satisfaction was also excellent regardless of Braille experience, except for one user. This result shows that even experts that are particularly attached to Braille are not reluctant to a sound based technology. In addition, the interactive map provides poor Braille readers with access to spatial information.

Satisfaction is one component of usability. Efficiency and efficacy of the interactive map also have to be evaluated. Relying on this prototype, we are designing an experiment to measure satisfaction, efficiency (exploration time) and efficacy (spatial learning) of the interactive map. We aim to show that all three components of usability are higher for interactive maps than for regular (paper) maps with Braille legends.

A second aspect of our work currently consists in designing advanced interactions. Our observations showed that blind users perform specific haptic exploration strategies that impose adapted interaction. Interaction must, especially, be distinguished from regular map exploration and should promote spatial learning. Currently, most interactive maps use mono-touch displays that present important limitations concerning interaction (i.e. simple tap events only). Multi-touch displays would enable new possibilities based on multiple fingers or gestural interaction.

References

1. WHO: Visual Impairment and blindness Fact Sheet N° 282. (2011)
2. Hatwell, Y., Martinez-Sarrochi, F.: The tactile reading of maps and drawings, and the access of blind people to works of art. In: Hatwell, Y., Streri, A., Gentaz, É. (eds.) Touching for Knowing: Cognitive Psychology of Haptic Manual Perception, pp. 255–273. John Benjamins Publishing Company, Amsterdam (2003)
3. Jacobson, R.D.: Navigating maps with little or no sight: An audio-tactile approach. In: Proceedings of Content Visualization and Intermedia Representations, Montréal, Québec, Canada, pp. 95–102 (1998)
4. Buzzi, M.C., Buzzi, M., Leporini, B., Martusciello, L.: Making Visual Maps Accessible to the Blind. In: Stephanidis, C. (ed.) HCII 2011 and UAHCI 2011, Part II. LNCS, vol. 6766, pp. 271–280. Springer, Heidelberg (2011)
5. Rice, M., Jacobson, R.D., Golledge, R.G., Jones, D.: Design considerations for haptic and auditory map interfaces. Cartography and Geographic Information Science 32, 381–391 (2005)
6. Zeng, L., Weber, G.: Audio-Haptic Browser for a Geographical Information System. In: Miesenberger, K., Klaus, J., Zagler, W., Karshmer, A. (eds.) ICCHP 2010. LNCS, vol. 6180, pp. 466–473. Springer, Heidelberg (2010)
7. Shimada, S., Murase, H., Yamamoto, S., Uchida, Y., Shimojo, M., Shimizu, Y.: Development of Directly Manipulable Tactile Graphic System with Audio Support Function. In: Miesenberger, K., Klaus, J., Zagler, W., Karshmer, A. (eds.) ICCHP 2010, Part II. LNCS, vol. 6180, pp. 451–458. Springer, Heidelberg (2010)
8. Wagner, A.B.: Collaboratively Generated Content on the Audio-Tactile Map. In: Miesenberger, K., Klaus, J., Zagler, W., Karshmer, A. (eds.) ICCHP 2010, Part II. LNCS, vol. 6179, pp. 78–80. Springer, Heidelberg (2010)
9. Parkes, D.: NOMAD: An audio-tactile tool for the acquisition, use and management of spatially distributed information by partially sighted and blind persons. In: Tatham, A.,

Dodds, A. (eds.) Proceedings of Second International Conference on Maps and Graphics for Visually Disabled People, Nottingham, United Kingdom, pp. 24–29 (1988)

10. Miele, J.A., Landau, S., Gilden, D.: Talking TMAP: Automated generation of audio-tactile maps using Smith-Kettlewell's TMAP software. BJVI 24, 93–100 (2006)

11. Minatani, K., Watanabe, T., Yamaguchi, T., Watanabe, K., Akiyama, J., Miyagi, M., Oouchi, S.: Tactile Map Automated Creation System to Enhance the Mobility of Blind Persons—Its Design Concept and Evaluation through Experiment. In: Miesenberger, K., Klaus, J., Zagler, W., Karshmer, A. (eds.) ICCHP 2010, Part II. LNCS, vol. 6180, pp. 534–540. Springer, Heidelberg (2010)

12. Wang, Z., Li, B., Hedgpeth, T., Haven, T.: Instant tactile-audio map: enabling access to digital maps for people with visual impairment. In: Proceedings of ASSETS, pp. 43–50. ACM, Pittsburgh (2009)

13. Casiez, G., Roussel, N., Vanbelleghem, R., Giraud, F.: Surfpad: riding towards targets on a squeeze film effect. In: Proceedings of CHI, pp. 2491–2500. ACM Press, Vancouver (2011)

14. Tatham, A.F.: The design of tactile maps: theoretical and practical considerations. In: Proceedings of International Cartographic Association: Mapping the Nations, pp. 157–166. K Rybaczak and M Blakemore, London (1991)

15. Hatwell, Y.: Introduction: Touch and Cognition. In: Hatwell, Y., Streri, A., Gentaz, É. (eds.) Touching for Knowing: Cognitive Psychology of Haptic Manual Perception, pp. 1–14. John Benjamins Publishing Company, Amsterdam (2003)

16. Paladugu, D.A., Wang, Z., Li, B.: On presenting audio-tactile maps to visually impaired users for getting directions. In: Proceedings of CHI, pp. 3955–3960. ACM Press, Atlanta (2010)

17. New, B., Pallier, C., Ferrand, L., Matos, R.: Une base de données lexicales du français contemporain sur internet: LEXIQUE. L'année Psychologique 101, 447–462 (2001)

18. Perkins, C.: Tactile campus mapping: Evaluating designs and production technologies. In: 20th International Cartographic Conference, Beijing, China, pp. 2906–2913 (2001)

19. Brock, A., Truillet, P., Oriola, B., Jouffrais, C.: Usage of multimodal maps for blind people: why and how. In: International Conference on Interactive Tabletops and Surfaces, p. 247. ACM Press, Saarbruecken (2010)

20. Côté-Giroux, P., Trudeau, N., Valiquette, C., Sutton, A., Chan, E., Hébert, C.: Intelligibilité et appréciation de neuf synthèses vocales françaises. Canadian Journal of Speech-language Pathology and Audiology 35, 300–311 (2011)

21. Kane, S.K., Wobbrock, J.O., Ladner, R.E.: Usable gestures for blind people. In: Proceedings of CHI 2011, p. 413. ACM Press, Vancouver (2011)

22. Buisson, M., Bustico, A., Chatty, S., Colin, F.-R., Jestin, Y., Maury, S., Mertz, C., Truillet, P.: Ivy: un bus logiciel au service du développement de prototypes de systèmes interactifs. In: 14th French-speaking Conference on HCI, pp. 223–226. ACM, Poitiers (2002)

23. Brooke, J.: SUS: A "quick and dirty" usability scale. In: Jordan, P.W., Thomas, B., Weerdmeester, B.A., McClelland, I.L. (eds.) Usability Evaluation in Industry, pp. 189–194. Taylor & Francis, London (1996)

24. Bangor, A., Kortum, P., Miller, J.: An Empirical Evaluation of the System Usability Scale. International Journal of Human-Computer Interaction 24, 574–594 (2008)

A Mobile Application Concept to Encourage Independent Mobility for Blind and Visually Impaired Students

Jukka Liimatainen[1], Markku Häkkinen[2], Tuula Nousiainen[1],
Marja Kankaanranta[1], and Pekka Neittaanmäki[2]

[1] Agora Center, University of Jyväskylä, Finland
{jukka.t.liimatainen,tuula.j.nousiainen}@jyu.fi,
marja.kankaanranta@ktl.jyu.fi
[2] Department of Mathematical Information Technology,
University of Jyväskylä, Finland
{markku.t.hakkinen,pekka.neittaanmaki}@jyu.fi

Abstract. This paper presents a user-centric application development process for mobile application to blind and visually impaired students. The development process connects the assistive technology experts, teachers and students from the school for visually impaired together to participate to the design of the mobile application. The data for the analysis is gathered from interviews and workshops with the target group. The main goal of the project is to examine how mobile application can be used to encourage and motivate visually impaired students to move independently indoors and outdoors. The application allows the students to interact with their environment through use of sensor technology now standard on most smart and feature phones. We present a user-centric application development process, report on findings from the initial user trials, and propose a framework for future phases of the project.

Keywords: Mobile phone application, interactive technologies, blind, visually impaired, accessibility.

1 Introduction

Interactive mobile applications such as camera-based scanning of barcodes and Near-Field Communication (NFC) can give the end-user access to a variety of enhanced information services. These applications and improvements in device accessibility are turning off-the-shelf mobile phones into functional personal assistive tools for individuals with visual impairments, enabling innovative ways for the user to interact with their environment.

This paper presents an overview of research project developing a mobile application prototype for students at a school for blind and visually impaired. The primary goal of the project is to examine how a game-like mobile application can be used to encourage and motivate visually impaired students to move independently in and around the school premises. The secondary goal for the students is to learn new way-finding techniques to assist in forming a mental map of their surroundings.

K. Miesenberger et al. (Eds.): ICCHP 2012, Part II, LNCS 7383, pp. 552–559, 2012.

The first version of the application was implemented following user-centered design principles [1, 2]. We followed a process in which different stakeholders (assistive technology professionals, teachers and students) participated in the design process to define the required accessibility features and adaptations in the application prototype [3]. The result is a way-finding application that allows students with visual impairments to interact with their environment through use of digital camera and two-dimensional (2D) barcode reader technology [4], now available on most smart and feature phones. Accessibility features were implemented in the application user interface to enhance the usability of the mobile device by the students. We present a user-centered application design process, report on findings from the initial user trials, and propose a framework for future phases of the project.

2   Related Works

The use of 2D barcodes with a mobile phone by visually impaired and blind users has been previously proposed by Al-Khalifa [5], who described a system consisting of 2D barcodes which are affixed to an object and a mobile phone bar code scanning application that directs the phone's web browser to a URL that contains an audio description of the object when scanned.

A way-finding application using barcodes for people who are blind and visually impaired has been proposed by Coughlin et al. [6]. The system utilized barcodes with color targets and special algorithm to improve the detection and reading of the codes. The feasibility of the system was confirmed with preliminary field tests with blind subjects. Tekin and Coughlan [7] further demonstrated a computer vision algorithm augmented with an audio signal for mobile phones to improve the detection of barcodes.

Chang et al [8] have proposed a low-cost guidance system prototype based on geo-coded 2D barcodes and social computing for individuals with cognitive impairments. 2D barcodes are representing traffic signs in way-finding system and the user receives navigational photos when scanning codes on the route. The tracking system follows the visited positions and alerts when in case of anomalies such as deviation from the route.

López-de-Ipiña et al [9] presented a system called "Blindshopping", which is a RFID and 2D barcode based mobile solution for enabling an assisted shopping service for blind and visually impaired users. In the "Blindshopping" solution architecture the navigation system is implemented with RFID reader attached to a white cane. A blind user can navigate the RFID tag lines in the supermarket while receiving verbal navigation instructions through smartphone attached headphones. Product recognition is implemented with a smartphone 2D barcode reader. The code infrastructure can be managed using a web-based application solution.

Valente et al. [10] presented "The Audio Flashlight", a non-visual mobile phone game designed for blind and visually impaired users. The user interface of the game relies solely on audio, vibration, and gestural input. Results from their pilot study addressed the importance of audio design and the need to avoid overloading the user with too much sensory information.

There is growing recognition of the importance that smart phones can play in the lives of individuals with disabilities, and a growing number of off the shelf consumer devices, such as the Apple iPhone[1] offer built-in accessibility support. Mobile applications (or apps) that augment a phone's existing accessibility or add new functionality are increasing in number. Recommendations and initiatives for accessibility features in smartphones and feature phones have been proposed by The International Telecommunication Union and The Global Initiative for Inclusive ICTS [11]. In addition, there have been accessibility evaluations and assessments for mobile phone by expert groups and research organizations [12, 13].

Our application approach differs from previous work in that it was implemented using an off-the-shelf, feature phone with modification of the touch-screen user interface to better support the needs of visually impaired and blind end-users. The application utilizes freeware 2D barcode reader software in combination with software and pre-recorded audio files stored in internal memory card of the mobile phone. Upon successful scan, the application loads and plays the appropriate audio file containing way-finding information for the recognized location. The accessible user interface allows the user to access and control the application with repeatable tapping gestures anywhere on the phone's touch-screen. The audio files (voice instructions), created by teachers who design the way-finding paths, are installed to the phone using file transfer software provided by the phone's manufacturer.

3   Conducting the Study

In user-centered design approach the end users are participating in the early stages of the design process. The aim of this approach is to achieve user-friendly and accessible solutions. This chapter covers the user-centered approach for blind and visually impaired from initial planning phase to final evaluation phase.

3.1   User-Centered Design Approach

The application design process followed the user-centered design approach in which different stakeholders participated in the design process. It contained initial requirement, implementation and evaluation phases, conducted in iterative cycles where design goals and solutions gradually become more specific after each iteration [2]. Participants for these design phases included assistive technology professionals (N=6), teachers from school for visually impaired and blind (N=3) and students from school for visually impaired and blind (N=9, aged 10-16 years).

---

[1] Apple and iPhone are trademarks of Apple Corporation.

3.2   The Requirement Phase

In the present research, accessibility and user requirements for a mobile phone application concept were identified from interviews with 6 assistive technology professionals. The analysis of the concepts and interview data led to the categorization in terms of specific applications and features. At the requirement phase total of 17 mobile application concept ideas were identified and analyzed. Three main classes were derived from the original interview data as shown in Table 1. The main issue which arose from these interviews was the need to develop an application that could encourage independent mobility (70, 6%) of blind and visually impaired people. There was also interested to develop audio games (23, 5 %) for visually impaired end-users. One of the concept ideas related to rehabilitation application. It was also determined that strong emphasis would be placed on creating a fully accessible user interface features.

Table 1. Mobile application ideas from the requirement phase interview data

Mobile Application ideas (main classes)	
1. Mobile application to motivate independent mobility	12/17 (70, 6 %)
2. Mobile (audio) game application	4/17 (23, 5 %)
3. Rehabilitation application	1/17 (5, 9 %)

3.3   The Implementation Phase

Based on the requirements data gathered from the interviews, an initial prototype of way-finding application was implemented for the Nokia 5800 touch-screen mobile phone with Symbian series 60 operating system. The idea of game-like way-finding application is based on the model of routes within the physical environment. Voice cues and directions for following a route are provided via scannable 2D barcodes placed within the environment.   Users of the application locate and scan the tags, and receive a sound cue indicating a successful scan and spoken directions on how to find the next tag in the route.

The user interface was modified to be more accessible utilizing repeatable tapping (haptic) gestures on the touch-screen (Fig 1.). Using repetition of tapping gestures on the touch-screen the user can start the scanning application, listen to the instructions, or close the application. After a successful scan the code redirects to the internal memory card of the mobile phone and starts software application which has two main functions:

- play two audio (MP3 format) files (with sound effects & voice instructions)
- show accessible display, where user can control the application by tapping gestures (one tap plays the instructions again and two taps starts the barcode reader)

Voice instructions can be recorded, updated and stored into the memory-card of the phone using a standard computer and off-the- shelf software provided by the mobile phone manufacturer (i.e. the Nokia PC Suite). Teachers can design the route indoors and outdoors within school premises and modify the audio instructions which enable the students to follow new routes.

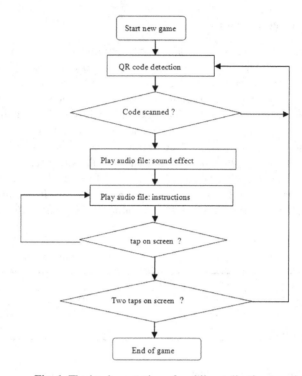

Fig. 1. The implementation of mobile application

3.4   The Field Tests

The field tests, conducted over multiple sessions at a school for the blind and visually impaired, included an initial session to introduce students and teachers to the application. After the introduction, the field trials were carried out on the school premises. The research survey was conducted before and after the field trials with the student participants.

Introduction to Test Session. After implementation and initial testing of the application, a field trial was held at a local school for the blind and visually impaired. The field trial involved 11 students (6 blind, 5 low vision). An initial session introducing the application was conducted by the lead researcher and presented to the students and 3 teachers of the visually impaired from the school. The students tested the application in a standard classroom with different sizes of printed 2D barcodes and, assisted by their teachers, learned how to locate the barcodes by touch and scan them with mobile phone camera. The tactile identifiability of the barcode tags were improved by covering them with plastic laminate.

Preliminary Questionnaires. The preliminary questionnaires were given to students before the field trials of the mobile application. The questionnaire covered the usage of mobile phones in everyday tasks and special questions about the mobile applications for physical activity. According the results of the preliminary survey most of the students either owned (36, 4 %) or had tried (54, 5 %) smartphones or feature phones with touch-screen. The average experience of using mobile phones was 6-9 years. More than half (54, 5 %) of the students had experience with mobile game applications. One of the students had tried physical activity or health-related computer or mobile applications before. The most popular daily usages of mobile phones were calling, text messages and listening music or radio (Fig. 2).

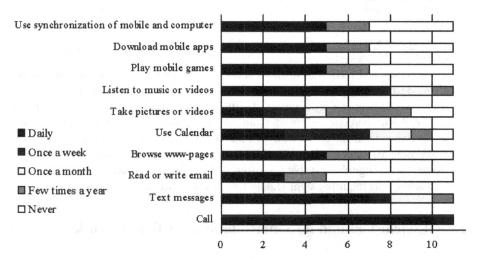

Fig. 2. The results of preliminary questionnaire

Conducting the Field Trials. After the initial session, the teachers designed a way-finding route within the school premises, marking the route with barcode tags. The students informed teachers about the places and buildings within the school area which they do not frequently visit. The teachers then created instructions on how to move between the marked locations, navigating a path from start to finish. These instructions were recorded by a teacher, stored as audio files (MP3 format) and transferred to each of the 11 test mobile phones. A test session was then conducted in which 11 students were introduced to the application and asked to follow a route by locating the barcodes, scanning them, and then following the audio instructions to locate the next bar code on the route. The students followed the route in pairs and used their own assistive devices for navigation (white cane).

4   The Results

The Results from the field trial indicate the prototype application provides an effective approach to introducing students to way-finding in the school premises. All students (N=11) in the pilot study successfully navigated the marked route within the premises using the application. After the field tests the usability survey and post test questionnaire were conducted. The System Usability Scale (SUS) test was used for assessment of perceived system usability. The usability score can vary from 0-100 with systems having a score higher than 50 considered to have favorable usability characteristics. In our study the usability test score was higher with blind students than with low vision (Table 2). The total SUS score was 57, 5.

Table 2. System Usability Test (SUS) results

Mobile Application ideas (main classes)	
Blind students (N=6)	64,6
Low vision (N=5)	47,5
Total score (N=11)	57,75

Observations and feedback of the field test have been reviewed and minor adjustments made in mobile application for evaluation in the next phase of the research. Scanning of 2D barcodes was improved with better placement near the light sources and updated with barcode reader with camera shutter sound effect when catching the code. As expected from our review of related research, the camera-based scanning required some assistance especially with blind students. Also the completion times of the route varied significantly between low vision and blind students, with the low vision participants requiring significantly less time to complete the route.

5   Conclusions and Recommendations for Future Work

A mobile application prototype combining common interactive technologies, an off-the shelf mobile phone, and an accessible application to way-finding was developed. The application prototype was designed to serve as a basic platform for future research activities, where we will explore new interactive elements, game-like features and interactions, and expand the navigation properties of the system.

Based on the positive results of the initial field test, we are continuing our research with an expanded group of blind and visually impaired students. Quantitative and qualitative data is being collected from the field tests, and focusing on the usability and motivational aspects of both the application used by the students and the route authoring tools used by the teachers.

We will be utilizing the results of our data analysis to continue to improve the motivational and accessibility features of the application. Because camera usage, and specifically the aiming of the camera, can be problematic for blind users, we are planning to enhance the usability of the application by replacing camera-based scanning with a NFC -based tag reading and WLAN/WIFI- positioning system. In addition, we will be including a screen-reader application with the phone to improve the overall usability of the touch user interface.

Acknowledgement. The work presented in this paper is being carried out as a part of the project "Personal Mobile Space", funded by the Finnish Funding Agency for Technology and Innovation (TEKES).

References

1. Norman, D., Draper, S.: User Centered System Design; New Perspectives on Human-Computer Interaction. L. Erlbaum Assoc. Inc., Hillsdale (1986)
2. ISO 13407: Human-centered design processes for interactive systems. Geneve: International Organization for Standardization (1999)
3. Thimbleby, H.: Understanding User Centred Design (UCD) for People with Special Needs. In: Miesenberger, K., Klaus, J., Zagler, W.L., Karshmer, A.I. (eds.) ICCHP 2008. LNCS, vol. 5105, pp. 1–17. Springer, Heidelberg (2008)
4. Upcode Ltd., http://www.upc.fi/en/upcode
5. Al-Khalifa, H.: Utilizing QR Code and Mobile Phones for Blinds and Visually Impaired People. In: Miesenberger, K., Klaus, J., Zagler, W.L., Karshmer, A.I. (eds.) ICCHP 2008. LNCS, vol. 5105, pp. 1065–1069. Springer, Heidelberg (2008)
6. Coughlan, J., Manduchi, R., Shen, H.: Cell Phone-based Way-finding for the Visually Impaired. In: 1st International Workshop on Mobile Vision, in Conjunction with ECCV 2006, Graz, Austria (2006)
7. Tekin, E., Coughlan, J.: A Mobile Phone Application Enabling Visually Impaired Users to Find and Read Product Barcodes. In: Miesenberger, K., Klaus, J., Zagler, W., Karshmer, A. (eds.) ICCHP 2010. LNCS, vol. 6180, pp. 290–295. Springer, Heidelberg (2010)
8. Chang, Y., Tsai, S., Chang, Y., Wang, T.: A Novel Wayfinding System Based on Geocoded QR codes for Individuals with Cognitive Impairments. In: 9th International ACM SIGACCESS Conference on Computers and Accessibility, pp. 231–232. ACM, New York (2007)
9. López-de-Ipiña, D., Lorido, T., López, U.: Indoor Navigation and Product Recognition for Blind People Assisted Shopping. In: Bravo, J., Hervás, R., Villarreal, V. (eds.) IWAAL 2011. LNCS, vol. 6693, pp. 33–40. Springer, Heidelberg (2011)
10. Valente, L., Clarisse, S., Feijo, B.: An exploratory study on non-visual mobile phone interfaces for games. In: VIII Brazilian Symposium on Human Factors in Computing Systems, Brazil, pp. 31–39 (2008)
11. Making Mobile Phones and Services Accessible for Persons with Disabilities, A joint report of ITU –the international telecommunication union and G3ICT – The initiative for inclusive ICTs (2011)
12. Treviranus, J., Richards, J., Silva, J.: Mobile Wireless Handset Accessibility Assessment. In: Inclusive Design Research Centre (IDRC), OCAD University (2011)
13. Billi, M., Burzagli, L., Catarci, T., Santucci, G., Bertini, E., Gabbanini, F., Palchetti, E.: A unified methodology for the evaluation of accessibility and usability of mobile applications. Univ. Access Inf. Soc. 9, 337–356 (2010)

Do-It-Yourself Object Identification
Using Augmented Reality for Visually Impaired People

Atheer S. Al-Khalifa[1] and Hend S. Al-Khalifa[2]

[1] Electronic and Computer Research Institute, King Abdulaziz City for Science and Technology
[2] Information Technology Department, College of Computer and Information Sciences,
King Saud University, Riyadh, Saudi Arabia
aalkhalifa@kacst.edu.sa
hendk@ksu.edu.sa

Abstract. In this paper, we present a Do-It-Yourself (DIY) application for helping Visually Impaired People (VIP) identify objects in their day-to-day interaction with the environment. The application uses the Layar[TM] Augmented Reality (AR) API to build a working prototype for identifying grocery items. The initial results of using the application show positive acceptance from the VIP community.

Keywords: Augmented Reality, Visually Impaired, Object Identification, Layar[TM], Assistive Technology.

1   Introduction

Visually Impaired People (VIP) face problems in identifying day-to-day objects. The outer shape of an object is not enough to help VIP recognize its content. VIP usually apply different techniques to recognize objects based on their features such as: texture, size, or sound. Therefore, object identification is a very challenging task that depends on the VIP experience.

Many Object identification assistive technologies, either hardware or software, were built to help VIP in recognizing surrounding objects. These assistive technologies help them in describing the environment. The description usually comes in the form that is suitable for VIP; It could be oral description or tactile.

Given the fact that most of these assistive technologies are specialized to perform a specific task e.g. Talking Scales, yet, it is best to integrate the technology into already found and used devices. One of the most popular and widely used technologies nowadays is smart phones. Smart phones are becoming ubiquitous and have high processing power. All people regardless of their disabilities are using mobile phones for their daily communication. Actually, smart phones are becoming popular and their capabilities have increased in terms of processing power and memory capacity. At the same time, their costs have fallen down which make them available for all individuals whether they are healthy or disabled.

K. Miesenberger et al. (Eds.): ICCHP 2012, Part II, LNCS 7383, pp. 560–565, 2012.
© Springer-Verlag Berlin Heidelberg 2012

In this paper we present a Do-It-Yourself (DIY) application for helping VIP identify real world objects using Augmented Reality (AR) technology. AR is defined as merging digital-generated graphics that are perfectly aligned to real world view [1]. This technology can be utilized to augment not only digital graphics but also sounds.

In the market we have several AR software used in mobile phones whether they are open source or proprietary. Mixare Browser (mixare.org) is an example of an open source AR framework while Layar™ (layar.com) is its proprietary counterpart.

The main contribution of this work is to present a DIY guide for creating a personalized augmented reality layer for VIP using Layar™. The guide does not involve advanced programming skills; any novice programmer can easily implement it.

The rest of the paper is organized as follows: section 2 sheds the light on some previous work in the area of object identification for VIP. Section 3 presents in detail the implemented DIY application. Section 4 reports the results of the preliminary evaluation of the application. Finally, section 5 concludes the paper with the application limitation and future work.

2 Previous Work

Different mobile applications have been created to help VIP in identifying objects; whether using image processing algorithms e.g. LookTel or depending on human identification e.g. VizWiz. These contributions made a solid start in using mobile phones for helping VIP.

LookTel is an example of using image processing for identifying objects. It is a visual assistance platform developed by Sudol et al. for VIP [2]. It performs currency identification, Optical Character Recognition (OCR) on texts, landmark and location recognition and packaged goods and tagged object identification. Tagging objects using unique vinyl stickers is an added function for recognizing problematic objects that lacks distinctive features for the scale-invariant feature transform (SIFT) recognition engine to recognize. The user can apply the pre-trained sticker on an object, for example medication bottle or glass jar, then add it to the system using the mobile phone along with the recorded audio description.

On the other hand, an example of human identification system can be seen in Bigham et al. [3] VizWiz iPhone mobile application. The application assists VIP in their visual environments by asking general questions answered by paid human workers. The application is used to identify and locate objects, where a user take a picture of the designated item using the mobile's camera followed by recording the spoken question. The photo and audio files are then uploaded to the server, which posts them as a job for recruited human workers in the Amazon Mechanical Turk (www.mturk.com/mturk/welcome). After identifying the object by speaking its name, the user will receive the audio answer on the mobile phone.

3   The Proposed DIY Application

Our proposed AR personalized helper DIY application uses LayarTM environment which provides a platform that supports end-users in creating their own real-time AR environments. It creates a layer of digital objects over physical Points Of Interest (POI) that can trigger a series of actions. These POIs can be geo-location (using GPS), Layar VisionTM objects or both [4].

Layar Vision^{TM} [4] is a client-side extension of the Layar^{TM} environment that enables visual detection, tracking and augmentation of real world objects based on associated preloaded fingerprint into the application's layer. When a user points a mobile phone camera at a Vision POI physical object, the Layar^{TM} client will detect it instantly and triggers different set of actions by sending a getPOI request to the layer service provider. This auto-trigger property can be used to create a personalized visual assistant by having the users create their own layer with their choice of objects that satisfy the specification of Layar^{TM} vision's POI. Following is a step by step guide on how to build a VIP personalized helper using Layar^{TM} AR.

The application demonstrates a simple case of identifying five grocery items. These objects are divided into two physical forms with the same attributes (length, width, height, weight and texture) but different product types– three potato chips bags (of different flavors) and two milk boxes (low fat and regular).

The application Requirements are as follows:

- Layar Vision^{TM}: applicable on the 6.0th version of Layar^{TM} Reality browser on Android 2.2 along with iPhone iOS 4.0 platform and above.
- Layar^{TM} developer account.
- Public web server.

After creating a developer account and a new Vision enabled layer, the five items' images were uploaded as reference images into Layar^{TM} publishing website. The service then analyze these images to rate their appropriateness to be recognized by the application. These images were taken using a Samsung Galaxy S II. Each image was then edited by cropping its background to the item's canvas using the painter program. Actually, Layar^{TM} has presented the best practices for creating reference images [5]; where a target object's photo must be of a flat surface, cropped background, non-blurry, non-light reflected and front angled photo.

Next, we used the code example published in Make magazine [6] by modifying it to adapt to our experiment. The example contains an "index.php" page and JavaScript Object Notion (JSON) file along with the page header and footer. The index file concatenates the POI or hotspot of each item into a single JSON response for the layer. Each hotspot object has: "ID", "anchor" for the reference image name, and actions. The ID must be unique for each item and the reference image name is identical to the name assigned to it in LayarTM publishing website.

Since we need the audio description of the specific item to play once an item reference image is detected, we have to modify the Action object of the GetPOI-JSON response found in each item file, as shown in Figure 1.

```
"actions": [
        {
                "uri": "audio://atheer.googlah.com/p-salt.mp3",
                "autoTrigger": true,
                "label": "RIYAL",
                "contentType": "audio/mpeg",
                "activityType": 2,
                "showActivity": true
        }
```

Fig. 1. The modified action for automatically playing an audio of an item description

Then we modified the main directory's index.php file by adding each POI's JSON response instance to the POIs array. At the same time we added a small audio icon that appears when recognizing an object that is identified in the Object Dictionary (Figure 2).

Fig. 2. The application running on Samsung Galaxy S II phone (left) and iPhone 4GS (right), the volume icon indicate that the object name is being spoken

Finally, we linked our created layer with the web server containing our application code by providing the API endpoint URL field with the path of index.php file [7].

4   Preliminary Evaluation

A group of three VIP were asked to try the application using two smart phones: (1) Samsung Galaxy S II phones running Android version 2.3.4 and (2) iPhone 4GS running iOS5.

The participants varied in age between 20-30 years old with a good experience in using mobile phones. The three VIP were given an introduction to the application explaining how to use it. They were then asked to perform the recognition tasks on a 3G connection.

After trying out the application, the VIP were asked a set of questions with answers ranging from strongly agree to strongly disagree. Table 1 shows the responses to the survey questions.

Table 1. Average response for three VIP. 1 is strongly disagree, 5 is strongly agree.

Usefulness as a grocery item reader.	3
Ease of pointing to regions of interest.	2
Reliability of the application.	4

By looking at the survey results, we can find that a positive feedback was reflected in the first and third questions; however the second question regarding the ease of pointing was below midpoint. One blind user comment was "the application is really needed, but for me to be able to use it I need to estimate the distance and angle of pointing the mobile camera in order to get the application recognize the object".

We can see from this preliminary evaluation that the application is both useful and needed for the VIP community, yet it needs to be improved in terms of reliability and ease of pointing.

5   Conclusion, Limitations and Future Work

Several assistive technologies aim to help visually impaired people in eliminating the barriers formed as a result of disregarding their disabilities in human's daily needs. These assistive technologies take different orientations whether used in object identification, individual navigation or creating accessible environments. In this paper we presented a DIY Object Identification application using LayarTM Augmented reality API. The application utilizes available end-user application for helping VIP in recognizing real world items.

One of the major limitations in the resulted application resides in the limited number of POI. No more than 50 POI can be registered in a layer. Also, we noticed that in low lighting Environments the application cannot identify the objects properly, i.e. it shows wrong results for similar objects. Moreover, sometimes the auto-trigger feature in Layar^{TM} would be fired once and cannot be re-fired again unless the user reloads the layer. The final limitation was realized in the volume of the played audio. In the Android OS compared to iOS 5, the audio played was low.

Despite all these limitations, creating a DIY was easy, straight forward and did not require deep technical skills. Our future work will include crowd-sourcing the process of populating the Object Dictionary. This can be done by developing a platform that enables ordinary people to send images of objects along with their audio description using their mobile phones.

References

1. Haller, M., Billinghurst, M., Thomas, B.H.: Emerging technologies of augmented reality: interfaces and design. Idea Group Inc, (IGI) (2007)
2. Sudol, J., Dialameh, O., Blanchard, C., Dorcey, T.: Looktel—A comprehensive platform for computer-aided visual assistance. In: 2010 IEEE Computer Society Conference on Computer Vision and Pattern Recognition Workshops (CVPRW), pp. 73–80 (2010)
3. Bigham, J.P., et al.: VizWiz: nearly real-time answers to visual questions. In: Proceedings of the 23nd Annual ACM Symposium on User Interface Software and Technology, New York, NY, USA, pp. 333–342 (2010)
4. Layar Reality Browser / Layar Vision Overview, http://layar.pbworks.com/w/page/43908786/Layar%20Vision%20Overview (accessed: January 17, 2012)
5. Layar Reality Browser / Reference Image Best Practices, http://layar.pbworks.com/w/page/43909057/Reference%20Image%20Best%20Practices (accessed: January 20, 2012)
6. Layar Augmented Reality for MAKE. vol 28. (and How to Make Your Own), http://boingboing.net/2011/11/21/layar-augmented-reality-for-ma.html
7. The example's source code explained, can be found on the following link, http://faculty.ksu.edu.sa/hend.alkhalifa/documents/resources/AR-example.rar

An Assistive Vision System for the Blind That Helps Find Lost Things

Boris Schauerte[1,*], Manel Martinez[1,*], Angela Constantinescu[2,*],
and Rainer Stiefelhagen[1,2]

Karlsruhe Institute of Technology
[1] Institute for Anthropomatics, Adenauerring 2
[2] Study Center for the Visually Impaired Students, Engesserstr. 4,
76131 Karlsruhe, Germany
forename.surname@kit.edu

Abstract. We present a computer vision system that helps blind people find lost objects. To this end, we combine color- and SIFT-based object detection with sonification to guide the hand of the user towards potential target object locations. This way, we are able to guide the user's attention and effectively reduce the space in the environment that needs to be explored. We verified the suitability of the proposed system in a user study.

Keywords: Lost & Found, Computer Vision, Sonification, Object Detection & Recognition, Visually Impaired, Blind.

1 Introduction

According to recent estimates of the World Health Organization, 285 million visually impaired people live in the world of which 39 million are blind [13]. Although 80% of all visual impairment could be avoided or cured, the unfortunate fact that the majority of blind people lives in developing countries in combination with the aging global elderly population leads to a huge innovation pressure for affordable and intuitive tools that aid visually impaired people. With the decreasing costs of digital camera technologies and mobile computing power, which is closely related to the wide distribution of mobile phones[1], computer vision is an increasingly cost-effective technology that allows visually impaired people to perceive (more) visual information in their environment. Furthermore, computer and robot vision algorithms are getting more robust and thus applicable in real-world applications (see, e.g., Google Goggles [7]). Research in the area indicates that computer vision is, for example, able to help blind people navigate in urban and indoor environments [11,3] or assist in shopping scenarios [12].

In this paper, we introduce a novel vision system that can help blind and visually impaired people find objects that were misplaced or have unexpectedly

---

* Equal contribution.
[1] According to strategy analysts, more than 1 billion camera phones were sold in 2011 (the first time that annual volumes have exceeded 1 billion units).

K. Miesenberger et al. (Eds.): ICCHP 2012, Part II, LNCS 7383, pp. 566–572, 2012.
© Springer-Verlag Berlin Heidelberg 2012

changed their location (e.g., they may have fallen to the ground or been relocated by another person). To this end, the user has to hold a small camera, which can also be attached to his wrist if he prefers to have both hands free in order to allow for unhindered grasping and haptic perception. The corresponding hand is then guided towards potential target object locations using computer vision for object detection and sonification for acoustic feedback. This way, we are able to guide the user effectively towards plausible object locations and reduce the search space. At each object location, the user can then use his accustomed senses to conclusively identify the object. Using this methodology, following our idea that we want to enhance the capabilities of the user and not replace or interfere with his intact senses, we aid the user in detecting the searched object without interfering with his sense of orientation and leave the final search strategy and decisions to the user.

2   Related Work

Most closely related to our work are the systems by Hub et al. [8], Caperna et al. [3], and Bigham et al. [2]. In 2004, Hub et al. [8] presented a system that assists blind users in orienting themselves in indoor environments. However, their system requires a world model of landmarks and objects in the target environment, because it seemed "impossible to realize object identification of arbitrary objects using systems that are only based on [...] image interpretation" [8]. Furthermore, Hub et al. do not use sonification, but rely on text-to-speech communication. Caperna et al. [3] combined a global positioning system, inertial navigation unit, computer vision algorithms, and audio and haptic interfaces. In their system, computer vision makes it possible to identify and locate objects such as signs and landmarks. To this end, they rely on the Scale-Invariant Feature Transform (SIFT) by D. Lowe (see [10]). However, the corresponding evaluation has been performed in a simplified scenario and computer vision was left as major aspect for future work. Bigham et al. [2] use Speeded Up Robust Features (SURF; see [10]) for object identification, but instead of training an object database (see, e.g., [3]), they send images with user requests (e.g., where is the object in the image) to Amazon's Mechanical Turk [1] where humans can outline the objects. The outlines of the object can then be used to estimate the object's location in the environment and guide the user towards the object by informing the user how close he is to the target [2].

3   Main System Components

3.1   Visual Object Detection

Specific Objects: We use SIFT (see [10]) to detect known objects. To this end, our system provides a simple training interface, which makes it possible to train new objects by holding them in front of the camera and triggering snapshots. Trained objects can then be searched for in the environment using common SIFT feature matching and classification methods (see, e.g., [4]).

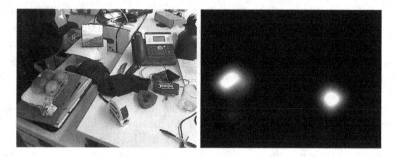

Fig. 1. Illustration of the object detection using color attributes. Image of a typical desktop environment (left) and the corresponding normalized target probability map for color "red" (right). The probability map is calculated at a lower scale than the original image to save computational resources. Here, two potential target objects are clearly identified.

Color Attributes: When using local features such as SIFT and SURF, it is only possible to detect specific, known objects (i.e., existent in the database) with a distinctive texture. As a complementary approach, we propose to use visual attributes to help find things in a broader range of scenarios; e.g., to help find a specific colored shirt in a pile of shirts or to find objects that have only been verbally described by other persons. To this end, in our prototype implementation, we use probabilistic models of the 11 basic English color terms [9], see Fig. 1, which can also be used to name the color of an object in front of the camera.

3.2 Sonification

Two sound properties – pan and pitch – are used to map the information about the object's location that is received from the vision module as follows (also see [5]): The location on the image's x-axis is mapped to pan, such that the perceived sound source location (left-front-right) corresponds with the object location relative to the image center. The location on the y-axis maps to pitch (see [6]). Here, objects located closer to the bottom of the image frame correspond to lower sounds, and objects located closer to the top of the frame correspond to higher sounds. In order to allow the user to rate how confident the system is about the detection, we map tempo to detection confidence with a more continuous sound (i.e., shorter time between "beeps") for higher detection confidence.

4 Evaluation

4.1 Procedure

To examine the suitability of the presented system, we first performed a pilot study to assess the complexity of two application scenarios with two blind users

Fig. 2. Example of an evaluation trial (the participant is shown at two locations in the room), i.e. a person searching for an object inside a room. The image shows the office room and an exemplary distribution of the items. Furthermore, the image illustrates several challenges our system had to cope with such as, for example, varying lighting conditions.

(one of which is blind from birth) and subsequently we performed our main study with 12 users (1 blind person). In both studies, the task was to find items in an office environment, see Fig. 2. In each trial, they had to find one specific item that was placed at a random location in the environment. In our evaluation we distinguish between two scenarios: In the first scenario, the object was placed randomly inside the room, thus the user had no information about the expected location. In the second scenario, the item was placed at a random location on the desks in the room, among other distractor items, and the user was told that the object is on a desk. In this scenario, the information about the object being placed on one of the desks limits the search space substantially and allows for efficient manual, unassisted exploration of the search area. In order to accustom the users with the system, we used a single initial trial for instructions and explanations. During the tests, the users wore open headphones that leave the hearing sense mostly unaffected. As camera, we used an off-the-shelf webcam without any calibration, control of imaging features, or user intervention.

For evaluation, we recorded the time durations that were required to find the target object and performed a pre- and post-test questionnaire. The results of the second scenario's post-questionnaire (12 participants; main evaluation) is shown in Tab. 1.

4.2 Discussion

In the first scenario, if the search space is unrestricted, the system allows to rapidly find the target objects. This is especially interesting, because the users reported that they usually – i.e., without the help of our system – would have given up the search. However, in the second scenario in which the search space is restricted the search times were not always better when using the system.

Table 1. Results of our post-questionnaire. Except for question 4 and 7, which allowed free answers and comments, we used an ordinal scale of $\{1, ..., 5\}$ to let the users rate specific aspects of our system. To improve the readability ↑ indicates that a higher value is better and ↓ indicates that a lower value is better. Since we have an even number of participants, there is no single middle value and we report the mean of the two middle values as median. (*) The users answered 3× "yes", 3× that it was less useful than color search, 1× that it would help more if the latency would be lower, 1× "not really", and 3× "no".

Question	↓↑	Median	Mean	Var
1. Which approach did you find better: searching with the system, or without it? (1: much better with, 5: much better without)	↓	2.0	2.67	1.00
2. How easy to use did you think the system was? (1: very difficult, 5: very easy)	↑	4.0	3.75	0.21
3. How intuitive did you find the system? (1: very intuitive, 5: very unintuitive)	↓	2.0	2.44	0.53
5. Which approach did you find better: searching with the color search, or without it? (1: much better without, 5: much better with)	↑	4.0	4.08	1.36
6. Which one did you think was faster, color search or searching without the system? (1: much faster with, 5: much faster without)	↓	2.5	2.58	1.54
8. Which approach did you find better: searching with the object search, or without it? (1: much better with, 5: much better without)	↓	3.0	3.33	1.15
9. Which one did you think was faster, object search or searching without the system? (1: much faster with, 5: much faster without)	↓	3.5	3.50	1.36
10. Please rate the sonification (sound output), in terms of how intuitive you think it was (1: very unintuitive, 5: very intuitive)	↑	3.5	3.50	1.36
11. Please rate how easy it was for you to interpret the sound (1: very easy, 5: very difficult)	↓	2.0	2.33	0.97
4. Did you find the color search useful?		\multicolumn 10× "yes", 2× "no"		
7. Did you find the object search useful?		conditionally*		

Nevertheless, the system was reported to be intuitive and easy to use, even though we only allowed a single training trial. Interestingly, the user reports indicated a different user experience depending on the usage of either the color attributes or the SIFT features. Due to the ambiguous results in the second scenario, we decided to further investigate it in our main evaluation.

The results of our main evaluation are shown in Tab. 1. As in our pilot study, the majority of the users reported the system as being very intuitive and easy to use (see the results for question 2 (Q2) and Q3, i.e. "How easy to use did you think the system was?" and "How intuitive did you find the system?", respectively). This is despite the fact that we only allowed the users a single trial for training and performed the post-questionnaire after three evaluation trials. Here, the chosen sonification mechanism plays a very important role and is crucial to achieve a good user experience, because it is the user's only source of information that is provided from the system, see Q10 and Q11 ("how intuitive you think [the sonification] was" and "how easy it was for you to interpret the sound", respectively). One third of the users reported that – in this scenario – they would prefer to search without the system (Q1). However, as can clearly be seen in the answers to Q5 ("with the color search, or without it?") and Q8 ("with the object search, or without it?") as well as in the answers to Q4 ("Did you find the color search useful?" – 10 out of 12 users did) and Q7 ("Did you find the object search useful?"), this depends on the features and the users prefer the color search over the search using SIFT features. As has been noted by one user in response to Q7, this is most likely caused by the fact that the SIFT approach takes more time for computation[2]. This leads to higher latencies and a decreased responsiveness, which in the end is best described as a slightly "sluggish" or "laggy" feeling when handling the system. This demonstrates that the computational complexity of algorithms and the resulting responsiveness have to be taken into account when designing and implementing such a system in order to allow for a good user experience. Using color as feature, 6 out of 12 people achieved on average better search times when using the system, which is slightly in contrast to the users' perception that they achieved better results using the system, see Q6 ("Which one did you think was faster, color search or searching without the system?"). This was likely caused by the following aspects: First, limiting the search space to the space directly above the desk surfaces made it possible for the users to rapidly detect most objects on the tables. For example, users do not have to fully orient themselves in the room and have to keep in mind all locations they already inspected and furthermore they do not need to first detect possible locations on which an object could be stored such as, for example, cupboards. Second, the users were still learning to handle the system (we observed that some users were still experimenting with features or, for example, kept misinterpreting aspects of the sonifications). Third, although seldom, false object detections did occasionally confuse the users.

5   Conclusion

We presented our current implementation of a computer vision system that is able to help visually impaired people find misplaced items. We experimentally demonstrated that the system makes it easier for visually impaired users to find misplaced items, especially if the target object is located at an unexpected location. As future work, we intend to integrate further visual attributes and, most importantly, to improve the overall system in order to reduce the average time that is required to find objects.

---

[2] The SIFT feature calculation and matching is computationally more expensive than calculating the color probability maps.

Acknowledgements. This work is supported by the German Research Foundation (DFG) within the Collaborative Research Program SFB 588 "Humanoide Roboter" and the VIPSAFE project by the German Federal Ministry of Education and Research (BMBF).

References

1. Amazon: Mechanical turk, https://www.mturk.com/
2. Bigham, J.P., Jayant, C., Miller, A., White, B., Yeh, T.: VizWiz:LocateIt - enabling blind people to locate objects in their environment. In: Proc. CVPR Workshop: Computer Vision Applications for the Visually Impaired (2010)
3. Caperna, S., Cheng, C., et al.: A navigation and object location device for the blind. Tech. rep., University of Maryland, College Park (2009)
4. Collet, A., Martinez, M., Srinivasa, S.S.: The MOPED framework: Object recognition and pose estimation for manipulation. Int. J. Robotics Research 30(10), 1284–1306 (2011)
5. Constantinescu, A., Schultz, T.: Redundancy versus complexity in auditory displays for object localization - a pilot study. In: Proc. Int. Conf. Auditory Display (2011)
6. Durette, B., Louveton, N., Alleysson, D., Hrault, J.: Visuo-auditory sensory substitution for mobility assistance: Testing thevibe. In: Workshop on Computer Vision Applications for the Visually Impaired (2008)
7. Google Mobile: Google Goggles, http://www.google.com/mobile/goggles/
8. Hub, A., Diepstraten, J., Ertl, T.: Design and development of an indoor navigation and object identification system for the blind. In: Proc. Int. ACM SIGACCESS Conf. Computers and Accessibility (2004)
9. Schauerte, B., Fink, G.A.: Web-based learning of naturalized color models for human-machine interaction. In: Proc. Int. Conf. Digital Image Computing: Techniques and Applications (2010)
10. Tuytelaars, T., Mikolajczyk, K.: Local invariant feature detectors: a survey. Found. Trends. Comput. Graph. Vis. 3, 177–280 (2008)
11. Wenqin, S., Wei, J., Jian, C.: A machine vision based navigation system for the blind. In: Proc. Int. Conf. Computer Science and Automation Engineering (2011)
12. Winlock, T., Christiansen, E., Belongie, S.: Toward real-time grocery detection for the visually impaired. In: Proc. CVPR Workshop: Computer Vision Applications for the Visually Impaired (2010)
13. World Health Organization: Visual impairment and blindness, http://www.who.int/mediacentre/factsheets/fs282/en/

Designing a Virtual Environment to Evaluate Multimodal Sensors for Assisting the Visually Impaired

Wai L. Khoo, Eric L. Seidel, and Zhigang Zhu

Department of Computer Science, CUNY City College
Convent Avenue and 138th Street, New York, NY 10031
khoo@cs.ccny.cuny.edu, {eseidel01,zzhu}@ccny.cuny.edu

Abstract. We describe how to design a virtual environment using Microsoft Robotics Developer Studio in order to evaluate multimodal sensors for assisting visually impaired people in daily tasks such as navigation and orientation. The work focuses on the design of the interfaces of sensors and stimulators in the virtual environment for future subject experimentation. We discuss what type of sensors we have simulated and define some non-classical interfaces to interact with the environment and get feedback from it. We also present preliminary results for feasibility by showing experimental results on volunteer test subjects, concluding with a discussion of potential future directions.

1 Introduction

Based on the 2002 world population survey, there are more than 161 million visually impaired people in the world today, of which 37 million are blind [2], [6], [7]. Research into alternative perception will have direct impact on these people with regards to navigation and orientation. We define alternative perception as using machines or devices to sense the environment and present the user with meaningful information about his or her surroundings, allowing the user to navigate the area. The machine then adapts based on the decisions made, so that it can intelligently present meaningful information (i.e. based on user's preference).

To realize alternative perception, we must determine what kinds of sensors (or combination of sensors) are better suited as "input" devices. In addition, we must also address the inherited limitations of these sensors and what compromises are needed, e.g., infrared has limited sensing distance. An efficient and robust system must be able to present meaningful information to the user without overloading their senses, which is the downfall of current electronic travel aid (ETA) technologies [1], [2]. The question boils down to which human senses can best be exploited for alternative perception without overloading the user, which is the main scope of this project. In the process of doing this project, some comparisons will be drawn on a sensor's pros and cons with other types.

The remainder of the paper is organized as follows. In Sect. 2 we present an overview of our approach and comparisons to related works. In Sect. 3 we

K. Miesenberger et al. (Eds.): ICCHP 2012, Part II, LNCS 7383, pp. 573–580, 2012.

describe the design of the experiment and environment. In Sect. 4 we show some preliminary results based on volunteer subjects. Finally, in Sect. 5 we discuss future work and extensions.

2   Overview of Our Approach

How is our research different from the state of the art ETAs? We need to define the fine line between human and computers. In other words, how much influence should we place on the computer for decision-making? If we rely heavily on the computer, then a minor error in the system or decision-making process will result in a potentially catastrophic error. Conversely, if we rely heavily on the human, then the enormous amount of raw data will overwhelm the user and potentially affect his or her decision adversely, making them ignore the technology all together [1], [6].

As such, we want to study this fine line by testing out various sensors and various non-classical interfaces ("display"). One metric that we can use to compare various approaches of different "display" is to measure a subject's brain [13] and motor activities [14]. Beauchamp, et al measured brain responses to vibrotactile somatosensory, auditory, and visual stimuli using magnetic resonance imaging [13], while Prilutsky, et al discussed how to quantify motor cortex function and the movement kinematics of the corresponding limb [14]. In order to measure human performance in navigation, an accurate tracking system is needed and ground truth of the environment is needed. This will be very hard for a real environment. Torres-Gil, et al [12] have developed a virtual reality simulator that will track the user's head orientation and position in a designated room and generate a virtual view of what the user is seeing. However, instead of presenting the view to the user graphically, an auditory representation of the scene is transduced to the user. Their results are mostly empirical. To have a better understanding of how virtual reality can help us evaluate multimodal sensors for the visually impaired, we are going to look at different brain scans and action measurements, and see which method the users show affinity for or respond well to, thus allowing us to quantify the results. However, brain activity can only be accurately measured when the subject is stationary, which is another reason why we decided to use virtual reality. To do this, we can have the user sit in front of a computer and perform a navigation task in the virtual environment while we obtain brain scans as well as action recordings of the user. The user reach his or her specified destination by relying on various stimulators on his or her body. Further details on simulated sensors and stimulators will be discussed in Sect. 3. The subject is, of course, blindfolded (or is actually blind) so that he or she has to rely on the devices. Using virtual reality not only allows us to determine which "display" is suitable, but also allows us to determine which combination of sensors (homogeneous and/or heterogeneous) is optimal.

We use Microsoft Robotics Developer Studio [15] to construct the 3D virtual environment with an avatar sitting on a wheelchair to approximate a real setting. The user will use an XBox controller to steer the wheelchair. He or she will be sitting on a chair in front of a computer with electrodes on his or her head and various sensors will be strategically placed on the avatar's body, the "display" device will be placed on the user's corresponding body parts. The user (who is either blindfolded or visually impaired) will have to navigate the avatar in an obstacle course and the virtual sensor readings will be translated to the real "display" devices. The user will have to make navigation decision based on the feedback received. Figure 1 illustrates the basic idea and setup of our approach.

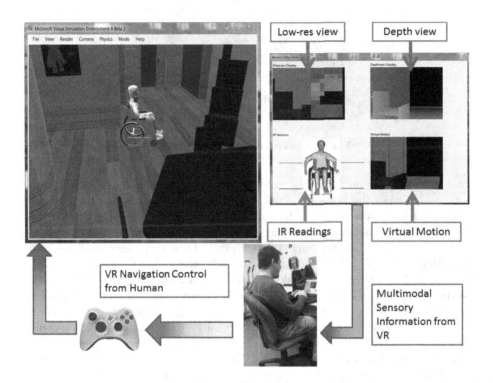

Fig. 1. Sensing and navigating a virtual environment

3   Sensors and Stimulators: Experiment Design

In the setup of Fig. 1, the overlooking view on the left provides the tester (and other sighted people) progress of the testee (subject). The sensor data window on the right shows some of the sensors we are simulating and will be programmatically fed into the corresponding stimulators on the subject. Currently the setup includes simulating low resolution image, a depth view, a simulated motion map, and infrared (IR) sensors.

The low resolution image will be fed into a tongue stimulating array such as Brainport's vision technology [11] (2). The Brainport is a limited clinical trial device; the white rectangular plastic house the 20 × 20 stimulating array, the

Fig. 2. Brainport tongue stimulation

signal is obtained from a camera mounted in the center of the glasses and processed on-board in the black handheld device. The depth view is obtained from
a simulated Microsoft Kinect. The simulated motion map is derived from the
depth view using known intrinsic and extrinsic parameters of Microsoft Kinect,
i.e. calculating the disparity value of each pixel. Then two views are generated
by shifting all of the pixel locations to the left (and right) by its disparity divided by 2. These two views are displayed consecutively such that you can see
objects nearer to you shifting more than objects furthest from you. This map is
also an alternative data that we can feed into the tongue stimulating array in an
attempt to capture object's presence by virtually "moving" it. The IR sensors
(on arms and legs) will be sensing the virtual environment and trigger the corresponding vibrators based on the scene [18]. This method of "display" is called
vibrotactile [5]. Figure 3 shows a prototype designed by our lab [18], where the
frequency of vibration corresponds to the measured distance (i.e. obstacle that
is very closer to the user will have stronger/faster vibration).

3.1 Sensors

We also plan to simulate other sensors including stereo cameras, laser range
sensors and ultrasonic range (sonar) sensors. We will simulate more sensors as
we come across them and if it is necessary to the study of this project. The
stereo cameras will be used as a comparison to the Microsoft Kinect, studying
its tradeoff in depth of field and computation complexity with regards to aiding
the visually impaired. In two pieces of accompanying work, our lab has developed a segmentatation-based stereo vision algorithm for obaining high-level 3D
description that can be provided to users [17], and people and obstacle detection

Fig. 3. Vibrotactile Prototype

algorithms using the Kinect [19]. Similarly, the laser range and sonar sensors will be used as a comparison to IR sensor, studying its tradeoff in range and field of view.

3.2 Stimulators

In addition to vibrators and tongue stimulating array as stimulators (or "display"), we can use braille to indicate range or intensity [16], auditory representation [12], converting 3D space into vibration array [9], and haptic feedback [16]. Braille is a traditional method for visually impaired people to communicate. However, it may be too slow (user "reading" speed may vary as well) to convey all of the spatial information needed for navigation and orientation. Auditory representation is similar in principle to echolocation, as used by bats. We can convert distance information into stereophonics which can be used to localize an objectc's location [9]. However, it may overwhelm the user since he/she will have to constantly "listen" to the scene. This may pose a danger to their safety especially in an urban area.

4   Experimental Results

Here we show the feasibility of the design and prototype mentioned in Sect. 3. As shown in Fig. 4(a), the user were able to navigate the virtual environment with an easy-to-use XBox controller. The controller is an intuitive tool to use for navigation compared to using a mouse and keyboard. Figure 4(a) also show what a typical experiment setup will look like. The user will sit in front of a computer with the controller in hand while wearing a set of stimulators, in this case a set of vibrators. The monitor will mainly be used by the test administrator(s) to monitor the progress of the subject.

Although the vibrotactile device (Fig. 3) is still in the prototyping phase, we were able to demonstrate that IR readings in the virtual reality can be interface out to Arduino, which can be used to control the vibrators on the user's body (Fig. 4(b)).

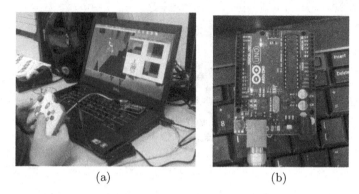

(a)   (b)

Fig. 4. Setup. (a).Example of a physical setup. (b). IR data extracted to Arduino.

5   Future Work

In order to show the capacity of our virtual environment sensor simulation, our next step is to generate a whole body simulation of range sensors. As an illustration, Fig. 5 visualizes the sensor setup of what we have in mind - including 12 IR rangers, 4 sonar sensors, and 4 laser rangers. The IR ranges are from 10 cm to 80 cm, mounted on arms and legs, which can be used for measuring proximity of doors, walls and close-by obstacles and will be transduced to vibrotactile stimulators with increasing levels of vibrations based on the measured distance. The sonar ranges up to 12 meters, while mounted on the user's wrists, two facing front and two facing back, could be used to detect farther obstacles with wider field of view. The laser range sensors are more accurate in both distance and angle, ranging up to 80 meters, which are mounted on user's head (2) and chest (2) for far environment obstacle detection.

To begin our experiments, we will be recruiting some human subjects and collaborating with our colleagues in the psychology department who will collect and analyze brain scans while we configure the sensors-stimulators setup. We will run several experiments with various sensor combination and placements, and various groups of subjects (sighted but blindfolded, low-vision, and totally blind). Finally, with the collected brain scan results and analysis, we will study the optimal combination and placements of sensors, and user's learning curve.

The goal of this project is to provide a research platform for the development of assistive devices for the visually impaired. Specifically, this project aims to determine which interface method (i.e. what type of information and how to present to the user) is the most efficient, reliable, and robust based on the various brain and action measurements that we will collect and study. This is different from mainstream assistive devices which focus on the technological and mechatronics aspects of the design. The key idea here is to test how visual and non-visual stimulation can enhance vision through understanding the underlying neural mechanisms, enhancing effects of the specific non-visual stimulation on vision.

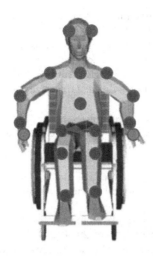

Fig. 5. Range field visualization: IR rangers (blue), sonar rangers (green) and laser rangers (red)

Acknowledgements. This work is supported by U.S. National Science Foundation Emerging Frontiers in Research and Innovation Program under Award No. EFRI-1137172 and City College 2011 Grant for Interdisciplinary Scientific Research Collaborations. We thank Mr. Nathan Slobody and Ms. Ania Wisniewska for their assistance in connecting the XBox controller and Arduino to the Microsoft Robotics Developer Studio.

References

1. Electronic Travel Aids:New Directions for Research, Working Group on Mobility Aids for the Visually Impaired and Blind, Committee on Vision (1986)
2. Dakopoulos, D., Bourbakis, N.G.: Wearable Obstacle Avoidance Electronic Travel Aids for Blind: A Survey. IEEE Trans. On Systems, Man, and Cybernetics 40(1) (January 2010)
3. Meijer, P.: An Experimental System for Auditory Image Representations. IEEE Trans. On Biomedical Engineering, 9(2) (February 1992)
4. Gonzalez-Mora, J.L., et al.: Development of a new space perception system for blind people, based on the creation of a virtual acoustic space, http://www.iac.es/proyect/eavi
5. Johnson, L.A., Higgins, C.M.: A navigation aid for the blind using tactile-visual sensory substitution. In: Proc 28th Annu. Int. Conf. IEEE Eng. Med. Biol. Soc., New York, pp. 6298–6292 (2006)
6. Liu, J., Sun, X.: A Survey of Vision Aids for the Blind. In: Proceedings of the 6th World Congress on Intelligent Control and Automation, Dalian, China, June 21 - 23 (2006)
7. American Foundation for the Blind, http://www.afb.org/
8. Ito, K., et al.: CyARM: an alternative aid device for blind persons. In: Proceedings of CHI Extended Abstracts 2005, pp. 1483–1488 (2005)

9. Bourbakis, N.: Sensing surrounding 3-D space for navigation of the blind. IEEE Eng. Med. Biol. Mag. 27(1), 49–55 (2008)
10. Hirose, M., Amemiya, T.: Wearable Finger-Braille Interface for Navigation of Deaf-Blind in Ubiquitous Barrier-Free Space. In: Proc. of 10th International Conference on Human-Computer Interaction (HCI International 2003), Universal Access in Human Computer Interaction, Crete, Greece, June 2003, vol. 4, pp. 1417–1421 (2003)
11. Wicab, Inc., Brainport Vision Technology, http://vision.wicab.com/technology/
12. Torres-Gil, M.A., Casanova-Gonzalez, O., Gonzalez-Mora, J.L.: Applications of virtual reality for visually impaired people. W. Trans. on Comp. 9(2), 184–193 (2010)
13. Beauchamp, M.S., Yasar, N., Frye, R., Ro, T.: Integration of touch, sound and vision in human superior temporal sulcus. NeuroImage 41, 1011–1020 (2008)
14. Prilutsky, B.I., Sirota, M.G., Gregor, R.J., Beloozerova, I.N.: Quantification of motor cortex activity and full-body biomechanics during unconstrained locomotion. Journal of Neurophysiology 94, 2959–2969 (2005)
15. Microsoft Robotics Developer Studio, http://www.microsoft.com/robotics/
16. Amemiya, T., Hirota, K., Hirose, M.: Wearable Tactile Interface for Way-Finding Deaf-Blind People using Verbal and Nonverbal Mode. Trans. of VRSJ 9(3), 207–216 (2004) (in Japanese)
17. Tang, H., Zhu, Z.: A Segmentation-based Stereovision Approach for Assisting Visually Impaired People. In: Miesenberger, K., et al. (eds.) ICCHP 2012, Part II. LNCS, vol. 7383, pp. 581–587. Springer, Heidelberg (2012)
18. Palmer, F., Zhu, Z., Ro, T.: Wearable Range-Vibrotactile Field: Design and Evaluation. In: Miesenberger, K., et al. (eds.) ICCHP 2012, Part II. LNCS, vol. 7383, pp. 125–132. Springer, Heidelberg (2012)
19. Khan, A., Lopez, J., Moideen, F., Khoo, W.L., Zhu, Z.: KinDectect: Kinect Detecting Objects. In: Miesenberger, K., et al. (eds.) ICCHP 2012, Part II. LNCS, vol. 7383, pp. 588–595. Springer, Heidelberg (2012)

A Segmentation-Based Stereovision Approach for Assisting Visually Impaired People

Hao Tang and Zhigang Zhu

Department of Computer Science, CUNY City College
Convent Avenue and 138th Street, New York, NY 10031
{tang,zhu}@cs.ccny.cuny.edu

Abstract. An accurate 3D map, automatically generated in real-time from a camera-based stereovision system, is able to assist blind or visually impaired people to obtain correct perception and recognition of the surrounding objects and environment so that they can move safely. In this paper, a segmentation-based stereovision approach is proposed to rapidly obtain accurate 3D estimations of man-made scenes, both indoor and outdoor, with largely textureless areas and sharp depth changes. The new approach takes advantage of the fact that many man-made objects in an urban environment consist of planar surfaces. The final outcome of the system is not just an array of individual 3D points. Instead, the 3D model is built in a geometric representation of plane parameters, with geometric relations among different planar surfaces. Based on this 3D model, algorithms can be developed for traversable path planning, obstacle detection and object recognition for assisting the blind in urban navigation.

1 Introduction

Using portable or wearable systems to assist blind or visual impaired for navigation attracts more and more attention during last decade. The algorithms can be categorized into three main groups: Electronic travel aids (ETAs), electronic orientation aids (EOAs) and position locator devices (PLDs). We are mostly interested in ETAs that could be used in a GPS denied environment.

In this paper, we propose a rapid segmentation-based stereovision approach to generate dense 3D maps. It is efficient since it is a feature-based matching approach. The dense 3D map is accurate because it is propagated from accurate 3D measurements of some well related salient features. The outcome of the system is not just an array of individual 3D points that are usually produced by a typical stereovision system. Instead, it is a geometric representation of plane parameters, with geometric relations among neighboring planar surfaces.

The 3D maps should be transduced to users, blind/or visually impaired, thorough auditory description and other types of "displays", such as vibrotactile or Braille, so that they can make a decision for navigation. Therefore, it is useful to provide uncertainty measurements of those planar regions to tell users how reliable the 3D map is.

K. Miesenberger et al. (Eds.): ICCHP 2012, Part II, LNCS 7383, pp. 581–587, 2012.

The paper is organized as the following. Section 2 discusses a few closely related works. In Section 3, we present our segmentation-based stereo vision approach. Section 4 provides some experimental results, with discussions in transducing stereovision results to some novel simulation devices. Finally we conclude our work in Section 5.

2   Related Work

There are various sensors used in ETA systems, such as video cameras [2], [10], [11], [15], ultrasound rangers [12], [20], and sonars [1], [3], [5]. Video camera become popular sensors in such systems due to the availability of low-cost, small CCD or CMOS cameras and recent advance in the computer vision algorithms. Coughlan et al. [7], [8] propose systems for helping visually impaired to find a path to a machine-readable sign using a cellphone camera. Using stereo cameras [2], [10], depth maps are produced to aid navigation. Staircases [14], [16], [17] and zebra-crossings [18] are detected using stereo cameras. However, above methods require a textured environment, and will not work well in textureless area because matching in textureless areas is ambiguous. Though stereovision using global optimization frameworks [4] may obtain more robust results, the computation is expensive and is not suitable for this application.

3   Our Algorithm

Before we go into more details of the algorithm, here is an overview. For a pair of stereo images, the left view is used as the reference view, color segmentation is performed on this image, and the so-called natural matching primitives (Fig.1a, details explained later) are extracted. Multiple natural matching primitives are defined for each homogeneous color image patch, which approximately corresponds to a planar patch in 3D. Then the matches of those natural matching primitives are searched for in the right image, a plane is fitted for each patch, and its planar parameters are estimated. To improve the robustness of stereo matching, each planar patch is warped between views to evaluate the matching accuracy, and uncertainty values are generated.

There are three major steps in our algorithm for the segmentation-based stereo matching: (1) matching primitive extraction; (2) patch-based stereo matching and plane fitting; and (3) plane merging, splitting and refinement. We will discuss them in the next three subsections.

3.1   Matching Primitive Extraction

First, the reference image is segmented, using a mean-shift based approach [6]. The segmented image consists of image patches with homogeneous colors, and each of them is assumed to be a planar patch in 3D space. For each patch, its boundary is extracted as a closed curve. Then we use a line fitting approach to extract feature points for stereo matching. The boundary of each patch is first fitted with connected straight-line segments using an iterative curve splitting method. The connecting points (with large curvature) between line segments are defined as interest points around which the natural matching primitives are defined (Fig. 1a).The representations are effective for urban scenes with objects of largely textureless regions and sharp depth boundaries.

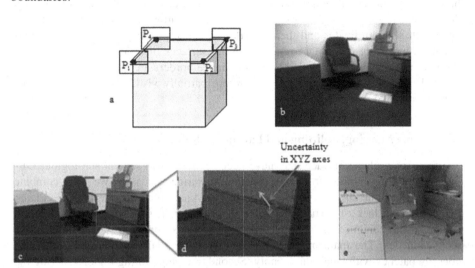

Fig. 1. a. Natural matching primitives around four interest points on a patch (the top of a rectangular object in this illustration); b: The left stereo image (reference image); c: The segmented image of the reference image (b); d: In a cropped window, boundary and features are drawn in a patch on a cabinet. Gaussian uncertainty measurement of a feature is drawn. e. Depth image with the boundaries and plane parameters of some patches overlaid.

3.2   Stereo Matching and Plane Fitting

On each patch of the reference image, the match for each interest point is searched along its epipolar line in the target image. We define a matching mask centered at each interest point, which only includes points on the patch (Fig.1a). The size of the mask is adaptively changed depending on the actual size of the patch. A few more pixels (e.g., 1-2) around the region boundary (but not belonging to the region) are also included so that we have sufficient salient image features to match. A sub-pixel search is performed in order to improve the accuracy of 3D reconstruction. For an interest point in the reference image, (x_l, y_l), we use the epipolar geometry to find its possible matches, using correlation. Then based on the correlation curve (in both the epipolar line and a few pixel above and below), we find a range of possible matches in the target image, and we then sample a number of points $\{(x_r, y_r)\}$. Finally we obtain the 3D coordinates $\{(X_i, Y_i, Z_i)\}$ of the points, and fit a 3D Gaussian distribution so the mean and variance values in X, Y, and Z can be obtained (Fig. 1d).

Assuming that each homogeneous color region is a planar patch in 3D, a plane

$$aX + bY + cZ + d = 0 \qquad (1)$$

is fitted to each patch after obtaining the 3D coordinates of the interest points of the patch. We use a robust RANSAC method to fit a plane. In the voting step, interest points with higher confidences are able to vote more tickets, the uncertainty values of the interest points are also updated using the plane fitting result. The result of a patch after the above steps is in the form of a 3D planar equation and the boundary of each patch with 3D coordinates and their uncertainties. The process is very efficient, particularly for a large textureless region, like the surfaces of a desk, walls and doors. The interest points of a patch that lie on the image borders are not taken into account (marked with very large uncertainty) therefore partially visible regions can also be correctly handled.

3.3   Plane Merging, Splitting and Parameter Refinement

One real-world planar surface may have been segmented to several sub-regions during segmentation. In order to recover meaningful surface structure, we try to combine them back into one surface. On the other hand, a patch may include multiple planar surfaces due to lack of texture. To solve the problem, first we perform a modified version of the neighboring plane parameter hypothesis approach [21] to infer better plane estimates. The main modifications are: first the plane hypothesis is only provided by patches with small uncertainty. Second, the neighboring regions sharing the same or very close plane parameters are merged into one larger region. This procedure is performed recursively till no more merging or spitting occurs.

(a)   (b)

Fig. 2. (a) The left stereo image (reference image); (b) Depth image with the boundaries and plane parameters of some patches overlaid, regions with large uncertainty (wrong estimate) are marked in color

4   Experimental Results

Experiments have been performed to test our approach. Image sequences were captured by the stereovision head Bumblebee. The baseline distance between the left and the right cameras is 12 cm, and focal length of each is 3.8 mm. The stereo system has been pre-calibrated and image pairs rectified.

In Fig. 1b, all objects (a table, a chair, a cabinet, walls and some boxes) are about 1-4 meters away from the camera. A depth map (the brighter, the closer) rendered from the results of the plane parametric estimation has been shown in Fig. 1e. Several large surfaces are annotated by their normalized surface normal vectors – using arrows and values (a,b,c), and distances of the centers of the patches to the camera (d, in meters), labeled with their boundaries. These plane estimation results are consistent with the results measured by hand. For the textureless regions in the experiment, e.g. the doors, the box and even the ground surface, full 3D results are also obtained. Fig. 2 shows another example of indoor scene, including a person sitting in front of camera, 3D models of large surface/objects (walls, door, ground are person) are corrected recovered.

One of our ongoing works is to apply the stereo vision results into visual prosthetic approaches. A retinal implant is used to partially restore vision for blind and visually impaired, especially who lost their vision due to retinitis pigmentosa or macular degeneration. Currently the state of art retina implants have limited resolution (60 – 100 channels) [22]. As another example, Brainport technique [23] invented by Wicab Inc. captures an image and processes the image by converting it into impulses which are sent via electrode array on the tongue (tongue simulation) to brain that is able to interpret the impulses into visual signals. The tongue simulation has 400 channels (20x20). Both methods are facing a problem of low resolutions. If we simply subsample an original image into a 20x20 or lower resolution array to drive the retinal or tongue stimulation, is would be hard to identify small objects that are close to the user.

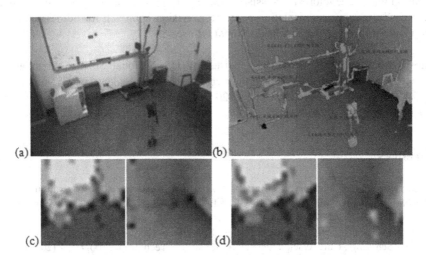

Fig. 3. (a) an indoor scene (left view) is captured in an office with a number of objects (note: a tripod is in a close range); (b) 3D depth map of the indoor scene; pixels with large uncertainty are marked in green; (c) sampling results of 2D image and 3D depth map using uniform sampling method: the tripod is missing after regular sampling; (d) sampling results of 2D image and 3D depth map using smart sampling method: the tripod is kept after sampling.

Therefore we applied a special sub-sampling method (refer smart sub-sampling) to sample 2D images and 3D depth maps and transduce the sampled results into the above devices that have limited resolutions so blind or visual impaired people can better 'see' surrounding environments through alterative perceptions. Instead of uniformly sampling, the smart sub-sampling method can convey more important information with a limited resolution. The main idea is to use both the segmentation and 3D reconstruction results to keep the small but close objects in the sub-sampled images. Fig. 3 shows an example after applying smart sub-sampling. Fig. 3a and 3b are left view of a stereo images and recovered depth map using the proposed method, respectively; Fig. 3c shows that the tripod, which is about 1.55 meters from the user, is missing after uniform sampling, but it is still preserved using the proposed smart sub-sampling (Fig 3d).

5   Conclusion

In both indoor and outdoor urban environments, most of the surfaces of man-made objects are planes; therefore a 3D reconstruction method that directly produces plane surfaces is an appropriate approach to solve the navigation problem for blind or visually impaired individuals. In this paper, we have proposed a segmentation-based stereo approach that features natural matching primitives, three-step efficient matching and accuracy parametric 3D estimation. Planar surfaces are represented by their plane parameters (orientations, distances, boundaries), and their relations, Based on this 3D model, algorithms in traversable path planning, obstacle detection and object recognition will be developed for assisting the blind in urban navigation. In our future work, we will test our segmentation-based stereovision approach for both 3D reconstruction and transducing with visually impaired users.

Acknowledgments. This work is supported by US National Science Foundation Emerging Frontiers in Research and Innovation Program under Award No. EFRI-1137172, and City Seeds: City College 2011 President Grant for Interdisciplinary Scientific Research Collaborations.

References

1. Aguerrevere, D., Choudhury, M., Barreto, A.: Portable 3D sound / sonar navigation system for blind individuals. In: The 2nd LACCEI Int. Latin Amer. Caribbean Conf. Eng. Technol. Miami, FL, June 2–4 (2004)
2. Audette, R., Balthazaar, J., Dunk, C., Zelek, J.: A stereo-vision system for the visually impaired, Sch. Eng., Univ. Guelph, Guelph, ON, Canada, Tech. Rep. 2000-41x-1 (2000)
3. Bouzit, M., Chaibi, A., De Laurentis, K.J., Mavroidis, C.: Tactilefeedback navigation handle for the visually impaired. In: ASME Int. Mech. Eng. Congr. RD&D Expo., Anaheim, CA, November 13–19 (2004)
4. Boykov, Y., Veksler, O., Zabih, R.: Fast approximate energy minimization via graph cuts. IEEE Trans. Patten Analysis and Machine Intelligence 23(11) (November 2001)

5. Cardin, S., Thalmann, D., Vexo, F.: A wearable system for mobility improvement of visually impaired people. Vis. Comput. 23(2), 109–118 (2007)
6. Comanicu, D., Meer, P.: Mean shift: a robust approach toward feature space analysis. IEEE Trans. Patten Analysis and Machine Intelligence (May 2002)
7. Coughlan, J., Manduchi, R., Shen, H.: Cell phone-based wayfinding for the visually impaired. In: 1st International Workshop on Mobile Vision (2006)
8. Manduchi, R., Coughlan, J., Ivanchenko, V.: Search Strategies of Visually Impaired Persons Using a Camera Phone Wayfinding System. In: Miesenberger, K., Klaus, J., Zagler, W.L., Karshmer, A.I. (eds.) ICCHP 2008. LNCS, vol. 5105, pp. 1135–1140. Springer, Heidelberg (2008)
9. Dakopoulos, D., Bourbakis, N.: Wearable obstacle avoidance electronic travel aids for blind: a survey. IEEE Trans. on Systems, Man, and Cybernetics, January 1 (2010)
10. Gonzalez-Mora, J.L., Rodrıguez-Hernandez, A., Rodrıguez-Ramos, L.F., Dıaz-Saco, L., Sosa, N.: Development of a new spaceperception system for blind people, based on the creation of a virtual acousticspace. Tech. Rep., May 8 (2009)
11. Hub, A., Diepstraten, J., Ertl, T.: Design and development of an indoor navigation and object identification system for the blind. In: Proc. ACMSIGACCESS Accessibility Computing, vol. 77–78, pp. 147–152 (September 2003/January 2004)
12. Ifukube, T., Sasaki, T., Peng, C.: A blind mobility aid modeled after echolocation of bats. IEEE Trans. Biomed. Eng. 38(5), 461–465 (1991)
13. Liu, J., Cong, Y., Li, X., Tang, Y.: A stairway detection algorithm based on vision for UGV stair climbing. In: IEEE Networking, Sensing and Control (2008)
14. Lu, X., Manduchi, R.: Detection and localization of curbs and stairways using stereo vision. In: IEEE International Conference on Robotics and Automation, ICRA (2005)
15. Meijer, P.B.L.: An experimental system for auditory image representations. IEEE Trans. Biomed. Eng. 39(2), 112–121 (1992)
16. Pradeep, V., Medioni, G., Weiland, J.: Piecewise planar modeling for step detection using stereo vision. In: Workshop on Computer Vision Applications for the Visually Impaired (2008)
17. Se, S., Michael, B.: Vision-based Detection of Stair-cases. In: Asian Conference on Computer Vision, ACCV (2000)
18. Se, S.: Zebra-crossing detection for the partially sighted. In: IEEE Computer Society Conference on Computer Vision and Pattern Recognition, CVPR (2000)
19. Shah, C., Bouzit, M., Youssef, M., Vasquez, L.: Evaluation of RU-netra–tactile feedback navigation system for the visually impaired. In: Proc. Int. Workshop Virtual Rehabil, New York, pp. 71–77 (2006)
20. Shoval, S., Borenstein, J., Koren, Y.: Mobile robot obstacle avoidance in a computerized travel aid for the blind. In: Proc, IEEE Int. Conf. Robot. Autom., San Diego, CA, May 8–13, pp. 2023–2029 (1994)
21. Tao, H., Sawhney, H.S., Kumar, R.: A global matching framework for stereo computation. In: Proc. Int. Conf. Computer Vision (2001)
22. Second Sight, http://2-sight.eu/en/home-en (last visited April 2012)
23. BrainPort Vision Technology, http://vision.wicab.com/technology (last visited April 2012)

KinDectect: Kinect Detecting Objects

Atif Khan, Febin Moideen, Juan Lopez, Wai L. Khoo, and Zhigang Zhu

Department of Computer Science, City College of New York, New York, NY 10031
{akhan14,fmoidee00,jlopez14}@ccny.cuny.edu,
{khoo,zhu}@cs.ccny.cuny.edu

Abstract. Detecting humans and objects in images has been a very challenging problem due to variation in illumination, pose, clothing, background and other complexities. Depth information is an important cue when humans recognize objects and other humans. In this work we utilize the depth information that a Kinect sensor - Xtion Pro Live provides to detect humans and obstacles in real time for a blind or visually impaired user. The system runs in two modes. For the first mode, we focus on how to track and/or detect multiple humans and moving objects and transduce the information to the user. For the second mode, we present a novel approach on how to avoid obstacles for safe navigation for a blind or visually-impaired user in an indoor environment. In addition, we present a user study with some blind-folded users to measure the efficiency and robustness of our algorithms and approaches.

1   Introduction

According to American Foundation for the Blind, the number of legally blind in the US is 1.3 million and the total number of blind and visually impaired is 10 million (100,000 students), and these numbers are increasing with the aging population in US and around the world. If we can accomplish a reliable and robust vision solution for blind people with cutting edge technology, at an affordable cost, then it will have a tremendous impact. The goal of this project is to develop a wearable computerized system that assists blind and visually impaired individuals in detecting multiple humans, and in detecting and avoiding obstacles.

Blind and visually impaired individuals encounter many challenges. One of the most common challenges is the inability to detect obstacles along their walking path. Kinect can be and has been used as a tool to help the blind and visually impaired people to detect humans and objects along their paths [1]. Xtion Pro Live by Asus is a sensor capable of acquiring both RGB color images and depth images in real-time. By combining the RGB camera and depth sensor, Xtion Pro Live offers a whole array of capabilities including: motion capture, object recognition and detection, facial recognition, voice recognition, 3D mapping, and others features which are fundamental and required to achieve our project idea. Furthermore, it can be run on USB power, which results in an ideal sensor for a wearable system.

The above features can be interconnected together to develop a robust visual guidance system which could help the blind on their daily tasks. For instance, walking by

K. Miesenberger et al. (Eds.): ICCHP 2012, Part II, LNCS 7383, pp. 588–595, 2012.

a corridor, detecting and avoiding obstacles, recognizing a human or object, finding a particular path, and many others, without the use of a walking dog (extremely expensive) or the white cane. In this paper, we utilize the depth information that Xtion Pro Live provides to detect humans and obstacles on the path of a blind or visually impaired person.

The paper is organized as the following. Section 2 discusses related work on various methods on obstacle and object detection for the blind. In Section 3, we discuss two algorithms using the 3D sensor: human detection and obstacle avoidance. In the first part, we focus on how to track and/or detect multiple humans and moving objects and then convey the information to the user. In the second part, we present a novel approach on how to avoid obstacles or objects for safe navigation of the blind or visually-impaired user in an indoor environment. In Section 4, we present a user study with some blind-folded and blind users to measure the efficiency and robustness of our algorithms and approaches. Finally, Section 5 concludes our work.

2   Related Work

There are a number of groups who have used various 3D vision techniques to solve the problem of object detections to guide blind people. Zöllner and Huber [1] designed a vibrotactile waist belt and markers from the AR-Toolkit by leveraging the Microsoft Kinect camera. Tyflos [2] is a prototype device consisting of two tiny cameras, a microphone, and ear speaker, mounted into a pair of dark glasses and connected into a portable PC for blind individuals. The overall idea is to detect changes in a 3D space by fusing range and image data captured by the cameras and creating the 3-D representation of the surrounding space.

Meers and Ward [3] proposed an electro-tactile stimulus approach with stereo video cameras and GPS for providing the user with useful 3D perception of the environment and landmarks without using the eyes. Authors in [4] used Kinect sensor on a wheeled indoor service robot for elderly assistance. The robot makes use of a metric map of the environment's walls, and manipulates the depth information of the Kinect camera to detect the walls and localize itself in the environment.

Dakopoulos and Bourbakis [5] aim to achieve obstacle avoidance and navigation in outdoor environments with the aid of visual sensors, GPS, and electrotactile simulation. Chen and Aggarwal [6] propose a segmentation scheme using Kinect to separate the human from his or her surroundings, and extract the whole contours of the figure based on the detection point.

Drishti [7] employs a precise position measurement system, a wireless connection, a wearable computer, and a vocal communication interface to guide blind users and help them travel in familiar and unfamiliar environments independently and safely. The system in [8] detects the nearest obstacle via a stereoscopic sonar system, and sends back vibro-tactile feedback to inform users about their localization at increasing the mobility of visually impaired people by offering new sensing abilities.

3   Human and Obstacle Detection

The Xtion Pro Live is built for gaming, so in most of the applications, the sensor is stationary. In our experiments, up to three people can be easily identified using the OpenNI framework, if the sensor is stationary. However, if the sensor is in motion while the user is walking, it is difficult to use the OpenNI's existing functions to detect and track people. It would be an interesting research topic to identify and track people when the sensor is in motion. In this paper we assume that the system will keep stationary when the user wants to identify people, and when the user walks, we switch to a different mode - obstacle detection and avoidance.

3.1   Human Detection and Transducing

We use the OpenNI framework [9] of the Xtion Pro Live to detect humans. We were able to identify the number of people and their relative positions in real-time from the Xtion Pro Live in millimeters (mm). For system debugging, we integrated and configured the OpenNI framework with OpenCV, an open source computer vision library [10].The program has the following key components:

1. Generate and show depth and RGB information using the OpenNI framework, which provides an application programming interface (API) for writing applications utilizing natural interaction. It covers communication with vision and audio sensors, as well as high-level middleware solutions (e.g. for visual tracking using computer vision).
2. Tracking people, and estimate distances and positions in 3D space. For tracking and estimation we take the depth value and display on the user torso.
3. People's depth data labeling and coloring for debugging.
4. Making OpenNI data (depth & RGB) accessible and compatible with OpenCV (RGB to BGR conversion)

Figure 1 shows one of the detection results, where three persons are detected. For showing that our algorithm can separate each person from the background, we use a unique color for each person that the algorithm detects.

Fig. 1. Depth data: people tracking. Each colored region represents the image of a person, and the 3D location of the centroid of each person is annotated on the region of each person.

Based on this result, our system can notify the blind user about the number of people which happens to be in his or her field of view, and their respective distances and positions (in millimeters, mm). Therefore, the user gains knowledge about people in front of him/her. This information can also be conveyed to user using text to speech function via headphone [11].

3.2   Obstacle Detection and Avoidance

The obstacle detection algorithm will work mainly on the depth component of RGB-D data. In the future, we plan to fuse the depth information with the color information to improve the system's performance in obstacle detection. To improve the efficiency, we divide the original range array of 640 (H) x 480 (V) into blocks of 32 (H) x 40(V) pixels (Fig. 2). Thus, each block consists of 1280 pixels resulting in a total of 20x12 blocks of entire field of view, and we calculate an average depth within each block. Then, we further group the 20x12 blocks into 5x3 regions with each region containing 4x4 blocks. Horizontally, we have 5 directions: middle, left, far left, right, far right, and vertically we have 3: top, middle, bottom. In each region, the average of the 16 blocks will be used to give a metric that an obstacle in the region should be avoided. In our experiment, we sort the 16 average depths and calculate the average (Z) of the middle 10 values. Then, the metric of obstacle is calculated as $M = Z/Z_m$, where Z_m is the minimum depth that an object can be to the user; in our experiments, we set $Z_m =$ 1.0 meter. After we calculate the metric of obstacle for each region, then in each direction, the largest of the three metric values are assigned as the metric of obstacle in that direction. We note this metric as M_d, d = (-2, -1, 0, 1, 2), representing far left, left, middle, right, far right.

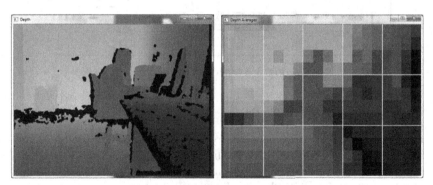

Fig. 2. Obstacle detection in 5x3 regions

We use two approaches in prompting the blind user about obstacles. In the first naive approach, we use the direction with the smallest probability of obstacle, and inform the user to turn to that direction if it is different from the previous one. This is searched in the order (far-left, left, middle, right, far-right). This raises issues that the changes of directions may be too frequent, and when two directions have the same probability, the direction that is first noted is always reported as the safe direction, with far-left is the more preferred direction.

In the second approach, in order to make the path smooth, we could use a direction update approach to give the current direction based on the previous direction, which asks the user to go to the closest direction that is still safe, e.g. $>1.5Z_m = 1.5$meters. This eliminates the problem of always preferring the far-left - here we prefer the directions in the order panning out from the middle.

4   Implementation and Experimental Results

4.1   System Architecture

The diagram in Fig. 3 shows the system schematic components. The main components are the Xtion Pro Live, the Laptop, and Bluetooth. The Xtion Pro Live, being smaller and having USB power cord, is connected to the laptop for scanning purposes. The laptop processes the depth data from the real world, and performs the detection algorithms as the blind walks along his or her passage. The computer notifies the blind person of objects ahead, and provides the user with an alternative route to avoid a possible collision. The laptop notifications are text-to-speech technology, and the user is listening to them through a Bluetooth. The user can also interact with the computer by asking if there are any people around. And the system will remind the user to stand still for a while when the system is trying to figure out how many and where the persons are.

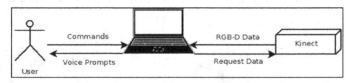

Fig. 3. System Schematic

4.2   System Integration and Testing

We installed the Xtion Pro Live on a belt for testing purposes. The prototype system includes these modules (Fig. 4), Xtion Pro live (Kinect), waist assembly to mount the Kinect, laptop for processing and transducing the data, laptop backpack to hold the laptop and headphone for giving the user directions.

We performed a user study with four blind-folded users walking in an indoor environment to validate the efficiency and robustness of our algorithms and approaches. Fig. 5 shows a picture of the scene where the users are asked to go from a start point roughly to an end point along a path. Fig. 6 shows the directions that the four users were instructed by our system using the simple one-step approach. You could see the unsmooth paths of most of the users. Fig. 7 shows the directions that the four users were instructed by our system using the direction update approach, where the paths are much smoother.

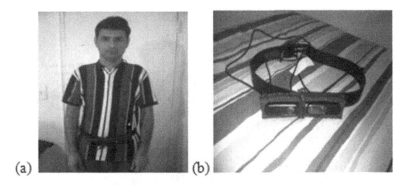

(a)   (b)

Fig. 4. Xtion Pro Live-Waist assemblies

Fig. 5. An indoor scene with the expected path labeled

The graph in Figure 6 represents obstacle avoidance paths of 4 blind-folded users using the first approach. In this diagram, the crosses represent the 4 different objects that we have: 2 trash-cans and 2 waste baskets. The X-axis shows the walking steps, each step covering 2 25cm tiles. The Y-axis demonstrates the actual number of tiles to get to that object. The coordinate (1, 12) represents the starting point; we see the viewpoint from this coordinate in Figure 5. The shifts represent the directional movements that the system prompted the blind-folded user in real time to avoid the obstacles. We observed that in this one-step approach, the algorithm favored the left-hand side first before the right-hand side. This is the reason why for some paths there is more left-turns that in others.

The plot in Figure 7 represents the experiment results of the direction update approach. In one step approach we observed that our algorithm favors the left hand side. In this plot, we observe that the middle direction is suggested to the user as long as there are no obstacles in the way. We can certainly conclude that this approach is better than one-step approach because it does not ask user to go left/right unless obstacle detected.

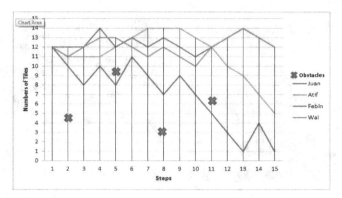

Fig. 6. Real paths of four users guided by the one-step approach

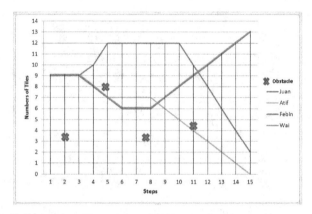

Fig. 7. Real paths of four users guided by the direction update approach

5   Conclusion and Discussions

In general, this system has the potential to replace the walking dog, which is extremely high cost, or even the white cane. As a result, this would facilitate the walking of a blind person by eliminating the fear of experiencing a collision. Compared to the current state of the art techniques that involve heavy computation to derive the depth information to achieve a simple task as obstacle avoidance, our proposed technique will be computationally simpler: Instead of building a global map, we are simply interested in a local map and we do not need a persistent map since the obstacle avoidance decision is made on the spot (i.e. locally). We also have found that the people detection function is a useful one for blind users.

However, obstacle detection and object avoidance has many limitations. For instance, most of the algorithms traditionally used for obstacle detection and navigation might work well, but when used in real time and integrated with Xtion Pro Live, they might result slow execution. Furthermore, the SAPI feature of our system reduces the computational efficiency output. Overall, obstacle detection and avoidance is still a difficult task to accomplish completely and make suitable 100% for blind users.

For people detection, the current algorithm requires the user to stand still to detect and track people, which have some constrained to the use of the sensor in real life. We hope to develop human detection algorithm when the sensor is in motion. This will create a lot of challenging issues since the sensor is in motion. All the background objects are in constant motion, thus making human detection using 3D and motion very difficult.

Acknowledgments. This paper was based on a computer science undergraduate senior design project at the City College of New York. The work is partially supported by US National Science Foundation Emerging Frontiers in Research and Innovation Program under Award No. EFRI-1137172, National Collegiate Inventors and Innovators Alliance (NCIIA) Course and Program Planning Grant (8281-10), and City SEEDs: City College 2011 Grant for Interdisciplinary Scientific Research Collaboration.

References

1. Zöllner, M., Huber, S., Jetter, H.-C., Reiterer, H.: NAVI – A Proof-of-Concept of a Mobile Navigational Aid for Visually Impaired Based on the Microsoft Kinect. In: Campos, P., Graham, N., Jorge, J., Nunes, N., Palanque, P., Winckler, M. (eds.) INTERACT 2011, Part IV. LNCS, vol. 6949, pp. 584–587. Springer, Heidelberg (2011)
2. Bourbakis, N.: Sensing Surround 3-D Space for Navigation of the Blind. IEEE Engineering in Medicine and Biology Magazine 27(1) (January-February 2008)
3. Meers, S., Ward, K.: A Substitute Vision System for Providing 3D Perception and GPS Navigation via Electro-Tactile Stimulation. School of IT and Computer Science University of Wollongong, Wollongong, NSW, Australia (2005)
4. Cunha, J., et al.: Using a Depth Camera for Indoor Robot Localization and Navigation. DETI/IEETA- University of Aveiro, Portugal (2011)
5. Dakopoulos, D., Bourbakis, N.: Wearable Obstacle Avoidance Electronic Travel Aids for Blind: A Survey. IEEE Trans. on Systems, Man, and Cybernetics, January 1 (2010)
6. Xia, L., Chen, C.-C., Aggarwal, J.K.: Human Detection Using Depth Information by Kinect. In: International Workshop on Human Activity Understanding from 3D Data in Conjunction with CVPR (HAU3D), Colorado Springs, CO (June 2011)
7. Ran, L., Helal, S., Moore, S.: Drishti: An Integrated Indoor/Outdoor Blind Navigation System and Service. In: PerCom, pp. 23–32 (2004)
8. Cardin, S., Thalmann, D., Vexo, F.: Wearable Obstacle Detection System for visually impaired People. Visual Computer: International Journal of Computer Graphics archive 23(2) (January 2007)
9. OpenNI Program Guide, http://www.openni.org/Documentation/
10. OpenCV, http://www.opencv.itseez.com
11. MSDNS. SAPI Function. Microsoft, August 28 (2008),
    http://msdn.microsoft.com/en-us/library/aa911241.aspx

A System Helping the Blind to Get Merchandise Information

Nobuhito Tanaka[1], Yasunori Doi[1], Tetsuya Matsumoto[1], Yoshinori Takeuchi[2],
Hiroaki Kudo[1], and Noboru Ohnishi[1]

[1] Graduate School of Information Science, Nagoya University,
Furo-cho, Chikusa-ku, Nagoya 464-8603 Japan
{nobuhito_tnk,yasunori,matsumoto,takeuchi,
kudo,ohnishi}@ohnishi.m.is.nagoya-u.ac.jp
[2] Department of Information Systems, School of Informatics, Daido University,
10-3 Takiharu-cho, Minami-ku, Nagoya 457-8530 Japan
ytake@daido-it.ac.jp

Abstract. We propose a system helping the blind to get best-before/use-by date of perishable foods. The system consists of a computer, a wireless camera and an earphone. It processes images captured by a user and extracts character regions in the image by using Support Vector Machine (SVM). Processing the regions by Optical Character Recognition (OCR) and the system outputs the best-before/use-by date as synthesized speech.

1 Introduction

From our interview to 14 blinds (10 males and 4 females) on merchandise purchase, we have found the following: 1) they can get rough location of shelf in stores where they often visit. 2) however, they cannot get merchandise name, price, and best-before/use-by date of perishable foods. Therefore the blind need help by a clerk or accompanying person in shopping. They, however, want to freely shop without relying on others. We propose a portable system which provides the blind with best-before/use-by date.

2 System Overview

This system consists of a note-computer (Intel Core i5 2.67GHz CPU, 4GB RAM, Windows 7 OS) , a wireless camera (SONY, DSC-W350) , OCR (Panasonic, Ver. 13.01) and an earphone. When users want to know best-before/use-by date of perishable foods, they take an image of merchandise by picking up it. After capturing the image, the system extracts the best-before/use-by date, by image processing. Finally the system provides the obtained information to the user as synthesized voice through an earphone.

K. Miesenberger et al. (Eds.): ICCHP 2012, Part II, LNCS 7383, pp. 596–598, 2012.

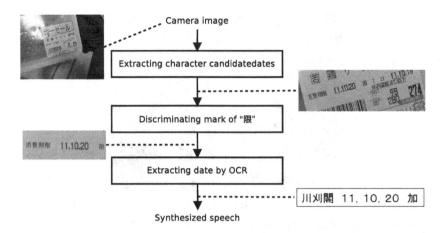

Fig. 1. Flowchart of best-before/use-by date recognition

3 Best-before/Use-by Date Recognition

Figure 1 illustrates the processing flowchart. First, the system extracts character candidates consisting of edges. Next, it finds the special mark appeared in best-before/use-by date by applying Support Vector Machine (SVM) to the character candidates and extracts a rectangular region surrounding the extracted mark. Finally, Optical Character Recognition (OCR) is applied to the region, and the best-before/use-by date is recognized. In a case of perforation printing, the recognition using OCR is difficult. Therefore, to resolve this problem, we apply the dilation processing before OCR.

4 Evaluation Experiment

For SVM training, we prepared 193 images as positive dataset and 32,741 images as negative dataset. We applied the proposed method to 70 images of perishable foods and drink in paper pack (40 perishable food images and 30 paper pack images). If the recognition result of OCR includes correct best-before/use-by date, we classify it as successful recognition.

The number of images for which the method successfully could extract date region is 37 for perishable foods and 27 for drink in paper pack. Among these images, the date recognition was succeeded for 33 perishable food images and 13 paper pack images. The rate of date recognition is 0.825 (33/40) for perishable foods and 0.433 (13/30) for drink in paper pack. The processing time is about 1.128 sec. in average. Figure 2 shows an example of best-before recognition results.

(a) Input image

(b) Extracted region image   (c) Processed image

Fig. 2. Example of best-before date recognition

5   Conclusion

This paper has presented a portable system to provide the blind with the merchandise information. Evaluation experiments show that users can know merchandise information and pick up the specified merchandise by using the system. Our future subject is to evaluate how the developed system helps the blind.

This work was supported by JSPS Grant-in-Aid for Scientific Research (c) (23500647).

References

1. Ye, Q., Jiao, J., Huang, J., Yu, H.: Text Detection and Restoration in Natural Scene Images. J. Visual Communication and Image Representation 18(6), 504–513 (2007)
2. Gllavata, J., Ewerth, R., Freisleben, B.: Text Detection in Images based on Unsupervised Classification of High-frequency Wavelet coefficients. In: ICPR 2004, pp.425–428 (2004)
3. Pan, Y., Hou, X., Liu, C.: Text Localization in Natural Scene Images Based on Conditional Random Field. In: ICDAR 2009, pp. 6–10 (2009)
4. Suzuki, Y., Takeuchi, Y., Matsumoto, T., Kudo, H., Yamamura, T., Ohnishi, N.: Improving the Character Extraction Rate and Ranking Voice Output in Systems Assisting Vision Impaired People Acquire Character Information from the Environment. The Journal of the Institute of Image Information and Television Engineers 58(12), 1800–1807 (2004)

Accessibility for the Blind on an Open-Source Mobile Platform

MObile Slate Talker (MOST) for Android

Norbert Markus[1], Szabolcs Malik[1], Zoltan Juhasz[2], and András Arató[1]

[1] Laboratory of Speech Technology for Rehabilitation,
Institute for Particle and Nuclear Physics, Wigner Research Centre for Physics,
Hungarian Academy of Sciences, Budapest, Hungary
[2] Dept of Electrical Engineering and Information Systems,
University of Pannonia, Veszprem, Hungary

Abstract. As Android handsets keep flooding the shops in a wide range of prices and capabilities, many of the blind community turn their attention to this emerging alternative, especially because of a plethora of cheaper models offered. Earlier, accessibility experts only recommended Android phones sporting an inbuilt QWERTY keyboard, as the touch-screen support had then been in an embryotic state. Since late 2011, with Android 4.X (ICS), this has changed. However, most handsets on the market today -especially the cheaper ones- ship with a pre-ICS Android version. This means that their visually impaired users won't be able to enjoy the latest accessibility innovations. Porting MObile SlateTalker to Android has been aimed at filling this accessibility gap with a low-cost solution, regarding the special needs of our target audience: the elderly, persons with minimal tech skills and active Braille users.

Keywords: (e)Accessibility, Blind People, Assistive Technology, Braille, Usability and Ergonomics, (e)Aging and Gerontechnology, Mobility, Android.

1   Introduction

MOST for Android is a follow-up of the earlier MOST projects [1][4] aimed at porting MObile SlateTalker (MOST) to Android. It was launched in early 2011 and at the time of writing, it is just being made publicly available.

The MOST development team has spent the last year exploring the potential of the Android operating system. During this time, the team has migrated the MOST framework to the Android platform, fixed known bugs in the open-source eSpeak TTS, ported our own BraiLab speech engine to Android and updated the design of the special Braille mask for the touch-screen to include the D-pad navigation controls and holes for extra functions in addition to the usual Braille holes. This mask is an essential part of any MOST powered device and has been evolving along with the subsequent MOST versions over the last decade.

K. Miesenberger et al. (Eds.): ICCHP 2012, Part II, LNCS 7383, pp. 599–606, 2012.
© Springer-Verlag Berlin Heidelberg 2012

The existing users of the pre-Android MOST devices are a poorly represented segment of the community, visually impaired smartphone users. These users may have little or no experience with computers or be elderly but they can communicate using Braille. Such persons remain the target audience for the new version of MObile SlateTalker.

2   State of the Art

MObile SlateTalker (MOST) [1] is a specially designed mobile software suite for the blind with dozens of useful applications making use of the phone's touch screen. It offers an unified menu system and promotes the daily usage of Braille by a proprietary input method that provides fast text entry, especially when entering non-English texts.

The MOST Consortium maintains and develops the MOST software and related hardware since 2004 with the active contribution of about 100 blind users in Hungary. Most of them are elderly or persons with minimal tech skills.

BrailleTouch [5] is an eyes-free text entry application for multi-point touchscreen mobile devices developed by Mario Romero and his team at Georgia Institute of Technology. It uses the chorded system of Braille and swipe gestures to input text. It does not involve any TTS. On Android, it can perform any text entry task. On iOS, it is a stand alone application that does not input text to the phone. It is and will always be free for any platform. Practically, it's not going to work on MOST Android handsets having a touch-screen hardware capable of handling only the most basic one- and two-finger gestures. As of 17th April, BrailleTouch is not yet publicly available.

Mobile Accessibility for Android [6] by Code Factory is an Android home screen application that incorporates a program suite of 10 applications simplified for the blind, a screen reader and an embedded Nuance Vocalizer TTS engine. Its concept is somewhat similar to that of MOST, in that it offers an unified environment for blind users, but it does not provide on-screen Braille input. Instead, the user is encouraged to use simplified gestures anywhere on the touch screen and a dynamic virtual keyboard for text entry. A full version can be downloaded from the Android Market for 70 Euros, or its 30-day trial version for free. The purchased app ships with a TTS whose language is included in the name of the app version.

3   How It Works

MOST is not a screen reader and does not require the presence of a screen reader installed on the same device. While using it, no graphical information is presented to the user. Instead, any pieces of data are channeled via pre-recorded and synthetic speech.

The MObile Slate Talker framework [1] provides a user interface that allows blind users to operate their device by simple touch actions, while getting an immediate audio feedback. In the MOST system, all applications, settings and features are organized into a unified menu tree that can be explored by the sole use of the four arrows. Character entry is realized by an on-screen Braille input method. A special mask is placed over the touch screen, turning it into a digital Braille slate. During Braille text input, the arrows are used for cursoring in the text.

Our 2010 survey[4] showed that both this simplicity of operation and the availability of the Braille entry mode were praised by an overwhelming majority of our users.

4   Background and Objectives

A growing number of smartphones today have a highly graphical user interface based on interacting with the touch-screen dominating the front side of the device. At the same time, many blind users (mostly the women and the elderly) worry that smartphones having physical numeric keys and buttons are on the verge of extinction

On a "traditional" smartphone, the physical keys and buttons are somewhat elevated, thus they remain tactile. In addition, their location is fixed all the time regardless of the application or in which mode the phone is currently being used. These factors give the blind user a feeling of a higher degree of security when interacting with the device. Consecutive MOST projects [3][4] have addressed this issue from the earliest stages of the design and development. MObile SlateTalker has always been used on touch-screen based hand-held devices (first on Pocket PC and Windows Mobile powered PDAs, and now also on Android handsets).

The special user interface for visually impaired users is provided by a transparent mask template placed over the touch-screen. Holes on this mask guide the users' fingers to dedicated areas of the screen. Thereby MObile SlateTalker turns a touch-screen operated smartphone into a device with quasi push-buttons and keys that become tactile and preserve their location on the screen throughout the operation. As opposed to this, designers of the most recent screen-readers seem to be forced to assign more complicated gestures for their visually impaired audience than the ordinary sighted smartphone users use.

Complications culminate around the problem of text input. Entering text (especially when abound with accented letters or special characters), on a flat glass surface, remains a partially resolved issue even with the best effort and concerted haptic, auditory and speech support. Perhaps this is why even the most advanced users cannot resist the temptation to obtain an external keyboard of some kind to couple it with their "accessible" smartphone.

MObile SlateTalker's Braille-mask-based input method is effective enough to eliminate this temptation on all target devices. Our 2006 paper [2] details the characteristics of the learning process of our test users and lists the typical entering speeds for sequential Braille dot entry on the MOST Braille mask. Recently the average entering speed for Hungarian uncontracted Braille is around 13 words per minute with a maximum at around 19 wpm.

5   Market Assessment of Accessible Smartphones in Hungary

Apple appears to be the sole manufacturer so far to have come up with a mobile product family offering a fully integrated, fully functional gesture based screen reader (VoiceOver) free of charge in all the languages supported by the iOs operating system. On the other hand, iOs devices occupy the high-end of the cell phone market and this fact is reflected in their prices. This may contribute to the fact that according to our recent survey, there are only about 30 blind iPhone users in Hungary and they are all men.

The elderly and female smartphone users are known to prefer the more conventional Symbian phones having physical keys and pushbuttons, and MObile SlateTalker powered devices.

5.1   Methodology Used for Conducting the Survey

Data for the survey comes from two technically separate sources. a) basic pieces of data (e.g., age, gender and device model used) from 90 of our registered users have been selected, updated and verified. b) Over 100 members of a smartphone oriented mailing list operated by a foundation under the umbrella of the Hungarian Association of the Blind and Partially Sighted have been selected for inclusion in the study, based on their public statements within a period of approx. 13 months (from Feb. 10 2011 through Apr. 15 2012). The information collected has recently been updated and verified. Eventually 82 list members have provided sufficient data qualifying them for inclusion in this study.

5.2   Findings of the Survey

In the table below, numbers represent actual persons or device ownership rather than percents. The "Persons" column on the left contains numbers refering to individuals (phone users), while in the subsequent four columns to the right, you can find the number of certain types of handsets owned by these individuals. In the column labeled "MOST", numbers refer to pre-Android MObile SlateTalker devices. The "Android" column shows the number of pre-ICS Android handsets used only with the standard accessibility features enabled. Among the iOs devices listed, only 32 are actual iPhones, the remaining two are iPod Touch models.

In each column, the number of males (m) and females (f) is listed along with the total (t) number of users in all age groups. The row labeled "Only" at the bottom of the table shows the number of users that -according to the data available- only have a single smartphone of the kind specified by the column.

The survey provided data about 154 visually impaired individuals using accessible mobile devices in Hungary. 109 of them are male and 45 are female. Assessing the totals, MObile SlateTalker appears to be the most favored by women, followed by Symbian. It is striking to find no females among the iOs and Android users (probably the former being less affordable, while the latter considered to be too experimental).

The age distribution in the "Persons" column yields a peak at the 30-39 year age group, with the number of females dropping sharply over the age of 60.

In the "Symbian" column, the ages are more smoothly distributed with a modest peak at the age group of 30-39 years, but the number of women already drops over the age of 50.

In our aspect, the most interesting is the "MOST" column. It differs from the other columns almost in all possible ways. First of all, the peak appears in an older age range, namely between 50 and 59 years. Actually the majority of this user group are above the age of 50. Women constitute one third of the MOST users which is the highest representation of females among the user groups. The 20-29 age range is unique because this is the sole age group of the entire survey of which females constitute the majority.

Table 1. Results of the Survey on Visually Impaired Smartphone Users in Hungary

Age	Persons			Handsets											
				MOST			Symbian			iOs			Android		
	F	M	T	F	M	T	F	M	T	F	M	T	F	M	T
10 - 19	1	2	3	0	1	1	1	1	2	0	1	1	0	0	0
20 - 29	11	17	28	5	4	9	8	12	20	0	4	4	0	2	2
30 - 39	12	28	40	8	10	18	6	19	25	0	11	11	0	4	4
40 - 49	8	20	28	4	10	14	6	16	22	0	7	7	0	2	2
50 - 59	9	20	29	9	15	24	1	6	7	0	0	0	0	1	1
60 - 69	3	18	21	3	16	19	0	4	4	0	3	3	0	0	0
70+	1	4	5	1	4	5	0	0	0	0	0	0	0	0	0
Total	45	109	154	30	60	90	22	58	80	0	26	26	0	9	9
Only				55			42			8			1		

The results of this survey show that addressing the special needs of the target users (in our case the elderly and women) in the design and ergonomics, the simplicity and affordability are reflected in the users' preferences and in their choice of product.

6   Porting MOST to Android

As the first technical details of the Android operating system were unveiled several years ago, it occurred to be an appropriate choice to migrate the next generation of the MOST software to. Android seemed to be a promising target especially because it had been declared to be an open-source cell phone platform.

Before the first actual Android phones hit the shops, technical reviews kept emphasizing Android's inherent advantages, its flexible nature and novel system architecture, and brand new ways the system and the applications could interact with each other. Any system components (home screens, widgets, services, input methods, etc.) might be replaced with third-party alternatives or custom-built ones.

At that stage, one could have the impression that a third-party developer would have full control over the operating system. We certainly hoped that any of its behaviors might be modified for the benefit of the visually impaired users. In the subsequent sections, we are going to discuss these issues in detail with regard to their accessibility implications, how such obstacles can be overcome, and deal with the question whether Android can finally be considered an open system or not.

As real Android handsets became available, soon it was obvious that the promises and the reality weren't in perfect unison. The practices introduced then persist still today. Handsets from the major manufacturers ship with a locked system ROM, which means that the pre-installed factory image cannot be modified at all, and the owner of the phone is degraded to a simple user with restricted rights in the system.

MOST relies on a fixed screen layout determined by the Braille mask placed over the touch screen. This fixed layout must be kept persistently on the screen within MOST. The Braille mask will not and cannot be moved or removed for the sake of individual user operations. Therefore MOST does what it can to prevent the screen layout from changing unexpectedly.

However, certain system dialogs and activities cannot be prevented from showing on the screen or be replaced by custom ones or it just makes no sense to do so without the required permissions.

For instance, a long press of the POWER button brings up the shutdown dialog that cannot be suppressed or replaced with a custom one. Anyway, invoking a call to shut down the device is bound with a permission not granted to a third-party app.

A long press of the HOME button brings up the recent apps list dialog, that cannot be dismissed from within a third-party app although what it provides could be reproduced with the standard SDK. It is the same with the "Battery is low", "An application is not responding" and "An application has kept the device awake for a long time" dialogs.

Defining a fixed screen layout that persists all over the system feels to be a bumpy road. For entering characters in Braille whenever it is needed, the best choice is to develop and install a custom Braille input method. However, it is a multistep procedure to allow a custom input method to be available all across the system, and even then it will only show up when the user moves the focus onto an input field. Further on, an input method can get covered or hidden unpredictably by a number of things.

As an alternative, a custom built application widget with a fixed size and screen location may hold an unchanging layout within the boundaries of the widgets own context while shifting the rest of the screen content out of the way. Blind-friendly input methods and a fixed location virtual D-Pad have been introduced by the Eyes-Free Project with Android 4.X and through a compatibility package they are meant to work on earlier Android platforms as well. However, on several pre-ICS devices, both these input methods and the virtual D-Pad get easily swept away by opening the default home screen's application menu, or when a system dialog mentioned earlier or a dialing screen or in-call activity is shown.

All this means that whenever the user moves (or is moved) outside the MOST environment, keeping the fixed Braille layout on the screen becomes a challenge. At this time, the only workaround seems to be to enable targeted accessibility services or the system's default accessibility feature as a last resort and to use the inbuilt physical keyboard of the phone.

Another complicating factor is that the handset manufacturers and even some carriers tend to "temper" with the top layer of the Android system. Most often it affects the look and feel of the user interface but these manufacturer-designed layers are usually more than simple custom skins, and they always constitute a non-open-source portion of the system. In certain cases, the custom layer even affects the performance of the accessibility functions and services.

Recording a phone call using the standard android.media.AudioRecord functions is not possible. However, this is an undocumented "feature" that comes with unexpected consequences. In the best case, the recording will simply be unusable. If a phone call is answered or initiated while an audio recording is in progress, the sound file being created may be left incomplete and therefore unusable. In the worst case, the system may crash so severely that it can't even be restarted.

The workaround involves pausing the recording when a call is answered or placed and resuming the recording after the call has ended.

On Motorola handsets, a double tap on the HOME button performs the so-called "default operation" that may be chosen from a list found among the application settings in the system. There is no way to suppress or replace this feature.

When one enables the system's accessibility service, it implicitly sets the "Caller ID readout" setting affecting the phone ringer to "Caller ID repeat" and this is applied every time the phone is rebooted. The workaround involves fumbling around with the system-wide stream volume settings and playing phone and alarm ringtones from within the MOST program.

Certain operations that an Android app may want to perform rely on a related system permission. Most such permissions may be granted by the application to itself, but a number of these self-issued permissions are rejected by the system. This is a rather poorly documented area of the system APIs and the SDK and hindered our development work already at the design stage.

Some of these rejected permissions are related to quite trivial functions such as setting the system clock's date/time, calling privileged numbers (i.e., placing emergency calls directly), enabling the speakerphone, muting the microphone or feeding DTMF codes into the phone line.

As an alternative to the regular consumer phones mentioned above, Google provides the Nexus family as a so-called Dev Phone product line for advanced developers. These phones are SIM-unlocked and system unlocked, but they are located in the higher price segment of the smartphone market and are not available in all regions. Such phones' ownership is restricted to registered Android developers and copy protected apps are not available for Dev Phones for download. These circumstances make them largely inadequate for most non-developer users.

With the restrictions on a regular consumer phone, the environment in which an Android app must run tends to resemble the conditions on an iOs device, but it must be stated that even so there is a lot more freedom for a third-party developer on the Android platform.

7   Conclusion

As PDAs went out of fashion, the MOST Consortium had to find a new range of target devices for MObile SlateTalker. By Q3 2011 Gartner estimated more than half (52.5%) of the smartphone market belonged to Android. The same research company also estimated that Android was going to dominate the entire mobile market soon. Therefore Android handsets appeared to be the best choice for us.

Since affordability was known to be among the main priorities of our users, we had to extend our software support to handsets sold at more modest prices. These tend to run on pre-ICS android versions on which the in-built accessibility functions are still in a kind of half-baked state.

The recent Android port of MObile SlateTalker with its own input method via a special mask template provides an affordable solution for our target audience who are otherwise poorly represented on the accessibility market and whose special needs are still to be addressed by the major players, at least in Hungary. This paper summarizes our efforts and results in overcoming the often unforeseen obstacles and unleashing the potentials of Android.

References

1. Arato, A., Juhasz, Z., Blenkhorn, P., Evans, G., Evreinov, G.: Java-Powered Braille Slate Talker. In: Miesenberger, K., Klaus, J., Zagler, W.L., Burger, D. (eds.) ICCHP 2004. LNCS, vol. 3118, pp. 506–513. Springer, Heidelberg (2004)
2. Juhasz, Z., Arato, A., Bognar, G., Buday, L., Eberhardt, G., Markus, N., Mogor, E., Nagy, Z., Vaspori, T.: Usability Evaluation of the MOST Mobile Assistant (SlatTalker). In: Miesenberger, K., Klaus, J., Zagler, W.L., Karshmer, A.I. (eds.) ICCHP 2006. LNCS, vol. 4061, pp. 1055–1062. Springer, Heidelberg (2006)
3. Markus, N., Juhasz, Z., Bognar, G., Arato, A.: How Can Java Be Made Blind-Friendly. In: Miesenberger, K., Klaus, J., Zagler, W., Karshmer, A. (eds.) ICCHP 2008. LNCS, vol. 5105, pp. 526–533. Springer, Heidelberg (2008)
4. Márkus, N., Arató, A., Juhász, Z., Bognár, G., Késmárki, L.: MOST-NNG: An Accessible GPS Navigation Application Integrated into the MObile Slate Talker (MOST) for the Blind. In: Miesenberger, K., Klaus, J., Zagler, W., Karshmer, A. (eds.) ICCHP 2010. LNCS, vol. 6180, pp. 247–254. Springer, Heidelberg (2010)
5. Romero, M.: Brailletouch Mobile Texting for the Visually Impaired. Georgia Institute of Technology (USA), http://calebsouthern.com/papers/frey_southern_romero_2011.pdf
6. Mobile Accessibility for Android by Code Factory, http://www.codefactory.es/en/products.asp?id=415

Accessibility of Android-Based Mobile Devices: A Prototype to Investigate Interaction with Blind Users

Sarah Chiti[1] and Barbara Leporini[2]

[1] Intecs, Pisa, Italy
sarah.chiti@intecs.it
[2] ISTI – CNR, Pisa, Italy
barbara.leporini@isti.cnr.it

Abstract. The study presented in this paper is part of mobile accessibility research with particular reference to the interaction with touch-screen based smartphones. Its aim was to gather information, tips and indications on interaction with a touch-screen by blind users. To this end we designed and developed a prototype for an Android-based platform. Four blind users (two inexperienced and two with experience of smartphones) were involved from the early phase of prototype design. The involvement of inexperienced users played a key role in understanding expectations of smart phones especially concerning touch-screen interaction. Skilled users provided useful suggestions on crucial aspects such as gestures and button position. Although the prototype developed is limited to only a few features for the Android operating system, the results obtained from blind user interaction can be generalized and applied to any mobile device based on a touch-screen. Thus, the results of this work could be useful to developers of mobile operating systems and applications based on a touch-screen, in addition to those working on designing and developing assistive technologies.

Keywords: mobile accessibility, touch-screen, blind users.

1 Introduction

The use of mobile devices is rapidly increasing especially with smartphones, which can provide additional functionalities compared to traditional phones. Generally speaking, it is a challenge for the visually-impaired to use these mobile devices. The interaction modality which is increasingly used for these devices is mainly via a touch-screen display. The absence of hardware keys makes the interaction with smartphones more difficult and complex for those who are blind. Interaction modalities based on gestures and taps can be a practicable solution, provided they are well designed and simple to use. Apple has already put on the market devices accessible to users with disabilities, such as iPhone 3G, 4 and 4S (http://www.apple.com/accessibility/). At the same time there are also some active projects aimed at studying how to provide access to devices based on the Android (http://eyes-free.googlecode.com/svn/trunk/documentation/android_access/index.html). However, all these solutions and studies are still at the early stages. It is therefore important to understand the suitability

K. Miesenberger et al. (Eds.): ICCHP 2012, Part II, LNCS 7383, pp. 607–614, 2012.

of the new interaction modalities with touch-screen devices for people with vision impairment. Our aim is to evaluate if there are still aspects to be made more accessible and usable for user interaction. In [8] the authors observed some usability issues encountered by blind users while interacting with the tablet iPad, although the Voiceover support seems to be generally accessible. This implies that there are still mobile accessibility issues to be analysed and evaluated in order to enhance blind user interaction with a touch-screen.

Our objective is to understand how a blind person – especially a beginner user - can interact easily with a mobile device through a touch-screen. This was done by involving the end users in the collection of preliminary information and comments useful for designing the interface. The Android platform is the system developed by Google as its solution for the mobile world. Devices based on this platform are still not particularly accessible and usable by blind people. By selecting the Android platform, we wanted to contribute to research in connection with this widely-used device. Furthermore, this system is very suitable for development due to the fact that it is more open. However, the main features identified and proposed can be generalised apart from the mobile operating system.

This study is part of the European project "Smarcos" (http://www.smarcos-project.eu/) that includes among its goals the development of services which are specifically designed and accessible for blind users. In this paper we present the prototype application designed to make the main phone features available in a way which is accessible for a blind user – especially for an unskilled one. The prototype has been developed to firstly evaluate the interaction modalities based on gestures, audio and vibro-tactile feedback. A preliminary evaluation with blind people was conducted in order to involve end users at an early stage of the prototype development.

After a brief related work section, the prototype will be introduced by describing the main features and functionalities. In particular, the preliminary evaluation results obtained by observing and interviewing a group of blind users will be discussed.

2   Related Work

A multimodal approach can be a valuable way to support various interaction modes, such as speech, gesture and handwriting for input and spoken prompts. The tests described in [2] showed that user performance significantly improves when haptic stimuli are provided in order to alert users to unintentional operations (e.g. double clicks or slips during text insertion). However, the study mainly focuses on the advantages of exploiting the haptic channel as a complement to the visual one and is not concerned with solutions for blind users. By combining various interaction modalities, it is possible to obtain an interactive interface suitable for users with varying abilities. A well-designed multimodal application can be used by people with a wide variety of impairments. Multimodal approaches and gesture-based apps can certainly facilitate interaction for users with impairments; however, creating accessible touch screen interfaces for the blind user still remains a challenge [1], [4] and [5]. Several studies investigate on multimodal interaction for people with disabilities using mobile devices. In [3] the authors evaluated a combination of audio and vibro-tactile feedback on a museum guide, which had a positive response for the user with vision impairments. With regard to user interface (UI) design, the work presented in [10] suggests an important principle which should be considered when designing a product: developers should focus on ability rather than disability. This interesting concept has been considered in several pilot projects, including Slide Rule which aimed to study touch screen access for blind users. In particular, Slide Rule is a prototype utilizing accuracy-relaxed multi-touch gestures, "finger reading," and screen layout schemes to enable blind people to use unmodified touch screens [6]. The study [7] found out preliminary results concerning gestures preferred by blind persons. Evaluated gestures include screen corners, edges, and multi-touch (enabling quicker and easier identification). Also new gestures in well-known spatial layouts (such as a qwerty keyboard) have been considered in the study. In our work we would like to further investigate on this kind of interaction modality by using an Android touch-screen based device.

More precisely, in our work we intend to investigate if gestures and voice and vibro-tactile feedback can be useful for the blind to confirm an action on an Android-based smartphone. The Android platform includes a built in text-to-speech engine and a screen reader to enable phone manufacturers to deliver accessible smartphones. Android phones can also be highly customized by downloading third-party accessibility applications that make nearly every function possible without sight, including making phone calls, text messaging, emailing and web browsing (http://www.google.com/accessibility/products/). [9] describes an example application developed for the blind using an Android-platform device. However, the proposed work on accessibility support is still in progress and input/output modalities need to be investigated in order to identify the most appropriate modalities to interact with a touch-screen.

3   Methodology

As mentioned, this research is aimed at investigating the accessibility and usability of interaction with a touch-screen-based smartphone for blind users. For this purpose, we developed a prototype application which makes some essential smartphone features available and accessible. An Android platform was used for this. The functionalities we included in our prototype were chosen according to the interaction modalities to be investigated. This application was used as a starting tool to gather evidence and evaluate user interaction involving a group of blind people. In this way, we applied a user-centred design approach to our study. The methodology used can be summarised as follows:

- Analysis of the interaction between blind users and a smartphone touch-screen. In order to identify users' requirements, a small group of four totally blind people was involved in the design-development cycle;
- Development of a prototype for the Android system able to give access to the functionalities chosen during the analysis. The prototype works on the basis of the main interaction gestures to be investigated;

- Collection of preliminary data and first impressions of the prototype by the end users. To this aim, the group was closely observed and interviewed for their feedback;
- Evaluation of the feedback collected during the interviews, which could be useful to improve user interface design.

4   User Requirements and Main Interaction Features

To gather information useful to identify the main features to be included as well as the main interaction aspects to be evaluated; four totally blind users were involved in our study. All four had knowledge of using ITC technologies and smartphones with screen readers. However, only two had experience of devices with a touch screen. The two less experienced users were included in the group in order to record their expectations of interacting with a touch-screen smartphone. The two more skilled members of the group were involved in order to gather suggestions and comments for more usable and appropriate interaction modalities.

All the users showed interest in a smartphone based on the Android platform for a number of reasons. One important aspect is the wide range of smartphone models available on the market with a variety of prices and features. Furthermore the users agreed on the basic functionalities necessary on a smartphone: first of all the phone functionalities such as calls, contacts and short messages should be accessible and easy to use. If these functionalities are provided, then the users would consider evaluating more complex features.

On the basis of feedback from users, it was clear that some aspects of interacting with a touchscreen needed to be considered when designing the prototype. Therefore we took into account (1) how the commands should be organised and sequenced, and (2) how the interactive elements should be designed and developed. The main issues and aspects observed by the user can be summarised as:

- **Keys and touchable elements as reference points:** The users pointed out that the hardware keys as well as all the elements clearly felt by a finger (e.g. buttons, edges, points, etc.) play a crucial role for a blind person. he main problems encountered by the users are related to the absence of hardware keys on the smooth screen of a smartphone. In particular the less experienced users were apprehensive about their ability to find their way around the screen as well as the different options. Using the numpad is one of the most worrying issues for the users. In particular, editing a phone number is considered to be the first functionality that should be not only accessible but especially usable. Furthermore, although a screen reader is generally available to announce the number touched, the users said that they usually rely on the "marked" five (5) key to find their way around the numpad when editing a number. As a result they requested this important feature on the touchscreen as well as. They also stated that because the hardware keys are clearly perceivable and the "five" key can help in moving around the numpad, a blind user can edit a number even in situations when there is a lot of noise, and a screen reading voice would not be heard very well. A similar option should also be available on a touch-screen device.

- **Organisation of commands and functionalities**: The two less experienced participants said that the commands and actions on the Nokia phones are organised in a way which makes it simple for a blind user who is familiar with menus and submenus. This means that they gave a positive evaluation of the opportunity to use a hierarchical menu for commands and actions.
- **Simplicity and usability of common functions**: The most widely used functions and commands need to be carried out as easily and naturally as possible. Some examples locating the main buttons quickly, exploring the objects following a logical pattern, and learning to use the smartphone for the first time with little effort. The more experienced users suggested placing some specific command buttons in a fixed position to make it easier to detect them. Furthermore they also proposed the idea of exploiting multimodal interaction in order to provide alternative and complementary forms of interaction with the smartphone. Particular attention should be paid to two particular aspects. First the way the UI elements are explored. Secondly the method used to select and confirm an action in order to avoid activating an undesired command involuntarily.

5   The Application Prototype

This prototype is an application for the Android system on mobile devices. It was tested on Samsung Galaxy S, Samsung Nexus S and Huawei IDEOS. The application is not in any way intended to replace screen reading software. Instead it implements the set of features and functionalities used to observe and assess how the users interact with the touch-screen. Thus, when designing the Android application we considered the following aspects with reference to user requirements:

1. Organization and arrangement of the UI items and the instructions to use the phone. The following points were analysed:

   - The structure and the logical order employed to organize the information (e.g. flat or nested in macro topics);
   - The division of the UI so that it contains all the elements needed to exploit the application. Two aspects were important in choosing the position and size of the elements on the screen (I) making identification of elements simple and (II) making use of previous knowledge of the usual positions for elements (e.g. exit/back button element on the top left which is similar to the typical ESC key position on a computer). In order to facilitate some main actions, four buttons were placed at the four corners of the screen. For most cases, these buttons are used to: (I) identify the current position (II) repeat the last action performed (III) confirm the last action performed (IV) close the current task.

— The way to define interaction modalities, i.e. (I) the accepted gestures for the screen (e.g., scrolling, flicking, tapping, double tapping) in order to navigate and access information and (II) the resulting feedback (e.g., vibration, vocal messages). Working together with the users, we identified the appropriate gestures to adopt. We associated a category of actions to each gesture. For instance, a left or right flick for scrolling through elements such as SMSs or contacts, or tables. Another example is the double tap to select a command or confirm critical actions, such as sending or deleting an SMS. As regards the feedback, we tried to do the following (I) associate voice messages only to crucial stages in order to avoid confusing the user with too much feedback (II) formulate short but clear phrases to describe the actions taken by the user (III) use similar phrases for similar activities. Both expert and non-expert users requested the option to decide how much vocal feedback is provided. In fact, in the early stages of learning, it is useful to have voice assistance, but with practice the voice can become irritating and unnecessary.

2. Implementation of the basic functionalities (contacts, call, read/write an SMS and read information in table format).Particular attention was paid to virtual keyboards as regards: (I) the layout of keyboard keys on the screen (II) the selection mode of a key. In order to satisfy the request by users for easy identification of the number 5 our proposal was to place this virtual number at the point where you first tap the screen. On the basis of this first tap the user can move around to locate the position of the other numbers. However, this solution does not exploit the prior knowledge of users who can find the position of a key by remembering its location on the screen. As a result we decided to use a keypad with numbers in fixed positions on the screen. Even though using a standard layout could have been more user friendly, we decided to maximize the size of the numeric keys in order to exploit the full screen. This solution was immediately found to be effective and fast to use. Regarding the voice feedback, this required more detailed analysis. While scrolling, the user received very quick vocal feedback when moving from one number to another. Therefore we decided to introduce a silent gap between the keys in order to have an interval between the vocalization of two adjacent numbers. The result was a significant decrease in errors when selecting a number. During the analysis and implementation of software keyboards, interesting results were obtained from the choice of selecting keys. Users were offered two options for selecting the desired key once it was located. These were (I) double tapping on the screen, or (II) only lifting the finger. Experienced users immediately chose the second solution. Although they could use both methods without difficulty, the finger lifting gesture proved to be more rapid and led to a smaller number of errors. The novice users initially preferred the double touch option, but after testing it for a short time, they switched preference. For this and other reasons, we decided that the two modes of selection were to co-exist in the application. Regarding key selection, we again addressed the number 5 question. To this end, we associated a vibro-tactile feedback

when touching the number 5 on the screen. The users were very positive about this additional feature. For this reason, we are currently researching the idea of associating different vibration patterns to the different keys.

3. Implementation of more complex features in order to evaluate advanced functionalities and opportunities for users with vision impairments. Although this study is mainly devoted to the analysis of user-touchscreen interaction we wanted to analyze how the potentialities provided by a smartphone can be exploited by blind users. In this context, providing a QR code reader that vocalizes the result seemed to be a good starting point. This QR reader could be used to identify household objects known to the user or to label the aisles and shelves of a supermarket. Experienced users were very interested in this as a further opportunity to increase their autonomy and independence.

During this study we tried to exploit the user settings in order to allow the user to choose how to provide and receive information using the phone.

This prototype relies on the (`https://market.android.com/details?id=com.svox.langpack.installer&hl=it`) text-to-speech engine in order to generate the audio feedback, i.e. all the audio messages are created on the spot using a voice synthesizer.

6   Conclusions

This study investigated the interaction between blind users and touch screen mobile devices. To this end, we chose Android-powered devices and we developed a prototype application to implement some targeted functionalities. Involving four totally blind users who interacted with the application, we analysed and evaluated different gestures and feedback. Although the study is based on the Android system, the interaction mode is independent of the operating system and platforms. This means that many of the results discussed can be taken into consideration both by people who develop systems for mobile devices, and those who produce assistive applications.

In the future we plan to develop an advanced version of the prototype using the suggestions from the users as well as our own observations. In addition, the study highlighted the need for a thorough analysis of the following topics: (I) Editing text using the QWERTY keyboard and (II) More extensive use of vibration as feedback. With regard to the first point, the main difficulties were the limited size and proximity of the keys. In addition it would be worth studying an efficient way to correct errors made when writing. For the second aspect, a wider use of vibration could be useful to better distinguish between UI elements.

Following this additional research, we will carry out a more structured user test based on specific tasks in order to collect further data.

References

1. Arroba, P., Vallejo, J.C., Araujo, Á., Fraga, D., Moya, J.M.: A Methodology for Developing Accessible Mobile Platforms over Leading Devices for Visually Impaired People. In: Bravo, J., Hervás, R., Villarreal, V. (eds.) IWAAL 2011. LNCS, vol. 6693, pp. 209–215. Springer, Heidelberg (2011)

2. Brewster, S.A., Chohan, F., Brown, L.M.: Tactile Feedback for Mobile Interactions. In: ACM CHI 2007 San Jose, CA, USA, pp. 159–162. ACM Press Addison-Wesley (2007)
3. Ghiani, G., Leporini, B., Paternò, F.: Vibro-tactile Feedback to Aid Blind Users of Mobile Guides. The Journal of Visual Languages and Computing (JVLC), Special Issue on Multimodal Interaction Through Haptic Feedback 20(5) (2009)
4. Guerreiro, T., Oliveira, J., Benedito, J., Nicolau, H., Jorge, J., Gonçalves, D.: Blind People and Mobile Keypads: Accounting for Individual Differences. In: Campos, P., Graham, N., Jorge, J., Nunes, N., Palanque, P., Winckler, M. (eds.) INTERACT 2011, Part I. LNCS, vol. 6946, pp. 65–82. Springer, Heidelberg (2011)
5. Jayant, C., Acuario, C., Johnson, W., Hollier, J., Ladner, R.: V-braille: haptic braille perception using a touch-screen and vibration on mobile phones. In: Proc. of the 12th International ACM SIGACCESS Conference on Computers and Accessibility (ASSETS 2010), pp. 295–296. ACM, New York (2010)
6. Kane, S.K., Bigham, J.P., Wobbrock, J.O.: Slide Rule: Making mobile touch screens accessible to blind people using multi-touch interaction techniques. In: Proc. of the ACM SIGACCESS Conference on Computers and Accessibility (ASSETS 2008), pp. 73–80. ACM Press (2008)
7. Kane, S.K., Wobbrock, J.O., Ladner, R.E.: Usable gestures for blind people: understanding preference and performance. In: Proc. of CHI 2011, pp. 413–422. ACM (2011)
8. Leporini, B., Buzzi, M.C., Buzzi, M.: INTERACTING with the iPad via VoiceOver: accessibility and usability issues. In: Proc. of the Workshop on Mobile Accessibility at INTERACT 2011, Lisbon, Portugal (2011)
9. Shaik, A.S., Hossain, G., Yeasin, M.: Design, development and performance evaluation of reconfigured mobile Android phone for people who are blind or visually impaired. In: The Proc. of the 28th ACM International Conference on Design of Communication, SIGDOC (2010)
10. Wobbrock, J.O., Kane, S.K., Gajos, K.Z., Harada, S. and Froelich, J.: Ability-based design: Concept, principles and examples. ACM Trans. Access. Comput. (2011)

TypeInBraille: Quick Eyes-Free Typing on Smartphones

Sergio Mascetti, Cristian Bernareggi, and Matteo Belotti

University of Milan

Abstract. In recent years, smartphones (e.g., Apple iPhone) are getting more and more widespread among visually impaired people. Indeed, thanks to natively available screen readers (e.g., VoiceOver) visually impaired persons can access most of the smartphone functionalities and applications. Nonetheless, there are still some operations that require long time or high mental workload to be completed by a visually impaired person. In particular, typing on the on-screen QWERTY keyboard turns out to be challenging in many typical contexts of use of mobile devices (e.g., while moving on a tramcar). In this paper we present the results of an experimental evaluation conducted with visually impaired people to compare the native iPhone on-screen QWERTY keyboard with *TypeInBraille*, a recently proposed typing technique based on Braille. The experimental evaluation, conducted in different contexts of use, highlights that *TypeInBraille* significantly improves typing efficiency and accuracy.

1 Introduction

The accessibility to smartphone devices by visually impaired users has recently significantly improved, hence rendering most of existing applications accessible to these users. Despite these achievements, there are still some operations that require a longer time or higher mental workload to be completed by a visually impaired person. In particular, in this paper we consider the problem of typing. Since the large majority of smartphone devices do not have a physical keyboard, typing is enabled by the on-screen QWERTY keyboard that appears on the device screen.

In this paper we show that this operation is time-consuming and error-prone for visually impaired users. To address this problem, we previously proposed *TypeInBraille*, a novel approach to text typing that is specifically designed for blind users [1]. The core idea is to insert text using the Braille code, by inserting each Braille cell with a sequence of at most three gestures. In this contribution we experimentally show that this solution has a number of advantages with respect to the on-screen keyboard. In particular, we show that: (a) *TypeInBraille* allows the users to improve their typing performances with respect to the on-screen keyboard both in terms of typing efficiency (words per minute) and accuracy (error rate); (b) learning to use *TypeInBraille* takes only a few minutes by people who already know the Braille code; (c) and differently from what happens with the on-screen keyboard, when using *TypeInBraille* the typing performance is

K. Miesenberger et al. (Eds.): ICCHP 2012, Part II, LNCS 7383, pp. 615–622, 2012.

not significantly affected by an uncomfortable environment in which the audio-feedback is unreliable and the user is subject to sudden movements.

2   Related Work

Two main families of text entry techniques have been proposed for the visually impaired. One family is based on the idea to allow the user to navigate through the characters using, for example, directional gestures ([2,3,4]). The different approaches differ in the layout of the letters and in the navigation technique. The main limitation of these solutions resides in the slow typing efficiency. For example, with "No-look notes" the average typing efficiency is 1.32 wpm (words per minute) [4]. As we show in this contribution, skilled iPhone users can type with an on-screen keyboard about 3 times faster.

The second family of techniques is based on Braille. In a preliminary paper we present *TypeInBraille*[1], that we briefly describe in Section 4 and that we experimentally evaluate in Section 5. Another Braille-based solution was proposed by Romero et al. in [5]. The user holds the device with the touchscreen facing away from him/her. The touchscreen is divided into six buttons which correspond to dot positions in the Braille cell. Each character is entered by pressing the buttons corresponding to the raised dots in the Braille representation of the character. Intuitively, this solution seems to enable users to achieve high typing efficiency. However, at present, efficiency and accuracy of this typing technique have not been evaluated. In a recent contribution the "BrailleType" solution is proposed [6]. The idea is to select the raised dots of a Braille cell and to confirm the character. The average typing efficiency with this solution is $1.49wpm$ and the error rate is about 7.5%. As we show in the following sections, our solution outperforms "BrailleType".

3   Problem Analysis

The iPhone[1] text entry technique is based on the spatial position of keys on the touchscreen. The iPhone on-screen keyboard arranges keys in three layers. In the first layer a QWERTY layout is displayed, whereas in the second and in the third layer are displayed numbers, punctuation marks and other special characters (e.g., the "+" or "#" symbols). A key is available for changing layer.

The process of entering a key with VoiceOver (i.e., the screen reader) is divided into two stages: *identification* of the target key and its *confirmation*. In the identification stage, the blind user scans the keyboard searching for the target key while the names of the touched keys are read by speech as soon as the keys are touched. Two modes are available to confirm a key: in the *keypad* mode confirmation is performed by tapping with another finger on the touchscreen while in the *touch* mode a key is confirmed when the user picks up the finger.

---

[1] Our analysis focuses on iPhones, but it also applies to other smartphones without a physical keyboard.

This technique turns out to be usable in many scenarios and by many categories of vision impaired users. Nonetheless, in some scenarios, users meet some problems which highly affect typing efficiency and accuracy. This is due to five main problems we identified during the experiments we conducted with blind users. (1) Since a single key has a small size, also a skilled blind user can rarely identify a target key without first exploring the keys around it. (2) In the target key confirmation stage it is relatively frequent that the user trying to enter a key inadvertently slides the finger over another close-by key, thus causing a typing mistake. (3) Moving among layers is time consuming as it additionally requires to identify and confirm the key to change the layer. (4) No shortcut exists to enter the keys that are used more frequently like the "blank space" and the "delete". (5) The input technique is fully dependent on speech output.

4   Our Solution: *TypeInBraille*

In Braille each character is represented by a cell made up of six dots organized into three rows of two dots each. *TypeInBraille* enables the user to input a character through its Braille representation by inserting the three rows of each cell from the top to the bottom. To enter a row the touchscreen is divided into two rectangles (left and right) and four gestures are defined. A tap on the left part of the screen corresponds to the left dot raised and the right dot flat (Figure 1(a)). Similarly, a tap on the right part corresponds to the right dot raised and a left dot flat (Figure 1(b)). A double tap (i.e., a tap with two fingers) represents two raised dots (Figure 1(c)) while a triple tap stands for two flat dots (Figure 1(d)). After a character is entered, it is read by speech to the user and/or a vibration effect can be triggered. We defined an additional gesture to represent the end of a character i.e., all the following rows contain flat dots only. This gesture is the "one finger right flick", a movement with one finger from left to right. Since the letters "a" and "c" have raised dots on the first row only, they can be represented with two gestures, while the blank space, which contains no raised dots, can be represented by one gesture only (i.e., the one finger right flick). For example the letter "a" followed by a blank space can be entered by the left dot gesture followed by two end of character gestures, the former indicating the end of the "a" character, the latter representing the blank space. Since the flick gesture is

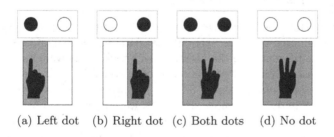

(a) Left dot   (b) Right dot   (c) Both dots   (d) No dot

Fig. 1. Gestures defined to enter a pair of dots

easy to remember and quick to perform, our technique adopts it also to insert a new line (one finger down flick) and to perform undo/delete operations (one finger left flick).

TypeInBraille overcomes the issues identified for the on-screen keyboard. (1) The user does not have to explore the touchscreen to search for a target key, since the two wide rectangles (i.e., the left or the right one) can be instantaneously identified thanks to the tactile feedback given by the physical borders of the device. (2) A key confirmation is not required. (3) No layer is involved in *TypeInBraille*. (4) Blank spaces, delete and new lines can be inserted with a single and easy-to-perform gesture. (5) We show in the following that *TypeInBraille* turns out to be partially or even totally independent on speech output. Actually, we experimentally show that the audio feedback is not indispensable, because the characters are entered through gestures that are almost position independent.

5   Experimental Evaluation

In this section we discuss the results of the experimental evaluation we conducted with blind users. We first describe how we designed and conducted the experiments and then we report the results of our evaluation.

5.1   Experimental Setting

The aim of the experimental evaluation is to assess the efficiency and accuracy of the *TypeInBraille* typing technique compared to writing with the on-screen QWERTY keyboard available on the iPhone mobile device. To this purpose, a within-subject experiment was designed and administered to a sample group of ten users with the following characteristics:

- Congenitally blind. We focused our attention only on congenitally blind users in order to minimize the effect of confounding variables (e.g., differences in mental representations of spatial structures).
- Skilled in reading 6-dot Italian literary Braille.
- Skilled in writing with an iPhone on-screen QWERTY keyboard assisted by speech output via VoiceOver.
- Never used *TypeInBraille* before.

Before starting the experimental evaluation, a ten minute *TypeInBraille* training session was conducted with the participants. Afterwards, five unconstrained text entry tasks were presented to the users. In each task, users were required to type a complete phrase set either with the on-screen QWERTY keyboard (tasks 1 and 4) or with *TypeInBraille* (tasks 2, 3 and 5). Since mobile device users operate both at the desk and on the move, the tasks were performed both while sitting at a desk (tasks 1, 2 and 3) and standing in a noisy urban tramcar (tasks 4 and 5). All the five phrase sets are designed respecting the characteristics of the English language; More specifically, according to the definition provided in [7], the correlation with English is always greater than 0.92. Each phrase set contains approximately 250 characters, namely 50 words on average.

Based on [7], in order to assess the efficiency and accuracy of both the on-screen QWERTY keyboard and *TypeInBraille*, the following metrics are measured: *words per minute* and *MSD error rate*. Intuitively, words per minute measures the typing efficiency of the user, independently of the typing accuracy. Vice versa, MSD error rate measures the accuracy of the transcribed text, computed as the minimum string distance to the "presented text" (i.e., the text that users are asked to type).

5.2   Experimental Results

We start analyzing the experimental results we obtained for the "desk" scenario. As shown in Figure 2(a), the typing speed for each user monotonically increases from task 1 to 3. In other words this means that after the 10 minutes training, the participants can write more words per minute using *TypeInBraille* than using the on-screen QWERTY. In more details, on average, efficiency increases by about 10%, with a minimum of about 2% (user 4) and a maximum of about 18% (user 2). The observation of the results for tasks 2 and 3 highlights that the experience acquired in the second task enables the users to further increase their typing speed. Indeed, on average, efficiency increases by about 9% with a minimum of about 6% (user 2) and a maximum of about 15% (user 3). Comparing tasks 1 and 3, we can observe that, after about 20 minutes of practice, using *TypeInBraille* the participants have been able to increase the typing efficiency with respect to the on-screen QWERTY by about 20% on average, with a minimum of about 9% (user 4) and a maximum of about 34% (user 3). The analysis of variance highlights a statistically significant difference between tasks 1 and 3 (applying a one-way repeated measure analysis of variance we obtained $p < 0.001$).

One question arises from the experimental results presented above: how fast could the users type after practicing with *TypeInBraille* as much as they have done with the on-screen QWERTY? Although we still do not have extensive experimental data to answer this question, we can report that one blind user that practiced almost daily for about 2 months, is able to write more than 10 wpm with *TypeInBraille*.

Typing efficiency in terms of words per minute is not a meaningful metric by itself to evaluate typing performance. Indeed, this metric should be at least evaluated together with the typing accuracy. Figure 2(b) shows that, while some users have been able to improve their accuracy in task 2 with respect to task 1 (3 users out of 10), the other users have increased their error rate. However, this is probably due to the fact that the users have only trained with *TypeInBraille* for 10 minutes. Indeed, in task 3 almost every user have improved the accuracy with respect to task 1 (9 users out of 10) and only one user obtained nearly the same accuracy. Also in this case the analysis of variance shows that there is a statistical significant difference between the two tasks (running the Wilcoxon Signed Rank Test $p(2 - tail) < 0.008$).

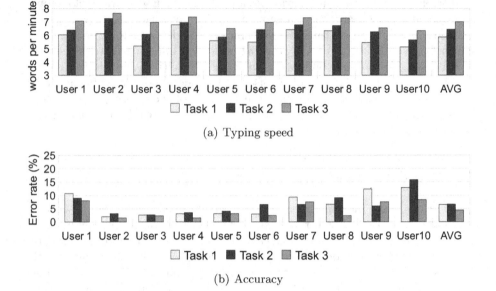

(a) Typing speed

(b) Accuracy

Fig. 2. Comparison in the "desk" scenario

One observation about the accuracy is that, in particular in the second task, many users committed mistakes due to the fact that they typed blank spaces when not needed. For example, in the first sentence of task 2 the average accuracy was about 10% while, ignoring the errors involving blank spaces, the accuracy drops to 3%. We have two motivations for this fact. First, during the 10 minute training, users practiced with single characters (e.g., the alphabet or the digits) but have not been asked to write any phrase and hence did not practice with blank spaces. Second, it could be observed that our technique uses the same gesture for ending a character and to insert a blank space and this may be misleading for the users, at least in the first stage of the training.

We now consider the "tramcar" scenario. Figure 3(a) shows that the increase in the typing efficiency between *TypeInBraille* and the on-screen QWERTY is more evident than in the "desk" scenario. Indeed, on average, *TypeInBraille* allows the users to type about 36% faster, with a minimum of about 24% (user 6) and a maximum of about 57% (user 1). This result is motivated by the fact that, in an uncomfortable environment, the average typing speed with the on-screen QWERTY decreases of about 20% (compare task 1 in Figure 2(a) with task 4 in Figure 3(a)). Vice versa, using *TypeInBraille*, the decrease in typing speed caused by the uncomfortable environment is about 8% (compare task 3 in Figure 2(a) with task 5 in Figure 3(a)). An analogous reasoning applies to the accuracy analysis. Indeed, using the on-screen QWERTY, the error rate in the "tramcar" scenario is about 150% than in the "desk" scenario (compare

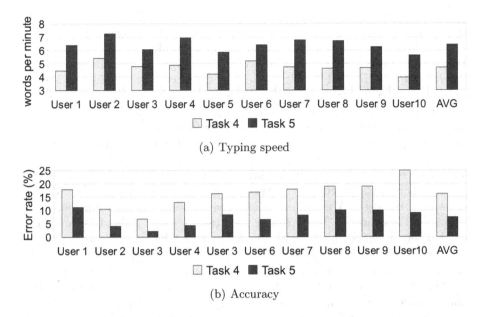

(a) Typing speed

(b) Accuracy

Fig. 3. Comparison in the "tramcar" scenario

task 1 in Figure 2(b) with task 4 in Figure 3(b)). Vice versa, the uncomfortable environment reduces the typing accuracy of *TypeInBraille* by about 65% (compare task 3 in Figure 2(b) with task 5 in Figure 3(b)). Consequently, in the "tramcar" scenario, *TypeInBraille* improves the typing accuracy with respect to the on-screen QWERTY by about 55%. Also in this scenario there is a significant difference between tasks 1 and 3 ($p < 0.001$)) and between tasks 4 and 5 ($p(2 - tail) < 0.006$).

The feedback from the users helps us understand why the performances of *TypeInBraille* are less degraded in an uncomfortable environment with respect to the on-screen QWERTY. There are two main reasons. First, typing with the on-screen QWERTY strongly relies on the speech feedback that is only partially audible in the "tramcar" scenario. Vice versa, using *TypeInBraille* the speech feedback is helpful but it is not indispensable. The second reason is that searching for a key while using the on-screen QWERTY requires a continuous exploration gesture. This movement is negatively affected by the sudden movements in a tramcar that often either require the user to start searching again for the target key or result in a typing mistake.

6   Conclusions and Future Work

In this paper we briefly illustrate *TypeInBraille*, and we compare this eyes-free typing technique with the use of the iPhone on-screen QWERTY supported by voice over. Our analysis, conducted with the help of blind users, identifies the main hindrances that arise while typing on a on-screen QWERTY keyboard. The experimental evaluation presented in this paper shows that *TypeInBraille* alleviates or totally solves most of these problems. In particular, there is a statistically significant improvement in terms of typing efficiency and accuracy granted by *TypeInBraille*. In the analysis of these results, it is necessary to also consider that the users involved in the experiments were all experienced with the on-screen keyboard while they were only trained with *TypeInBraille* for about 10 minutes. Additionally, *TypeInBraille* has benefits other than the writing performances. For example, as shown by the experiments, it can also be efficiently used also in uncomfortable environments in which the user is subject to sudden movements and the speech feedback is only partially audible.

The experiments we conducted also allowed us to collect a number of feedbacks from the users. We intend to use these feedbacks to improve the typing technique. For example, *TypeInBraille* requires the use of at least three fingers. Consequently, it is not possible to use this technique holding the device in one hand and typing with the thumb. We intend to investigate how to re-define the gestures so that all of them can be performed using the thumb only. Another direction to improve the experimental analysis consists in automatically and remotely collecting usage metrics (e.g., typing efficiency) from the *TypeInBraille* application that is available on the Apple Store. Since the number of users that have already downloaded this app is in the order of hundreds (and growing), the amount of collected data could be at least one order of magnitudes higher than the data we collected for the experiments presented in this paper.

References

1. Mascetti, S., Bernareggi, C., Belotti, M.: TypeInBraille: a braille-based typing application for touchscreen devices. In: Proc. of the 13th Int. ACM SIGACCESS Conf. on Computers and Accessibility, ASSETS 2011. ACM (2011)
2. Guerreiro, T., Lagoá, P., Nicolau, H., Santana, P., Jorge, J.: Mobile text-entry models for people with disabilities. In: Proc. of the 15th European Conference on Cognitive Ergonomics, ECCE 2008, pp. 39:1–39:4. ACM (2008)
3. Yfantidis, G., Evreinov, G.E.: Adaptive blind interaction technique for touchscreens. Universal Access in the Information Society, pp. 328–337 (2006)
4. Bonner, M.N., Brudvik, J.T., Abowd, G.D., Edwards, W.K.: No-Look Notes: Accessible Eyes-Free Multi-touch Text Entry. In: Floréen, P., Krüger, A., Spasojevic, M. (eds.) Pervasive 2010. LNCS, vol. 6030, pp. 409–426. Springer, Heidelberg (2010)
5. Frey, B., Southern, C., Romero, M.: BrailleTouch: Mobile Texting for the Visually Impaired. In: Stephanidis, C. (ed.) HCII 2011 and UAHCI 2011, Part III. LNCS, vol. 6767, pp. 19–25. Springer, Heidelberg (2011)
6. Oliveira, J., Guerreiro, T., Nicolau, H., Jorge, J., Gonçalves, D.: Blind people and mobile touch-based text-entry: acknowledging the need for different flavors. In: Proc. of the 13th Int. ACM SIGACCESS Conf. on Computers and Accessibility, ASSETS 2011. ACM (2011)
7. MacKenzie, I.S., Tanaka-Ishii, K.: Text Entry Systems: Mobility, Accessibility, Universality. Morgan Kaufmann Series in Interactive Technologies. Morgan Kaufmann Publishers Inc., San Francisco (2007)

Real-Time Display Recognition System for Visually Impaired

Irati Rasines[1], Pedro Iriondo[2], and Ibai Díez[1]

[1] TECNALIA. HealthTech Unit. Parque Tecnológico de Bizkaia, c/ Ibaizabal Bidea,
48160 Zamudio, Spain
{irati.rasines,ibai.diez}@tecnalia.com
[2] University of the Basque Country, Department of Systems and Automation Engineering,
48013 Bilbao, Spain
pedro.iriondo@ehu.es

Abstract. Currently, electronic devices incorporating displays to present the information to the user are ubiquitous common, and visually impaired people might have problems to use these devices. This article focuses on developing a real time display detector and digital character recognition application using techniques based on the connected components approach. The display zone detection accuracy rate is about 85% and the recognition rate greater than 88%. The system was implemented on both a desktop and a cell phone.

Keywords: Display, OCR, Connected Components, Android, Real-time.

1 Introduction

People with vision impairments might have problems in different situations in daily life, requiring vision, affecting their quality of life and independence. Some years ago, during the analog device era, every electronic device had a knob that provided affordance for visually impaired to determine the unit's status, but currently electronic devices (fridges, HiFi, ovens...) incorporating digital displays to present the information to the user have become increasingly common.

This drives research making this information available to the visually impaired important for this significant minority of users.

There are two different ways to transmit the information shown in the displays to the user: the first is for the manufacturers to include in their devices the option to transmit the information in audibly to the user. However, incorporating text to speech translators make the product much more expensive, so they become high-end products out of reach for many. The second option is to create an external and device independent interface capable of reading the information shown in the display.

There have been several approaches to this problem, but the state of art in this field is not very extensive. There is a 7-segment display reader application for those

K. Miesenberger et al. (Eds.): ICCHP 2012, Part II, LNCS 7383, pp. 623–629, 2012.

displays with their own illumination [1] and another application specifically for 7 digit displays of measuring instruments [2]. Another approach, the Clearspeech system [3] requires special markers on the borders of the display to align the device to work. Focusing on mobile applications there is an application running on a Nokia N95 cell phone [4] but is only oriented to 7-segment display detection and reading.

We have developed a prototype display reader system which initially finds the display thus reducing the computational cost since only the selected area is processed. A digital character recognition system is also implemented which reads the characters aloud to the user with synthesized speech.

2   Display Recognition System

We built a demonstration prototype of the real time display detector system which is able to find illuminated LCD/LED displays on PCs and cell phones running Android OS independent of the background. It implemented a simple Optical Character Recognition (OCR) engine using connected-components and an unsupervised learning algorithm based on dimensionality reduction, Principal Component Analysis (PCA), which reads digital type characters.

2.1   Databases

To test and validate the display detection system required a display image database with representative data both in quantity and quality. Since there was no existing database, it was necessary to create one consisting on 700 images of different types and color of illuminated displays. Every one of the photographed electronic device's displays has its own illumination, the selection of the devices was base on the types of displays commonly found in daily life. The experiments for display localization were performed using color images of size 640x480 pixels.

In order to train and test the OCR, we developed another database, consisting on 96 (42x24pixels) images of the hexadecimal system for training and 10 images for each digit for testing. The images of the training set were clean images while the OCR engine was tested with images from the display image database.

2.2   Selection of Parameters

There were no previous studies to base the setting of parameters for display detection. We choose the YUV [5] color space because it gives more reliable information about the lighted areas when finding the display and discriminating no display zones.

2.3   YUV Color Space

In the YUV color space the images take human perception into account. It defines a color space in terms of one luminance (Y) and two chrominance (U,V) components. The conversion between RBG and YUV color spaces is given by the following matrix:

$$\begin{pmatrix} Y \\ U \\ V \end{pmatrix} = \begin{pmatrix} 0.299 & 0.587 & 0.114 \\ -0.147 & -0.289 & 0.436 \\ 0.615 & -0.515 & -0.100 \end{pmatrix} \begin{pmatrix} R \\ G \\ B \end{pmatrix} \qquad (1)$$

In order to determinate what is display data and what is background a threshold was established for each color. Having set the thresholds, we can obtain a binary image where the white zones are candidate zones to be displayed, and the coordinates of these zones are shown on the screen of the device to determine whether the application is acting correctly.

$$Display \quad Color \ = \ \begin{cases} Blue & if & U > 50 \ \& \ U < 150 \\ Red & if & U < -30 \ \& \ V > 30 \ \& \ V < 110 \\ Green & if & U < -25 \ \& \ V < -10 \\ Yellow & if & U < -65 \ \& \ V < 20 \end{cases} \qquad (2)$$

Once the display zone is detected, we extract the original image and process the color image until we get an optimal binary image. Different image processing techniques were used to achieve this.

2.4   Image Enhancement

An image is considered optimal when the characters inside it are readable. To ensure we have a clean suitable image for the OCR to process, it was necessary to process the detected display zone.

Initially, a channel mixture was performed in order to increase the contrast of the image and get better results in the binarization step. The proportion that each channel provides to the optimal grey image to is the following one:

$$Grey \quad image \ = 0.1 * Green \ _{channel} \ + Blue \ _{channel} \qquad (3)$$

The chosen method for binarization is Optimum Global Thresholding (Otsu). Another 14 different binarization methods have been implemented, but as can be observed in the table below, Otsu method is the one that has higher score when measuring accuracy vs. processing speed.

Table 1. Computational cost of the binarization algorithm vs. accuracy of the results for the fifteen tested methods

Binarization Method	Computational Cost (seconds)	Accuracy (over 10)
Basic Global Thresholding	0.0425545	7.1
Optimum Global Thresholding (OTSU)	0.0294325	6.9
BCV	0.2840241	7
Criterion Functions Equivalent to BCV	0.0548060	6.8
Variable Thresholding Based on Statistic	0.7376767	5.6
Thresholding Using Moving Averages	0.0787855	6.2
Minimum Error Thresholding	0.0362351	5.8
1D Entropy	0.0417808	5.7
2D Entropy: Brink's Method	0.3389573	0.4
2D Entropy: Sahoo's Method	0.7894348	4.3
K means clustering	0.8488577	6.6
Fuzzy C means clustering	2.8823924	7.2
Markov Random Field: Gibbs	8.3744330	6.7
Markov Random Field: Gibbs	14.7551304	7
Markov Random Field: Gibbs	15.2448980	7

Once the image is binarized, the particles with small areas are removed from the image, as well as those components that satisfy the following condition, since they are unlikely to be characters and we are going to believe they are noise:

$$\frac{Width}{Heigh} > 0.25 \tag{4}$$

After removing the noise in the image, a dilatation is performed to join the segments of the characters. Using connected components, each character is extracted, sent to OCR for recognition.

2.5 OCR

A small OCR engine was created to recognize the digital characters. For this task we have used an unsupervised learning algorithm called dimensionality reduction. The main reason for applying dimensionality reduction is data compression [6].

Data compression not only allows us to compress the data and use less computer memory and less space, it also allows us to speed up our learning algorithms. The goal is to eliminate the redundant features of our dataset. Further, this dimensionality reduction gives us a way of visualizing the data better (as we can easily figure out, it is easy to plot 2D data, but not 50D data).

Principal Component Analysis. The dimensionality reduction algorithm we have chosen is one of the most popular one: the principal component analysis (PCA). The PCA algorithm builds a linear transformation that chooses a new coordinate system for the original data set based on the covariance matrix. The transformation leading from the old to the new coordinates is precisely the linear transformation required to reduce the dimensionality of the data.

In our case, as we have said, the data set for training the PCA consists on 96 (42x24pixels) images of the hexadecimal system (6 different images for each character). Before applying PCA we first performed mean normalization of our data in order to have a data set whose mean is zero (feature scaling had not been necessary since our data already had comparable range of values).

Dimensions were reduced from the initial 96 to 30 after making sure that with 30 eigenvectors the elements of the dataset base could get rebuilt satisfactory. In the figure bellow, we can observe the OCR recognition rate in our test database set (scores over 10):

	0	1	2	3	4	5	6	7	8	9	A	B	C	D	E	F
0	8													2		
1		10														
2			10													
3				10												
4					10											
5						7				1		2				
6							7		1			3				
7								10								
8									10							
9										10						
A											9	1				
B			2									8				
C													9		1	
D			2									4		4		
E															10	
F																10

Fig. 1. OCR performance results

Order to Send Images to the OCR. The order in which the detected characters are passed to OCR is essential because the result of the recognition step will be saved for later reading in the same order. Thus, we start by passing the connected component whose bounding box has the smaller coordinates (x, y) in the image, and that way we ensure that the first element of the display (and all the row after this) is sent to the OCR in the first place. After the first row is recognized, the next row is the one with a bigger y coordinate than the first element, and smallest x coordinate (all the components in that row are sent after this). Using this method, we ensure that in the case of having displays with several rows, components will be read in the correct sequence.

3   Experiments Performed and Results

The detection technique has been tested with 700 images and finds the display zone correctly the 85,14% of the cases without detecting any false positives. The detection rate increases up to 96,71% if the algorithm becomes more flexible about false positives. However, this increase in the detection rate is not an improvement in the system since the number of false positives is high.

We also tested the algorithm directly on the cell phone (Android OS). Even though displays are missed in some frames, since the processing is made on real time shortly the display is found again.

Fig. 2. Captured image, thresholded binary image and how the display gets detected

Figure 2 shows a captured image, the thresholded binary image and how the detection is shown on the mobile device allowing determination whether the detection is being done correctly. The detection performs well even far from the display, but for recognition, the image must not be taken so far from the display that the characters are not recognizable.

Figure 3 shows the display zone binarized using Otsu method, the result of the cleaning process and the connected components detected. Each element with different colour is the one that will be the input for the OCR.

The OCR recognizes the characters inside the display zone with an accuracy of 88.75%.

Fig. 3. Binarized image, cleaned image and detected connected componets

4   Conclusions and Future Work

We proposed a novel, fast color space based algorithm to detect LED/LCD self illuminated displays. We have developed a real time running algorithm, achieving 20 frames per second on a Samsung Galaxy S i9000, running Android OS on a 1000MHz processor. Android SO was chosen because of it is easy to share and install applications for this OS.

At this point, the characters inside the display are communicated to the user as they are recognized. We do not take into account the validity of the result obtained according to the preceding or subsequent characters, as the most recognized are numbers. When we train our OCR with the complete alphabet, we must define a grammar to determine the validity of a character going behind another (for example, both in English and Spanish is much more likely to have an "u" after a "q" rather than an "a").

In the future, we will integrate our detector with a commercial OCR to be able to detect and read any type of display, as there is no way to read non-digital characters without a complex OCR. Next, we will implement an option to guide and orientate the blind/visually impaired user providing different type of beeps depending the distance to the display to acquire the most suitable images for the recognition step.

Acknowledgements. The research developments presented in this paper are partially promoted by Fundación Centros Tecnológicos – Iñaki Goenaga.

References

1. Shen, H., Coughlan, J.: Reading LCD/LED Displays with a Camera Cell Phone. Smith-Kettlewell Eye Research Institute, San Francisco (2006)
2. Ghugardare, R.P., Narote, S.P., Mukherji, P., Kulkarni, P.M.: Optical character recognition system for seven segment display images of measuring instruments. In: TENCON, IEEE Region 10 Conference, pp.1–6, 23–26 (2009)
3. Morris, T., Blenkhorn, P., Crossey, L., Ngo, Q., Ross, M., Werner, D., Wong, C.: Clearspeech: A display reader for the visually handicapped. IEEE Transactions on Neural Systems and Rehabilitation Engineering 14(4), 492–500 (2006)
4. Tekin, E., Coughlan, J., Shen, H.: Real-Time Detection and Reading of LED/LCD Displays for Visually Impaired Persons. In: Proceedings IEEE Workshop Applications on Computer Vision (2011)
5. Gonzalez, R., Woods, R.: Digital Image Processing. Prentice-Hall (2008)
6. Hinton, G.E., Sejnowski, T.J.: Unsupervised Learning: Foundations of Neural Computation. MIT Press (1999)

A Non-visual Interface for Tasks Requiring Rapid Recognition and Response

An RC Helicopter Control System for Blind People

Kazunori Minatani[1] and Tetsuya Watanabe[2]

[1] National Center for University Entrance Examinations, Tokyo, Japan
`minatani@rd.dnc.ac.jp`
[2] University of Niigata, Faculty of Engineering, Niigata, Japan
`t2.nabe@eng.niigata-u.ac.jp`

Abstract. To implement a user interface for blind people, auditory and tactile outputs have mainly been used. However, an auditory interface is ineffective for tasks that require the rapid recognition that vision enables. Thus, this paper presents a method to achieve rapid recognition with a non-visual user interface. This user interface is implemented to achieve a prototype fully controllable system of an RC helicopter for blind people by using a braille display as a tactile output device. This paper also explains the system integration software, named brl-drone, and hardware components of that system including the AR. Drone. The AR. Drone is a controlled helicopter that uses an auxiliary magnetic sensor and a game controller to solve the problems that arise when a braille display is used as a tactile indicating device.

Keywords: Blind People, Non-visual Interface, RC Helicopter, Braille Display, AR. Drone.

1 Background and Objective

To implement a user interface for blind people, auditory and tactile outputs have mainly been used. Information can be obtained faster by listening to speech (auditory recognition) than by reading braille (tactile recognition). Nevertheless, intrinsically, speech is constructed from a time series of phonemes, so it requires certain definite time.

This fact does not totally change even if blind people can understand something said at a faster speech rate than sighted people can [1]. Thus, an auditory interface is ineffective for tasks that require the rapid recognition that vision enables. We tried to solve this problem by using a braille display as a tactile output device.

Our primary purpose is to achieve a fully controllable system of an RC helicopter for blind people. An event called the Jump to Science Summer Camp 2010 [2] was held to increase blind students' interest in science. We hosted a workshop in which they tried to control an RC helicopter. Blind students who joined that workshop enjoyed this attempt to learn how to fly helicopters. Such attempts may also be

K. Miesenberger et al. (Eds.): ICCHP 2012, Part II, LNCS 7383, pp. 630–635, 2012.
© Springer-Verlag Berlin Heidelberg 2012

signifi-cant if the report of a sound localization deficit in early-blind people [3] is taken into account. The students seemed to be very satisfied with the workshop.

That workshop was a purely educational activity, not a kind of experiment in a controlled environment. However, the author recognized problems that must be solved by developing a proper user interface. The workshop's attempts had a critical limitation. Even without sight, a person can detect the position of a flying RC helicopter relative to himself/herself by the sound generated by its rotors. The position of the flying RC helicopter can be known, but the direction because an RC helicopter makes the same sound no matter which direction it faces. Generally, an RC helicopter's control systems are designed to command horizontal moves in the relative direction of the fuselage's head (i.e. turn left or right, move forward in the current direction, etc.). Thus without sight, horizontal moves are impossible to command. The control is limited to only vertical moves (go up or down).

We try to overcome this limitation by indicating the direction of a helicopter's head on a braille display. In our view shaped by the experience of the summer camp, the direction of a helicopter must be recognized immediately, so using speech (an information media constructed from a time series of phonemes) requires too much time. Furthermore, one's auditory sense should be allowed to concentrate on the sound generated from a helicopter's rotors.

Another problem with controlling an RC helicopter arises when a braille display is used as a tactile indicating device. If information that must be recognized rapidly appears on a braille display, the user must put his/her fingers on it. RC helicopters, which are sold as toys, are usually designed to be controlled by a pair of joysticks. This user interface is designed on the assumption that both hands will grasp the joysticks. This is incompatible with our interface using a braille display. For our interface, the commands generated by at least one joystick must be input another way. Therefore, we adopted a method to use the user's own head as a joystick-like device.

2   Development Platform

Fig. 1 illustrates the system's components and the relationship between them.

2.1   Controlled Helicopter and Its Attached Additional Sensor

We choose the AR. Drone from the Parrot [4] as the target. Generally, RC helicopters have no programmability, so they are unfit for our development. On the other hand, the AR. Drone has sufficient potential. It was originally designed to be controlled with iOS devices (iPhone, iPad, and iPod touch) through a Wi-Fi connection. Users can not only send commands to an AR. Drone but also receive data of sensors and images captured by cameras on the AR. Drone. Commands and data are exchanged as UDP packets on a Wi-Fi connection established between iOS devices and the AR. Drone. This means devices with a TCP-IP stack, such as all modern PC operating systems, can play the role of a third-party control system of an AR. Drone.

The AR. Drone has an accelerometer and a gyro, the data from which enables pitch, roll, and yaw to be calculated. However, the gyro used as an MEMS sensor tends to make certain errors that lead to miscalculation of the yaw value. For our purpose, the direction of an AR. Drone's head must be calculated precisely. For this calculation, the yaw value is critical data.

Thus, this error is not tolerable. To avoid undesirable characteristics of the gyro sensor and acquire more accurate information on the direction of an AR. Drone's head, we decided to attach a magnetic sensor to the AR. Drone to obtain richer information from it during its fly. As a magnetic sensor we adopted the WAA-010 9 axis sensor [5].

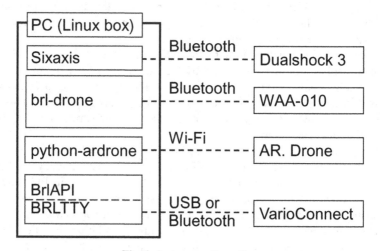

Fig. 1. System configuration

2.2   Controlling Platform

Base Platform and Peripherals: Linux Operating System (Debian 6.0 Squeeze) on a PC acts as the core of controlling platform. The PC must have Wi-Fi, Bluetooth, and USB interfaces for connecting to the AR. Drone, WAA-010, and peripherals (explained below).

As already mentioned, a braille display is required. This time, we choose the VarioConnect 40 braille display from BAUM [6]. Reasons for this choice are:

1. It has one joystick-like device named Navistick on the front center of the braille display that can be used an input device to command an AR. Drone.
2. BAUM's communication protocol between a PC and a braille display allows more than two cursor routing keys to be sent simultaneously [7]. This feature may make our system's user interface more user-friendly.

A head-tracking sensor is needed. As explained above, we planned to use the user's own head as the second joystick required to control an AR. Drone so that the position of the head can be tracked. We decided to use the PlayStation 3's game controller, named Dualshock 3 [8], from Sony Computer Entertainment as the sensor. Fortunately, the base shape of that controller can be placed on a cap.

Thanks to the Dualshock 3's accelerometer, if the user wears a cap attached to the Dualshock 3 controller, by how much and in what direction the user should tilt his/her head can be detected. This controller supports connection to the PC through not only USB but also Bluetooth, so there are no wires to obstruct the user's body and head movement.

System Integration Software: Elements explained above are integrated by the application software running on a Linux PC. This software is written in Python scrip-ting language. It is tentatively named brl-drone.

Brl-drone uses some open source software. It uses python-ardrone [9] for sending commands to and receiving data from an AR. Drone. To control a braille display, Brl-drone uses the Python binding of BrlAPI [10], which is a part of the BRLTTY [11]. Here, we focus on using the VarioConnect as a braille display, but thanks to the BrlAPI, it is possible to support braille displays that can be used with the BRLTTY with the least amount of effort.

The software that receives the Dualshock 3's sensor data is implemented in an independent process. Sixaxis [12] is a user space daemon that supports Bluetooth connection between Sixaxis, which is early version of the PlayStation 3 game controller, and Linux. On the basis of Sixaxis's source code, we developed a user space daemon to read the Dualshock 3's sensor data through Bluetooth. Using UNIX's named pipe, this daemon sends Dualshock 3 sensors' values to brl-drone.

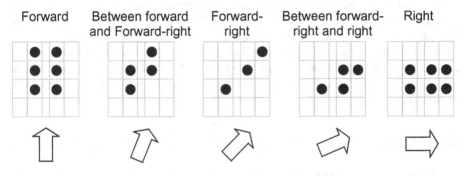

Fig. 2. Tactile symbols showing the direction

User Interface: Apart from the user's head with Dualshock 3, interaction between the user and the system is put all together on a braille display.

Information about an AR. Drone's current state is indicated using braille. Such information includes the battery usage, the altitude, the pitch-rolls of an AR. Drone and user's head, and the direction of an AR. Drone's head. The battery usage (percentile) and altitude (centimeter) are displayed as digits, while the others are represented as icons that occupy two cells each.

The symbol of the direction of an AR. Drone's head, which we judged the most important value, is put at the center of a braille display. On a braille cell array, that place is nearest to the Navistick, which may be often manipulated by the user. The direction of an AR. Drone's head is represented as symbols such as those shown in Fig. 2. 360 degrees are divided into 16 directions and each direction is mapped to a unique symbol.

All controlling commands to an AR. Drone can be input with buttons on the braille display. Such commands include takeoff, move forward/backward/left/right/down/up, turn left/right, and change speed.

For reasons of practicality, move forward/backward/left/right are also assigned to commands generated by the user's head. Like Linux console's PC cursor, the Vario-Connect's Navistick can generate only one direction key code at a time. During a flight, it is expected to move in a medium direction (i.e. forward-left, backward-right). By calculating Dualshock 3's sensor value, the user's head can command the AR. Drone to move in any arbitrary direction.

3   Conclusions and Future Works

Brl-drone is guaranteed to show information about a controlled AR. Drone in 0.25 seconds. We consider this rapidity to be not only fit for tactile recognition but also sufficient to control RC helicopters. Preliminary demonstration videos are uploaded to a video sharing site [13]. Actual demonstration flights will be performed at the ICCHP conference venue if circumstances permit.

Carrying out subjective experiments can hopefully produce good results. However, this evaluation has particularly troublesome characteristics because controlling an RC helicopter is itself a hard task even for sighted persons. Events like the Jump to Science Summer Camp 2010 mentioned above should be utilized for evaluation.

In January 2012, the Parrot announced to release the AR. Drone 2.0 which will be a successor of the AR. Drone. The AR. Drone 2.0 will have own magnetic sensor, and it may be accessible through an SDK. If such an SDK will be released, our system can be simplified.

References

1. Asakawa, C., et al.: Maximum Listening Speeds for the Blind. In: Proc. Conf. of Int. Community for Auditory Display 2003, pp. 276–279 (2003)
2. Jump to Science (in Japanese), http://www.jump2science.org
3. Zwiers, M.P., Van Opstal, A.J., Cruysberg, J.R.M.: A Spatial Hearing Deficit in Early-Blind Humans. Journal of Neuroscience 21, 1–5 (2001)
4. AR.Drone.com, http://ardrone.parrot.com/
5. Wireless Technologies Inc. (in Japanese), http://www.wireless-t.jp/support.html
6. BAUM Retec AG, http://www.baum.de/cms/en/braille/
7. BAUM Retec AG, http://www.openbraille.org/documents/VarioConnect-comm-prot-public-V6.pdf

8. DUALSHOCK3 wireless controller,
http://uk.playstation.com/ps3/peripherals/detail/item113530/
DUALSHOCK%C2%AE3-wireless-controller/
9. venthur / python-ardrone GitHub,
http://github.com/venthur/python-ardrone
10. BrlAPI: let applications write braille!, http://brl.thefreecat.org/
11. BRLTTY, http://mielke.cc/brltty/
12. PdaXrom embedded, http://www.pdaxrom.org/index.php/
PS3_sixaxis_bluetooth_uinput_driver
13. (in Japanese), http://www.youtube.com/watch?v=C30QafU88x0,
http://www.youtube.com/watch?v=oRQUt1RgJUU

Reaching to Sound Accuracy in the Peri-personal Space of Blind and Sighted Humans

Marc J.-M. Macé[1,2,*], Florian Dramas[1,2], and Christophe Jouffrais[1,2]

[1] IRIT, University of Toulouse, Univ. Paul Sabatier, 31062, Toulouse cedex 9, France
[2] IRIT, CNRS, Univ. Paul Sabatier, 31062, Toulouse cedex 9, France
CA: marc.mace@irit.fr

Abstract. With the aim of designing an assistive device for the Blind, we compared the ability of blind and sighted subjects to accurately locate several types of sounds generated in the peri-personal space. Despite a putative lack of calibration of their auditory system with vision, blind subjects performed with a similar accuracy as sighted subjects. The average error was sufficiently low (10° in azimuth and 10 cm in distance) to orient a user towards a specific goal or to guide a hand grasping movement to a nearby object. Repeated white noise bursts of short duration induced better performance than continuous sounds of similar total duration. These types of sound could be advantageously used in an assistive device. They would provide indications about direction to follow or position of surrounding objects, with limited masking of environmental sounds, which are of primary importance for the Blind.

Keywords: Sound localization, Blindness, assistive device, augmented reality.

1   Introduction

Humans are able to localize distant [1 - 2] and proximal [3 - 4] sound sources with a fair accuracy. This capability has been used previously in assistive devices for the Blind to guide them with virtual beacons [5] along a path. In the present study, the issue of sound localization is included in the context of an assistive device for the Blind [6, 7] that could assist both in navigation tasks and object localization tasks. As this assistive device is intended to be used in daily life, the sounds it produces must be designed to minimally interfere with the sounds of the environment. This could be achieved by using sounds as short as possible while still allowing good localization performance. Another important feature of this assistive device is that it should be able to orientate users with distant sounds as well as to guide reaching movements towards close-by objects with proximal sounds.

The usability of this device relies heavily on the sound localization capabilities of the Blind. A preliminary step before generating virtual sounds to indicate a position in the proximal space would be to verify that blind people are able to localize close-by

---

* Corresponding author.

K. Miesenberger et al. (Eds.): ICCHP 2012, Part II, LNCS 7383, pp. 636–643, 2012.

sound sources as accurately as sighted people despite the lack of vision to calibrate their acoustic space. Some studies were conducted on this issue and no definitive answer emerges as blind people show better [8, 9], identical [10] or worse [11] performance compared to sighted people depending on the experimental protocol. Also, most of these sound localization studies with blind persons had concentrated on the localization of distant [12 - 13] or continuously presented [14] sounds and little is known of their localization capabilities with very short stimuli presented in the peri-personal space.

As an assistive device for the blind based on sound localization should be able to indicate directions precisely, the first objective of this study was to determine if blind persons are able to localize brief nearby sounds and if their accuracy is comparable to the accuracy of sighted persons [4]. The second objective was to determine the most important characteristics for a sound to be correctly localized in the proximal space -to guide reaching movements- while being the least intrusive, an aspect of the auditory stimuli which had been largely overlooked in the past.

We tested a group of blind subjects and a group of sighted subjects with seven auditory stimuli, varying the number of bursts and stimulus duration. The task for the subject consisted in pointing at the perceived location of the sound with the index finger.

2   Material and Methods

2.1   Subjects

8 legally blind subjects (mean age 40.7) and 9 sighted subjects (mean age 25.8) were involved in this experiment. Half of the blind subjects were born blind; the four others lost vision between the age of 1 and 8 years. All subjects were right handed and fourteen out of seventeen subjects had normal hearing. The three subjects whose audiogram showed a deficit of 20 to 50 dB at one or two frequency bands above 4000 Hz were still included in the study as the stimuli used were all broad-band. These subjects showed no statistical differences in performance compared to the others.

2.2   Protocol

Sighted subjects didn't see the setup before the experiment and were blindfolded to follow the exact same protocol as blind subjects. An experimental platform (half-disc, radius 1 m) was equipped with 35 loudspeakers (ref.: CB990, 8 Ohm, 3 W) disposed on 5 semi-circular rows of 7 speakers each (See Fig 1), covering 180°.

The subjects were seated in the hollow part at the center of the platform, in front of the second column of speakers (0°). Subjects were pointing to the targets with the right hand. The orientation of the head was monitored with a magnetic sensor (Flock of Bird, Ascension Technology) and the pointing movements were measured with a home-made video-based tracking system (maximum RMS error inferior to 3 cm).

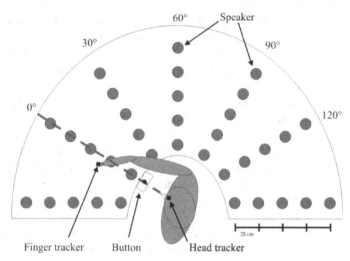

Fig. 1. The semi-circular platform was covered by 7 columns and 5 rows of loudspeakers. The subject was seated in front of the column labeled 0° (dotted line) and had to press a button to start the trial. After a delay, one of the loudspeakers emitted a sound. The subject had to point with its forefinger to the perceived sound and bring back his hand to the start button.

A trial started when the subject pressed the button of a mouse (at the starting position, Fig 1), with the additional condition that his head was orientated towards the 0° column (with +/- 2.5°). A brief auditory stimulus was then presented via a single loudspeaker. The subject had to point with the forefinger at the perceived location of the sound source before coming back to the starting position to trigger the next trial.

There were seven auditory conditions according to the number and the duration of the bursts within the sound stimulus: 1*10 ms, 1*25 ms, 1*50 ms, 1*200 ms, 2*25 ms with a 30 ms pause (50 ms of sound / 80 ms of total stimulus duration), 3*25 ms with a 30 ms pause (75 ms / 135 ms) and 4*25 ms with a 30 ms pause (100 ms / 190 ms). Each burst in the stimuli consisted of a Gaussian white noise covering 20 to 20000 Hz at approximately 60 dB.

To avoid border effects found in a previous experiment, only the results from speakers between 0 and 120° were used. Each subject performed 4 pointing movements to each stimulus on each loudspeaker, corresponding to a total of 700 trials. These trials were arranged in a complete random design within and across subjects. Subjects never had feedback on their performance during the experiment. Before the recording session, they performed a trial session with 10 pointing movements towards some of the stimuli used during the experiment.

2.3   Data Analysis and Statistics

After removing the front-back errors which were analyzed separately (2.5% of the trials; data not shown), we measured the pointing accuracy across two components: azimuth error and distance error relative to the subject. Azimuth error was computed as the absolute value (in degrees) of the difference between the azimuth of the sound source and the pointed azimuth. Distance error was computed as the absolute value (in mm) of the difference between the distance of the sound source and the pointed distance.

Analysis of variance was performed on the two groups of subjects (BLIND and SIGHTED) using the azimuth error and distance error as data. We also calculated 2-factors ANOVAs: CONDS*GROUPS for the same two measurements, to assess the performance across stimulus conditions for BLIND and SIGHTED groups. Tukey post-hoc tests were performed to assess the significant differences within factors. Significance level was set at 0.05 for all the analysis.

The data of one blind subject was removed from the analysis as her performance was at least 3 standard deviations below the performance of other blind subjects for most of the measurements.

3   Results

3.1   Azimuth and Distance Error across Groups

The average error in azimuth was significantly different between blind and sighted GROUPS ($F(1, 11532)=8.96$, $p=0.003$) with blind subjects being in average half a degree more precise in azimuth than sighted subjects (Fig 2A).

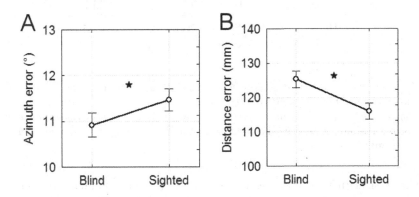

Fig. 2. Mean azimuth error in degrees (A) and mean distance error in mm (B) for Blind and Sighted subjects for all stimulus conditions together. Error bars are IC95. Blind subjects had a better accuracy than sighted subjects to evaluate the azimuth of a sound source but were less accurate to evaluate its distance.

The average error in distance was also significantly different between the two groups of subjects ($F(1, 11532)=28.63$, $p<10^{-5}$): sighted subjects were in average slightly better (close to 10 mm) to evaluate the distance of the sound source than blind subjects (Fig 2B).

3.2   Azimuth Error across Stimulus Conditions

For the two groups, the azimuth error depended both on sound duration and number of repetitions (Fig 3) and there was no GROUP*CONDITION interaction $(F(6, 11520)=0.36, p=0.90)$ as the azimuth accuracy across conditions was similar for blind and sighted subjects.

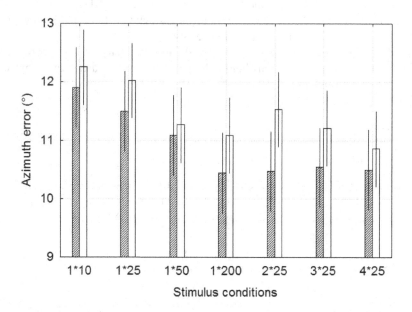

Fig. 3. Mean azimuth error in degrees for blind (hatched) and sighted (white) subjects across stimulus conditions. From conditions 1*10 to 1*200, the azimuth error decreased with sound duration. The repetition of a sound burst also resulted in an accuracy increase from 1*25 to 2*25 before reaching a plateau with 3 and 4 repetitions of the sound, especially for blind subjects. Error bars are IC95.

When considering conditions with 1 burst only (1*Sound duration), azimuth error linearly decreased with sound duration from 12.1° (1*10) to 10.8° (1*200) for both groups, meaning that pointing accuracy significantly increases with stimulus duration $(F(3, 6564)=5.78, p=0.0006)$. Pointing accuracy also significantly increased with the number of 25 ms bursts $(F(3, 6615)=3.94, p=0.008)$, but a Tukey post-hoc analysis revealed that the only significant difference was between 1*25 ms and the other N*25 conditions, which indicates that pointing accuracy in azimuth was already at best with only two repetitions of the sound.

Interestingly, the stimulus in condition 2*25 had a total duration of 80 ms (2*25 ms + 30 ms of silence) and induced similar accuracy in azimuth than the longer 1*200 ms stimulus, especially for blind subjects.

3.3   Distance Error across Stimulus Conditions

For the two groups, the distance error depended both on sound duration and the number of repetitions (see Figure 5) and there was no GROUP*CONDITION interaction ($F_{(6, 11520)}$=0.83, p=0.55), revealing that distance estimation across conditions was similar for the two groups of subjects.

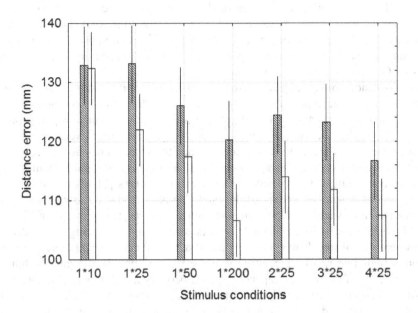

Fig. 4. Mean distance error in degrees for blind (hatched) and sighted (white) subjects across stimulus conditions. From conditions 1*10 to 1*200, the distance error decreased with sound duration. The repetition of a sound burst also resulted in an accuracy increase from 1*25 to 2*25 before reaching a plateau with 3 and 4 repetitions of the sound. Error bars are IC95.

When considering conditions with 1 burst only (1*Sound duration), distance error linearly decreased with sound duration from 133 mm (condition 1*10) to 113 mm (condition 1*200) for both group together, meaning that pointing accuracy significantly increased with stimulus duration ($F_{(3, 6564)}$=13.06, $p<10^{-5}$). The number of 25 ms bursts did also significantly increased the pointing distance accuracy ($F_{(3, 6615)}$=7.76, p=0.00004). However a Tukey posthoc analysis revealed that the only significant difference was between 1*25 ms and the other N*25 conditions, which indicates that pointing accuracy in distance was already at best or close to best with only two repetitions of the sound.

4   Discussion

In average, the performance of blind subjects to localize nearby short sounds matched the performance of sighted subjects. For sounds with a unique burst, pointing accuracy of blind subjects increased with sound duration up to a plateau around 10.5° and 120 mm when pointing to a 200 ms sound. Interestingly, the same performance was reached when only two bursts of 25 ms were presented. The total duration of this double burst stimulus was 80 ms (2*25 ms + 30 ms silence), compared to the 200 ms of the unique burst. This advantage of multiple sound bursts over continuous sounds can be attributed to the localization cues specifically present in the onset and offset of a sound [15]. As a direct conclusion of this result, the sounds used in an assistive device for the Blind should be composed of short bursts to maximize the localization performance while preserving normal hearing of the environment. Preserving the surrounding sounds is especially important as blind persons heavily rely on auditory cues for Orientation and Mobility skills.

In conclusion, blind subjects were able to locate short sounds in peri-personal space with a good accuracy. The average accuracy for the optimal condition (2*25 ms white noise burst) was around 10° in azimuth and 12 cm in distance, which is precise enough to orientate the subjects towards a specific goal and could even guide a grasping movement until tactile feedback occurs when the object is reached. Coupled with an artificial vision system, this approach, where nearby targets could be sonified with good accuracy, could well complement navigation systems [5] where only far-field targets and landmarks are indicated. It could also be extended by using short sounds designed to convey additional information such as earcons [16] or spearcons [17].

This performance with real sounds is a first step towards designing an assistive device where virtual sounds will be used instead of real sounds. It is possible to generate virtual sounds that will be perceived at any spatial location by filtering the binaural signal in a specific way that depends on each person's morphology [18]. This set of transfer function are called HRTF's (Head Related Transfer Functions) and are obtained by recording different sounds with a microphone inserted inside the ear. The next step in the development of our assistive device will be to evaluate the sound location capabilities of nearby and distant short virtual sounds by blind people.

Acknowledgements. This work has been supported by the French Foundation for Medical Research (FRM-INE2005) and by the French National Research Agency (ANR) through TecSan program (project NAVIG n°ANR-08-TECS-011). The authors thank BFG Katz for helpful comments on the design of the setup and experiment.

References

1. Middlebrooks, J.C., Green, D.M.: Sound localization by human listeners. Annual Review of Psychology 42, 135–159 (1991)
2. Blauert, J.: Spatial hearing: the psychophysics of human sound localization. MIT Press (1997)
3. Brungart, D.S.: Auditory localization of nearby sources. III. Stimulus effects. The Journal of the Acoustical Society of America 106, 3589–3602 (1999)

4. Brungart, D.S., Durlach, N.I., Rabinowitz, W.M.: Auditory localization of nearby sources. II. Localization of a broadband source. The Journal of the Acoustical Society of America 106, 1956–1968 (1999)
5. Loomis, J.M., Golledge, R.G., Klatzky, R.L., Speigle, J.M., Tietz, J.: Personal guidance system for the visually impaired. In: Proceedings of the First Annual ACM Conference on Assistive Technologies, Assets 1994, pp. 85–91. ACM Press, New York (1994)
6. Katz, B.F.G., Dramas, F., Parseihian, G., Gutierrez, O., Kammoun, S., Brilhault, A., Brunet, L., Gallay, M., Oriola, B., Auvray, M., Truillet, P., Thorpe, S., Jouffrais, C.: NAVIG: Guidance system for the visually impaired using virtual augmented reality. Technology and Disability (in press, 2012)
7. Kammoun, S., Parseihian, G., Gutierrez, O., Brilhault, A., Serpa, A., Raynal, M., Oriola, B., Macé, M.J.-M., Auvray, M., Denis, M., Thorpe, S.J., Truillet, P., Katz, B.F.G., Jouffrais, C.: Navigation and space perception assistance for the Visually Impaired: The NAVIG project. BioMedical Engineering and Research 33, 182–189 (2012)
8. Röder, B., Teder-Sälejärvi, W., Sterr, A., Rösler, F., Hillyard, S.A., Neville, H.J.: Improved auditory spatial tuning in blind humans. Nature 400, 162–166 (1999)
9. Lessard, N., Paré, M., Lepore, F., Lassonde, M.: Early-blind human subjects localize sound sources better than sighted subjects. Nature 395, 278–280 (1998)
10. Zwiers, M.P., Van Opstal, A.J., Cruysberg, J.R.: Two-dimensional sound-localization behavior of early-blind humans. Experimental Brain Research 140, 206–222 (2001)
11. Zwiers, M.P., Van Opstal, A.J., Cruysberg, J.R.: A spatial hearing deficit in early-blind humans. The Journal of Neuroscience 21, RC142, 1–5 (2001)
12. Lewald, J.: Vertical sound localization in blind humans. Neuropsychologia 40, 1868–1872 (2002)
13. Voss, P., Lassonde, M., Gougoux, F., Fortin, M., Guillemot, J.-P., Lepore, F., Postale, C.: Early- and late-onset blind individuals show supra-normal auditory abilities in far-space. Current Biology 14, 1734–1738 (2004)
14. Wanet, M.C., Veraart, C.: Processing of auditory information by the blind in spatial localization tasks. Perception And Psychophysics 38, 91–96 (1985)
15. Rakerd, B., Hartmann, W.M.: Localization of sound in rooms, III: Onset and duration effects. The Journal of the Acoustical Society of America 80, 1695 (1986)
16. Blattner, M., Sumikawa, D., Greenberg, R.: Earcons and Icons: Their Structure and Common Design Principles. Human-Computer Interaction 4, 11–44 (1989)
17. Walker, B.N., Nance, A., Lindsay, J.: Spearcons: speech-based earcons improve navigation performance in auditory menus. In: Proceedings of the International Conference on Auditory Display, pp. 95–98 (2006)
18. Katz, B.F.G., Parseihian, G.: Perceptually based head-related transfer function database optimization. JASA 131 (2012)

Hapto-acoustic Scene Representation

Sebastian Ritterbusch[1], Angela Constantinescu[2], and Volker Koch[3]

[1] Karlsruhe Institute of Technology, Engineering Mathematics and Computing Lab.,
Karlsruhe, Germany
[2] Karlsruhe Institute of Technology, Study Centre for the Visually Impaired Students,
Karlsruhe, Germany
[3] Karlsruhe Institute of Technology, Building Lifecycle Management,
Karlsruhe, Germany
{sebastian.ritterbusch,angela.constantinescu,
volker.koch}@kit.edu

Abstract. The use of the Phantom Omni force feedback device combined with sonification is evaluated in applications for visually impaired people such as medical engineering, numerical simulation, and architectural planning.

Keywords: haptic, acoustic, force feedback, sonification, visually impaired.

1 Introduction

Advances in computing technologies make it possible for ever greater amounts of data to be automatically gathered, stored, processed and interpreted. Many fields, such as medicine or urban planning take advantage of computer simulations and visualizations in order to improve their activities: highly accurate and fast-changing 3D city models are available, and medical CT scans yield virtual 3D scenes. However, in some cases, the amount of data gathered is so substantial that a meaningful visual representation cannot be generated. Moreover, access to this information is severely limited to visually impaired people, unnecessarily restricting their life and job opportunities. We believe that the combination of haptic devices with 3D acoustics and annotations shows a promising approach of how to generally represent complex virtual spatial scenes without the need for vision.

2 Related Work

Hapto-acoustic applications have been used so far in fields such as medical training and simulation, arts and design, video games or robotics. For visually-impaired people, some applications specifically addressing their needs have been developed in fields such as mathematics, maps and mobility, non-visual display of graphics and games. Some systems even deal with collaborative spaces shared between sighted and visually impaired users.

K. Miesenberger et al. (Eds.): ICCHP 2012, Part II, LNCS 7383, pp. 644–650, 2012.
© Springer-Verlag Berlin Heidelberg 2012

Among the systems most closely related to ours, we note Omero [2] - a framework for the active exploration of VRML[1] models based on a multimodal interaction in which visual, auditory, verbal and tactile interfaces were combined. Omero does not seem to make use of spatial sound, and the models are mainly static, with the exception of objects which could change state such as opening/closing doors. Also, the testing reported poor results with blind users (when the visual interface was missing). A subsequent study based on Omero [3] tests an audio-haptic scenario with blind users. The models used depict concepts of plane (2D) geometry such as basic shapes and areas. Crommentuijn et al. [1] use a Phantom Desktop device in order to evaluate several auditory displays in an object localization task in a virtual haptic 3D environment. Heuten et. al. [5] use interactive 3D sonification (without any haptic interaction) for the exploration of city maps. Preliminary tests report that blind users could successfully reproduce the parts of a city map that were sonified. Yet another interesting study is that of Magnusson et al [6], who used a Phantom device in combination with 3D audio in a virtual environment in a navigation and object location scenario. Within the MICOLE project [12], a multimodal software architecture SDK (Micole-Lib) together with sample applications have been developed. The SDK allows for the creation of applications that make use of graphics (virtual environments), audio and haptics (force feedback, Braille devices and the VTPlayer haptic mouse). While the results of the MICOLE project such as design recommendations for haptic and audio development and collaborative software were useful to us, the project itself addresses children and their inclusion in mainstream education, while our focus is instead on scientific and academic scenarios.

3   System Description and Applications

In our application, we used the Sensable PHANTOM Omni® force-feedback device combined with spatial sound enhanced with additional mappings of sound attributes to scene attributes. The sound was used to guide the user to the closest point of interest such as object or part of an object, while the haptics enabled him or her to experience shape, firmness and texture. Moreover, objects possess a magnetic force which slightly pulls the user's hand towards the object, when the cursor is within a certain distance range. For the sound feedback, we used the "ears-in-hand" metaphor, assuming that the user's ears are on the tip of the pointing device. Here are the sound mappings used:

- X axis maps to pan: if the closest point of interest is right of the cursor, the sound is stronger on the right side, and vice versa
- Y axis maps to pitch: the higher the cursor is in the space model, the higher the sound's pitch is. A reference sound can also be turned on to help the user
- Z axis maps to wave shape: in front of the object (closer to the user) the sound is represented by a sine wave, while behind the object (further away from the user) it is a square wave
- Distance maps to tempo: the closer the cursor is to the closest point of interest, the fastest the tempo of the sound is - similar to a sonar.

---

[1] VRML: Virtual Reality Modeling Language, a standard for describing 3D models, especially suited to be used on the World Wide Web.

The proposed method is evaluated in three areas:

- Pre-operative assessment of the operation field for key-hole surgery,
- Experiencing virtual 3D city and architecture models for planning and navigation purposes,
- Analysis of numerical simulations with high dimensional information for each point.

Keyhole operation methods have large advantages of often significantly shorter operation times, and often lower risks for the patients. Typically, the surgeon has no direct view into the field of operation, and is relying on tomography methods for pre- and inter-operative supervision. In the specific case of minimally invasive implantation of aortic heart valves, the pre-operative analysis of the shape of the aorta and the calcification distribution is fundamental. Especially the visual identification of calcification is challenging, since visualization methods are often implicitly threshold based. The sonification of surrounding material density could lead to a better understanding of the distribution of calcification and could therefore extend the pre-operative analysis, supported by visually impaired assistants.

In the context of architecture and the build environment in general the developed methods and tools could lead to significant improvements of accessibility for visually impaired people. As the build environment is not static but constantly changing and developing itself, highly dynamic virtual models can communicate changes easier, faster and more effective by hapto-acoustic channels. Furthermore, the conveyance of more qualified and detailed information about the environment, such as specific road condition and traffic flow allows ad-hoc allocation of individual and time sensitive semantic aspects to the model.

The increasing performance of computing resources leads to a data explosion and increasing data complexity in numerical simulation. Often, for each point in space, there are high-dimensional resulting vectors, which cannot be displayed visually at the same time. Acoustics offer the opportunity to reflect each dimension of the result in varying frequency, modulation and amplitude, which can be analyzed by the human ear. The use of hapto-acoustic methods for analysis of highly dimensional numerical simulations have the potential to offer deeper and more-combined insight into the results compared to visual representations.

4   Evaluation

4.1   Procedure

A pilot study with five users, two of whom were blind, has been performed in order to assess our system. For each scenario, one model was used as follows:

- Medicine (Med): true model of an aorta obtained from a real patient
- Architecture (Arch): the complex of buildings that belongs to the Department of Mathematics at KIT
- Mathematics (Math): flow simulation in the lungs

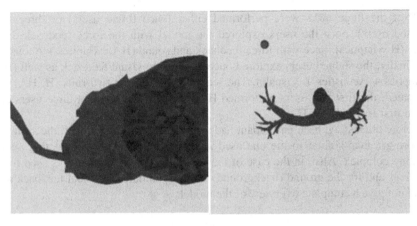

Fig. 1. Snapshots of the models used. Left: Aorta (Med). Right: Flow simulation in the lungs (Math); the red dot is the cursor (Phantom Stylus).

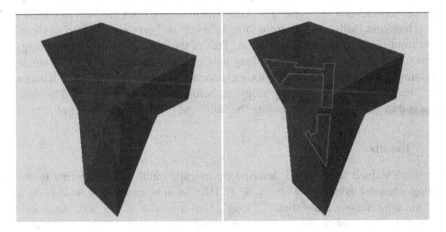

Fig. 2. Snapshots of the models used. Complex of buildings (Arch), as it was used in the testing (left), and with the buildings highlighted in red (right); based on the 3D-City model of Karlsruhe, © Stadt Karlsruhe, Liegenschaftsamt.

All models are based on true data, obtained for instance from the local authority real estate office (Liegenschaftsamt Karlsruhe) in the case of the maps, or CT measurements from patients who agreed that the data be used for research purposes in the case of medical data.

For each of the three models, the users had to perform three tasks:

- Reach the object by touching the closest point or the first point of interest in the model that they could find
- Describe the model
- Find a certain part in the model, given a verbal description of it

Each of the three tasks were performed either twice (blind users) or three times (sighted users): once the users explored the model with the force feedback device alone (H = haptics); once with force feedback and sound (HA = Haptics + Acoustics); and finally, the sighted users explored once more using visual feedback as well (HAV = Haptics + Acoustics + Visuals). The sequence of the first two runs (H, HA) were alternated: the first two users performed H before HA and the next three users completed first HA and then H.

Before the testing, each participant had time to get familiarized with the system by exploring a map similar to the one used in the actual testing, but depicting another building complex. Also, in the case of the maps, the colors and patterns used for the buildings and for the ground (background) were so similar, that visual feedback alone could not give a complete overview of the model.

4.2   Participants

The five users who participated in the experiment, three men and two women, had ages between 23 and 44; computer skills which ranged from medium to expert user; and orientation skills ranging from "not so good" to "very good". One of them was blind from birth, another one late blind. Two of them play instruments and sing, one of them used to play an instrument long ago, and two neither play an instrument nor they sing. Two users had no previous experience whatsoever with the Phantom device, while three had previously seen one before, and briefly tried it. The group of users is thus heterogeneous regarding the skills and previous knowledge of the users.

4.3   Results

The three sighted users could describe on average quite well the forms they were feeling when not using visual feedback (H, HA). In some cases, they would only identify one attribute (such as "round", "long", "has a hole in it, like a donut"). In other cases, they could make out a rather good mental model of the objects ("like a tree branch" for Math, "like a round cup" for Med). Yet in other cases, they would make a wrong mental image. The two blind users gave up much faster in trying to describe the model, and identified less attributes than the sighted users. The times they spent on the task are accordingly smaller. According to one user, it is difficult for people who are blind from birth to experience 3D maps. They can only interpret maps in a bird's eye view or profile view. Surprisingly, even the users who found describing the object a very difficult task - could successfully complete the third task (finding a part), at least once out of six trials, without visual feedback.

In the questionnaire following the evaluation, four out of five users found the system difficult to use, while one user, who had had the most experience with the Phantom Omni before, found it easy to use. However, three out of five users found it intuitive, and the other two answered with "I don't know". All users found the sound feedback useful or very useful, at least in some cases (like when reaching objects), or conditionally ("not in combination with haptics"). All users rated the sound intuitive (3) or very intuitive (2) and agreed that it was easy (4) or very easy (1) to interpret.

However, two out of five users preferred to explore the models without sound - only using haptic feedback.

Most users gave suggestions for improving the prototype and mentioned that they would like to try the system again and maybe even use it after their suggestions are implemented.

5 Conclusion

Previous research has shown that using hapto-acoustic interfaces in virtual 3D environments can enhance the users' experience in tasks such as navigation, object location and more. In our research, we used a combination of force feedback and sonification in three scenarios from medicine, architecture and mathematics in order to allow for a better exploration and analysis of the data sets. For blind and partially sighted people in particular, such an approach could allow them to study and work in areas previously restricted to them, such as mathematics or architecture.

Aknowledgements. We would like to thank the Clinic for Heart Surgery in Karlsruhe for providing some of the research data used in this project. We would also like to thank the City of Karlsruhe and the local real estate office for providing the maps data. We must also mention that this project is supported by funds from the Excellence Initiative I, sphere of competence: "Technology, Culture and Society".

References

1. Crommentuijn, K., Winberg, F.: Designing auditory displays to facilitate object localization in virtual haptic 3D environments. In: Proceedings of the 8th International ACM SIGACCESS Conference on Computers and Accessibility (Assets 2006), pp. 255–256. ACM, New York (2006)
2. Felice, F.D., Renna, F., Attolico, G., Distante, A.: A haptic/acoustic application to allow blind the access to spatial information. In: WHC 2007: Proceedings of the Second Joint EuroHaptics Conference and Symposium on Haptic Interfaces for Virtual Environment and Teleoperator Systems. IEEE Computer Society, Washington (2007)
3. De Felice, F., Attolico, G., Distante, A.: Configurable Design of Multimodal Non Visual Interfaces for 3D VE's. In: Altinsoy, M.E., Jekosch, U., Brewster, S. (eds.) HAID 2009. LNCS, vol. 5763, pp. 71–80. Springer, Heidelberg (2009)
4. Grunwald, M.: Human Haptic Perception, Basics and Applications. Birkhäuser, Basel (2008)
5. Heuten, W., Wichmann, D., Boll, S.: Interactive 3D sonification for the exploration of city maps. In: Proceedings of the 4th Nordic Conference on Human-Computer Interaction: Changing Roles (NordiCHI 2006), pp. 155–164. ACM, New York (2006)
6. Magnusson, C., Danielsson, H., Rassmus-Gröhn, K.: Non Visual Haptic Audio Tools for Virtual Environments. In: McGookin, D., Brewster, S. (eds.) HAID 2006. LNCS, vol. 4129, pp. 111–120. Springer, Heidelberg (2006)
7. Moll, J., Huang, Y., Sallnäs, E.-L.: Audio makes a difference in haptic collaborative virtual environments. Interacting with Computers 22(6), 544–555 (2010)

8. Rassmus-Gröhn, K.: Enabling Audio-Haptics. Licentiatuppsats Certec, LTH. Certec, Lund (2006)
9. Robin King, A.: Re-presenting visual content for blind people (2006), http://www.alasdairking.me.uk/research/PhD.htm
10. Shen, X., Shirmohammadi, S.: Tele-Haptics - Introduction, Haptics Applications, Haptic Rendering, Stable Haptic Interaction, Architecture of Haptics Applications, – Networked Haptics, http://encyclopedia.jrank.org/articles/pages/6909/Tele-Haptics.html
11. Sodnik, J., Tomazic, S., Grasset, R., Duenser, A., Billinghurst, M.: Spatial sound localization in an augmented reality environment. Proceedings of the 20th Conference of the Computer-human Interaction Special Interest Group (CHISIG) of Australia on Computer-Human Interaction: Design: Activities, Artefacts and Environments, Sydney, Australia (2006)
12. The MICOLE project, http://micole.cs.uta.fi/

Efficient Access to PC Applications by Using a Braille Display with Active Tactile Control (ATC)

Siegfried Kipke

Handy Tech Elektronik GmbH
Brunnenstraße 10
72160 Horb-Nordstetten
Germany
ski@handytech.de

Abstract. Braille displays are providing tactile access to information shown on a screen. The invention of Active Tactile Control (ATC) allows detecting the tactile reading position on a Braille display in real time. Based on ATC new computer interactions have been implemented. Braille frames allow the simultaneous display of various independent sources of information on a Braille display and are used to improve access to complex applications. A task-overview for handling of multiple tasks with direct access to the activated tasks triggered by the reading position has been implemented. A tactile notification of a spelling mistake triggered by the tactile reading position provides blind users assistance when editing text. A new rule set for blind users' PC interaction based on Active Tactile Control needs to be defined.

Keywords: tactile reading position, Braille, computer access, Braille frames, assistance, computer interaction, e-learning, blind PC users.

1   Braille Displays in a Glance

Since Braille was invented 187 years ago, it became the common tool for blind and visually impaired people all around the globe. Lately, we can see a shift towards speech output today. Nevertheless there are great advantages in using Braille. Blind people not only have access to text structure and format, it also enables them to read self determinedly, is an excellent literacy tool and on top of that, Braille is a discreet way to access information.

For blind computer users, Braille displays, on which Braille is presented refreshable as a combination of raised dots, are a very important way to access information. A standard Braille Display uses between 40 and 80 Braille cells for the tactile presentation of Braille characters. Each Braille cell is made up of a 2 by 4 Dot matrix.

To blind users, there are crucial benefits in reading texts in Braille. Not only does a Braille display present information shown on a computer screen in Braille in real time, it also has a set of control elements like command keys, courser routing keys and navigation keys.

K. Miesenberger et al. (Eds.): ICCHP 2012, Part II, LNCS 7383, pp. 651–658, 2012.

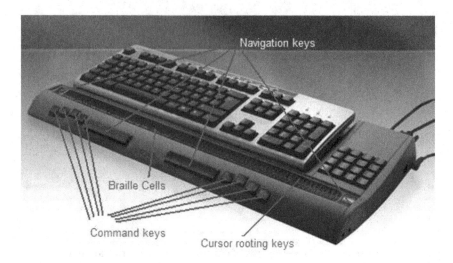

Fig. 1. Braille display with a set of control elements like Command keys, Cursor Rooting keys and Navigation keys

2   State of the Art in the Use of ATC Technology

With the invention of Active Tactile Control (ATC) new interactions with computer systems are made possible. ATC detects the reading position on a Braille display in real time. This information is used to improve the access to various applications. The Active Braille from Handy Tech is the first portable Braille display with patented ATC technology.

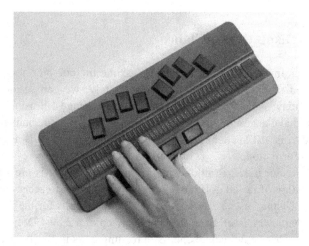

Fig. 2. Active Braille with ATC Technology

The reading position is defined as the position of attention when reading on a Braille display. Typically, the reading position moves from the left to the right. Often, at around the middle of the Braille display, the reading position moves from the index finger of the left hand to the index finger of the right hand. It is also common to use the right hand for a tactile pre-orientation while the reading position stays at the index finger of the left hand.

To detect the tactile reading position on a Braille display in real time using ATC, the force applied to each tactile pin of a Braille display is analyzed 100 times per second. In the case of an Active Braille there are 320 Pins to be monitored.

Based on the knowledge of the reading position, the first implication of ATC was automatic scrolling. This function allows blind readers a continuous reading flow, since there is no more need in having to press the navigation keys at the end of every line of text.

Over all, each application based on detecting the reading position will help to improve the interaction of a blind PC user with their computer. A set of assistive functions based on ATC have already been implemented: reading words or letters, announcing text attribute changes. These functions can be assigned to individual reading beha-viors. At the moment we can distinguish between four reading behaviors (reading, fast reading, resting and reading backwards).

The detected reading position can be saved to a Log File and be analyzed with the ATC-LogAnalyser later on. The Log File therefore is a great tool for teachers to support students learning Braille well-directed.

The ATC-LogAnalyser allows teachers to analyze the reading behavior of a student during a lesson and provides an objective tool to determine information on the reading flow. Statistics on how many words per minutes, respectively how many characters per minute have been read, how many changes in reading speed within a session, how often the student read backwards, and how many characters or words have not been read by the student as well as the overall reading flow can be collected and analyzed.

3 Methodology for Improved PC Interaction for Blind Users Based on ATC

New approaches have been developed to investigate how ATC could improve the productivity of Braille readers in a work environment. An international group of experts, mainly Braille display users, have defined areas in which ATC could be turned into an effective tool to improve blind people's interaction with a PC.

A typical situation for Braille display users is correcting spelling mistakes. Normally, a Braille display can either show the context of the spelling mistake or the suggested corrections. With the introduction of Braille frames for Braille displays using Active Tactile Control, the simultaneous display of various independent sources of informa-tion on a Braille display was made possible for the first time. Braille frames create a most effective way for blind computer users to access several applications running multitasking on a computer system.

4   Efficient Access to Complex PC Application with ATC

ATC enabled Braille displays like an Active Braille used in combination with a screen reading program, present various examples of reading-position-triggered computer interactions. The knowledge of the reading position not only allows to indicate text attributes at the reading position like the font size, also control elements to interact with a computer application like the mouse, can be placed using the reading position.

In order to improve the handling of multiple tasks, a task-overview with direct access to the activated tasks, triggered by the reading position, has been implemented. An example for the direct access to content that is linked with a text position triggered by the tactile reading position would be the indication of spelling mistakes. As the read-ing finger reaches a misspelled word a separate Braille frame with the correction op-tions will be displayed automatically. This feature will assist blind users with the editing process of text files. For the screen reading program Window-Eyes, the read-ing-position PC interaction has been implemented as scripts.

Various approaches of using ATC technology to improve the accessibility of com-plex PC applications for blind users have been implemented already. Often, various infor-mation is presented simultaneously in individual areas on the screen. Control-ling the content of multiple Braille frames by the reading position detected by ATC, improves the access to these information.

4.1   Multiple Sub-windows Access

A good example to improve access to complex applications by ATC is the Windows Explorer. Here, the two Braille frames shown on the Braille display are the directory tree and the file list. When the tactile reading position is at the directory-tree frame the controls can be used to scroll in the folder list. When reading in the file-list frame, the controls are for scrolling within the list of files.

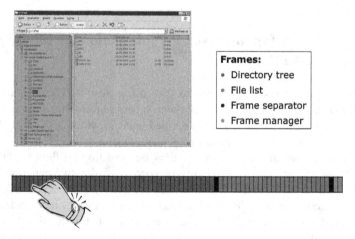

Frames:
- Directory tree
- File list
- Frame separator
- Frame manager

Fig. 3. Example of how a directory tree and a file list are presented on a Braille display in sepa-rate Braille frames

Using this Braille frame technology, a blind computer user can benefit of the pre-sen-tation of multiple applications or frames shown as Windows on a screen.

Frames:
- Folder list
- Mail list
- Mail
- Frame separator
- Frame manager

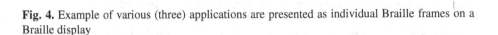

Fig. 4. Example of various (three) applications are presented as individual Braille frames on a Braille display

4.2   Presenting Additional Information Depending on the Reading Position

Braille Frames can also be used to show additional information on a Braille display depending on the reading position. The implementation of QuickSpell as a script for the screen reader Window-Eyes is a good example for this. When a spelling mistake is detected at the reading position an additional Braille frame appears on the Braille display showing the selection of possible alternatives. By selecting the correct option the Braille frame will vanish from the Braille display. Following, the Braille display shows the whole content of the original text field.

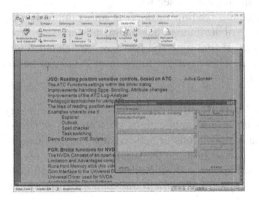

Frames:
- Document
- Spell checker
- Frame separator
- Frame manager

Fig. 5. Example of the presentation of a pop-up window on a Braille display

4.3   Manipulation of Tactile Content Using the Detected Reading Position

Similar to the idea of using cursor rooting bottoms at the Braille output to be able to place the cursor at the corresponding position, it is possible to use the ATC Technology to directly interact with the content shown on the Braille display. This enables blind users to communicate their feedback directly to the PC whilst reading information presented on the Braille display without the need of having to reach for the PC keyboard.

One simple example is to track or place the mouse pointer along with the reading position. This mechanism, implemented as assistant function for ATC, is especially helpful when on-screen magnification is used in combination with a Braille display. It allows to synchronize the magnified area on the screen with the corresponding Braille reading position on the Braille display.

Another implementation of a PC interaction controlled by the reading position is that after activation, e.g. by tapping twice on a selected position on the Braille display, the section of text covered by the reading position will be marked.

Providing Background Information on the Tactile Reading Position. Braille characters can only be displayed in a uniformed size on a Braille display. Text properties like text attributes and font size are not tactile detectable simultaneously to the actual textual information on the Braille display. With the knowledge of the tactile reading position, detected by ATC, it is now possible to provide the Braille reader with additional information about the context of their reading position.

There are two general approaches of how to present this background information. The first option is to show additional information as modification of the tactile presentation. The second option is to have the context information announced by a speech output.

The first approach uses various sections of the Braille display, the so-called Braille frames, for displaying individual information in each section.

Announcing the attribute changes at the reading position is an example for the second approach. When there is a change of attribute at the reading position, e.g. from normal to bold text, "bold" is announced. If font type and font sizes are changed too, then e.g. "bold, 12, Arial" is announced. This assistant function of ATC can be assigned to the different reading behaviors.

Reading Position Sensitive Controls Using Braille Framing. The ATC Technology allows blind users the direct control of several applications presented as windows parallel on the screen for the first time. Applications or sub-windows of applications are displayed as Braille frames in dedicated sections on the Braille display.

Depending on the tactile reading position on the Braille display the focus will position on the corresponding frame. The current frame is the frame with the current reading position detected by ATC.

Handling of Multiple Tasks on a Braille Display. It is common that only the active task running on a computer is presented on a Braille display. When using a multi tasking operating system, such as Microsoft Windows, the blind user also wants quick access to the various tasks running.

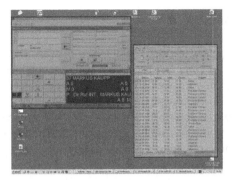

Frames:
- Telephony app
- Excel
- Frame separator
- Frame manager

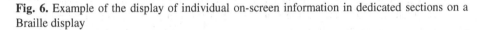

Fig. 6. Example of the display of individual on-screen information in dedicated sections on a Braille display

ATC is able to provide quick access to different tasks. Implemented as a script for the screen reader Window-Eyes, the various tasks running are presented by a self explaining letter of the alphabet, e.g. o for Outlook, w for MS Word and so on. For example, if 5 Tasks are running, 5 letters representing them are shown on the Braille display in the order in which they were started. This task indication is followed by a blank Braille cell. This means that on a Braille display with 88 Braille cells, six are occupied by the task representation. The remaining Braille cells of the Braille display act like an 82 character Braille display. The active task is presented in addition to the letter with the Braille dots 7 and 8. By touching the different letters, ATC enables the System to announce each task. By clicking on a task with cursor rooting the task presented is shown in the foreground. When cursor rooting is activated for the active task all other tasks will be minimized.

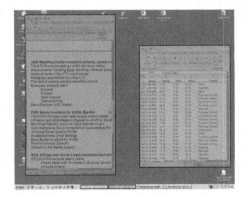

Frames:
- Word
- Excel
- Outlook
- IExplorer

Fig. 7. Example of the parallel presentation of active and running tasks on a Braille display using Braille frames

5   Conclusion and Next Steps

Active Tactile Control (ATC) opens up new methods of interaction with a PC for blind users. This technology in the field of computer access for blind users is comparable with the introduction of touch screens for sighted users. Computer interaction based on ATC allows blind people to use their computers more efficiently.

After the complete implementation of the described new methods the next area for implementing ATC is to develop a new rule set of PC interaction for blind users. Based on described implementations more research is needed to develop a complete new rule set for PC interaction for Blind users.

References

1. Kipke, S.: New Concepts of PC Interaction for Blind Users Based on Braille Displays with ATC Technology (Active Tactile Control). In: Miesenberger, K., Klaus, J., Zagler, W., Karshmer, A., et al. (eds.) ICCHP 2010. LNCS, vol. 6179, pp. 131–134. Springer, Heidelberg (2010)
2. Kipke, S.: From basic to advanced Braille display function. CSUN (2009)
3. Kipke, S.: Sensitive Braille Displays with ATC Technology (Active Tactile Control) as a Tool for Learning Braille. In: Miesenberger, K., Klaus, J., Zagler, W.L., Karshmer, A.I. (eds.) ICCHP 2008. LNCS, vol. 5105, pp. 843–850. Springer, Heidelberg (2008)
4. Kipke, S.: New Methods of Learning Braille by using the Active Tactile Control (ATC) Technology. CSUN (2007)
5. Schutzrecht Handy Tech Elektronik GmbH.: DE102004046526A1 2004-04-06

Applications of Optically Actuated Haptic Elements

Branislav Mamojka and Peter Teplický

Slovak Blind and Partially Sighted Union, Bratislava, Slovak republic
{mamojka,p.teplicky}@unss.sk

Abstract. There are missing commercially available large area dynamic tactile displays providing access to high-resolution graphic and Braille for the blind people. This is not solved by currently available displays in the form of a Braille line. The objective of the project NOMS (Nano-Optical Mechanical Systems) is to solve this problem by using optically activated haptic actuators. These will require no hard to assembly moving mechanical parts and have the potential for finer resolution. Recently developed carbon nanotube enriched photoactive polymers provided the starting technology for this purpose. There will be presented development of materials of this kind and their integration into tactile displays.

Keywords: Braille, display, tactile, haptic, photo actuation.

1   Introduction

Most of the information is presented in visual form which is inaccessible to blind people. To make it accessible the synthetic speech and tactile displays are used. Tactile displays are the most suitable means to present exact writ-ten form and layout of a text and perhaps the only possibility to present graphics to blind people. Unfortunately, there are still missing commercially available large area refreshable tactile displays providing access to high-resolution graphic and larger blocks of Braille texts. Blind readers, as well as sighted people, need possibility to backtrack and review Braille text larger than one line and to review information units that takes more than one line like equations or tables. Even more serious problem is access to tactile graphics like maps, plans, diagrams, and schemes in real time. This problem is not solved by currently available displays in the form of a Braille line. Tactile graphics is obviously available in various forms of a relief print, which are not at disposal in real time; production process is complex, long and obviously not automatic. Exceptional special devices presenting graphics part-by-part on small refreshable tactile areas of fingertip size need hard training, excellent manual skills, good imagination and memory and therefore also do not represent satisfactory solution. Finally, more recently there occurred two-dimensional refreshable tactile graphical displays [1-2] based on the same principle as Braille displays using piezo electric elements. Although working very nice they are still extremely expensive not only for individual users, but even for institutions providing education and other services to the blind people. Thus, the current tactile technology for the blind people significantly limits their access to information,

K. Miesenberger et al. (Eds.): ICCHP 2012, Part II, LNCS 7383, pp. 659–663, 2012.

in particular graphics and more complex texts, needed for education, work, and everyday life in rapidly developing information society. Therefore revolutionary technologies are needed to improve the lives of blind people providing better access to information.

The project NOMS - Nano-Optical Mechanical Systems [3] offers one promising solution - the use of actuators that can be activated optically, using materials changing their size by influence of light. These require no bulky moving parts and have the potential for much finer resolution than current technology. The most challenging task of the project is research and development of suitable optically active materials [4-6]. Recently developed carbon nanotube enriched photoactive polymers have provided the starting technology for this purpose. Liquid Crystal Elastomers (LCE) and also other polymers are examined.

2   NOMS: Objectives

The main objective of NOMS project is research and development of proto-type of photo-actuated large area, high resolution, and fast refreshable, tactile display - tablet - working as follows:

- The original video signal from a computer screen will be transformed into pulses that will trigger the appropriate emitters in the tablet.
- The light emitted by LED/LD-like platform will be focused by microlenses on a polymer NANO-composite film
- The photo-actuation of the film will be tailored to enable tactile graphic representation.
- The final tablet will have the following features:
- 80x80 blisters tactile display with 1.25 mm mutual distance
- Full text and graphical capability
- Tactile distances below human touch resolution enabling more smooth tactile graphics
- Rapid refresh rate. The estimated actuation speed of one blister is 100 ms, which will yield a maximum reaction delay for changing the whole display contents of a 100x100 mm display of approximately 1 second, assuming sequential actuation.
- Easy modular integration for larger display capability (A4 format by 6 modules)
- Fully integrated electronic circuitry
- Wireless Capability to connect to a PC and other devices
- Portability

Photomechanical actuation is preferred to electromechanical transduction also due to following technical and safety reasons:

- Wireless actuation
- Electrical-mechanical decoupling
- Low noise
- Easy scaling up/down

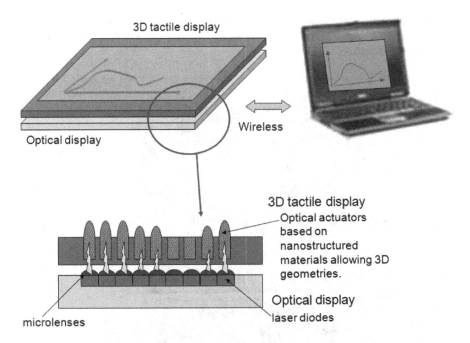

Fig. 1. Schematic of proposed visual-aid NOMS, showing computer wireless interface along with subjacent optical technology (source: Project NOMS)

3   The Work Performed So Far

The work covers the research and production of photoactive NANO-materials, blister and tablet design, communications and control software, optics and microsystem integration, as well as end user evaluation and neuro-cognitive studies.

A very important task has been the research and choice of actuating material [4]. However, only few materials actually exhibit photo-actuation. Initially, we favored carbon nanotube-polymer composites because of expected decreased manufacturing costs and true photo-actuation. But better results were found for liquid crystals elastomers. Actuation parameters (magnitude of the stroke, needed exerted force in tactile applications, etc.) in liquid crystal elastomer (LCE) materials have outperformed those of carbon nanotube polymer systems. Also, one of the initial disadvantages of the LCE materials, their transparency to visible light, has been overcome by incorporating carbon nanotubes in the elastomer to produce absorption over the complete visible spectrum, allowing successful actuation of LCE-CNT material using a visible LED light source. Nevertheless, we are not fully satisfied with some characteristics and stability of those materials needed for construction of haptic displays. Therefore the material research continues. At present we work with materials doped by laser welding dyes which seem to be more promising.

The work continues on an intermediate deliverable, a prototype of 10x10 tactile tablet with a pitch of 2.5 mm to allow standard Braille representation using different photo-actuated materials.

Fig. 2. 10x10 light emitting layer and driver boards (the LEDs are lit by random data). (source: Project NOMS)

The interface between the PC and the NOMS tablet has required development of software to perform the visual to tactile transformation, Wireless communication to transmit the tactile image to the display, to control electronics to operate the tablet. A first version of the software has been re-leased and the wireless communication protocol has been chosen.

4   Potential Impacts and Use of Final Results

Knowledge gained by studying photo-active NANO materials during NOMS project development will open new horizons for practical as well as research purposes not only for blind people, but for general public as a means of design for all.

The NOMS graphical display will be for instance suitable for use as a novel research tool for neuropsychologists allowing major progress in this field which has so far been limited by existing tactile technology which is either non-refreshable (e.g. embossed on paper) or just new very expensive devices [1-2] with lower resolution than proposed by the NOMS project.

Another hopeful application is a single tactile element resembling LED. It might be used for the same signaling purposes as LED, parallel with it or instead of it. This technology could be applied for signaling purposes (power on/off, recording on/off, heating on/off, waiting message etc.) to support or substitute visual perception.

The work proposed here identifies a new direction leading to Implementation of NOMS technology in non-assistive applications which will also be of great interest to the general public judging by the advent of multiple tactile interfaces in PDAs, cell phones, music players and large surface personal computers. Research of photo active NANO-materials will support also development in multiple adjacent fields such as medicine or robotics through artificial muscle technology.

5   Conclusion

The proposed device will comprise an invaluable added advantage over current assistive technology by provision of graphic and text information on a large area fast refreshable tactile display. Moreover NOMS is addressing also other specific needs of visually impaired people since that technology is readily adaptable to the latest and most common technical developments like e-books, i-phones and all featuring flat screens without classic key-boards. It could really improve accessibility of electronic information every-where. The results of the material research will also provide significant contribution to nano-technologies in general.

Acknowledgement. Project Coordinator: DrJaumeEsteve, Consejo Superior de InvestigacionesCientíficas (CSIC), Spain, Tel: + 34 93 594 7700 E-mail: info@noms-project.eu, Timetable: September 2009 to August 2012, Instrument: Small or Medium Scale Focused Research Project, Project NOMS is funded by the European Union within 7th Frame Program, Project Reference: 228916, Website: http://www.noms-project.eu

References

1. HyperBraille, http://www.hyperbraille.de/?lang=en
2. KGS Corporation, http://www.kgs-jpn.co.jp/eindex.html
3. Project NOMS, http://www.noms-project.eu/
4. Project NOMS, http://www.noms-project.eu/
   index.php?option=com_docman&task=cat_view&gid=42&Itemid=71
5. Spitalsky, Z., Tasis, D., Papalis, K., Galiotis, C.: Progress in Polymer Science 35, 357 (2010)
6. Albuerne, J., Boschetti-de-Fierro, A., Abel, V.: Journal of Polymer Science Part B: Polymer Physics 48, 1035 (2010)

Trackable Interactive Multimodal Manipulatives: Towards a Tangible User Environment for the Blind

Muhanad S. Manshad[1], Enrico Pontelli[1], and Shakir J. Manshad[2]

[1] Computer Science Department, New Mexico State University (NMSU), New Mexico, USA
{mmanshad,epontell}@nmsu.edu
[2] Math Adoptive Technology Lab for Students with Disabilities, NMSU, New Mexico, USA
smanshad@nmsu.edu

Abstract. This paper presents the development of Trackable Interactive Multimodal Manipulatives (TIMM). This system provides a multimodal tangible user environment (TUE), enabling people with visual impairments to create, modify and naturally interact with graphical representations on a multitouch surface. The system supports a novel notion of active position, proximity, stacking, and orientation tracking of manipulatives. The platform has been developed and it is undergoing formal evaluation.

Keywords: Haptic Feedback, Graphing, Accessibility, Blind and Visually Impaired, Multitouch, Multimodal, TUI, Diagrams, Tangible User Environment (TUE), NASA TLX, Subjective Workload, Manipulatives, Fiducials, Markers.

1 Introduction

Through their K-12 years, blind and visually impaired students are taught to construct, manipulate and browse the physical world using the sense of touch through free hands. This method is ubiquitous in reading braille and in all learning interactions (Fig. 1 and 2). Fundamentals of science and math are taught using simple inexpensive materials, requiring little to no learning curve. Dominant materials used in everyday classrooms are manipulatives, such as cubes, number lines, and combinations of corkboards, pins and rubber bands [13]. Manipulatives are tangible objects that are part of a hands-on learning environment. Through design and constant manipulation, a student can create mental models "images" of important concepts in algebra, geometry, measurements, and science. It is through multiple experiences that students gain true conceptual understanding [13]. There are, however, several concerns. E.g., each manipulative must be easily distinguishable, color properties have to be replaced by braille, and an unambiguous area for placement of manipulatives must be provided, to render interaction without distress for loss of position, orientation, and proximity of cubes. Another type of commonly used manipulatives relies on corkboards, pins and rubber bands (Figure 2). This form is used to create graphs, charts, and geometric shapes. This involves inserting pins on a wooden board with a raised grid and wrapping rubber bands around the pins to form a touchable graph. This is a simple method, but has

K. Miesenberger et al. (Eds.): ICCHP 2012, Part II, LNCS 7383, pp. 664–671, 2012.

several drawbacks. Pins can fall off if not placed correctly. If a pin is removed by mistake, the rubber bands can also fall off, causing the loss of the representation and possible injuries. The setup of this form is tedious and lacks feedback (e.g., audio) to denote correct or incorrect interactions. The static nature of manipulatives requires continuous manual intervention and validation (e.g., by the teachers).

Fig. 1. Two-handed uses for Braille and manipulatives [2], [10], [13], [14]

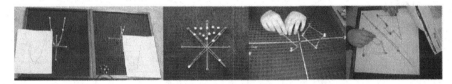

Fig. 2. Two-handed interaction when constructing diagrams/graphs [13]

The emergence of digital manipulatives [11] offers a new approach to address some of these issues. These manipulatives are based on the concepts of Tangible User Interfaces (TUIs), which provide a new compelling approach to enhance people's interaction with digital information [12]. The concept of TUI was first introduced in 1997, by Ishii and Ullmer – they define a user interface that can "augment the real physical world by coupling digital information to everyday physical objects and environments" [5]. TUIs naturally employ a two handed approach, which fits perfectly with the existing classroom practices for blind and visually impaired students. However, the technological developments and the associated research implications of TUIs for these groups of students are still in their infancy. McGookin et al. developed a TUI system that tracks markers on a table-top surface [9]. Their results demonstrate the potential offered by this approach in providing non-visual access to charts. However, their system only allows for data browsing of statistical data, without construction and other types of interaction. Subjective workload evaluations were not provided. In this project, we investigate TUIs for students with visual impairments further.

2   Background and Motivation

This paper presents an extension of our previous work (abstract): MICOO (Multimodal Interactive Cubes for Object Orientation) [7]. The limitations of existing approaches and the belief that TUIs might provide break-through ways to engage blind and visually impaired students in learning mathematical and scientific graphical concepts are at the foundation of TIMM. With TIMM we provide a general digital tangible manipulatives platform with the following characteristics:

1. It is general and programmable: we envision TIMM as a set of manipulatives that are flexible and provide an open API – allowing them to be programmed to meet the needs of different applications (e.g., presentation and manipulation of different concepts from algebra, geometry, and other scientific domains);
2. It is capable of providing multi-modal feedback;
3. It supports both presentation of graphical structures as well as their manipulation (e.g., creation and transformation).
4. It maintains a visual component, to enable interaction between blind, visually impaired students and sighted students/instructors.

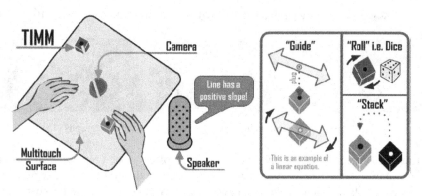

Fig. 3. TIMM Tangible User Environment

3   TIMM for Tangible User Environments (TUE)

Manipulatives are defined as a set of objects (e.g. blocks) that a student is instructed to use in a way that teaches or reinforces a lesson [4]. In a class room setting, manipulatives demand an environment that requires an interaction space (e.g., table-top, desk), active guidance/feedback (e.g., teacher), and a set of rules (e.g., lesson). Moreover, manipulatives in their class room setting provide a complete learning environment. We define a set of TUIs (manipulatives), their tangible interaction space (multitouch table-top), and a set of rules (applications) with active feedback (multi-modal), in a system which renders all interactions and user intention; thus, a tangible user environment.

We have developed a collection of manipulatives called *TIMM (Trackable Interactive Multimodal Manipulatives)* and a custom multitouch table-top to identify and track TIMM surface movements and interactions. This system renders active interactions by reading and tracking markers underneath each TIMM. In Figure 3, on the left we show the system. In this setup we provide an environment that is non-intrusive, providing look and feel of a typical table of a classroom setting. On the right of Figure 3, we describe the types of interactions that are possible with TIMM: "Guide", "Roll", and "Stack". The novel concept of "Guide" provides the ability to plug a tactile representation into a TIMM. This representation can be for example, a miniaturization of a graphical representation; in this case we show a line or a linear equation. Once a tactile representation is plugged into a TIMM, the system is then to actively rotate the representation to provide instant tactile feedback that matches a graphical object on that location. The "Roll" ability allows a roll action on the surface while accurately tracking the face of the object. This ability for example can be used to represent a virtual dice. The "Stack" ability allows several TIMMs to be stackable while actively track which TIMM is on top/bottom. The design of TIMM is guided by the following criteria:

1. *Natural active interaction:* Any system will naturally require a learning curve. However, employing a two handed input interaction approach (natural to students with visual impairments) will yield a reduced learning curve.
2. *Multiple points of interaction:* Existing research has extensively investigated uses of haptic technology (e.g., Wingman, PHANToM, Falcon). These devices require a user's whole palm and hand-grip, leaving other receptors on the hand unemployed (single point of interaction). Manshad and Manshad designed a haptic glove, which provides vibration feedback through natural movement and position [8]. Their evaluations highlight the significance of providing multiple points of interaction – students browsed a mathematical graph faster than using single point interaction. McGookin et al. evaluations also supported this notion [9].
3. *Independence:* the system should provide active feedback in support of correct and incorrect interactions. This will lessen the need for manual intervention. (e.g., teachers).

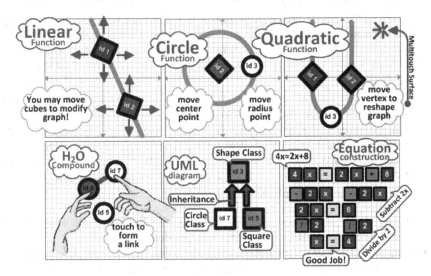

Fig. 4. Sample applications of TIMM

The initiative of TIMM is to develop a novel platform that adapts to a wide range of applications, particularly those found in everyday classrooms for blind and visually impaired students using manipulatives. The form and outer shape of TIMM is also meant to be adaptable and to serve as a generic platform for TUI-based interaction with graphical structures. As a generic platform, the system provides a novel notion of active position, proximity and orientation tracking of all objects. With this information we create a tangible user environment that reasons with user intent and validate their manipulation. Thus, provide continuous feedback to the user while guiding and instructing him/her to complete their task without the need of a 3rd person.

Consequently, the system also provides active tracking of TIMM against components of interest (e.g., diagram relation markers, entities, or graphs). If the orientation and position of a TIMM matches a component, then a user is allowed to modify that component by moving the TIMM (Fig. 4). Conversely, if a TIMM does not match the orientation or it is far from a component, audio feedback will be activated to direct and help the user to reach that component. A user may also use his fingers to quickly touch and browse the surface while listening for audio feedback. If a component is found, a user may put a TIMM on that position. This notion is called "bread crumbs", which allows the user to leave several TIMMs behind to form a tactile presentation and meaning that is configurable. As summarized in Fig. 4, multitouch can be used to detect or create links among entities (e.g., connect two nodes in a graph), manipulate graphical structures or construct expressions and equations. Thus, there are two general modes of interaction:

- Construction Mode:
  - Graphing: During construction of a graph (e.g., linear equation) a blind or visually impaired student typically locates two points (i.e. point A & point B) on a corkboard then inserting a pin on each point, and then wraps a rubber band around them to construct a tactile line. Using TIMM, a user will also locate two points through moving a TIMM and verifying the point of interest by reasoning with feedback (e.g., music, speech). Once points are located, a user can tie a piece of yarn or wikki-stix to form a tactile line between both TIMM points as shown in fig 3.
  - Diagram: Pins and rubber bands on a corkboard are also used to form an outline of a geometric shape. Similarly, TIMM graph construction method can be used to form outlines of shapes. However, when constructing more complex representations (e.g., UML, flow chart, compounds), a user must place several TIMMs to form a representation, and can link each object with a relation object. Once placing a TIMM, a user is then asked to describe or provide a description using a standard or a braille keyboard.

- Browsing Mode: (this mode is activated once a user finishes construction, loads a diagram representation from file, or inputs a function to graph).
  - Graphing: If a user enters a function, then he will be asked to place a TIMM to locate a point (e.g., x-intercept, y-intercept, vertex, center of circle, etc…) while listening to directions (e.g., "go upper left", "go lower left", "go up", "go down", "you are on the line", "you are on x-intercept", etc…). The system will continue to ask to user to locate the least amount of point to construct a tactile representation of the graphed function. Once all TIMMs are in place, the user can then manipulate the function by moving any TIMM. With every new move, audio feedback will be given to describe the change in the graph (e.g., "negative slope", "positive slope", "area of circle", etc…) as seen in scenario 1 of fig 5.

Alternatively, a user may use the "Guide" TIMM to quickly represent a function after locating only a single point. Then, the user can manipulate the graph either by moving the TIMM or rotating the "Guide" tactile representation as seen in scenario 2 of fig 5.

- Diagram: Similarly with TIMM graph manipulation, the user will also receive directions to place a TIMM to match a loaded diagram. Once all TIMM objects are in place, the user is free to manipulate the diagram, add to it, or remove links and relationships. User is also able to change the description of each object and rotate to change orientation.

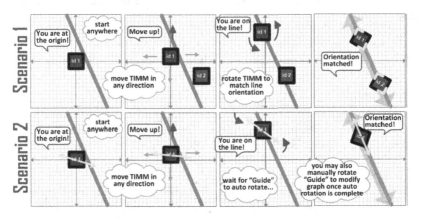

Fig. 5. Graph browsing and manipulation example

3.1 Hardware and Software Implementation

TIMM has been developed from scratch, using affordable off-the-shelf hardware components. The system allows for natural interaction using TIMM on a multi-touch surface. The current surface is controlled through a single infrared camera for TIMM movement and orientation tracking. Through the open-source Community Core Vision 1.5 (CCV) platform [3] we are extending our initial design to support multiple cameras for higher precision tracking of markers (Fig 6). Through CCV we can configure camera video stream and select tracking data to publish as UDP packets.

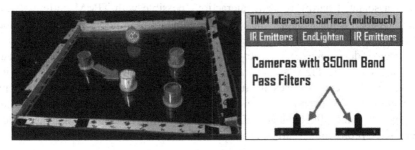

Fig. 6. Side view layers (right) and current design (left)

Current software implementation is a custom C# application which extends the open source reacTIVision TUIO framework [6]. New TIMM API provides active proximity and orientation of TIMM against components of interest. API for direction feedback, "Guide" control and "Roll" ability are also provided. The software subscribes to the CCV UDP packets, then plots position and orientation of each TIMM. Depending on the current application of TIMM that the user selected (e.g. graph, diagram), the software provides a graphical representation of the table-top surface. This representation can be saved and printed. The software also keeps track of overall time taken to complete each task, correction or incorrect movement of each TIMM, and time taken to move a single object, to later be used for evaluation and usability testing.

Fig. 7. Hardware design of TIMM

Since our system is to serve as a generic platform, there is no limit on the look and feel of TIMM objects. The intent is to make use of everyday manipulatives found in classrooms, and convert them to trackable objects. This can easily be done by placing a fiducial marker underneath any object. Software must then be configured to understand new objects on the surface and correctly predict user intention of manipulation, since current software only supports graph and diagram construction. Figure 7 describes associated hardware with interactions possible with TIMM currently developed: "Guide": using a stepper motor and volume knob to provide rotation feedback and input; "Roll": six markers placed on each side of a TIMM are used to determine the current side facing the surface; and "Stack": two IrDA transceivers are used to sense any stackable TIMMs. Generally, each TIMM sends wireless data to our interaction software and receives instructions (e.g. stepper motor movement, vibration feedback, etc...). Currently we are adding a speech/audio player component to provide speech and audio feedback. Each TIMM is programmable using the Arduino open-source prototyping platform [1].

4   Current Status

A number of formal evaluation activities are currently underway, including NASA TLX (Task Load Index) workload assessment and Neurosky's MindWave attention and meditation data. Current participants include students from the Alamogordo New Mexico School for the Blind and Visually Impaired. Participants will be tasked to browse, modify and construct a graph (on a Cartesian plot) and a diagram. Completion times and errors will be recorded and analyzed.

Acknowledgments. Many thanks to the NUI (Natural User Interface) Group Community forums for answering questions during the system building process.

References

1. Arduino, http://www.arduino.cc
2. Braille Math Blocks,
   http://www.unclegoose.com/products/braille-math-blocks
3. Community Core Vision Information, http://nuicode.com
4. Definition of Manipulatives,
   http://mw3.merriam-webster.com/dictionary/manipulatives
5. Ishii, H., Ullmer, B.: Tangible bits: towards seamless interfaces between people, bits, and atoms. In: Proc. CHI 1997: Conference on Human Factors in Computing Systems, Atlanta, GA, USA (1997)
6. Kaltenbrunner, M.: reacTIVision and TUIO: a tangible tabletop toolkit. In: Proc. ITS 2009: Conference on Interactive Tabletops and Surfaces, Banff, Canada (2009)
7. Manshad, M.S., Pontelli, E., Manshad, S.J.: MICOO (multimodal interactive cubes for object orientation): a tangible user interface for the blind and visually impaired. In: Proc. ASSETS 2011: Conference on Accessibility and Computers, Dundee, Scotland (2011)
8. Manshad, M.S., Manshad, A.S.: Multimodal vision glove for touchscreens. In: Proc. ASSETS 2009: Conference on Accessibility and Computers, Nova Scotia, Canada (2009)
9. Mcgookin, D.K., Robertson, E., Brewster, S.A.: Clutching at straws: using tangible interaction to provide non-visual access to graphs. In: Proc. CHI 2010: Conference on Human Factors in Computing Systems, Atlanta, GA, USA (2010)
10. Reading Braille, http://www.aph.org/devel/donoresp.htm
11. Resnick, M., Martin, F., Berg, R., Borovoy, R., Colella, V., Kramer, K., Silverman, B.: Digital manipulatives: New toys to think with. In: CHI 1998: Proc. of the ACM Conference on Human Factors in Computing Systems, Los Angeles, CA, USA (1998)
12. Shaer, O., Hornecker, E.: Tangible User Interfaces: Past, Present, and Future Directions. In: Foundations and Trends in HCI vol. 3(1-2), pp. 1–137
13. Texas School for the Blind and Visually Impaired,
    http://www.tsbvi.edu/presentations
14. Wikki-Stix, http://www.wikkistix.com

Introduction of New Body-Braille Devices and Applications

Satoshi Ohtsuka[1], Nobuyuki Sasaki[2], Sadao Hasegawa[3],
and Tetsumi Harakawa[4]

[1] Gunma National College of Technology, Maebashi, Japan
ohtsuka@ice.gunma-ct.ac.jp
[2] Tsukuba University of Technology, Tsukuba, Japan
nsasaki@cs.k.tsukuba-tech.ac.jp
[3] Ouunkai, Shinjukuku, Japan
pbb00564@nifty.ne.jp
[4] Maebashi Institute of Technology, Maebashi, Japan
harakawa@maebashi-it.ac.jp

Abstract. In this paper, two new Body-Braille devices are described. After the Body-Braille system and its current development status is explained, first, a new device for Braille-based real-time communication over internet (via Skype) is introduced and second, a new device for autonomous learning, which adopts wireless communication, is explained. The former is already developed and being used in the field test stage; the latter one is being developed now.

Keywords: Body-Braille, vibration, Helen Keller phone, autonomous learning, visually impaired, deaf-blind.

1 Introduction

The Body-Braille system transmits Braille characters to disabled people by vibration at any point on the body. Two vibration motors (vibrators) are driven three times to express the six points of each Braille cell. We have experimented with Body-Braille in several systems such as the "Tele-support system", which is a remote support system for deaf-blind people [1], an independent support system for deaf-blind people's walking around town using RFID, and a communication system between deaf-blind people and non-disabled people using infrared technology. In this paper, we describe two new devices implemented in the Body-Braille system. The first one is a Braille-based phone system for deaf-blind people over an audio telephone channel. We call it the "Helen Keller phone". We developed this device using Skype for the signal channel instead of mobile phones. The second device is a system in which a deaf-blind person can learn Body-Braille autonomously. In order to use this system, it is necessary to drive the vibration modules by wireless communication. In the current stage, we have finished designing the circuit modules of a Body-Braille device for the learning system and continue to develop the application.

K. Miesenberger et al. (Eds.): ICCHP 2012, Part II, LNCS 7383, pp. 672–675, 2012.

2   Body-Braille and Related Devices

2.1   Body-Braille

The Body-Braille system allows a user to read Braille characters through six micro-vibrators settled on the surface of the body such as the back, head or arms. It is designed to support the daily lives of deaf-blind people. Body-Braille has several merits: (1) Any part of the body can receive Braille data; (2) Both text and symbol information can be transmitted; (3) It is wearable; (4) Information is received passively; and (5) It supports the study of Braille. However, it is very hard to place 6 vibrators on the surface of the body, and the dispersed vibration sometimes causes read errors by phantom sensation. Reducing the number of vibrators would solve this problem. For this purpose, we are studying a simplified Braille system, in which Braille characters are presented using only two points instead of the original six. With this new simpler Braille code, called "two-point system", we can use fewer vibrators. As a result, the equipment size becomes much smaller than in earlier versions.

2.2   Devices in the Body-Braille System

We have been developing several Body-Braille devices in each stage of the research. The first generation used large equipment with six vibrators for the basic measurement and system experiment. The second generation used smaller equipment with two vibrators for the same purposes as the first generation. The third generation also uses smaller equipment with two vibrators for the practical use test of the Helen Keller phone. The fourth generation will have equipment with two vibrators and wireless communication to drive the vibrators and will be used for deaf-blind people's learning of Body-Braille. The third generation's equipment has been developed and is in the field test stage. The fourth generation's equipment is currently being developed. In this paper we introduce the devices used in the third and fourth generation.

3   Helen Keller Phone

3.1   Helen Keller Phone System

The Helen Keller phone system is a communication system for deaf-blind people via Skype. In this system, a deaf-blind person can talk with another disabled person without any support, just like the audio communication of non-disabled people. When a deaf-blind person wants to communicate with another deaf-blind person, he or she makes an internet connection with another deaf-blind person and chats with them using Braille and DTMF (Dual Tone Multiple Frequency) tone signals which compose the Braille code. DTMF signals which are mapped to six points of a Braille cell are transmitted through the audio channel of Skype to another deaf-blind person's Body-Braille device which outputs the vibrations corresponding to a recomposed Braille cell. Fig. 1 shows the schematic diagram of the Helen Keller phone system.

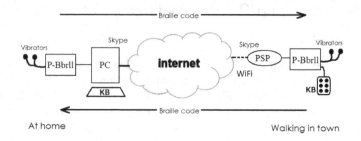

Fig. 1. The Schematic Diagram of the Helen Keller Phone System

3.2   Device of Helen Keller Phone

The third generation equipment is smaller than that in previous generations and is called "P-Bbrll (Pocket size Body-Braille equipment)". It drives two vibrators and consists of infrared, serial line, and DTMF tone signal communication interfaces. P-Bbrll is 100mm × 18mm × 58mm and weighs about 100g, so it is very portable. For the input of Braille code, 6 keys (F,D,S,J,K and L) of a PC keyboard or a tone generater are used to generate the combination of DTMF tone signals corresponding to the points of one Braille cell. These tones are transmitted through the audio channel of Skype on a PC or a Sony PSP go (Play Station Portable go) to the other person's P-Bbrll, activating the attached vibrators. The two vibrators express the 6 points of one Braille cell by being driven three times — once for each of the three lines of one cell. When the left or right (or both) point of one line is convex, the corresponding vibrator(s) emits a long vibration. If neither point is convex, the right vibrator emits a short vibration.

4   New Wireless Device and Application

4.1   Needs of Wireless System

Body-Braille is intended as a communication system for deaf-blind people and a support system for the independent life of deaf-blind people. In order to test its effectiveness for this purpose, we need an extended field test with many deaf-blind people, but we have not had many subjects so far. In order to get more subjects, we need a Body-Braille learning system so that users can learn to read Braille cells using vibrators. For this purpose, we have to supply very easy-to-use experimental equipment including such features as wireless connections between the main equipment and vibration modules. We are currently developing a wireless device using XBee (ZigBee) technology. It consists of a primary device which communicates with a host machine and transmits the driving information of vibrators and a vibration module which receives the driving information and then drives the vibrators. The primary device has a six-key mini keyboard and memory chip which records the learning results. The vibration module has a

Fig. 2. The Picture of the Wireless Equipment

micro-battery which can be charged through a USB terminal. The size of the vibration module is 80mm × 60mm × 30mm, and it is supposed to be settled around both wrists of a subject. The Fig. 2 shows the picture of the equipment.

4.2 Application — System for Autonomous Learning

The subject operates the six-key mini keyboard, first selecting a genre. We supply several sets of simple words from many genres. The subjects receive a word by Body-Braille vibrations and then input the reading result using the mini keyboard. After the presentation of feedback (i.e., correct/incorrect), the result is logged in the primary device and is referred to by a host machine later. This wireless device is also being studied as an entertainment application, such as a vibration system which expresses an interpretation of a musical atmosphere.

5 Conclusion

Two new Body-Braille devices for the Helen Keller phone and an autonomous learning system were described. The device for the Helen Keller phone has been developed in the commercial base and now it is being tested with several deaf-blind subjects all over Japan. We have obtained very positive feedback on it. Now we are summarizing the result, which will be reported at the conference. The other device, for autonomous learning, is still being designed now. We will be able to report the test result several months later. But we are sure to get much more subjects by using the wireless technology, and we can also supply an entertainment application.

Acknowledgment. A part of this work was supported by JSPS KAKENHI 20500497 and 23500667.

References

1. Ohtsuka, S., Sasaki, N., Hasegawa, S., Harakawa, T.: Body-Braille System for Disabled People. In: Miesenberger, K., Klaus, J., Zagler, W.L., Karshmer, A.I. (eds.) ICCHP 2008. LNCS, vol. 5105, pp. 682–685. Springer, Heidelberg (2008)

Author Index